Grails in Action, Secon

Grails in Action
Second Edition

GLEN SMITH
PETER LEDBROOK

MANNING
SHELTER ISLAND

For online information and ordering of this and other Manning books, please visit www.manning.com. The publisher offers discounts on this book when ordered in quantity. For more information, please contact

Special Sales Department
Manning Publications Co.
20 Baldwin Road
PO Box 261
Shelter Island, NY 11964
Email: orders@manning.com

Manning Publications Co.
20 Baldwin Road
PO Box 261
Shelter Island, NY 11964

Development editor: Cynthia Kane
Copyeditors: Katie Petito, Lianna Wlasiuk
Proofreader: Elizabeth Martin
Typesetter: Dennis Dalinnik
Cover designer: Marija Tudor

ISBN: 9781617290961
Printed in the United States of America
1 2 3 4 5 6 7 8 9 10 – EBM – 19 18 17 16 15 14

To Kylie, who sacrifices daily to let me chase such crazy dreams.
Love you so much, matie!

—G.S.

To my parents, for always being there.

—P.L.

brief contents

contents

foreword

No matter how powerful your web framework, or how well-documented it may be, and independent of all of those tutorials, tips, and blog posts you find on the web, there is no replacement for a book that thoroughly introduces you to the topic. For many years *Grails in Action* has been the guide for the growing number of Grails developers.

Whenever I visit a team that uses Grails I look around to see what books they have available, and I'm always delighted to see *Grails in Action,* since I can rely on the solid foundation they got from the book, and I can easily refer to it for best practices and background knowledge.

But the world is ever-changing and the Groovy and Grails worlds particularly so. Web technologies rise and fall quickly these days and Grails adapts mostly through its immense plugin community, but also by carefully evolving the framework itself.

All these changes called for a second edition of our beloved Grails book, and I am so glad to finally have it in my hands!

Glen and Peter have managed to bring in all the new while retaining the characteristics of the first edition: it's very approachable for the beginner, short and clear for the impatient, covers all bases for the practitioner, and drives the ball deep for the expert—all this with their special touch of humor for an enjoyable read.

Have fun using Grails in action with *Grails in Action, Second Edition*!

DIERK KÖNIG
AUTHOR, *GROOVY IN ACTION*

preface

"Hey, Peter. I think we should throw together a second edition. What do you think?"

"Are you serious? You know how much work we put into the first edition, it nearly killed us both."

"No, come on. Don't be thinking major rewrite; be thinking a light-touch iteration just to refresh a few things. It'll be a snap, done in a couple of months."

"I'm tired already."

And so began our journey toward this volume you now hold. It was as far from a light-touch rewrite as any second edition could be. Experts recommend a second edition should have at least 20% new content; I think ours is more like 50%, with a refresh of the rest. So we're very tired right now!

So much has happened since the first edition. Grails is now owned and backed by an industrial heavyweight, forms a core part of the Spring portfolio, and has seamlessly embraced diverse technologies such as single page web apps, NoSQL, and the Cloud (all of which get special chapters in this new edition). Various plugins have come and gone, having been embraced into the core—and excised from it. Through it all, Grails has remained on the cutting edge of all things web development, and has now developed a loyal following among the larger Java web crowd. This little hipster framework has now become relatively mainstream. And that's exciting to see.

I remember a military leadership guy once saying to me at a business function, "Glen, great things don't just happen. They are brought about." I think that's probably true. And everything great about this second edition has been brought about by Peter Ledbrook. He carried this idea through to completion, rewrote vast sections of many chapters, and fixed so many source code errors he should have unlocked a special GitHub badge. He sustained this project on the days I was totally over it. And he carried the responsibility for this effort being a worthy second edition. Anything good here is his fault. So if you see him at a conference, make sure to buy him a drink!

We really hope you enjoy this much expanded and updated second edition of *Grails in Action*. We're confident you will find it even more pragmatic and brimming with the many best practices we've learned from a bunch more years of experience working in the field.

GLEN SMITH

acknowledgments

Last time we were here, it was a new undertaking and we didn't know what we were getting ourselves into. This time we were supposed to know better, and yet the support shown from the team at Manning was once again vital to this endeavor. We would like to thank everyone involved in the publication of this book. Particular thanks go to our development editor, Cynthia Kane, who put up with some rather sleepy authors during the conference calls and kept our motivation high. The production team also did a marvelous job of tightening up our prose and clearing up all those ambiguities and inconsistencies that inevitably appear even with just one author.

No technical book is worth a penny unless it's accurate. There is a lot of detail inside *Grails in Action, Second Edition* with plenty of scope for error. It is thanks to the persistence of our technical proofreader, Doug Warren, and his attention to detail, that the code we present in this book works. Many thanks to him.

We'd also like to thank our reviewers for sending detailed feedback on the manuscript at various stages in its development: Aiden Mark Humphreys, Alvin Scudder, Antonio Mas Rodriguez, Cynthia Pepper, Daniel Miller, David Madouros, Debra Miller, Ivan Todorović, Jack Frosch, Jeffrey Yustman, Jerry Gaines, Koray Güclü, Marc Weidner, Michael A. Angelo, Mike Spencer, Phillip Warner, Pratap Chatterjee, Shiloh Morris, and Toby Hobson.

The early MEAP subscribers also did a sterling job of pointing out typos, grammatical errors, confusing explanations, and other issues. If you're interested, you can find much of that feedback on GitHub in the book's repository there. Equally important for us was all the positive feedback we received. That was a great motivator to complete the book and ensure it was as good as we could make it.

Thanks also to Dierk König for his encouragement and for agreeing to write the foreword to our book. And last, but not least, we would like to thank Graeme Rocher and the rest of the Grails team and contributors for producing such a wonderful framework that has made software development fun again.

Glen Smith

When I was a kid, one of my mentors, Paul Le Lievre, said to me, "Glen, there's no such thing as a free lunch. It's only free because someone else pays." That's good advice. Someone always pays. And the main person who paid for this book to happen was my amazing and long-suffering wife, Kylie. This time, the project took more than 18 months, which is a long time to endure an absentee author husband. Thanks for putting up with my grumpy and stressed manner as *Grails in Action, Second Edition* was reworked, rewritten, reshaped, and endlessly edited into an almost completely different book. Matie, you are the best! Consider this book a voucher for unlimited childcare-free weekends redeemable at your leisure. Bubble bath will be supplied.

My beautiful children, Isaac and Zoe, also paid a hefty price for this tome. Love you guys so much. Daddy is home, and months of extended bike rides and endless cuddles await!

My parents, Alby and Jan Smith, and parents-in-law, Steve and Joy Salter, have been a great encouragement for this second edition project and a great help with childcare. Thanks again for your support!

Once again, Peter Ledbrook, my coauthor, was a calm voice of encouragement when I was drowning in an ever-growing to-do list. He's a very humble and low-profile guy who is always willing to help without any kind of bravado or drama. He knows more about Grails than any non-Graeme person and has written all the technically challenging stuff in this book. Our friendship has now survived two major book projects, and the books have been significantly better for his partnership.

Peter Ledbrook

No one warned us how much work a second edition would involve. And yet once again, my coauthor, Glen Smith, brought energy and enthusiasm to the project despite getting up at 5 a.m. for our calls. Together, we somehow pulled through and the result lies before you. We hope you like it!

I'd also like to thank Graeme Rocher, the Grails project lead, for responding quickly to my many questions about the framework's internals, while continuing to push the boundaries on the project. The framework has changed a lot since the first edition, even while we were writing the book, so those insights were invaluable in keeping the content up to date.

Last, but definitely not least, many thinks to all our early adopters who provided both valuable feedback and encouragement at all stages. They were vital to keeping our spirits up.

about this book

Grails in Action, Second Edition is a comprehensive introduction to the Grails framework covering the nuts and bolts of all core Grails components: controllers, views, services, taglibs, and plugins. But much more than an introduction, *Grails in Action, Second Edition* is jam-packed with skills, techniques, and insights from the trenches: solving the challenges you're likely to face developing your next killer web app.

Roadmap

Grails in Action, Second Edition gives you a fast-paced and accessible introduction to the world of agile web development.

The book is divided into four parts:

- Part 1: Introducing Grails
- Part 2: Core Grails
- Part 3: Everyday Grails
- Part 4: Advanced Grails

Part 1 will introduce you to Grails by taking you through building your first Grails application—a simple Quote of the Day application. You'll get a taste for all the parts of the Grails ecosystem and for how all the parts hang together to create a complete application. But in order to make any sophisticated use of Grails, you'll need an appreciation for Groovy—the dynamic language that forms the foundation of your Grails coding. So we'll spend some time training you on all the basics in chapter 2.

Part 2 begins our deeper exploration of the core Grails artifacts. You'll learn how models, views, and controllers interact, and you'll gain a deep understanding of all the core features that make up the heart of Grails applications. We'll introduce you to Hubbub, our sample social-networking application, and implement all the features that you'll commonly find in Grails applications: domain modeling, querying, skins and layout, form handling, and more. By the end of part 2, you'll be confidently developing your own basic applications.

Because real-world web applications involve a lot more than just forms and databases, part 3 will tackle the skills you'll need to take your application to the world. We'll explore testing strategies to ensure your code is implemented correctly, and we'll show how to give your application that Web 2.0 feel through time-saving third-party plugins. Few applications can face the outside world without some kind of security model, so we'll explore the security implications of taking your Grails application online. Finally, we'll look at strategies for designing RESTful APIs and conclude with a survey of the asynchronous technologies that are becoming increasingly popular in developing scalable applications.

In part 4, we conclude our tour of Grails with the most advanced features of the framework. We'll look deep inside Grails' underlying technologies, Spring and Hibernate. We'll also show you how to integrate Grails with your existing build processes and run your applications in the cloud.

Three appendixes address reference issues and XML and Spring builders. Two bonus chapters, "Advanced GORM kung fu" and "Developing plugins," are available online from the publisher's website at www.manning.com/gsmith2 or www.manning.com/GrailsinActionSecondEdition.

Who should read this book

Whether you're a seasoned Java developer ready to dip your toes in the waters of dynamic web frameworks, or a hardcore web developer making the switch to the latest Convention over Configuration paradigm, *Grails in Action, Second Edition* will give you the tools to get productive quickly and the deep knowledge to handle the corner cases when you get stuck.

Some experience with web development (in particular CSS, HTML, and JavaScript) is assumed, along with a basic knowledge of programming. Previous experience with Java web development is an advantage, but we take the time to explain core Java web concepts in sidebars where applicable. If you're coming from another language background (such as Ruby, Perl, or PHP), you should find the move to Grails quite natural.

Code conventions

This book provides copious examples that show how you can make use of each of the topics covered. Source code in listings or in text appears in a `fixed-width font like this` to separate it from ordinary text. In addition, class and method names, object properties, and other code-related terms and content in text are presented using the same `fixed-width font`.

Code and command-line input can be verbose. In many cases, the original source code (available online) has been reformatted; we've added line breaks and reworked indentation to accommodate the page space available in the book. In rare cases, when even this was not enough, line-continuation markers were added to show where longer lines had to be broken.

Code annotations accompany many of the listings, highlighting important concepts. In some cases, numbered cueballs link to additional explanations that follow the listing. We also use *italics* to highlight new code that has been added or changed from an earlier listing.

Getting the source code

You can access the source code for all of the examples in the book from the publisher's website at www.manning.com/GrailsinActionSecondEditon. All source code for the project is hosted at GitHub (github.com)—a commercial Git hosting firm. We will maintain the current URL via the publisher's website. The source is maintained by chapter, so, for example, you can download /source-code/ch06 and you will have a full copy of the source up to that point in the book.

Keeping up to date

The Grails world moves very quickly. There have been substantial changes in Grails in the time it took us to develop *Grails in Action, Second Edition.* Even moving from Grails 2.2 to 2.3 caused us to make significant changes!

Although the book targets Grails 2.3, a new version of Grails (2.4) is already available. Fortunately, everything in here is still valid for the new version. You may notice a difference in the initial state of files such as grails-app/conf/BuildConfig.groovy, but the code we add will still work.

Speaking of Grails 2.4, you will find some interesting changes.

- It now comes with Spring Framework 4 rather than 3.2.
- Hibernate 4 is now the default, although you can switch to the older Hibernate 3 plugin, which has the dependency name `hibernate`.
- You can enable static compilation of your controllers, services, and other artifacts via the new `@GrailsCompileStatic` annotation.
- New Grails projects use the Asset Pipeline plugin instead of Resources, but you can easily switch back to Resources.
- The Maven plugin now works much better for multiproject builds and you can use it with any 2.x Grails version.
- Where queries (chapter 5) have improved support for subqueries and projections.

Of these, the only one that has an immediate impact is the Asset Pipeline plugin. We recommend you remove those dependencies and replace them with the appropriate Resources plugins while you work through the book. That said, we recommend you use Asset Pipeline for real projects. The Grails user guide has good coverage of it.

If there are portions of source code needing modification for a future release, you'll be able to find information on the *Grails in Action, Second Edition* Author Online forum (www.manning.com/GrailsinActionSecondEdition).

Author Online

Purchase of *Grails in Action, Second Edition* includes free access to a private web forum run by Manning Publications where you can make comments about the book, ask technical questions, and receive help from the authors and from other users. To access the forum and subscribe to it, point your web browser to www.manning.com/GrailsinActionSecondEdition. This page provides information on how to get on the forum once you are registered, what kind of help is available, and the rules of conduct on the forum. It also provides links to the source code for the examples in the book, errata, and other downloads.

Manning's commitment to our readers is to provide a venue where a meaningful dialog between individual readers and between readers and the authors can take place. It is not a commitment to any specific amount of participation on the part of the authors, whose contribution to the Author Online remains voluntary (and unpaid). We suggest you try asking the authors some challenging questions lest their interest stray!

The Author Online forum and the archives of previous discussions will be accessible from the publisher's website as long as the book is in print.

About the authors

GLEN SMITH started "stunt programming" the day his school took delivery of its first set of Hitachi Peach computers (in the early '80s) and has been doing it ever since. He's worked as a Unix/C systems programmer, Perl hacker, and even Visual Basic dude (but he tells everyone it was just a phase). When Java came along, he lost interest in everything else. These days, he spends most of his time consulting in Java EE technologies to the Australian government.

He has been involved in the Grails community since Grails 0.1 and launched the first public-facing Grails app (an SMS gateway) on Grails 0.2. He is a regular on the Groovy and Grails speaking circuit, the cohost of the Grails podcast (http://grailspodcast.com), and the man behind groovyblogs.org.

Glen lives in Canberra, Australia, with his wife, two children, and an exuberant labradoodle. He blogs at http://blogs.bytecode.com.au/glen and twitters at http://twitter.com/glen_a_smith.

PETER LEDBROOK started his software development career as a teenager learning to program in the comfort of his bedroom. After surviving the trials and tribulations of C and C++, he switched to Java during his first job and has stayed with it ever since.

An avid fan of open source software since those early days, he has always looked to that community for innovative and useful solutions. He discovered Grails while investigating Ruby on Rails and was astonished at how easy it was to write web applications using the framework. The love affair began.

He wrote several popular plugins (Remoting, Shiro, and GWT) and then became a core Grails committer when he joined G2One as a consultant at the end of 2007. He also has plenty of battle scars from actively working on several public-facing applications and helping teams make the most of Grails.

About the technical editor

DOUG WARREN is a consultant, architect, and developer specializing in Java, Spring, Grails, Ruby, and open source technologies. He was leader of both a Java and a Web Services user group for many years. Over the past 14 years, he has also been a very active technical proofreader and reviewer for Manning Publications.

about the title

By combining introductions, overviews, and how-to examples, Manning's *In Action* books are designed to help learning and remembering. According to research in cognitive science, the things people remember are things they discover during self-motivated exploration.

Although no one at Manning is a cognitive scientist, we are convinced that for learning to become permanent, it must pass through stages of exploration, play, and, interestingly, retelling of what is being learned. People understand and remember new things, which is to say they master them, only after actively exploring them. Humans learn in action. An essential part of an *In Action* guide is that it is example-driven. It encourages the reader to try things out, play with new code, and explore new ideas.

There is another, more mundane, reason for the title of this book: our readers are busy. They use books to do a job or solve a problem. They need books that allow them to jump in and jump out easily and learn just what they want, just when they want it. They need books that aid them *in action*. The books in this series are designed for such readers.

about the cover illustration

The figure on the cover of *Grails in Action, Second Edition* is a "Jeune Fille de Plouneour-Trez," or a young woman from a town in the province of Bretagne in northern France. The illustration is taken from a French book of dress customs, *Encyclopedie des Voyages,* by J. G. St. Saveur, published in 1796. Travel for pleasure was a relatively new phenomenon at the time and illustrated guides such as this one were popular, introducing both the tourist as well as the armchair traveler to the inhabitants of other countries of the world, as well as to the regional costumes of France.

The diversity of the drawings in the *Encyclopedie des Voyages* speaks vividly of the uniqueness and individuality of the world's towns and regions just 200 years ago. This was a time when the dress codes of two regions separated by a few dozen miles identified people uniquely as belonging to one or the other, and when members of a social class or trade or profession could be easily distinguished by what they were wearing.

Dress codes have changed since then, and the diversity by region, so rich at the time, has faded away. It is now often hard to tell the inhabitant of one continent from another. Perhaps, trying to view it optimistically, we have traded a world of cultural and visual diversity for a more varied personal life…or a more varied and interesting intellectual and technical life.

At a time when it is hard to tell one computer book from another, Manning celebrates the inventiveness and initiative—and the fun—of the computer business with book covers based on the rich diversity of regional life of two centuries ago, brought back to life by the pictures from this collection.

Part 1

Introducing Grails

The field of Java-based web application frameworks has made great strides in usability, but creating an application with them is still hard work. Grails's core strength is developing web applications quickly, so you'll jump into writing your first application right away.

In chapter 1, we expose you to the core parts of Grails by developing a simple Quote of the Day (QOTD) application from scratch. You'll store to and query from the database, develop business logic, write tests, and add Ajax functionality. By the end of it, you'll have a feel for the parts of Grails.

To develop serious Grails applications, you need a firm grasp of Groovy—the underlying dynamic language that makes Grails tick. In chapter 2, we take you on a whirlwind tour of core Groovy concepts and introduce the syntax.

By the end of part 1, you'll understand the power of Groovy and Grails and be ready to take on the world. Feel free to do so—Grails encourages experimentation. But you might want to stick around for part 2, where we take you deeper into the core parts of Grails.

1 Grails in a hurry . . .

This chapter covers

- What is Grails?
- Core Grails philosophy
- Grails installation
- Key components of a Grails application
- Your first Grails application—developing and deploying it

"Help, I've lost my Mojo!" That statement is a concise summary of what developers feel when working with any of the plethora of Java web frameworks. Each change requires time spent editing configuration files, customizing web.xml files, writing injection definitions, tweaking build scripts, modifying page layouts, and restarting apps. Aaaahhhh! "Where has all the fun gone? Why is everything so tedious? I wanted to whip up a quick app to track our customer signups! There must be a better way . . . " We hear you.

Grails is a next-generation Java web development framework that draws on best-of-breed web development tooling, techniques, and technologies from existing Java frameworks, and combines them with the power and innovation of dynamic language development. The result is a framework that offers the stability of technologies you know and love, but shields you from the noisy configuration, design complexity, and boilerplate code that make existing Java web development tedious. Grails allows you to spend your time implementing features, not editing XML.

But Grails isn't the first player to make such claims. You're thinking, "Please don't let this be YAJWF (Yet Another Java Web Framework)!" Because if the Java development world is famous for one thing, it's having an unbelievably large number of web frameworks. Struts, WebWork, JavaServer Faces (JSF), Spring MVC, Seam, Wicket, Tapestry, Stripes, Google Web Toolkit (GWT), and the list goes on and on—all with their own config files, idioms, templating languages, and gotchas. And now we're introducing a new one?

The good news is that this ain't your grandma's web framework. We're about to take you on a journey to a whole new level of getting stuff done—and getting it done painlessly. We're excited about Grails because we think it's time that Java web app development was fun again! It's time for you to sit down for an afternoon and crank out something you'd be happy demoing to your boss, client, or the rest of the internet. Grails is that good.

In this chapter, we take you through developing your first Grails app. Not a toy, either. Something you can deploy and show your friends. An app that's data-driven and Ajax-powered that has full CRUD (create, read, update, delete) implementation, a template-driven layout, and even unit tests. All in the time it takes to eat your lunch, with less than 100 lines of code. Seriously.

But before you fire up your IDE and get your hands dirty writing code, you may need more convincing about why Grails is such a game-changer and should be on your radar.

1.1 Introducing Grails

Grails is a next-generation Java web development framework that generates developer productivity gains through the confluence of a dynamic language, a convention over configuration philosophy, powerfully pragmatic supporting tools, and an agile perspective drawn from the best emerging web development paradigms.

1.1.1 Why Grails changed the game

Grails entered the Java Web Application landscape in 2006 and has grown steadily in adoption since. Taking full advantage of Groovy as the underlying dynamic language, Grails made it possible to create a `Book` object and query it with dynamic methods such as `Book.findByTitle("Grails in Action")` or `Book.findAllBy-DatePublished-GreaterThanAndTitleLike(myDate, "Grails")`, even though none of those methods existed on the `Book` object.

Even better, you could access any Java code or libraries you were already using, and the language syntax was similar enough to Java to make the learning curve painless. But best of all, at the end of the day you had a WAR file to deploy to your existing Java app server—no special infrastructure required, and no management awareness needed.

The icing on the cake was that Grails was built on Spring, Hibernate, and other libraries already popular and used by enterprise Java developers. It was like turbocharging existing development practices without sacrificing reliability or proven technologies.

Grails's popularity exploded. Finally, Java web developers had a way to take all the cool ideas that Rails had brought to the table and apply them to robust enterprise-strength web application development, without leaving behind any of their existing skills, libraries, or infrastructure.

1.1.2 *Seven big ideas*

That's enough history about how Grails came to be such a popular Java web framework. But if you (or your manager) need further convincing that Grails is an outstanding option for your next big web app project, the following subsections discuss seven of the big ideas (shown in figure 1.1) that drove Grails to such a dominant position in the emerging next-gen Java web frameworks market.

BIG IDEA #1: CONVENTION OVER CONFIGURATION

One of the things you'll notice about developing with Grails is how few configuration files exist. Grails makes most of its decisions based on sensible defaults drawn from your source code:

- Add a controller class called `ShopController` with an action called `order`, and Grails will expose it as a URL of /yourapp/shop/order.
- Place your view files in a directory called /views/shop/order, and Grails will link everything for you without a single line of configuration.
- Create a new domain class called `Customer`, and Grails will automatically create a table called customer in your database.
- Add fields to your `Customer` object, and Grails will automatically create the necessary fields in your customer table on the fly (including the right data types based on the validation constraints you place on them). No SQL required.

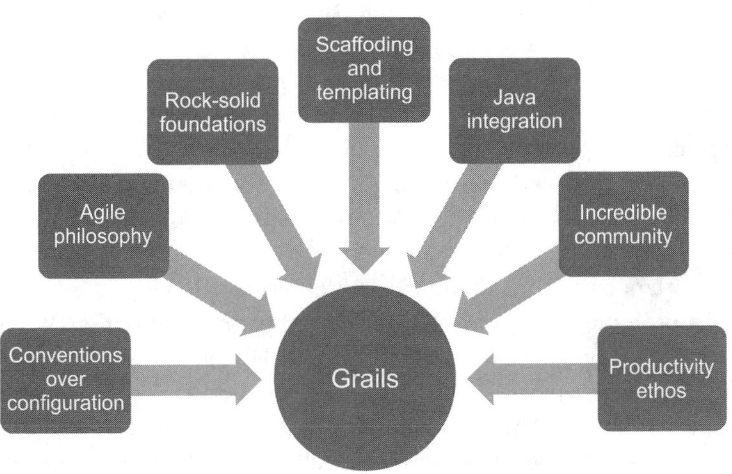

Figure 1.1 The Grails ecosystem is a powerful confluence of people, ideas, and technology.

Grails is about convention *over* configuration, not convention *instead of* configuration. If you need to tweak the defaults, the power is there. Grails makes overriding the defaults easy, and you won't need any XML. But if you want to use your existing Hibernate configuration XML files in all their complex glory, Grails won't stand in your way.

BIG IDEA #2: AGILE PHILOSOPHY

Grails makes a big deal about being an agile web framework, and by the time you finish this chapter, you'll understand why. By making use of a dynamic language (Groovy), Grails makes things that were a real pain in Java a complete joy. Whether it's processing form posts, implementing tag libraries, or writing test cases, Grails offers a conciseness and expressiveness to the framework that make these operations easier and more maintainable at the same time.

The Grails infrastructure adds to the pleasure by keeping you iterating without getting in the way. Imagine starting up a local copy of your application and adding controllers, views, and taglib features while it's running—without restarting it! Then imagine testing those features, making tweaks, and clicking refresh in your browser to view the updates. It's a joy.

Grails brings a whole new level of agility to Java web application development, and when you've developed your first complete application, which you'll do over the next 30 minutes or so, you'll start to appreciate some of the unique power Grails provides.

BIG IDEA #3: ROCK-SOLID FOUNDATIONS

Even though Grails itself is full of innovation and cutting-edge ideas, the core is built on rock-solid proven technologies: Spring and Hibernate. These are the technologies that many Java shops use today, and for good reason: they're reliable and battle-tested.

Building on Spring and Hibernate also means there's no new magic going on under the hood if you need to tweak things in the configuration (by customizing a Hibernate configuration class) or at runtime (by getting a handle to a Spring `ApplicationContext`). None of your learning time on Spring and Hibernate is wasted.

It doesn't matter if you're new to Grails and don't have a background in Spring or Hibernate. Few Grails development cases fall back to that level, but know it's there if you need it.

This same philosophy of using best-of-breed components has translated to other areas of the Grails ecosystem—particularly third-party plugins. The scheduling plugin is built on Quartz, the search plugin is built on Lucene and Compass, and the layout engine is built on SiteMesh. Wherever you go in the ecosystem, you see popular Java libraries wrapped in an easy-to-use instantly productive plugin. Peace of mind plus amazing productivity!

Another important part of the foundation for enterprise developers is having the formal backing of a professional services, training, and support organization. When SpringSource acquired G2One in November 2008, Groovy and Grails inherited the backing of a large company with deep expertise in the entire Groovy and Grails stack. In recent times, SpringSource was acquired by VMware and spun off into a dedicated big data and Spring-related development and support organization called Pivotal (http://gopivotal.com/).

This has also introduced a range of support options to the platform that are useful to organizations looking for 24/7 Groovy and Grails support backup.

Big idea #4: Scaffolding and templating

If you've ever tried bootstrapping a Spring MVC application by hand, you know it isn't pretty. You need a directory of JAR files, bean definition files, web.xml customizations, annotated POJOs (plain old Java objects), Hibernate configuration files, database-creation script, and a build system to turn it all into a running application. It's hard work, and you may burn a day in the process.

By contrast, building a running Grails application is a one-liner: `grails create-app myapp`, and you can follow it up with `grails run-app` to see it run in your browser. All the same stuff happens behind the scenes, but based on conventions and sensible defaults rather than on hand-coding and configuration.

If you need a new controller class, `grails create-controller` will generate a skeleton for you (along with a skeleton test case). The same goes for views, services, domain classes, and all the other artifacts in your application. This template-driven approach bootstraps you into a fantastic level of productivity, where you spend your time solving problems, not writing boilerplate code.

Grails also offers an amazing feature called *scaffolding*. Based on the fields in your database model classes, Grails can generate a set of views and controllers on the fly to handle CRUD operations without a single line of code.

Big idea #5: Java integration

One of the unique aspects of the Groovy and Grails community is that, unlike some other Java virtual machine (JVM) languages, we love Java! We appreciate that problems and design solutions are better implemented in a statically typed language, so we have no problem writing our web form processing classes in Groovy and our high-performance payroll calculations in Java. It's all about using the right tool for the job.

We're also in love with the Java ecosystem and don't want to leave behind the amazing selection of Java libraries we know and love. Whether that's in-house data transfer objects (DTO), JARs for the payroll system, or a great new Java library for interfacing with Facebook, moving to Grails means you don't have to leave anything behind—except verbose XML configuration files. And as we've said before, you can reuse your Hibernate mappings and Spring resource files if you're so inclined!

Big idea #6: Incredible community

One of the most compelling parts of the Grails ecosystem is the fantastic and helpful user community. The Groovy and Grails mailing list is a hive of activity where both die-hard veterans and new users are equally welcome. The Grails.org site hosts a Grails-powered wiki full of Grails-related information and documentation.

A wealth of third-party community websites has also sprung up around Grails:

- Groovyblogs.org aggregates what's happening in the Groovy and Grails blogosphere and is full of interesting articles.
- Sites such as Facebook and LinkedIn host Grails social networking options.

- A Groovy podcast (search for groovypodcast on YouTube) runs every so often to keep you up to date with news, interviews, and discussions in the Groovy and Grails world.

But one of the coolest parts of the community is the amazing ever-growing list of third-party plugins for Grails. Whether it's a plugin to implement full-text search, Ajax widgets, reporting, instant messaging, or RSS feeds, or to manage log files, profile performance, or integrate with Twitter, there's something for everyone. You'll find literally hundreds of time-saving plugins. (We introduce you to the most popular ones in chapter 10.)

BIG IDEA #7: PRODUCTIVITY ETHOS

Grails is about more than building web applications. It's about executing your vision quickly so that you can get on to more important "life stuff": hanging out with your family, walking your dog, learning rock guitar, or getting your veggie patch growing big zucchinis. Web apps come and go; zucchinis are forever. Grails productivity gives you that sort of sage-like perspective.

For us, productivity is the new black, and developing in Grails is about getting your life back one feature at a time. When you realize that you can deliver in one day work that used to take two weeks, you start to feel good about going home early. Working with such a productive framework even makes your hobby time more fun. You can complete all those Web 2.0 startup website ideas you've dreamed about, but that ended up as half-written Struts or Spring MVC apps. Through the course of this chapter, we'll give you a taste of the kind of productivity you can expect when moving to Grails.

Most programmers we know are the impatient type, so in this chapter we'll take 30 minutes to develop a data-driven, Ajax-powered, unit-tested, deployable Web 2.0 website. Along the way, you'll get a taste of the core parts of a Grails application: models, views, controllers, taglibs, and services. Buckle up—it's time to hack.

1.2 Getting set up

To get Grails up and running, review the installation process shown in figure 1.2.

1. Install a Java Development Kit (JDK) (version 1.6 or later).

   Run `javac -version` from your command prompt to verify the version you have. Most PCs come with Java preinstalled, so you may not need this step.
2. After your JDK is installed, download the latest Grails distro from grails.org and unzip it to your favorite installation area.
3. Set the `GRAILS_HOME` environment variable, which points to your Grails installation directory, and add GRAILS_HOME/bin to your path.

   On Mac OS X and Linux, edit the ~/.profile script to contain lines such as these:

   ```
   export GRAILS_HOME=/opt/grails
   export PATH=$PATH:$GRAILS_HOME/bin
   ```

   On Windows, go into System Properties to define `GRAILS_HOME` and update your `PATH` setting.

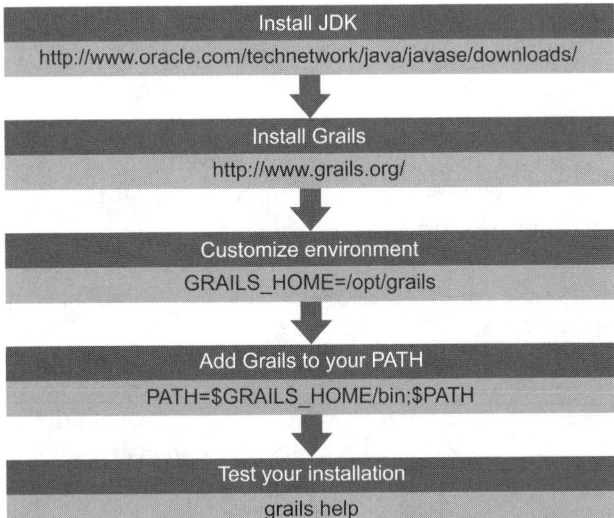

Figure 1.2 The Grails installation process

4. Set the `JAVA_HOME` environment variable to the location of your JDK, in the same way as you did for `GRAILS_HOME` in the previous step.
5. To verify that Grails is installed correctly, run `grails help` from the command line. This will give you a handy list of Grails commands and confirm that everything is running as expected.

> **Note on Grails versions**
>
> The book is based on Grails 2.3.7, but the latest version of Grails may be different by the time you read this. The best way to ensure that you're running the correct version of Grails with all our sample code is via the Grails wrapper:
>
> ```
> ./grailsw <command>
> ```
>
> You don't need the starting ./ on Windows, it's only for Unix-like systems. The wrapper is a script that downloads and caches the appropriate version of Grails for the current project. Projects based on the same version of Grails use the same cached version, so don't worry about losing lots of disk space!
>
> New projects created by Grails 2.3 and above already contain the wrapper, but for Grails 2.1 and 2.2 you need to explicitly run `grails wrapper` if you want it for your own projects.

As your Grails applications become more sophisticated, you'll want to take advantage of the fantastic IDE support available for Grails projects. You can find Grails plugin support for your preferred IDE—IntelliJ, NetBeans, or Eclipse—or you can use the dedicated Groovy/Grails Tool Suite[1] from Pivotal. We won't develop much code in

[1] Download the tool suite from https://spring.io/tools/ggts.

this chapter, so a text editor is all you need. Fire up your favorite editor, and let's talk about your sample application.

1.3 QOTD: your sample program

If you're writing a small application, you may as well have fun. This example is a Quote-of-the-Day web application in which you'll capture and display famous programming quotes from development rock stars throughout time. You'll let the user add, edit, and cycle through programming quotes, and add a dash of Ajax sizzle to give it a modern feel. You'll want a short URL for your application, so make qotd your application's working title.

> **NOTE** You can download the sample apps for this book, including CSS and associated graphics, from the book's site (www.manning.com/gsmith2). To view the latest issues and check out the latest sources, see the GitHub project (https://github.com/GrailsInAction/graina2) for details.

It's time to start your world-changing quotation app, and all Grails projects begin the same way. First, find a directory to work in. Then create the application:

```
grails create-app qotd
cd qotd
```

Well done. You've created your first Grails application. You'll see that Grails created a qotd subdirectory to hold your application files. Change to that directory now, which is where you'll stay for the rest of the chapter.

Because you've done the hard work of building the application, it would be a shame not to enjoy the fruit of your labor. To run the app, enter:

```
grails run-app
```

Grails ships with a Tomcat plugin used to host your application during the development and testing lifecycle. When you run the `grails run-app` command, Grails compiles and starts your web application. When everything is ready to go, you'll see a message like this on the console:

```
Server running. Browse to http://localhost:8080/qotd
```

This means it's time to fire up your favorite browser and take your application for a spin: http://localhost:8080/qotd/. Figure 1.3 shows your QOTD application running in a browser.

After you've taken in the home page, you can stop the application by pressing Ctrl-C or running `grails stop-app` from another terminal/command prompt. Alternatively, you can leave the application running and issue Grails commands from a separate terminal/command prompt in your OS.

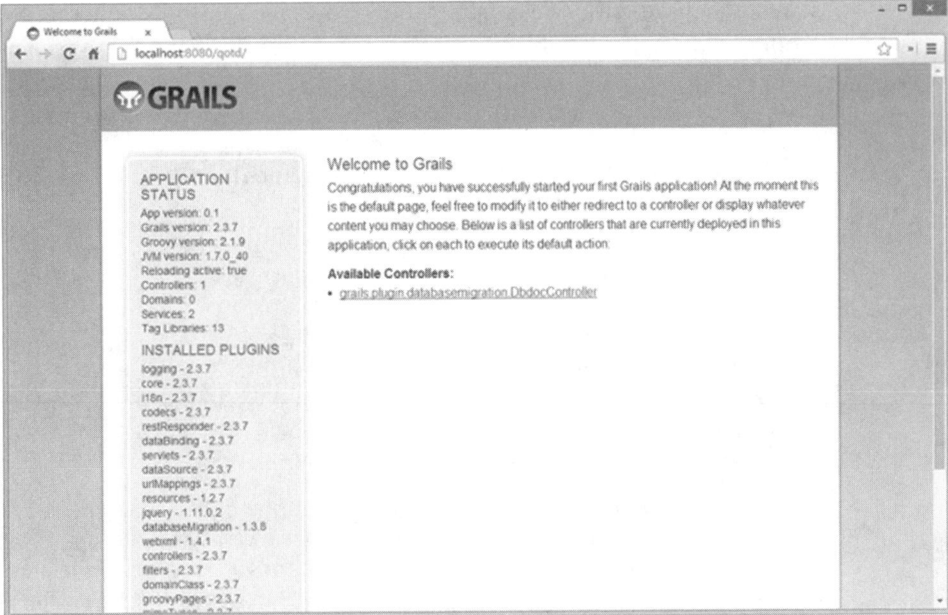

Figure 1.3 Your app is up and running.

> **Running on a custom port (not 8080)**
>
> If port 8080 isn't for you (because you have another process, such as Tomcat, running), you can customize the port that the Grails embedded application server runs on using the `-Dserver.port` command-line argument. If you want to run Grails on port 9090, for instance, you could run your application like this:
>
> ```
> grails -Dserver.port=9090 run-app
> ```
>
> If you decide to always run a particular application on a custom port, you can create a custom /grails-app/conf/BuildConfig.groovy file with an entry for `grails.server.port.http=9090` to make your custom port the default. Or make a system-wide change by editing the global $HOME/.grails/settings.groovy file. You'll learn more about these files in chapter 15.

1.3.1 Writing a controller

You have your application built and deployed, but you're short on an engaging user experience. Now is a good time to learn that Grails handles interaction with users via a *controller*.

Controllers are at the heart of every Grails application. They take input from your user's web browser, interact with your business logic and data model, and route the user to the correct page to display. Without controllers, your web app would be static pages.

Like most parts of a Grails application, you can let Grails generate a skeleton controller by using the Grails command line. Let's create a simple controller for handling quotes:

```
grails create-controller quote
```

Grails will respond with a list of the artifacts it generated:

```
| Created file grails-app/controllers/qotd/QuoteController.groovy
| Created file grails-app/views/quote
| Created file test/unit/qotd/QuoteControllerSpec.groovy
```

A word on package naming

If you omit the package name for a Grails artifact, it will default to the name of the app (in the previous example, if you do a `grails create-controller quote`, it creates an artifact called /grails-app/qotd/QuoteController.groovy).

For production code, the Grails community has settled on the standard Java-based convention where your artifacts should be created with your org domain name. Grails lets you change the default package name for your app in /grails-app/conf/Config.groovy. For this chapter's example, you might choose to change the setting in that file to read:

```
grails.project.groupId = "com.grailsinaction.qotd"
```

With such a setting in play, when you do `grails create-controller quote` it will create the class in /grails-app/controller/com/grailsinaction/qotd/QuoteController.groovy. It's a great key saver change to make at the start of a new Grails project. To prevent surprises for people picking up this chapter halfway through, we're going to stick with the default package name of qotd for now.

Grails creates this skeleton controller in /grails-app/controllers/qotd/QuoteController.groovy. You'll notice that Grails sorted out the capitalization for you. Here is the skeleton:

```
package qotd

class QuoteController {
     def index() { }
}
```

Not so exciting, is it? The previous index entry is a Grails *action*, which we'll return to in a moment. For now, let's add a home action that sends text back to the browser:

```
package qotd

class QuoteController {
    def index() { }

    def home() {
        render "<h1>Real Programmers do not eat Quiche</h1>"
    }
}
```

Grails provides the `render()` method to send content directly back to the browser. This will become more important when you dip your toes into Ajax waters, but for now let's use it to deliver your "Real Programmers" heading.

How do you invoke your action in a browser? If this were a Java web application, the URL to get to it would be declared in a configuration file, but not in Grails. This is where the convention over configuration pattern comes in.

Ruby on Rails introduced the idea that XML configuration (or configuration of any sort) can be avoided if the framework makes opinionated choices for you about how things fit together. Grails embraces the same philosophy. Because your controller is called `QuoteController`, Grails will expose its actions over the URL /qotd/quote/youraction. Figure 1.4 gives a visual breakdown of how URLs translate to Grails objects.

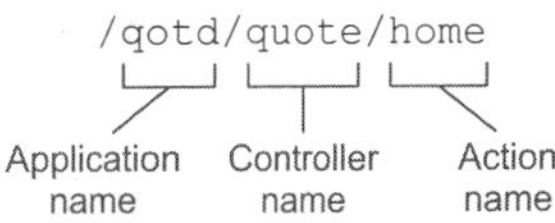

Figure 1.4 How URLs translate to Grails objects

In the case of our `hello` action, we need to navigate to: http://localhost:8080/qotd/quote/home.

Figure 1.5 shows your brand-new application running without a single line of XML.

If you're wondering about that `index()` routine in the skeleton controller code, that's the method called when the user omits the action name. If you decide all references to /qotd/quote/ should end up at /qotd/quote/home, you need to tell Grails about that with a default action such as the one in the following listing.

Listing 1.1 Handling redirects

```
package qotd
class QuoteController {
    static defaultAction = "home"
    def home() {
        render "<h1>Real Programmers do not eat Quiche</h1>"
    }
}
```

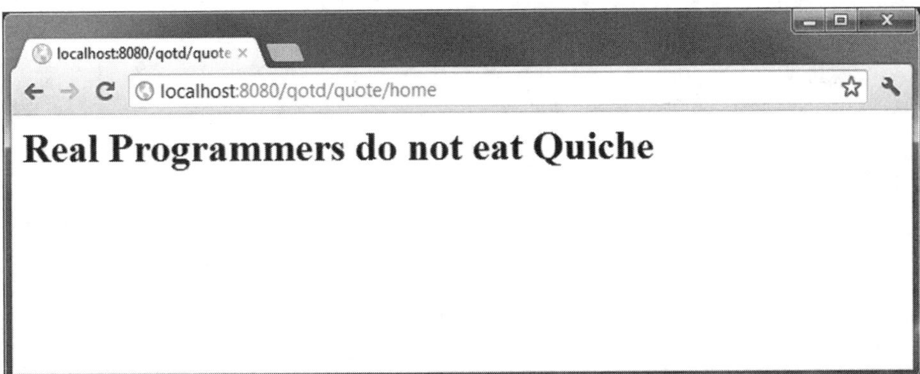

Figure 1.5 Adding your functionality

The app looks good so far, but having that HTML embedded in your source is nasty. Now that you've learned about controllers, it's time to get acquainted with views.

1.3.2 Generating an HTML page: the view

Embedding HTML inside your code is always a bad idea. Not only is it difficult to read and maintain, but your graphic designer will need access to your source code to design the pages. The solution is to move your display logic to a separate file known as the *view*. Grails makes it simple.

If you've done any work with Java web applications, you'll be familiar with JavaServer Pages (JSP). JSPs render HTML to the user of your web application. Grails applications make use of Groovy Server Pages (GSP). The concepts are similar.

We've already discussed the convention over configuration pattern, and views take advantage of the same stylistic mindset. If you create your view files in the right place, everything will hook up without a single line of configuration.

Begin by implementing your random action as shown in the following code. We'll handle the view next.

```
def random() {
    def staticAuthor = "Anonymous"
    def staticContent = "Real Programmers don't eat much quiche"
    [ author: staticAuthor, content: staticContent]
}
```

What's with those square brackets? That's how the controller action passes information to the view. If you're an old-school servlet programmer, think of it as request-scoped data. The `[:]` operator in Groovy creates a `Map`, so you're passing a series of key/value pairs through to your view.

Where does your view fit into this, and where will you put your GSP file so that Grails can find it? Use the naming conventions you used for the controller, coupled with the name of your action, and place the GSP in /grails-app/views/quote/random.gsp. If you follow that pattern, no configuration is required.

Let's create a GSP file that references your `Map` data, as shown in the following code:

```
<html>
<head>
    <title>Random Quote</title>
</head>
<body>
    <q>${content}</q>
    <p>${author}</p>
</body>
</html>
```

The `${content}` and `${author}` format is known as the GSP expression language, and if you've worked with JSPs, it will be old news to you. If you haven't worked with JSPs, you can think of those `${}` tags as a way of displaying the contents of a variable. Let's fire up the browser and give it a whirl. Figure 1.6 shows your new markup in action.

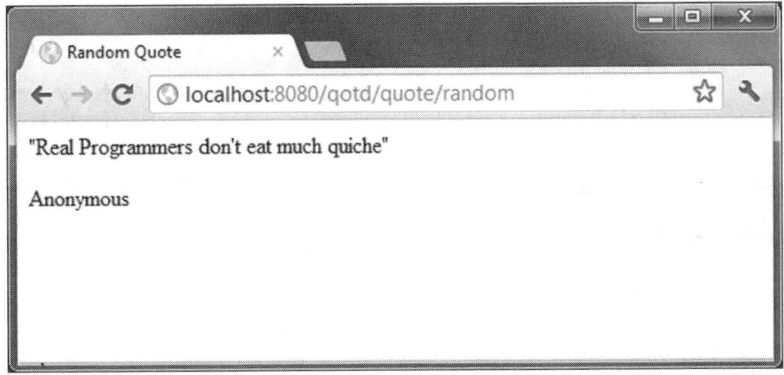

Figure 1.6 Your view in action

1.3.3 Adding style with Grails layouts

You've now written your piece of backend functionality, but the output isn't engaging—no gradients, no giant text, no rounded corners. Everything looks mid-90s.

You think it's time for CSS, but let's plan ahead. If you mark up random.gsp with CSS, you're going to have to add those links to the header of every page in the app. Grails has a better way: layouts.

Layouts give you a way to specify layout templates for certain parts of your application. For example, you may want all of the quote pages (random, by author, by date) styled with a common masthead and navigation links; only the body content should change. To do this, let's mark up your target page with IDs you can use for your CSS:

```
<html>
<head>
    <title>Random Quote</title>
</head>
<body>
    <div id="quote">
        <q>${content}</q>
        <p>${author}</p>
    </div>
</body>
</html>
```

Now, how do you apply those layout templates (masthead and navigation) we discussed earlier? Like everything else in Grails, layouts follow a convention over configuration style. To have all your `QuoteController` actions share the same layout, create a file called /grails-app/views/layouts/quote.gsp. Grails doesn't have shortcuts for layout creation, so you've got to roll this one by hand. The following listing shows your attempt at writing a layout.

Listing 1.2 Adding a layout

```
<html>
    <head>
        <title>QOTD &raquo; <g:layoutTitle/></title>       ❶ Merges title from target page
```

```
        <g:external dir="css" file="snazzy.css"/>        ❷ Creates relative link to CSS file
        <g:layoutHead />                                 ❸ Merges head elements from target page
        <r:layoutResources />                            ❹ Merges in JavaScript, CSS, and other resources
    </head>
    <body>
        <div id="header">
            <g:img dir="images" file="logo.png" alt="logo"/>
        </div>
        <g:layoutBody />                                 ❺ Merges body elements from target page
    </body>
</html>
```

Let's break down the use of angle brackets. Because this is a template page, the contents of your target page (random.gsp) will be merged with this template before you send any content back to the browser. Under the hood, Grails uses SiteMesh, the popular Java layout engine, to do the merging for you. Figure 1.7 shows the merge process.

To make your layout template in listing 1.2 work, it needs a way to access elements of the target page (when you merge the title of the target page with the template, for example). It's time to introduce you to taglibs because access is achieved through Grails's template taglibs.

If you've never seen a tag library (taglib) before, think of them as groups of custom HTML tags that can execute code. In listing 1.2, you took advantage of the `<g:external>`, `<g:layoutHead>`, and `<g:layoutBody>` tags. When the client's browser requests the page, Grails replaces those tag calls with real HTML, and the contents of the HTML will depend on what the individual tag generates. For instance, that `<g:external>` tag ❷ will generate an HTML `<link>` element that points to the URL for snazzy.css.

In the title block of the page, you include your QOTD title and follow it with chevrons (>>) represented by the HTML character code `»`, and add the title of the target page itself ❶.

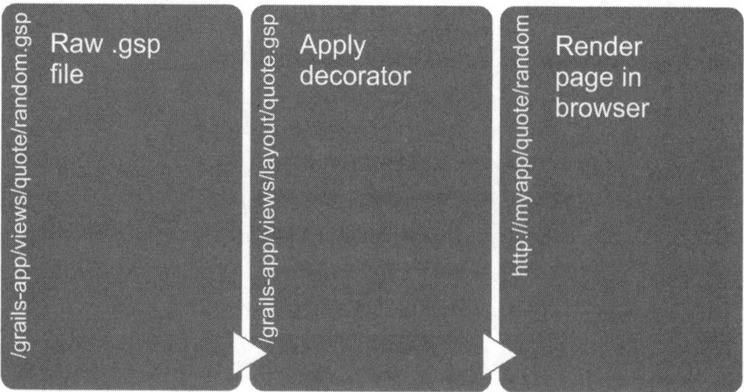

Figure 1.7 SiteMesh decorates a raw GSP file with a standard set of titles and sidebars.

After the rest of the head tags, you use a <g:layoutHead> tag to merge the contents of the HEAD section of any target page ❸. This can be important for search engine optimization (SEO) techniques, where individual target pages might contain their own META tags to increase their Google-ability.

With your head metadata in place, it's time to lay out any other HEAD-bound resources that your page might need in the head section with a <g:layoutResources> tag ❹. This is any other CSS or JavaScript that the Grails resources infrastructure requires in the HEAD section of this page. More on this magic in the Advanced UI chapter!

Finally, you get to the body of the page. You output your common masthead <div> to get your Web 2.0 gradient and cute icons, and then you call <g:layoutBody> to render the BODY section of the target page ❺.

Refresh your browser to see how you're doing. Figure 1.8 shows your styled page.

> **Getting the CSS and artwork**
>
> If you're following along step-by-step at your workstation, you'll be keen to grab the CSS and image files that go along with the styling shown previously (so your local app can look the same). You can grab the few files you need (/web-app/css/snazzy.css and /web-app/images/) directly from the chapter 1 source code available for download from www.manning.com/gsmith2 or directly from the current source code on GitHub (https://github.com/GrailsInAction/graina2).

Your app is looking good. Notice how you've made no changes to your relatively bland random.gsp file. Keeping view pages free of cosmetic markup significantly reduces your maintenance overhead. And if you need to change your masthead, add more JavaScript includes, or incorporate a few additional CSS files, do it all in one place: the template.

Fantastic. You're up and running with a controller, view, and template. But things are still static in the data department. You're overdue to learn how Grails handles

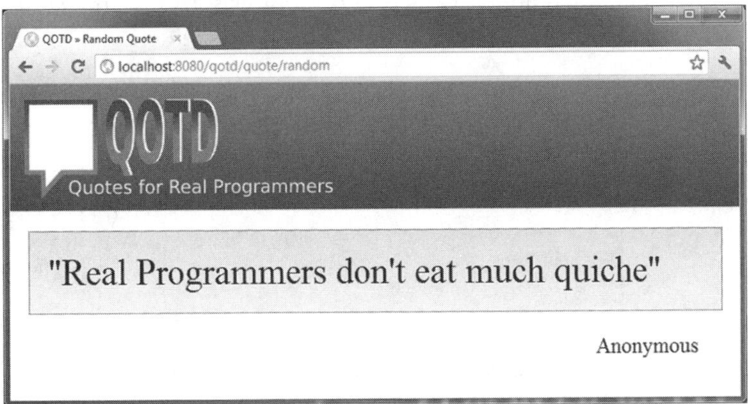

Figure 1.8 QOTD with some funky CSS skinning

information in the database. When you have that under your belt, you can circle back and implement a real random action.

1.4 Creating the domain model

You've begun your application, and you can deploy it to your testing web container. But let's not overstate your progress—Google isn't about to buy you yet. Your app lacks a certain pizzazz. It's time to add interactivity allowing users to add new quotations to the database. To store those quotations, you'll need to learn how Grails handles the data model.

Grails uses the term "domain class" to describe objects that can be persisted to the database. In your QOTD app, you're going to need a few domain classes, but let's start with the absolute minimum: a domain class to hold your quotations.

Let's create a `Quote` domain class:

```
grails create-domain-class quote
```

You'll see that Grails responds by creating a fresh domain class. Here's a matching unit test to get you started:

```
| Created file grails-app/domain/qotd/Quote.groovy
| Created file test/unit/qotd/QuoteSpec.groovy
```

In your Grails application, domain classes always appear under the /grails-app/domain. Look at the skeleton class Grails created in /grails-app/domain/qotd/Quote.groovy:

```
package qotd

class Quote {

    static constraints = {
    }
}
```

That's uninspiring as it appears now. You'll need fields in your data model to hold the various elements for each quote. Let's beef up your class to hold the content of the quote, the name of the author, and the date the entry was added:

```
package qotd

class Quote {
    String content
    String author
    Date created = new Date()

    static constraints = {
    }

}
```

Now that you've got your data model, you need to create your database schema, right? Wrong. Grails does all that hard work for you behind the scenes. Based on the definitions of the types in the previous code sample, and by applying simple conventions,

Grails creates a quote table, with `varchar` fields for the strings, and `Date` fields for the date. The next time you run `grails run-app`, your data model will be created on the fly.

But how will it know which database to create the tables in? It's time to configure a data source.

1.4.1 Configuring the data source

Grails ships with an in-memory database out of the box, so if you do nothing, your data will be safe and sound in volatile RAM. The idea of that makes most programmers a little nervous, so let's look at how to set up a more persistent database.

In your /grails-app/conf/ directory, you'll find a file named DataSource.groovy. This is where you define the data source (database) that your application will use. You can define different databases for your development, test, and production environments. When you run `grails run-app` to start the local web server, it uses your development data source. The following code shows an extract from the standard DataSource.groovy file, which shows the default data source.

```
...
environments {
    development {
        dataSource {
            dbCreate = "create-drop"                    <-- Recreates database on every run
            ➥ url = " jdbc:h2:mem:devDb;MVCC=TRUE;LOCK_TIMEOUT=10000;
;DB_CLOSE_ON_EXIT=FALSE"                    <-- Specifies an in-memory database
        }
    }
    ...
}
```

You have two issues here. The `dbCreate` strategy tells Grails to drop and recreate your database on each run. This is probably not what you want, so let's change that to `update`. This change lets Grails know to leave your database table contents alone between runs (but we give it permission to add columns if it needs to).

The second issue relates to the URL—it's using an H2[2] in-memory database. That's fine for test scripts, but not for product development. Let's change it to a file-based version of H2 so that you have real persistence.

The updated code is shown here:

```
...
environments {
    development {
        dataSource {
            dbCreate = "update"                    <-- Preserves tables between runs
            url = "jdbc:h2:devDb;MVCC=TRUE;LOCK_TIMEOUT=10000;
➥ DB_CLOSE_ON_EXIT=FALSE"                    <-- Specifies file-based database
        }
    }
    ...
}
```

[2] H2 (the Java SQL database) database engine, www.h2database.com.

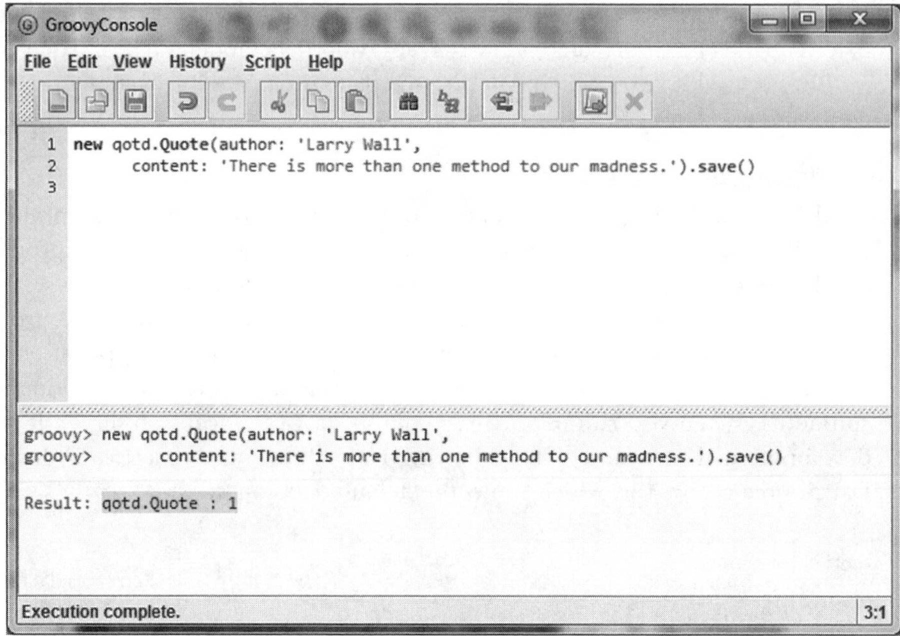

Figure 1.9 The Grails console lets you run commands from a GUI.

Now that you have a database that persists your data, let's populate it with sample data.

1.4.2 Exploring database operations

You haven't done any work on your UI yet, but it would be great to save and query entries in your quotes table. To do this for now you'll use the Grails console—a small GUI application that starts your application outside a web server and gives you a console to issue Groovy commands.

You can use the `grails console` command to tinker with your data model before your app is ready to roll. When you issue this command, your QOTD Grails application is bootstrapped, and the console GUI appears, waiting for you to enter code. Figure 1.9 shows the process of saving a new quote to the database via the console.

For your exploration of the data model, it would be nice to create and save those `Quote` objects. Type the following into the console window, then click the Run button (at the far right of the toolbar):

```
new qotd.Quote(author: 'Larry Wall',
      content: 'There is more than one method to our madness.').save()
```

The bottom half of the console will let you know you're on track:

```
Result: qotd.Quote : 1
```

Where did that `save()` routine come from? Grails automatically endows domains with certain methods. Let's add two more entries to get a taste of querying:

```
new qotd.Quote(author: 'Chuck Norris Facts',
➥ content: 'Chuck Norris always uses his own design patterns,
➥ and his favorite is the Roundhouse Kick.').save()

new qotd.Quote(author: 'Eric Raymond',
➥ content: 'Being a social outcast helps you stay concentrated
➥ on the really important things, like thinking and hacking.').save()
```

Let's use another dynamic method, `count()`, to make sure that your data was saved to the database correctly (we show the script output after `>>>`):

```
println qotd.Quote.count()
>>> 3
```

Looks good so far. It's getting tedious typing in that `qotd` package name before each command, so let's put an import into your script to cut down on the boilerplate and get on with business:

```
import qotd.*
println Quote.count()
>>> 3
```

Much clearer. Next it's time to roll up your sleeves and query your `Quote` database. To simplify database searches, Grails introduces special query methods on your domain class called *dynamic finders*. These special methods use the names of fields in your domain model to make querying as simple as this:

```
import qotd.*
def quote = Quote.findByAuthor("Larry Wall")
println quote.content
>>> There is more than one method to our madness.
```

Now that you know how to save and query, it's time to get your web application running. Exit the Grails console, and you'll learn how to get those quotes onto the web.

1.5 Adding UI actions

Let's get something on the web. To begin, you'll need an action on your `QuoteController` to return a random quote from our database. You'll work out the random selection later—for now, let's cut corners and fudge your sample data:

```
def random() {
    def staticQuote = new Quote(author: "Anonymous",
                content: "Real Programmers don't eat much Quiche")
    [ quote : staticQuote]
}
```

You'll also need to update your /grails-app/views/quote/random.gsp file to use your new `Quote` object:

```
<q>${quote.content}</q>
<p>${quote.author}</p>
```

You've got a nicer data model, but nothing else is new. This is a good time to refresh your browser and see your static quote passing through to the view. Give it a try to convince yourself it's working.

Now that you have a feel for passing model objects to the view, and now that you know enough querying to be dangerous, let's rework your action in the following listing to implement a real random database query.

Listing 1.3 A database-driven `random`

```
def random() {
    def allQuotes = Quote.list()                          // 1 Obtains list of quotes
    def randomQuote
    if (allQuotes.size() > 0) {
        def randomIdx = new Random().nextInt(allQuotes.size())   // 2 Selects random quote
        randomQuote = allQuotes[randomIdx]
    } else {
        randomQuote = new Quote(author: "Anonymous",      // 3 Generates default quote
            content: "Real Programmers Don't eat much Quiche")
    }
    [ quote : randomQuote]                                // 4 Passes quote to the view
}
```

With your reworked `random` action, you're starting to take advantage of real database data. The `list()` method ❶ returns the complete set of `Quote` objects from the quote table in the database and populates your `allQuotes` collection. If the collection has entries, select a random one ❷ based on an index into the collection; otherwise, use a static quote ❸. With the heavy lifting done, return a `randomQuote` object to the view in a variable called `quote` ❹, which you can access in the GSP file.

Now that you've got your QOTD random feature implemented, let's head back to http://localhost:8080/qotd/quote/random to see it in action. Figure 1.10 shows your random feature in action.

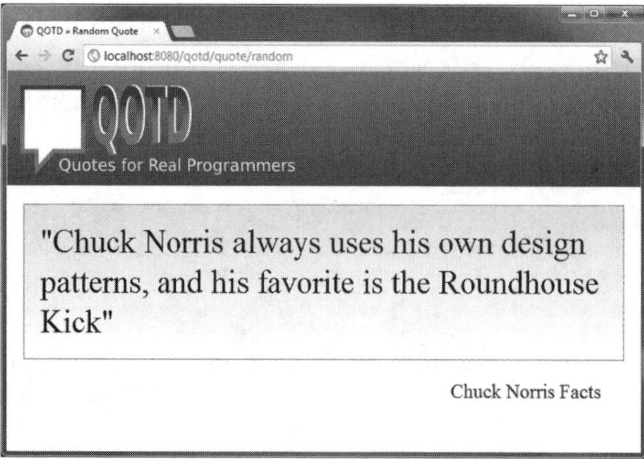

Figure 1.10 Your random quote feature in action

1.5.1 Scaffolding: adding rocket fuel

You've done all the hard work of creating your data model. Now you need to enhance your controller to handle all the CRUD actions to let users put their own quotes in the database.

That's if you want to do a slick job of it. If you want to get up and running quickly, Grails offers a fantastic shortcut called *scaffolding*. Scaffolds dynamically implement controller actions and views for the common things you'll want to do when adding CRUD actions to your data model.

How do you scaffold your screens for adding and updating quote-related data? It's a one-liner for the `QuoteController`, as shown in following code.

```
class QuoteController {
    static scaffold = true
   // our other stuff here...
}
```

That's it. When Grails sees a controller marked as `scaffold = true`, it creates controller actions and GSP views on the fly. If you'd like to see it in action, head to http://localhost:8080/qotd/quote/index and you'll find something like the edit page shown in figure 1.11. (Note that this used to be called in the `list()` action if you come across code written in Grails 2.2 and earlier.)

Click the New Quote button, and you're up and running. You can add your new quote as shown in figure 1.12.

See how much power you get for free? The generated scaffolds aren't tidy enough for your public-facing sites, but they're absolutely fantastic for your admin screens and

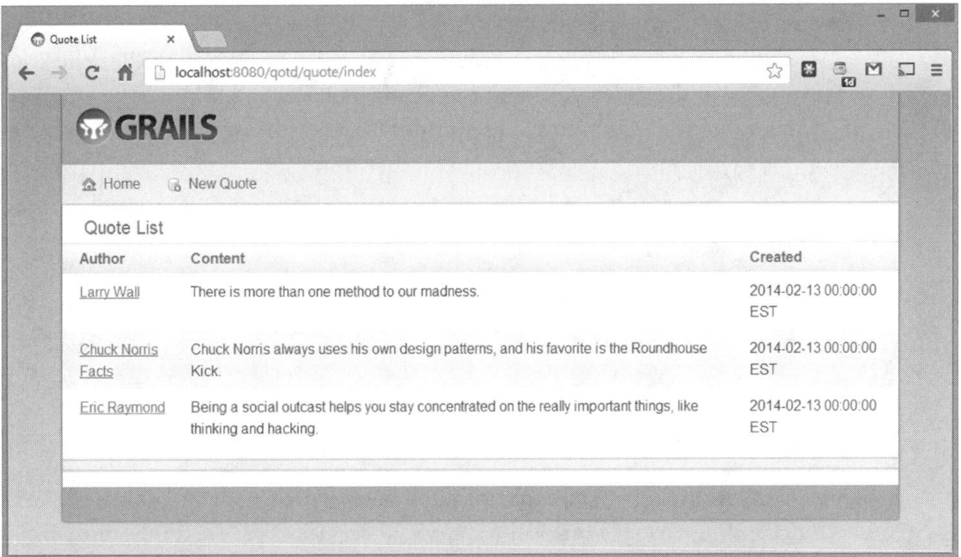

Quote List
localhost:8080/qotd/quote/index
GRAILS
Home
New Quote
Quote List
Author
Content
Created
Larry Wall
There is more than one method to our madness.
2014-02-13 00:00:00 EST
Chuck Norris Facts
Chuck Norris always uses his own design patterns, and his favorite is the Roundhouse Kick.
2014-02-13 00:00:00 EST
Eric Raymond
Being a social outcast helps you stay concentrated on the really important things, like thinking and hacking.
2014-02-13 00:00:00 EST

Figure 1.11 The `index()` scaffold in action

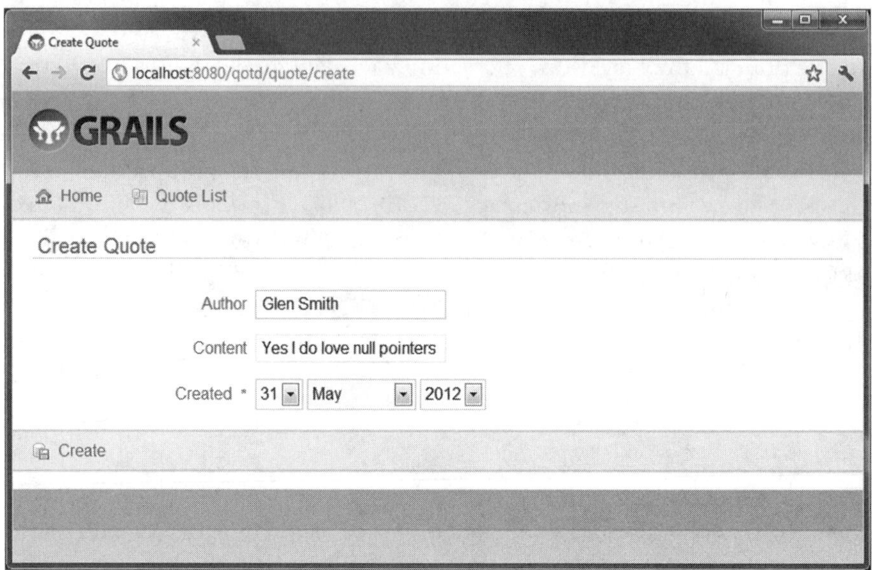

Figure 1.12 Adding a quote has never been easier.

perfect for tinkering with your database during development (where you don't want the overhead of mocking together multiple CRUD screens).

1.5.2 Surviving the worst-case scenario

Your model looks good and your scaffolds are great, but you're still missing pieces to make things more robust. You don't want users putting dodgy stuff in your database, so let's explore validation.

Validation is declared in your `Quote` object, so you need to populate the `constraints` closure with all the rules you'd like to apply. For starters, make sure that users always provide a value for the author and content fields, as shown in the following code:

```
package qotd

class Quote {
    String content
    String author
    Date created = new Date()

    static constraints = {
        author(blank:false)
        content(maxSize:1000, blank:false)
    }
}
```

Enforces data validation

These constraints tell Grails that neither `author` nor `content` can be blank (neither `null` nor `0` length). If you don't specify a size for `String` fields, they'll be defined `VARCHAR(255)` in your database. That's probably fine for `author` fields, but your content may expand on that. That's why you added a `maxSize` constraint.

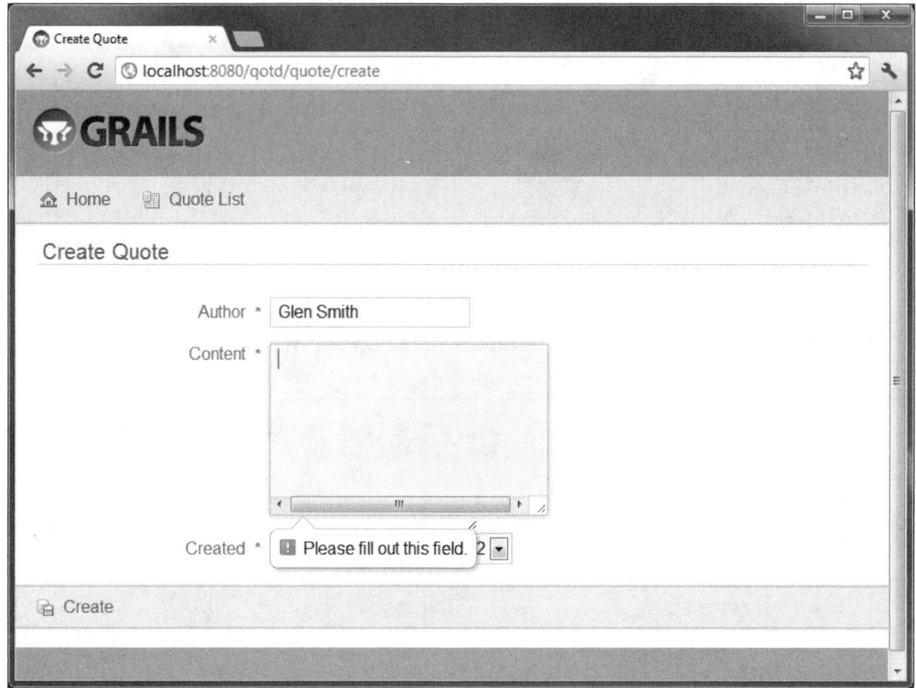

Figure 1.13 When constraints are violated, error messages appear in red.

Entries in the `constraints` closure also affect the generated scaffolds. (The ordering of entries in the `constraints` closure also affects the order of the fields in generated pages.) Fields with constraint sizes greater than 255 characters are rendered as HTML `<textarea>` elements rather than `<input>` fields. Figure 1.13 shows how error messages display when constraints are violated.

1.6 *Improving the architecture*

Spreading logic across your controller actions is all well and good. It's easy to track down what goes where in your small app, and maintenance isn't a concern right now. But as your quotation app grows, you'll find that your structure gets more complex. You'll want to reuse logic in different controller actions and even across controllers. It's time to tidy up your business logic, and the best way to do that in Grails is via a service.

Let's create your service and learn by doing:

```
grails create-service quote
```

which echoes back the familiar Grails artifact creation messages to let you know it's done:

```
| Created file grails-app/services/qotd/QuoteService.groovy
| Created file test/unit/qotd/QuoteServiceSpec.groovy
```

This command creates a skeleton quote service in /grails-app/services/qotd/QuoteService.groovy:

```
package qotd

import grails.transaction.Transactional

@Transactional
class QuoteService {
    def serviceMethod() {
    }
}
```

With your service created, let's rehome your random quote business logic into its own service method, as shown in the following listing.

Listing 1.4 Beefing up service

```
package qotd

import grails.transaction.Transactional

@Transactional
class QuoteService {

    def getStaticQuote() {
        return new Quote(author: "Anonymous",
            content: "Real Programmers Don't eat much quicheQuiche")
    }

    def getRandomQuote() {
        def allQuotes = Quote.list()
        def randomQuote = null
        if (allQuotes.size() > 0) {
            def randomIdx = new Random().nextInt(allQuotes.size())
            randomQuote = allQuotes[randomIdx]
        } else {
            randomQuote = getStaticQuote()
        }
        return randomQuote
    }
}
```

Now that your service is implemented, how do you use it in your controller? Again, conventions come into play. You'll add a new field to your controller called `quoteService`, and Grails will inject the service into the controller:

```
class QuoteController {
    static scaffold = true
    def quoteService
    // other code omitted
    def random = {
        def randomQuote = quoteService.getRandomQuote()
        [ quote : randomQuote ]
    }
}
```

Doesn't that feel much tidier? Your `QuoteService` looks after all the business logic related to quotes, and your `QuoteController` helps itself to the methods it needs. If you have experience with Inversion of Control (IoC) containers, such as Spring or Google Guice, you'll recognize this pattern of application design as dependency injection (DI). Grails takes DI to a new level by using the convention of variable names to determine what gets injected. But you have yet to write a test for your business logic, so now's the time to explore Grails's support for testing.

> **Services pre-Grails 2.3**
> The @Transactional annotation is new to Grails 2.3. In earlier versions, services were transactional by default. Don't try to add the annotation to your services if you are using one of those earlier versions.

1.6.1 Your Grails test case

Testing is a core part of today's agile approach to development, and Grails's support for testing is wired right into the framework. Grails is so insistent about testing that when you created your `QuoteService`, Grails automatically created a skeleton unit-test case in /test/unit/qotd/QuoteServiceSpec.groovy to encourage you to test.

Grails tests are written in a testing framework called Spock. You'll learn the basics of Spock testing in chapter 2, where we give you a proper introduction to the framework. For now, just consider Spock a "JUnit-like" testing framework where tests follow a more formal given/when/then structure.

> **Tests pre-Grails 2.3**
> Versions of Grails prior to 2.3 created standard JUnit tests rather than Spock ones. Chapter 2 shows you how to use Spock with those earlier versions.

Let's look at the skeleton test case that Grails generated.

```
package qotd

import grails.test.mixin.TestFor
import spock.lang.Specification

/**
 * See the API for {@link grails.test.mixin.services.ServiceUnitTestMixin}
     for usage instructions
 */
@TestFor(QuoteService)
class QuoteServiceSpec extends Specification {

    def setup() {
    }

    def cleanup() {
    }
```

```
    void "test something"() {
    }
}
```

It's not much, but it's enough to get started. The same convention over configuration rules apply to tests, so let's beef up your `QuoteServiceSpec` case to inject the service that's under test as shown in the following listing.

Listing 1.5 Adding real tests

```
}
package qotd

import grails.test.mixin.TestFor
import spock.lang.Specification

@TestFor(QuoteService)                                          // 1 Type of service to inject
class QuoteServiceSpec extends Specification {

    void "static quote service always returns quiche quote"() {

        when:
        Quote staticQuote = service.getStaticQuote()            // 2 Injects service dynamically at runtime

        then:
        staticQuote.author == "Anonymous"
        staticQuote.content == "Real Programmers Don't eat much quicheQuiche"

    }
}
```

Not much can go wrong with the `getStaticQuote()` routine, but let's give it a workout for completeness.

The Grails testing framework makes heavy use of Groovy Mixins at runtime (you'll learn about these in chapter 2) to decorate your test class with magic handles. In this example we've declared this test a `@TestFor(QuoteService)` ❶. This ❷ tells Grails to automatically inject a service object to the test scope that points to an instance of a real `QuoteService` object.

To run your tests, execute `grails test-app QuoteServiceSpec`. If you omit the test name, test-app runs all the tests, but in this case you're after only your newly minted test case. You should see something like the following results:

```
| Tests PASSED - view reports in target\test-reports
```

This code shows that your tests run fine. Grails also generates an HTML version of your test results, which you can view by opening /target/test-reports/html/index.html in a web browser. From there you can visually browse the entire project's test results and drill down to individual tests to see what failed and why, as shown in figure 1.14.

You'll learn how to amp up your test coverage in chapter 9, but for now you have a test up and running, and you know how to view the output.

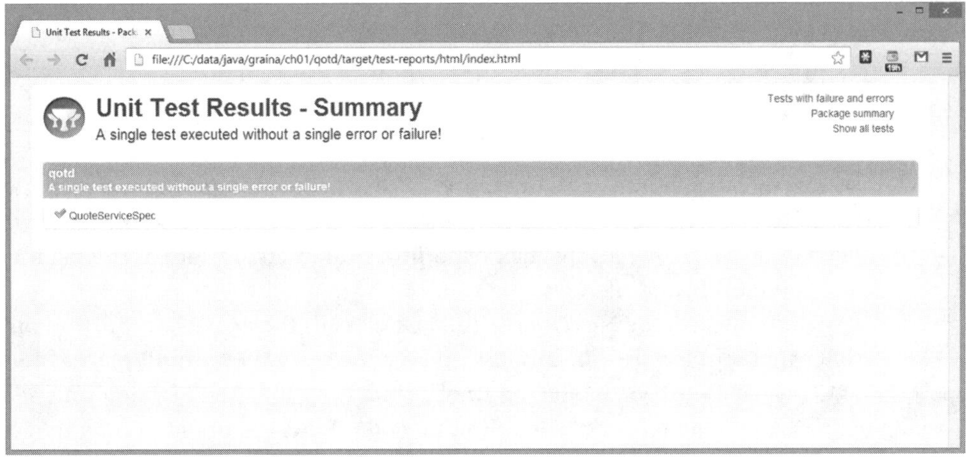

Figure 1.14 HTML reports from the unit test run

1.6.2 *Going Web 2.0: Ajaxing the view*

Our sample application wouldn't be complete without adding a little Ajax (Asynchronous JavaScript and XML) secret sauce to spice things up. If you don't know Ajax, it's a way of updating portions of a web page using JavaScript. Use Ajax to make your web application more responsive by updating the quote without having to reload the masthead banners and other page content. It also gives you a chance to look at Grails tag libraries.

Let's Ajaxify your random.gsp view:

- Add the Ajax library to the `<head>` element.

  You'll use jQuery, but Grails also lets you use Yahoo! Interface Library (YUI), Dojo, or others:

```
<head>
    <title>Random Quote</title>
    <g:javascript library="jquery" />
</head>
```

- In the page body of random.gsp, add a menu section that allows the user to display a new quote or navigate to the admin screens.

  You'll use Grails's taglibs to create both your Ajax link for refreshing quotes and your standard link for the admin interface. The following code shows your new menu HTML. Add this snippet before the `<div>` tag that hosts the body of the page:

```
<ul id="menu">
    <li>
        <g:remoteLink action="ajaxRandom" update="quote">
            Next Quote
        </g:remoteLink>
    </li>
```

```
        <li>
            <g:link action="index">
                Admin
            </g:link>
        </li>
    </ul>
```

You saw these tag library calls in section 1.3.3, where you used them to generate a standardized layout for your application. In this example, you introduce a `g:remoteLink`, which is Grails's name for an Ajax hyperlink, and `g:link`, which is the tag for generating a standard hyperlink.

When you click the Next Quote link, Grails calls the `ajaxRandom` action on the controller that sent it here—in this case, the `QuoteController`—and places the returned HTML inside the `<div>` that has an ID of `quote`. But you haven't written your `ajaxRandom` action, so let's get to work. The following code shows the updated fragment of `QuoteController.groovy` with the new action:

```
def ajaxRandom() {
    def randomQuote = quoteService.getRandomQuote()
    render {
        q(randomQuote.content)
        p(randomQuote.author)
    }
}
```

You've already done the heavy lifting in your quote service, so you can reuse that here. Because you don't want your Grails template to decorate your output, you're going to write your response directly to the browser (we'll talk about more elegant ways of doing this in later chapters).

We take advantage of Grails's HTML Builder to generate an HTML fragment on the fly. To satisfy your curiosity about the markup this code generates, go to http://localhost:8080/qotd/quote/ajaxRandom and see the generated HTML, which should look like this:

```
<q>Chuck Norris always uses his own design patterns, and his favorite is the
     Roundhouse Kick. </q><p>Chuck Norris Facts</p>
```

Whoa, there! What's with the embedded HTML?

In the previous sample, your render method call takes advantage of a Grails builder—a dynamic way of constructing objects of various sorts including XML, HTML, and JSON (more on these in chapter 2).

Grails also offers several other methods to achieve the same result here, including partial templates, which provide a more elegant and externalized way of achieving reusable HTML fragments. We'll talk more about this approach in chapter 8 when we discuss fragment layouts in detail.

Let's take your new Ajax app for a spin, as shown in figure 1.15.

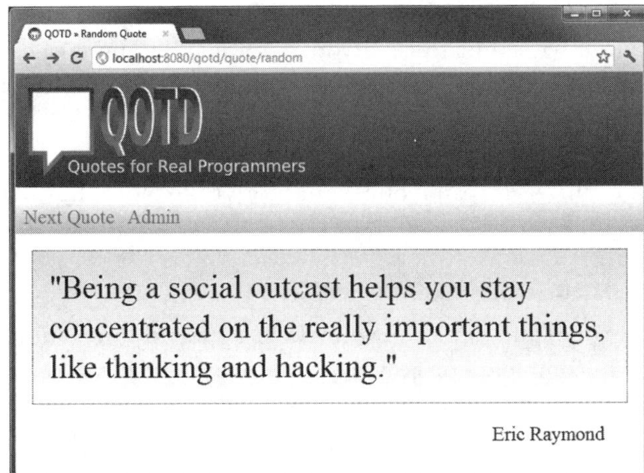

Figure 1.15 Your Ajax view in action

To convince yourself that all the Ajax snazziness is in play, click the Next Quote menu item several times. Did you notice there's no annoying repaint of the page? You're living the Web 2.0 dream.

1.6.3 Bundling the final product: creating a WAR file

Look how much you've achieved in half an hour! But it's no good running the app on your laptop—you need to set it free and deploy it to a real server on the cloud. For that, you'll need a WAR file, and Grails makes its creation a one-liner:

```
grails war
```

Watch the output, and you'll see Grails bundling up all the JARs it needs, along with your Grails application files, and creating the WAR file in your project's root directory:

```
| Done creating WAR target\qotd-0.1.war
```

Now you're ready to deploy.

1.6.4 And 80 lines of code later

You've learned about Grails. And you've created plenty of code, too. But don't take my word for it; let's have Grails crunch the numbers with a `grails stats` command. Table 1.1 shows the `grails stats` command in action.

Table 1.1 Crunching numbers: the `grails stats` command in action

```
grails stats

    +----------------------+-------+-------+
    | Name                 | Files |  LOC  |
    +----------------------+-------+-------+
    | Controllers          |     1 |    20 |
    | Domain Classes       |     1 |    10 |
    | Services             |     1 |    21 |
    | Unit Tests           |     3 |    39 |
    +----------------------+-------+-------+
    | Totals               |     6 |    90 |
    +----------------------+-------+-------+
```

Only 90 lines of code (LOC)! Not too shabby for an Ajax-powered, user-editable, random quote web application with unit tests. If you removed the empty skeleton test cases that Grails created for your domain, controller, and service classes, you would trim it down to 51 lines.

This Grails introduction has given you a taste of models, views, controllers, services, taglibs, layouts, and unit tests. And you've got more to explore. But before you go further, let's explore Groovy.

1.7 Summary and best practices

Congratulations, you've written and deployed your Grails app, and now you have a feel for working from scratch to completed project. The productivity rush can be addictive.

Here are a few key tips you should take away from this chapter:

- *Rapid iterations are key.* The most important takeaway for this chapter is that Grails fosters rapid iterations to get your application up and running in record time, and you'll have fun along the way.
- *Noise reduction fosters maintenance and increases velocity.* By embracing convention over configuration, Grails eliminates XML configuration that used to kill Java web frameworks.
- *Bootstrapping saves time.* For the few cases where you do need scaffolding code (for example, in UI design), Grails generates all the skeleton boilerplate code to get you up and running—another way Grails saves time.
- *Testing is inherent.* Grails makes writing test cases easy. It even creates skeleton artifacts for your test cases. Take the time to learn Grails's testing philosophy (which we'll look at in depth in chapter 7), and practice it in your daily development.

We'll spend the rest of the book taking you through the nuts and bolts of developing full-featured, robust, and maintainable web apps using Grails, and we'll point out the tips, tricks, and pitfalls along the way.

The Groovy essentials

2

This chapter covers

- Basics of the Groovy language
- Differences between Java and Groovy
- Groovy's power features

As you saw in chapter 1, you can get a Grails application running in no time. You can even take the principles you learned in that chapter to add extra features. But if you want to develop something more complex, such as the Twitter-clone we use as the example project in this book, you'll need to have a good grasp of the Groovy language.

Groovy is a dynamic, object-oriented language with a Java-like syntax. Furthermore, it integrates well with Java and the Java ecosystem: it runs on the JVM and uses JAR files for libraries. Java classes can depend on Groovy classes and vice versa. It's also fun! This chapter is an introduction to the language based on a couple of worked examples. We do assume that you already know at least one object-oriented language such as Java, Ruby, or PHP.

The aim of this chapter is to prepare you for the examples throughout the rest of the book, but the information contained in the chapter is practical enough that you can start using Groovy day-to-day for other projects or as a portable language for writing scripts. We're sure you'll find plenty of uses for it! We also introduce the Spock testing framework, which we use throughout the book. If you know Groovy but not Spock, we recommend that you read section 2.2 before moving on to the next chapter.

2.1 Writing your first script

Practical examples are one of the best ways to learn a new language, so we're going to take our Quote of the Day application from chapter 1 and add features that a developer or app administrator would likely find useful.

One problem you may have noticed while coding the QOTD app is that it's short of data. We're going to show you a technique for setting up sample data in chapter 5, but you still have to manually define the data or generate it somehow. We're feeling lazy, so we're going to write an automatic quote generator.

2.1.1 Using lists, loops, and methods

Remember the Grails console UI from the previous chapter? We used it to try out the persistence features of Grails, saving to and querying the database. This console UI can also be used to write plain Groovy scripts, which is what we're going to do now.

The idea behind your first script is to take a set of quote parts (a subject, a verb, and an object) and randomly combine them into distinct quotes. You then attribute each quote to a randomly selected author. The initial iteration of this script prints the generated quotes.

Fire up the console UI with the command

```
grails console
```

then type the code from the following listing into the upper window. You can find this example as dataGenerator.groovy in the chapter source code on GitHub.

Listing 2.1 Writing a Groovy script to generate quotes

```
def authors = [
    "Peter Ledbrook",
    "Glen Smith"
]

def quoteParts = [
    ["Time", "waits", "for no man"],
    ["The roundhouse kick", "solves", "all problems"],
    ["Groovy", "is", "the bees knees"]
]

for (int i in 0..<10) {
    def quote = createQuote(quoteParts, authors)
    println quote
}

String createQuote(List quoteParts, List authors) {
    def rand = new Random()
    def n = quoteParts.size()
    def m = authors.size()
```

Declares an untyped local variable, `authors`, and initializes it with a list of strings.

You can nest lists (and maps). This is a list of lists.

Loops over the numbers 0 to 9 inclusive. 0..<10 is a literal of type groovy.lang.Range.

A simple method call.

Defines a reusable method in the script, with the method body bounded by curly braces, {}.

```
    return quoteParts[rand.nextInt(n)][0] + ' ' +
        quoteParts[rand.nextInt(n)][1] + ' ' +
        quoteParts[rand.nextInt(n)][2] + ' by ' +
        authors[rand.nextInt(m)]
}
```

Accesses list elements by index using square brackets, [].

When you run this script, you'll see random quotes and awful grammar. That's the price of laziness. Fortunately, your English teacher will almost certainly never see them.

> **The two consoles**
>
> Grails occasionally leaves ambiguity in its naming. One instance of this is the name "console". It can refer to either the console UI for writing scripts (started with the `grails console` command) or the interactive console for speedy execution of Grails commands (started with `grails`). We use the terms "console UI" for the former and "interactive console" for the latter to differentiate them.
>
> If you have Groovy installed separately, you can use its `groovyConsole` command to start a similar console UI. The main difference is that it doesn't give you access to the classes in your Grails application, though it's great for trying out standalone Groovy code.

We've highlighted the most important elements of the example application in the code sample itself, but a few of the things we've introduced deserve more attention. What else should you take away from this first iteration?

OPTIONAL TYPES

Unlike almost any other language, Groovy has the concept of optional types. That means you can declare variables, arguments, and method returns as having a specific type, or you can leave types out. It's up to you. It's a powerful feature but can lead to confusion.

Let's take another look at the `createQuote()` method from the example. We declared that it takes two `List` arguments:

```
String createQuote(List quoteParts, List authors) { … }
```

What happens if we try to pass an argument that's not a list? Try replacing the line

```
def quote = createQuote(quoteParts, authors)
```

with

```
def quote = createQuote(quoteParts, "test")
```

and running the script again. What you'll see is the result of an exception:

```
groovy.lang.MissingMethodException: No signature of method:
     ConsoleScript1.createQuote() is applicable for argument types:
     (java.util.ArrayList, java.lang.String) values: [[[Time, waits, for no
     man], [The roundhouse kick, ...], ...], ...]
```

```
Possible solutions: createQuote(java.util.List, java.util.List)
at ConsoleScript1.run(ConsoleScript1:13)
at
org.springsource.loaded.ri.ReflectiveInterceptor.jlrMethodInvoke(ReflectiveIn
     terceptor.java:1254)
```

That's not a pretty sight, but the key here is that you get a runtime exception not a compiler error (even Groovy scripts are compiled before they're run, but you don't see the compilation step). If that's the case, why bother with explicitly declaring types? Well, the types are still enforced at runtime, which can lead to errors that are easier to diagnose. On top of that, it acts as helpful documentation for the user of the method or API.

This is an important topic that we come back to later in this chapter when we discuss compiler type-checking and best practice. In the meantime, we strongly recommend that you read fully the error messages from `MissingMethodExceptions` and the related `MissingPropertyExceptions`. They usually provide all the information you need to understand why they occurred.

THE FOR LOOP

If you don't come from a Java background, you may wonder why we want to discuss the humble `for` loop. It's because the most common Groovy `for` loop doesn't match the syntax of the standard Java versions. You can use the Java syntax if you wish, but we encourage you to use the `in` keyword instead:

```
for (int i in 0..<10) { … }
```

The Java-style counting loop (typically used for iterating numbers) can be handy if you want a step size of anything other than one, but it doesn't offer performance benefits and is plain ugly. On top of that, you can't include other variables in the `for` declaration. This is completely invalid Groovy, even though it's valid Java:

```
for (int i = 0, n = someList.size(); i < n; i++) { … }
```

Put simply, stick to the idiomatic Groovy `for` loop.

There's one last thing we want to mention before moving on. We talked about Groovy's optional types, so it's a good time to mention that this feature also applies to `for` loops. You can write

```
for (i in 0..<10) { … }
```

and get exactly the same behavior as before. But if you declare an incompatible type for the variable `i`, such as `Date`, you get a `GroovyClassCastException`.

You'll see more example loops in this chapter, so you'll quickly pick up how to use them.

The autocoercion minefield

In certain circumstances, Groovy will automatically coerce values of one type to another. We mention this now because you may try code like this:

```
for (String i in 0..<10) { … }
```

expecting a `GroovyClassCastException`. But in fact, `i` takes the values `"0"`, `"1"`, `"2"`, and so on. You'll only ever see auto-coercion between different number types or when `String` is the target. Even then, it's rarely a problem except when you're trying to demonstrate enforcement of types to readers or students.

VARIABLE SCOPE IN SCRIPT METHODS

Defining methods in scripts is convenient for introducing reuse without going the whole nine yards and creating custom classes. It also helps keep scripts understandable. One little issue that you need to be aware of is that methods can't see local variables defined in the script.

To demonstrate the issue, change the signature of the `createQuote()` method to

```
String createQuote() { … }
```

and replace the line that calls the `createQuote()` method with

```
def quote = createQuote()
```

You might expect that `createQuote()` will still work because it looks like the script's `quoteParts` and `authors` variables are visible to the method, but when you run the script with the changes, you'll see a `MissingPropertyException` for `quoteParts`.

A full explanation for this behavior is too advanced for this chapter. Instead, we'll leave it as an exercise for the keen among you to investigate how scripts are turned into instances of `groovy.lang.Script`. For everyone else, all you need to know is that methods inside scripts don't have access to local variables declared outside of them.

USE OF JAVA CLASSES

Most major languages have their own class library geared toward that language. Groovy is different in that it piggybacks on the standard Java class library. Your strings are of type `java.lang.String`, your dates of type `java.util.Date`, and so on. That means when you develop in Groovy, you should always keep the Java API docs[1] open.

You might think that this limits the language somewhat. Don't worry. Not only does Groovy add its own classes into the mix, such as the `groovy.lang.Range` type we mention in our example, but it also enhances the standard Java classes, as you'll see shortly.

While we're on the topic of the standard Java classes, it's useful to note that you don't have to explicitly import them. In Java, the only classes you don't have to explicitly import are in the `java.lang` package. Groovy automatically imports those classes

1 Java Platform, Standard Edition 7 API Specification, http://docs.oracle.com/javase/7/docs/api/.

and everything in `java.util`, `java.net`, `java.io`, and `groovy.lang` as well (among others). This explains why you didn't have to import `java.util.List` in the example.

That's enough about the first example. We've gone into detail about several of the features it presents, and you've learned useful nuggets of information, such as how the types work. Let's get back to the fun stuff by introducing string manipulation.

2.1.2 Working with strings

The next iteration of our example sees us converting the generated quotes into a form of Pig Latin. This is a fun little word game that involves simple manipulation of words, turning them into something unrecognizable to the average English speaker. The rules for modifying words vary, but in this case we're going to use Wikipedia[2] as our source.

For words that begin with consonant sounds, the initial consonant or consonant cluster is moved to the end of the word, and "ay" is added, as in the following examples:

- "happy" becomes *appyhay*
- "duck" becomes *uckday*
- "glove" becomes *oveglay*

For words that begin with vowel sounds or silent letter, "way" is added at the end of the word:

- "egg" becomes *eggway*
- "inbox" becomes *inboxway*
- "eight" becomes *eightway*

It's difficult to deal with the silent letter requirement, so we treat those words as if they start with a consonant group. Otherwise that's it. You can easily implement the nice and straightforward logic with a few distinct methods. Add the code in the following listing to the previous example (new code is in italics).

Listing 2.2 Converting quotes into Pig Latin

```
. . .
for (int i in 0..<10) {
    def quote = createQuote(quoteParts, authors)
    println quote

    def pigLatinWords = []
    for (String word in quote.split(/\s+/)) {
        pigLatinWords << pigLatinize(word)
    }

    println pigLatinWords.join(' ')
}
```

Creates new, empty list (`def pigLatinWords = []`)

Splits quotes into words and turns each word into Pig Latin (the inner `for` loop)

2 Learn to speak Pig Latin: http://en.wikipedia.org/wiki/Pig_Latin.

```
String createQuote(List quoteParts, List authors) {
    . . .
}

def pigLatinize(String word) {
    if (isVowel(word[0])) {
        return word + "way"
    }
    else {
        def pos = firstVowel(word)
        return word[pos..-1] + word[0..<pos] + "ay"
    }
}

def firstVowel(String word) {
    for (int i in 0..<word.size()) {
        if (isVowel(word[i])) return i
    }

    return -1
}

boolean isVowel(String ch) {
    return ch.toLowerCase() in ["a", "e", "i", "o", "u"]
}
```

Extracts a character through the array-style accessor

Extracts substrings using a range; a negative index applies from the end of the string, where -1 is the last character of the string

Uses the result of a method as the upper bound of a range

Uses the `in` keyword as a Boolean condition

This extended example demonstrates a couple of points about strings in Groovy: first, manipulating them is easy; and second, they're treated as sequences of characters. The latter means you get a uniform API for working with arrays, lists, and strings so you don't have to exercise your memory so hard. As an example, the syntax for extracting a substring, `word[pos-1]`, can also be used to get a slice of a list or an array.

Before we talk a bit more about strings, we want to satisfy your curiosity about the new `for` loop we added:

```
def pigLatinWords = []
for (String word in quote.split(/\s+/)) {
    pigLatinWords << pigLatinize(word)
}
```

This is the first `for` loop that iterates over an array or collection rather than a range, yet you'll see the syntax is the same. Of more interest are the new Groovy features that you'll become gradually more familiar with as we go through the book:

- Slashy strings
- The Groovy JDK
- Operator overloading

Slashy strings are string literals that have a unique property: you don't need to escape the backslash (\) character. If you were to use double-quotes instead of slashes, you'd end up with `"\\s+"` as the argument to `split()` in the example. This makes slashy strings particularly useful for regular expressions, which tend to have plenty of backslashes in them.

The `split()` method is part of the standard Java class library, and you'll find it in the Java API docs, but the left-shift operator (`<<`) and the `join()` method are different: they apply to Java lists and arrays, but they aren't provided by the Java runtime. These are examples of Groovy *enhancing* the Java class library to provide useful extra features. If you're a Java developer, you'll soon wonder how you lived without them! These extensions to the Java class library are listed and described in the Groovy JDK documentation.[3]

When you look for `<<` in the documentation, though, you won't find it. That's because its implementation is in the method `leftShift()`. The Groovy JDK docs for `Collection` tell you this method adds an item to the collection. But you'll also see the method defined on `StringBuilder`, `File`, and `OutputStream`, among others. The `<<` operator generally has the semantics of appending, whether that's adding an item to a collection, appending text to a `StringBuilder`, or writing data to a stream.

The relationship between `<<` and the `leftShift()` method is important because it underpins Groovy's operator overloading. If a class implements a method that has the right name and signature, you can also use the corresponding operator with objects of that class. Imagine you have a class representing a matrix: you could add a `plus()` method to it that would then allow you to use the `+` operator for adding matrices together. We provide a list of operator-to-method mappings in appendix A.

Be careful with adding operator support to your own classes. It can be a recipe for confusion and result in users always referring to your API docs. You have to be sure that your class closely matches the standard semantics of the operators you want to use. For example, don't use `<<` to send an email. The concept of sending something doesn't match the standard semantics of adding or appending data. The mail server isn't aggregating the emails but routing them to a destination. An explicit `send()` method is much better in this case. When in doubt, avoid operator overloading.

We covered many of the basics of Groovy with this one example and had fun with Pig Latin, too. As you can see, Groovy makes a great cross-platform language for writing scripts—as long as you have a JDK installed. It's also a nice language for developing more structured applications, such as a Grails app! In the next section we'll look at the building blocks of such applications: classes. We'll also introduce you to even more Groovy goodness.

2.2 Creating a quote analyzer class

Our Quote of the Day application contains several quotes now, and it might be interesting to get statistics from those quotes. How many quotes are there? What's the average number of words per quote? How many quotes are there for each author? This information could be useful in the QOTD app itself, in another web application sharing the same database, or in a system admin's script. It makes sense to encapsulate the required analysis and data in a reusable class.

---

[3] "Groovy JDK API Specification Version 2.2.1, describing methods added to the JDK to make it more groovy," http://groovy.codehaus.org/groovy-jdk/.

We could start coding the analysis engine straightaway, but one of our primary goals for the second edition of this book is to hardwire testing into every chapter. We're not test-driven development (TDD) snobs, nor are we "one true way" advocates, but we do think you'll see great benefits from writing tests.

Seeing your tests pass is a great confidence booster, and when you constantly run tests, you feel as if your app is making progress. You also gain confidence when refactoring, because if you introduce any errors, the tests tell you what you've broken long before a user does! Finally, writing tests helps you focus on what the behavior of the code should be before you've written it, and your classes become easy to test because the test case already exists.

Your first step is writing the `QuoteAnalyzer` test case. You could use JUnit for this, but we recommend Spock. We use it throughout the book, so now is a good time to learn about it. Due to its high readability, it's also a great tool for teaching you about all the features of Grails.

2.2.1 Introducing Spock properly

As you discovered in chapter 1, Grails 2.3 creates unit tests based on a framework called Spock. If you come from a Java background you're likely comfortable with the JUnit style of testing. After all, JUnit is the granddaddy of Java unit testing tools. The Grails community has largely moved to Spock (www.spockframework.org), which we consider more powerful, concise, and expressive than JUnit. Spock marries behavior-driven development (BDD) techniques with JUnit mechanics and adds plenty of extra sauce.

Spock in Grails 2.2 and earlier

If you're using a pre-2.3 version of Grails, you need to install a plugin in order to use Spock. We'll cover Grails plugins in more detail in chapter 10, but for now you need to add some dependencies to your project's grails-app/conf/BuildConfig.groovy file. The exact syntax depends on your Grails version. For 2.0.x and 2.1.x use

```
plugins {
    . . .
    test ":spock:0.7"
}
```

The syntax for Grails 2.2.x is more involved:

```
dependencies {
    test "org.spockframework:spock-grails-support:0.7-groovy-2.0"
}
plugins {
    . . .
    test(":spock:0.7") {
        exclude "spock-grails-support"
    }
}
```

(*continued*)

Spock has different JARs for different versions of Groovy, hence the different syntaxes (Grails 2.2.x was the first Grails version to use Groovy 2). When you next execute `grails compile` or `grails refresh-dependencies`, Grails will download and install the Spock plugin and all the dependencies it needs.

CREATING YOUR FIRST SPECIFICATION

In this section, you'll create a simple class that performs analysis on a set of quotes. The class doesn't need access to the database because you'll pass in the quotes as method arguments, so a simple unit test will suffice. All it does is process quotes and determine things such as the average character length of the quotes and the number of quotes per author.

To get started, run the command

```
grails create-unit-test qotd.QuoteAnalyzer
```

to create a skeleton Spock specification in the file QuoteAnalyzerSpec.groovy under the directory test/unit/qotd. This file includes an `@TestMixin` annotation, but you don't need it in this case because `QuoteAnalyzer` is a plain, standalone class. It's not a Grails artifact, like a domain class or a controller. We'll talk in more depth about the test mixins in chapter 9, so don't worry about it right now.

Packages and file paths

Packages are the namespace mechanism for Java and Groovy. The combination of class name and package must be unique within a project, but it's a good idea to have unique class names even across packages to avoid confusion and make it easier to work with the project in an IDE.

You've probably noticed by now that Grails commands create files in a directory structure that matches a class's package; for example, qotd/QuoteAnalyzer.groovy for the class `qotd.QuoteAnalyzer`. That's intentional. Although Groovy doesn't require them to match, Grails makes that assumption when determining whether the source file for a class has been modified. If files in your project are constantly being recompiled even if they haven't been modified, you probably have a mismatch between the source file's path and the name of the package or class.

After you open the specification file in an editor, replace its content with listing 2.3. The code includes a single test, which allows us to focus on the structure of Spock specifications.

Listing 2.3 Your first Spock specification

```
package qotd

import spock.lang.*
```

```
class QuoteAnalyzerSpec extends Specification {
    @Shared quotes = [
            new Quote(author: "Peter Ledbrook",
                    content: "Time waits for no man"),
            new Quote(author: "Glen Smith",
                    content: "Groovy solves all problems")]

    def "Total number of quotes"() {
        given: "An analyzer initialized with known quotes"
        def analyzer = new QuoteAnalyzer(quotes)

        when: "I ask for the quote count"
        def quoteCount = analyzer.quoteCount

        then: "The number of quotes in the test list is returned"
        quoteCount == 2
    }
}
```

Spock tests extend spock.lang.Specification.

Variables shared between feature methods are annotated this way.

Feature method names are plain English—with spaces!

Initial conditions.

Execution.

Result verification. This is an implicit assert.

The key point to take away from this example is that Spock feature methods (the methods that test a single feature each) have an inherent structure based on these `given`, `when`, and `then` blocks. You set up the test's initial conditions in `given`, call the method or property you're testing in `when`, and verify that the result is what you expect in `then`.

The order of the blocks is fixed—`given` -> `when` -> `then`—but otherwise you can write code as you like. In particular you can create local variables as you would in any other Groovy method, and those variables can be accessed from subsequent blocks.

Note that the string literals after each block label are documentation and have no impact on the test code. The only requirement is that they must be on the same line as their corresponding label.

This approach may take a little while to get used to, and you may wonder why this structure is important, but we believe you'll soon discover that formulating test cases using this structure is much easier. On top of that, Spock has genuine power features that will undoubtedly delight you, such as parameterized feature methods.

TESTING MULTIPLE DATA SETS

Whenever you test code, you want to make sure you're exercising it with a variety of inputs. What happens if the quote analyzer is created with an empty list of quotes? Or what if the list is `null`? More complex code often has additional special cases that you need to test. Copying and pasting the test code with the different inputs and expected outputs isn't uncommon, but it's a maintenance nightmare and guarantees tests that are hard to read.

What you need is a way to parameterize the inputs and outputs so that the testing tool reruns the same code with the different data. Spock has exactly what you need: data-driven feature methods. The best way to explain these is through example, so let's see in the following listing how to add extra data sets to the existing test case.

Listing 2.4 Adding multiple data sets to a test

```
package qotd

import spock.lang.*

class QuoteAnalyzerSpec extends Specification {
    @Shared quotes = [
            new Quote(author: "Peter Ledbrook",
                      content: "Time waits for no man"),
            new Quote(author: "Glen Smith",
                      content: "Groovy solves all problems") ]

    @Unroll
    def "Total number of quotes"() {
        given: "An analyzer initialized with known quotes"
        def analyzer = new QuoteAnalyzer(inputQuotes)

        when: "I ask for the quote count"
        def quoteCount = analyzer.quoteCount

        then: "The number of quotes in the test list is returned"
        quoteCount == expected

        where:
        inputQuotes       |    expected
           []             |       0
         quotes           |       2
    }
}
```

Reports each data set as a separate test (highly recommended)

Initialize using an undeclared variable, `inputQuotes`

Compare against another undeclared variable, `expected`

Tabulate the data with the header row containing the parameterized variable names

How good is that? You can add as many data sets as you like by adding extra rows to the table, and you can add more parameterized variables in extra columns (separated by the vertical bar, "|"). The test is incredibly readable and even developers who don't know Spock will be able to work out what's going on.

Spock tests give us a consistent structure for the specifications and allow you to document them through the feature method names and the string literals attached to each block. Even if you exclude the power features, these basic attributes of Spock tests make it far easier to write and read test cases. That's why we strongly recommend you use Spock yourself and why we think it serves as a great base for explaining features of both Groovy and Grails. You can still run Spock specifications as JUnit test cases in your IDE, so you're not losing any convenience!

For now, run the test case using the command

```
grails test-app unit:
```

The test will fail, but we fix that next.

2.2.2 Creating the initial class

The current specification will fail because it tries to instantiate a class that doesn't exist. You need to create the class. The question is, where? You saw several different classes in chapter 1, but they were all Grails *artifacts*, that is, classes with a special role understood by Grails. Our quote analyzer has no special role, so there's no command to run or artifact directory to put it in.

Such classes do have a home in a Grails project: either src/groovy or src/java depending on what language you write them in. We prefer to write Groovy, so create the file QuoteAnalyzer.groovy in the directory src/groovy/qotd and put this code in it, as shown in the following listing.

Listing 2.5 Implementing the quote analyzer

```
package qotd

class QuoteAnalyzer {
    private final List<Quote> quotes

    QuoteAnalyzer(List<Quote> quotes) {
        this.quotes = new ArrayList(quotes)
    }

    int getQuoteCount() {
        return this.quotes.size()
    }
}
```

Declares a field (not a property) that's accessible only to the methods in the class.

Adds custom constructor (or object initializer).

The getter method is treated as a read-only property.

Note that this class is in the same package as the specification class. That's not required, but it's common practice, and we recommend you follow the convention.

This short bit of code, which satisfies the requirements of our specification, introduces a couple of important concepts in Groovy: classifiers and properties. Let's look at them in turn.

CLASSIFIERS

The `quotes` field (we'll explain why it's a field and not a property next) has two special keywords attached to its declaration: `final` and `private`. These keywords are known as *classifiers*, which aren't required for the declaration of a field but allow you to control certain elements of behavior. What do they do? Table 2.1 describes them and other common classifiers.

Table 2.1 Classifiers for classes, fields, properties, and methods

Keyword	Description
`final`	Declares either that a property can't be modified once initialized or that a method can't be overridden. Often combined with static to define constants.
`private`	Property or method is accessible only in the class.
`protected`	Property or method is accessible only in the class, from subclasses, or from classes in the same package.
`public`	Default scope; property or method is globally accessible from any code.
`static`	Property or method can be accessed without a corresponding instance of the class. Another way to look at it (in the case of properties) is that the state is shared between all instances of the class.

The only tricky concept in the table is perhaps the meaning of `static`, but PHP and Ruby, for example, both have the same idea, PHP with its own `static` keyword and Ruby with class variables and methods.

> **Honoring classifiers**
>
> Groovy is lax in enforcing the behavior you specify through classifiers. For example, `private` fields and methods can still be accessed from other classes. Enforcement of `final` is also a touch patchy. Still, it's worth using classifiers if only for documenting the intended behavior.

That leaves the question of whether fields and properties are the same thing.

PROPERTIES

Fields are the repositories of state for objects, and so are properties. The syntax for accessing fields is the same as for properties. Here's how the quote analyzer specification gets the quote count:

```
def quoteCount = analyzer.quoteCount
```

From the perspective of the caller, `quoteCount` could be a field or a property. In this case it's a property. In fact, it's a read-only property. You may have already worked out why: properties are defined by getter and setter methods, such as `getQuoteCount()`. You can only change the value of a property if it has a setter method. Otherwise it's read-only.

Most of the time, you don't bother to create getter and setter methods unless you want to do something special, such as calculate a property's value on demand. You're more likely to declare the property like a field:

```
class Person {
    String name
    int age
}
```

These are properties because they lack an explicit classifier, such as `public` or `private`. And unlike a field, you can call the getter and setter methods even though they're not explicitly defined:

```
def person = new Person(name: "Peter Ledbrook", age: 38)
println person.getName()
```

Try it out in the Grails or Groovy console to be sure.

That last fragment of code introduces a complementary feature of properties: the GroovyBeans constructor. It allows you to initialize an object on creation without explicitly declaring any constructors. You provide a comma-separated list of `propertyName: initialValue` pairs. Note that this works only with properties, not fields! If you try it with a field, you'll get a `MissingMethodException` for the corresponding getter or setter method.

The structure of classes and properties is important, but it's hardly interesting. Let's instead move on to problem-solving code by calculating other quote statistics. You'll get the hang of classes and properties from the numerous examples in the book!

2.2.3 Working with maps

Much of programming is about data structures and algorithms. Our first example in this chapter made use of lists, which are instances of an important data structure that crops up time and again in Grails code. An equally important structure is the map, sometimes known as an associative array in other languages. Our next example demonstrates how handy maps are and how easy they are to work with in Groovy.

Your analyzer already calculates the total number of quotes (not a particularly hard job), so why not extend that to calculate the number of quotes per author? Your method can return a map containing pairs of authors and quote count. Let's first describe how it should work by adding an extra feature method called `getQuoteCountPerAuthor()` to the analyzer's specification, as shown in the following listing.

Listing 2.6 Adding a test method for the `getQuoteCountPerAuthor()` method

```
. . .
class QuoteAnalyzerSpec extends Specification {
    @Shared quotes = [ … ]
    . . .
    @Unroll
    def "Number of quotes per author"() {
        given: "An analyzer initialized with known quotes"
        def analyzer = new QuoteAnalyzer(quoteList)

        expect: "The per-author quote count is correct"
        expected == analyzer.quoteCountPerAuthor

        where:
        quoteList     | expected
        []            | [:]
        quotes        | ["Peter Ledbrook": 1, "Glen Smith": 1]
    }
}
```

expect allows you to combine when and then in one block.

Source data contains only two authors with one quote each.

You can implement the `getQuoteCountPerAuthor()` method (remember it can be accessed as the read-only property `quoteCountPerAuthor`) any number of ways, but we'll stick to a simple loop that iterates over the quotes and updates a map containing the quote counts. The following listing shows the implementation we propose.

Listing 2.7 Implementing `getQuotePerAuthor()`

```
. . .
class QuoteAnalyzer {
    . . .
    Map<String, Integer> getQuoteCountPerAuthor() {
        def result = [:]
```

Integer must be used instead of int in parameterized types.

Creates new, empty map.

```
        for (Quote quote in quotes) {
            if (result.containsKey(quote.author)) {
                result[quote.author] = result[quote.author] + 1
            }
            else {
                result[quote.author] = 1
            }
        }
        return result
    }
}
```

Uses square-bracket array-like access to get and put key values.

Just as lists in Groovy are instances of `java.util.List`, maps are instances of `java.util.Map`. Yet creating and working with maps in Groovy is far nicer than in Java. Not only do you get useful syntax sugar, but Groovy also adds a host of useful methods to maps that aren't provided by the JDK class itself.

One oddity that crops up in this example is the use of the type `Integer` in the parameterized return type. This occurs because Java's generics don't support primitive types, such as `int` and `double`, and Groovy inherits this restriction. Otherwise, Groovy is flexible because you can treat even primitive types as objects. Try this in the Grails or Groovy console UI:

```
int i = -101
i = i.abs()
println i
```

You can call methods even on instances of primitive types.

When you declare integer properties or method arguments, you can safely choose either `int` or `Integer`. For all practical purposes, the only difference between them (in Groovy) is that `Integer` variables can be `null`.

Before we look at some of the advanced features of Groovy, we'll round out this section with an example of error handling and file manipulation. If you come from a Java background, we're sure to impress you with how easy it is!

2.2.4 Taking the analyzer for a spin

The `QuoteAnalyzer` class isn't much use unless you use it. We're going to write another script that analyzes the quotes in the database, produces a report from the statistics, and writes that report to a file. It's straightforward and plays to Groovy's strengths.

Enter the content shown in the following listing into the Grails console UI and run the script.

Listing 2.8 Creating the `quoteStatistics.groovy` script

```
import qotd.QuoteAnalyzer
import qotd.Quote

new Quote(
    author: "Peter Ledbrook",
    content: "Time waits for no man").save()
```

```
new Quote(
    author: "Glen Smith",
    content: "Groovy solves all problems").save(flush: true)

def analyzer = new QuoteAnalyzer(Quote.list())          <-- Loads all quotes from the database.
try {
    def reportFile = new File("report.txt")
    reportFile.withPrintWriter { w ->
        w.println """\                    <-- Triple-quotes allow for multiline strings: "\" is the line-continuation character.
Quote report
------------

Total: ${analyzer.quoteCount}            <-- Embeds a Groovy expression in a double-quote string.

Number of quotes by author:
"""
        for (entry in analyzer.quoteCountPerAuthor) {
            w.println "  " + entry.key.padRight(20) + entry.value    <-- Each map entry's key is the author name; the value is the quote count.
        }
    }

    println reportFile.text
}
catch (IOException ex) {                 <-- try/catch/finally blocks are the main mechanism for error handling.
    println "Unable to write to the 'report.txt' file!"
}
```

This example has so much to talk about—where should we start? Let's begin with running the script, because you can't run it with the `groovy` command or in the Groovy console UI. That's for two reasons:

1. The `Quote` and `QuoteAnalyzer` classes must be on the classpath of the script, otherwise they won't be found.
2. The script uses Grails Object-Relational Mapping (GORM) to retrieve the quotes from the database. We dive into GORM properly in chapter 3.

The Grails console UI solves both these problems by including all the project's classes on the classpath and enabling GORM.

RUNNING THE SCRIPT

What if you want to run this script regularly? You definitely don't want to type it out each time. Instead, you can save it to a file from the console UI. We typically save such scripts into files in the root of the project with camel-case names, such as quoteStatistics.groovy. You can load the script into the console UI at a later date and run it from there.

When you run the script, it should print a simple report to the console indicating two quotes, one for each author. You can then readily view the saved report by opening the generated report.txt file in an editor.

One thing to note is that we suggested you save the script in the root of the project directory. So then what's the "scripts" directory for? It has a special role in that any scripts inside it are treated as part of the Grails build system. This means you can write your own Grails commands. We talk more about the build system in chapter 17.

> **The run-script command**
>
> You can also run plain Groovy scripts directly from their files by using the run-script command:
>
> ```
> grails run-script quoteStatistics.groovy
> ```
>
> This is broken in early Grails 2.3 versions but works fine in 2.3.4 and above and Grails 2.2.x and earlier.

What about the script code itself? We'll discuss saving and querying domain classes more fully in chapters 3 and 5, so we'll skip straight to exception handling.

ERROR HANDLING WITH EXCEPTIONS

Exceptions are *de rigeur* in object-oriented languages, and Groovy is no exception (pardon the pun). In the example, we handle only instances of `IOException` or its subclasses—all other exceptions bubble up to the Java runtime, which stops execution and dumps the exception stack trace to the console. You can also add a `finally` block after all of your `catch` clauses to do something regardless of whether or not an exception was thrown.

You have flexibility in what exceptions you catch and handle. With Groovy 2 (and hence Grails 2.2+), you can even declare multiple exceptions in a single `catch`. Ultimately, all exceptions and errors must inherit from the class `java.lang.Throwable`, as shown in figure 2.1.

On the whole, you don't need to worry about the difference between `Exception` and `RuntimeException` in Groovy. You're not required to catch checked exceptions (unlike in Java) or runtime (unchecked) ones. The only time it becomes important is when you integrate with Java libraries, such as Spring and its transaction processing (as you'll see in chapter 14). We do recommend that you extend `RuntimeException` whenever you create your own exceptions, though. It makes for the smoothest integration with Java and Java libraries.

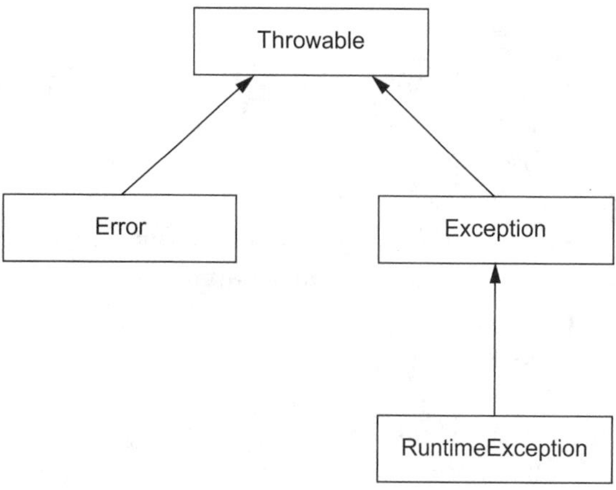

Figure 2.1 The base Groovy exception class hierarchy

Speaking of creating your own exceptions, how do you raise your own errors? With the throw statement:

```
throw new IllegalArgumentException("<error message>")
```

As you can see, you have to pass an *instance* of an exception to throw. Here we use a standard exception class provided by the Java class library, but you can throw your own custom exceptions too.

Next up is more on string literals, as this is the first example in the chapter that introduces embedded Groovy expressions as well as multiline strings.

MORE ON STRING LITERALS

You've already seen three different types of string literals, although we only brought attention to one: the slashy string. Double quotes and single quotes are also valid string delimiters, with double-quote string literals allowing you to embed Groovy expressions inside ${}.

Groovy evaluates these expressions, converting the results into strings before inserting them into the final string. Instead of code like this:

```
String greeting = "Hello " + name
```

you can use

```
String greeting = "Hello ${name}"
```

In fact, for simple variable expansion like this, you can drop the curly braces:

```
String greeting = "Hello $name"
```

Single-quote strings don't do anything special, so they're useful if you want to include the dollar symbol without having to escape it. Otherwise, we tend to prefer the double-quote version in day-to-day Groovy coding.

You can also use single- or double-quotes for multiline strings, and they behave the same way. Use three quotes instead of one as we do in the previous simple example, but remember that any newline inside the quotes will result in a newline in the resulting string. That's why the backslash is particularly handy: it allows you to split lines in the source code without splitting them in the actual string. Hence its name: the line-continuation character. To see what we mean, try executing the following code in the console UI:

```
def msg = """Hi,            <-- Triple quotes start a multiline string.

Welcome to \                <-- The backslash joins the next line to this one.
the jungle!
"""

println msg
```

You'll see that the printed message looks like this:

```
Hi,

Welcome to the jungle!
```

We'll finish off this section with a quick word about the file manipulation work the example does because it sets you up nicely for the discussion about closures in the next section on advanced Groovy.

FILE MANIPULATION

We'll admit it: the file manipulation we perform in our latest script will likely impress only Java developers, but that's mainly because of the lack of richness in the Java class library. The Groovy JDK provides the following methods and properties that we use in the example to make our lives easier:

- *`File.withPrintWriter`*—Opens the file for writing and automatically closes it afterward.
- *`File.text`*—Returns or sets the entire contents of a file as or from a string.
- *`String.padRight`*—Adds spaces to the end of a string up to a fixed width; useful for tabulation and alignment.

Of these, the most interesting is `File.withPrintWriter` because it uses a powerful feature of Groovy that we haven't yet encountered: closures. We'll explain closures in the next section, but for now we want to show one example of why they're so useful.

The usual paradigm in Java for working with a file looks like this:

```
def reportFile = new File("report.txt")
def output
try {
    output = new FileOutputStream(reportFile)
    // Write to the output stream
    . . .
}
finally {
    if (output) output.close()
}
```

This is horribly verbose and requires you to declare an uninitialized variable, `output`, all so the file stream is closed properly whether or not an exception is thrown. It's boilerplate that helps obfuscate the real code.

In Groovy, we can pass a block of code to `withPrintWriter()`. The method opens the stream, executes the block of code we pass to it, and closes the stream safely, regardless of whether or not the block of code throws an exception. That block of code we pass to `withPrintWriter()` is the closure. And `withPrintWriter()` passes the open stream/writer into the closure so the encapsulated code can write to that stream.

After you get comfortable with Groovy, you'll use closures and the associated Groovy JDK methods on a daily basis. Closures add an extra dimension to the way you solve problems in code and make it much easier to express certain concepts. That's why Java 8 has its own variant in the form of lambda expressions.

You've done useful work in this chapter, from learning how to incorporate scripts into a Grails project to using the core features of Groovy. Rather than teach you how to program in Groovy, the aim of this chapter is to familiarize you with the syntax and discuss the most useful features while showing practical uses of the language. If you plan to do significant Groovy and/or Grails development, it's worth learning the language properly, perhaps through a book such as *Groovy in Action* by Dierk Koenig et al., (Manning, 2007). Book details are at http://www.manning.com/koenig2/.

We'll finish the chapter with a theoretical section that introduces advanced concepts of the language. We'll also discuss when and how you should incorporate these concepts into your applications.

2.3 Going to the next level

Thus far, you've seen a language that isn't dissimilar to Java. That's for good reason: the creators of Groovy wanted it to be as close to Java as possible. As a result, you can already code anything you need using the syntax and techniques we've shown you. But you're missing out on the real power and expressiveness of the language.

In this section, we'll look at the more advanced parts of Groovy that distinguish it from Java and make it a more productive (in our biased opinion) language. And if there's one feature that enhances the developer experience, it's closures. They make it easier to focus on *what* you want to do rather than *how* to do it.

2.3.1 Discovering closures

One of the greatest limitations of Java is the lack of what is known as first-class functions. You can't have a function without a class wrapping it. This leads to single-method interfaces and classes, such as `java.util.Comparator`. Is the interface necessary? Couldn't we treat a function as an object defined by its signature (arguments and return type)? This is what closures do for us.

At the simplest level, closures represent anonymous functions that can be passed as arguments to other functions, assigned to variables, and called with arguments. You saw an example closure with `File.withPrintWriter()`, but let's use another one to reinforce how they're used. Imagine that you want your quote analyzer to report the average number of characters per quote. As a first attempt you may try

```
def getAverageQuoteLength() {
    if (!quotes) return 0.0

    def totalSize = 0
    for (Quote q in quotes) {
        totalSize += q.content.size()
    }

    return totalSize / quotes.size()
}
```

Sure, this works, but you must read several lines of code together to understand what's going on. What are you trying to achieve here? You want to sum together the number of characters in each quote and then divide the result by the number of quotes. In effect, the code has two parts: the summing and the evaluation of the number of characters in a quote.

The algorithm for summing is always the same: add a bunch of numbers together. The only variation is where the numbers come from. That's why Groovy adds a `sum()` method to collections that allows you to specify which value you want to sum for each element of a collection. Without further ado, here's our preferred implementation of the previous method:

```
def getAverageQuoteLength() {
    return quotes.sum { it.content.size() } / quotes.size()
}
```

Not only is this much more succinct, but the intention of the code is much more obvious. In this case you're summing `content.size()` for each of the quotes, with `it` representing each element of the quotes list.

Understandably, the collections probably have the highest density of methods that use closures. Another classic example is the `findAll()` method, which returns a new collection containing only the elements that match a particular condition—specified as a closure that returns a Boolean. If you want only the quotes from Peter Ledbrook, you can use the code

```
def peterQuotes = quotes.findAll { it.author == "Peter Ledbrook" }
```

The method `findAll()` executes the closure for every element in the list of quotes and passes in the current element as the closure argument (remember, a closure is like an anonymous function and hence can have arguments). In this case, the argument is implicitly available as the variable `it`. You can also explicitly declare the closure arguments, as you saw with the iteration over a map in the quoteStatistics .groovy example:

```
analyzer.quoteCountPerAuthor.each { String author, int count ->
    w.println "   " + author.padRight(20) + count
}
```

The arguments can be either typed or untyped, and you must demarcate the end of the argument list with `->` if you do declare them.

It may help you to understand the syntax of methods with closures if you see the signature method. Let's take `findAll()` as an example:

```
List findAll(Closure conditionFunction)
```

As you can tell from the signature, these closures have their own type and are, in fact, objects. That's why they can be used as arguments and assigned to variables.

Those are the basics of closures. For those of you with Ruby experience, they correspond to Ruby's code blocks. They aren't a complicated concept, but it can be hard to move away from the "use a loop" mentality if you've never used a language with a similar construct (we're looking at you, Java). Once you get the hang of them, you'll wonder how you ever lived without them!

There's certainly more to closures than we can possibly cover here, but with these basics you'll be able to learn the rest as you work with the language, and you'll see them pop up in examples throughout the book. Before we move on, there's one trap we want to warn you about that newcomers fall into.

In an effort to be as Groovy as possible, some developers always use the `each()` method for iterating over collections. The trouble with this approach is that neither `break` nor `continue` work in this context, even though they work fine in `for` and `while` loops, and it's not obvious why the code isn't working.

The solution is either to use a `for` loop or an appropriate Groovy JDK method. The `break` keyword is often used to break out of a loop once an item is found. In such scenarios, the Groovy JDK `find()` method is a much better approach.

You can find several other methods in the Groovy JDK that work for different use cases. Appendix A has descriptions of the most useful ones, and we recommend you try them out because they make for much more succinct and understandable code.

We're nearly done with this introduction to Groovy. You've seen all the important constructs of the language, enough to begin coding. There are only two things left to discuss: the dynamic nature of Groovy and when to use explicit types. The first of these is targeted at Java developers rather than Rubyists, Pythonistas, PHP developers, or others that have a dynamic language background. That's because Java developers sometimes struggle with the dynamic nature of Groovy, particularly when explicit types don't behave as expected.

2.3.2 Programming dynamically

Dynamic languages sound exciting, don't they? It's built into their name: "dynamic." But what do we mean by that term? The definition comes in two parts:

- Properties, variables, and arguments don't need to have explicit types.
- Behavior can be modified at runtime.

Let's take a look at examples that illustrate these points.

CHANGING THE BEHAVIOR OF EXISTING CLASSES AT RUNTIME

In section 2.1.1 we highlighted that the method call

```
def quote = createQuote(quoteParts, "test")
```

doesn't result in a compiler error but in a runtime `MissingMethodException`. Why? Because you can add behavior at runtime, so the method may exist by the time it's called.

To demonstrate the impact this has, we'll modify the previous script that we wrote to generate data (listing 2.1) by adding a new method to the `List` class at runtime. The method randomly selects one of its elements. The following listing shows the required code changes to the script.

Listing 2.9 Implementing a method at runtime

```
List.metaClass.random = {->
    delegate[new Random().nextInt(delegate.size())]
}
. . .
```

Adds a zero-argument random() method to instances of List

```
String createQuote(List quoteParts, List authors) {
    return quoteParts.random()[0] + ' ' +
        quoteParts.random()[1] + ' ' +
        quoteParts.random()[2] + ' by ' +
        authors.random()
}
. . .
```

Calls the new random() method as if it were a method on the List class

At this point we're not interested in the mechanics of how the `random()` method is added to the `List` class. The key point to take away is that it's *possible* to add methods and properties at runtime, so Groovy can't raise errors about unknown properties and methods at compile time.

This behavior of resolving properties and methods at runtime has its advantages. Here are some of the ones we particularly like:

- *Correct selection of overloaded methods*—When you call an overloaded method, Groovy selects the appropriate one based on the actual types of the arguments at runtime. This is far more useful than selecting based on declared type.
- *Generating data from code*—Writing data as code is powerful, particularly as you can incorporate conditions, loops, and other bits of flow logic. The classic Groovy example is the `MarkupBuilder` class, which allows you to generate XML incredibly easily. We show an example after this list.
- *Duck typing*—Duck typing is particularly useful for testing as it allows you to pass any type of object as an argument as long as it implements the required properties and methods. For this to work, the method arguments must be untyped because Groovy does enforce types at runtime. The name comes from the phrase "if it walks like a duck and quacks like a duck, it's a duck." See figure 2.2 for a diagrammatic view of duck typing.

Other advantages include loading and instantiating classes at runtime; you don't need their types on your classpath when you compile your application, allowing for

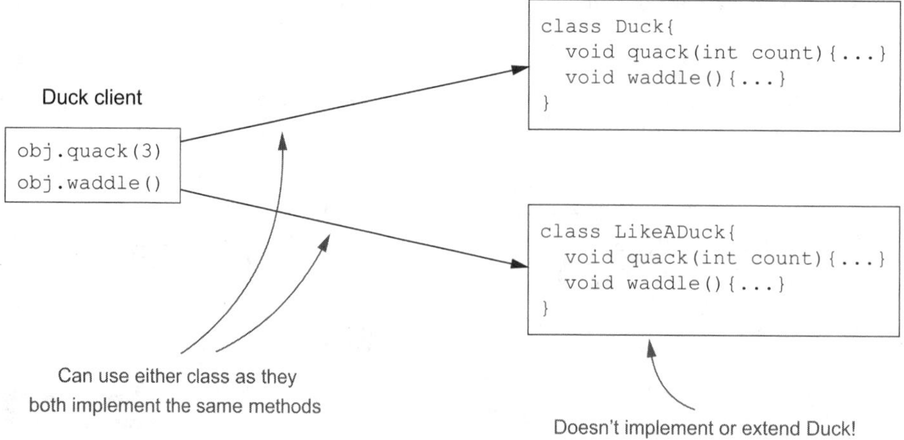

Figure 2.2 An example of duck typing

easier modularization. But the advantages mentioned previously are definitely our favorites.

Given the freedom that comes with dynamic languages, you need to be careful not to abuse that flexibility. Adding dynamic behavior everywhere guarantees confusion and hard-to-diagnose errors.

Let's finish off this section with the example XML generation we promised.

GENERATING DATA FROM CODE

Type this code into the Grails console UI:

```
def mkp = new groovy.xml.MarkupBuilder()
def items = ["Oranges", "Bananas", "Cereal", "Milk"]

mkp.shoppingList {
    for (itm in items) {
        item(itm)
    }
}
```

When you run it, you'll see the following in the output:

```
<shoppingList>
  <item>Oranges</item>
  <item>Bananas</item>
  <item>Cereal</item>
  <item>Milk</item>
</shoppingList>
```

You can probably guess what's happening: the calls to the methods `shoppingList()` and `item()` are turning into XML elements of the same name. Those methods don't exist on the `MarkupBuilder` class, though. They're only evaluated at runtime. Groovy also has a `JSONBuilder` class for generating JavaScript Object Notation (JSON).

Hopefully it's clear that Groovy is a dynamic language, because this point is important for understanding the discussion over whether or not to use explicit types. There's no right answer to the question, but you can make an informed decision as to when and when not to use types based on what we present next.

2.3.3 To type or not to type

Should I declare my properties with explicit types? What about method arguments? What are the implications of each? Newcomers to Groovy often find themselves asking questions such as these when they start coding. In most languages you don't have a choice: you're stuck with explicit types everywhere or nowhere.

What do explicit types buy you in Groovy? They neither result in compiler errors, as we explained in the previous section, nor do they make the code run faster. Maybe we should just ignore them.

Not so fast! Despite the lack of compilation errors, explicit types do have their uses:

- They document your code, making it easier for other developers to follow and use.
- APIs are easier to use when they include type information because you know, at a glance, what argument types are required.

- Runtime errors due to type mismatches are easier to diagnose than the alternative `MissingPropertyExceptions` and `MissingMethodExceptions`.
- Code can use the type information to do clever things. For example, GORM relies on explicit types to map properties to database column types.

The first three of these points argue for using explicit types for method signatures and public properties, and in general, that's what we recommend. But be aware that explicit types break duck typing: Groovy enforces the types at runtime. This can make testing harder with concrete types such as `File`.

As for local variables, we don't use explicit types because they offer little advantage. As long as methods are a sensible size (say less than 15 lines or so), it's clear what type local variables are without the noise of an explicit type. With all that in mind, here's our general *guideline* for explicit types. Note "guideline," not rule!

Guideline on using explicit types

For method signatures and properties, we recommend that you use explicit types unless doing so makes testing significantly harder or your code relies on duck typing in another way. We recommend that you leave local variables untyped.

This guideline will cause disagreements, and that's fine. Go with whatever you or your team chooses. This guideline is more for those who have no strong opinions and want a "safe" option based on others' experience.

Static type checking

With the advent of Groovy 2, it's possible to add compile-time type checking to your classes via the `@groovy.transform.TypeChecked` annotation. This doesn't change the way the code behaves at runtime, but at compile time Groovy generates errors for variables, methods, and properties it can't resolve.

We haven't heard of it being used much, but if you're a Java developer you may find it easier to work with Groovy when using the annotation. A companion annotation, `@groovy.transform.CompileStatic`, exists, but don't use this in Grails applications at the moment because it doesn't work for several types of artifacts. It's fine, though, for standalone, nonartifact Groovy classes.

As you can see from this section, Groovy is a powerful and flexible language that happens to be more accessible than Java. Closures allow for a new approach to solving problems and can make your code more expressive than it would be otherwise. Combine them with the Groovy JDK methods and you have an entire chest of toys to play with.

The language also provides flexibility in the way that you use types. Hopefully we've given you useful guidance on when to use explicit types and when not, but as we said, you'll find your own preferences as you gain experience. Or you may be forced to use your team's style guidelines!

With that, we're done with this Groovy primer. Remember, you can always refer to this chapter at any time to refresh your memory on specific points of syntax or Groovy feature we discussed. All that's left to do now is wrap up.

2.4 Summary and best practices

We covered Groovy at a rapid pace, so let's stop and take stock. From the early sections and examples in this chapter, you should feel confident and excited about programming in Groovy. We covered the basic syntax and the most common constructs that you'll use for Grails development. A single chapter is never going to be exhaustive, but anything that isn't covered here will be explained in later chapters.

Before we move on to the Grails fundamentals, here are some general guidelines to make your Groovy experience as enjoyable and productive as possible:

- *Learn more about the language.* Your Grails expertise will be only as good as your Groovy chops. For a comprehensive look at the language itself, check out *Groovy in Action*, by Dierk Koenig et al. (Manning, 2013), at http://manning.com/koenig2/.
- *Become familiar with the Groovy JDK and the Java class library, particularly the classes under* `java.lang`, `java.io`, *and* `java.math`. As you become more experienced, it's worth getting to know the Groovy API too, which includes things such as `groovy.xml.MarkupBuilder`, `groovy.sql.Sql`, `groovy.lang.Range`, `groovy.lang.Closure`, and more.
- *Practice, practice, practice!* The more you use any language, the better you become with it. Consider installing Groovy and using it to write scripts. You can also include it in other Java projects, for example, for the unit tests.
- *Don't overuse closures.* If a standard Groovy method suffices, use that. Closures should be used where they add value, such as arguments to other methods.
- *Embrace a test-first philosophy.* This approach quickly picks up logic errors as well as typos, while also helping you to produce reliable software. We give this area thorough coverage in chapter 9.
- *Use a Groovy-aware IDE.* Tools such as Eclipse, Intellij IDEA, and NetBeans offer many features, such as underlining unknown properties and methods (to catch typos) and debugging support.

Groovy is a flexible language with powerful constructs that allow you to write solutions the way you want. It also has a relatively simple syntax, so the learning curve isn't that great. One of the great strengths of developing with Grails is that you code in Groovy.

With this small diversion out of the way, it's time to get back to dedicated Grails work and start exploring the fundamentals of the framework that we touched on in chapter 1.

Part 2

Core Grails

In part 1, we gave you a whirlwind introduction to both the core parts of Grails and the underlying Groovy language that powers it. In part 2, we'll start a more thorough exploration of the three core parts of the Grails ecosystem: models, controllers, and views.

In chapter 3, we'll look at domain modeling—the heart of any Grails application. You'll learn about saving and updating domain classes, explore the many facets of validation, and cover all basic relationships for domain classes (1:1, 1:m, m:n).

Chapter 4 will put your modeling skills to work by taking you through the numerous query mechanisms that Grails offers for searching your domain model. We'll also investigate Grails's fantastic scaffolding features, which allow you to build a functional UI in record time.

Chapter 5 introduces ways to query a database in Grails without using SQL. You'll learn how to generate sample data and explore advanced querying techniques by building a basic search form for Hubbub that provides a basis for trying different types of query.

In chapter 6, you'll be ready to explore some of the web-oriented features of Grails. In particular, how you can route a user around the different features in your application using Grails controllers. We'll also cover binding data from web forms, writing a request filter, and even creating custom URL mappings to add user-friendly permalinks to your application.

Chapter 7 builds on your knowledge of controllers by introducing the Grails Service object, which helps free controllers from the heavy lifting of application logic, and lets controllers do what they do best—control the flow of the user through the application. We'll also discuss data binding, error handling, URL mappings, and filters.

In chapter 8, we'll turn our attention to the user interface components of a Grails application, exploring Grails tags for UI construction. We'll show you how to quickly add a consistent and sophisticated look and feel to your applications, and even how to build custom skins for your application. Finally, we'll introduce Grails's Ajax support, and show you how to add slick animations to your applications.

Once you've finished this part of the book, you'll have a comprehensive understanding of all the basics of Grails and be well on your way to becoming a productive Grails developer. In part 3, we'll introduce more sophisticated Grails features that will really make your application ready for production.

3 Modeling the domain

This chapter covers

- What GORM is and how it works
- How domain classes are saved and updated
- Techniques for validating and constraining fields
- Domain class relationships (1:1, 1:m, m:n)

In this chapter, we explore Grails's support for the data model portion of your applications (getting stuff into the database and querying to get it back), and if you're worried we'll dig deep into complex outer joins, you'll be pleasantly surprised how straightforward Grails makes data access. We won't write a line of SQL, and you won't find any Hibernate XML mappings here either. We'll take full advantage of the convention over configuration paradigm we introduced in chapter 1, which means less time configuring and more time getting work done.

We'll spend most of our time exploring how Grails persists domain model classes to your data store of choice (be it a relational database or a shiny new NoSQL store) using GORM, mentioned briefly in chapter 2. You'll also learn how GORM models various relationships (one to many, many to many, and so on.)

But we're practitioners, not theorists, so we'll discuss these topics while building the heart of the sample application you'll use throughout this book: Hubbub. You won't spend much time on the UI in this chapter, but the concepts we'll cover are fundamental for building the rock-solid data models that back our applications.

Without further ado, let's look at your sample application.

3.1 Introducing the Hubbub sample application

Our goal in this book is to take you to the stage where you could work as a productive Grails developer. We'll mentor you in the skills you need to produce world-class applications in record time by showing you how to develop a real application. Our plan is that everything you learn while developing Hubbub you can apply in your workplace developing the next Facebook (or other world-beating web app).

The example we'll use for the rest of the book is Hubbub, a simple microblogging application similar to Twitter. Think of it as a system that lets you write short posts about what you're hacking on right now. Friends can follow your posts to see what you're geeking out on and get motivated to check things out for themselves. You can follow your friends' posts, too. Figure 3.1 shows a complete version of Hubbub in action.

> **TIP** No doubt you're already well-versed in how common social network apps work, but if you need friends to follow, check out @glen_a_smith and @pledbrook on Twitter. Our tweets may be geeky, but we're mostly harmless.

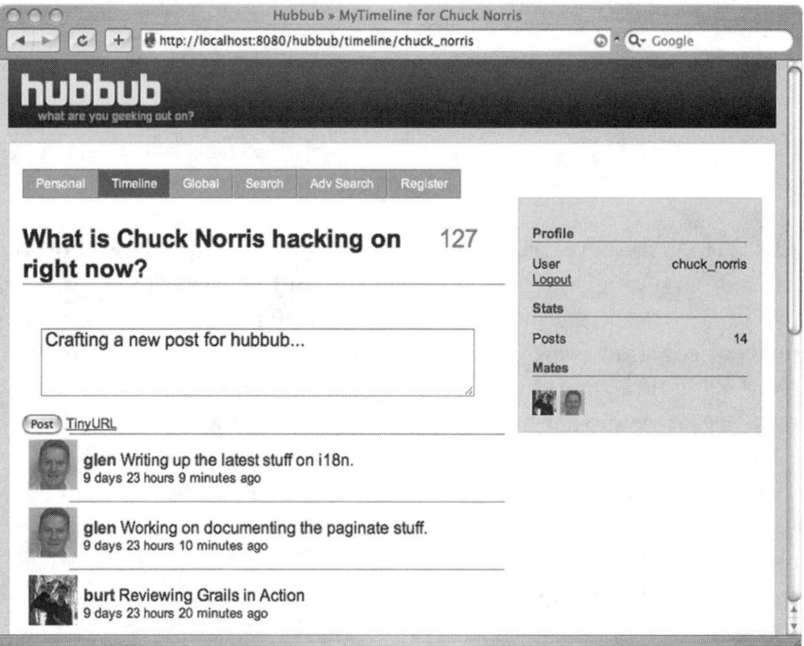

Figure 3.1 The Hubbub we're heading toward

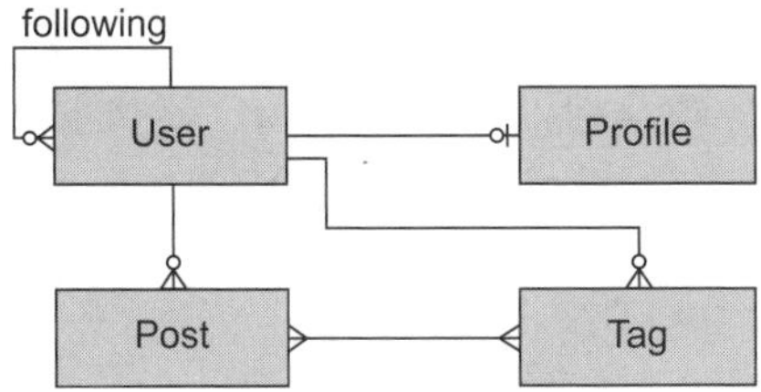

Figure 3.2 The basic Hubbub data model demonstrates the most used relationship types.

The domain model for Hubbub is simple. Figure 3.2 shows the Hubbub entity relationship (ER) model in all its glory.

The `User` class holds the user's authentication details (user ID and password), but all good social networking applications let you associate bio information with each user (profile pic, email, blog, time zone, and favorite rock star, for example). We model that in a `Profile` class (which is an optional 1:1 relationship—each `User` may optionally have one `Profile` and each created `Profile` relates to one, and only one, `User`).

Hubbub's purpose is to let users create posts—one-line blog entries that describe what they're hacking on right now. A user can write many posts, and each post has a single author, so that's a classic 1:m (one-to-many) relationship.

But what's a social networking application without hashtags? Applications such as Twitter make great use of #hashtags to see what topics are "trending" or "so hot right now" among users. Each time a user creates a `Post`, he can apply hashtags to it, and a given `Post` can have many tags. But that means the reverse is also true. Each `Tag` can also relate to many `Posts`. We have an m:n (many-to-many) relationship. You can also link the `Tag` back to the `User` object, because it's handy to see all the tags a user has available without searching all their posts.

We've saved the trickiest part until last: the `User` object has self-references. A `User` can follow many other `Users` (which we call a "following" relationship). That sounds as if it would be exhausting to implement, but it turns out to be straightforward.

Don't worry about getting it straight in your head yet. We'll spend plenty of time with these classes over the next few chapters. You'll get a feel for the function of the main objects and be on your way.

3.1.1 Domain-driven design

If you're as impatient as we are, you probably wonder why we're starting with all this domain-model design stuff here. Why not something a little sexier, such as an autocompleting Ajax-powered search gizmo? Don't worry, we'll get to that.

Grails is designed to be an interactive agile development framework. That means you can start anywhere you like, refactor, make changes, and still end up with a fantastic app. You can start with the UI, domain modeling, service classes, or even the test cases, if you like.

When we work on Grails apps, the first thing we usually do is sketch out screen designs on graph paper, as shown in figure 3.3. This gives us a good feel for how the

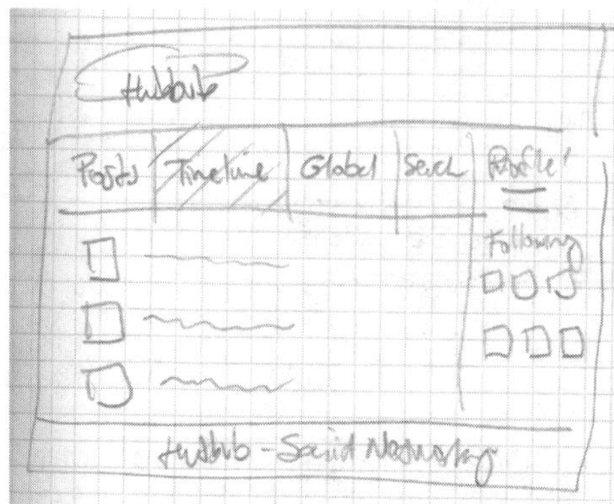

Figure 3.3 Early screen designs for the Hubbub UI

user will interact with the system, and a sense of how the finished product may look. This gets us in the headspace of the application and gives us ideas about the user experience. Peter likes to do this kind of stuff on his iPad, but I'm a little more low-tech, so I'll scratch out something on paper.

When developing any kind of web app, the UI is only part of the story. Once we have our UI sketches mocked up, we move on and define the domain model: how all the persistent data in the system fits together. This gives us a good feel for how the core parts of the system will collaborate, and it helps us flesh out our thinking. Grails makes domain modeling so easy that we usually do this bit directly in code without any real data model on paper. In fact, that's why this chapter is the first to cover its topic in greater depth: domain modeling is a great place to start your Grails application development journey.

During this section you'll start defining your data model, then you'll use Grails to generate a quick-and-dirty scaffold UI (we introduced you to these autogenerated UI artifacts in chapter 1, and we'll look more closely at them in the next chapter). With the autogenerated UI, you'll feel like you're making progress because you'll have an app that runs and persists to a database. This will motivate you to move to the app's next level of functionality and start implementing graph paper scratchings as a real UI.

You may be more disciplined than we are and not need the carrot of seeing things up and running, but you're stuck with us for this chapter, so let's get Hubbub to the point where you can see it running in a browser.

3.1.2 Hubbub kick-start: from 0 to first hit

You've completed the rough version of your screens on paper, and you have a "napkin-level" data model to work from, so it's time to generate the application. Let's create the app:

```
grails create-app hubbub
```

We find it's good encouragement to do a `cd hubbub` followed by an initial `grails run-app` to start a newly created application. Point your browser at http://localhost:8080/hubbub/ to see things up and running, as shown in figure 3.4.

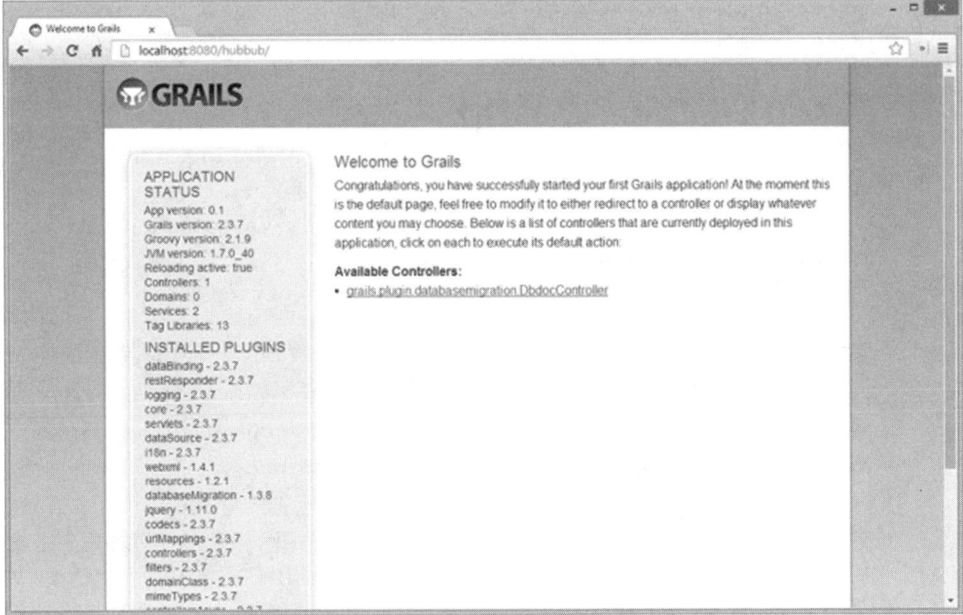

Figure 3.4 The newly created Hubbub application

With the shell of Hubbub in place, it's time to put meat on the bones. The next section explains how to generate your first domain class.

3.1.3 *Introducing GORM*

Before we generate our first domain class, let's take a quick look at the GORM implementation.

Object-relational mapping (ORM) is the process of getting objects into and out of a persistent data source (you may use a relational database, an object database, or one of the new NoSQL databases—but Grails abstracts most of these details for you). Having an ORM layer such as GORM means you can be (mostly) oblivious to the SQL/NoSQL that happens behind the scenes and get on with coding. For example, if you call `user.firstName = "Glen"`, the ORM may create the SQL `UPDATE` statement to ensure that the object's `firstName` field is persisted in your relational database, or it might generate the JSON to send it to a NoSQL store. In Java applications, that role is usually handled by an ORM such as Hibernate or the Java Persistence API (JPA); in Grails, it's done by GORM, which takes full advantage of Groovy's dynamic typing to make data access simple.

If you've used Hibernate, EclipseLink, or another Java ORM library, you know that configuration is required. Often, you have to write XML mapping files or add annotations to each persistent class, and you may have to configure transactional behavior, too. GORM, like most of Grails, is based on convention over configuration to get you up and running without a single line of XML.

Now that you know a bit about GORM, it's time to define your first domain model object and see things in action.

3.2 Your first domain class object

We outlined the preliminary domain model at the beginning of this chapter, and you have your application shell in place, so it's time to define your domain model classes. One of the first things you need to define is a `User` object so your users can sign up and start using the system.

The first step is to ask Grails to create a skeleton of your domain class:

```
grails create-domain-class com.grailsinaction.User
```

This creates a new class file in /grails-app/domain/com/grailsinaction/User.groovy (and a corresponding unit test in /test/unit/com/grailsinaction/UserTests.groovy). As we discussed in chapter 1, it's good practice to store classes in packages rather than in the default scope, so you'll keep all source in a package called `com.grailsinaction`. Now it's time to think about the fields you want to define for new `User` accounts. You don't want the signup process to be onerous, but you need a few basics from your users:

```
package com.grailsinaction

class User {
    String loginId
    String password
    String homepage
    Date dateCreated
}
```

Types that can be used in domain classes

We've used `Strings` and `Dates` in our `User` object so far, but you can use an extensive range of Java types: `Integer`, `Long`, `Float`, `Boolean` (and their corresponding primitive types), `Date`, `Calendar`, `URL`, and `byte[]` are all in the list of supported types. Grails will also make sensible choices about an appropriate database type to map what you're storing. See the Hibernate documentation for a full set of supported types.

Grails provides special support for date fields named `dateCreated` and `lastUpdated`. If you have fields with such names, Grails automatically sets the current timestamp value on first save to `dateCreated` or on every save to `lastUpdated`. We take advantage of `dateCreated` to preserve the user's registration time.

Now you can store a user's details. You don't have a UI to enter anything into yet, but you do have the skeleton of a test case that Grails created, which should make it easier to begin writing tests for your code. Before you write your first real test, let's discuss the amazing world of Grails testing.

3.2.1 Saving and retrieving users via tests

The whole testing infrastructure (and particularly unit testing) had a massive overhaul in Grails 2.0. If you've been around the Grails block, you know that unit testing support in Grails 1.x was clunky, tedious, and often incomplete, creating friction when writing solid tests for your app. Unit testing was rewritten completely in Grails 2.0, so even if you're a Grails 1.x veteran burned by Grails testing, it's worth following along the next few sections to start your transition to Spock and Grails 2.0 and find a reason to get excited about testing again.

We first introduced you to the idea of Grails automated testing in chapter 1, when you created tests for `QuoteService`. Tests are useful across your application—so useful, in fact, that chapter 9 discusses testing strategies for all development lifecycle phases.

For now, though, tests give us a chance to show how GORM saves your objects to the database and how you get them back. Let's write the first test case.

> **Unit versus integration tests?**
>
> When you create any artifact from the command line, Grails automatically generates a corresponding unit test in /grails-app/test/unit/YourArtifactSpec.groovy. Unit tests run in isolation and rely on fairly sophisticated mocking techniques using Groovy mixins (which we introduce in the next few chapters and deep dive into in chapter 7). For most of your everyday Grails hacking, you'll work with unit tests. Why didn't we start there?
>
> Given that we're testing database-related logic, integration tests are the "right way to do it," and you may as well learn the right way! Yes, Grails does provide mocking support for the data tier, but in this chapter we want to test the data tier, not mock it out! Grails calls this *integration testing*.
>
> For integration tests, Grails bootstraps the real database and wires up all components as it would for a running application. That means you can see what happens when you create, save, and delete domain objects into a real database, and you don't have to mess with any tricky mocking features yet. Integration tests are much slower to run, but they're fantastic for the learning and experimenting you'll do in chapter 9. They're also the right way to test transactional code, because no one deploys to a mock database!

As we discussed previously, Grails creates a unit test case skeleton in /test/unit/com/grailsinaction/UserSpec.groovy. But you want an integration test, because you want to run it against your database. Recall from chapter 1 that you create integration tests with this command:

```
grails create-integration-test com.grailsinaction.UserIntegration
```

This command generates /test/integration/com/grailsinaction/UserIntegrationSpec.groovy.

Next, create and save a `User` object in the database (for the user joe). Then see if you can query the database to find the user based on the user ID. The following listing introduces your first saving test.

Listing 3.1 Saving and retrieving a domain object from the database

```
package com.grailsinaction
import spock.lang.*
class UserIntegrationSpec extends Specification {

    def "Saving our first user to the database"() {

        given: "A brand new user"
        def joe = new User(loginId: 'joe', password: 'secret',
                homepage: 'http://www.grailsinaction.com')

        when: "the user is saved"
        joe.save()                                              ❶

        then: "it saved successfully and can be found in the database"
        joe.errors.errorCount == 0                              ❷
        joe.id != null                                          ❸
        User.get(joe.id).loginId == joe.loginId                 ❹
  }

}
```

❶ Calls save() to persist object
❷ Ensures save() was error free
❸ Confirms save() set database ID
❹ Retrieves User object by ID

The process of creating a new domain object instance normally consists of constructing the object, then invoking the `save()` method ❶. When you invoke `save()`, GORM generates the SQL code to insert your `User` object into the database. GORM returns the saved `User` object (or `null` if `save()` fails, which we'll talk about later) and sets an `errors` object to hold any validation errors ❷. Once the `User` is saved to the database, it's assigned an `id` field in the database ❸. We can then use this `id` with the `get()` method ❹ to query for the object (you can also use the `read()` method if you want a read-only copy of the object).

Much snazzier ways exist for querying for objects than `get()` and `read()`, and we cover them when we get to dynamic finders in the next chapter, but `get()` works for now.

It's time to confirm that your test case works, so let's ask Grails to execute your test case:

```
grails test-app integration:
```

You can use `grails test-app` if you want to run both unit and integration tests, but we're only interested in integration tests for now. Normally you'd follow the colon with the particular test name you wish to run, but you can leave it blank to run all integration tests. You get brief output in the console that gives you the good news you've been looking for:

```
| Completed 1 spock test, 0 failed in 24ms
| Tests PASSED - view reports in C:\TEMP\hubbub\target\test-reports
```

And you're all green (that's what people say when tests pass because most IDEs display passing tests with a green bar). That "PASSED" tells us your Spock assertions passed, as

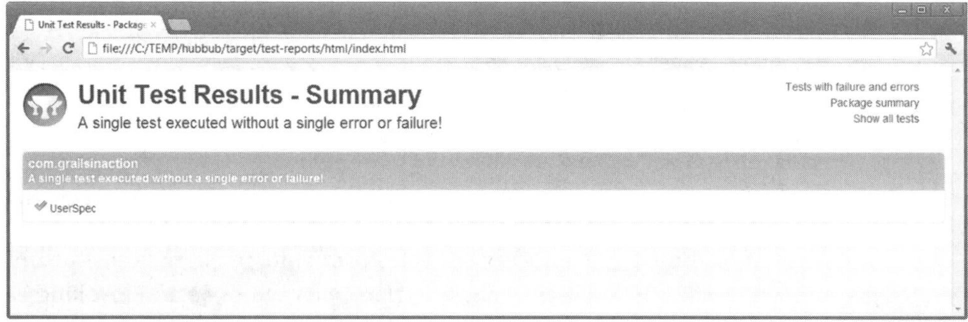

Figure 3.5 You can open the test report in your browser.

expected. Grails also writes a nicely formatted HTML report in target/test-reports/html/index.html. Figure 3.5 shows the output from your previous test run.

> **What does save() do behind the scenes?**
>
> Behind the scenes, `save()` uses the Hibernate session that Spring puts on the current thread, then adds your `User` object to that session. In Hibernate lingo, this means the `User` object moves from being a transient to a persistent object.
>
> The flush to the database (the real SQL inserts) from the Hibernate session occurs at the end of the thread's lifetime, but if you want to force your object to persist immediately, you can do an explicit `user.save(flush: true)`.
>
> But we're getting ahead of ourselves. We'll cover this in more detail in chapter 12.

3.2.2 Updating user properties

You've completed your first save, so try implementing an update routine. Update is a special case of saving, so let's try updating joe's password programmatically.

> **NOTE** You have to create your "joe" user every time you run a test cycle, because integration tests always return the database to the way they found it. Your changes execute in a transaction that's rolled back at the end of each test to ensure that the database is clean for each test.

Start with `save()` and `get()` as in your previous test, and then you'll modify user fields and repeat the `save()` and `get()` to make sure the update worked. The following listing takes you through the save-and-update test cycle.

Listing 3.2 Updating users by changing field values and calling `save()`

```
def "Updating a saved user changes its properties"() {

    given: "An existing user"
    def existingUser = new User(loginId: 'joe', password: 'secret',
        homepage: 'http://www.grailsinaction.com')
    existingUser.save(failOnError: true)
```

```
    when: "A property is changed"
    def foundUser = User.get(existingUser.id)
    foundUser.password = 'sesame'
    foundUser.save(failOnError: true)

    then: "The change is reflected in the database"
    User.get(existingUser.id).password == 'sesame'
}
```

❶ Modifies retrieved User object directly

❷ Updates database

❸ Checks that password has been persisted

You're used to the `save()` and `get()` cycle from your previous test. But notice how executing an update is a matter of changing property values ❶ and invoking `save()` ❷ to persist the change to the database. Setting the `failOnError:true` option to `save()` means Grails will throw an exception if the object fails any validation tests. An exception causes the test to fail instantly, so using this option means you don't have to look at the errors property later in your test results. Save your updated object, then requery the database to confirm that the password change was applied ❸.

To confirm that your change is working as you expect, invoke another `grails test-app integration`:

```
| Completed 2 spock tests, 0 failed in 292ms
| Tests PASSED - view reports in C:\TEMP\hubbub\target\test-reports
```

You can now see that your two tests are running successfully with no failures! With your updates running successfully, it's time to turn your attention to deleting users.

3.2.3 Deleting users

You now have a feel for loading and saving, but those pesky bots will soon fill your database with dodgy user registrations, so you need to delete `User` objects, too.

It's time for your third and final test case. The following listing shows how to use the `delete()` method to remove an object from the database.

Listing 3.3 Deleting objects from the database is a one-liner

```
def "Deleting an existing user removes it from the database"() {

    given: "An existing user"
    def user = new User(loginId: 'joe', password: 'secret',
        homepage: 'http://www.grailsinaction.com')
    user.save(failOnError: true)

    when: "The user is deleted"
    def foundUser = User.get(user.id)
    foundUser.delete(flush: true)

    then: "The user is removed from the database"
    !User.exists(foundUser.id)
}
```

❶ Removes the user immediately

❷ Checks for object ID in database

Deleting gives us a chance to introduce two new domain class methods: `delete()` and `exists()`. You can call `delete()` on any domain class that you fetch from the database ❶. We use the `flush:true` option because we want your test to delete it from the database immediately and not batch up the change.

Even though `flush:true` removes the object from the database, your instance handle won't nullify, which is why you can reference `foundUser.id` in the later `exists()` call, even after `foundUser` is deleted from the database.

You can check for the existence of any domain instance with the `exists()` method ❷. As you would expect, `exists()` returns `true` if that ID exists in the database. Spock lets you specify "`then:`" block assertions as Booleans, so you don't need the full form of `User.exists(foundUser.id) == false`.

Before you move on, you can confirm nothing is broken with a `grails test-app integration`:

```
| Completed 3 spock tests, 0 failed in 99ms
| Tests PASSED - view reports in C:\TEMP\hubbub\target\test-reports
```

You now have a good handle on saving, updating, and deleting your `User` objects. But although you tested that your `save()` calls work correctly, we haven't encountered any reason for a `save()` call to fail! The main reason for such failure is a domain class field constraint-validation failure (such as not providing a value for a field that's non-nullable, or providing an invalid email address for an email type field). Now it's time to introduce you to the features Grails offers for validation.

3.3 Validation: stopping garbage in and out

You created your new `User` object and successfully tested saving it to the database, so you may already think a little defensively: "What keeps clients from putting all sorts of junk (including nulls and blanks) into my domain object and saving them?" The answer is, nothing yet. That's our cue to talk about validation.

Grails goes out of its way to make all the common validations easy, and when things don't match your validation needs, it's not hard to customize them. Say you want to make sure that all passwords have at least six characters but not more than eight. You can apply this sort of constraint through a special `constraints` closure that uses a comprehensive domain-specific language (DSL) to specify constraints. You can use a validator to limit the size of fields, enforce non-nullability, or check (via patterns) whether a field contains a URL, email address, credit card number, or other data.

Let's add basic constraints to your `User` object. We'll make sure the `loginId` and `password` fields have size limits and that the `homepage` contains a valid URL. The following listing shows your updated domain class with the new constraints.

Listing 3.4 Adding constraints in Grails

```
package com.grailsinaction
class User {
    String loginId
    String password
    String homepage
    Date dateCreated
```

```
    static constraints = {
        loginId size: 3..20, unique: true, nullable: false
        password size: 6..8, nullable: false
        homepage url: true, nullable: true
    }
}
```

❶ Specifies min and max field lengths

❷ Checks against a URL pattern, which may be null

The `size` constraint ❶ makes sure the `loginId` field is between 3 and 20 characters (inclusive). When applied to a `String` field, `size` checks the length of the string. But if you apply it to a numeric field, it ensures the number entered is within the range. For example, an `Integer` field called `quantity` could be constrained to ensure the user doesn't order more than 10 items with `quantity (size: 0..10)`. You also specified a `unique` constraint on the `User` to ensure that two users don't have the same `loginId`.

> **The one true style of constraints**
>
> Grails constraints can be specified in two different styles. Optionally, you can put parentheses around the list such as:
>
> ```
> loginId(size:3..20, unique: true)
> ```
>
> Or drop the parentheses entirely and use the style in listing 3.4. We like using the style without the parentheses because it means less visual clutter, but you might see either style in production code. Previous versions of Grails required the parentheses, so we thought we'd warn you about it here.

You don't have to list all fields in your `constraints` block—only those you want to supply specific validations for. One thing to note is that fields aren't nullable by default, so if you want a field to be optional, you have to specify the `nullable` constraint explicitly. You allow the homepage field ❷ to be optional (`nullable`), but if it's supplied, you force it to match a URL pattern. This kind of combination gives you more power to specify validations concisely yet expressively.

What happens if the user tries to save an object that doesn't satisfy the constraints on an object? Let's write a test case and see. It's time to introduce you to the `validate()` method that's available on every domain class. When you call `validate()`, Grails checks whether or not the constraints have been satisfied and provides an `errors` object that you can interrogate to see which fields failed.

The following listing augments your UserIntegrationSpec.groovy file with a new test that attempts to save an instance that doesn't satisfy the constraints.

Listing 3.5 Interrogating the results of a failed validation

```
def "Saving a user with invalid properties causes an error"() {

    given: "A user which fails several field validations"
    def user = new User(loginId: 'joe',
        password: 'tiny', homepage: 'not-a-url')
```

```
    when:  "The user is validated"
    user.validate()                                   ❶ Validates constraints.

    then:
    user.hasErrors()

    "size.toosmall" == user.errors.getFieldError("password").code    ❷ Errors collection contains code describing failure.
    "tiny" == user.errors.getFieldError("password").rejectedValue
    "url.invalid" == user.errors.getFieldError("homepage").code
    "not-a-url" == user.errors.getFieldError("homepage").rejectedValue   ❸ Errors collection holds failing value.
    !user.errors.getFieldError("loginId")             ❹ Checks that valid fields are not in errors collection.
}
```

As we mentioned, `validate()` ❶ checks the constraints on the domain class to see if they've been satisfied, and it returns `true` or `false`. As a result, this is a common idiom you see in Grails controllers:

```
if (user.validate()) {
    user.save()
    redirect action: "show", id: user.id
} else {
    // go and give them another crack at it in the original page
    render view: "edit", model: [user:user]
}
```

After you check for validation, you can access the domain object's `errors` property to see what went wrong. The returned `errors` object holds a collection of `fieldError` objects, each representing a different field in your domain object. Each `fieldError` object has a `code` ❷ describing the type of validation that failed and a `rejectedValue` ❸ containing the data the user entered. If the field has no errors, its `fieldError` object is `null`, which is the case for `loginId` ❹.

In case you want to know more about those error codes, we give you a full set of them in table 3.1. But for now, know that you can find out exactly what's failing the validators. In chapter 7, we'll show you how to do all these checks in a unit test, which makes things more concise.

Now that you know how to cause an error (by violating a constraint), write a test case that repairs the damage after a bad save attempt. This isn't something you'd typically do when processing a web request, but it helps demonstrate how these validations work. The following listing shows a test case that first attempts a `save()` with invalid data and then repairs the damage and performs a valid `save()`.

Listing 3.6 Recovering from a failed validation

```
def "Recovering from a failed save by fixing invalid properties"() {

    given: "A user that has invalid properties"
    def chuck = new User(loginId: 'chuck',
        password: 'tiny', homepage: 'not-a-url')        ❶ Uses invalid URL and password
    assert chuck.save() == null
    assert chuck.hasErrors()                            ❷ Returns true
```

```
    when: "We fix the invalid properties"
    chuck.password = "fistfist"
    chuck.homepage = "http://www.chucknorrisfacts.com"
    chuck.validate()

    then: "The user saves and validates fine"
    !chuck.hasErrors()                           ❸ Removes errors
    chuck.save()                                 ❹ Returns the saved object on success
}
```

Our original `User` object had an invalid URL and password ❶, which caused the object to fail validation ❷. After correcting the troublesome fields, `validate()` is happy again and the `errors` object resets ❸. Once the user is in a valid state, `save()` returns the saved object ❹.

You've now exercised constraints, and you've gained confidence that your database fields will persist consistently. Until now, we've exposed you to size and URL constraints only, but we'll explore additional Grails validators next.

3.3.1 Standard validators

Now that you know how the basic constraint mechanism works, you may wonder what Grails validators are available out of the box. Plenty exist, and table 3.1 lists the most common ones.

Table 3.1 Grails validators available out of the box

Name	Description	Example	Error properties
`blank`	Ensures string isn't blank (or null).	`password(blank:false)`	`blank`
`email`	Ensures field is a well-formed email address.	`userEmail(email:true)`	`email.invalid`
`inList`	Ensures value appears in supplied range or collection.	`country(inList:['Australia', 'England'])`	`not.inList`
`matches`	Ensures field matches the supplied regular expression.	`loginId(matches: '[0-9]{7}[A-Za-z]')`	`matches.invalid`
`maxSize`	Ensures size of field in database doesn't exceed supplied value.	`orderQuantity(maxSize:100)`	`maxSize.exceeded`
`minSize`	Ensures size of field in database always exceeds supplied value.	`orderQuantity(minSize:10)`	`minSize.notmet`

Table 3.1 Grails validators available out of the box *(continued)*

Name	Description	Example	Error properties
`nullable`	Specifies whether the property is allowed to be null.	`password(nullable: false)`	`nullable`
`size`	Specifies a range for min and max length of a string or size of an int or collection.	`loginId(size:3..20)`	`size.toosmall` or `size.toobig`
`unique`	Specifies whether the property must be unique.	`loginId(unique:true)`	`unique`
`url`	Ensures that the field contains a valid URL.	`homepage(url:true)`	`url.invalid`
`validator`	Allows custom validation by supplying a closure.	See section 3.3.3	`validator.invalid`
`bindable`	Affects whether a property will bind via automatic data binding.	See chapter 11 on security	N/A

You can find a complete set of validators in the Grails reference documentation at http://grails.org/doc/latest/guide. To find the names of the codes, click Constraints from the Quick Reference list, then click a specific constraint type.

Blank isn't null?

You may have noticed in table 3.1 the separate validators for `nullable` and `blank`. This is important, because when you submit HTML forms with empty fields, they're presented to Grails as "blank" fields that would pass a `nullable:true` validation. The rule of thumb is that if you always want the user to supply a value, use `blank:false`. If you don't mind if a user provides a value or not, use `nullable:true`.

3.3.2 *Custom validation with regular expressions*

What if your validation rules are different, and you need to customize them?

If your validation is a variation on a regular expression pattern, the `matches` constraint will probably do. Say you're writing a student system for your local university, and all student IDs are seven numbers followed by a letter. You may implement that with a straight regular expression:

```
static constraints = {
    loginId matches: '[0-9]{7}[A-Za-z]'
}
```

Regular expressions unlock power, but they may not be powerful enough in certain situations.

3.3.3 Cross-field validation tricks

Regular expressions can take you a certain distance, but won't help if you need to do cross-field validations. Take the business rule that a user's `password` must not match their `loginId`. For these sorts of situations, you need the `validator` closure constraint. It's a little trickier to understand, but it gives you the power to do anything!

When you specify the `validator` constraint, you supply a closure with one or two parameters. The first parameter is the value that the user tried to place in the field, and the second, if you supply one, references the instance of the domain class itself. The closure should return `true` if the data entered is valid for that field.

In our case, we need the two-argument version because you want to confirm that what the user typed in their `password` field doesn't match their `loginId`:

```
static constraints = {
    ...
    password size: 6..8, blank: false, validator: { passwd, user ->
        passwd != user.loginId
    }
    homepage url: true, nullable: true
}
```

Things are getting tricky. When you save the domain class, the password validators now ensure that the password is between six and eight characters inclusive and that the supplied password doesn't match the user's `loginId`. You can get as creative as you like with custom validators, because they give you the power to check programmatically nearly anything.

> **TIP** Several of the constraints (such as `size`, `maxSize`, and `nullable`) have a direct impact on how Grails generates the fields in your database. If you specify a `maxSize` of eight, Grails generates a database field with a column size of eight. Check out the reference guide for specific advice on how certain constraints affect database generation.

3.3.4 Keeping validation DRY by importing constraints

Constraints are a powerful way to specify declaratively the business rules that relate to your domain objects. But what if you need to use the same set of constraints across several objects? What if you decide that passwords need to have the same rules across all objects that have a password?

New in 2.0: Sharing constraints between objects

In Grails 1.x there was no clean way of sharing constraints between objects, leading to a great deal of workaround hackery. Grails 2.0 restores DRYness with the new `importFrom` statement.

You could copy and paste, but that violates the DRY (don't repeat yourself) principle and gives you many points of update. Grails 2.0 introduced a constraints-sharing mechanism that lets you import constraints between objects. Suppose you want an external application to consume Hubbub API services. We'll create an `ApplicationUser` domain class to model that role, but we want to preserve the same password business rules for passwords as our standard `User`. With that scenario in mind, let's examine the following listing, which shares constraints between two domain objects: `User` and `ApplicationUser`.

Listing 3.7 Sharing constraints between objects

```
package com.grailsinaction

class ApplicationUser {

    String applicationName
    String password
    String apiKey

    static constraints = {

        importFrom User, include: ['password']

        applicationName blank: false, unique: true
        apiKey blank: false

    }
}
```

❶ Shares constraints between classes

In this example you import the rules related to the `password` property to the new `ApplicationUser` object ❶. You use the `include:` style, which lets you whitelist the properties to import. Grails also supports an `exclude:` style, which blacklists property constraints that you don't want to import. For ultimate flexibility, it also supports a regular expression style importer that matches wildcards on imported names. To round out the import options, it offers a fourth "no args" style that imports all property constraints from the target object that have names matching the current object. Because your `User` and `ApplicationUser` objects share the same name for their `password` field, you can use the more terse `importFrom User` version.

3.4 Defining the data model—1:1, 1:m, m:n

You now know how CRUD operations work, how to apply validations to your domain class fields, and even how to generate a quick-and-dirty UI. But Hubbub needs more than a `User` class to get work done, so it's time to learn about modeling relationships in the data model.

Figure 3.6 Each `User` object has an optional `Profile` object.

Using an ORM doesn't mean you have to compromise on how you model domain classes. Grails gives you the flexibility to use whatever relationships make sense for you: one-to-one (1:1), one-to-many (1:m), or many-to-many (m:n). Even better, GORM looks after creating the appropriate table structures using sensible naming conventions.

3.4.1 One-to-one relationships

You'll first model a one-to-one relationship. This is probably the easiest relationship to understand.

In the Hubbub example, it's time to refactor out the user's authentication fields (`loginId`, `password`) and profile information (homepage, email, photo, and whatever else comes along). You're moving toward your original Hubbub data model (shown in figure 3.2), which includes a `Profile` object. The relevant section of the data model is shown in figure 3.6.

Start by creating a `Profile` domain class:

```
grails create-domain-class com.grailsinaction.Profile
```

Next, update your newly created object to handle the `Profile`-related features of the existing `User` class. You pull out the `homepage` field and add entries for `email` and even a `photo`. The following listing shows the refactored `Profile` class.

Listing 3.8 Refactored `Profile` class with a 1:1 relationship with the `User` class

```
package com.grailsinaction
class Profile {
    User user
    byte[] photo
    String fullName
    String bio
    String homepage
    String email
    String timezone
    String country
    String jabberAddress
    static constraints = {
        fullName blank: false
        bio nullable: true, maxSize: 1000
        homepage url: true, nullable: true
        email email: true, blank: false
        photo nullable: true, maxSize: 2 * 1024 * 1024
        country nullable: true
        timezone nullable: true
        jabberAddress email: true, nullable: true
    }
}
```

❶ Declares Profile is attached to a User object. (`User user`)

❷ Models binary data in a byte[ ] (`byte[] photo`)

Photo can be up to 2 MB in file size. (`photo nullable: true, maxSize: 2 * 1024 * 1024`)

The most obvious new feature in this domain class is the addition of a `user` field ❶. This field tells GORM that `Profile` has a relationship to the `User` domain class (meaning GORM stores the `User`'s `id` value against the corresponding profile in the database).

> **Refactoring homepage and breaking tests**
>
> With your homepage property moved from the `User` class to `Profile`, several of your tests will now fail. That's a good thing—it's your safety net to make sure your logic still works how you expect. To fix things, make sure you update any references to `user.homepage` (which is now `user.profile.homepage`), including `User`() constructors!

You introduced several new fields and constraints on the `Profile` object, and added placeholders for `fullName` (which is a required field), `bio`, `country`, and `timezone`. You added fields for `homepage` and `email` and used the built-in validators to make sure they conform. Because most of these fields are optional (except for `email` and `fullName`), you marked them `nullable` right from the get-go. Jabber addresses have the same form as email addresses, so you can apply a validator to that field, too.

You also want to store the user's photo with their profile as a BLOB (binary large object). In this case, marking the `photo` field as a byte array (`byte[]`) tells GORM to store it as a BLOB ❷.

Now that you set up the `Profile` class, it's time to link it to your `User` class. The next listing shows the code to create a `hasOne` link to `Profile` in your `User` class and specify constraints for how the relationship works.

Listing 3.9 Adding a 1:1 relationship from `User` to `Profile`

```
package com.grailsinaction
class User {
    String loginId
    String password
    Date dateCreated
    static hasOne = [ profile : Profile ]          ❶ Declares Profile part of User
    static constraints = {
        loginId size: 3..20, unique: true, blank: false
        password size: 6..8, blank: false, validator: { passwd, user ->
            passwd != user.loginId
        }
        profile nullable: true          ❷ Marks Profile as optional
    }
}
```

You introduce new features to your `User` class in the 1:1 refactoring. First, you added a `hasOne` relationship to your `Profile` field for the `User`, so Grails knows the link is 1:1 ❶. It needs to be a set (or list) of `Profiles` to be 1:m.

You also added a constraint to make the profile `nullable` ❷. If you don't specify this, Grails forces you to create a `Profile` instance every time you create a `User` object, which is overhead you can avoid for now.

> **Eager and lazy fetching strategies**
>
> By default, GORM uses a lazy fetching strategy to retrieve attached collections as they're accessed. Most of the time, that's exactly what you want. But in the case of `hasOne` mapping, if your access strategy involves accessing the linked object immediately (as you do with your `Profile` object), it makes sense to have Hibernate retrieve the `Profile` at the same time as the related `User`. This is an *eager fetching* strategy, and Hibernate defaults to eager loading in `hasOne` scenarios to improve performance.
>
> If you use a 1:1 relationship with eager fetching, it may make sense to use Grails's composition feature instead. This allows you to embed the `Profile` object into the same table as the `User` object (but still use different object references to talk to each). We'll talk more about this in online chapter 19 on advanced GORM use.

Now that you have experience with 1:1 mappings, it's time to turn to the more common one-to-many (1:m) modeling scenario.

3.4.2 One-to-many relationships

In our Hubbub example, each user is capable of making many *posts* or *entries*, and each post belongs to one (and only one) user, as shown in figure 3.7. That's a classic one-to-many (1:m) relationship.

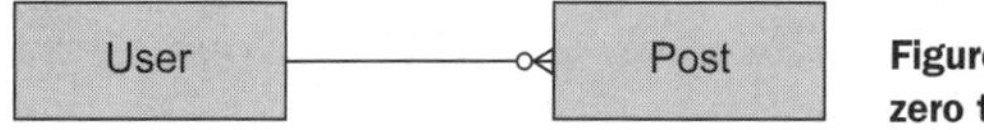

Figure 3.7 Each `User` can have zero to many `Post` objects.

First, create the relationship, and then we'll look at how you can apply sorting to the many sides of the relationship.

CREATING THE ONE-TO-MANY RELATIONSHIP

You need to create a new domain class for `Post`:

```
grails create-domain-class com.grailsinaction.Post
```

Grails introduces two domain class property types to model the relationship: `hasMany` (on the "one" side of the relationship) and `belongsTo` (on the "many" side of the relationship). Implement the `Post` side first, because it needs only a content field and the date it was created. The following listing shows the class.

Listing 3.10 `Post` class models all posts for a given `User`

```
package com.grailsinaction
class Post {
    String content
    Date dateCreated
    static constraints = {
        content blank: false
    }
    static belongsTo = [ user : User ]
}
```

❶ Points to the owning object

In our `Post` example, you see the `belongsTo` property ❶ for the first time. This property is vitally important in both 1:m and m:n relationships because it tells GORM how to implement cascading operations. In particular, when the `User` is deleted, all their matching `Post` objects are deleted, too.

> **BelongsTo and cascading**
>
> GORM cascades only to objects marked with `belongsTo`. In listing 3.10, `Post` `belongsTo` `User`, so if any `User` is deleted, the matching `Post` object is also deleted. `belongsTo` has a special meaning in m:n relationships, where `addTo*()` methods can be persisted only from the owning side. But more on that later.
>
> In listing 3.10, you used the *map style* of `belongsTo`, where you created a bidirectional link between `User` and `Post` classes. This creates a new field on `Post` called `user` that's the bidirectional mapping back to the owning `User`. This lets you move backward to `post.user.loginId`, for example. This is handy later, when you query for posts and want to show the associated user's ID.

You told Grails that `Post` belongs to a `User`, so now you need a way to tell it that your `User` object should link to many `Post` objects. That's done with a `hasMany` property:

```
class User {
    // existing code here
    static hasMany = [ posts : Post ]
}
```

With `hasMany` and `belongsTo` in place, you have all the basics of the one-to-many relationship. But how do we tell Grails to add new `Posts` for a given `User`? With more GORM magic.

Once you have a one-to-many relationship between `User` and `Post`, Grails automatically adds two new methods to your `User` class: `User.addToPosts()` and `User.removeFromPosts()`. You need to create an integration test for `Post` so you can exercise these new capabilities. Start with the usual process:

```
grails create-integration-test com.grailsinaction.PostIntegration
```

With the shell of our test case in place, write code to create a user and add new posts to their account. In the following listing, you'll take full advantage of the new `addToPosts()` method to make your `User` more prolific.

Listing 3.11 The `User.addToPosts()` method makes 1:m relationships easy

```
package com.grailsinaction

import spock.lang.*

class PostIntegrationSpec extends Specification {

    def "Adding posts to user links post to user"() {
```

```
        given: "A brand new user"
        def user = new User(loginId: 'joe', password: 'secret')     ❶ Creates User
        user.save(failOnError: true)                                   to hold Posts

        when: "Several posts are added to the user"
        user.addToPosts(new Post(content: "First post... W00t!"))   ❷ Persists Post
        user.addToPosts(new Post(content: "Second post..."))           by adding to
        user.addToPosts(new Post(content: "Third post..."))            a User

        then: "The user has a list of posts attached"
        3 == User.get(user.id).posts.size()
    }
}
```

Notice that you have to call `save()` on the `User` object to persist it in the database ❶. Once the `User` is attached to the database, though, any additions you make to its object graph (such as adding new `Post` objects via `addToPosts()` ❷) are automatically persisted. For this reason, you don't need to call `save()` on each `Post` you create. If you feel skeptical, rerun your test cases to make sure everything works as you expect:

```
grails test-app integration:
```

By taking advantage of GORM's magic dynamic properties, you added your user and a few posts. But how do you retrieve those posts when you want to work? A typical approach is to get a handle to the `User` object and iterate through their posts. The following listing shows a test case that accesses all posts for a given user.

Listing 3.12 Accessing a `User`'s posts by walking the object graph

```
def "Ensure posts linked to a user can be retrieved"() {

    given: "A user with several posts"
    def user = new User(loginId: 'joe', password: 'secret')
    user.addToPosts(new Post(content: "First"))                    Adds posts
    user.addToPosts(new Post(content: "Second"))                   to User
    user.addToPosts(new Post(content: "Third"))
    user.save(failOnError: true)

    when: "The user is retrieved by their id"                      ❶ Loads User
    def foundUser = User.get(user.id)                                 via ID
    def sortedPostContent = foundUser.posts.collect {
        it.content                                                 ❷ Iterates through
    }.sort()                                                          User's posts

    then: "The posts appear on the retrieved user"
    sortedPostContent == ['First', 'Second', 'Third']              ❸ Sorts posts
}                                                                     alphabetically
```

In this example, you load the user via `id` ❶, then use the Groovy `collect()` method ❷ to iterate through each post, retrieving the content. The `collect()` returns a list of `Post` content, which we compare to ensure the list value matches your known values.

By default, you won't know the ordering of 1:m collections (because they're mapped as `Sets`), so for this test case, we sort them alphabetically to make the comparison meaningful ❸.

To present the user's posting history, you typically want to sort their posts by descending creation date, but sorting by hand every time gets old quickly. In the next section, we look at a way to return posts already sorted.

KEEPING THE MANY SIDE SORTED

When using one-to-many relationships, you often won't care about the ordering on the many side, such as for items on an invoice. For these situations, it makes sense to use the default Grails ordering. When you do need to apply ordering, take advantage of Grails's more sophisticated search options (such as Where and Criteria queries, which we cover in chapter 5) to do the ordering at the same time.

Sometimes you want to access the many side of a relationship in a prescribed order. In a blog application you likely want to keep entries in descending date order (so your front page displays the most recent entries). For these situations, Grails lets you specify your own ordering mechanism using the mapping closure (which you used in our `Profile` example in listing 3.10).

To implement this type of sorting, let Grails know that your `Posts` need to be returned in a sorted order based on the date they were created. Do this by adding a new mapping block to your `Post` domain class, as shown in the following listing.

Listing 3.13 Sorting `Posts` by creation date

```
package com.grailsinaction
class Post {
    String content
    Date dateCreated
    static constraints = {
        content blank: false
    }
    static belongsTo = [ user : User ]
    static mapping = {
        sort dateCreated:"desc"        <-- Specifies sort order for Post
    }
}
```

You can specify the sort order as either ascending or descending. In this example, all queries to the `Post` object return in a descending order.

But what if you want the posts sorted when accessing them via the `User` object (such as when iterating over `user.posts.each`)? For those scenarios, Grails lets you specify the sort on the relationship itself, rather than on the `Post` object. You can update your `User` class (instead of the `Post` class) with a mapping block like this:

```
static mapping = {
    posts sort:'dateCreated'
}
```

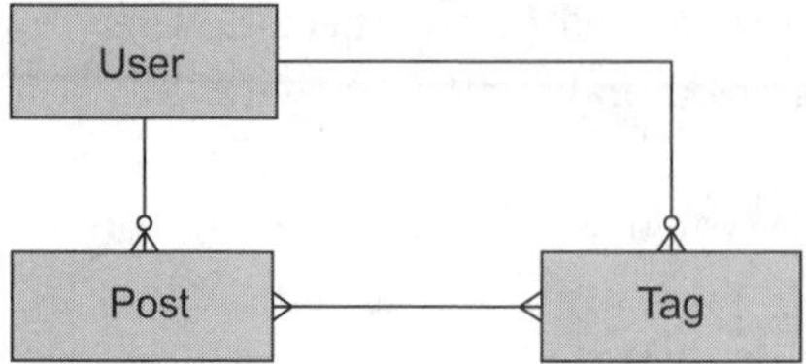

Figure 3.8 A tricky many-to-many scenario between `Users`, `Posts`, and `Tags`

This form of the mapping tells Grails that you want to sort by `dateCreated` when accessing the `posts` collection via a user.

Now that we've looked at sorting, it's time to move on to the trickiest relationship of them all: many-to-many.

3.4.3 Many-to-many relationships

Where would your social networking application be without tags? Tags give users the chance to group and cluster their posts, browse posts associated with particular tags, and generally categorize their posts. Let's make a provision in the domain model for tagging.

It's also time to consider how you may want to use tags. Let's imagine these are your requirements:

- Generate a tag cloud for the user on their home page
- Provide an RSS feed for all posts with a given tag
- See all tags for a given post

To include those requirements in your domain model, you need to model two relationships:

- A `User` creates many `Tags`, so each `Tag` relates to one `User` (1:m)
- A `Post` has many `Tags`, and each `Tag` may relate to many `Posts` (m:n)

That's a mouthful, but the model in figure 3.8 may make things clearer.

The good news about many-to-many relationships is there's little new syntax to learn. If two objects are in a many-to-many relationship, they both have a `hasMany` clause pointing to the other object. The following listing updates your `Post` class to add the new `hasMany` relationship with your `Tag` class.

Listing 3.14 Modeling a `Post` that can have many `Tags`

```
class Post {
    String content
    Date dateCreated
    static constraints = {
        content blank: false
    }
    static belongsTo = [ user : User ]
    static hasMany = [ tags : Tag ]            <- Models a Post with many Tags

    static mapping = {
        sort dateCreated:"desc"
    }
}
```

We've seen `hasMany` before in one-to-many scenarios, and this is the same beast. The `[ tags : Tag ]` map tells us that a `Post` relates to many `Tag` objects and that the relationship is stored in a property named `tags`.

Let's introduce the `Tag` domain model, which you can link back to our `Post` object. In the following listing you'll specify that a `Tag hasMany Posts`.

Listing 3.15 The `Tag` object models relationships to both `Post` and `User`

```
class Tag {
    String name
    User user
    static constraints = {
        name blank: false
    }
    static hasMany = [ posts : Post ]
    static belongsTo = [ User, Post ]
}
```

Affects the side objects that can be added from

You can see the `hasMany` relationship in listing 3.15 this time linking back to the `Post` class. The other important difference in this class is that the `Tag belongsTo` both `User` and `Post`. This `belongsTo` relationship is important in the many-to-many context: it affects how `addTo*()` methods work (see the following sidebar for more information).

> **How belongsTo affects many-to-many relationships**
>
> The `belongsTo` field controls where the dynamic `addTo*()` methods can be used from. In listing 3.15, we can call `User.addToTags()` because `Tag belongsTo User`. We can also call `Post.addToTags()` because `Tag belongsTo Post`. But `Post` doesn't `belongTo Tag`, so we can't call `Tag.addToPosts()`.

The last change that we need to make relates to the `User` object, which now needs to be updated to reference the `Post` and `Tag` classes. The following listing updates the `hasMany` clause.

Listing 3.16 `User` now `hasMany Posts` and `Tags`

```
package com.grailsinaction
class User {
    // .. existing code
    static hasMany = [ posts : Post, tags : Tag ]
}
```

Specifies User has many Posts and Tags

You referenced both `Post` and `Tag` in the `User` class's `hasMany` clause. With all the pieces of the many-to-many relationship in place, let's write a test case to make sure that your assumptions still hold true. The following listing presents a test case for a post with one or more tags, which you can add to `PostIntegrationSpec`.

Listing 3.17 A complex many-to-many scenario for posts and tags

```
def "Exercise tagging several posts with various tags"() {

    given: "A user with a set of tags"
    def user = new User(loginId: 'joe', password: 'secret')
    def tagGroovy = new Tag(name: 'groovy')
    def tagGrails = new Tag(name: 'grails')
    user.addToTags(tagGroovy)
    user.addToTags(tagGrails)
    user.save(failOnError: true)

    when: "The user tags two fresh posts"
    def groovyPost = new Post(content: "A groovy post")
    user.addToPosts(groovyPost)
    groovyPost.addToTags(tagGroovy)

    def bothPost = new Post(content: "A groovy and grails post")
    user.addToPosts(bothPost)
    bothPost.addToTags(tagGroovy)
    bothPost.addToTags(tagGrails)

    then:
    user.tags*.name.sort() == [ 'grails', 'groovy']
    1 == groovyPost.tags.size()
    2 == bothPost.tags.size()

}
```

Sets up tags, adds them to user

❶ Adds post to user, tag to post

❷ Adds multiple tags to post

Because your `Tag` class is 1:m to `User` and m:n to `Post`, you have to add the tag to the user and the tag to the post. Behind the scenes, Grails manages both the `users` and `posts` properties on the newly added `Tag` object, ensuring that all the relationships are kept bidirectional.

In listing 3.17, you have a `groovyPost` ❶ with one tag ("groovy") and a `bothPost` ❷ with two tags ("groovy" and "grails"). By making numerous calls to `post.addToTags()`, you can add as many tags to each post as the user wants.

As you can see, many-to-many relationships are the trickiest of the standard relationships, so you need to get a good handle on how the `addTo*()` methods work. Listing 3.17 gets you started, but we encourage you to experiment with your own use cases.

Cascading: the rules for deletes and updates

GORM works behind the scenes to make all those 1:m and m:n relationships work smoothly. We've explored the `addTo*()` methods, but we haven't looked into how GORM handles the cascading.

The rules around 1:m relationships are straightforward. In our Hubbub example, if you delete a `User`, GORM automatically deletes all associated `Post` objects.

But let's take the trickier situation of `Tags`. A `Post` may have many `Tags`, and each `Tag` may relate to more than one `Post`. In this case, GORM settles things by looking at the `belongsTo` clause. If there's no `belongsTo` clause defined on the object, no cascades will happen in either direction, and you're on your own.

3.4.4 *Self-referencing relationships*

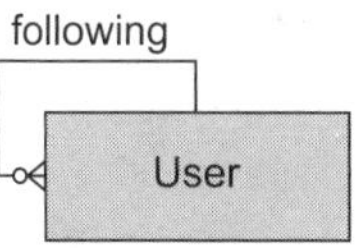

Figure 3.9 Modeling the "follows" relationship

The final part of the Hubbub data model models the "follows" process—how a `User` can follow other `Users`. The data model includes it as a self-referencing relationship, as shown in figure 3.9.

There's nothing special about the self-referencing part. It's a specialized version of the one-to-many relationship you've already seen. You can update the `User` class's `hasMany` reference to model the relationship, as shown here:

```
class User {
    //... other code omitted
    static hasMany = [ posts : Post, tags : Tag, following : User ]
}
```

As usual, write a test case to make sure you know how things will work. The test in the following listing adds people the user is following. It goes in `UserIntegrationSpec`.

Listing 3.18 A simple test case for adding followers

```
def "Ensure a user can follow other users"() {

    given: "A set of baseline users"
    def joe = new User(loginId: 'joe', password:'password').save()
    def jane = new User(loginId: 'jane', password:'password').save()
    def jill = new User(loginId: 'jill', password:'password').save()

    when: "Joe follows Jane & Jill, and Jill follows Jane"
    joe.addToFollowing(jane)
    joe.addToFollowing(jill)
    jill.addToFollowing(jane)

    then: "Follower counts should match following people"
    2 == joe.following.size()
    1 == jill.following.size()

}
```

Works on self-references, too

As you can see, `addToFollowing()` works the same way for self-references as in the previous one-to-many scenario.

You explored relationship types in Grails, and you have a full set of integration tests to prove it. Grails has been busy also, generating the tables and fields behind the scenes (including the foreign key relationships). If you look inside the Hubbub database, you'll see that it now consists of five tables that hold all the data and relationships in our application. Figure 3.10 shows the full layout of the database, which makes sense when you match it up with the domain model fields you created to date.

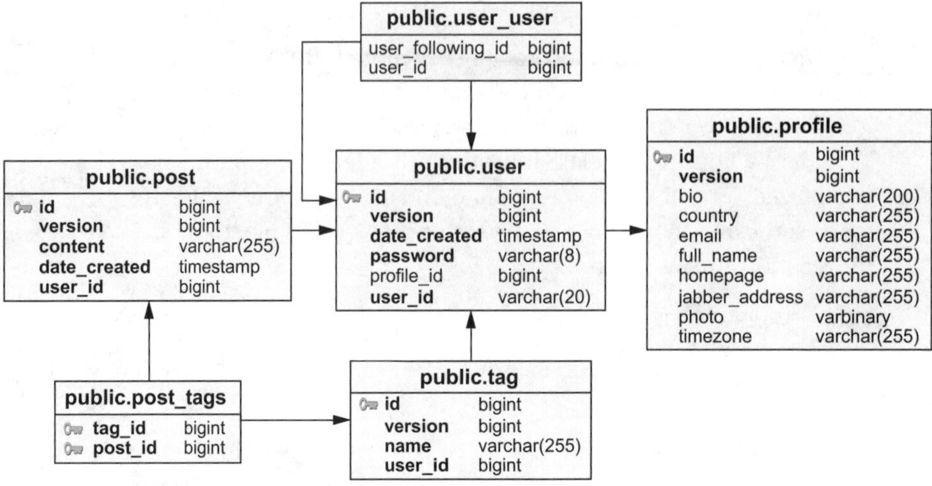

Figure 3.10 The final Hubbub data model after all changes

3.5 Summary and best practices

We covered an immense amount of material in this chapter. Many of the concepts we introduced are foundational and are reinforced in the next few chapters where we cover controllers and views.

We introduced the domain model class, including the common domain model relationships. You learned about validation and how to create custom constraints.

Best practices covered in this chapter:

- *Use domain-driven design.* Create your basic domain model classes as the first step in your application, and use scaffolding to get them online. This helps you stay motivated and understand your domain better.
- *Learn the basic modeling options.* You'll spend time setting up Grails models in your future development work. Take the time to learn all the basic relationship types presented in this chapter. The test cases give you valuable experimentation fodder.
- *Use tests to experiment.* Domain model test cases provide a great way of experimenting with tricky `save()` scenarios and testing your validations.
- *Don't trust users—validate.* Make use of validators to keep your domain objects in order. Custom validators aren't hard to implement, so don't be afraid to roll your own if the situation demands. It's better to encapsulate the validation logic in your domain class than to use dodgy controller hacks.

Armed with those basics, you need to develop a little more UI kung fu to be ready for your first fully functional version of Hubbub, which is only a few short chapters away.

4 Creating the initial UI

This chapter covers

- Generating UIs instantly with scaffolding
- Restyling the scaffolding
- Customizing the scaffolding for your project

We spent most of the last chapter on domain modeling. It's time to reward that effort with an instant working web application based on the scaffolding you first saw in chapter 1. In this chapter, you'll create that UI and take a closer look at how it works and how to customize its look.

Do you need scaffolding? No. Few live web applications are based on such UIs because they aren't particularly user-friendly. Why not start working on a fancy UI for Hubbub? We have several reasons.

First, it's nice to have a working web application quickly. It allows you to experiment with the domain model and show off progress to your boss, and it works brilliantly with a release early, release often approach. Getting to the same stage with a custom UI requires more of an investment in HTML, CSS, and back-end implementation. And the larger the domain model, the longer it takes to get to that point!

Second, scaffolding isn't exclusive. You can develop a custom UI side by side with the scaffolding and even integrate the two. In the case of Hubbub, this allows you to create posts, add tags, and edit the content of posts, all while still developing the main timeline page. That makes it easier to test features and debug problems without inspecting the database directly.

Finally, this approach introduces you to the main components of a Grails application and illustrates how they interact without code getting in the way. So let's get started and scaffold the domain classes you created in chapter 3.

4.1 Creating instant UIs with scaffolding

In chapter 3, you created a `User` class and explored CRUD operations and querying by hand. That's important stuff that you'll use soon, but scaffolding allows you to create, edit, and delete user instances from your browsers without any need to work with the domain classes directly. These first steps require a single Grails command (`create-scaffold-controller`), refinement of the domain class constraints, and judicious changes to a properties file.

4.1.1 Scaffolding Hubbub's domain classes

We introduced Grails's scaffolding in chapter 1, but that time we created the controller and then edited it to enable scaffolding. This time, we need to scaffold four domain classes, so we'll take a shortcut and create a scaffolding-enabled controller in one step. Start the Grails interactive console and execute this series of commands:

```
create-scaffold-controller com.grailsinaction.User
create-scaffold-controller com.grailsinaction.Profile
create-scaffold-controller com.grailsinaction.Post
create-scaffold-controller com.grailsinaction.Tag
```

You can use tab completion on the command name and domain class.

These commands create a corresponding controller file for each domain class, such as grails-app/controllers/com/grailsinaction/UserController.groovy, that looks like this:

```
package com.grailsinaction

class UserController {
    static scaffold = true
}
```

Scaffolds by convention (UserController -> User domain class)

Now start the Grails application to see the scaffolding in action. Execute `run-app` from the interactive console and point your browser at http://localhost:8080/hubbub. Clicking on the `UserController` link on the home page brings up an empty list of users (there's no data in the database yet), but you can follow the Create User link to add a user to the system. You'll see an editing screen that allows you to populate the user's details, as shown in figure 4.1.

You may ask how does Grails determine the order in which to display the domain class fields in the show, create, and edit views? Perhaps it's the order in which the fields are declared in the class itself? In fact, the order is random unless you declare constraints.

Fields in random order often look weird because data typically has a logical order to it, so controlling the order in which they appear is a useful feature. Fortunately, the

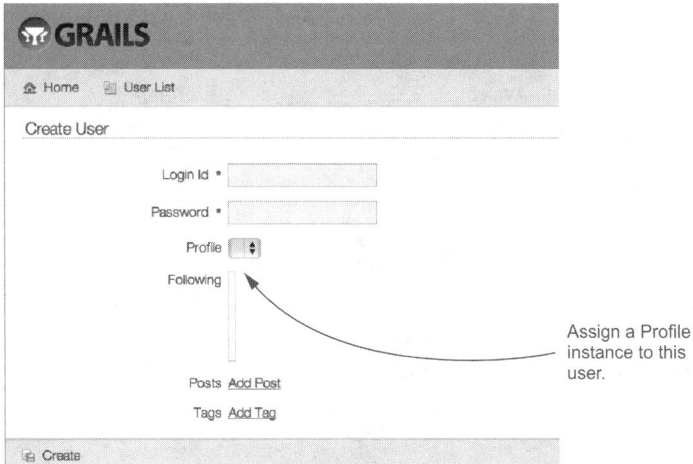

Figure 4.1 Scaffolding also includes relationships to other domain classes.

scaffolding displays the fields in the order in which they're declared in the constraints block. Recall the user constraints from chapter 3:

```
static constraints = {
    loginId size: 3..20, unique: true
    password size: 6..8, validator: {
        passwd, user -> passwd != user.userId
    }
    profile nullable: true
}
```

Compare the ordering of these constraints with the generated form in figure 4.1. The order of the form fields in that figure matches the ordering of the constraints shown in the previous code. You can even control the ordering of fields that have no validation constraints (new code in italics):

```
static constraints = {
    loginId size: 3..20, unique: true
    password size: 6..8, validator: { passwd, user ->
        passwd != user.loginId
    }
    tags()                          Controls ordering of associated fields
    posts()                         without any validation constraints
    profile nullable: true
}
```

Of course, constraints aren't for decoration. In the previous chapter, we mentioned how they can affect the schema generated in the database. They're also an integral part of Grails's validation mechanism, which is fully incorporated into the scaffolding.

4.1.2 Improving the validation

In the coming sections, you're going to need a valid profile in the system. This will give you an ideal opportunity to explore how the scaffolding handles validation failures. Let's start by looking at how validation errors manifest themselves in the scaffolding pages.

USING THE DEFAULT VALIDATION BEHAVIOR

Figure 4.2 contains the results of trying to submit the Create Profile form with an invalid home page URL and invalid email address.

The most striking thing to note in this figure is that Chrome and Safari behave differently. The form fields use new HTML5 types, such as `email` and `url`, which the browsers know how to validate, and it's up to the browser how it deals with validation failures on those fields. Safari always submits the form to the server, whereas Chrome won't. Such browser differences are something you should get used to.

One immediate area of improvement is in the server-side generated errors, as seen with Safari. If the form is submitted, the Create Profile page displays again with these error messages at the top:

- Property [homepage] of class [class `com.grailsinaction.Profile`] with value [not a URL] is not a valid URL
- Property [email] of class [class `com.grailsinaction.Profile`] with value [invalid email] is not a valid e-mail address

These are far too geeky for the average user, so let's change them into something closer to plain English.

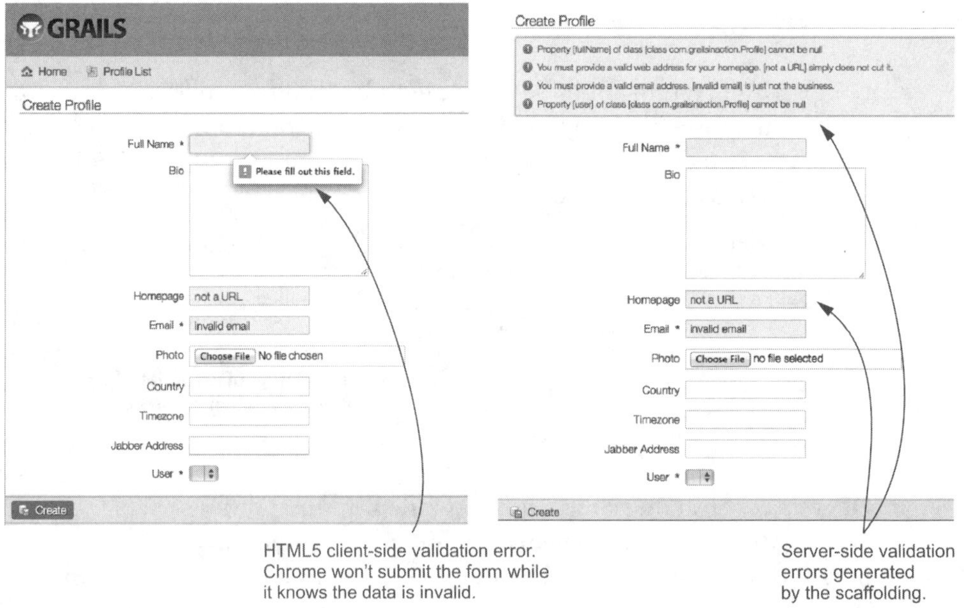

Figure 4.2 How validation errors look in the scaffolding; shown in Chrome (at left) and in Safari (at right).

CUSTOMIZING ERROR MESSAGES

Validation error messages are one example of text that's visible to the user but should be easy to find and modify in your project. You don't want text embedded in your code, and in these days of globalization, it makes sense to localize such text as well. That's easily done in Grails using properties files known as *resource bundles.*

Our exploration starts in the grails-app/i18n/messages.properties file. You'll see many entries in this file, but the following are those we're interested in currently:

```
default.invalid.url.message=Property [{0}] of class [{1}] with value [{2}] is
    not a valid URL
default.invalid.email.message=Property [{0}] of class [{1}] with value [{2}]
    is not a valid e-mail address
```

Recognize from figure 4.2 that these are the error messages displayed for the Homepage and Email fields. They apply to any property that fails to validate against the `url` and `email` constraints. As is, they're fine for development, but context is required to clearly communicate the problem to end users. Your users shouldn't need to know about class names and properties.

To make the messages more relevant, create an entry in `messages.properties` specifically for them:

```
profile.homepage.url.invalid=You must provide a valid web address for your
    homepage. [{2}] simply does not cut it.
profile.email.email.invalid=You must provide a valid email address. [{2}] is
    just not the business.
```

That's all you have to do—Grails automatically selects these messages for your profile fields based on conventions. To leverage those conventions, use message keys (the text to the left of the =) of the form shown in figure 4.3.

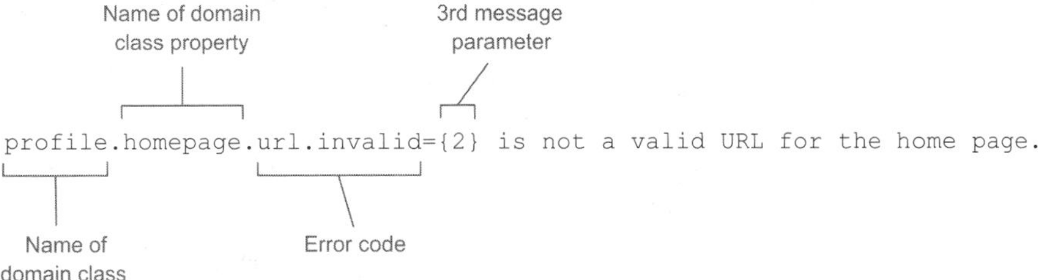

Figure 4.3 Declaring custom messages in resource bundles

That was easy, but how did we know that the invalid value substitutes the parameter `{2}` in the message text? It can be inferred from the default validation messages, but it isn't documented in the Grails user guide. That isn't particularly helpful for people learning the framework, so here are the parameter numbers and what those parameters contain:

- `{0}`—The name of the domain class property.
- `{1}`—The name of the domain class.
- `{2}`—The invalid value.

- {3}—The limiting value in the constraint, such as a maximum value or a matching pattern. Applies to `match`, `max`, `min`, `maxSize`, `minSize`, `inList`, and `equals` constraints.
- {4}—The upper bound for a constraint ({3} is the lower bound). Applies to `range` and `size` constraints.

This mechanism extends beyond the error messages to the scaffolding labels. If you look at `messages.properties` again, you'll see message keys such as the following:

```
default.home.label=Home
default.list.label={0} List
```

You can, for example, change the text for the Home link on the top navigation bar by modifying the `default.home.label` value.

Customizing error messages is one of the first things you should do if you plan to have users interact with the scaffolding UI. It's a small change, but it improves the user experience.

> **Localization**
> You'll see many properties files under grails-app/i18n. You can provide language-specific custom messages to your application by adding them to the appropriate messages_<lang>.properties file. Messages in French would go in messages_fr .properties, messages_fr_FR.properties, or messages_fr_CA.properties. These properties files use UTF-8 for the encoding, so you can use non-Latin characters. For more in-depth information, research Java resource bundles.

With the scaffolding in place and useful error messages for failed validation, you could feasibly move on and start building Hubbub's proper UI. If the application developers are the only ones who'll see and use the scaffolding, why invest more time and effort?

Now imagine that you retain the scaffolding as an administrative UI or that you make the application available to end users early to get feedback. In these cases, you want the scaffolding to fit with the look of the final application and with the company branding. In the next section, we dive into customizing the look of the scaffolding UI.

4.2 Restyling the scaffolding

Although the default scaffolding is powerful, the generic Grails look begs to be tweaked. You might want to do it to show off progress to your managers, who'd appreciate a unique look with the company branding. Alternatively, you may want to make the scaffolding UI available to end users, in which case it must look like a company product. Looks do count as part of the user experience and brand identity.

Grails gives you several options for customizing the look of the scaffolding UI, from simple changes to colors, images, fonts, etc., to completely changing the underlying

HTML markup. Start with the simplest approach: updating the style of the pages using Cascading Style Sheets (CSS).

4.2.1 Changing the skin you're in

Once upon a time, HTML markup not only determined the structure of content but also the look of the resulting page. You'd use the `<b>` tag to display things in bold or `<font>` to change the typeface. If you were really hip, you'd throw in the `<blink>` text (which has, thankfully, been consigned to the dustbin of history). Life was simple, that is, unless you needed to change the look of the footer across a whole set of pages, or change the color of level 2 headings. Then life became hard quickly.

Wise people decided that the inability to customize pages easily was holding back the web as a presentation platform, so they introduced a transformative technology called CSS. As shown in figure 4.4, the idea is simple: keep the semantic meaning of a document in the markup where it belongs, but move styling into style sheets that can be applied to multiple documents. Changing the look of a particular category of heading across multiple pages is now a simple case of modifying a single CSS rule in a separate file: the style sheet.

Many readers are already aware of CSS and comfortable working with it. If you aren't one of those people, don't worry. We'll introduce examples to get you started.

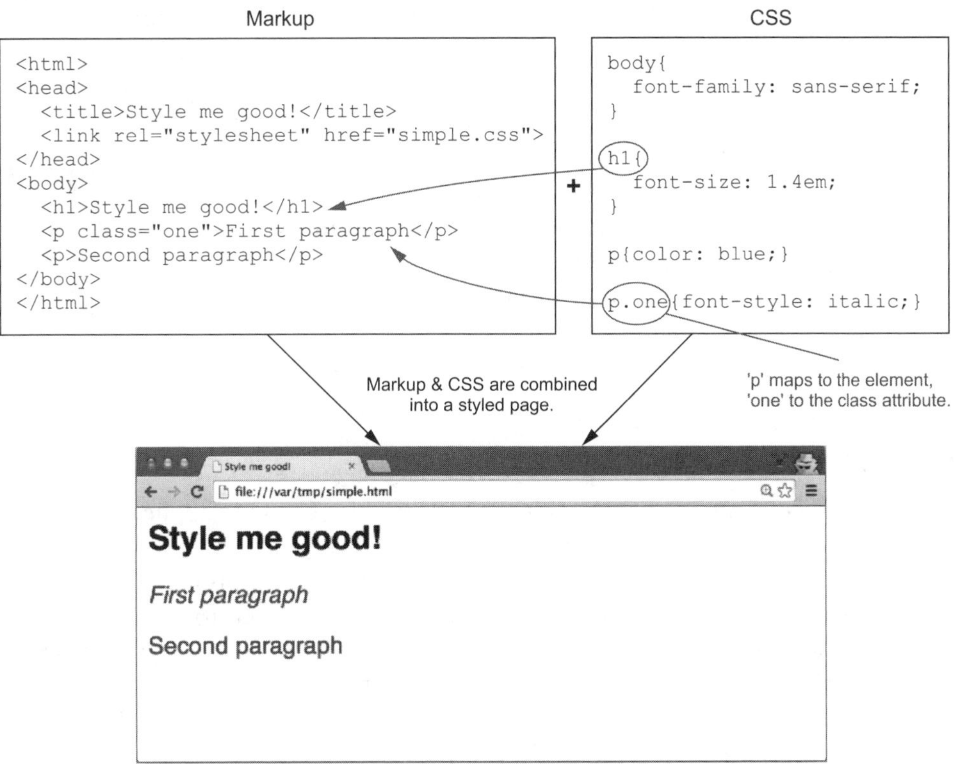

Figure 4.4 HTML + CSS = good-looking pages

You may not even need to work on CSS if your team has dedicated front-end developers, but it's still useful to understand how it works in case you need to fix something urgently, and those front-end developers aren't around.

As for the scaffolding, you can find all the styles for it in the web-app/css/main.css file in your Grails project. All you have to do is edit that file to add your own flair. Let's say you want to change all the major headings, `<h1>` elements, to appear in bright red and italic bold. Find the `h1` rule in main.css and update it to look like this:

```
h1 {
    color: red;
    font-style: italic;
    font-weight: bold;
    font-size: 1.25em;
    margin: 0.8em 0 0.3em 0;
}
```

Modifies the text color from green to red, the font from normal to italic, and the font weight from normal to bold.

The CSS attributes we've changed are fairly easy to work with, but main.css does contain attributes that are more complex. One of the best ways to learn is to make changes to existing rules and see what happens! It's also worth trying out the browser's developer tools, such as Firebug for Firefox and Developer Tools for Chrome and Safari. Even Internet Explorer has decent developer tools these days. They allow you to see what styles are active on particular elements of the markup as well as change CSS values on the fly. They even provide autocompletion for colors, font styles, and many other CSS attributes. Such tools are invaluable when working on browser-based UIs.

We've touched on CSS here, but it's an amazingly powerful technology that enables you to change the look of the scaffolding beyond recognition. Beyond modifying fonts and colors, you can also affect the way parts of the page are laid out with CSS. Still, it does have limitations. You can't, for example, add extra links and images to the header and footer of the pages, because those additions require markup. And if you want to add branding to your pages, you'll almost certainly want custom links and images.

4.2.2 Branding your pages

Say you want to add your company logo and slogan to the application pages, and perhaps your legal department asked you to add a disclaimer and copyright message to the bottom of each page. For all its power, you can't do this with CSS. You should use a layout, and in this section, we'll show you how to add custom headers and footers to the scaffolding with a minimum of fuss. In chapter 8 you'll learn more about the details of layouts.

As it happens, the scaffolding already uses a layout: grails-app/views/layouts/main.gsp, which you can modify to add your own banner. You can see the result in the following listing.

Listing 4.1 Changing the standard layout decorator for Hubbub

```
<html>
<head>
  <title>Hubbub &raquo; <g:layoutTitle default="Welcome" /></title>
  <g:external dir="css" file="hubbub.css"/>        <-- Adds a custom CSS file
  <g:external dir="css" file="main.css"/>
  <g:layoutHead />
</head>
<body>
  <div>
    <div id="hd">
      <g:link uri="/">
        <g:img id="logo" uri="/images/headerlogo.png"
➥ alt="hubbub logo"/>
      </g:link>
    </div>
    <div id="bd"><!-- start body -->
      <g:layoutBody/>
    </div>  <!-- end body -->
    <div id="ft">
      <div id="footerText">Hubbub - Social Networking on Grails</div>
    </div>
  </div>
</body>
</html>
```

Uses custom masthead image

Adds a simple custom footer

With this modified layout file and the hubbub.css style sheet (which you can find on GitHub), you end up with scaffolding that looks like figure 4.5.

Using this technique, you can quickly change the layout for your entire site. Even better, once you learn more about how layouts work, you can override the layouts on a per-controller or even per-action basis. This allows you to fine-tune the look of different sections of the site. Let's say you want to include text in the banner that identifies whether the current page is related to posts, users, or profiles. You could add these layout files:

- *grails-app/views/layouts/post.gsp*—This would contain a banner labeled Posts that would be displayed on all pages implemented by `PostController`.
- *grails-app/views/layouts/user.gsp*—The banner would be labeled Users.
- *grails-app/views/layouts/profile.gsp*—The banner would be labeled Profiles.

For the layouts to take effect for the pages of a particular controller, the name of the layout file must match the logical property name of the controller, that is, `PostController` becomes post.gsp.

You've gotten rid of that default feel to the scaffolding for the Hubbub application, and you haven't had to do much work to get there. You could leave the scaffolding UI as is and go straight to developing that user-friendly UI we talked about; however, if the scaffolding works well for your situation, but you need more control over the individual screens, you have more customization options that we'll discuss in the next section.

Figure 4.5 You can change the scaffolding to use your own layouts and style sheets.

4.3 Working with the scaffolding code directly

Until now, we've looked at only dynamic scaffolding and how to influence the look and feel through changes to the domain class constraints, error messages, styles, and layouts. You haven't in any way changed the hidden code that underpins the scaffolding. Can you do that? If you can, you'll have greater flexibility in customizing not only the look of the UI but also the behavior.

Grails provides two options to reveal that hidden code and modify it:

- Expose the scaffolding templates
- Generate the physical code for all your scaffolding controllers

Both approaches have advantages and disadvantages, so we'll look at them in turn and then discuss which to use and when in the best practice section of the chapter.

4.3.1 Customizing the dynamic scaffolding

There's only one way to customize the HTML markup used by the dynamic scaffolding: modifying the scaffolding templates. To demonstrate how to do this, consider a simple change that you want to make to the scaffolding UI. It's currently difficult for a user to select the appropriate profile for a new Hubbub user, as you can see in figure 4.6.

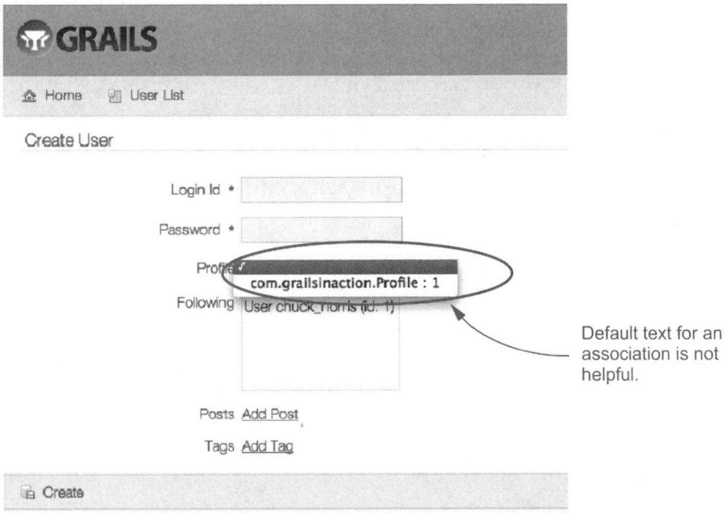

Figure 4.6 The default scaffolding page for creating a new user.

Unless you know which profile has a particular instance ID, you have to guess which one to pick! Ideally the drop-down list should display identifying information such as the `fullName` field of the profile, as shown in figure 4.7.

As you can see, that's much more user friendly. The simplest way to implement this is to add a `toString()` method in the `Profile` domain class that returns the full name:

```
class Profile {
    String fullName
    . . .

    String toString() { return fullName }
}
```

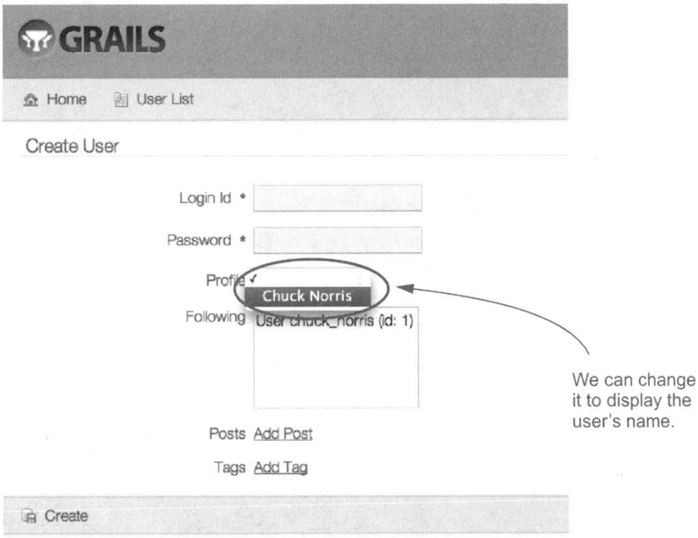

Figure 4.7 The improved Create User page lets you select a Profile by its full name.

That will fix the Create User page right away. So why wouldn't you want to do this? After all, it certainly fits the principle of Keep It Simple, Stupid (KISS). The problem is that `toString()` is used in many other circumstances as well, such as in logging, inside debuggers, and in simple `println()` statements. In those situations, you typically want information that's more useful for diagnostics, which conflicts with the needs of the UI.

We'll take a different, more involved, approach that relies on modifying the underlying scaffolding code. The idea is to use a special `displayString` property that the scaffolding uses when displaying an association. All you have to do then is add the property to every domain class involved in scaffolding, as we show here for the `Profile` class:

```
class Profile {
    String fullName
    . . .

    String toString() { return "Profile of $fullName (id: $id)" }

    String getDisplayString() { return fullName }
}
```

Returns a diagnostic string for log messages and debugging (annotates `toString()`)

Creates a read-only displayString property for the scaffolding (annotates `getDisplayString()`)

Before you can modify the scaffolding templates, you must first install the template files into the project. The scaffolding uses these files to generate the UI on the fly.

INSTALLING THE TEMPLATE FILES

Run the command

```
grails install-templates
```

and look in the newly created src/templates directory. You'll see a set of directories and files matching those shown in figure 4.8.

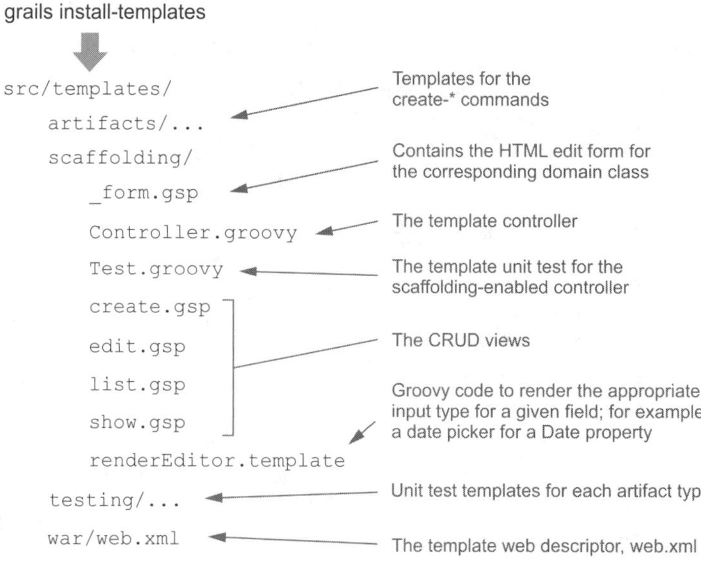

Figure 4.8 The files added to your project via the `install-templates` command

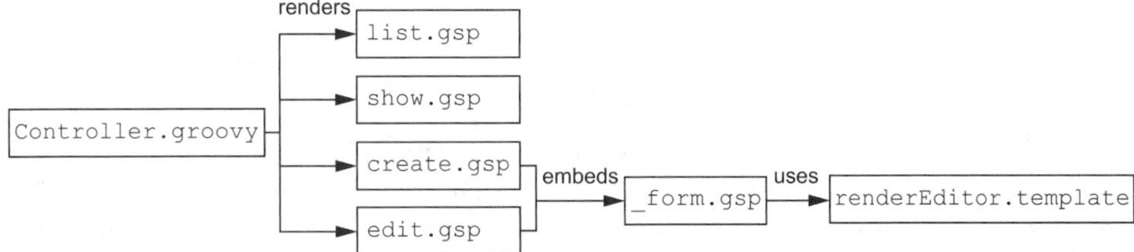

Figure 4.9 How the different scaffolding templates fit together

Once you have those template files in your project, you can start customizing them.

> **NOTE** Customization of the scaffolding templates is a fairly advanced topic for this early in the book, so feel free to skip to the next section and come back when you're more comfortable with Grails.

For those who want to stay for the ride, let's make the scaffolding use the `displayString` property. The key initial question is which files need changing. To answer that, you need to understand each template file's role. We show the relationships in figure 4.9. As you can see, they aren't complicated.

Which files do you need to modify? The controller has nothing to do with how associations are rendered, so you can ignore that. The list and show views do render the values of associations, so they require tweaking. You may think the create and edit files also need changes because they display drop-down lists and list boxes for associations, but hopefully you can see from figures 4.8 and 4.9 that the actual rendering of those widgets happens in `renderEditor.template`, which means you can safely ignore the create and edit views as well as the `_form.gsp` partial template.

MODIFYING THE TEMPLATES

The three files you need to modify—list.gsp, show.gsp, and renderEditor.template—are all fairly long, so we show only enough in the code samples to identify what code you add and where. Let's start with the list view in the following listing, in which the extra code is marked in italics.

Listing 4.2 Required changes to the template list.gsp

```
. . .
<tbody>
  <g:each in="\${${propertyName}List}" status="i" var="${propertyName}">
  <tr class="\${(i % 2) == 0 ? 'even' : 'odd'}">
    <%  props.eachWithIndex { p, i ->
          if (i == 0) { %>
    . . .
    <%     } else if (p.manyToOne || p.oneToOne) { %>
    <td>\${${propertyName}?.${p.name}?.displayString?.encodeAsHTML()}</td>
    <%     } else { %>
    <td>\${fieldValue(bean: ${propertyName}, field: "${p.name}")}</td>
    <%  }    }    } %>
```

Renders displayString for single-ended associations

```
  </tr>
  </g:each>
</tbody>
. . .
```

The code you need to add may look a little arcane, but it helps to understand this is a template file that's first converted to a GSP file, which is then used by the standard Grails view renderer. During the conversion of the template to a valid GSP file, only code inside `<% %>` markers and `${}` expressions are resolved and executed. That's why a few of the dollar signs are escaped with a backslash: to ensure they end up in the GSP as is and not evaluated.

With that knowledge in hand, you should be able to tell that the `propertyName` and `p` variables exist only during the parsing of the template. They don't exist in the generated GSP. The first of them, `propertyName`, resolves to the logical property name of the domain class that this view is for. The second one, `p`, resolves to a property of that domain class and comes from the `props.eachWithIndex()` loop at line 5 of the listing.

The change to the show view is similar, as shown in the following listing.

Listing 4.3 Using the `displayString` property in the show view

```
...
<%  } else if (p.oneToMany || p.manyToMany) { %>
  <g:each in="\${${propertyName}.${p.name}}" var="${p.name[0]}">
    <span class="property-value" aria-labelledby="${p.name}-label">
      <g:link controller="${p.referencedDomainClass?.propertyName}"
              action="show" id="\${${p.name[0]}.id}">
      \${${p.name[0]}?.displayString?.encodeAsHTML()}
      </g:link>
    </span>
  </g:each>
<%  } else if (p.manyToOne || p.oneToOne) { %>
<span class="property-value" aria-labelledby="${p.name}-label">
  <g:link controller="${p.referencedDomainClass?.propertyName}"
          action="show" id="\${${propertyName}?.${p.name}?.id}">
    \${${propertyName}?.${p.name}?.displayString?.encodeAsHTML()}
  </g:link>
</span>
<%  } else if (p.type == Boolean || p.type == boolean) { %>
<span class="property-value" aria-labelledby="${p.name}-label">
  <g:formatBoolean boolean="\${${propertyName}?.${p.name}}" />
</span>
...
```

Adds a link for *-to-many associations

Adds a link for *-to-one associations

We've dealt with the views, so we're now left with the form fields:

- Drop-down lists for many-to-one and one-to-one associations
- List boxes for one-to-many and many-to-many associations

As we mentioned earlier, the code for generating these fields resides in `renderEditor.template`. This file contains a set of Groovy functions used by the `_form.gsp` partial template.

The bits of `renderEditor.template` we're interested in are the `render*()` methods. There's a method for Boolean fields, one for enums, and several for associations of different types: `renderOneToMany()`, `renderManyToOne()`, and `renderManyToMany()`. The first of these renders a list of links with an `Add` link at the end. The other two render HTML `<select>` elements.

Remembering that you want to use the `displayString` property for the user-visible text, what do you do next? For the `<select>` elements, you add an extra line so that the generated `<g:select>` tag uses the `displayString` property for the content of the `<option>` elements, as shown in the following listing.

Listing 4.4 Using the `displayString` property

```
. . .
private renderManyToOne(domainClass,property) {
    if (property.association) {
        def sb = new StringBuilder()
        sb << '<g:select'                                    ◁ Renders a <g:select> GSP tag
        sb << ' id="' << property.name << '"'
        sb << ' name="' << property.name << '.id"'
        sb << ' from="${' << property.type.name << '.list()}"'
        sb << ' optionKey="id"'
        sb << ' optionValue="displayString"'                 ◁ Sets the property to use for the <option> content
        if (isRequired()) sb << ' required=""'
            sb << ' value="${' << "${domainInstance}?.${property.name}" <<
  '?.id}"'
        sb << ' class="many-to-one"'
        sb << renderNoSelection(property)
        sb << '/>'
        sb as String
    }
}
```

You can do something similar for `renderOneToMany()` and `renderManyToMany()` to get the result you want, but we won't go into the details here. Once you're comfortable with Grails and all its parts, this example should give you an idea of what you can achieve with such customizations.

Changing the way associations are displayed in the scaffolding is a small yet practical example of customizing the scaffolding templates to your needs. You can take this further and rewrite the scaffolding completely to generate a rich UI based on HTML/JavaScript tools such as AngularJS. In fact, someone has already done this.[1]

Whether you should invest energy in the scaffolding depends on the size of your domain model and how usable you want to make the generated UI. The larger the model, the greater the return on the investment. And if people use the scaffolding UI regularly, making them more productive through improvements to the scaffolding can be cost-effective. In the end, it's a decision to make on a project-by-project basis.

---

[1] A Grails plugin for scaffolding views using Angular.js, https://github.com/robfletcher/grails-angular-scaffolding.

> **Scaffolding and bidirectional relationships**
> Unfortunately, default scaffolding can't handle bidirectional one-to-one relationships that require both sides. If `User` requires a `Profile` and `Profile` requires a `User`, you end up with a classic catch-22: to create a profile you need a user, but to create a user you need a profile. You can work around this by modifying the template Create User page to submit both the user and profile information together.

We dived deep into the internals of the scaffolding, and you may need a break. Don't worry if it's a little overwhelming right now. By the end of the book, it'll make more sense. We recommend you come back then and experiment with changing the templates to see what effect those changes have. It's a great way to learn.

The templates we worked on also form the basis of another type of scaffolding that Grails calls *static* scaffolding. The technique serves a completely different purpose that we'll look at next.

4.3.2 Scaffolding as a starting point

Dynamic scaffolding creates a UI on the fly that's responsive to changes in your domain model. This is effective while you're developing the domain model, but it also hides the code from you. You can't fiddle with the code to see how it works if the code isn't there. It's a shame, because that was one of the ways that we, the authors, learned how to use Grails. Fortunately, Grails gives us static scaffolding to satisfy this use case.

The idea is that the scaffolding templates are generated as files in your project for whichever domain classes you want. Figure 4.10 shows exactly what files are created for Hubbub's `User` domain class. To generate these files, execute this command:

```
grails generate-all com.grailsinaction.User
```

You can also generate the controller and views independently through the `generate-controller` and `generate-views` commands, but those are much less common.

Play with these generated files to your heart's content. The files are easier to understand than the scaffolding templates you saw in the previous section, but be aware that once you generate these files, you have to update them manually if the corresponding domain class changes.

grails generate-all com.grailsinaction.User

```
grails-app/
  controllers/com/grailsinaction/UserController.groovy
  views/user/
    _form.gsp
    create.gsp
    edit.gsp
    list.gsp
    show.gsp
```

Figure 4.10 The generated files from static scaffolding

The views make a good starting point for experimenting with the code because markup is fairly easy to understand, and even small changes typically have an immediate, visible effect on the UI.

As for the generated controller, we listed all its actions in table 4.1 so that you can see their roles and how they interact with the corresponding views.

Table 4.1 Scaffolding controller methods

Action name	Function	Rendered view
`index`	Shows paginated list of domain class instances. Prior to Grails 2.3, this action redirected to a `list` action, which no longer exists.	N/A
`show`	Shows the properties for one instance of the domain class.	`show.gsp`
`create`	Shows a blank editing form for a new domain class instance, and submits it to `save`.	`create.gsp`
`save`	Saves new instances of domain classes. Redirects to `list` if the data is valid or renders the `create` view.	N/A or `create.gsp`
`edit`	Displays an editing form for a domain instance, and submits it to `update`.	`edit.gsp`
`update`	Updates a given instance of a domain class with new values. Redirects to `list` if the submitted data is valid, otherwise it renders the `edit` view.	N/A or `edit.gsp`
`delete`	Deletes a given ID, then redirects to `list`.	N/A

We won't go any further into static scaffolding, because you won't be using it as the basis for Hubbub's UI, but don't be afraid to use it as a starting point for your own projects. It's particularly useful for those who are new to web development. That said, scaffolding takes shortcuts in the code that aren't appropriate for normal application development, leading to the following warning.

Scaffolding isn't best practice

The scaffolding code isn't an example of best practice in terms of structuring an application—it doesn't use services, for one thing—and we don't encourage you to blindly use scaffolding code in your production applications. Don't worry, we'll teach you best practice in the rest of the book!

The last thing we want to warn you about is switching between dynamic and static scaffolding. If you use one of the `generate-*` commands and then want to switch back to dynamic scaffolding, be sure to delete all the generated views! The generated views override the views provided by the dynamic scaffolding, leading to changes in your domain classes not appearing in the UI. It's easily done.

With that, we end our coverage of scaffolding. As you've seen, working with the underlying code for the scaffolding, whether it's via the templates or the generated files, gives you flexibility in customizing the UI. A scaffolding UI is never ideal in terms of user experience, but that experience can be improved dramatically while still getting a cheap-to-build UI for a large domain model.

4.4 Summary and best practices

In this chapter, we explored Grails scaffolding and you saw how to use scaffolding to create an instant UI for an application. You also saw how to skin the application with your own CSS and layouts, customize the error messages, and change the look completely by modifying the scaffolding templates.

Scaffolding is a cheap way to get a web UI, so there's a temptation to use it for the final product, particularly when the domain model is large. We normally discourage this, because we think a UI should be tailored to the user and not the domain model. But we recognize that it's sometimes more beneficial to get a UI in the users' hands quickly than invest the time in a custom UI. Dynamic scaffolding also has the key benefit that it automatically keeps in sync with the domain model—a huge win if your domain model changes frequently.

What do we recommend?

- *Use scaffolding to get going quickly and to stay motivated.* Scaffolding gives you a feeling of progress and keeps you focused on getting your app out the door. It's also a great support while building a custom UI, because it allows you to interact fully with the data, making it easier to test the new UI.
- *Use scaffolding for administration screens.* It's difficult to anticipate everything that might happen in your running application, so having access to all the production data through a web UI can make your life much easier. Rather than disposing of the dynamic scaffolding once your web UI is done, why not keep it and make sure that only administrators can access it? See chapter 11 for how to add access control to your app.
- *Customize the scaffolding if it's the final product.* If you do decide to base your application on scaffolding, be sure to customize the look and update the templates to ensure they can handle all of your relationships. Remember that the default scaffolding can't handle certain types of relationships. And you definitely don't want your application looking like an out-of-the-box Grails app.
- *Use static scaffolding appropriately.* Static scaffolding isn't currently an example of best practice for Grails applications, so you shouldn't use it as such. If you're new to web application development, using the `generate-*` commands and playing with the resulting code is a great way to learn. But you should make sure your code follows best practice at a later point. Experienced web

developers probably shouldn't generate the static scaffolding. Instead, keep the dynamic scaffolding to support development of a custom UI developed from scratch.

In the next chapter, you will return to the domain model and learn how to interact with it through database queries. You'll also start on that custom UI we kept talking about in this chapter. This is where the real fun begins!

5 Retrieving the data you need

This chapter covers

- Generating sample data
- Querying the database without SQL
- Unlocking the power of advanced querying features

After a few chapters you have a fully working web application that stores and retrieves data in a relational database. This forms a great base for further development, because you can fully interact with the data model before the real application is ready. You can, for example, make changes to the data via the scaffolding UI to test a feature that you're developing, such as a search form.

Where do you go next? You don't want to expose users to the scaffolding UI because it doesn't exactly provide a great user experience. You need to build a friendlier UI. Let's start with a simple home page. What should go on that page? A good starting point is a list of Hubbub posts, and for that you need to query the database.

This chapter introduces various ways of querying a database in Grails. Once you've finished it, you'll know how to fetch posts from the last 24 hours submitted by people whom the current user is following! You'll also develop a basic search form for Hubbub that provides a basis for exploring the different types of queries.

Before we begin, it's useful to have data in the database so that your queries can return results. A convenient way to do that is to populate the database on application startup.

5.1 Setting up the data and search form

Testing a data-dependent application that has no data is painful. If you don't have data, most pages will be empty and you'll be unable to test the features you've implemented. You could manually add test data every time you start the server, but it won't take long before you try to automate the process. That's why the first step in implementing your search form is to create sample data automatically when the application starts.

5.1.1 Loading sample data

The most convenient way to initialize such sample data in a Grails application is via the `BootStrap` class in grails-app/conf because its `init` closure is executed every time the application starts. This happens regardless of whether the application is started via the `run-app` command, `run-war`, or when it's deployed to a separate servlet container as a WAR file. The best thing about this approach is that you can use standard GORM to generate the data—so you still don't need any SQL!

Before you code the sample data, you need to consider under what circumstances this code is going to run. Three factors are involved:

- Whether you're using an in-memory database
- What `dbCreate` setting you're using
- What environment is active

We'll start by looking at the first two factors, then incorporate the active environment afterward.

HANDLING DATA DURABILITY

Understanding the relationship between the durability of the database (whether the data persists between server restarts) and the `dbCreate` setting in DataSource.groovy is crucial to knowing how you should set up your sample data; otherwise, you may end up with no data, duplicate data, or errors on startup. Figure 5.1 explains how this relationship affects the longevity of your data.

As you can see, data longevity boils down to two scenarios: the data is wiped between server restarts or it's preserved. We don't want to recreate the data if it's already there, because that results in either duplicate records (if the domain class constraints allow duplicates) or failed saves. To avoid that, you first do a quick check to see whether the data exists, as shown in listing 5.1. We've left out sample data from the listing because the code is long, repetitive, and not particularly educational. You can find the complete code on GitHub.[1] You'll need to copy it if you're building Hubbub yourself locally.

1 The example BootStrap code on GitHub, https://github.com/GrailsInAction/graina2/blob/master/ch05/hubbub/grails-app/conf/BootStrap.groovy.

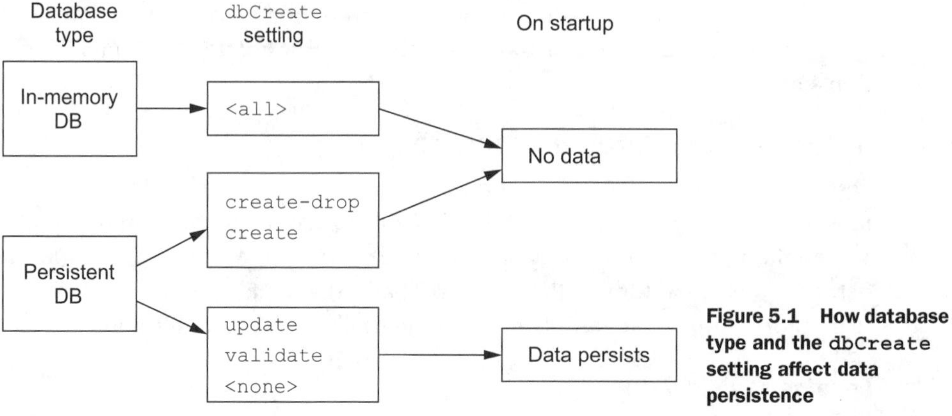

Figure 5.1 How database type and the `dbCreate` setting affect data persistence

Listing 5.1 Initial attempt at generating sample data

```
import com.grailsinaction.*

class BootStrap {
    def init = { servletContext ->
        if (!Post.count()) {
            createSampleData()
        }
    }

    private createSampleData() {
        ...
    }
}
```

- Makes domain classes available; BootStrap is not in a package.
- Checks for Posts in database.
- Doesn't need destroy property, which is called on application shutdown.

In this case, checking the number of posts is a good test for whether the sample data is already loaded in the database. You could feasibly do the check on any of the domain classes in the model because the sample data is either there or it's not.

Another consideration when creating sample data is how you'll deal with validation errors. You don't expect them, but that doesn't stop validation errors from happening and ruining your sample data set.

THROWING EXCEPTIONS ON SAVE()

If you look at the source code on GitHub, you'll see code that calls the `save()` method:

```
phil.save(failOnError: true)
```

What's that `failOnError` argument about? By default, the `save()` method quietly fails and returns `null` if the domain instance does not satisfy the class's validation constraints. It won't be until the application is running and you test your features that you'll notice the missing data. It may even take a few hours to debug what the problem is!

The `failOnError` argument solves this issue by throwing an exception if the validation fails. That means you'll see right on application startup whether any data has failed to save to the database. It's well worth using this argument whenever you save a domain instance in `BootStrap`.

USING ENVIRONMENT BLOCKS

The last factor we mentioned when contemplating the sample data was the active environment. The sample data makes sense for development, but what about for production? Your users probably wouldn't appreciate seeing dummy posts from dummy users. It makes sense to load the sample data only for the development environment.

You can achieve this in one of two ways. The first is via environment blocks, which are special demarcated blocks of code that are executed only for a particular environment. The following code loads the sample data only if the application is running in the development environment:

```
import com.grailsinaction.*

class BootStrap {
    def init = { servletContext ->
        environments {                                   <-- Starts environment blocks
            development {
                if (!Post.count()) createSampleData()    <-- Creates sample data in the development environment
            }
        }
    }
    ...
}
```

The syntax is simple: you declare an `environments` block as shown and nest as many named environments as you want inside it. Each named environment is another block inside which you put the code you want to execute. Grails defines standard environments—`development`, `test`, and `production`—but you can also add custom ones.

Imagine that you have a set of staging servers that you deploy the application to before it goes into production. You want to ensure your reference sample data is set up so any tests that run against the staging servers work properly. Simply add a nested `staging` block inside the `environments` block like so:

```
environments {
    staging {
        ...
    }
}
```

To then activate this staging environment when you package the application as a WAR file, you pass the `-Dgrails.env` option on the command line:

```
grails -Dgrails.env=staging war
```

No other configuration is needed. You don't have to declare the environment anywhere or specify the name on the command line. If any code is conditional on that environment, it'll be executed. The downside is that if you mistype the environment name, you won't get a warning. Instead, Grails quietly loads the default configuration.

> **Execution order**
>
> You have no guarantees when the code in the `environments` block will be executed relative to other code in `BootStrap`. It seems that, at present, the block is executed after everything else in the `init` closure. But that may change in the future as this behavior isn't documented anywhere.

It's important to note that every Grails command has a particular environment that it defaults to. Usually this is `development`, but the `test-app` command defaults to the `test` environment (unsurprisingly), and the `war` command defaults to `production`. You'll see in the next subsection how to activate specific standard environments from the command line.

USING THE ENVIRONMENT CLASS FOR MORE COMPLEX SCENARIOS

The second way to conditionally create data is by a straightforward `if` statement that checks the current environment via the Grails `Environment` class:

```
import grails.util.Environment

class BootStrap {
    def init = { servletContext ->
        if (Environment.current != Environment.DEVELOPMENT) {
            // Set up reference data for
            // non-development environments
            . . .
        }
        else if (Environment.current.name == "staging") {
            . . .
        }
    }
}
```

Checks the current active environment using Environment instances

Compares environments by name (required for custom environments)

Although this isn't as elegant as the environment blocks, it's useful in many scenarios. The previous code sample shows how you can execute code for any environment *except* the specified one, something that you can't properly achieve with environment blocks.

One ugly spot in Grails that can confuse newcomers is an inconsistency in how you activate environments and reference them within your code. The previous example even showed two different ways to test the current environment! To help you get a handle on environments, we've listed their different forms in table 5.1.

Table 5.1 The different faces of environments

Name	Constant	Command line activation
development	`Environment.DEVELOPMENT`	`grails dev . . .`
test	`Environment.TEST`	`grails test . . .`
production	`Environment.PRODUCTION`	`grails prod . . .`
<user-defined>, for example, `myEnv`	`Environment.CUSTOM`	`grails -Dgrails.env=myEnv . . .`

Figure 5.2 Hubbub search form

The environment name is the string you use in environment blocks and when you want to check for a particular custom environment. The constants are instances of `Environment` that you can use instead of the names when checking for the standard environments.

With these techniques, you can easily control which data is loaded under what circumstances. Now you have your sample data loading on startup, you can send queries and get back useful results. It's time to set up that search form.

5.1.2 *Implementing the search*

The search feature you're going to implement has three parts:

- The search form that allows users to enter a search string in the UI
- The code to execute the search
- The results page

Only the second part involves executing a database query, but the corresponding HTML page provides the context for that query. Don't worry if you can't follow the logic of the page generation because you'll dive into that side of things in the following chapters. For now, focus on the relationship between the search form and the database query.

CREATING THE SEARCH FORM

The search form is a web page that contains a text box for the search string and a button to execute the search. The aim is to end up with a form like the one in figure 5.2. As you saw in chapter 1, you can implement pages like this with GSP views.

First, create the file grails-app/views/user/search.gsp and add the code shown in the following listing, which contains the HTML form that's displayed to the user.

Listing 5.2 A search form for Hubbub

```
<html>
<head>
    <title>Search Hubbub</title>
    <meta name="layout" content="main"/>
</head>
```

Uses the same layout as the scaffolding for consistency.

```
<body>
    <formset>
        <legend>Search for Friends</legend>
        <g:form action="results">
            <label for="loginId">Login ID</label>
            <g:textField name="loginId" />
            <g:submitButton name="search" value="Search"/>
        </g:form>
    </formset>
</body>
</html>
```

Submits form to the results action of UserController. (annotates `<g:form action="results">`)

Lets the user enter the ID to search for; value available in controller as "loginId" parameter. (annotates `<g:textField name="loginId" />`)

A few special <g:> tags exist in the listing that you're probably not familiar with unless you've used something such as JSP tags in the past. These tags generate HTML based on their attributes, and you can see what impact each tag has in figure 5.3. It's worth getting used to looking at the generated HTML because it's useful in debugging rendering issues and seeing exactly what the GSP tags do.

With this search form in place you can add an empty `search` action to `UserController`, which renders the search.gsp page by convention (see listing 5.3). Once that action is in place, you'll be able to point your browser at /hubbub/user/search, enter any search criteria, and submit the form. The next step is to process the form submission.

When the user enters a user ID, or part of a user ID to search for, and clicks Submit, what happens? As you'll learn in the next few chapters, the data is submitted to the URL specified in the `action` attribute of the `<form>` element. That URL is handled (at the moment) by the `results` action on `UserController`, which needs implementing.

IMPLEMENTING THE RESULTS PAGE

To deal with the form submission, you need your `results` action to perform the necessary database query and render the results of that query back to the browser. For the query, you're going to use the `where()` method that's added to all domain classes. You can see it in action in the following listing.

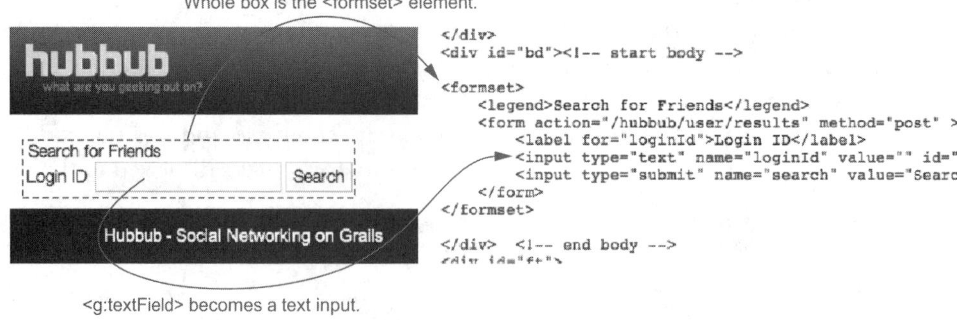

Figure 5.3 The basic Hubbub user search page and its underlying HTML

Listing 5.3 Adding the search logic to `UserController`

```
package com.grailsinsaction

class UserController {
    static scaffold = true

    def search() {}

    def results(String loginId) {
        def users = User.where {
            loginId =~ loginId
        }.list()
        return [ users: users,
                 term: params.loginId,
                 totalUsers: User.count() ]
    }
}
```

- The action for the "search" form page
- Argument name matches name of the text field in the form
- Queries the DB for all users with a loginId that's like the search string

The first thing that strikes you is the lack of any SQL, or even any SQL-like, terms. Don't worry, it's still sending a SQL query to the database, but you can express that query in terms of the language constructs you're used to in Groovy. That's convenient if you haven't yet learned SQL.

A second interesting aspect of this bit of code is how it appears to compare the `loginId` variable with itself. In fact, the `loginId` on the left-hand side refers to the property of that name on the `User` class, whereas the one on the right-hand side refers to the action's argument. This will be clearer once we dissect the behavior of such queries.

How does this query work? It breaks down into the three parts shown in figure 5.4. You should see that the criteria go inside a closure—that's the argument to the `where()` method. The content of that closure does need more discussion, so we'll come back to Where queries (the name for this type of query) in the next section. For now, let's finish off this search form.

> **Adding to the scaffolding**
>
> Notice how you've kept the scaffolding in `UserController` but augmented it with your new search operation? The scaffolding pages for CRUD remain, so you can still manipulate the data. You have additional custom pages now for the search form and its results. Eventually you can remove the scaffolding or use it later as an administrative UI once the application is ready.

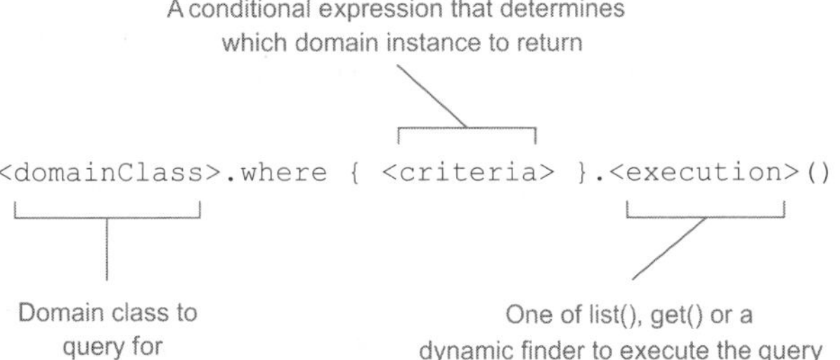

Figure 5.4 Breakdown of a Where query

At the moment, users must include the SQL wildcard character, `%`, in the search string if they want wildcard matching. It's impractical to force users to do this in their searches because few people know what SQL is, let alone a SQL wildcard. Instead, let's incorporate the wildcards directly in the query:

```
def users = User.where { loginId =~ "%${loginId}%" }.list()
```

Any login ID that includes the search term will be returned in the results. For those who know SQL, the `=~` operator represents a SQL `ILIKE` comparison, meaning that it's case insensitive.

The last step in implementing the search form is to create the page that displays the search results. Listing 5.4 implements a `results.gsp` view for this purpose. The file goes into the same directory as the search view (grails-app/views/user) and it's rendered by convention—the name of the view matches the name of the controller action.

Listing 5.4 A results screen for the search

```
<html>
<head>
  <title>Search Results</title>
  <meta name="layout" content="main"/>
</head>
<body>
  <h1>Results</h1>
  <p>
    Searched ${totalUsers} records
    for items matching <em>${term}</em>.
    Found <strong>${users.size()}</strong> hits.
  </p>
  <ul>
    <g:each var="user" in="${users}">
    <li>${user.loginId}</li>
    </g:each>
  </ul>
  <g:link action='search'>Search Again</g:link>
</body>
</html>
```

Displays total number of users in the system (annotation on `Searched ${totalUsers} records`)

Iterates over all matched users (annotation on `<g:each ...>`)

Now when you search for a user you'll see all the matching results. That's another useful feature implemented with a minimum of fuss. You can try other queries in the `results` action because you'll see the results in the browser without restarting the server! It's a great way to experiment.

We could continue demonstrating how queries work through adding more features to the app, but that's a pretty inefficient approach—all the extra controller and view code would swamp the chapter! Instead, we're going to explore a greater range of queries through focused integration tests.

5.2 Writing Where queries

Where queries—those executed via the `where()` method—are particularly approachable for Groovy developers because they're based on Groovy operators. They're also powerful, enabling you to query on associations, use aggregate functions such as `avg()`, and more. That's why we see them as your first port of call when you need to query the database.

We'll start by explaining the syntax of the `where()` method and criteria closure with an extensive set of examples. You'll soon get a feel for how to write your own queries. We'll then delve deeper and show you how to interpret errors and find out what SQL the Where queries are sending to the database. This information is invaluable when you write queries that don't behave as you expect—something that happens to the best of us!

5.2.1 The query syntax

You saw the overall syntax for Where queries previously when you created the results page for the user search, but we didn't explain at the time what form the individual conditions should take. To recap, figure 5.5 shows that structure again.

The criteria block is probably the most important and flexible part of a Where query, so let's take an in-depth look at it. We start with the example from the previous section:

```
User.where { loginId =~ loginId }.list()
```

Why isn't Grails confused about which `loginId` we mean? If you remember, we said that the one on the left-hand side of the operator refers to the property on `User`, whereas the other one refers to the action's argument. That's an implicit assumption made by Grails for all Where criteria expressions and criteria expressions aren't commutative. Swapping the left-hand side with the right-hand side changes the behavior of the query, as explained in figure 5.6.

Fortunately, as long as you stick to the following rule, you'll find most criteria work as you'd expect.

> **The Where criterion rule**
> The domain class properties that you want to compare against must be declared on the left-hand side of the criteria.

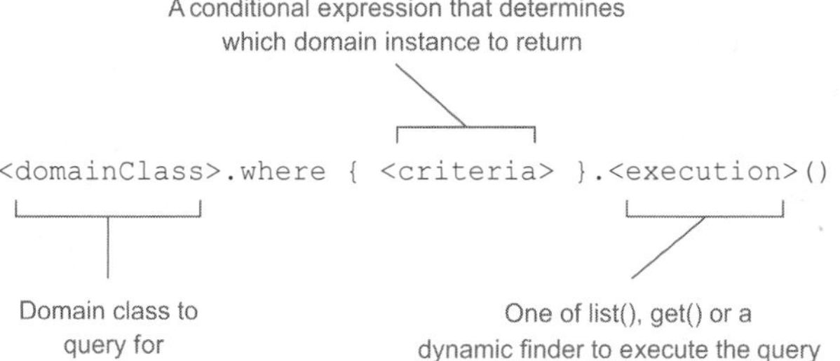

Figure 5.5 Breakdown of a Where query

Working

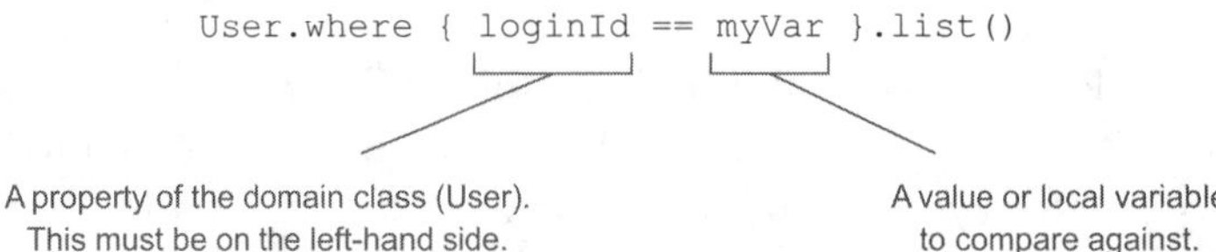
User.where { loginId == myVar }.list()
A property of the domain class (User).
This must be on the left-hand side.
A value or local variable
to compare against.

Broken

```
User.where { myVar == loginId }.list()
```

Results in compilation error:
User domain class does not have a 'myVar' property.

Figure 5.6 The placement of variables in Where criteria is important

You can see examples in listing 5.5 that follow the basic rule, demonstrating different types of conditions. You can see how to query associations, perform the equivalent of SQL's `BETWEEN` constraint, and return a single instance.

To test the examples, first create an integration test

```
grails create-integration-test com.grailsinaction.QueryIntegration
```

then replace the content of your newly created test (QueryIntegrationSpec.groovy in the test/integration/com/grailsinaction directory) with the code from the following listing. All the queries run against a real database, because this is an integration test. Note that this test will only pass if you're using the BootStrap.groovy file from the chapter source on GitHub.

Listing 5.5 Where queries in action

```
package com.grailsinaction

import spock.lang.*

class QueryIntegrationSpec extends Specification {

    void "Simple property comparison"() {
        when: "Users are selected by a simple password match"
        def users = User.where {
            password == "testing"
        }.list(sort: "loginId")

        then: "The users with that password are returned"
        users*.loginId == ["frankie"]
    }

    void "Multiple criteria"() {
        when: "A user is selected by loginId or password"
        def users = User.where {
            loginId == "frankie" || password == "crikey"
        }.list(sort: "loginId")
```

Combines conditions with logical operators.

```
        then: "The matching loginIds are returned"
        users*.loginId == ["dillon", "frankie", "sara"]
    }

    void "Query on association"() {
        when: "The 'following' collection is queried"
        def users = User.where {
            following.loginId == "sara"
        }.list(sort: "loginId")

        then: "A list of the followers of the given user is returned"
        users*.loginId == ["phil"]
    }

    void "Query against a range value"() {
        given: "The current date & time"
        def now = new Date()

        when: "The 'dateCreated' property is queried"
        def users = User.where {
            dateCreated in (now - 1)..now
        }.list(sort: "loginId", order: "desc")

        then: "The users created within the specified date range
➥ are returned"
        users*.loginId == ["phil", "peter", "glen", "frankie",
➥ "chuck_norris", "admin"]
    }

    void "Retrieve a single instance"() {
        when: "A specific user is queried with get()"
        def user = User.where {
            loginId == "phil"
        }.get()

        then: "A single instance is returned"
        user.password == "thomas"
    }
}
```

Queries on single- and multi-ended associations via standard "." Syntax.

Uses `in` operator plus a range to do a SQL BETWEEN query.

Returns a single instance rather than list via get(). Throws an exception if there's more than one matching result.

Any simple database query can be written using Groovy syntax with the `where()` method. Listing 5.5 shows a few operators you can use in conditions, but you can also use `!=`, `<`, `>`, `<=`, and `>=`. You can even use `==~` for case-sensitive pattern matching (`=~` is the case-insensitive form). You can also combine these with logical operators such as `!` (negation), `&&` (logical `AND`), and `||` (logical `OR`), all in a form that's highly readable to any developer.

Writing queries such as these in code, as opposed to writing SQL directly, brings other benefits. What happens when you mistype `loginId` on the left-hand side of any of the criteria in listing 5.5? You get a *compilation error* rather than an exception when you run the tests! This is useful early feedback. The only slight downside is that you can't use Where queries if you don't know at compile time what properties you want to query. It can be useful occasionally to determine those properties at runtime, perhaps based on user input, and you'll see an example of such dynamic queries in section 5.3.3.

Another big advantage of Where queries is the ability to have *optional criteria*. Consider the user search discussed previously and imagine that a user can optionally choose to limit the results to only those users who were added to the system after a specified date. This is completely doable with two separate queries inside a condition block, as we demonstrate inside this sample method:

```
def fetchUsers(String loginIdPart, Date fromDate = null) {
    def users
    if (fromDate) {
        users = User.where {
            loginId =~ "%${loginIdPart}%" && dateCreated >= fromDate
        }.list()
    }
    else {
        users = User.where { loginId =~ "${loginIdPart}" }.list()
    }
}
```

However, part of the query is duplicated and the overall code is too verbose. More to the point, you now have two separate queries to maintain. What if you want to make the query case-sensitive? You'd have to update both instances of the query. It's much better to do this instead:

```
def fetchUsers(String loginIdPart, Date fromDate = null) {
    def users = User.where {
        loginId =~ "%${loginIdPart}%"
        if (fromDate) {
            dateCreated >= fromDate        <-- This criterion is included
        }                                      only if the fromDate
    }.list()                                   parameter has a value.
}
```

You now only have a single query to maintain! You're also not limited to two expressions as multiple expressions *on separate lines* are implicitly ANDed together. That's why you can include `if` statements, loops, or any other bit of flow control logic you want. There's also a related method, `whereAny()`, that behaves exactly the same except it implicitly ORs expressions on separate lines.

You'll use plenty of Where queries as you build up Hubbub, so you'll see more examples later in the book. Where queries even extend to nonrelational data stores, as you'll see in chapter 16. For the moment, it's a good time to try different queries with different domain properties. Gaining familiarity with the syntax and learning what is or isn't possible is important; a large number of Grails applications are driven by data stored in a database. That's why you'll experiment with more queries next.

5.2.2 *Exploring Where queries*

Writing test cases as you did in the last section is a great way to ensure that your code is working as you expect. But there's a delay in feedback between making changes and seeing the results. That's not ideal when you want to play with code and see what's possible. The quickest and simplest way to try out different queries is to take advantage of the Grails GUI console that we introduced in chapter 1. From within the project directory, run

```
grails -reloading console
```

The `-reloading` argument is important because it ensures that any changes you make to your application code take effect in the console!

GET ME DATA

You're now ready to go. All you need is data to query—queries that return no data aren't much fun and aren't useful. If you remember, you set up sample data at the beginning of the chapter, so it makes sense to use that. At the time of writing, the console UI doesn't automatically execute `BootStrap.init` on startup, but it's easy to load it once the console is running. Enter the following code in the upper window of the console and run the script (Script > Run from the menu):

```
import com.grailsinaction.Post
import grails.util.Environment

Environment.executeForCurrentEnvironment(new BootStrap().init)
println "There are ${Post.count()} posts in the database"
```

The last line is there so you can check that the data was loaded correctly. If it states a non-zero number of posts, you're all set. If it's reporting no posts, there's probably something wrong with your `BootStrap` class: verify it against the sample code from online.

As `init` is an instance property, the previous code first instantiates `BootStrap`, then passes the `init` closure to the `executeForCurrentEnvironment()` method. You do this because the `init` closure has environment blocks that won't work correctly otherwise. In fact, the power user can take advantage of this technique to execute any closure that includes environment blocks.

TYPES OF ERRORS

Now that you have data loaded into the in-memory database, you can start experimenting with your own queries. At some point, one of your queries will fail. What happens then? Learning to recognize and diagnose issues with Where queries saves head scratching.

What kinds of problems are you likely to encounter? Let's start with compilation errors, which we mentioned briefly in the previous section. Clear out or comment out whatever code is in the upper window of the console UI and add

```
import com.grailsinaction.Post

Post.where {
    contnt =~ /%BBQ%/
}.list()
```

A typo on the property name results in a compilation error.

When you run the script again, you'll see a compilation error:

```
Cannot query on property "contnt" - no such property on class
com.grailsinaction.Post exists
```

This is expected as the property name is `content`, not `contnt`. The type-checking even works across associations, as you can see if you try this example:

```
import com.grailsinaction.Post

Post.where {
    user.lognId == "peter"
}.list()
```

The compilation error this time is that no property `lognId` exists on `User`, because that's the type of the `user` association you're querying on.

> **How do they work?**
>
> Where queries happen through a powerful feature of Groovy called *AST transformations*. The code inside the braces is transformed at compilation time into the equivalent Criteria syntax (see section 5.3.2). Because this happens at compilation time, the transforms can check property names and throw compilation errors, even though Groovy is a dynamic language. It's cool, but can lead to interesting error messages.
>
> If you're interested and not scared of low-level stuff, the Grails console offers a menu option for an AST browser: Script > Inspect Ast. This allows you to see exactly what syntax the Where query transformation generates. A side benefit is that it shows any compilation errors clearly, so you can use it to work around the problem of the console not displaying the compilation error messages in Grails versions prior to 2.3.

Compilation errors are straightforward to deal with, so what else could you encounter when dealing with Where queries? Try this query in the console:

```
Post.where {
    user.dateCreated > "2 weeks ago"
}.list()
```

This time you'll see a `ConversionFailedException` explaining that you can't convert a `String` to a `Date`. This is because `dateCreated` is a date property, meaning you can only compare it to another date. Most type mismatches between the domain class property and the value you're comparing it against result in such an exception.

NOTE If the property on the left-hand side is a string, the right-hand side will always be converted based on the result of its `toString()` method. This can introduce subtle bugs if you're not careful.

The other exception that may result from type mismatches is `ConverterNotFoundException`. This one appears when you're comparing a property whose type is a domain class against a value with a different type. For example:

```
Post.where {
    user == 12
}.list()
```

results in the error

```
No converter found capable of converting from type java.lang.Integer
to type com.grailsinaction.User
```

Finally, you may occasionally see references to the `DetachedCriteria` class in exceptions resulting from your query. If this is the case, it generally means that you're trying to do something that can't be achieved through Where queries. It's a good indicator that you need to try one of the other query types we introduce in section 5.3.

CONTROLLING THE NUMBER OF RESULTS

It's rarely a good idea to ask for results from the database without putting a limit on what comes back, otherwise you might find yourself inundated with tens or hundreds of thousands of domain instances—and a crashed application. To mitigate the risk of such a catastrophe, you can pass in extra parameters to the `list()` method, such as `max` and `offset`. We provide a comprehensive list of options in table 5.2.

Table 5.2 Named arguments supported by `list()`

Option	Description
`max`	Specifies the maximum number of rows to return
`offset`	Specifies the number of elements into the `ResultSet` to start at when returning values (useful for pagination)
`sort`	Specifies the field to sort on in the returned list
`order`	Specifies the order of the sort: "`asc`" or "`desc`" (default is "`asc`")
`ignoreCase`	Sets sorting to ignore case (`true` by default)
`fetch`	Specifies eager/lazy fetch strategy as a `Map` of options

These options are particularly useful when you want to implement paging functionality. For example, let's say you want posts 6 to 10 for the user "phil" ordered by most recent first. The corresponding query is

```
def posts = Post.where {
    user.loginId == "phil"
}.list(max: 5, offset: 5, sort: "dateCreated", order: "desc")

println posts
```

Simple. This can even be extended to single instance results. Let's say this time you want Phil's most recent post. You could use the `list()` method, but then you'd get a list back as a result. We know in this case that you're going to get at most one post back, so you can use an alternative method, `get()`, that returns the domain instance directly:

```
def latestPost = Post.where {
    user.loginId == "phil"
}.get(max: 1, sort: "dateCreated", order: "desc")

println latestPost
```

max value of 1 ensures the query only returns one or zero objects

Note that if the query returns more than one instance, `get()` throws a great big `NonUniqueResultException`, which explains why you use a value of 1 for `max`.

> **Session is closed!**
> You might see an exception in the console UI when executing queries that says "Session is closed!" It happens with the list query you've just seen if you don't have the `println()` statement after the query. For this reason, we recommend that you never have a query as the last statement of the script. A simple `println()` at the end will ensure that you're never disturbed by this exception.

You've now seen the important parts of the Where query syntax and certainly know enough to cover 80% or more of your requirements. To round off that knowledge, it's worth knowing how to diagnose and debug your queries through the generated SQL.

SHOW ME THE SQL

Even though Grails and GORM successfully hide the underlying SQL used for querying and updating domain classes, ultimately you'll need to know what's happening so you can tune queries, debug queries that aren't working as expected, and so on. And if you're not familiar with SQL at this point, seeing what Grails generates for queries and updates is a great way to learn it.

How do you get to see the SQL? You have a couple of options. The one mentioned in the user guide and often suggested in mailing lists and forums is to add a `logSql = true` line to your DataSource.groovy file:

```
dataSource {
    pooled = true
    driverClassName = "org.h2.Driver"
    username = "sa"
    password = ""
    logSql = true
}
```

Enables SQL logging for queries and updates

This is a straightforward way to get what you want, and you can see it in action simply by rerunning the Grails console UI and executing queries. Every time you run a query, the corresponding SQL is displayed in the output pane. You'll even see a whole load of SQL `insert` statements when you run the `BootStrap` initialization code. But if you look closely at the printed SQL statements, you'll notice something missing: the values that are inserted into the database or used in criteria. All you see instead are question marks.

Whether or not the values are important to you depends on what you're doing. If you simply want to see whether you're executing too many queries, for example, to check for the classic N + 1 select problem (we'll show an example of that at the end of the section), then the values are irrelevant. But if you want to investigate data corruption, the values are critical. Fortunately, it's easy to display the values as well by adding these lines to your logging configuration in `Config.groovy`:

```
log4j = {
    . . .
    debug "org.hibernate.SQL"
    trace "org.hibernate.type.descriptor.sql.BasicBinder"
}
```

This ensures that all your database updates are logged with the values. If you do use these two log settings, we recommend you remove the `logSql = true` setting, otherwise you end up with duplicate entries in your log.

You can also make the SQL statements more readable by adding these extra settings to `DataSource.groovy` in the `hibernate` block:

```
hibernate {
    . . .
    format_sql = true
    use_sql_comments = true
}
```

You're all set to diagnose any issues you have with persistence. You can try this out with the following example in the console UI:

```
def posts = Post.list()

for (p in posts) {
    println p.user.profile.fullName
}
```

Assuming that you've already loaded the sample data in the console UI, you should see several queries executed even though there appears to be only one query in the code. This is an example of the N + 1 select problem. The +1 is the initial query for the posts, while the N represents the extra queries to get the users for each post. In fact, this example also has N queries to fetch the profiles!

> **Source for logging information**
> Before we move on, we'd like to take this opportunity to give credit to the source of these tidbits of information about logging: Burt Beckwith, our technical reviewer from the first edition. His blog at http://burtbeckwith.com/blog is well worth following, particularly for its content about Hibernate and its use with Grails.

Everything we've covered so far sets you up nicely to use Where queries when they make sense, which is for the majority of your data access needs. In fact, you can safely skip the rest of the chapter if you want to get on with developing Hubbub and come back when you're ready to digest more advanced querying options. For those of you that are ready, we look in the next section at the scenarios in which Where queries don't work or aren't the best mechanism.

5.3 When Where queries aren't suitable

Where queries are concise, powerful, and easy to read for us developers, making them a good first port of call for your query needs. Still, that doesn't mean they're suitable for all occasions, so it's good to know that Grails gives you other options. These range from the simple `count()` method to the ultra-powerful Hibernate Query Language (HQL).

The later parts of this section take advantage of advanced query skills in Grails, so don't get discouraged if it seems tricky the first few times. The primary aim of this section is to give you an overview of what's available. The Grails user guide has much of the necessary detail. You can come back to this section at any time, particularly if you encounter situations in which Where queries don't do what you need. We start, though, with several simple query methods that have great utility.

5.3.1 Cheap and cheerful listing and counting

On many occasions, you'll want information from the database without any criteria whatsoever. Perhaps you want all the Hubbub posts in the system (with constraints on how many are returned). Or perhaps you need to know how many exist. Two static methods on domain classes that work well for these use cases are `list()`, which returns all instances of a domain class, and `count()`, which returns the total number of instances in the database.

Returning all the records from a database table is a quick way to bring your application to a grinding halt, so it's no surprise you can fine-tune this. In fact, the standalone `list()` method supports exactly the same options as the `list()` method you saw for Where queries. Imagine you want to see the first five users ordered by ascending `loginId`. You'll also access the associated posts for each user, so you want to eagerly fetch those posts at the same time. The required query is simple:

```
def users = User.list(sort: 'loginId',
                      order: 'asc',
                      max: 5,
                      fetch: [posts: 'eager'])
```

Sorts the users
Limits results to 5
Fetches each user's posts eagerly

Even the no-nonsense `count()` method has a bigger brother with additional flexibility. For example, let's say you want to find out how many users have a particular poor password in your application. The ideal solution is the `countBy()` method:

```
def poorPasswordCount = User.countByPassword("password")
```

It's a rather contrived example, but it demonstrates how `countBy()` works. The name of the method determines what criteria are used in the query. In this case, "Password" in the method name tells Grails to count all users with a `password` property that matches the given value.

You can also find other magic methods in the Grails user guide: `findBy()` and `findAllBy()`. These behave in a similar fashion to `countBy()`, returning the first matching domain instance and all matching instances respectively. Taking an example from earlier, you can return all users whose login IDs match a particular pattern using

```
def users = User.findAllByLoginIdIlike("%${loginId}%")
```

As you can see, the comparators as well as property names are included in the method name. These dynamic finders (as they're called) have been superseded by Where queries, so we won't delve further here. If you prefer this approach to Where queries, the Grails user guide covers them nicely. You can also see examples of all the query types in this subsection in this chapter's source code on GitHub (see the `SimpleQueriesIntegrationSpec` class).

5.3.2 Introducing Criteria queries

You get good bang for your buck with Where queries, but situations exist where they don't fit the bill. Perhaps you're building a query dynamically from user input in a search form, such that you don't know ahead of time what properties to query on. Or you may need to group results or perform other more advanced operations. To make sure you're ready for such occasions, it's time to experience the power of GORM Criteria queries.

You'll start with an example that does the same as a previous Where query: return all users whose login IDs match a given string, and optionally were created in the system after a given date. Here's the Criteria version of the query:

```
def fetchUsers(String loginIdPart, Date fromDate = null) {
    def users = User.createCriteria().list {          <-- Creates query object and executes it with list()
        and {
            ilike "loginId", "%${loginIdPart}%"       <-- Defines criteria via named methods, such as ilike() and ge()
            if (fromDate) {
                ge "dateCreated", fromDate
            }
        }
    }
}
```

The syntax is similar to that of Where queries, but significant differences exist:

- Combining criteria is done through `and()` and `or()` methods that group together all the criteria in their blocks.
- The criteria are based on methods rather than operators, where the first argument is the name of the property you want to query on. See appendix B for a full list of Where query operators and Criteria query methods.

As with Where queries, you can also include conditions, loops, or other standard Groovy structures.

To finish off this introduction to Criteria queries, we'd like to point out a couple of useful variants. First, you can replace the `list()` with either `get()` (if you want a single result) or `count()` (if you want the number of records selected by the query).

Second, there's a special `withCriteria()` method you can use in place of `createCriteria().list()`:

```
def fetchUsers(String loginIdPart, Date fromDate = null) {
    def users = User.withCriteria {                          ◁— A shortcut for
        and {                                                   createCriteria().list()
            ilike "loginId", "%${loginIdPart}%"
            if (fromDate) {
                ge "dateCreated", fromDate
            }
        }
    }
}
```

Why would you want to use a Criteria query in place of a Where query? The examples we've shown so far can easily be done with the latter. The answer lies in two special types of query: dynamic and report-style. Let's start with dynamic queries.

5.3.3 Dynamic queries with criteria

Criteria queries allow you to construct complex criteria without using SQL. One of the situations where it shines is when you want to query on properties that are determined at runtime.

Imagine that you want to generate a basic search form for Hubbub profiles. You'll provide the user with input fields for a set of profile properties (maybe their full name, email, and homepage), and a radio group allowing them to apply the `AND`, `OR`, or `NOT` logical operators to their criteria. Figure 5.7 shows an example HTML form.

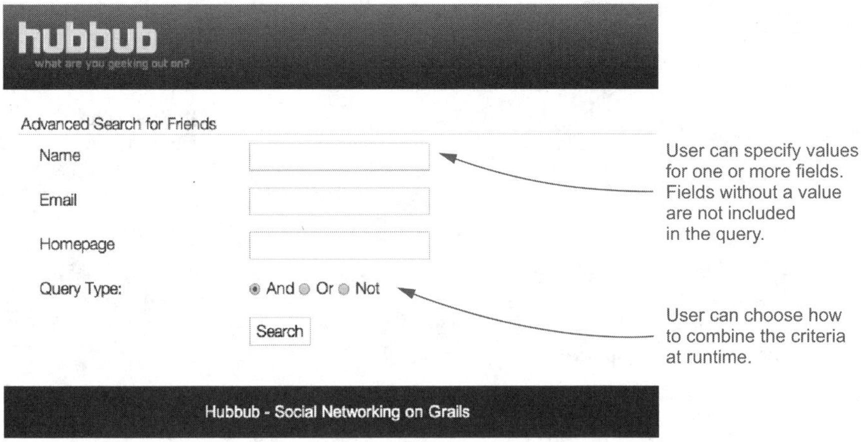

Figure 5.7 A more advanced search screen with Boolean operators

You can take the values submitted with this form and use them to build a Criteria query on the fly. Here's what such a dynamic query might look like inside a controller action:

```
def advResults() {                                            Works out what
    def profileProps = Profile.metaClass.properties*.name  ◁— properties Profile has
```

```
    def profiles = Profile.withCriteria {
        "${params.queryType}" {
                                                    Applies the conjunction from the
                                                    queryType form field: and, or, or not
            params.each { field, value ->
                if (profileProps.contains(field) && value) {
                    ilike field, "%${value}%"
                }                                   Adds an ilike criterion for each
            }                                       submitted field, as long as it
        }                                           matches a property on Profile
    }
    return [ profiles : profiles ]
}
```

This example uses advanced techniques, such as evaluating the properties that exist on a class. But it's not important for you to understand these techniques. The key point is that you can use the values from the form (`queryType`, `field`, and `value`) to build the criteria for the query at runtime. If you'd like to experiment with this code, you can find it in the chapter source code on GitHub. The advanced search form is in the grails-app/views/user/advSearch.gsp file and the `advResults` action is in UserController.groovy.

Before moving on, we'd like to clarify one aspect of the previous Criteria query. Groovy allows you to invoke any method at runtime using a GString. The GString is evaluated first and then Groovy uses the result as the name of the method you want to invoke. So in the example

```
"${params.queryType}" { … }
```

becomes

```
and { … }
```

if the `queryType` parameter has the value `"and"`.

Grails has even more powerful features for creating report-style Criteria queries. These allow you to aggregate query results, producing information that would be useful in a business report. It's time to explore `groupBy` functionality.

5.3.4 Creating a tag cloud using report-style query projections

Most of the time when you're querying, all you want back is a set of records that matches the criteria you specify. You've seen several ways of doing this, and we've stated our preference for Where queries in such cases. But sometimes you want to extract more information from the data in your database, such as how many posts contain the text "BBQ" on a per-user basis. You could do this with multiple queries, but it's usually better to use as few queries as possible as database access is often a bottleneck in application performance. The solution is to use *projections*.

Projections are aggregating, reporting, and filtering functions that can be applied after the query has finished. A common use case is to summarize data from a normal query. To demonstrate what projections can do, you're going to build a tag cloud for a user. In this case, you're not only interested in the tags they have used, but how many posts are linked to each tag. You don't care about which posts, only the total number.

Where queries usually aren't an option for this kind of reporting because they don't give you access to the full range of projections. In this case, you can't retrieve the number of tags for a given post as part of the query. So use a Criteria query instead:

```
def tagList = Post.withCriteria {
   createAlias "tags", "t"

   user { eq "loginId", "phil" }

   projections {
      groupProperty "t.name"
      count "t.id"
   }
}
```

Define aliases for associations so you can use them in projections

Group the results by tag name and calculate how many posts have each tag

This is power querying and we're introducing a couple of new concepts to you, so don't worry if you can't get this in one go. As you become familiar with querying in general, reading and understanding such code becomes second nature.

What's happening here? At first glance, you're querying for `Posts` that match a simple criterion: `loginId` matches `"phil"`. But what are the `createAlias()` declaration and projections block for? An alias is required if you want to reference the properties of associations (in this case, the `name` and `id` properties on the `Tag` instances in the `tags` collection) from projections. If you were to replace `t` with `tags` in the projections, you'd see this exception message:

```
could not resolve property: tags.name of: com.grailsinaction.Post
```

The `projections` block is required when declaring your query projections. For this query, the `groupProperty` projection collects all posts that have a tag with the same name. The count projection then produces the number of posts collected for each tag. You can see how the projections relate to the domain classes and how they affect the query results in figure 5.8. It's important to note how the results take the form of a list of lists rather than a list of domain instances.

All you need to do now is convert that list of tag names and counts into a map of the same. It's time to dust off those Groovy skills and use a new Groovy JDK method for lists:

```
def tagcloudMap = tagList.collectEntries { pair -> pair as List }
```

This little piece of magic converts a list of pairs into a map of key-value entries, where the first element of each pair is the key, and the second is the value.

More projections are available in GORM. In addition to `count()`, you can use `max()`, `min()`, `avg()`, `sum()`, and other statistical methods. The GORM projections are merely enhancements to the standard Hibernate projections. Check out the Hibernate Javadocs[2] on the `Projections` class to see a full list.

[2] Details of Hibernate projections, http://docs.jboss.org/hibernate/orm/3.6/javadocs/org/hibernate/criterion/Projections.html.

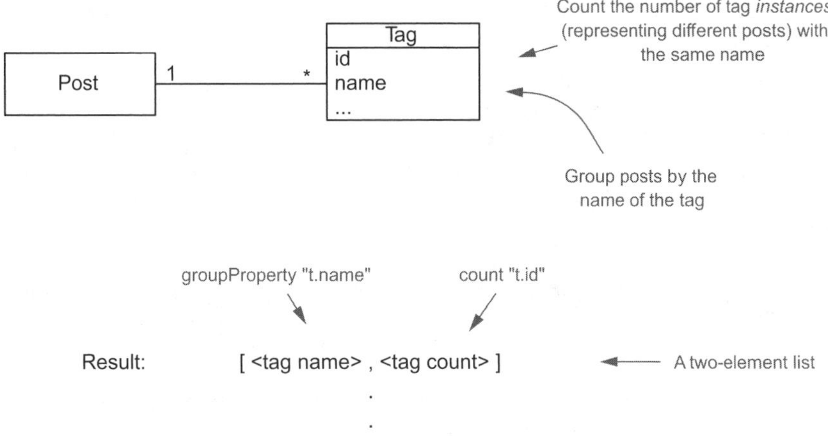

Figure 5.8 How projections affect query results

Criteria queries are a powerful tool that abstracts you away from the underlying SQL, while still providing access to the power features. This is good if you're not a SQL aficionado, but as we've mentioned before, it *is* still SQL under the hood. If you prefer one less layer of abstraction, or are simply more comfortable with SQL, then you've got one final option for writing your queries.

5.3.5 *Using HQL directly*

If you've come from a Hibernate background, you're probably used to expressing complex Hibernate queries using HQL, Hibernate's SQL-like query language. Even if you don't know Hibernate but are familiar with SQL, you'll feel comfortable with HQL. It's for those cases where none of the other options suffice or where HQL is simply easier to write. Be aware though that if you go down this route, you'll tie yourself to Hibernate. You can't use the queries with a different data store, such as MongoDB.

You can take full advantage of HQL directly from the static `find()`, `findAll()`, `executeQuery()`, and `executeUpdate()` methods on domain classes. A basic HQL query looks like figure 5.9:

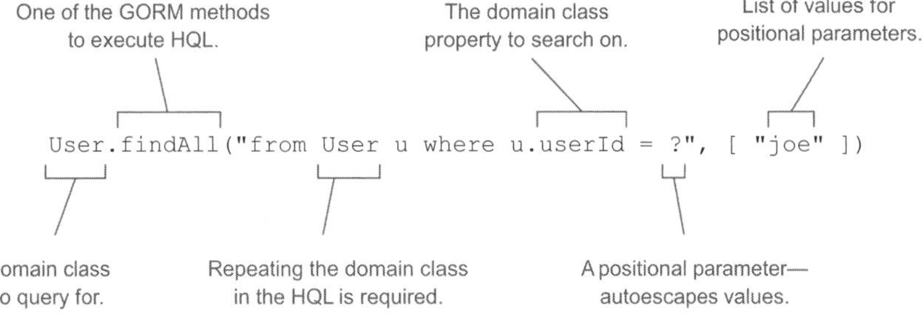

Figure 5.9 Basic HQL query

In figure 5.9, we've supplied `"joe"` as a positional parameter value, but in a real application you'd be more likely to supply a dynamic value, such as `params.loginId`.

> **Mitigating against SQL injection attacks**
>
> One of the most common web security vulnerabilities is the SQL injection attack. In this type of attack, the user passes in malicious query parameters to alter the queries sent to the database (for example, `...?loginId=abc123;delete+from+users;`). This is why you should never do your own concatenations of HQL query strings. If you use the property placeholder (`?`) form of HQL queries, you'll always be protected from these sorts of attacks.

The main difference between HQL and SQL is the use of domain class names and domain properties instead of table names and column names. Otherwise they're closely aligned. You can even do projections:

```
Post.executeQuery("select t.name, count(t.id) from Post p " +
    "join p.tags as t where p.user.loginId = ? group by t.name", ['phil'])
```

This is the HQL version of the projections-based Criteria query from the previous section. It's more succinct and more readable. Whether you should use Criteria queries or HQL comes down to personal preference, but you should also consider whether you want the queries to be portable to other datastores, such as MongoDB. Remember that HQL doesn't work with nonrelational databases. That said, many of the advanced features available to Criteria queries aren't supported by nonrelational databases, such as projections! We'll talk more on this in chapter 16.

Why does the first example in this section use `findAll()` and the second one use `executeQuery()`? The `find()` and `findAll()` methods return instances of the corresponding domain class, whereas `executeQuery()` allows you to specify which properties or aggregates you want in your result set. Where you'd use projections in a Criteria query you'd use `executeQuery()` with HQL. And if you want to insert, update, or delete records via HQL, you *must* use `executeUpdate()`.

Full coverage of HQL would probably take the rest of the book, and it's time you got back on track with your Hubbub application. Fortunately the Hibernate user guide[3] is pretty good on HQL, so we refer you to that for more about this powerful query syntax.

That concludes your whirlwind journey through Grails query options. We've focused heavily on Where queries because we think those are the ones you should be using most. But we've also introduced the other query options because Where queries don't work in all situations. Those options have much more depth to them than we've covered here, but we've laid out the path for you to get started and learn more. This

---

[3] "HQL: The Hibernate Query Language," http://docs.jboss.org/hibernate/orm/3.6/reference/en-US/html/queryhql.html.

last section may have been heavy going, but sit safe in the knowledge that you can still progress with the rest of the book without fully understanding how Criteria or HQL queries work. You have time later to become familiar with those options.

5.4 Summary and best practices

In this chapter, you've explored the options that Grails offers for querying the database. These range from the simple `list()` and `count()` methods, through to the flexible Where queries, up to the all-powerful Criteria and HQL queries. As we've said throughout the chapter, we think Where queries, with their programmer-friendly syntax and basic type checking, are the go-to syntax for most of your querying needs, but they don't work in all cases. That's why you have the other options.

You also looked at getting data into the system via the `BootStrap` class. This is important because most applications are difficult to use without data in them. That said, sample data usually only makes sense in the context of testing and development, so it's good to know that you can conditionally load data based on the currently active environment.

Let's revisit the key ideas from this chapter, which you can take away and apply to your own Grails apps:

- *Use Where queries by default.* Where queries are easy to understand by programmers of all abilities and backgrounds. No knowledge of SQL is necessary to read and understand the code. They also allow for `if` statements!
- *Use the Grails console UI.* The Grails console UI is ideal for prototyping tricky queries and it lets you try options without recompiling.
- *Use the most appropriate query type for the job.* Knowing which query type to use in any given situation takes experience, but if you find yourself struggling with a Where query, don't be afraid to switch to Criteria queries or HQL. Remember that complex projections or dynamic queries *require* you to use one of the other query types. Also, try to be consistent: use either Criteria queries or HQL for the advanced stuff. Using both requires more effort on the part of you and your teammates.
- *Use bootstraps conditionally.* Grails lets you perform different bootstrap operations in each environment, so use that. Don't assume that your user's development database is an in-memory one and always check whether your sample data exists before re-creating it.

In the next chapter, you'll take your domain modeling skills and apply them to working with forms and controllers in the UI layer. It'll be a refreshing break from all this heavy-duty database work.

6 Controlling application flow

This chapter covers

- Introducing mocking
- Unit testing your view code
- Exploring scopes
- Working with redirects

In chapters 3 and 5, you learned how Grails handles domain objects as you went about creating, updating, saving, deleting, and querying all kinds of domain classes. Along the way, you used scaffolding controllers to route the user around the application, and you implemented a few GSP views to host your forms. But, for the most part, you ignored how controllers do their work. It's time to set that right.

In this chapter, we'll focus exclusively on controllers—and all the important roles they play in dealing with data from the web tier, routing it to services, and shipping off results to the view. And all those Spock testing skills you've been learning along the way? Well, you'll extend those into the controller space, learning a whole swag of new techniques for controller-specific testing to make sure all the new code you write is rock solid. By the end of the chapter, you'll be ready to implement all the common controller use cases in your own applications as well as many of the edge cases.

We'll get the chapter underway by pulling together all you've learned so far about controllers, forms, and domain classes. Then we'll show you how to modify Hubbub to add and display user posts on a Twitter-style timeline.

6.1 Controller essentials

In our exploration of the Grails ecosystem so far, we've been focused more on the model (saving and querying domain objects) and passed over the gritty details of how controllers, views, and taglibs work together. Let's take a detailed look at form-controller interactions with a focus on the controllers.

Imagine that you want to display a timeline of a user's recent posts. You'd need to implement a controller action (perhaps `timeline` in the `Post` controller) to retrieve the posts for a user, then pass them to a view (/views/post/timeline.gsp) to display them in the browser. As you discovered in chapter 1, Grails exposes controller actions as URLs using conventions. Here's how Grails translates controller action names into URLs:

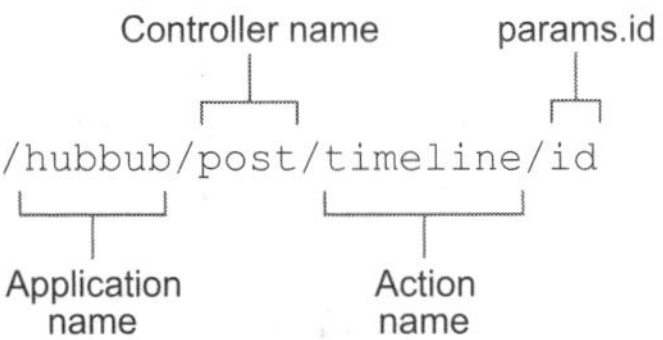

When the user points the browser at http://localhost:8080/hubbub/post/timeline/chuck_norris, Grails will fire the `timeline` action on the `Post` controller, passing `chuck_norris` as the `id`. Typically, that action will retrieve data from the database and pass it to the view to display. Under Grails conventions, the view name matches the action name (but with a .gsp extension), so the `timeline` action will retrieve the data and pass it to /views/post/timeline.gsp to be rendered. Figure 6.1 demonstrates this flow.

You saw this flow in action in chapter 1 and in the search form examples in chapter 4. Let's apply our knowledge of controllers to add a timeline to Hubbub.

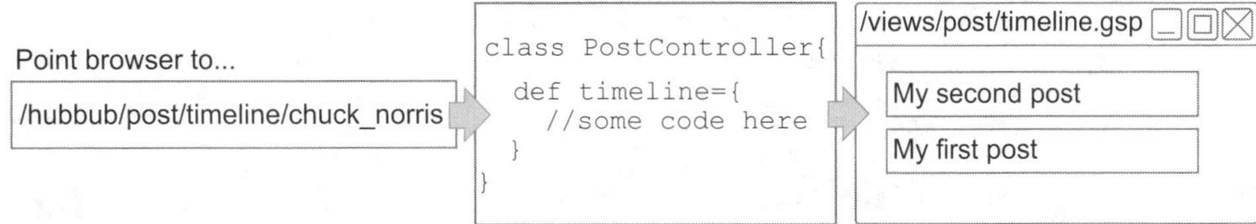

Figure 6.1 From URL to controller to view

6.2 Implementing a timeline for Hubbub

A timeline for a user should display a list of posts for the user mixed with posts by everyone they follow. But let's start small and implement the capability to display all the posts for one user.

You'll start by updating your `PostController` to implement a `timeline()` action. The following listing shows your first implementation of a user timeline.

Listing 6.1 Adding the timeline action to your `PostController`

```
package com.grailsinaction
class PostController {
    static scaffold = true

    def timeline() {
        def user = User.findByLoginId(params.id)          ❶
        if (!user) {
            response.sendError(404)                        ❷
        } else {
            [ user : user ]                                ❸
        }
    }
}
```

❶ Retrieves user based on id parameter

❷ Sends error code for nonexistent users

❸ Passes matched user to view

As you've seen in earlier chapters, actions typically process form parameters and use them to interact with the data model. In this case, we're using the optional `id` parameter to hold the user's ID, and we use it to retrieve the entire `User` object from the database ❶. For now, if we can't find the user ❷, we're going to send an HTTP 404 status message back to the browser (which the browser will render as a "Not Found" message). We'll add fancier error handling later in the chapter.

Once you've successfully retrieved the `User` object, the action's result gets placed into a map that's returned to the view ❸, which is typically a GSP file. The view can access any objects in the map to display them to the user. You could use an explicit `return` statement at the end of your action, but there's no need. Groovy always considers the last line of a closure or method as the return value, and it's common for Grails programmers to omit `return` in controller actions.

> **The optional id param**
>
> You may not have seen the `id` field in action yet. As illustrated at the beginning of section 6.1, the conventional URL-to-controller mapping is /controller/action/id, where the `id` portion is passed into the `params.id` field. Because the format of the field is free-form, it gives you cool options for permalinks.
>
> For example, /user/profile/chuck_norris would fire the `profile()` action on the `User` controller, passing in `chuck_norris` to the `params.id`. This was how people commonly did permalinking before Grails implemented custom URL mappings, which we'll get to later.

(continued)

Grails scaffolds use the `id` field to represent the database ID, so you'll often see URLs such as /user/show/57 used to display the user with `id` 57 from the database. It's practical, but it sure ain't pretty.

6.3 Testing controller actions: an introduction to mocking

You've now written your first serious bit of controller logic, and you may be tempted to launch a browser and test things by typing in URLs, but that's going to quickly become tedious. You'd have to populate your `User` objects in the database, get a user `id` out of the database to look up, and spend more time doing busywork. And even after you've done all that, you still haven't written any view code to display the timeline, so you'd have to wait even longer to get feedback that your new code is working nicely.

Let's work a bit smarter and write a Spock test that will exercise your new code immediately, so you'll know you're making good progress, while it provides a regression test suite for making bold changes later in the chapter.

Up to this point you've learned only about integration tests—tests that spark up the whole Grails infrastructure, including the database, but it's time to introduce you to unit tests, which are much faster to run and perfect for testing controller actions.

6.3.1 About unit tests

Unit tests mock out the database layer of your Grails application by using an in-memory GORM database layer. That means no transactions, at least for now, but it also means a super-fast start time, and in situations where the goal of the tests isn't the persistence layer itself, it's the ideal way to go.

Unit tests are generated automatically for any Grails artifacts you create using the Grails shell commands (`grails create-controller` for example). If you create an artifact by hand in a text editor or by copy/paste, you can create a shell test using the `grails create-unit-test` command.

6.3.2 @TestFor and @Mock mixins

Groovy Mixins, which you learned about in chapter 2, handle Grails unit testing support. Using abstract syntax tree (AST) transformation magic (low-level class compilation fiddling), mixins take code from another class and import it into your current class (without changing your class hierarchy).

The two most important mixins you need to learn about for Grails unit testing are the `@TestFor` and `@Mock` mixins:

- *`@TestFor`*—Tells your unit test what kind of Grails artifact you're testing. In our case, it's a controller.
- *`@Mock`*—Tells your test which domain (database) objects you need to save and query in your test.

6.3.3 *Applying @TestFor and @Mock*

Let's look at a real `PostController` test case in the following listing, then we'll debrief on what magic those mixins are doing.

Listing 6.2 A basic controller unit test

```
package com.grailsinaction

import grails.test.mixin.Mock
import grails.test.mixin.TestFor
import spock.lang.Specification

@TestFor(PostController)
@Mock([User,Post])
class PostControllerSpec extends Specification {

    def "Get a users timeline given their id"() {
        given: "A user with posts in the db"
        User chuck = new User(
                loginId: "chuck_norris",
                password: "password")
        chuck.addToPosts(new Post(content: "A first post"))
        chuck.addToPosts(new Post(content: "A second post"))
        chuck.save(failOnError: true)

        and: "A loginId parameter"
        params.id = chuck.loginId

        when: "the timeline is invoked"
        def model = controller.timeline()

        then: "the user is in the returned model"
        model.user.loginId == "chuck_norris"
        model.user.posts.size() == 2
    }

}
```

1. Imports controller test artifacts
2. Adds mock save() and find() methods to User
3. save() method now available on object
4. params property introduced by @TestFor
5. controller property introduced by @TestFor

Congratulations! You've written your first Grails unit test. What's so different from the integration tests you know and love? Less than you might think:

- You mark this test as an `@TestFor` a controller ❶, meaning Grails will create and insert a `params` object ❹ and wire up a controller object ❺ that points to an instance of your `PostController` class.
- You mark the class with an `@Mock` annotation ❷, which automatically creates the GORM dynamic query and `save()` methods on your `User` domain class ❸ and performs all save/update/query operations against an in-memory hashmap rather than a real database. You also mock the `Post` class because you add instances of it to the `posts` collection. In fact, you should mock any domain class that's in any way used from the test case or the method under test.

For completeness, we should also show you how to test for the nonexistent user—remember you were sending a 404 (Not Found) status to the browser? For that test you'll need to use the implicit response object to get a handle to the returned status. Here's how you'd express that in a Spock test:

```
def "Check that non-existent users are handled with an error"() {

    given: "the id of a non-existent user"
    params.id = "this-user-id-does-not-exist"        <-- An invalid user id

    when: "the timeline is invoked"
    controller.timeline()

    then: "a 404 is sent to the browser"              (1) Confirm a 404
    response.status == 404                            <-- error code

}
```

In this case you're using the mock response object (1) to confirm that your 404 status property is correctly returned.

> **New in Grails 2.0: Actions as functions (not closures)**
>
> In the old Grails 1.x days, all controller actions had to be defined as closures. This means you'll see code like this:
>
> ```
> def timeline = {
> }
> ```
>
> This approach caused problems with serialization, and also meant extra class generation, putting pressure on JVM permanent generation (permgen) memory. The new Grail 2.x action parameter work, which you'll read about presently, introduced a new method-based approach to controller actions (though closures are still supported for backward compatibility). Using methods gave the opportunity to do more complex action-based binding, which we'll introduce you to shortly.

6.4 From controller to view

Because you've now written the code to retrieve the user from the database, and you've written the tests to make sure that code is working, it makes sense to implement a view to display the information in a browser.

6.4.1 Creating the view

Following Grails conventions, you'll implement your view in a file that has the same name as your controller and action. In this case, the view will be named /grails-app/views/post/timeline.gsp. The following listing shows your first effort to display the user's timeline.

Listing 6.3 Displaying a user's timeline

```
<html>
    <head>
        <title>
            Timeline for ${ user.profile ? user.profile.fullName :
    user.loginId }
        </title>
        <meta name="layout" content="main"/>
    </head>
    <body>
        <h1>Timeline for ${ user.profile ? user.profile.fullName :
    user.loginId }</h1>
        <div id="allPosts">
            <g:each in="${user.posts}" var="post">
                <div class="postEntry">
                    <div class="postText">
                        ${post.content}
                    </div>
                    <div class="postDate">
                        ${post.dateCreated}
                    </div>
                </div>
            </g:each>
        </div>
    </body>
</html>
```

(1) Accesses nested domain objects
(2) Iterates through user's posts
(3) Displays each post

By using the `User` object that the controller placed into your request scope, you can read the `User`'s fields and display the data in the browser. In this example, you check if the `User` has a `Profile` object, and if they do, you display the full name, otherwise you display their `loginId` (1).

You can reference objects in request scope by enclosing the name in Groovy's interpolation syntax, `${}`. If you pass complex objects to your view (such as a domain object with relationships to other domain objects), you can access them as you would in any other setting. In listing 6.3, you render `${user.profile.fullName}` (1).

You also iterate over each of the `User`'s `Post` objects (2), displaying the `content` and `dateCreated` of each post (3).

Figure 6.2 shows your new timeline view in action. You've worked hard, and it's time to see something running in the browser, so feel free to issue a `grails run-app` and get this party started.

> **What about unit testing your view code?**
>
> You've written unit tests for your controller, but what about your GSP code in the view? At the time of writing, Grails' support for testing GSPs is fairly clumsy, but support for unit testing taglibs is excellent. Taglibs should be the artifact that you're using to encapsulate any complex view-tier logic. The rest of your GSP code is probably presentation concerns that are better tested in a real browser. But how do you automate that?

(continued)

Most people approach the problem of automated exercising of their views by writing functional tests in Geb (a Groovy-based functional testing tool we'll take you through in detail in chapter 9). Functional tests exercise your running Grails application end-to-end using a real web browser and are probably what you're looking for in testing your view tier.

With the timeline in place to show all the user's posts, you can now work on adding new posts to the timeline. This gives you a chance to create and save domain objects.

Breaking view name conventions

If you don't want your view name to match your action name, you can use the `render()` method. For instance, if you want to use user_timeline.gsp to generate the output for your timeline action, you can use the `view` argument to `render()`:

```
render(view: "user_timeline",
       model: [ user: user ])
```

Notice that you omit the .gsp extension when referring to the view.

6.4.2 *Adding new posts*

In chapter 3, you learned how to create and save `Post` objects from a unit test, but it'll be more fun when you can create them through a browser. Now that you know a little about how controllers work, let's apply your knowledge to the UI to give you a way to create posts from the app.

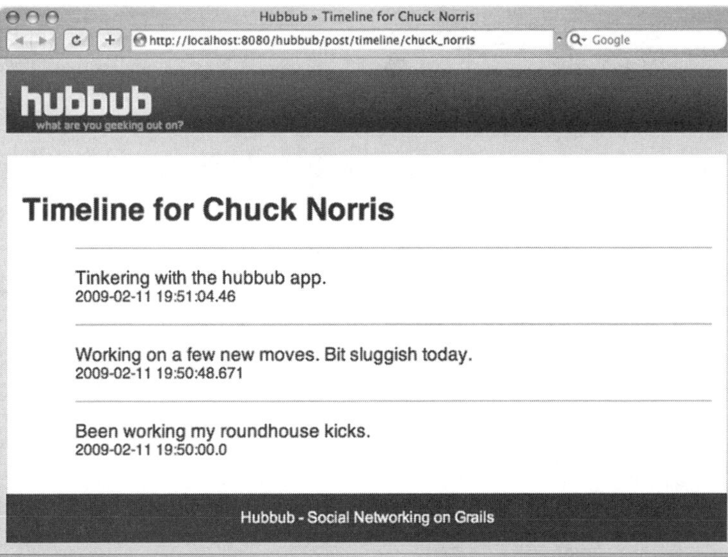

Figure 6.2 Your first timeline in action

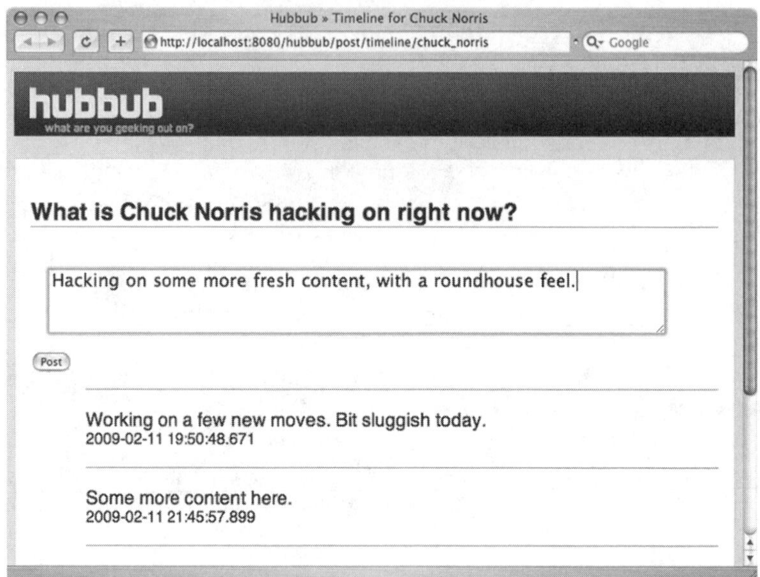

Figure 6.3 Adding posting capabilities to Hubbub

First, let's enhance your view to give your user the ability to add new posts. You want to end up with the capability shown in figure 6.3.

For this to work, you need to add a form to timeline.gsp to capture the new content for the post.

ADDING A FORM

You'll need a `textArea` component so the user can enter the body of the post. Italics in the following listing show the `div` you'll add to your timeline.gsp file to handle the new input.

Listing 6.4 Adding a form for new posts

```
...
<body>
    <h1>Timeline for ...</h1>
    <div id="newPost">
        <h3>
            What is ${user.profile.fullName} hacking on right now?
        </h3>
        <p>
            <g:form action="addPost" id="${params.id}">          ❶
            <g:textArea id='postContent' name="content"
                rows="3" cols="50"/><br/>                        ❷
            <g:submitButton name="post" value="Post"/>
        </g:form>
    </p>
</div>

<div id="allPosts">
...
```

❶ Retains id from current URL

❷ Provides textArea to enter post

In the listing you added a new form to the page using the <g:form> tag, with the target of the form being the addPost action ❶.

You pass through the current id field to the form submission so that the addPost action knows which user ID it's being invoked for. For example, the form submission URL for the chuck_norris user ID is /post /addPost/chuck_norris.

You've also added the <g:textArea> tag to let the user enter their post contents ❷. Because the control is named content, you can expect params.content to turn up in your controller logic somewhere.

UPDATING THE CONTROLLER

The following listing shows your updated PostController code, which now handles adding new posts to the user's timeline.

Listing 6.5 The updated PostController handles new Post objects

```
package com.grailsinaction
class PostController {
    static scaffold = true

    def timeline() {
        ...
    }

    def addPost() {
        def user = User.findByLoginId(params.id)
        if (user) {
            def post = new Post(params)
            user.addToPosts(post)
            if (user.save()) {
                flash.message = "Successfully created Post"
            } else {
                flash.message = "Invalid or empty post"
            }
        } else {
            flash.message = "Invalid User Id"
        }
        redirect(action: 'timeline', id: params.id)
    }
}
```

❶ Finds user based on id param

❷ Binds params data to new Post object

❸ Links new post to existing user

❹ Returns false if Post validation fails

❺ Informs user of success or failure

❻ Returns user to timeline

When you saved domain models in chapter 3, you wrote integration tests. Now you're doing it for real from the UI. Like your timeline action, addPost starts by retrieving the User object based on its ID ❶, but here you've added error handling to test whether the user exists.

If the User exists in the database, you create a new Post object, passing in the params map ❷. When you pass a map into the constructor of a domain class, Grails binds the properties of the map to fields on the object, skipping the ones that don't match. In this case, params.content will be mapped to the Post's content field. Figure 6.4 shows how the content field of the params object maps to the Post object. Grails refers to this process as *data binding*.

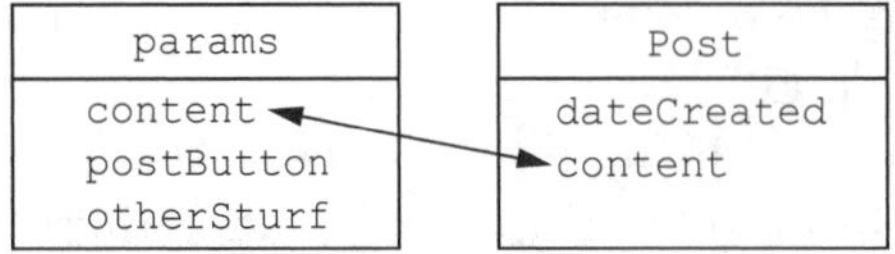

Figure 6.4 Binding a `params` map to a `Post` object

With the form data bound to your new `Post` object, the new `Post` is added to the `User` object ❸. Finally, you can attempt a `save()` to ensure that constraints on the `Post` object are satisfied ❹. We'll introduce more advanced data binding techniques in chapter 7 that allow you to perform all these operations in a single line, but for now let's use the basic data binding mechanism.

Whether things go well or fail dismally, you keep the user informed by providing feedback with `flash.message` ❺. We'll discuss flash scope in the next section, but, in short, it's a way to communicate information to the user. Later in the chapter, we'll show you a more robust way of handling validation errors, but `flash.message` is fine for now.

When everything is done, you redirect the user back to the `timeline` action ❻, which will rerender the timeline with the new post. Notice that the redirect includes the `id` param. This is important because the timeline action relies on having the user's ID, and when you redirect programmatically (rather than typing in a browser URL), you need to explicitly provide the value. You now need to update your timeline.gsp file to output those error or success messages to the user.

UPDATING THE VIEW

The following code fragment shows the updated `div` for your flash message:

```
...
<h1>Timeline for ...</h1>
<g:if test="${flash.message}">
    <div class="flash">
        ${flash.message}
    </div>
</g:if>
<div id="newPost">
...
```

> **TIP** You'll need to style the `div` with CSS so it stands out as a warning message. To view the CSS styling that matches the screen shots that follow, download the source for this chapter. You'll find the relevant CSS rule for .flash in web-app/css/hubbub.css.

With error handling in place, it's time to experiment with adding an invalid post so you can see what happens in the UI tier when you add an invalid post.

TESTING THE NEW FUNCTIONALITY

Figure 6.5 shows the result of attempting to add a blank post.

Great work! Your validation is firing, your error message is displaying correctly, and you've implemented the capability to add new posts to Hubbub. But you've skipped a step. Where's the matching unit test for your new feature?

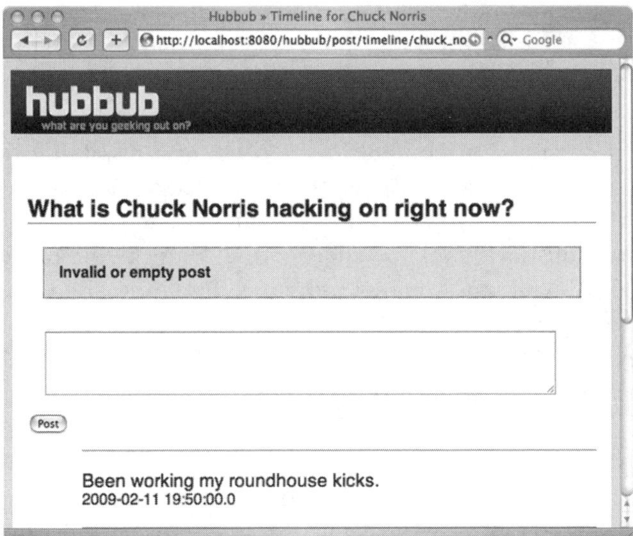

Figure 6.5 Adding a blank post generates an error.

ADDING A TEST CASE

Because you already include the Post class in the @Mock annotation, you can begin work on a new test case right away, as shown in the following listing. A mock save() method is already added to the Post class.

Listing 6.6 Test case for a successful post

```
...
class PostControllerSpec extends Specification {
    ...
    def "Adding a valid new post to the timeline"() {
        given: "A user with posts in the db"
        User chuck = new User(
                loginId: "chuck_norris",
                password: "password").save(failOnError: true)

        and: "A loginId parameter"
        params.id = chuck.loginId

        and: "Some content for the post"
        params.content = "Chuck Norris can unit test entire
➥ applications with a single assert."

        when: "addPost is invoked"
        def model = controller.addPost()

        then: "our flash message and redirect confirms the success"
        flash.message == "Successfully created Post"
        response.redirectedUrl == "/post/timeline/${chuck.loginId}"
        Post.countByUser(chuck) == 1                              <-- Ensure the post ended up in the DB
    }
}
```

For an exercise to do on your own, it would be great to write a test for the case when no content is provided and an error is generated (or even when an invalid user ID is provided). We've included a sample in the source code that comes with the book, but why not try writing one yourself?

You've now implemented two of Hubbub's major features: displaying the user's timeline and adding posts. You've also applied your knowledge of creating domain objects (from chapter 3) and used dynamic finders to query them (from chapter 4).

But a few things are still unexplained. Where did all these `flash` objects come from, and what do they do? And why aren't we using the standard validation messages we saw in chapter 4? Fear not. By the end of the chapter, you'll understand all these essential controller issues.

We'll start with the `flash` object, which relates to how Grails handles scope.

6.5 Exploring scopes

You've seen how controller actions can return a map that gets passed through to the view, and you've seen the `flash` object also passing data from the controller to the view. This passing of information, and the lifetime of the variables that you pass, is known as variable *scope*.

Grails supports different scopes to store information in, and each of them lasts a different length of time. When you passed data in a map from a controller to a view, you implicitly used *request scope*. But Grails lets you reference the different scopes explicitly so you can store data for as long as you need it. In particular, Grails offers four special map-like storage scopes that you can reference by name in every controller action (see table 6.1).

> **NOTE** The `request`, `flash`, `session`, and `servletContext` scope variables aren't Java `Maps`. For example, `request` is a Java `HttpServletRequest` object. But the underlying objects have been enhanced by advanced Grails metaclass operations to expose map-like storage, making things easier for the programmer.

Table 6.1 Grails supports four storage contexts for passing content between controllers and forms

Scope variable	Survival time for entries in this scope
`request`	Survive until the target GSP finishes rendering.
`flash`	Survive to the next page, and the one after that.
`session`	Survive until the current user closes the browser.
`servletContext`	Survive until the application is restarted (this map is shared by all users).

If you've worked with Java web applications before, you've probably seen request, session, and servlet context scopes. If you've dabbled in the latest Java Enterprise Edition spec (JEE6 and above), you may have even bumped into the new flash scope. Flash scope has been in Grails since the beginning and is used heavily in most Grails

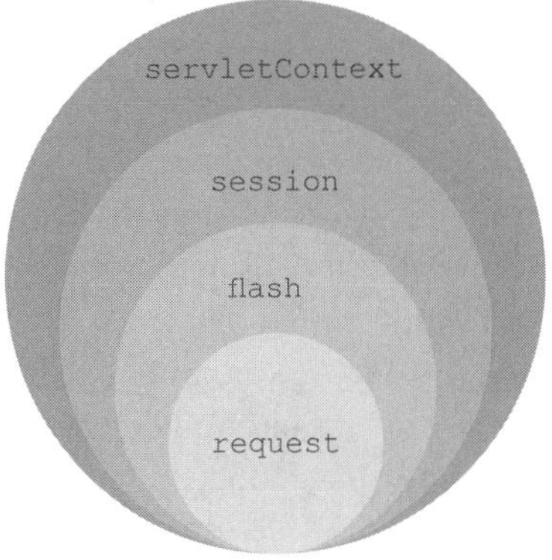

Figure 6.6 Request scope is the shortest lived, and servletContext the longest.

applications, because it's a real lifesaver. Figure 6.6 shows the relative lifespans of the different scopes.

Next, we'll look at each scope individually.

6.5.1 Request scope

Request scope is great when you want to store data that's shared only between your controller and the view (normally a GSP page). In this case, the server is said to "forward" the request to the page (meaning that the browser location doesn't change—it's all handled within the server itself). Even though you weren't aware of it, you've used request scope every time you returned a `Map` from your controller actions. Request scope is used to hold that data until the view finishes rendering it.

But what about your `addPost` action? You do the heavy lifting of adding a post, but then you want to redirect the browser to the user's timeline to display a Successfully added message. That means the browser is involved, which means your request scope is gone.

For these scenarios, Grails offers *flash scope.*

6.5.2 Flash scope

Entries in the flash map survive one (and only one) redirect, after that they're removed. That's exactly what you need for your `addPost` action. You can safely place a Successfully added message into your flash map and know that it'll survive the redirect back to your `timeline` action.

Like all of these scope maps, `flash` is a general-purpose map, but convention dictates that you put these kinds of UI messages in an attribute called `flash.message`. You'll commonly see flash scope referenced in GSP files wrapped in a condition to keep things tidy, as in our earlier `Post` example. Here's a sample of the kind of code you'll commonly encounter in a GSP:

```
<g:if test="${flash.message}">
    <div class="flash">${flash.message}</div>
</g:if>
```

For objects that you want to survive longer than a single redirect, you'll need to explore session scope.

6.5.3 Session scope

The next longest-lived scope is session scope. Objects that you place in session scope remain until the user closes their browser. Internally, servers use a session cookie called `JSESSIONID` to map a user to their session, and the cookie expires when they close their browser (or when the server times out the session due to inactivity).

Sessions are replicated in a clustered environment, so it's best to keep their contents to a minimum. A common use case is putting a logged-in `User` object into the session, so be sure you understand how detached domain objects work (see the sidebar).

Session gotchas: the mystery of the detached object

If you're storing a domain object in the session (such as the logged-in `User` object), the object will become *detached* from your Hibernate session. That means you can't access any uninitialized lazy-loaded relationships the object holds. For example, you can't call `session.user.following.each {}`. To reattach the object (so you can walk its object graph of relationships, for instance), use the `attach()` method that is available on all domain classes. For our `User` example, it would look like this:

```
def user = session.user
if (!user.isAttached()) {
    user.attach()
}
user.following.each { nextFollowing -> /* do stuff */ }
```

6.5.4 servletContext (application) scope

The final scope available is servletContext scope, sometimes called *application scope*. This map is shared across your whole application, and it's handy for storing state that's not dependent on any particular user, such as the number of logins since the application was started. This scope is also useful for loading resources from within your web application itself, for example through code like this:

```
servletContext.getResourceAsStream("/images/my-logo.gif")
```

Consult the standard `servletContext` Javadoc for details.

> **NOTE** More niche controller scopes exist, such as flow and conversation scopes (specific to Webflow) and the instance-affecting prototype and singleton. Check out the Grails user guide for details of the common ones (we rarely use any of these).

You now have a handle on how scopes work, and we've explained the mystery of that `flash` object. In summary, choose a scope based on the type of data you want to store:

- *Request scope*—For rendering in the view
- *Flash scope*—For surviving a redirect

- *Session scope*—For long-lived user-specific data
- *Application scope*—For long-lived application-specific data

Now that you've learned the underpinnings of the mysterious flash scope, it's time to turn your attention to other aspects of controller interaction, in particular, exploring how controllers can talk to other controllers to route the user around the application. When we introduced the `addPost` action, we called `redirect()` methods, so it's time to learn about controller redirects and flows.

6.6 Handling default actions

Grails lets you supply a default `index` action for each controller that you implement. When the user accesses the controller without specifying an action name, such as when accessing /hubbub/post, the `index` action handles the request, typically redirecting the user to another action.

Let's retrofit an `index` action to your `PostController`, so that when users navigate to /hubbub/post, they're immediately redirected to the `timeline` action. The following listing shows the updated `PostController` code.

Listing 6.7 Catching the `index` action and redirecting the user

```
package com.grailsinaction
class PostController {
    static scaffold = true
    def index() {
        if (!params.id) {
            params.id = "chuck_norris"
        }
        redirect(action: 'timeline', params: params)
    }
    ...
}
```

Passes params when redirecting

One of the gotchas when redirecting is that you lose your `params` map if you don't explicitly pass it through to your redirected action. If you hadn't passed `params` from the `index` action to the `timeline` action, the incoming `params` map would have been `null`.

Let's write a test for your new `index` logic.

6.6.1 One test, two use cases

You need a way to test the use case in which a `params.id` is supplied and also the case in which no `params.id` is supplied. Previously you'd have written two tests to cover both scenarios, but Spock offers a great time-saving feature for parameterized testing using the `where:` clause.

In listing 6.8, you set up a `where:` clause with a table that lists the `suppliedId` and the `expectedUrl`. Spock runs this test twice, once for each of the lines in the `where:` clause below the heading row, substituting the line's value into the relevant variables inside the body of the test. On the first run of given/when/then, Spock substitutes joe_cool for suppliedId, and /post/timeline/joe_cool for the expectedUrl. If the tests pass, Spock then moves on to the next combination.

Listing 6.8 Testing the index action with various parameter combinations

```
@spock.lang.Unroll
def "Testing id of #suppliedId redirects to #expectedUrl"() {

    given:
    params.id = suppliedId

    when: "Controller is invoked"
    controller.index()

    then:
    response.redirectedUrl == expectedUrl

    where:
    suppliedId  |   expectedUrl
    'joe_cool'  |   '/post/timeline/joe_cool'
    null        |   '/post/timeline/chuck_norris'

}
```

Because you now have this same test running twice, once for each combination, you might get yourself into a state where one of the tests passes (for example, the joe_cool line), but the other fails (for example, the null line). It would be handy to customize the output so the test appears as two different test cases. Enter the Spock @Unroll annotation. You can even use parameters from your where: clause in the name of the test itself, so the output is easy to distinguish. Look at figure 6.7, which shows the output of running the test in IntelliJ to see how the @Unroll annotation affected the final two lines of test output.

One major disadvantage of implementing your own index action in this case is that it overrides the one provided by the scaffolding. You'll lose access to the scaffolding view that displays a list of the posts! For that reason, the chapter source code on GitHub renames index to home and explicitly sets the default action as described in the sidebar. We updated the unit test specification as well, which now calls the home action.

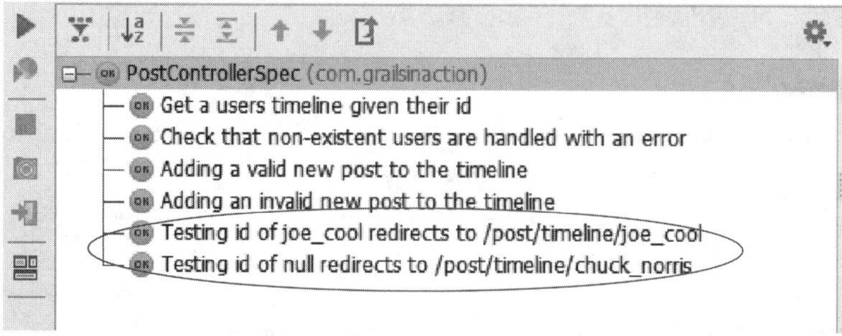

Figure 6.7 Results of running the test with the @Unroll annotation

> **A world of default-action alternatives**
>
> We've discussed using the `index` action to perform default actions when hitting the base controller URL, but you can handle default actions many other ways.
>
> If your controller has only one action on it, that will be interpreted as the default action. In listing 6.5, if `timeline` were the only action in the controller, you could have omitted the `index` action and the controller would handle requests for /hubbub/post.
>
> If your controller has multiple actions, you can explicitly declare your default action at the top of your controller:
>
> ```
> static defaultAction = 'timeline'
> ```
>
> Using an `index` action is common, so we showed you that technique first. But in most of these sorts of scenarios, using `defaultAction` makes more sense, because you don't have to repackage your `params`, and there's no client redirect involved.

The typical role of an `index` action is redirecting, but we haven't explained the options for handling redirects. It's time to get acquainted with the many redirect options.

6.6.2 *Working with redirects*

We've used `redirect()` calls throughout our code. For example, we redirect back to the timeline at the end of the `addPost` action. When a default `index` action is called, we redirect to another one.

All our `redirect()` uses so far have followed a particular pattern, like this:

```
redirect(action:'timeline')
```

For this form of redirect, the target action name must exist on the current controller.

But what if you want to refer to an action on a different controller? Perhaps after registering a user on the `User` controller, you want to send them to the timeline on the `Post` controller. For those situations, you can use the extended version of `redirect()`:

```
redirect(controller: 'post', action:'timeline', id: newUser.loginId)
```

The `id` field is optional, as is the action name. If you don't specify an action, it will go to the default action on the controller (as discussed in the previous section).

If you need to pass parameters during the redirect, you can pass in a map of parameters to be sent:

```
redirect(controller: 'post', action:'timeline',
    params: [fullName: newUser.profile.fullName,
             email: newUser.profile.email ]
           )
```

Finally, you can also redirect using the `uri:` or `url:` params to redirect to relative or absolute addresses. For example, instead of this:

```
redirect(controller: 'post', action:'timeline')
```

you can use the URI option:

```
redirect(uri: '/post/timeline')
```

And if you need to go to an external address, use the URL version:

```
redirect(url: 'http://www.google.com?q=hubbub')
```

That's about all you need to know about redirects. We'll use them frequently, so it's good to be familiar with their many flavors.

Our next step is to take what we've implemented in this chapter, and move it to a more maintainable application architecture. One of the most powerful tools Grails offers for doing that is the Grails service. We'll look at services in the next chapter, along with a deep dive into the many ways you can transport data between forms, controllers, and services.

But for now, let's review what we've learned about controllers.

6.7 Summary and best practices

In this chapter, you've explored a mountain of skills and techniques related to controllers.

You started by implementing a `timeline` page with a feature for adding new posts to Hubbub. You also saw three different ways an action can behave: returning a model for a view, rendering some content directly, and redirecting.

Let's pull out some of the key practices to take away from the chapter:

- *If it might break, test it.* You don't need to test everything, but test everything that can break. Experience will help you work out the low-hanging fruit, but while you're getting to know Grails it's good practice to test everything.
- *Mock out your data layer with @Mock.* Unit tests run so much faster than integration tests, and when working with controllers, it's the controller that you want to test, not the data layer.
- *Use Spock* `where:` *clauses to test edge cases.* The Spock `where:` clause gives you a concise way of testing all the edge cases of your dataset while still keeping tests maintainable. Make use of them for any controller flows that branch based on incoming data. Don't forget to use the `@Unroll` feature to make sure you have nice named tests for each condition.
- *Use flash scope.* Flash scope is ideal for passing messages to the user (when a redirect is involved).
- *Get to know redirects.* Using `redirect()` with flash scope gives you flexibility for passing data to your view and having it cleaned up automatically.

7 Services and data binding

This chapter covers

- Using services for more maintainable architecture
- Data binding and error handling
- Using command objects for tricky form validations
- Uploading and rendering images
- Working with URL mappings and filters

In the previous chapter you learned the basics about what controllers do, how to extend them with your own logic, and how to test them. We haven't yet introduced you to the best way to use controllers in building larger Grails applications.

In this chapter we examine the controller's best friend: the Grails service. Services help free controllers from the heavy lifting of application logic, and let controllers do what they do best—control the flow of the user through the application. In this chapter we'll take you through all the basics of Grails services, and provide insights to grow your application in a maintainable and testable way.

And if we free controllers from the tyranny of heavy business logic and return them to their flow controlling core business, it'll give us a reason to discuss taking data from an HTML form and binding it into variables and objects that you can process more conveniently in your application. Grails calls this operation *data binding* because you're binding form data to real Grails objects. In this chapter we'll take you through the various mechanisms for Grails data binding and show you when it's best to use each one.

Let's get this chapter underway by refactoring your post logic out of the controller and into a service; then we can start reusing post service throughout your application.

7.1 Services: making apps robust and maintainable

You learned about powerful controller techniques in the previous chapter: basic forms of data binding, params processing, controller routing, and even redirect magic. But before things get unmaintainable, and they will if you keep piling logic into your controllers, you'd better learn techniques to keep a clean application architecture for the long haul. In this section, we'll explore how services can dramatically simplify your controllers by moving all your business logic into a single place.

In `PostController`, you implemented an `addPost` action to handle the creation of new `Posts`. But later you'll want to create `Posts` from many different entry points—specifically from a Representational State Transfer (REST) service. As a result, you'll need to repeat your `Post` logic at each entry point, but because we're DRY people, that repetition sounds like a bad thing.

In this section, you'll extract all your functionality for creating new posts into a Grails service that you can call from anywhere you like. This approach makes things tidier and more maintainable.

7.1.1 Implementing a PostService

Services offer a simple, maintainable, and testable way of encapsulating reusable business logic. Services can participate in transactions, be injected almost anywhere in your application, and are easy to develop. It's time to abstract your `Post` operations into a `PostService` that you can access from anywhere in your application. You first saw services in chapter 1, where you wrote a simple `QuoteService` class to abstract the lookup process for quote generation.

Let's create a `PostService` for Hubbub. It won't surprise you that the process starts on the command line:

```
grails create-service com.grailsinaction.Post
```

This command creates a starter PostService.groovy file in /grails-app/services/com/grails-inaction.

In the following listing, you'll add logic to your service so you can add posts by supplying the `loginId` and `content` of the post.

Listing 7.1 PostService.groovy defines `PostService` and a related exception class

```
package com.grailsinaction
import grails.transaction.Transactional
```

```
class PostException extends RuntimeException {      ❶ Forces transactions to roll
    String message                                      back if exceptions occur
    Post post
}
                                                     ❷ Places Post-related logic
@Transactional                                          into reusable service
class PostService {
                                                     ❸ Rolls back database
    Post createPost(String loginId, String content) {    changes if errors occur
        def user = User.findByLoginId(loginId)
        if (user) {                                  ❹ Wraps Post-creation
            def post = new Post(content: content)       logic in method
            user.addToPosts(post)
            if (post.validate() && user.save()) {    ❺ Validates Post
                return post                             object during save
            } else {
                throw new PostException(
                    message: "Invalid or empty post", post: post)   ❻ Throws
            }                                                          exception if
        }                                                              validation
        throw new PostException(message: "Invalid User Id")            fails
    }
}
```

First, to handle any errors that you encounter with the save ❶, you define a new exception class, `PostException`. You'll use this exception to store an error message and any `Post` objects that fail validation. Groovy lets you define more than one class in a .groovy file, so you do that here to keep the exception with the service.

> **Services before Grails 2.3**
>
> If you use an older version of Grails than 2.3, your service won't have an annotation on the class, because services are by default transactional (even in Grails 2.3 without the annotation). You can disable the transactional behavior by adding this property to your service class:
>
> ```
> static transactional = false
> ```
>
> We recommend that for Grails 2.2 and older, you include the property in transactional services and simply set its value to true. This makes it clear the service is transactional.

Next, you define your service, which, following Grails conventions, always ends with the word `Service` ❸, and you mark it transactional ❷. The `createPost()` method takes a `loginId` and the post's `content` ❹ and returns a `Post` object or throws a `PostException` if things go bad.

NOTE Because `PostException` extends `RuntimeException` in listing 7.1, Grails will automatically roll back any database transactions that happen inside the `createPost()` method. You'll learn more about how this works in chapter 14.

This is a transactional service, so you can attempt the `validate()` ❺, which fails if validation errors occur, triggering your invalid-post exception ❻. With the exception, you pass back the `Post` object itself, because clients may want to inspect and display the exact validation errors. If the `save()` goes well, you return the persisted `Post` object. The theory looks sound, but let's exercise it in the following listing with a new unit test.

Listing 7.2 Exercising your new `PostService` (`PostServiceSpec`)

```
package com.grailsinaction

import spock.lang.*
import grails.test.mixin.TestFor
import grails.test.mixin.Mock

@TestFor(PostService)
@Mock([User,Post])
class PostServiceSpec extends Specification {

    def "Valid posts get saved and added to the user"() {

        given: "A new user in the db"
        new User(loginId: "chuck_norris",
                ➥ password: "password").save(failOnError: true)

        when: "a new post is created by the service"
        def newPost = service.createPost("chuck_norris", "First Post!")

        then: "the post returned and added to the user"
        newPost.content == "First Post!"
        User.findByLoginId("chuck_norris").posts.size() == 1
    }
}
```

This is all well and good when things go swimmingly, but what happens when your post is invalid and an exception is thrown? Now is a good time to introduce you to Spock's `thrown()` construct. Let's update your `PostServiceSpec` with a test for the exception in the following listing.

Listing 7.3 Testing exceptional outcomes to `PostServiceSpec`

```
def "Invalid posts generate exceptional outcomes"() {

    given: "A new user in the db"
    new User(loginId: "chuck_norris",
            ➥ password: "password").save(failOnError: true)

    when: "an invalid post is attempted"
    def newPost = service.createPost("chuck_norris", null)

    then: "an exception is thrown and no post is saved"
    thrown(PostException)

}
```

When exceptions are thrown that are part of your anticipated business logic, it'd be handy to reason about those exceptions. Spock provides the `thrown()` construct for such scenarios. If the code in listing 7.3 fails to throw a `PostException`, your `createPost()` logic is broken, and Spock will rightly fail the test; if everything is working correctly, your `createPost()` method will throw a `PostException` rightly complaining about the null content, and your Spock test will catch that exception so that the test completes normally.

With your `PostService` in place, you need to wire it up to the `PostController`.

7.1.2 Wiring PostService to PostController

As you saw in chapter 1, Grails injects or wires the service into the controller through a process called dependency injection (DI). You tell Grails that you want this injection to happen by declaring a property in the controller with the same name as the service (but with a lowercase first letter). In the following listing, you'll declare a `postService` property that Grails identifies as a place to inject your `PostService` class. The updated `PostController` code shows that all posting is now done through the injected `PostService`.

Listing 7.4 An updated `PostController` using `PostService`

```
package com.grailsinaction
class PostController {
    static scaffold = true
    static defaultAction = "home"

    def postService

    def home() { ... }

    def timeline(String id) {
        def user = User.findByLoginId(id)
        if (!user) {
            response.sendError(404)
        } else {
            [ user : user ]
        }
    }

    def addPost(String id, String content)  {
        try {
            def newPost = postService.createPost(id, content)
            flash.message = "Added new post: ${newPost.content}"
        } catch (PostException pe) {
            flash.message = pe.message
        }
        redirect(action: 'timeline', id: id)
    }
}
```

❶ Injects PostService instance into the controller

❷ Use arguments to bind form data as discussed in section 7.2.1

❸ Invokes service method

❹ Catches errors for display in UI

Your controller has been updated to inject the `PostService` automatically ❶. With your service in place, all you have to do is invoke the `createPost()` method ❸ and deal with any fallout from invalid posts ❹. One thing that may be new to you in the updated controller is the use of action arguments to bind data from the HTML form ❷. Grails 2.x introduces this new mechanism, which allows you to match the names of HTML form fields to action arguments and automatically binds the data to the appropriate types. You'll learn more about the many faces of Grails data binding in the next section, but the general rule of thumb for now is that if you have only a few HTML fields to bind to, action arguments provide the best (simplest and cleanest) way to get the job done.

The controller can now use the service, but you need to make sure that the right arguments get passed to the controller (your service tests will catch any errors that exist in the service layer itself).

It's time to rewrite your `PostControllerSpec` and learn how to mock out the service layer using Spock mocks. Using this approach allows you to test only the logic within the class itself, which means less code and faster setup. Here's how you can test the controller in isolation:

```
def "Adding a valid new post to the timeline"() {

    given: "a mock post service"
    def mockPostService = Mock(PostService)                    <-- ❶ Spock lets you mock any existing class.
    1 * mockPostService.createPost(_, _) >>
            new Post(content: "Mock Post")                     <-- ❷ Returns a given post object when mock is invoked.
    controller.postService = mockPostService                   <-- Injects the mock into the controller.

    when:  "controller is invoked"
    def result = controller.addPost(                           <-- Invokes controller method with args.
            "joe_cool",
            "Posting up a storm")

    then: "redirected to timeline, flash message tells us all is well"
    flash.message ==~ /Added new post: Mock.*/                 <-- Ensures flash message is correct.
    response.redirectedUrl == '/post/timeline/joe_cool'        <-- Makes sure app redirects correctly.
}
```

This testing sample introduces you to the Spock `Mock()` function ❶. `Mock()` lets you create an object that sits in for the real target object, while letting you test the number of times it's invoked (classic mocking), and even control what values get returned when it's invoked (typically called stubbing rather than mocking).

Once you create the mock, you can tell Spock to return a new `Post` object whenever the `createPost()` method is invoked ❷. That `1 *` prefix tells Spock that this mock object should be called only once from your code under test, so if it gets called 0 times, or more than once, Spock should throw an error. And those funny argument types to `createPost(_, _)`? Those are Spock placeholders. They mean "whenever `createPost()` is called with two arguments of any kind, return a new `Post`." This is a powerful operation because you can simulate a known return value that your mock service will return and make sure that the controller invoked it the right way. It also means you don't need to invest any energy mocking out the data layer (because your service tests will handle all that work).

If you want to test argument invocation to the service, you could enforce the argument matching exactly with something such as

```
1 * mockPostService.createPost("joe_cool", "Posting up a storm")
➥ >> new Post(content: "Posting up a storm")
```

in which Spock could verify the mock was invoked with exactly those arguments. But for now we're keen to show you the more general case first.

Creating the `PostService` involves significant refactoring, but the result is a tidy, reusable service that you can use in later chapters for posting from REST services and message queues, so it's worth the effort. As part of that effort, you'll need to update the unit test for invalid post data if you have it, otherwise you'll see a `NullPointerException` from the test.

Services invite more exploration, such as whether they're injected as singletons or prototypes, how transactions are preserved, and how to test them, so we'll come back to them in chapter 14. We gave you a taste of services here because controllers are the most common place to use them, and we're planning to take advantage of them later in the chapter.

Logging: a special case of injection

One special case of injection is the Grails logger. We haven't used it yet, but every controller, service, and domain class is automatically injected with a Log4j `log` object (which happens during compilation rather than through classic Spring injection, but the result is the same).

You can use a `log` object wherever it makes sense:

```
log.debug "The value of user is: ${user}"
```

The `log` object can be particularly useful in exception scenarios. If you pass the exception as the second parameter to the `log` method, you get a full stack trace in your logs:

```
try {
    user.punchChuckNorris()
} catch (e) {
    log.error "Failed to punch Chuck Norris", e
}
```

Logging configuration is controlled by entries in your /grails-app/conf/Config.groovy file. You can even use the Runtime Logging plugin to change log levels while your application is running. Grails will also happily mock out your logging calls when running in a unit test, so you don't need to use any of the old `mockLogging()` calls that were required in Grails 1.x.

With your posting functionality now tidily abstracted in its own service, it's time to explore other aspects of your controller that you can implement in more satisfying and maintainable ways.

The next vital area of controller operation that you need to be familiar with is data binding—how form data is parsed and validated and ends up in the database. You've used simple techniques so far, but it's time to introduce you to more powerful features.

7.2 Data binding

Now that you understand how services work, it's time to revisit the way you get form parameters into domain objects. Until now you've manipulated data in the `params` map, bound incoming parameters with a `new Post(params)` style constructor, and in the last section you used action arguments to bind a subset of the incoming parameters. In this section we'll deep dive on all the options you have for getting data out of your forms and into your objects (or another state that makes sense for your application).

The process of marshaling incoming HTML data into objects or other strongly typed parameters is known as data binding. We've given you a few tools for data binding, but it's time you know all the ins and outs, and by the end of this section you'll know which mechanisms are the best for any given scenario.

7.2.1 Action argument binding

The simplest version of data binding, which is new in Grails 2.x, is action argument data binding. This method of binding, which you've seen in listing 7.4, involves naming action arguments to match the names of the fields in your HTML forms. This binding method is perfect when you have one or two incoming parameters that you want to work with (such as an `id` to delete or a registration code to look up). Remember the latest implementation of the `addPost` action:

```
def addPost(String id, String content) {
    try {
        def newPost = postService.createPost(id, content)
        flash.message = "Added new post: ${newPost.content}"
    } catch (PostException pe) {
        flash.message = pe.message
    }
    redirect(action: 'timeline', id: id)
}
```

In this sample you bound the HTML elements `id` and `content` into string variables that you passed on to the service. But what if you had constraints that forced you to use different HTML field names (for example, if you have corporate standards around form field naming)? Grails provides an annotation (`grails.web.RequestParameter`) that lets you map your form field names onto your variable names. It's verbose, but it gets the job done:

```
import grails.web.RequestParameter

def addPost(@RequestParameter('frm_id') String id,
            @RequestParameter('frm_content') String content) {
    // your logic here…
}
```

In this example you map the incoming form field `frm_id` onto your `id` variable, and the incoming `frm_content` field onto your content variable.

What happens if errors occur in the binding? Say the user provides a string that you want to marshal into an integer? The answer is the controller's `errors` property. You can inspect the errors property to find the fine-grained details on where any particular bindings failed.

7.2.2 Binding to an existing object

Most of our data-binding explorations have focused on creating new domain objects from an incoming `params` object. But the update scenario is another common case—perhaps you're letting the user change their profile with an updated email address.

Imagine you have an `update` action, such as the one in the following listing, that updates the properties of an existing `User` based on the `params` data.

Listing 7.5 Data binding with properties can be perilous

```
def update() {
    def user = session.user?.attach()
    if (user) {
        user.properties = params
        if (user.save()) {
            flash.message = "Successfully updated user"
        } else {
            flash.message = "Failed to update user"
        }
        [ user : user ]
    } else {
        response.sendError(404)
    }
}
```

❶ Attaches existing user from session scope

❷ Updates fields based on matching params

❸ Validates user is still current

In this example, you reattached a `User` object that you stored in session scope during login ❶ to the current thread's Hibernate session. You then bound the `params` object to the user's `properties` ❷, so any parameter that matches the name of a user property will be updated on the `User` object. Finally, you validated the object by calling `save()` to make sure all your constraints still hold ❸.

You now have a strategy for updating existing domain classes, but you haven't looked at how to exclude or include specific parameters in the binding. For that, we need to introduce `bindData()`.

7.2.3 Working with blacklist and whitelist bind params

The `bindData()` method available in controllers lets you blacklist certain parameters from the marshaling process.

The two-argument version of `bindData()` is equivalent to a standard property assignment:

```
bindData(user, params)
```

This has the same result as the more familiar assignment style of data binding that you've already seen:

```
user.properties = params
```

But `bindData()`'s blacklisting power is introduced when using the three-argument version of the command, which takes a list of properties to exclude from the binding process. If you want to exclude your `loginId` and `password` parameters from the update, you could do something like this:

```
bindData(user, params, ['loginId', 'password'])
```

That solves half the problem—the blacklisting of certain properties. What if you want to specify certain parameters to be included in the bind? Since Grails 1.1, the `properties` object supports a subscript operator that you can use in whitelist binding scenarios.

For example, if you let the user update only their `email` and `fullName` values, you can do this:

```
user.profile.properties['email', 'fullName'] = params
```

This will update only the `email` and `fullName` properties on the user's `Profile` object, discarding all other parameters that match `User` property names.

Using bindData() outside controllers

`bindData()` offers powerful services for data binding; however, this method only works inside a controller because the feature is bound via the controller's `metaClass`. If you're looking for a `bindData()` style binding for use in Grails services or other artifacts, you can inject the `grailsWebDataBinder`[1] bean and use its `bind()` method. The Grails user guide has a simple example using it.

If you use a Grails version prior to 2.3, do a web search for workarounds using Grail's `BindDynamicMethod` object.

Now that you've explored data binding for single domain classes, let's explore how you can perform data binding on entire graphs of objects.

7.2.4 Complex forms: binding multiple objects

All of your examples so far have concentrated on binding a single domain class, but Grails also gives you the option to handle form submissions for nested objects. Consider user registration, for example. You need a `User` object (to handle the `loginId` and `password`), and a `Profile` object (to handle the `fullName`, `bio`, `homepage`, `email`, and other attributes).

[1] Jeff Brown, [Java] Interface DataBinder, http://grails.org/doc/latest/api/org/grails/databinding/DataBinder.html.

In the following listing, you'll implement a form that references fields on a `User` object and its `Profile` in a null-safe way. Submitting a form like this will allow you to create both the `User` and attached `Profile` in a single save. The code should go in the grails-app/views/user/register.gsp file.

Listing 7.6 A form that updates multiple domain objects in a single submit

```
<html>
<head>
    <title>Register New User</title>
    <meta name="layout" content="main"/>
</head>
<body>
    <h1>Register New User</h1>
    <g:hasErrors>
        <div class="errors">
            <g:renderErrors bean="${user}" as="list" />
        </div>
    </g:hasErrors>
    <g:if test="${flash.message}">
        <div class="flash">${flash.message}</div>
    </g:if>
    <g:form action="register">
        <fieldset class="form">
            <div class="fieldcontain required">
                <label for="loginId">Login ID</label>
                <g:textField name="loginId" value="${user?.loginId}"/>
            </div>
            <div class="fieldcontain required">
                <label for="password">Password</label>
                <g:passwordField name="password"/>
            </div>
            <div class="fieldcontain required">
                <label for="profile.fullName">Full Name</label>
                <g:textField name="profile.fullName"
                    value="${user?.profile?.fullName}"/>
            </div>
            <div class="fieldcontain required">
                <label for="profile.bio">Bio</label>
                <g:textArea name="profile.bio"
                    value="${user?.profile?.bio}"/>
            </div>
            <div class="fieldcontain required">
                <label for="profile.email">Email</label>
                <g:textField name="profile.email"
                    value="${user?.profile?.email}"/>
            </div>
        </fieldset>
        <fieldset class="buttons">
            <g:submitButton name="register" value="Register"/>
        </fieldset>
    </g:form>
</body>
</html>
```

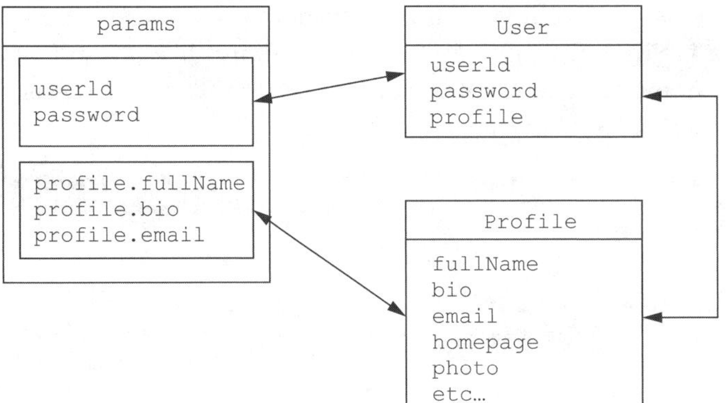

Figure 7.1 Parameters are split into bound objects based on their prefix.

The registration form in the listing contains a number of fields from both the `User` and `Profile` objects. Notice that the profile-related fields are kept in form controls with the prefix `profile`: `profile.fullName`, `profile.bio`, `profile.email`. Grails makes use of this prefix when the form is submitted to bind the field to a relation on the saved object. Figure 7.1 demonstrates how the single set of parameters is split off into the `User` object and its nested `Profile` object.

The next listing shows the new `register` action, which goes in the `UserController` class. Creating and saving a `User` object based on the incoming `params` object binds all those `Profile` fields as well.

Listing 7.7 Implementing a `register` action for the `UserController`

```
def register() {
    if (request.method == "POST") {
        def user = new User(params)
        if (user.validate()) {
            user.save()
            flash.message = "Successfully Created User"
            redirect(uri: '/')
        } else {
            flash.message = "Error Registering User"
            return [ user: user ]
        }
    }
}
```

Form submitted as POST, so create new user

GET request, so display user registration page

If `user.validate()` fails, you can return to the registration form, passing the failing `User` object.

You have one more thing to do for the action to work properly: make `Profile` belong to `User`. In other words, change this line in `Profile`:

```
User user
```

to this:

```
static belongsTo = [ user : User ]
```

The reason for this is that validation only cascades to `belongsTo` associations. Even though the `hasOne` on `User` ensures that saves are cascaded, it doesn't work for validation.

If you have an object with validation errors, you can use the `<g:hasErrors>` and `<g:renderErrors>` tags to display them. Recall the `errors div` in your registration form (listing 7.6):

```
<g:hasErrors>
    <div class="errors">
         <g:renderErrors bean="${user}" as="list" />
    </div>
</g:hasErrors>
```

The `<g:renderErrors>` tag renders validation messages for the named bean as an HTML unordered list (`<ul>`), which is convenient for informing the user about what's wrong. This is the same mechanism scaffolding uses to display validation errors, which you saw in chapter 4. Figure 7.2 shows your new registration form in action, rendering appropriate error messages.

TESTING MULTIPLE BINDING

Listing 7.7 gave us a sample of how multiple binding works in theory, but it would be nice to test the operation. You can test it with the standard use of the `params` object, as shown in the following listing.

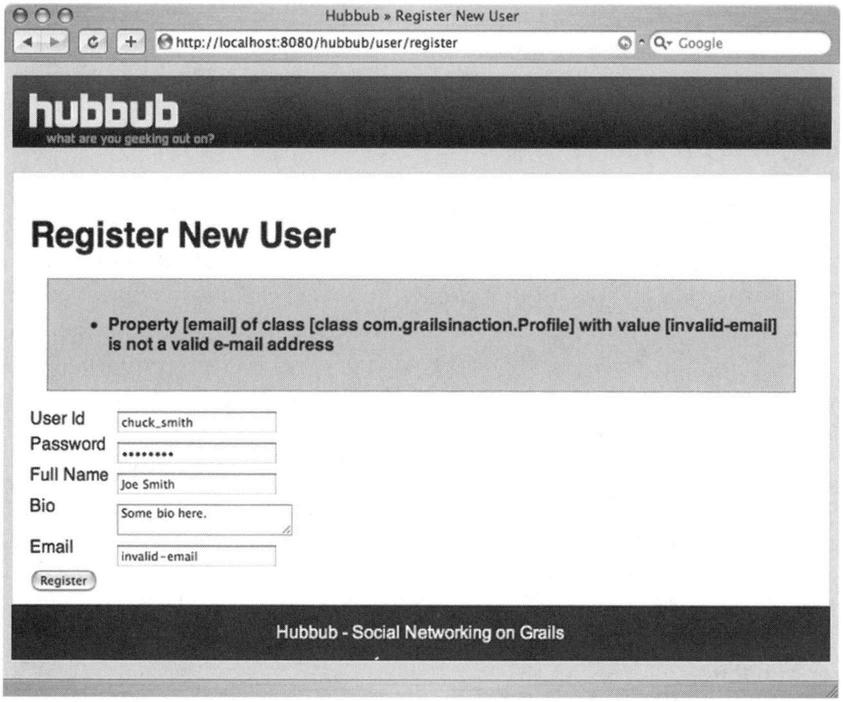

Figure 7.2 You can bind multiple domain objects on a single form and include error handling.

Listing 7.8 Unit testing the `register` action for the `UserController`

```
package com.grailsinaction

import spock.lang.Specification

@TestFor(UserController)
@Mock([User, Profile])
class UserControllerSpec extends Specification {

    def "Registering a user with known good parameters"() {

        given: "a set of user parameters"
        params.with {                                    // 1 Using with() to shorthand param creation
            loginId = "glen_a_smith"
            password = "winnning"
            homepage = "http://blogs.bytecode.com.au/glen"
        }

        and: "a set of profile parameters"               // 2 Setting nested properties on params
        params['profile.fullName'] = "Glen Smith"
        params['profile.email'] = "glen@bytecode.com.au"
        params['profile.homepage'] = "http://blogs.bytecode.com.au/glen"

        when: "the user is registered"
        request.method = "POST"                          // 3 Invoking your action as a POST request
        controller.register()

        then: "the user is created, and browser redirected"
        response.redirectedUrl == '/'
        User.count() == 1                                // 4 Confirm objects in the DB
        Profile.count() == 1

    }
}
```

In this sample, you used the Groovy `with()` method ❶ as a shorthand way of setting up your form parameters for the user object. But what about your nested `Profile` object? For setting up your nested profile, you used the `params` object in a map style, effectively setting up form variables for `user.profile.fullName`, `user.profile.email`, and `user.profile.homepage` ❷. With your params set up appropriately, you could invoke your `register` action as a method ❸, then confirm that your `User` and `Profile` objects were created in the database ❹.

You've now implemented a basic registration process and even thrown in error handling and unit testing to keep it tidy. But you may wonder how error handling works behind the scenes. It's important to understand how errors work, in case your application needs custom layout and rendering of error messages for particular fields. Let's take a look.

7.2.5 Error handling

In the previous section, you passed a `User` object that failed validation through to the view. The view then used the `<g:hasErrors>` and `<g:renderErrors>` tags to display the error messages (as in figure 7.2). You may be curious how those tags know what the failing validations are.

In chapter 3 (section 3.3), you saw that calling `user.validate()` populates a `user.errors` object with failing validations. The `hasErrors()` and `renderErrors()` methods use this object to iterate through the errors.

But what if you want to highlight the individual field values that are failing validation, rather than list them all at the top of the page? You can take advantage of a special version of the `hasErrors` tag that specifies a domain object in request scope as well as the field you're rendering. The following listing shows an example of rendering the email validation errors next to the `email` field.

Listing 7.9 Implementing field-level errors is hard work at the moment

```
<dt>Email</dt>
<dd>
    <g:textField name="profile.email" value="${user?.profile?.email}"/>
    <g:hasErrors bean="${user}" field="profile.email">
        <g:eachError bean="${user}" field="profile.email">
            <p style="color: red;"><g:message error="${it}"/></p>
        </g:eachError>
    </g:hasErrors>
</dd>
```

❶ Displays block when field is invalid

❷ Iterates through errors on email field

❸ Displays error text

You used the `<g:hasErrors>` tag to find any validation errors for the `email` field on the user's `Profile` object ❶. If any errors did exist, you used the `<g:eachError>` tag to iterate through them ❷. Remember that a given field may fail more than one validation. Finally, you resolved the error message from your resource bundle using the `<g:message>` tag ❸.

After seeing that example, you probably feel that `<g:renderErrors>` is pretty nice after all. But after seeing all that markup you must be thinking, "That's an awful lot of boilerplate code for displaying error messages against a single field! There must be a better way!" We hear you! And Grails has an elegant answer to make that markup go away by using the Fields plugin (http://grails.org/plugin/fields). For now, it's good to appreciate how errors are handled from first principles. Figure 7.3 shows you the kind of markup generated by the techniques in listing 7.9. As you can see, you can colocate the errors, but it's work, and a red asterisk next to the failing field is probably as effective.

Now that you understand the power of Grails's data binding, and you've learned how errors work, it's time to introduce you to one last technique for data binding that makes the whole operation more maintainable: Grails' *command objects*.

Figure 7.3 Field-level markup of errors is difficult but achievable.

7.3 Command objects

All this data binding and manipulation is wonderful, but what happens when there isn't a one-to-one mapping between the form data and a domain object? For example, a registration screen may have both `password` and `confirmPassword` fields that need to match to ensure the user hasn't made a mistake entering the password.

For these sorts of scenarios, Grails offers the command object. The command object's purpose is to marshal data from form parameters into a nondomain class that offers its own validation.

7.3.1 Handling custom user registration forms

User registration involves subtle validations that make sense only during the registration process (like the example of matching passwords). Let's cook up a `UserRegistrationCommand` object to see how you might capture both sets of data in a single command object.

Typically, command objects are single-use objects, so by convention they're created inside the same .groovy file as the controller that uses them. If you create them outside the controller that uses them, we recommend you mark the classes with a `@grails.validation.Validateable` annotation. This also allows you to use them as general validatable objects, not just as command objects.

For our example, let's enhance the `UserController` class to use this new command class, as shown in the following listing. Put this class definition in UserController.groovy after the controller class (not inside it).

Listing 7.10 A `UserRegistrationCommand` class

```
...
class UserController {
    ...
}

class UserRegistrationCommand {
    String loginId
    String password
    String passwordRepeat
    byte[] photo
    String fullName
    String bio
    String homepage
    String email
    String timezone
    String country
    String jabberAddress

    static constraints = {
        importFrom Profile
        importFrom User
        password(size: 6..8, blank: false,
                 validator: { passwd, urc ->
                    return passwd != urc.loginId
                })
```

Introduces field for password confirmation (annotates `passwordRepeat`)

Reuses the same business constraints as our domain class (annotates `importFrom Profile` / `importFrom User`)

```
        passwordRepeat(nullable: false,                    Checks confirmation field
                validator: { passwd2, urc ->               matches first password
                    return passwd2 == urc.password
                })
    }
}
```

Look at all the validation going on there! You incorporated all the validation from both the `User` and `Profile` objects in a DRY manner using `importFrom`. You also added a custom field and validation that are specific to the registration process (specifically, that `password` and `passwordRepeat` must match).

Command objects are particularly useful in scenarios where you have different or augmented validation rules firing for the form submission that aren't in your domain model. A password-confirmation field is a classic example.

With our command object in place, it's time to wire up a test case to exercise your validations (particularly your tricky cross-field validation portions). Let's use Spock's `@Unroll` annotation to create a data-driven test to exercise the corner-cases. We'll add this test to your existing `UserControllerSpec` because it relates to your command class that lives inside UserController.groovy. Also be sure to import the `@Unroll` annotation.

Listing 7.11 Unit testing `UserRegistrationCommand` class with `@Unroll`

```
@Unroll
def "Registration command object for #loginId validate correctly"() {

    given: "a mocked command object"
    def urc = mockCommandObject(UserRegistrationCommand)        (1) Grails special support for command objects

    and: "a set of initial values from the spock test"
    urc.loginId = loginId
    urc.password = password
    urc.passwordRepeat = passwordRepeat
    urc.fullName = "Your Name Here"
    urc.email = "someone@nowhere.net"

    when: "the validator is invoked"
    def isValidRegistration = urc.validate()

    then: "the appropriate fields are flagged as errors"
    isValidRegistration == anticipatedValid
    urc.errors.getFieldError(fieldInError)?.code == errorCode   (2) Standard Grails error fields still apply

    where:
    loginId  | password         | passwordRepeat | anticipatedValid
    ➥        | fieldInError     | errorCode
    "glen"   | "password"       | "no-match"     | false
    ➥        | "passwordRepeat" | "validator.invalid"
    "peter"  | "password"       | "password"     | true
    ➥        | null             | null
    "a"      | "password"       | "password"     | false
    ➥        | "loginId"        | "size.toosmall"
}
```

Most of this code will be familiar to you, the only variant invoked is `mockCommandObject()` ❶ when you created the command. This invocation will tell Grails to decorate your `UserRegistrationCommand` class with the standard `validate()` method and `errors` property that are added to command classes when they're invoked in the Grails runtime environment.

All of the standard error codes ❷ that you learned about in chapter 3 still apply when using command objects, so you don't have new tricks to learn when inspecting error conditions after validation fails.

The neatest part of the command object process is writing a controller action to consume the form submission. Reference the command as the first argument to the action closure, and the binding occurs automatically. The following listing shows your custom action `register2` for handling your command object.

Listing 7.12 A register action that uses command objects

```
def register2(UserRegistrationCommand urc) {
    if (urc.hasErrors()) {
        render view: "register", model: [ user : urc ]
    } else {
        def user = new User(urc.properties)
        user.profile = new Profile(urc.properties)
        if (user.validate() && user.save()) {
            flash.message =
                  "Welcome aboard, ${urc.fullName ?: urc.loginId}"
            redirect(uri: '/')
        } else {
            // maybe not unique loginId?
            return [ user : urc ]
        }
    }
}
```

❶ Binds data from params to command object

❷ Uses hasErrors to check validations

❸ Binds data to new user object

❹ Saves and validates new user

In this code, the command object is passed in as the first argument to the action's closure ❶, causing Grails to attempt to bind all incoming `params` entries to the command object's fields. Validations are then applied, and you can check the results by calling `hasErrors()` on the command object itself ❷.

If the data looks good, you can bind the command object's fields to the various domain classes. In listing 7.12, you bind to both `User` and `Profile` ❸ and then attempt to save the new user.

You have to confirm that the `save()` is successful ❹, because the constraints only make sense in a domain class and not in a command object. For example, your `User` class has a `unique` constraint on the `loginId`. Although you could attempt to simulate a unique constraint on your command object with a custom validator, even then the user isn't guaranteed to be unique until the real `save()` is committed to the database.

For the moment, you'll use the existing form and `register` action. In the next chapter, we'll show you an extended user registration form that has fields matching the properties of `UserRegistrationCommand`. That form will submit to the `register2` action.

TESTING COMMAND OBJECTS WITH CONTROLLERS

You've been through the process of testing your command objects in isolation (confirming that your constraints and validators work), but now you need to turn your attention to using command objects in conjunction with controllers. The most important thing you need to know here is that you must call `validate()` before you invoke the controller action! This listing is your test case in action.

Listing 7.13 Using controllers to test command objects

```
def "Invoking the new register action via a command object"() {

    given: "A configured command object"
    def urc = mockCommandObject(UserRegistrationCommand)
    urc.with {
        loginId = "glen_a_smith"
        fullName = "Glen Smith"
        email = "glen@bytecode.com.au"
        password = "password"
        passwordRepeat = "password"
    }

    and: "which has been validated"
    urc.validate()

    when: "the register action is invoked"
    controller.register2(urc)

    then: "the user is registered and browser redirected"
    !urc.hasErrors()
    response.redirectedUrl == '/'
    User.count() == 1
    Profile.count() == 1

}
```

You must call validate() manually when testing with controllers.

Pass your command object into your controller.

Apart from the manual calls to `validate()`, this should be a process you're familiar with.

You probably realized that command objects are great for this sort of form, where you don't have a one-to-one mapping with a domain class. But they also offer other features. Command objects can participate in injection, for example.

7.3.2 Participating in injection

Command objects aren't dumb value objects with a little validation. They're subject to the same bean-injection features as controllers, which means they can make fantastic encapsulators of business logic.

In the `UserRegistrationCommand` example, the user enters a clear-text password, but imagine you want to store it encrypted in the database. If you'd defined a `cryptoService`, you could inject it directly into the command object. You could do something like this:

```
class UserRegistrationCommand {
    def cryptoService
```

```
    String getEncryptedPassword() {
        return cryptoService.getEncryptedPassword(password)
    }
// our other properties and validators
}
```

You could then use the `cryptoService` to ensure there's only one class that knows how password encryption is implemented. Adding a convenience routine such as `getEncryptedPassword()` to your command class makes consuming the command class in your controller code tidier.

Now that we've covered data binding and controller logic, all that's left for this chapter is the sweet stuff. We'll move on to handling photo uploads, creating a basic security file, and customizing the site's URLs.

Let's look at how to upload user profile photos.

> **When to use which Grails binding method**
>
> We've introduced several methods of binding data to objects so far. You may wonder which to use where. The basic rule of thumb is that if you're creating a new domain object, use the `Constructor(params)` variant. If you have a few params on which you'd like to perform logic rather than data binding, use action arguments. If you have several related validatable params, use command objects. If you're updating an existing object with a subset of properties, use `bindData()` for white listing (or a straight params assignment if you don't care about white listing).

7.4 Working with images

You've now seen nearly every controller trick that you'll likely use in your next Grails project. But a few outliers exist. You won't need them in every application, but when you need them, you really need them.

In this section, we'll explore how to handle file uploads (your user's profile photo) and how to render custom content types (image data, in your case). Although your next application might not have much use for photos, the techniques are useful for whatever kind of content you want to render.

7.4.1 Handling file uploads

What's a social networking site without the ability to upload photos and avatars? If you've ever added file-upload capabilities to a Java web application, you know the complexities involved (not only the mess involved when handling byte streams, but also handling security issues, such as limiting file sizes to prevent denial-of-service attacks). Grails puts that complexity behind you. Let's implement a photo-upload capability for Hubbub.

You'll start by creating an `ImageController` to handle image uploading and rendering:

```
grails create-controller com.grailsinaction.Image
```

You have two ways to handle file uploads in a controller, and the one you select depends on what you want to accomplish. If you want to store the image in a domain class, your best option is to use a command object. The following listing shows how to use a command object for photo uploads. We look at storing images on the filesystem in the next subsection.

Listing 7.14 Handling image uploading via a command object

```
package com.grailsinaction
class PhotoUploadCommand {
    byte[] photo
    String loginId
}
class ImageController {
    def upload(PhotoUploadCommand puc) {
        def user = User.findByLoginId(puc.loginId)
        user.profile.photo = puc.photo
        redirect controller: "user", action: "profile", id: puc.loginId
    }

    def form() {
        // pass through to upload form
        [ userList : User.list() ]
    }
}
```

Holds uploaded photo data

Passes list of users to the view

The upload process for images using a command object binds the uploaded image data to a byte array.

To select a photo for upload in our browser window, you need a view with an upload control. Let's create /grails-app/views/image/form.gsp to host your upload form. The form also needs to be tagged to tell the browser that the form contains a file upload, so use the `<g:uploadForm>` tag, as shown in the following listing.

Listing 7.15 An image-upload form

```
<html>
<head>
    <title>Upload Image</title>
    <meta name="layout" content="main">
</head>
<body>
    <h1>Upload an image</h1>
    <g:uploadForm action="upload">
        User Id:
        <g:select name="loginId" from="${userList}"
            ➥ optionKey="loginId" optionValue="loginId" />
        <p/>
        Photo: <input name="photo" type="file" />
        <g:submitButton name="upload" value="Upload"/>
    </g:uploadForm>
</body>
</html>
```

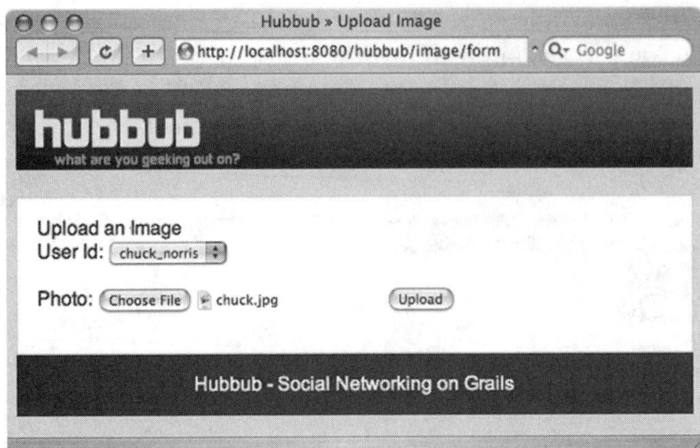

Figure 7.4 The image-upload form in action

Remember, the upload form needs to use `<g:uploadForm>` instead of `<g:form>`, and it needs an input box with `type="file"` to hold the image-upload data.

The browser will render the form in listing 7.15 with an upload box as shown in figure 7.4.

With your command object backing the upload, users are only a click away from getting their profile pictures into the database.

7.4.2 *Uploading to the filesystem*

If you want to store the uploaded image in the filesystem rather than in the database, you need access to the implementation of Spring `MultipartFile` that backs the upload process.

For this case, you have more options for storing the byte array:

```
def rawUpload() {
    // a Spring MultipartFile
    def mpf = request.getFile('photo')
    if (!mpf?.empty && mpf.size < 1024*200) {
        mpf.transferTo(new File(
            "/hubbub/images/${params.loginId}/mugshot.gif"))
    }
}
```

Ensures file size is less than 200 KB

The `MultipartFile` class has a `transferTo()` method for moving the picture data directly to a file, which is convenient if you're averse to storing BLOBs in your database. For a detailed discussion of `MultipartFile`, consult the Spring API documentation.

> **Image formats and transferTo()**
>
> It's important to remember that `transferTo()` doesn't do any magic image conversion—it copies bytes around. In the previous example we assumed the user is uploading a .gif file when we should look inside that `byte[]` to determine the image format. You can use the Burning Image plugin to perform these inspections. Check http://grails.org/plugin/burning-image for details.

7.4.3 Rendering photos from the database

Now that photos can be uploaded to the database or filesystem, you need a way to display them. You'll create `<img>` tags in your application and have Grails retrieve your profile photos and render them.

First, create a new profile view, so the `UserController` can view a profile, and include a link to the user's profile picture. Let's call the view /views/user/profile.gsp and give it an HTML image tag:

```
<html>
...
<body>
    <div class="profilePic">
        <g:if test="${profile.photo}">
            <img src="${createLink(controller: 'image', action:
➥ 'renderImage', id: profile.user.loginId)}"/>
        </g:if>
        <p>Profile for <strong>${profile.fullName}</strong></p>
        <p>Bio: ${profile.bio}</p>
    </div>
</body>
</html>
```

Creates link to renderImage action

This GSP page creates a link back to /image/renderImage/<id> based on the `loginId` of the current user. Once you implement the `renderImage` action in `ImageController`, you can link your image tags to /image/renderImage/chuck_norris or any other user ID.

We leave it as an exercise for you to implement the corresponding `profile` action in `UserController`. Find the user for the given ID and add the user's `Profile` object to the view model under the variable name `profile`. You can find an example implementation in the chapter source on GitHub, along with the full code for the profile view (we've left out the `<head>` section in the code snippet as it's not important for the discussion).

The following listing has the code for `ImageController`'s `renderImage` action, showing you how to send image data to the client.

Listing 7.16 Sending image data to the browser

```
def renderImage(String id) {
    def user = User.findByLoginId(id)
    if (user?.profile?.photo) {
        response.setContentLength(user.profile.photo.size())
        response.outputStream.write(user.profile.photo)
    } else {
        response.sendError(404)
    }
}
```

Sends 404 error if no photo

As the code shows, you can send content to the browser by writing the bytes directly to the response's output stream. When you do this, also tell the browser the size of the data.

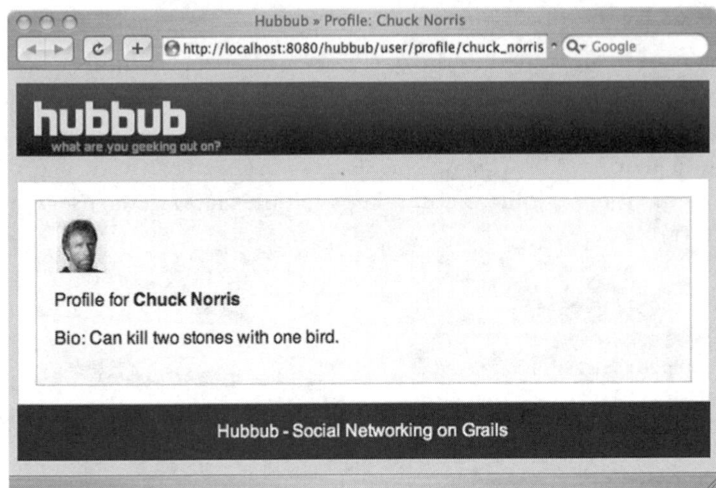

Figure 7.5 Rendering a profile picture

With your back-end rendering implemented, figure 7.5 shows the result for /user/profile/chuck_norris.

You now have a basic profile screen running, which completes your explorations of image rendering and all the UI functionality you'll do in this chapter. You'll learn more UI techniques in chapter 13, but for now you have two more important controller features to learn about: filters and URL mappings. Both affect how a user navigates your application, and it's essential to understand when developing powerful Grails applications.

Let's start with exploring filters.

7.5 *Intercepting requests with filters*

In this chapter, we've looked at the front-end user experience, but important techniques exist that you need to implement at the back end. In this section we'll explore the use of filters for augmenting the Grails request/response pipeline with your own custom processing.

7.5.1 *Writing your first filter*

Grails filters give you a powerful tool for intercepting every request (or a subset of requests) and for performing business logic before or after the controller action fires. If you've worked with Java servlet filters, you might recognize that the Grails filters provide similar functionality, although Grails filters only intercept controller requests, not static file requests for JavaScript, CSS, image files, and the like.

A classic example of where you might want this sort of approach is a security filter—you want to check that a user has access to a target resource (popular Grails security plugins use Grails filters for this purpose). Let's put a simple security filter together as an example.

First, you'll create a shell for your filter:

```
grails create-filters com.grailsinaction.LameSecurity
```

This command will write a starter template in /grails-app/conf/com/grailsinaction/LameSecurityFilters.groovy. (Note the plural Filters; if you name it with the singular form, it won't fire.)

Next you'll modify your filter to perform simple checks, as shown in the following listing.

Listing 7.17 A basic security filter implementation

```
package com.grailsinaction

class LameSecurityFilters {
    def filters = {
        secureActions(controller:'post',                          ❶ Names security rules
                   action:'(addPost|deletePost)') {               ❷ Limits filter to two actions
            before = {
                if (params.impersonateId) {                       ❸ Tests for presence of impersonateId param
                    session.user = User.findByLoginId(params.impersonateId)
                }
                if (!session.user) {                              ❹ Tests for existing user in session
                    redirect(controller: 'login', action: 'form')
                    return false                                  ❺ Stops subsequent filters from firing
                }
            }
            after = { model->
            }
            afterView = {
                log.debug "Finished running ${controllerName} -
➥ ${actionName}"                                                 ❻ Logs diagnostic data after view completes
            }
        }
    }
}
```

You can name the filters that you put into the file (for documentation purposes only), so it's good to choose names that summarize your filter logic. You called your set of rules `secureActions` ❶.

You can put as many filters as you like in the file, and all matching rules will fire in order from the top until one returns `false` from its `before` closure. As you'll learn soon, you can apply filters to wildcards (`controller: '*', action: '*'`), but in the previous listing, you want the filter to fire only for the `addPost` or `deletePost` actions ❷. Using Boolean operators lets you fine-tune the application of the filter.

We'll leave it as an exercise for you to implement `LoginController` and its form action. The HTML form needs fields for login ID and password. It should be submitted to a separate action, say `signIn`. That action should then check the password against the one stored in the database for the given user and, if they match, store the corresponding `User` instance in the session under the key "user". Otherwise `signIn` should redirect back to the login form. You can find a sample implementation in the chapter source code.

Inside the body of the filter, you can provide closures for `before`, `after`, or `afterView`. Table 7.1 outlines the filter lifecycle phases and their typical features.

Table 7.1 Lifecycle phases and their usage

Closure	Fires when?	Useful for
`before`	Before any controller logic is invoked	Security, referrer headers
`after`	After controller logic, but before the view is rendered	Altering a model before presentation to view
`afterView`	After the view has finished rendering	Performance metrics

Our `before` closure checks that the user provided an `impersonateId` parameter ❸ and, if so, and the corresponding user exists, it stores the `User` object in the session to signify a login. Otherwise it redirects to the login screen ❹.

If any `before` closure returns `false`, as happens at ❺, no other filters will fire and the controller action won't be invoked. This is typically done when you have a filter (such as a security filter) that has redirected the request.

You also added an `afterView` closure ❻ to demonstrate diagnostic options, and to show the variables that Grails provides in filters. Although filters don't have all the functionality of controllers, they expose the common controller variables that we covered earlier in the chapter (`request`, `response`, `params`, `session`, `flash`, and a few filter-specific extras). They also have two methods: `redirect()` and `render()`. Table 7.2 shows additional filter variables that you haven't used.

Although you didn't use it in listing 7.17, there's also a special case for the `after` closure that takes a model as an argument. That's the model map the controller returns from the action that handled the request. You can augment that model in your filter, and modify it if necessary.

Table 7.2 Variables exposed to filters

Variable	Description
`controllerName`	Name of the currently firing controller.
`actionName`	Name of the currently firing action.
`applicationContext`	The Spring application context—useful for looking up Spring beans, but filters support dependency injection, which is much cleaner.
`grailsApplication`	The current `grailsApplication` object—useful for finding out runtime information, such as the Grails version or application name.

TIP Modifying existing model values in your filters is a bad idea—it makes your code difficult to follow and inevitably introduces subtle bugs in your controller logic. Augment them, by all means, but leave your existing model values alone, lest you get support calls in the wee hours and have to debug things.

Handling injection in filters

What if you need a service inside your filter? Filters have the same injection rules as other Grails artifacts, so you can declare the service (or other artifact) as a property in your filter and it'll be injected for you. Here's an example:

```
class SecurityFilters {
    def authService
    def filters = {
        // then somewhere inside one of your filters
        authService.checkAccess(params.loginId,
                                    controllerName, actionName)
    }
}
```

7.5.2 Testing filters

You've written your first filter; it's time to exercise it with testing code. Because filters fire in the process of executing a controller action, Grails unit-testing support for filters is all handled through controller unit tests, albeit with a little bit of hackery, as shown in the following listing.

Listing 7.18 Testing your filter

```
...
@TestFor(PostController)
@Mock([User,Post,LameSecurityFilters])          <-- Adds the filter to the list of mocks
class PostControllerSpec extends Specification {

    /* other tests here */

    def "Exercising security filter for unauthenticated user"() {

        when:
        withFilters(action: "addPost") {                         <-- (1) Invokes action via withFilters
            controller.addPost("glen_a_smith", "A first post")
        }

        then:
        response.redirectedUrl == '/login/form'

    }
}
```

In this sample, you're expanding your `PostControllerSpec` to exercise the `addPost` (1) action when invoked through the security filter. The filter will catch that the user hasn't yet authenticated, and you can assert that they're redirected to your login form.

Roll your own security: don't try this at home

We're using the `LameSecurityFilters` example to introduce you to filter lifecycles (because it's a common example that you've probably implemented before). But we need to stress that you shouldn't roll your own security! Grails has several excellent security plugins, including Spring Security and Apache Shiro. We'll take you through Spring Security in depth in chapter 11.

7.5.3 Filter URL options

You've seen filters applied to controllers and actions, but you have more options for both fine- and course-grained filtering. First, both controller and action names are subject to wildcarding (and you can wildcard either or both). You can also use Boolean operators to be selective about what you capture.

Let's look at a few common filtering use cases. This example filters for all actions on all controllers:

```
myGreedyFilter(controller:'*', action:'*') {
}
```

This one filters for all actions on the User controller:

```
myControllerFilter(controller:'user', action:'*') {
}
```

And the following one filters for only a few actions on the User controller:

```
mySelectiveFilter(controller:'user', action:'(update|edit|delete)') {
}
```

But if thinking in terms of controllers and actions isn't your bag (perhaps because you've done URL mapping magic for permalinking), you can also use a URI style of mapping in your filters:

```
myGreedyUriFilter(uri:'/**') {
}
mySelectiveUriFilter(uri:'/post/**') {
}
myParticularUriFilter(uri:'/post/supersecret/list') {
}
```

The URI-matching mechanism uses Ant-style wildcarding. If you've never seen those double asterisks before, they mean "all subdirectories nested to unlimited levels." One thing to note is that URL mappings fire before filters, so if you were depending on a filter to catch a nonexistent URL, think again. It'll return a 404 error and not get to your filter.

That's your arsenal of tools for selective filtering. You've learned the skills to create all sorts of back end intercepting logic for your next application. Whether you implement a custom security mechanism or a stats-tracking filter, or you debug and profile, filters give you power for fine-grained request interception.

There's one final feature of controllers that we need to cover: URL mappings.

7.6 Creating custom URL mappings

You're following Grails convention with URLs translating to /controllerName/actionName/id. But even this convention is configurable through URL mappings.

The /grails-app/conf/UrlMappings.groovy file is shown in the following listing. You can configure rules in this file for routing incoming requests to particular controllers and actions.

Listing 7.19 UrlMappings.groovy holds URL routing information

```
class UrlMappings {
   static mappings = {
      "/$controller/$action?/$id?"{
         constraints {
            // apply constraints here
         }
      }
      "/"(view:"/index")
      "500"(view:'/error')
   }
}
```

The $ variables in the UrlMappings file can be confusing, so let's add a static mapping (permalink) to the file to see how things work:

```
"/timeline/chuck_norris" {
    controller = "post"
    action = "timeline"
    id = "chuck_norris"
}
```

With the permalink in place, you can now access the URL /hubbub/timeline/chuck_norris, and it'll route you to the `PostController` and fire the `timeline` action with an `id` parameter of `chuck_norris`. Note that this isn't a redirect: the browser's URL will stay the same, but the controller and action specified in the permalink will fire.

You can also use a more concise version of the syntax:

```
"/timeline/chuck_norris"(controller:"post",
                action:"timeline", id:"chuck_norris")
```

We find the block-based version more readable, and it also gives you more flexibility (as we'll see shortly).

Now that you've seen mapping blocks, it's time to get back to those variables you saw earlier.

7.6.1 myHubbub: rolling your own permalinks

You can define how custom variables in URL mappings are passed through as parameters to the controller. For example, it'd be great to have a permalink on the Hubbub site to give users a page for their recent posts. Maybe a URL such as /hubbub/users/glen could map to all of Glen's posts, and /hubbub/users/peter could send you off to Peter's.

One way to achieve this style of permalink is to create a URL mapping such as this:

```
"/users/$id" {
    controller = "post"
    action = "timeline"
}
```

This will still call the `timeline` action of the `PostController`, but with a `params.id` value of "glen", "peter", or whatever forms the last part of the URL.

In addition to this URL mapping, you should add one for My Timeline that displays the timeline for the currently logged in user:

```
"/timeline" {
    controller = "post"
    action = "personal"
}
```

All you then need to do is add a `personal` action in `PostController` that displays the current user's timeline or redirects to the login page if no user is logged in. See the chapter source on GitHub if you're not sure how to implement this.

Your new `UrlMappings` code will form a core part of your application's operation, so you need to think about testing again. You could fire up your web browser and test all the combinations, but by now you know that we're way too lazy to invest time in any boring operation that we can automate. Let's work smarter by writing testing code to exercise your new mapping goodness.

> **NOTE** You'll need to update `PostControllerSpec` as well, because the custom URL mapping affects the redirect URLs. Where the tests check for /post/timeline/<id>, check for /users/<id> instead.

First, you'll create a `UrlMappingsSpec` in the root directory of our testing tree (create the /test/unit/UrlMappingsSpec.groovy file manually). Then you can get busy exercising your new mappings, as shown in the following listing.

Listing 7.20 UrlMappingsSpec.groovy tests UrlMappings are working

```
import com.grailsinaction.*
import spock.lang.*

@TestFor(UrlMappings)
@Mock(PostController)
class UrlMappingsSpec extends Specification {

    def "Ensure basic mapping operations for user permalink"() {

        expect:
        assertForwardUrlMapping(url, controller: expectCtrl, action:
      expectAction) {
            id = expectId
        }

        where:
        url                         | expectCtrl| expectAction    | expectId
        '/users/glen'               | 'post'    | 'timeline'      | 'glen'
        '/timeline/chuck_norris'| 'post'    | 'timeline'      | 'chuck_norris'
    }
}
```

The class in this code checks your forward URL mappings when you move from a URL through to a given controller and action. You've also passed in a closure where you're testing that the parameters parsed out of the URL are working correctly. You can also exercise the reverse URL mappings (moving from controller and action back to a

URL). The reverse mapping can be handy when working with `<g:link>` taglib calls to make sure you end up with the right-looking URLs.

7.6.2 Optional variables and constraints

When you define custom variables in your mapping string, you can provide constraints to make sure the value matches a particular string or list.

Suppose you want to provide permalinks for a user's RSS or Atom feeds. You can implement a feed permalink with an entry like this:

```
"/users/$loginId/feed/$format?" {
    controller = "post"
    action = "feed"
    constraints {
        format(inList: ['rss', 'atom'])
    }
}
```

Notice two important things here. You've made the format portion of the URL optional (by suffixing it with `?`), so the user can omit it. If they do supply it, you've added a `constraints` section to ensure that they can only specify "rss" or "atom" as the format. This means /hubbub/users/glen/feed/atom is fine, as is /hubbub/users/glen/feed, but /hubbub/users/glen/feed/sneaky will return a 404 page-not-found error. You can use these constraints to define permalinks with fine-grained URLs.

The rules in your UrlMapping file are applied in the order in which they appear, so you can start with more specific rules and fall back to more general ones.

7.6.3 Handling response codes and exceptions

While we're on the topic of 404 pages, UrlMappings also gives you great flexibility in mapping response codes to custom pages. If you look in the default mapping file, you'll notice this entry:

```
"500"(view:'/error')
```

This maps the "Error 500: Internal Server Error" code to /views/error.gsp. You can use this mechanism to map any of the HTTP response codes to one of your pages. For example, you could map the standard 500 error to a page inspired by the classic "tweet of death" Twitter 500 page:

```
"500"(view:'/failWhale')
```

If you want your errors handled by a controller action instead of directly by a GSP, that's supported, too. This might be convenient for keeping stats on which URLs keep 404ing on your site. Here's how you could configure the 404 error code to be handled by a dedicated errors controller:

```
"404"(controller: "errors", action: "notFound")
```

You're not limited to catching response codes; you can also intercept exception conditions directly and pass them through to an appropriate handler. For example:

```
"500"(controller: "errors", action: "internalError",
      exception: NullPointerException)
```

You can get a handle to the exception itself in the target controller by accessing the `request.exception` property.

```
class ErrorController {
    def internalError() {
        log.error "Internal system error", request.exception
        // perhaps some stats action
    }
}
```

7.6.4 *Mapping directly to the view*

You'll have situations where you want to map a URL directly to a view and bypass any controller logic. The classic example is your application's home page, which you may implement like this:

```
"/"(view:"/homepage/index")
```

Notice that you don't include the .gsp extension when you construct the mapping.

7.6.5 *Wildcard support*

URL mappings can also support greedy wildcards using Ant-style wildcards. This is particularly useful when you impersonate filenames in your back end.

If you generate PDFs dynamically, but want to provide permalinks on your site, you may do something like this:

```
"/documents/$docname**.pdf"(controller:"pdf", action:"render")
```

The wildcard option lets you match /documents/release-notes/myproject.pdf as well as /document/manuals/myproject.pdf. In both cases, you'll get a `docname` parameter that you can use in the controller action. The `docname` will contain the relative path that `$docname` matches (for example, release-notes/myproject and manuals/myproject). This capability is convenient for developing content management systems (CMS) where you generate the PDF based on dynamic data in a domain object.

And that's the end of your exploration of UrlMappings. We've finished all you need to know about controllers. It's time to review what you've taken in.

7.6.6 *Named URL mappings*

You've nearly completed your tour of Grails URL mapping features, but there's one more feature to discuss: Named UrlMappings. Grails gives you a handy way of naming your URL mappings so they're easier to reference in your views. We'll talk more about view-tier concerns in the next chapter, but for now, we wanted to introduce you to the idea of naming mapping. Let's show you how to name a mapping:

```
name chuck: "/timeline/chuck_norris" {
            controller = "post"
            action = "timeline"
            id = "chuck_norris"
        }
```

Once you've named the UrlMapping as `chuck`, you can reference it later in your view pages when you want to create links to that controller. For example:

```
<g:link mapping="chuck">A Link to Chuck's Page</g:link>
```

You'll explore more link options in the next chapter, including how you can pass parameters to your link tags, but for now we want you to note that naming UrlMappings can be a handy way to reduce clutter in your view pages.

And that concludes your tour of URL mappings. When we explore RESTful architectures further in chapter 12, we'll discuss several other UrlMapping capabilities that pertain exclusively to RESTful operations. In particular, we'll talk about the ability to route GET/POST/UPDATE/DELETE HTTP methods to different Grails controller methods. But for now, let's review what you've learned and give you some practical takeaways.

7.7 Summary and best practices

In this chapter, you've explored a mountain of skills and techniques related to services.

You started by implementing a `timeline` and `addPost` feature for Hubbub. You then refactored your posting operations into a `PostService` that you'll reuse later in the book. After tidying up your posting logic, you looked at data-binding techniques, including action arguments, whitelisting, blacklisting, error handling, and command objects.

You then had fun with custom controller content types while implementing your profile page and handling photo uploads. Finally, you learned about back-end logic and using filters and UrlMappings.

Let's look at the key practices from the chapter:

- *Business logic goes in services.* Don't use controllers to do any heavy lifting. They are designed only for controlling application flow and doing data marshaling. All your data access and business logic should happen in transactional services.
- *Use the errors object wisely.* Make use of the errors object on your domain class to display validation messages. Take advantage of resource bundles to make error messages relevant to your application use cases.
- *Raw params is a last resort.* You have many great data-binding tricks in your Grails toolbox. Use them. If you're binding a few fields, use action arguments. If you're binding a bunch of fields, use command objects. Using the `params` object and doing magic is your last resort.
- *Learn to love command objects.* Take advantage of command objects for form submissions. Don't use them only for validation—they can also be handy for encapsulating tricky business logic.

- *Understand data binding nuances.* Data-binding options in Grails are plentiful and subtle. Understand how data binding works for child objects when form parameters are prefixed. Use whitelisting to ensure that data binding doesn't compromise sensitive fields.
- *Be forgiving with URLs.* Use default actions to make URLs more forgiving, and do the same for custom URL mappings. Permalink-style URLs are much easier to remember and not difficult to implement. Using UrlMappings can make your life easier when you get to the View tier.
- *Apply filters.* Employ filters when you need to selectively fire back-end logic based on URLs or controller-actions combos.

You've learned how controllers and services fit together in this chapter, and in the next chapter you'll build on your knowledge by implementing fine-looking views to give Hubbub visual sizzle.

8 Developing tasty forms, views, and layouts

This chapter covers

- Rendering and processing forms
- Writing custom tag libraries
- Creating stunning layouts
- Adding visual effects and animation
- Exploring interactive Ajax tags and remoting

You've spent most of the book building the heart of Hubbub: processing incoming requests; interacting with the data model; calling business logic; and creating posts, users, and timelines. It's been fun, but not visually satisfying. It's time to leave the core functionality behind and work on the UI of your web application.

A great-looking UI has all sorts of subtle impacts on the user. People think that a visually pleasing application is more robust, performs better, and is more productive than a bare-bones application, even though none of that may be true.

In this chapter, you'll focus on the front end. You'll cover the basics of putting forms together, and you'll investigate how to support multiple browsers with reusable layouts. You'll explore Grails's handy new resources infrastructure which manages all your visual assets. You'll also turn your attention to visual effects and implement slick animations and Ajax interactions. By the time you're done, Hubbub will sparkle.

You first need to get a good grasp of Grails's primary view technology, GSP, so your UI adventure begins with a tour of the core GSP form tags.

A brief word on testing the view tier

Because testing UI functionality is tricky (and not that beneficial) from Grails unit tests, you'll take a short hiatus from unit testing for the next few sections. In chapter 9, we'll introduce you to testing Grails views in a real browser using a functional testing tool called Geb. For now, get a feel for what these tags do when running in a real browser.

8.1 Understanding the core form tags

You've used GSPs to handle your HTML output since chapter 1, but we haven't given you a solid introduction to them. GSP is an evolution of view technology from JSP. The things that were difficult in JSP (particularly tag libraries) are simplified and accessible in GSP. When you catch yourself developing custom taglibs while your application is running (and not requiring a restart), you'll fall in love.

In this section, we'll cover all the basic GSP tags you'll use from day to day when designing forms and user interactions. Whether it's flow control, iteration, or complex form management with error handling, you'll find it all here. But it all starts with the "if" tests.

8.1.1 A handful of essential tags

You'll spend most of your time working with Grails views, using a few core GSP tags. It's time to learn a few of the most common tags.

The first ones you need to learn are the logical and iteration tags. Every programmer loves a good `if()` test, so the following listing introduces `<g:if>` to test usernames.

Listing 8.1 The basic `if` tag

```
<g:if test="${user?.name == 'Chuck Norris'}">
   Roundhouse Kicks welcome here.
</g:if>
<g:elseif test="${user?.name == 'Jack Bauer'}">
   Lock up your Presidents.
</g:elseif>
<g:else>
   Take a number. We'll call you when we're ready.
</g:else>
```

The `else` and `elseif` blocks are optional. Use `if`, `if ... else`, or `if ... elseif ... else` in whatever combinations you want.

Another common tag is <g:each>, which iterates through a collection or array. It's often used when accessing a domain class member collection, such as iterating through followers:

```
<g:each var="nextUser" in="${following}">
    <li>${nextUser.loginId}</li>
</g:each>
```

The <g:if> and <g:each> tags are the bread and butter of select and iteration, and you'll use them often. But you'll also need to combine them with basic link tags to keep your user moving through the application. Let's look at how to introduce workflow with the versatile <g:link> tag.

8.1.2 *A pocketful of link tags*

Another common set of tags is the linking tags. These give you convenient ways to generate URLs that link to controller actions.

LINK

Here's an example of the <g:link> tag:

```
<g:link controller="post" action="global" >Back to Hubbub</g:link>
```

You can omit the `action` attribute if you're linking to the default action. Similarly, if you're linking to another action in the current controller, you can omit the `controller` attribute. If the previous action was /post/edit, you could link back to the `timeline` action (/post/timeline) with this link:

```
<g:link action="timeline" >Back to Timeline</g:link>
```

But sometimes you don't want a full anchor tag—you want the target URL.

CREATELINK

Using target URLs can be handy for Ajax, which works in URL terms, but it's also handy for generating <img> tags. For example, when generating thumbnail tags for your followers, you could use something like this:

```
<img src="<g:createLink action="renderImage" controller="image"
    id="${nextUser.loginId}"/>" alt="${nextUser.loginId}"/>
```

This creates a URL such as /image/renderImage/glen. Remember that the last part of the URL forms the `params.id` attribute in your controller. All the linking tags support `action`, `controller`, and `id` attributes, so you have flexibility.

Although <g:link> and <g:createLink> are the most common link tags, there's another one that you'll use less frequently.

RESOURCE

The <g:resource> tag (which in older Grails versions was confusingly called `createLinkTo`) is handy for generating links to files within your application. Its most common use is with CSS and static images. It's also aware of the Resources plugin (which we discuss in chapter 13 when we talk about more advanced UI work), which makes mapping links to resources DRY. Here's a common example:

```
<link rel="stylesheet"
    href="${resource(dir:'css',file:'hubbub.css')}" />
```

That's not a tag; that's a method call!

You can reference all tags using a method-style syntax—with attribute maps as an argument—rather than using the more classic JSP-style invocation. The preceding code line is equivalent to this:

```
<link rel="stylesheet" href="
     <g:resource dir='css' file='hubbub.css'/>
"/>
```

In fact, Grails provides a dedicated tag for this niche case of resource linking.

EXTERNAL

To handle the case of CSS, JavaScript, and favicon links, use the `<g:external>` tag:

```
<g:external dir='css' file='hubbub.css'/>
```

Some people find this method-style invocation easier to read when nesting tags within other tags. In this example, it gets tricky to work out which `/>` belongs to which tag, but a good IDE goes a long way to making this clear.

The link tag names are similar, and this can be confusing. They're summarized in table 8.1.

Table 8.1 Link-related tags

Tag	Description
`link`	Generates an `<a href>` around the enclosed content.
`createLink`	Generates a URL for embedding in another tag.
`resource`	Generates a URL to a local file.
`external`	Used to create <link> tags for CSS, favicons, and JavaScript.

> **TIP** In chapter 7, we explored URL-mapping tricks with entries in UrlMappings.groovy. The good news is that the link tags are aware of your rewrite rules and honor those mappings.

Our next core set of tags involves form handling. Let's explore the flexibility available with the Grails form tags.

8.1.3 *A tour of the form tags*

Forms are the bread and butter of web interactivity. You'll spend time generating forms in GSPs and processing their results in controller actions, so it's important to understand how to use the HTML form-field tags in GSPs. You're free to mix and match regular by-hand HTML form fields with Grails tags, but you'll find that the form tags make things simpler and more maintainable.

In chapter 7, we introduced a user registration form that used a few of the standard Grails form tags. The following listing shows a revised attempt at that form using a greater variety of tags. It also submits the form to the `register2` action, which uses a command object with all the required properties. We've introduced a few fake fields so we can demonstrate what's available.

Listing 8.2 New registration form demonstrating core form tags

```
...
<g:uploadForm action="register2">                         <-- Marks form to support file uploads
    <fieldset class="form">
        <div class="fieldcontain required">
            <label for="loginId">Login ID</label>
            <g:textField name="loginId"/>                  <-- Creates plain text field
        </div>
        <div class="fieldcontain required">
            <label for="password">Password</label>
            <g:passwordField name="password"/>             <-- Creates obscured password field
        </div>
        <div class="fieldcontain required">
            <label for="passwordRepeat">Password (repeat)</label>
            <g:passwordField name="passwordRepeat"/>
        </div>
        ...                                                <-- Other fields from previous form
        <div class="fieldcontain required">
            <label for="country">Country</label>
            <g:countrySelect name="country"
                noSelection="['':'Choose your country...']"/>   Creates country selection box
        </div>
        <div class="fieldcontain required">
            <label for="timezone">Timezone</label>
            <g:timeZoneSelect name="timezone"/>            <-- Creates timezone select box
        </div>
        <div class="fieldcontain required">
            <label for="photo">Photo</label>
            <input type="file" name="photo"/>
        </div>
        <div class="fieldcontain required">
            <label for="referrer">Who introduced you to Hubbub?</label>
            <g:select name="referrer"
               from="${com.grailsinaction.Profile.list()}"
               optionKey="id"
               optionValue="fullName"
               noSelection="${['null':'Please Choose...']}" />   Populates select box from database
        </div>
        <div class="fieldcontain required">
            <label for="spamMe">Spam me forever?</label>
            <g:checkBox name="spamMe" checked="true"/>     <-- Creates check box
        </div>
```

```
        <div class="fieldcontain required">
            <label for="emailFormat">Email Format</label>
            <g:radioGroup name="emailFormat"
                labels="['Plain','HTML']"
                values="['P', 'H']"
                value="H">
                    ${it.label} ${it.radio}
            </g:radioGroup>
        </div>
    </fieldset>
    <fieldset class="buttons">
        <g:submitButton name="register" value="Register"/>
        <g:link controller="post">Back to Hubbub</g:link>
    </fieldset>
</g:uploadForm>
```

Creates group of radio buttons

Navigates around the app

Look at all those tags! We'll spend the rest of this section discussing these core tags, but this gives you a chance to see them in use first. Figure 8.1 shows how the form is rendered.

That's a fairly comprehensive survey of all the basic form tags. Let's take a look at each of them in turn.

THE FORM TAG

All Grails forms start with a `<g:form>` or `<g:uploadForm>`, depending on whether you're supporting file uploads or not. You configure the form tags with an optional `action` and `controller` name:

```
<g:form controller="user" action="register">
```

As with the `<g:link>` tag we discussed previously, you can usually rely on conventions. For instance, if you're inside another `User` action (such as /user/list), you can describe your form in terms of the target action, and it'll default to the current controller:

```
<g:form action="register">
```

If you want the form to submit to the current action, you can even omit the action name.

TEXTFIELDS, TEXTAREAS, AND PASSWORDFIELDS

The cornerstone of web form development is using text fields. The three basic variants include `<g:textField>` (single line), `<g:textArea>` (multiline), and `<g:passwordField>` (single line with asterisk placeholders).

Our registration form uses the single-line versions:

```
<g:textField name="loginId" value="${newuser?.loginId}"/>
<g:passwordField name="password" value="${newuser?.password}"/>
```

The `name` attribute refers to the name of the field in the `params` object being submitted to the target action. In this example, you have `params.loginId` and `params.password` holding the values.

All form fields support a `value` element that represents the prepopulated value of the form. In the preceding example, you use the safe dereference operator (`?.`) to keep your values null-safe for the initial form display.

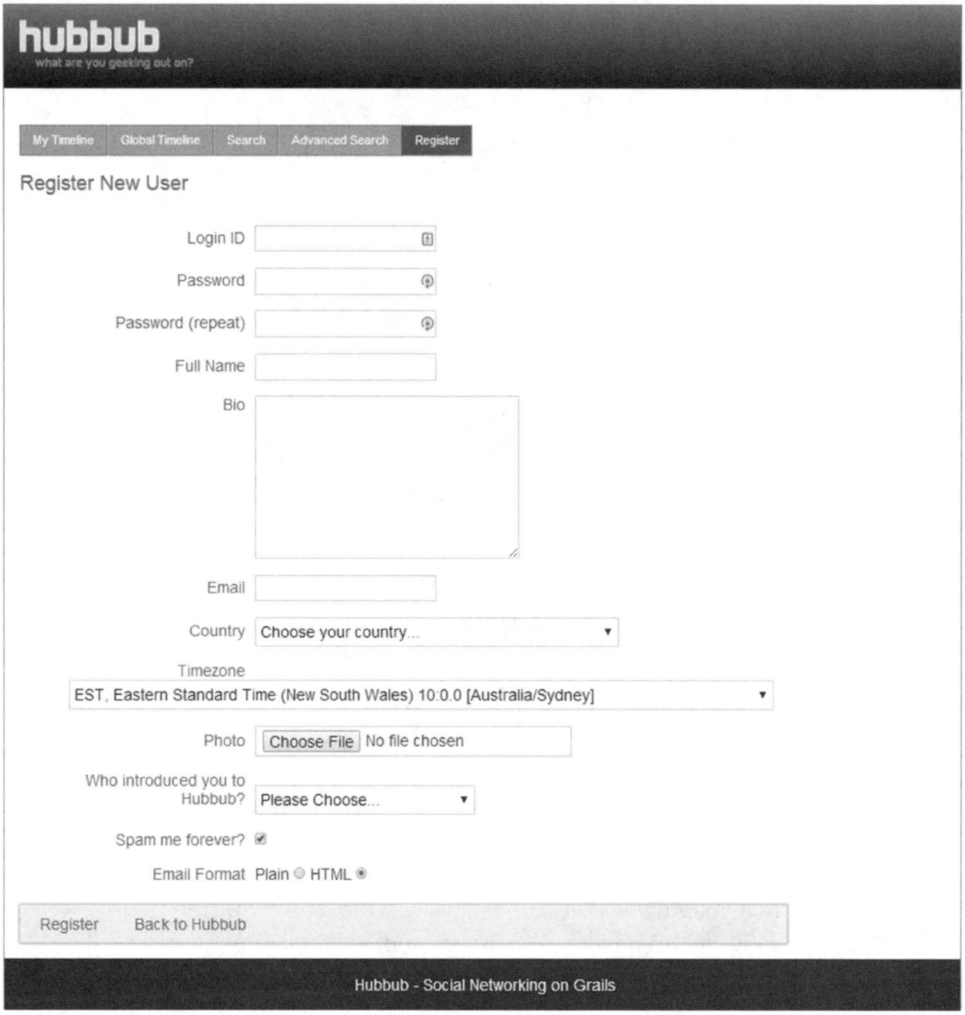

Figure 8.1 A registration form that uses the core form tags

Although you didn't use a `textArea` in listing 8.2, they follow the same basic format as the other text-based fields:

```
<g:textArea name="bio" value="${newuser.bio}" rows="10" cols="60"/>
```

This renders a `textArea` with the specified size, prebound to the target value of `newuser.bio`.

> **How can I pass custom HTML attributes to Grails taglibs?**
>
> The `textArea` tag only explicitly supports `name` and `value` attributes, but it passes through unknown attributes to the generated HTML tag. This means you can use the standard `rows` and `cols` attributes of HTML `textAreas`.

(continued)

This pass-through mechanism exists for all Grails tags, so if you want to render specific HTML attributes in the final tag output (perhaps a class attribute for CSS styling, or some of the new HTML5 data-* tags), add them to the tag's attributes and they'll be passed through.

THE DROP-DOWN JOY OF SELECT

One of the most complex (and sophisticated) Grails form tags is `<g:select>`. The select tag lets you generate drop-down boxes populated from back-end data sources or embedded lists and ranges.

The tag expects the `from` attribute to contain a list of objects (or a range, if you prefer). You then supply an `optionKey` and `optionValue` that represent the property on each object that should be used to generate the drop-down list.

Let's revisit the registration example from listing 8.2:

```
<g:select name="referrer"
              from="${com.grailsinaction.Profile.list()}"
              optionKey="id"
              optionValue="fullName"
              noSelection="${['null':'Please Choose...']}" />
```

The `from` attribute retrieves a list of profiles from a back-end domain class. The `optionKey` attribute represents the `Profile` object's `id` field, and it's the value that will be submitted for the `referrer` parameter. The `optionValue` attribute represents the string that will be displayed in the drop-down list itself—it displays the `Profile` object's `fullName` field.

The special case in which nothing is selected is handled by the `noSelection` attribute, which takes a map with a key of `null` (the string, not the value).

The `from` field is a piece of Groovy code, so you can use any sort of dynamic finder you like to generate the list, or you can provide a static list if that makes sense:

```
<g:select from="['Groovy', 'Java', 'Python']" name="preferredLanguage"/>
```

If you don't supply `optionKey` and `optionValue`, the tag does a `toString()` on each element in the list for both the key and the value, which is perfect when you need a static list.

CHECK BOXES AND RADIO BUTTONS

Check boxes are supported through a simple tag that consists of a name and a value representing the checked status:

```
<g:checkBox name="spamMe" value="${newuser.spamMe}"/>
```

Radio buttons give you more flexibility. The most common way to work with radio buttons is via a `radioGroup`. In listing 8.2, you implemented `emailFormat` using the `radioGroup` tag:

```
<g:radioGroup name="emailFormat"
              labels="['Plain','HTML']"
              values="['P', 'H']"
              value="H">
    ${it.label} ${it.radio}
</g:radioGroup>
```

Notice that you must supply both `labels` and `values` for the buttons.

The `radioGroup` tag is also different from `checkBox` in that the tag iterates through its contents once for each entry. That's why you need to supply those `${it.label}` and `${it.radio}` elements, which get rendered once for each radio button. This iterating approach gives you flexibility in how the radio buttons are marked up, but it's an oddity among the Grails form taglibs.

Grails also provides a `<g:radio>` tag for cases when you want to generate your radio buttons without iteration, but you need to set the same `name` attribute for each button in the group. For this reason, it's often safer to go with the `radioGroup` approach.

HIDDEN FIELDS

Although we didn't demonstrate hidden fields in listing 8.2, they're a special case of a `<g:textField>` that doesn't display in the browser. Here's an example:

```
<g:hiddenField name="dateRendered" value="${new Date()}" />
```

You're free to put whatever text values you like in a `hiddenField`, and they'll end up in the `params` map when the form is submitted.

HANDLING DATE SELECTIONS

One of the least-documented Grails tags is the `datePicker`. This tag creates a series of controls that allow the user to select a date value.

The tag renders a series of combo boxes for the user to select the day of the month, month name, and year (and optionally values for hours, minutes, and seconds), making it ideal for applications that take care of things such as hotel booking or flight dates. When the user submits the form, the Grails data binder turns the collection of controls into a Java `Date` object, making date handling straightforward.

Creating a `datePicker` is straightforward:

```
<g:datePicker name="arrivalDate"
             value="${myBooking.arrivalDate}"
             precision="day"/>
```

The `precision` field specifies which fields you want the user to enter. In the preceding example, the value of `day` provides fields for the day, month, and year. Setting the precision to `minute` would create additional fields for both hours and minutes in the `datePicker`. See the Grails reference guide for a complete set of configuration options.

One common gotcha when working with the `datePicker` is that your controller must use Grails's data binding mechanism (either via `bindData()` or a properties assignment) for the conversion of the `datePicker` controls to work. In practice, don't use Groovy-style property binding to do your initial save. For example, `new Booking(params).save()`

won't work when processing forms containing `datePickers`. Also, don't expect `params.arrivalDate` to return a date—the actual date is built up during data binding from the several HTML controls that the `datePicker` tag generates.

TAG SUMMARY

We've covered new ground and introduced many of the common tags that you're likely to use. Tables 8.2 and 8.3 summarize both the common and less-common tags that you'll encounter when developing with Grails.

Table 8.2 Summary of common form tags

Tag	Description
`g:form`	Creates a standard HTML form element.
`g:uploadForm`	Creates a form that supports nested file upload elements.
`g:textField`	Creates a single-line text field.
`g:passwordField`	Creates a single-line text field with opaque characters.
`g:textArea`	Creates a multiline text field.
`g:checkbox`	Creates a check box that returns a `true` or `false` value.
`g:radio` and `g:radioGroup`	Creates a radio button that can be nested in a radio group for scenarios where only one option can be selected.
`g:select`	Creates a drop-down box with prepopulated elements.
`g:hiddenField`	Creates a field that isn't visible in the browser.
`g:submitButton`	Creates a button for submitting the form to the server.
`g:actionSubmit`	Creates a button that submits the form to a particular controller action. This is not recommended. It's best to use one submit button per form. Use styled links for anything that doesn't submit the form, such as a cancel option.

Table 8.3 Less-common UI-related form tags

Tag	Description
`g:datePicker`	Creates a series of drop-down lists for current time and date selection.
`g:currencySelect`	Displays a user-selectable list of currencies.
`g:paginate`	Displays a series of page navigation links for multipage datasets.
`g:timezoneSelect`	Displays a user-selectable list of Java time zones.
`g:countrySelect`	Displays a user-selectable list of countries.
`g:message`	Displays a message from a message-bundle.
`g:hasErrors`	Tests whether an object has validation errors.

Table 8.3 Less-common UI-related form tags *(continued)*

Tag	Description
`g:renderErrors`	Renders all validation errors on an object as a list.
`g:javascript`	Used to embed inline JavaScript code. Can also be used to link to an external JavaScript file or library.
`g:img`	Creates a Resource-aware link to an image.

> **TIP** Grails lets you use legacy JSP taglibs in GSPs. If you use existing validation or utility taglibs, there's no need to rewrite them—add a `<% @taglib %>` directive to your GSP. Check out the Grails user guide for examples.

That completes your whirlwind tour of the core Grails form tags. You'll spend the rest of the book applying these tags, so don't feel too overwhelmed—you'll get plenty of practice!

One other tag deserves special consideration because it implements the tricky concept of pagination—datasets that you can browse through over multiple pages. In the next section you'll use this tag to add pagination to Hubbub's timeline feature.

8.1.4 *Adding pagination to the timeline*

One of the most unusual and useful core tags is `<g:paginate>`. It renders a series of navigation links so you can move through multiple pages of results.

To demonstrate this tag, you'll create a global timeline in Hubbub, which will show all the posts in the system. The list of posts is going to grow rapidly, so adding a `<g:paginate>` tag allows you to add navigation links to older posts, as shown in figure 8.2.

Provided that your controller has populated a count of the entries that can be paginated, using the tag is as simple as passing on this total. You can also tell it how many results you want displayed per page using the `max` parameter (`max` is optional, and it defaults to 10).

```
<g:paginate action="global" total="${postCount}" max="25" />
```

The tag divides the total number of entries by the maximum per page and creates links for each page. Each page link is sneakily marked up to point to the current controller, but you should almost always specify the action for the links and any other required parameters, such as `id`. The `<g:paginate>` tag also adds `max` and `offset` values (for example, `max = 25`, `offset = 50`) to the links. For example, when you click the link for the third page in the timeline, you'll navigate to `/post/global?max=25&offset=50`.

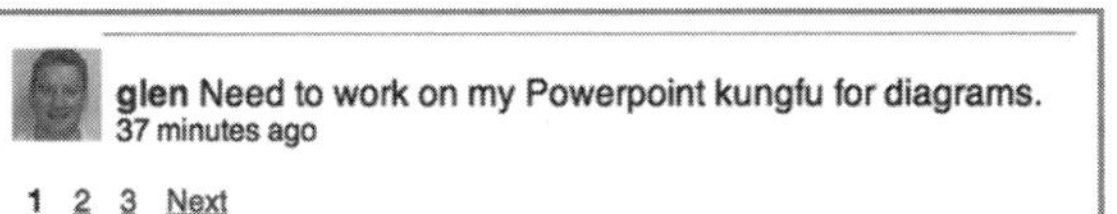

Figure 8.2 The `<g:paginate>` tag in action

Dynamic finders and `Where` queries know about the `max` and `offset` variables, so you can pass the `params` map directly to them. The timeline action passes `max` and `offset` values to `Post.list()`. The new global action looks like this:

```
def global() {
    [ posts : Post.list(params), postCount : Post.count() ]
}
```

The `list()` parameter honors those values in the query, offsetting the query result list and returning the next page of posts. We'll leave it as an exercise for you to create the corresponding view so you can see the tag in action. The view should be the same as timeline.gsp, except there is no `user` variable in the model. You need to display the contents of the `posts` variable directly.

You now have a good grasp of all the core Grails form UI elements. In situations for which none of the standard tags works, you'll need to write your own. That's next.

8.2 Extending views with your own tags

You've used many of the standard Grails tags for form elements, conditional branching, error handling, and even iteration. But what about when the built-in options aren't specific enough? To give you an idea of the options for developing your own tags, let's write a few.

Grails supports three different types of custom tags, as listed in table 8.4.

Table 8.4 Types of custom tags supported by Grails

Type	Description	Example
Simple tags	Outputs HTML	`<g:submitButton>`
Logical tags	Performs a conditional output based on a test	`<g:if test="">`
Iterative tags	Iterates through a collection, rendering content for each element	`<g:each in="">`

The good news is that you can write whatever simple, logical, and iterative tags you need. You'll write one of each type to give you some ideas.

8.2.1 Simple tags

The Hubbub timeline could use a date upgrade. Most Web 2.0 apps support those "5 minutes ago" dates, which look cool and solve time zone issues. Let's implement a `dateFromNow` tag that takes a date and outputs a nice format.

It comes as no surprise that you start with a template:

```
grails create-tag-lib com.grailsinaction.Date
```

This command generates the shell of a taglib in /grails-app/taglib/DateTagLib.groovy. Implementing simple tags involves processing the `attrs` parameter and rendering HTML to the output stream.

You invoke the tag like this:

```
<g:dateFromNow date="${post.created}"/>
```

Implementing the `dateFromNow` tag in the `DateTagLib` class involves creating a closure called `dateFromNow` and processing the `date` attribute. The following code snippet shows a first draft of the implementation.

```
class DateTagLib {
    def dateFromNow = { attrs ->
        def date = attrs.date
        def niceDate = getNiceDate(date) // implement this somehow...
        out << niceDate
    }
}
```

Accesses date attribute from custom tag

Writes formatted date to the page

NOTE Grails v2.3+ adds a static `defaultEncodeAs` property to new tag libraries. We'll explain encodings in chapter 11, but the tags in this section should not be encoding their output. That's why the property isn't shown.

You access `date` using `attrs.date`, pass it to your `getNiceDate()` method to turn it into the "x minutes ago" format, and then output the result to the stream. Groovy overloads the `<<` operator for streaming objects to perform a `write()`, so there's nothing more to do than implement your `getNiceDate()` business logic, which you add to DateTagLib.groovy as shown in the following listing.

Listing 8.3 Implementing a much nicer date format for Hubbub

```
protected String getNiceDate(Date date) {
    def now = new Date()
    def diff = Math.abs(now.time - date.time)
    final long second = 1000
    final long minute = second * 60
    final long hour = minute * 60
    final long day = hour * 24
    def niceTime = ""
    long calc = 0;
    calc = Math.floor(diff / day)
    if (calc) {
        niceTime += calc + " day" + (calc > 1 ? "s " : " ")
        diff %= day
    }
    calc = Math.floor(diff / hour)
    if (calc) {
        niceTime += calc + " hour" + (calc > 1 ? "s " : " ")
        diff %= hour
    }
    calc = Math.floor(diff / minute)
    if (calc) {
        niceTime += calc + " minute" + (calc > 1 ? "s " : " ")
        diff %= minute
    }
    if (!niceTime) {
        niceTime = "Right now"
```

```
    } else {
        niceTime += (date.time > now.time) ? "from now" : "ago"
    }
    return niceTime
}
```

You now have a reusable tag to use wherever you need to render a date in "x minutes ago" format. You used a single attribute (`date`) for this example, but your tags can have multiple attributes.

What's the g:? Using custom namespaces

All your sample tags have taken the form `<g:tagName>`. The `g:` prefix is referred to as the tag's *namespace*. If you don't specify a custom namespace for your taglibs, they use the `<g:>` prefix. How do you customize this? Add a new declaration to your DateTagLib.groovy file:

```
static namespace = "hub"
```

If you do this, you can refer to your tags as `<hub:dateFromNow ...>`. It's best to use short namespaces to reduce typing, but avoid single characters, which are informally reserved for platform taglibs. Use a namespace of "hub" for Hubbub tags so you can specify `<hub:dateFromNow>`.

You should always declare a namespace for your tags so they're less likely to collide with other tags—particularly with future Grails built-ins.

With your trusty `<hub:dateFromNow>` in place, it's time to enhance your timeline.gsp to use your funky new dates. In the next listing, let's refactor your timeline.gsp to use the new tag.

Listing 8.4 Invoking custom `dateFromNow` from timeline.gsp

```
<div id="allPosts">
    <g:each in="${user.posts}" var="post">
        <div class="postEntry">
            <div class="postText">${post.content}</div>
            <div class="postDate">
                <hub:dateFromNow date="${post.dateCreated}"/>    <-- Invokes custom date taglib
            </div>
        </div>
    </g:each>
</div>
```

It's one thing to create taglib logic, it's another thing to test it. Let's take a short diversion into testing taglibs

8.2.2 Testing taglibs

Grails provides support for taglib tests through use of the `applyTemplate()` method, which invokes your tag and returns its output as a string. If your tag takes method arguments, you can take advantage of `applyTemplate()`'s arguments to pass those in as a map. If you want to test that an invocation of the `dateFromNow` tag with the current time results in `"Right now"` returned, you could frame that assertion as:

```
applyTemplate('<hub:dateFromNow date="${date}" />',
              [date: new Date()]) == "Right now"
```

Let's combine your knowledge of Spock's parameterized `@Unroll` tests to pepper your `dateFromNow` taglib with a few different inputs and make sure that your business logic is implemented correctly. Add your new test to /test/unit/com/grailsinaction/DateTagLibSpec.groovy as shown in this listing.

Listing 8.5 `DateTagLibSpec` exercises taglib with numerous values

```
package com.grailsinaction
import grails.test.mixin.TestFor
import spock.lang.*

@TestFor(DateTagLib)                                    <-- Mix in all TagLib test helpers
class DateTagLibSpec extends Specification {

    @Unroll                                             <-- Tells Spock to parameterize this test in several runs
    void "Conversion of #testName matches #expectedNiceDate"() {

        expect:
        applyTemplate('<hub:dateFromNow date="${date}" />',
                      [date: testDate]) == expectedNiceDate    <-- Invokes tag with the supplied date

        where:
        testName         | testDate               | expectedNiceDate
        "Current Time"   | new Date()             | "Right now"
        "Now - 1 day"    | new Date().minus(1)    | "1 day ago"
        "Now - 2 days"   | new Date().minus(2)    | "2 days ago"
    }

}
```

For completeness, it's good to have parameterized assertions covering the "x minutes ago" and "x seconds ago," which we'll leave as an exercise for you; it may be a good opportunity to explore Groovy's amazing `TimeCategory`[1] DSL.

Now that you've implemented a simple tag and seen how to test it, let's explore Grails's support for building logical tags.

8.2.3 Logical tags

Sometimes you want to display a block of content conditionally. Let's say you want to display only certain content to Lynx browser users. You could do something like this:

```
<hub:certainBrowser userAgent="Lynx">
    <p>Best viewed in Internet Explorer. Just kidding, you hardcore Linux
     user! Lynx rocks! </p>
</hub:certainBrowser>
```

[1] Class TimeCategory, http://groovy.codehaus.org/api/groovy/time/TimeCategory.html.

You want Linux users to see this message, but all other browsers will pass on by. Let's implement a `UtilTagLib` as shown in the following code snippet.

```
class UtilTagLib {
    static namespace = "hub"

    def certainBrowser = {  attrs, body ->
        if (request.getHeader('User-Agent')
    =~ attrs.userAgent ) {
            out << body()
        }
    }
}
```

Checks that User-Agent header matches tag attribute

Displays any content that was inside original tag

Notice that logical tags take two arguments: `attrs`, which you've already seen, and body, which contains the `content` block inside the tag. If the test evaluates to `true`, you render the `body()` to the output stream; otherwise you send nothing.

This sort of tag is common for security scenarios. For example, when using the Apache Shiro security plugin, you'll often employ convenience tags such as `isLoggedIn` for conditional output:

```
<shiro:isLoggedIn>
    <div>Logged in as: <jsec:principal/>
         (<g:link controller="auth" action="signOut">
            sign out
          </g:link>)</div>
</shiro:isLoggedIn>
```

Notice that the contents of your logical tags may themselves be complex GSP fragments that call other tags in other taglibs. As a tag implementor, you don't need to worry because the `body()` call seamlessly handles everything for you.

With our exploration of logical tags complete, let's turn to the last style of custom tags Grails supports: iteration tags.

8.2.4 Iteration tags

The most complex of the custom tag types is the iteration tag. This type of tag performs multiple invocations of its `body()` with different input values for each iteration.

The Hubbub sidebar should contain images for the friends that you're following. You could implement it as a standard `<g:each>` tag, like this:

```
<!-- People I am following -->
<div id="friendsThumbnails">
    <g:each var="followUser" in="${following}">
        <img src="
            <g:createLink action="tiny" controller="image"
                id="${followUser.loginId}"/>
            "alt="${followUser.loginId}"/>
    </g:each>
</div>
```

An eachFollower tag would provide a more visually pleasing approach and let you do something like this:

```
<hub:eachFollower in="${following}">
   <img src="
      <g:createLink action="tiny" controller="image"
         id="${followUser.loginId}"/>
      " alt="${followUser.loginId}"/>
</hub:eachFollower>
```

The eachFollower tag can be implemented with an iterating call to the body method:

```
def eachFollower = { attrs, body ->
    def followers = attrs.followers
    followers?.each { follower ->
        body(followUser: follower)
    }
}
```

But that's work to replicate the standard behavior of <g:each>. To be honest, we can't think of many scenarios where you're not better off using the more explicit semantics of <g:each>. A smarter use of your time would be implementing a tag for user thumbnails, which you'll explore next.

8.2.5 *Calling one tag from another*

When you're developing your own custom tags, you often want to reuse standard Grails tags from within your own implementation. If you were building a custom tag that incorporated links to a standard controller action, you'd probably want to take advantage of the existing createLink tag.

Let's apply that thinking to a new custom tag so you can see this reuse in action. Take the example of generating URLs for those tiny follower images. As you saw in the last section, you're currently doing this in HTML with dynamic URL construction:

```
<img src="
   <g:createLink action="tiny" controller="image"
      id="${followUser.loginId}"/>
   " alt="${followUser.loginId}"/>
```

It would be much nicer to hide that in a custom tinyThumbnail tag, like this:

```
<hub:tinyThumbnail loginId="${followUser.loginId}"/>
```

When you implement your tinyThumbnail tag (which you'll do in /grails-app/taglib/com/grailsinaction/UtilTagLib.groovy), you want to reuse the functionality built into the standard g:createLink tag. And you can! Here's your custom implementation:

```
def tinyThumbnail = { attrs ->
   def loginId = attrs.loginId
   out << "<img src='"
   out << g.createLink(action: "tiny",              Reuses existing
      controller: "image", id: loginId)             Grails tag
   out << "' alt='${loginId}'"
}
```

As you saw previously, you can invoke an existing tag using method-style invocation. The `namespace` must be used as the object of the method call ("g" for the standard taglibs, as shown previously).

Now that you've learned how to create your own custom tags, the next step is to learn how to improve application layouts.

8.3 Adding delicious layouts

You've spent plenty of time implementing functionality for Hubbub, but you've spent none on its appearance. Grails makes implementing features fast and enables you to make your application look and feel good. At the heart of look-and-feel matters is Grails' support for layouts.

You've used templates since chapter 4 (and we even touched on them in chapter 1), but we never explained how they work. All the heavy lifting for layout functionality in Grails is done via a popular Java layout library called SiteMesh (www.sitemesh.org/). You may not have been exposed to SiteMesh before, so let's take a look at it.

8.3.1 Introducing SiteMesh

SiteMesh operates as a page decorator. You render plain HTML for your page, and it's passed through a SiteMesh decorator (to add the header, footer, sidebars, and so on), and the final merged page is rendered to the browser. Think of it like the example shown in figure 8.3.

One of the most powerful and sophisticated features of SiteMesh is merging elements from your target page into your decorator. This makes more sense with an example, so let's explore how SiteMesh is used to implement Hubbub's common look and feel.

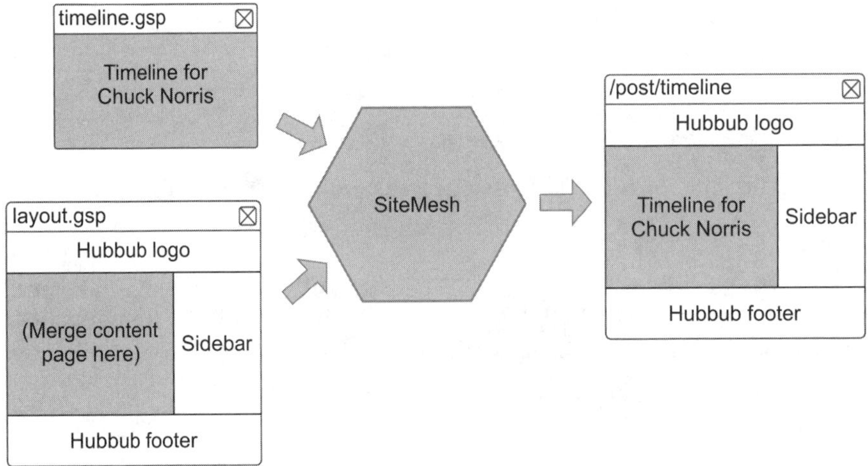

Figure 8.3 SiteMesh in operation merging pages

EXPLORING THE MERGING PROCESS

Let's review your template from chapter 4—a simple layout that adds a title field and a basic footer. You placed your layouts in /grails-app/views/layouts, but because you want your template to apply to your scaffolding code too, you edited the standard template, called /grails-app/views/layouts/main.gsp. The following listing reproduces that template.

Listing 8.6 A basic custom template for Hubbub

```
<html>
<head>
  <title>Hubbub &raquo; <g:layoutTitle default="Welcome" /></title>
  <g:external dir="css" file="hubbub.css"/>
  <g:external dir="css" file="main.css"/>
  <g:layoutHead />
</head>
<body>
  <div>
    <div id="hd">
      <g:link uri="/">
        <g:img id="logo" uri="/images/headerlogo.png" alt="hubbub logo"/>
      </g:link>
    </div>
    <div id="bd"><!-- start body -->
      <g:layoutBody/>
    </div>  <!-- end body -->
    <div id="ft">
      <div id="footerText">Hubbub - Social Networking on Grails</div>
    </div>
  </div>
</body>
</html>
```

❶ Merges <title> element from content page

❷ Merges <head> element from content page

❸ Merges <body> element from content page

You start by laying out the title. You prefix all title elements with "Hubbub >>", followed by the title value from the target page ❶. If the target page doesn't have a custom `<title>` element, you display "Welcome". This gives you a convenient way to change all the titles in one place.

Use the SiteMesh `<g:layoutHead>` tag ❷ to merge any content from your target page's `<head>` element and the `<g:layoutBody>` tag ❸ to merge in the contents of your target page's `<body>` element.

Once all those tags fire, your target view page will be merged with your layout template to give a consistent layout throughout the application. This approach to markup offers a double win. Your content pages become simple and uncluttered, and your layout pages make it easy to change the look and feel of your application with a single edit.

Displaying application versions in footers

The `<g:meta>` tag gives you access to all the entries in your Grails application.properties file in the root directory of your project. It's often convenient to display the version of your application in the footer, for reporting issues against, and to confirm that a new version has deployed successfully. You might display your current application and Grails version in a footer using code like this:

```
Version <g:meta name="app.version"/>
on Grails <g:meta name="app.grails.version"/>
```

You can change the version of your application at any time by using the `grails set-version` command from the command line, or by editing the application.properties file directly. The version number of your application affects the naming of your target WAR file, so it can be handy to bump the number with each deployed version to allow you to keep old copies of WAR artifacts around for an immediate rollback if things go bad. (This isn't a substitute for version control, but it's a cheap rollback option nonetheless.)

APPLYING LAYOUTS BY CONVENTION

In chapter 1, we introduced a simple way of applying layouts by convention. It's time to review the options and applications of them.

If you're dealing with pages produced by `PostController`, you could control its decoration with the techniques listed in table 8.5.

Table 8.5 Conventions for applying layout templates

Apply template to ...	Example of convention or technique
All actions in a controller.	Create layout in /layouts/post.gsp (or create a static field on the controller called layout). `static layout = 'post'`
A specific action in a controller.	Create layout in /layouts/post/list.gsp.
A portion of a target page.	Include tag in target page. `<g:applyLayout name="postFragment">Hi</g:applyLayout>`
Override any conventions explicitly for a single page ...	Include tag in target page. `<meta name="layout" content="vanilla"/>`
Or use a single default layout as a fallback for your entire application.	/layouts/application.gsp (You can even customize its name using the Config element.) `grails.sitemesh.default.layout = 'base.gsp'`

Using conventions eliminates the need to specify the `<meta>` tag and makes your application more maintainable. When you open a GSP file and don't see any meta magic, you know exactly where to look for a decorator (/views/layouts/<controllerName>), which makes maintenance more straightforward.

While we're on the subject of real-world approaches to page layouts, it's time to explore other ways to make them simpler.

8.3.2 Standardizing page layouts

If you've done any work laying out multicolumn web applications, you already know how complex a standard CSS layout can be. Browsers may not float the divs correctly to give you the right gutter, it's hard to get sections of your page to grow while others stay static, you have to contend with font-size issues, and the page never looks good in Internet Explorer.

You need to address all these issues in your application layouts, and it's time we showed you the best way to go about it. First, sketch out how you want Hubbub to look. Figure 8.4 shows a rough sketch for the app.

You can see the top header followed by a tabbed area with a right sidebar, followed by a full-width footer. If you were coding this by hand, you'd be in for a shock. This kind of CSS layout involves a massive amount of work and is difficult to keep consistent across browsers. In Grails, the smartest way to handle CSS layouts is with a gridding system such as Bootstrap or the 960 Grid System (960.gs).

Bootstrap gives you a simple CSS-based mechanism for fine-grained control of browser layouts. It's a small CSS (and optionally JavaScript) file that you can add to your application to solve your cross-browser layout and formatting dramas for good. Even on Internet Explorer.

You can download the CSS file and view comprehensive documentation from the Bootstrap page (http://getbootstrap.com/), where you'll also find great samples of all the different gridding, layout, and formatting components included in Bootstrap. You can even use the online builder to generate your basic template layout for you. Figure 8.5 shows a sample of Jetstrap, a third-party Bootstrap GUI builder which you can use directly from your browser to generate a basic template for your site. In this example, you're building your layout from the sketch in figure 8.4.

Once you've got the layout you want, click the CSS/HTML button and you'll be presented with your template ready to customize. The following listing shows the Bootstrap code generated by Jetstrap from the layout in figure 8.5.

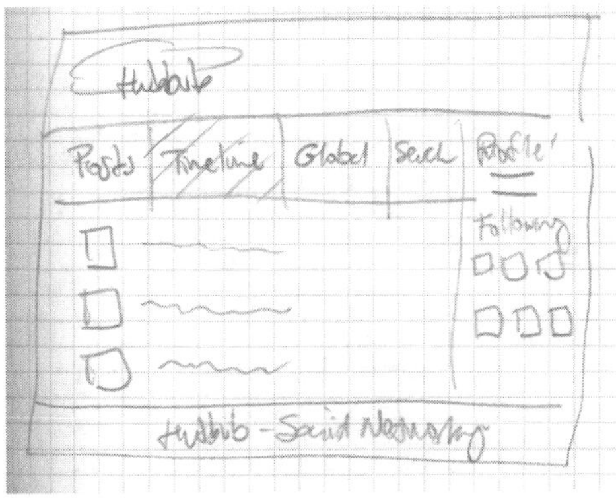

Figure 8.4 A mockup of the Hubbub UI

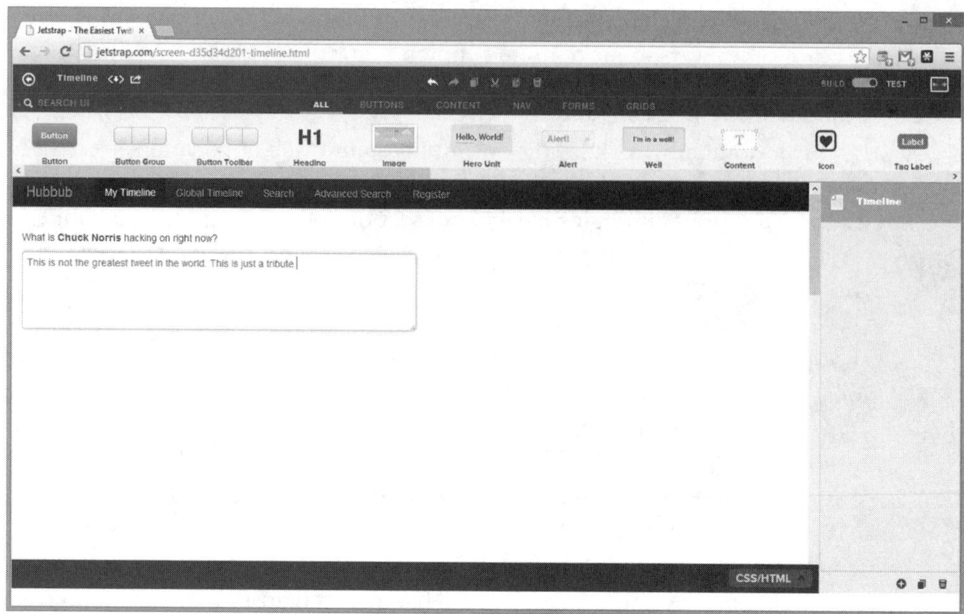

Figure 8.5 The Jetstrap builder makes cross-browser CSS layouts easy.

Listing 8.7 The Bootstrap-generated code

```
<div class="navbar navbar-fixed-top navbar-inverse">
  <div class="navbar-inner">
    <div class="container-fluid">
      <a class="brand" href="#">
        Hubbub
      </a>
      <ul class="nav">
        <ul class="nav nav-tabs">
        </ul>
        <li class="active">
          <a href="#">
            My Timeline
          </a>
        </li>
        <li>
          <a href="#">
            Global Timeline
          </a>
        </li>
        <li>
          <a href="#">
            Search
          </a>
        </li>
        <li class="">
          <a href="#">
            Advanced Search
```

```
          </a>
        </li>
        <li class="">
          <a href="#">
            Register
          </a>
        </li>
      </ul>
    </div>
  </div>
</div>
<div class="container-fluid">
</div>
<div class="row-fluid">
  <div class="span12">
    <div class="control-group">
      <label for="textarea1">
        What is
        <strong>
          Chuck Norris
        </strong>
        hacking on right now?
      </label>
    </div>
    <textarea id="tweetContent" name="textarea1"></textarea>
  </div>
</div>
```

With a few tagged Bootstrap divs, you have a cross-browser, safely degrading CSS layout that will look the same on any browser. All you need to do now is incorporate your <g:layout*> tags to merge in the head and body, and add CSS styling to give you a better idea of what it might look like.

For the rest of the book, we'll stick to the hand-coded layout in listing 8.6. It results in a less flexible and useful layout, but helps keep things simple. We do recommend using something such as Bootstrap on real projects.

An important part of Grails is its philosophy of DRY. Layouts are one aspect of this, because they allow you to decorate multiple pages with the same outline markup. But what if you have pieces of markup repeated inside views? That's where Grails templates come in.

8.3.3 Markup fragments with templates

When you want to reuse portions of your application layout throughout your application, that content is a candidate for a template. Templates encapsulate fragments of GSP functionality and can be incorporated in your pages using the <g:render> tag.

Consider the timeline pages you have. All of them display a list of Hubbub messages in the same way. You should factor that message list out into a separate GSP template. Create the file /grails-app/views/post/_postEntry.gsp (note the underscore) and set its content to the following:

```
<div class="postEntry">
    <div class="postText">${post.content}</div>
    <div class="postDate">
        <hub:dateFromNow date="${post.dateCreated}"/>
    </div>
</div>
```

As you can probably tell, this represents the markup for a single post. It's trivial to get a list of posts, though, by using this form of the `<g:render>` tag in the timeline views, such as timeline.gsp:

```
...
<div id="allPosts">
    <g:render template="postEntry" collection="${user.posts}" var="post"/>
</div>
...
```

This will apply the markup fragment to all the posts in the `user.posts` collection, ensuring that each post is made available to the template as the variable `post`. It's also worth noting that when you reference the name of a template, you leave out the underscore and the .gsp suffix.

The template can also be applied to a single post using either this syntax:

```
<g:render template="postEntry" bean="${singlePost}" var="post"/>
```

which is analogous to the collection-based variant we just showed, or:

```
<g:render template="postEntry" model="[post: singlePost]"/>
```

The advantage of this second form of the `<g:render>` tag is that you can pass multiple variables into the template.

What if you want to use the template form in a view that's not associated with `PostController`? You can still do that, but you have to specify an absolute path for the template:

```
<g:render template="/post/postEntry" bean="${singlePost}" var="post"/>
```

The leading slash marks the template name as a path relative to the views directory.

Templates are great for self-contained pieces of view functionality. You can even use them in controllers when rendering Ajax fragments—you'll get into that in section 8.4. If you want, have a go at moving the section of the page for posting a new message into its own template. That's everything inside the `<div id="newPost">` element.

With your standard layouts now in place, it's time to let the user choose their own look and feel for Hubbub. This is called *skinning*, and Grails makes it easy to implement.

8.3.4 Adding skinning

Hubbub looks great with its standard blue and gray design. But social-networking sites generally let users skin their timelines. Let's add skinning to Hubbub.

First, you'll need a way to select a preferred skin, and for that you'll need to add a new optional field to the `Profile` object, as shown in the following listing.

Listing 8.8 Setting up to select a preferred skin

```
package com.grailsinaction
class Profile {
    static belongsTo = User
    String fullName
    // ... other fields omitted
    String skin

    static constraints = {
        fullName(nullable: true)
        // ... other constraints omitted
        skin(nullable: true, blank: true, inList: ['blues', 'nighttime'])
    }
```

Adds support for per-user skinning

With the skin in place, you need to customize the user's timeline page to take advantage of it. If the user has a skin for their timeline, you'll apply it using CSS. The following code snippet shows an extract of the updated timeline.gsp view, with the new markup in italics.

```
<html>
    <head>
        <title>Timeline for ...</title>
        <meta name="layout" content="main"/>
        <g:if test="${user.profile?.skin}">
            <g:external dir="css" file="${user.profile.skin}.css"/>
        </g:if>
    </head>
    <body>
    ...
</html>
```

Checks whether user has a skin

Applies user's preferred skin

The updated timeline checks to see if the user has a skin configured, and, if so, it adds a link to the appropriate style sheet from the CSS directory. The CSS skin files override the background colors of body elements and heading styles. For skinning to work well, it's important that you make good use of CSS classes and IDs to mark up your view pages.

You can find the CSS style sheets for the "blues" and "nighttime" in the chapter source on GitHub. Have a look in the web-app/css directory. Figure 8.6 shows the "nighttime" skin in action.

If you need to support skinning site-wide rather than for individual pages, you're better off using filters, which we introduced in chapter 7. Set up your skin name in a filter and pass it using a session-scoped variable. Then configure the CSS skin in your main layout page, and you're set.

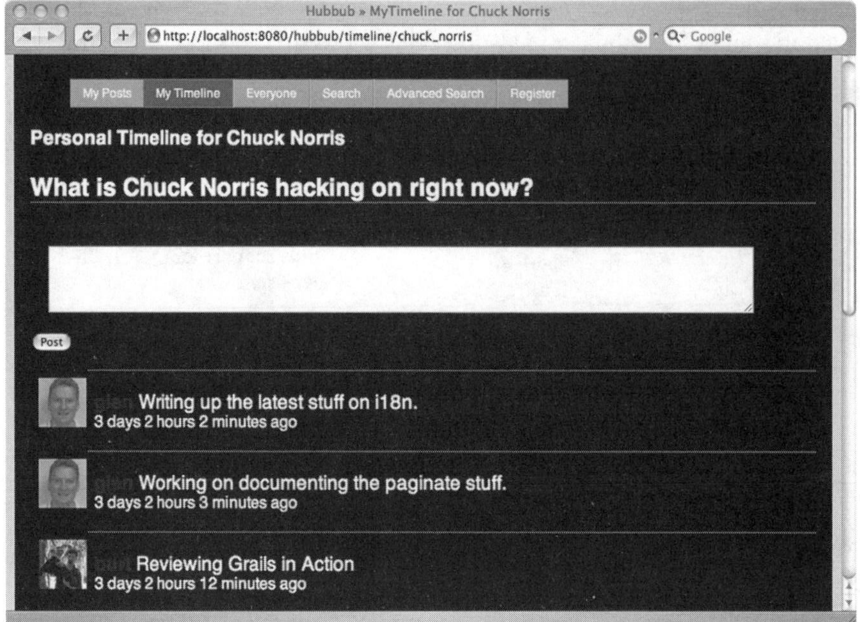

Figure 8.6 The nighttime theme in action

8.3.5 Implementing navigation tabs

With the skinning in place, it's time to turn your attention to navigation. Which UI elements will you provide to allow the user to navigate around the application? The most recognizable option is to display a series of navigation tabs at the top of the page.

In the early days of Grails, this tab-style navigation was done by hand. Typically you'd write a tag to generate menu items and do the hard work of highlighting the appropriate tab based on the current controller action. Things got messy quickly.

Since Marc Palmer's Navigation plugin came on the scene, generating navigation tabs has become straightforward. We're going to cover third-party plugins in depth in chapter 10, but for now we'll walk you through the basics of installing and using the Navigation plugin.

To install the plugin, update your /grails-app/conf/BuildConfig.groovy with the required plugin co-ordinates:

```
plugins {
    ...
    runtime ":navigation:1.3.2"
}
```

Once the plugin is installed, you can mark your controller classes with a new `navigation` property and tell the plugin which actions from your controller to display in your menu. You want to generate a menu for Hubbub that looks something like figure 8.7.

Figure 8.7 The planned navigation menu

The Navigation plugin makes generating the menu straightforward. The following listing shows extracts of the updated `UserController` and `PostController` with new navigation blocks that specify what to include in the menu.

Listing 8.9 Defining menu options in your controller

```
class PostController {
    static navigation = [
        [group:'tabs', action: 'personal', title: 'My Timeline', order: 0],
        [action: 'global', title: 'Global Timeline', order: 1]
    ]
    // ... other code omitted
}
class UserController {
    static navigation = [
        [group:'tabs', action:'search', order: 90],
        [action: 'advSearch', title: 'Advanced Search', order: 95],
        [action: 'register', order: 99, isVisible: { true }]
    ]
    // ... other code omitted
}
```

For each navigation block, you provide a series of maps, each representing one item in the menu. In each map, you provide the action that fires when the menu is clicked, along with an optional title. If you don't specify a title, the plugin uses a nicely formatted name of the action (`register` becomes "Register" and `advSearch` defaults to "Adv Search").

You can use the `order` property to control where in the menu your items are positioned. (In the future, third-party plugins may use this field to include their own items in your menus automatically.) You can even supply an `isVisible` property that's tested when the menu is rendered. For example, you might configure the Register menu to display only if the user isn't logged in.

Now that your menu blocks are defined, add two entries in your template to display the menu:

- In the `head` element of your main layout, add a `<nav:resources/>` element.

  ```
  <head>
      ...
      <nav:resources/>
  </head>
  ```

  This incorporates the menu CSS elements. (You can override default menu styling with your own styling, but the defaults look great.)

- In the body of your layout, position the menu on the page using a `<nav:render/>` tag; specify the group attribute from your navigation block:

```
<div id="bd"><!-- start body -->
    <nav:render group="tabs"/>
    <g:layoutBody/>
</div>
```

With those two changes, your menu is ready to roll. Figure 8.8 shows the new menu in operation.

With your menu looking slick, it's time to explore other ways to take your UI to the next level. One obvious way is to use Ajax to update the user's timeline in-place when they add a new post. But before you get started, you need to learn how Grails integrates Ajax.

8.4 Applying Ajax tags

We've saved the best UI work for last. In this section, you'll use Ajax to take the Hubbub UI experience to a whole new level. You'll get a taste for dynamically changing your Hubbub page in-place using remote calls to back-end code. Then you'll create visual sizzle with JavaScript animation and effects.

But first you need to lay the foundation by choosing a JavaScript library to do the heavy lifting.

8.4.1 Choosing a JavaScript library

Grails implements its built-in Ajax functionality through adaptive tag libraries. All the standard Ajax tags can be backed by whatever JavaScript library you prefer and still expose the same API to the client and server. jQuery is supported out of the box, and Dojo, YUI, and Prototype are supported using plugins. That means you're free to start with one library and change to a different one as your application fills out.

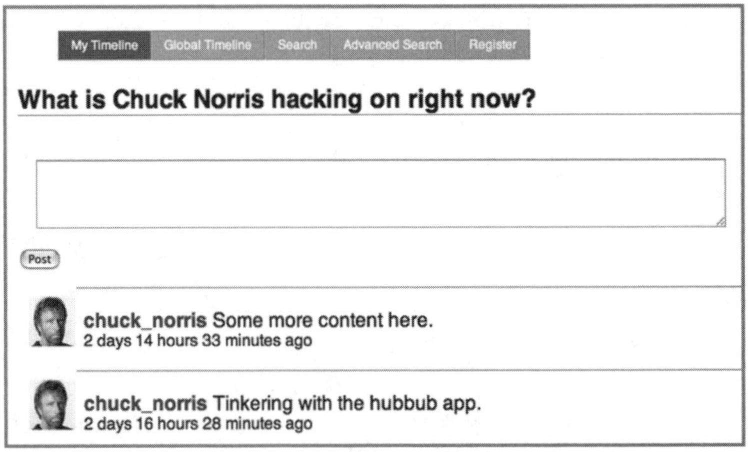

Figure 8.8 The Navigation plugin painlessly handles all your menu needs.

Not all JavaScript libraries play nicely together, so if any of your GSPs use a particular library, it makes sense to use that for your Ajax implementation, too. For instance, if you're planning any animation effects with Scriptaculous, it makes sense to choose Prototype (because that's what Scriptaculous uses under the hood). If you're planning to use YUI autocomplete, you may as well use YUI for your Ajax remoting, too, because you've already burned the page-load time bootstrapping the YUI infrastructure.

jQuery seems to be the most widely used by Grails developers (and because it comes bundled with Grails, there's low friction in getting up and running), so you'll use jQuery for the examples.

8.4.2 *Essential Ajax form remoting*

It's time to apply Ajax style to your user's timeline action. You'll restyle your posting form to submit post contents using Ajax, then update your timeline with the latest entries.

The first step in using an Ajax call is importing your preferred library. You'll start by updating your timeline.gsp `head` element to tell Grails that you want to use jQuery as your remoting library. Using the `library` attribute of the `javascript` tag generates HTML tags for the multiple source JavaScript files that comprise the specified library. The new markup is in italics:

```
<head>
    <title>Timeline for ${user.profile.fullName}</title>
    <meta name="layout" content="main"/>
    <g:javascript library="jquery"/>
</head>
...
```

At this point, you also need to update the layout because you're using the Resources plugin. If you don't add the following lines (in italics) to main.gsp, the relevant JavaScript code won't appear in your pages and the Ajax won't work!

Listing 8.10 Updating the layout

```
<html>
<head>
    ...
    <g:layoutHead />
    <r:layoutResources />
    <nav:resources/>
</head>
<body>
    ...
    </div>
    <r:layoutResources />
</body>
</html>
```

Resources plugin requires two <r:layoutResources> tags either in a view or its layout

With your library selected and the Resources plugin primed (we'll talk more on this in chapter 13), you can now update the posting form to submit the `Post` contents remotely. Grails provides the `<g:submitToRemote>` tag to bundle the contents of a form and send it via Ajax to a back-end service. The following listing shows the updated form definition.

Listing 8.11 Adding a new `Post` via Ajax

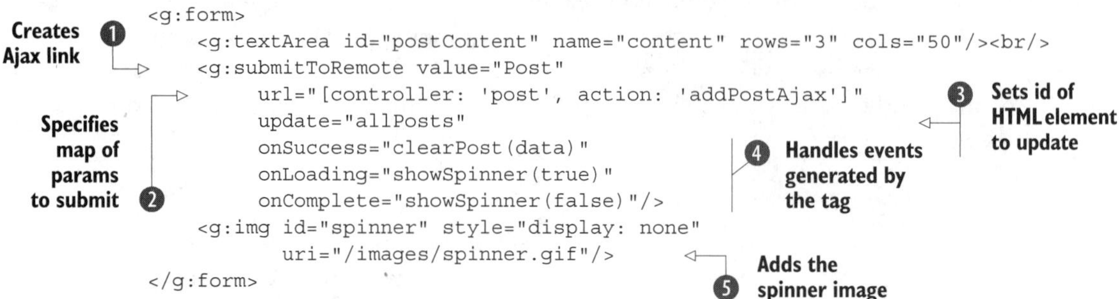

```
<g:form>
    <g:textArea id="postContent" name="content" rows="3" cols="50"/><br/>
    <g:submitToRemote value="Post"
        url="[controller: 'post', action: 'addPostAjax']"
        update="allPosts"
        onSuccess="clearPost(data)"
        onLoading="showSpinner(true)"
        onComplete="showSpinner(false)"/>
    <g:img id="spinner" style="display: none"
         uri="/images/spinner.gif"/>
</g:form>
```


The `<g:form>` and `<g:textField>` tags remain unchanged, other than the removal of the `action` attribute from the former. Only a `<g:submitToRemote>` tag has been introduced ❶. Its only required attribute is `url`, which is a map with `controller` and `action` values ❷. You'll add a new `addPostAjax()` action in the `PostController` to handle the new submission.

If the `update` attribute is specified ❸, it should be the `id` of the `div` to update when the call is complete. In this case, the `addPostAjax` action returns the updated HTML for the timeline, which is in a `div` with `id` `allPosts`.

If the `onSuccess` attribute is specified ❹, it should contain the JavaScript function to call after the form submission has finished successfully (no back-end 404s or other errors). Whatever function you supply to `onSuccess` takes an argument (`data`) which is the `XMLHTTPResponse` that represents the back-end call. In your case, use `clearPost()` to clear the `textArea` when the user has successfully posted the new item.

Finally, `onLoading` and `onComplete` are called before and after the Ajax call, which you take advantage of to show and hide an animated spinner image ❺.

If you're curious about those `clearPost()` and `showSpinner()` JavaScript calls, there's no magic in them—only a few lines of jQuery to keep the UI responsive. It's always good to show and hide an image when doing Ajax calls so that the user knows that something is happening. Add the JavaScript shown in the following code snippet to your timeline.gsp to keep the user up to date.

```
<g:javascript>
    function clearPost(e) {
        $('#postContent').val('');
    }
    function showSpinner(visible) {
        if (visible) $('#spinner').show();
                else $('#spinner').hide();
    }
</g:javascript>
```

With your client interface implemented, you need to implement the `addPostAjax` action in `PostController`. The following listing shows the back-end code you need.

Listing 8.12 Implementing the `addPostAjax()` back end

```
def addPostAjax(String content) {
    try {
        def newPost = postService.createPost(          ❶ Creates post via service
           session.user.loginId, content)
        def recentPosts = Post.findAllByUser(          ❷ Queries 20 most recent posts
           session.user,
           [sort: 'dateCreated', order: 'desc', max: 20])
        render template: 'postEntry',                  ❸ Renders postEntry template
           collection: recentPosts,                       for each query result
           var: 'post'
    } catch (PostException pe) {
        render {                                       ❹ Handles bad situations
            div(class:"errors", pe.message)               with error message
        }
    }
}
```

Because you did the hard work of abstracting the `PostService` in chapter 7, you can reuse it for your Ajax implementation here ❶. Note that we've assumed that your makeshift security filter is populating the `session.user` object—you will have to add the `addPostAjax` action to the filter definition to enable this. In the security chapter you'll revisit the login process to make this consistent. After you create your new `Post`, you retrieve the latest posts to send back to the timeline ❷. Then it's a matter of reusing the `postEntry` template you developed previously and passing it your collection of recent posts ❸. This sends the HTML of the timeline body back to the client for updating the `allPosts` div.

If an error happens in the process, you'll use the markup builder (discussed in chapter 2, section 2.4.4) version of `render` ❹ to send back a `div` with the error message (styled as an error, so the big pink warning box is displayed).

Figure 8.9 shows your Ajax timeline in progress with your stylish Ajax spinner giving the user feedback to indicate things are under way.

The `submitToRemote` tag you used in listing 8.9 has other options that you haven't explored yet, including the ability to handle server response codes such as `on404` and other event options. It can also handle JSON return values, which you'll use later in the chapter. For full coverage of its capabilities, check out the Grails user guide.

With your basic Ajax functionality in place, it's time to explore how to use animation libraries to make the entire app more visually stunning.

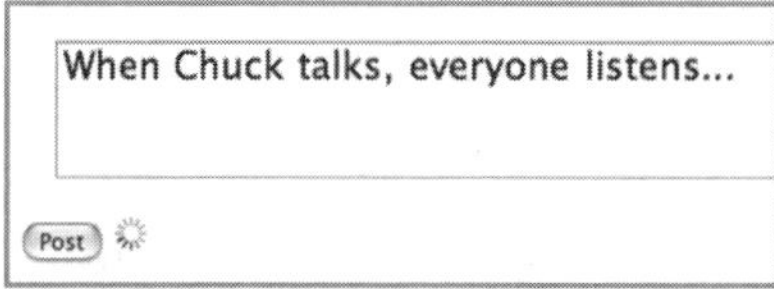

Figure 8.9 The Ajax spinner in action

8.4.3 Adding sizzle: animation and effects

You've already given Hubbub a makeover in this chapter, but it's time to go the whole nine yards and add animation effects for true Web 2.0 sizzle. If the last time you used JavaScript effect libraries was doing marquees in the late 90s, there's good news: things have come a long way.

Through libraries such as jQuery, YUI, and Scriptaculuous, visually stunning and cross-browser JavaScript has become a reality. A new level of engineering has created reusable libraries that degrade gracefully and integrate unobtrusively into your application.

You'll use jQuery for your visual effects. It comes with Grails, so there's nothing to install, and you can get straight to business. It also has many effects that can usually be implemented as one-liners.

INTRODUCING JQUERY ANIMATIONS

jQuery is a JavaScript library for a wide range of DOM manipulation techniques (including adding impressive visual effects to your application). Fading, appearing, flashing, resizing, and animating are all common UI interactions that jQuery offers.

If you haven't used a JavaScript animation library, you might be intimidated by the thought of complex animation code. Be comforted: jQuery provides good defaults for an incredible amount of behavior, making everything look great, even for the artistically challenged.

The first step in using the library is to include it in your page header (which you applied previously):

```
<head>
    ...
    <g:javascript library="jquery" />
</head>
```

With the library imported, using animation effects is a simple matter of invoking one of the numerous jQuery `effect` methods [for example, `$('myDiv').fadeIn()`]. Let's take it for a test drive by adding a `TinyURL` bar to Hubbub.

> **TIP** If you're chasing a full list of jQuery animations, you can find them on the jQuery website at http://api.jquery.com/category/effects/.

SLICK FADES ON TINYURLS

If you've ever used Twitter, you'll notice that any URLs you place in your messages are automatically compressed via URL shrinking sites such as TinyURL.com. Because URLs can be long, this URL-shrinking process helps keep posts that incorporate URLs under the 140-character limit that Twitter imposes. It's high time you added a TinyURL feature to Hubbub. And while you're at it, you'll add JavaScript effect know-how to make it look slick.

To make it easy for users to add URLs to their posts, you'll add a TinyURL entry box to the posting form. But users need a TinyURL entry box onscreen only when they want to include a URL in their post. So let's make a `div` to hold the TinyURL entry form on your timeline.gsp but have it fade in and dissolve out as required.

To make the div invisible by default, use a `display:none;` CSS tag:

```
...
<g:form>
    ...
</g:form>
<div id="tinyUrl" style="display:none;">
    <g:formRemote name="tinyUrlForm" url="[action: 'tinyUrl']"
                  onSuccess="addTinyUrl(data);">
        TinyUrl: <g:textField name="fullUrl"/>
      <g:submitButton name="submit" value="Make Tiny"/>
   </g:formRemote>
</div>
...
```

You've also taken advantage of the Grails `<g:formRemote>` tag in this code. The `formRemote` tag takes the contents of the form, serializes all the fields, and submits them as an Ajax request.

With your Ajax form now submitting, add a JavaScript link on your form to fade the div in and out as required. A simple link next to the Post button is fine:

```
...
<g:submitToRemote ... />
<a href="#" id="showHideUrl" onclick="toggleTinyUrl(); return false;">
    Show TinyURL
</a>
...
```

Then you need a little JavaScript to implement the appearing and dissolving. The code shown in the following listing can go almost anywhere in timeline.gsp, but it's a good idea to keep it close to the TinyURL form.

Listing 8.13 Implementing appearing and dissolving

```
...
<div id="tinyUrl">
    ...
</div>
<r:script disposition="head">
function toggleTinyUrl() {
    var toggleText = $('#showHideUrl');
    if ($('#tinyUrl').is(':visible')) {
        $('#tinyUrl').slideUp(300);
        toggleText.innerText = 'Hide TinyURL';
    } else {
        $('#tinyUrl').slideDown(300);
        toggleText.innerText = 'Show TinyURL';
    }
}
</r:script>
...
```

You'll dive deeper into that `r:script` tag in chapter 13, but for now note that the magic `disposition="head"` call ensures that this piece of JavaScript is pushed to the top of the page in the `<head>` section of the HTML, which means you can happily take advantage of it later in the page knowing that it's already been loaded into the browser.

The jQuery animation calls are one-liners, `$('myDiv').slideDown()` and `$('myDiv').slideUp()`, which pass the `div id` of your TinyURL form. This `effect` pair causes the TinyURL bar to smoothly appear and disappear from the top down.

You can also customize the time it takes for the effects to complete. We like to keep effects fairly quick to ensure they don't distract from the workflow. For example, we tuned the `slideDown()` to take half the default time:

```
$('tinyUrl').slideDown(300)
```

Consult the jQuery documentation (http://api.jquery.com/category/effects/) for the details of the `effect` parameters. Each API page on the jQuery side includes examples at the bottom, so you can see the effect running in your browser.

jQuery has shortcuts for most of the common UI features you'll want to animate. Now that you know how effects work, let's refactor your example with a one-liner:

```
<a href="#" id="showHideUrl"
    onclick="$('tinyUrl').slideToggle(300); return false;">
    TinyURL Bar
</a>
```

`$.slideToggle()` does all the appear and fade work you implemented in your custom JavaScript in a single call. Notice that we explicitly return `false` from `onclick` to ensure the browser doesn't follow the # link.

HANDLING JSON RETURN VALUES

It's good to have your TinyURL bar fading in and out, but what about when the user wants to use it? You'd like them to enter a URL, click the Make Tiny button, and have the post field automatically append the tiny URL to the current post's `textArea`.

To implement that, you need a way to do the following:

1. Bundle up the current full URL from the text field and send it to the back end via Ajax.
2. Calculate the TinyURL in some back-end controller action, and return the value.
3. Catch the return value in your view and append it to the `textArea` of the post.

You already have the code for the first step in the `<g:formRemote>` tag. The form submits the URL (as the `fullUrl` parameter) to the `tinyUrl` action on `PostController`. When the remote call completes, the `onSuccess` attribute contains the JavaScript function to be called on success.

The gee-whiz aspect is that the `onSuccess` target gets passed the result of the remote action. If your action returns text, XML, or JSON, you can use it in your client-side JavaScript function.

Let's implement your controller. The following code snippet shows your TinyURL implementation, which you add to `PostController`. You'll take the `fullUrl` the user passes in, and hand it off to the TinyURL website for shrinking.

```
def tinyUrl(String fullUrl) {
    def origUrl = fullUrl?.encodeAsURL()
    def tinyUrl =
        new URL("http://tinyurl.com/api-create.php?url=${origUrl}").text
    render(contentType:"application/json") {
        urls(small: tinyUrl, full:fullUrl)
    }
}
```

A Groovy enhancement to the URL class lets you access the contents of a URL by calling on the `text` property. In listing 8.14, you call the TinyURL endpoint, which returns a compressed version of the incoming `${origUrl}` value. Once you have the compressed URL, you can take advantage of the versatile `render()` method to return a small piece of JSON. The returned JSON contains properties for both large and small versions of the URL. You're only interested in the small version for display, but you wanted to demonstrate how to return multiple values.

Let's complete the picture by implementing the client-side JavaScript to process the returned JSON in your `addTinyUrl(data)` callback. The following listing, also from /view/post/timeline.gsp, shows the JavaScript for our handler.

Listing 8.14 Implementing JavaScript to process the returned JSON

```
<head>
    ...
    <g:javascript>
    ...
    function addTinyUrl(data) {
                var tinyUrl = data.urls.small;
                var postBox = $("#postContent")
                postBox.val(postBox.val() + tinyUrl);
                toggleTinyUrl();
                $("#tinyUrl input[name='fullUrl']").val('');
    }
    </g:javascript>
</head>
...
```

When the back end returns a content type of application/JSON, Prototype automatically `evals()` the return value into a native JavaScript object. From there, you can access the `small` property value you returned from your controller in the previous code snippet to display your tiny URL. Figure 8.10 shows the new feature in operation.

You've now got a good handle on jQuery eye candy, and you've even combined it with funky back-end Ajax and JSON magic.

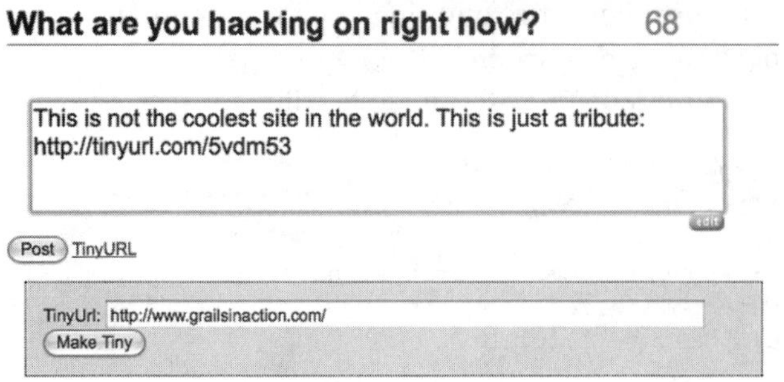

What are you hacking on right now? 68

This is not the coolest site in the world. This is just a tribute: http://tinyurl.com/5vdm53

Post TinyURL

TinyUrl: http://www.grailsinaction.com/

Make Tiny

Figure 8.10 The TinyURL feature in action

That completes your tour of Grails's Ajax functionality. We've covered an incredible amount about Grails UI features in this chapter, so let's wrap up.

8.5 Summary and best practices

You started this chapter by touring the basic Grails form tags and learning about more form tags than you'll probably ever need to use in one application. You also looked at how to develop your own custom tags for situations where the standard tags don't provide enough flexibility.

You then toured all the different options Grails gives you for layouts and templates, and you even implemented your own skins and navigation menus.

Finally, you explored advanced Grails Ajax concepts, implementing a dynamic timeline and a TinyURL codec that uses JSON to communicate with back-end services. Along the way, you picked up JavaScript animation skills to make it all sizzle.

You're learning and developing a few best practices:

- *Apply pagination.* Paginating large datasets creates a much better user experience and it's easy to implement.
- *Develop custom tags.* Take the time to develop reusable tag components for common parts of your UI. It'll save you time, simplify maintenance, and enable you to reuse them in future projects.
- *Use convention-based layout.* Favor convention-based layouts over explicit meta tags. Often a specific layout for one particular action can make things much more maintainable than doing meta-magic branching. Take advantage of meta tag styles when you need to style a subset of pages for a controller, but use convention layouts for the rest.
- *Lay out smarter.* Handle basic flash message display in your layout rather than repeating it for each view. Use templates for common HTML fragments, passing in explicit model elements. Inside Ajax calls, resist the urge to render HTML directly, and do any rendering via a template call.
- *Pick a JavaScript library.* Gain an appreciation of the strengths and weaknesses of the various JavaScript libraries. They all have different approaches and are

worth exploring. Choose an Ajax library that makes sense for the rest of your app. It takes time to download libraries, so minimize the number of libraries in play.

- *Use a layout library.* When developing complex CSS layouts, use Bootstrap. It'll save you time and look great on all browsers.

This section has taught you Grails's core concepts, so we'll move on to part 3, which discusses how to apply all this information to build the necessary pieces of a real-world application. Part 3 begins with chapter 9, which covers testing the view. You'll dive deep into Grails support for functional testing and make sure everything works great when deployed to a real browser.

Part 3

Everyday Grails

In part 2 of this book, you learned about the basic building blocks of Grails applications, ending with chapter 8, which discussed developing tasty forms, views, and layouts. In part 3, you apply your core knowledge to building all the necessary pieces of a real-world application.

In chapter 9, we'll teach you how to build robust tests for your newly developed code so you can make sure everything works properly before your code is deployed. We'll start with unit tests for all the basic Grails artifacts you've developed so far. We'll then build on those fine-grained testing skills with the broader ideas of integration and functional testing. By the end of chapter 9, testing will be your middle name.

Chapter 10 introduces Grails plugins—ways of extending your applications using third-party code modules. You'll use plugins to give Hubbub important functional enhancements such as email integration and full text search. You'll also solve performance and deployment pain points such as effective caching and database schema migration.

Security is a vital topic in deploying any kind of application on the internet, so chapter 11 gives you a thorough grounding in web security issues. After learning about the common vulnerabilities in web applications, you learn how to mitigate them and keep everything secure. We'll also take you on a tour of a popular Grails security plugin that allows you to add all sorts of access-control features to Hubbub.

Exposing your application to the world via a RESTful API has become standard practice for most successful modern web applications. In chapter 12, we talk about the ideas behind RESTful APIs and give you the tools to quickly build REST-style features into your application.

With a comprehensive set of back-end architecture knowledge in place, we turn our attention to the latest front-end techniques in chapter 13 and look at building Grails single-page apps using the popular Angular.js JavaScript MVC library. You'll wire up your shiny new front end to the RESTful services you developed in chapter 12 to consolidate all these technologies and see how they fit together in a Grails environment.

Rounding out part 3 is chapter 14, which takes you into the heart of Spring integration in Grails. You learn different ways of defining and interacting with Spring-managed beans in your application. Then you tour transactions—how they work and what they're useful for.

Upon completing part 3, you'll have all the knowledge required to deliver robust, full-featured Grails web applications.

9 Building reliable applications

This chapter covers

- The mechanics of running tests in Grails
- Test types and phases
- How to write unit tests with mocks
- Browser-based testing with Geb

You've made good progress with the Hubbub application, and you've seen all the core elements that make up a standard Grails application. The question now is how to further develop the application while ensuring that you don't introduce bugs—or at least as few as possible.

The answer is through testing! Throughout the first part of the book we used test cases to explain how bits of Grails work and to help you get into the testing habit. It's time to take stock and learn more about Grails' support for writing various tests so that your own projects can benefit from them. You'll find out how the unit test framework works and how to decide between different types of tests. And throughout you'll continue to use Spock, because it's ideal for all levels of testing.

Let's begin by looking at the testing infrastructure.

9.1 Running tests

When you run the tests for Hubbub, you see that Grails first executes the project's unit tests and then the integration tests. If the project were to have functional tests, those would run as well (after the integration tests). This is great before you push to production, because a simple call to `grails test-app` ensures that the application is ready. But for day-to-day development, running all the tests every time you invoke `test-app` slows your development cycle down to a crawl. That's not what you want!

Fortunately, the `test-app` command gives you control over what tests are run at varying levels of granularity. If you want to run the unit tests, that's easy. What about a single test case? Again, you can do that. By exploring the mechanics of the `test-app` command, you'll understand the Grails view of the world when it comes to testing.

9.1.1 Mastering test execution

When Grails runs the unit tests and then the integration tests, what determines that order? How does it know which test cases are unit tests and which ones are integration tests? How does it handle both Spock and more traditional JUnit test cases? The answers lie in the test execution framework, of which we're only going to scratch the surface.

Let's start with the ordering of unit tests and integration tests. Both are examples of what Grails calls test *phases*, and these phases have a specific ordering built into the framework. Figure 9.1 shows you the four standard phases and the order in which they run.

We'll discuss several of the phases in more depth in section 9.1.2 so that you can make an informed choice about which type of test to use for each part of your application. For the moment, let's focus on the mechanics of `test-app`. Think of the phases as one axis of choice: you can run any or all of the phases. Another axis provided by the test framework is the test *type*.

Type as a name is a bit generic, but in this context, type refers to the library that underpins a particular test case. What do we mean by library? Spock is a library for writing test cases, as are JUnit and TestNG. Hence Spock and JUnit are test types.

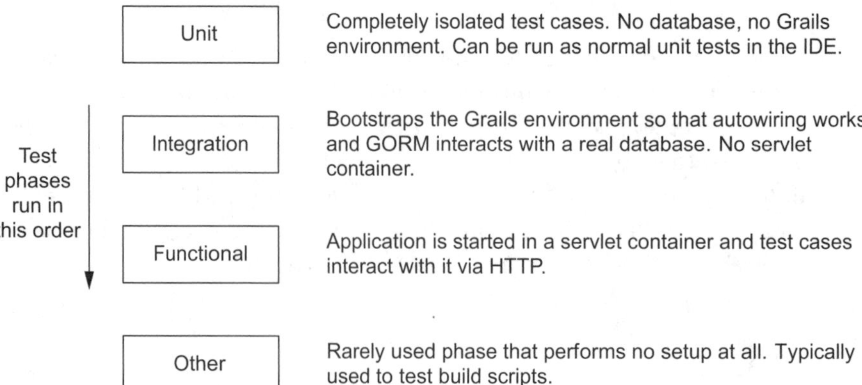

Figure 9.1 The four standard test phases

Why this talk of axes? They're one mechanism that allows you to choose what tests to run. When you execute `test-app` without any arguments, all types of tests are run in all phases. But to run only your Spock unit tests, you can use this simple incantation:

```
grails test-app unit:spock
```

The `unit:spock` argument is a directive of the form `<phase>:<type>` that tells `test-app` to restrict the executed tests to those that match the given phase and type. Here are more examples:

```
test-app unit:                                  <-- Run all tests in unit phase
test-app :spock                                 <-- Run Spock tests in all phases
test-app unit:unit integration:spock            <-- Run JUnit unit tests and Spock integration tests
```

Do you see the flexibility there? You can specify any number of directives, mixing phases and test types. And as you can probably infer from these examples, an empty string before or after the colon (:) acts as an implicit match all wildcard.

In reality, most projects stick to a single testing library the same way that Hubbub is using Spock exclusively, so you're unlikely to use the test type axis. But the first command shown previously for running the unit tests will likely become a regular fixture in your day-to-day development.

> **Where are my reports?**
>
> Grails prints useful output about test failures to the console as you run your test suite, but if you have many failures or you want more information about those failures, then more extensive reports are handy. You can find a beautifully presented HTML report at target/test-reports/html/index.html, or you can readily open it from the interactive console via the command
>
> ```
> open test-report
> ```
>
> which opens the report in your default browser.

The phase and test type axes are useful for controlling which tests are executed, but sometimes you want to execute a particular test case. Or perhaps even a single test method within a test case. For such fine levels of control, you need to pass an extra argument to the `test-app` command.

Let's say you want to run the `PostController` unit tests, because that's the class you're working on. You don't care about the tests for other classes. Use this command line:

```
grails test-app com.grailsinaction.PostControllerSpec
```

A quick look at the test reports confirms that `PostControllerSpec` is the only test case run. That's what you want, right? Yes, but two spots of ugliness are here: there's too much typing for the test case name (although autocomplete in the interactive console helps) and Grails starts the integration tests, slowing down the overall execution.

You may consider the long class name a minor inconvenience, but it doesn't have to be even that. If you don't specify a package with the name, Grails will automatically search for the class in *all* packages. And if your test cases have a conventional suffix ("Tests" for JUnit tests and "Spec" for Spock tests), you can leave that out, too. Now the command becomes

```
grails test-app PostController
```

Much better! As for the initialization of the integration tests when running the command, if you know the test case is a unit test you can add a phase directive:

```
grails test-app unit: PostController
```

Combined with the interactive console, command lines like this offer quick feedback on test failures. The basic form of this last argument is

```
<package>.<class>.<testMethod>
```

where both the package and the method name are optional. You can also use the wildcard "*" in place of the package or class. For example `com.grailsinaction.*` will match any test case in the `com.grailsinaction` package. We've included more examples in table 9.1 to give you a clear idea of what you can do and how to use wildcards. (Note that `SomeTests` and `HelperTests` don't exist in the Hubbub project.)

Table 9.1 Example test case patterns for the `test-app` command

Pattern	Example matches
`PostController`	`com.grailsinaction.PostControllerSpec`
`SomeTests`	`SomeTests` `org.example.util.SomeTests`
`com.*.*`	`com.grailsinaction.PostControllerSpec`
`com.**.*`	`com.grailsinaction.PostControllerSpec` `com.grailsinaction.util.HelperTests`

These examples cover the most common use cases for patterns. Other combinations are possible, but rarely useful. Note that you can even specify Spock test methods by using quotes. For example, from the standard command line you can execute

```
grails test-app unit: PostService.\"Invalid posts generate exceptional
➥ outcomes\"
```

Alternatively, you can use this from the Grails interactive console:

```
grails> test-app unit: PostService."Invalid posts generate exceptional
➥ outcomes"
```

In other words, you only need to escape the quotes when you aren't using the interactive console.

Before moving on, we should clarify the difference between the "*" and "**" wildcards in package names. If you think of packages as hierarchical names, then "*" represents exactly one package level, whereas "**" represents zero or more levels. Hence, using ** matches a wider result set (see table 9.2).

Table 9.2 Example test case patterns for wildcard usage

Pattern	Example matches
`*.SomeTests`	`util.SomeTests`, but not `util.other.SomeTests`

`**.SomeTests`	`SomeTests`
	`com.grailsinaction.SomeTests`
	`com.grailsinaction.util.SomeTests`

You now have full control over which test cases to run, allowing you to focus on the ones appropriate to the job. Specifying a single test to run when developing a new class is particularly useful. What phase should you target when writing a test—unit, integration, functional, or something else—is covered next.

9.1.2 *Choosing a test phase*

Whether you conscientiously follow the test-driven development (TDD) philosophy or not, it's important to decide what types of tests you want to write for different parts of the application. Your choices will determine how much test code you write, the length of your development cycle, and how robust your tests are in the face of changing application code. Don't worry. We'll guide you through the decision-making process.

The first order of the day is to learn how each test phase behaves and the implications for your own tests.

UNIT TEST PHASE

The majority of tests you have seen so far have been unit tests. What differentiates these is the speed with which they run because almost no setup is required by Grails to

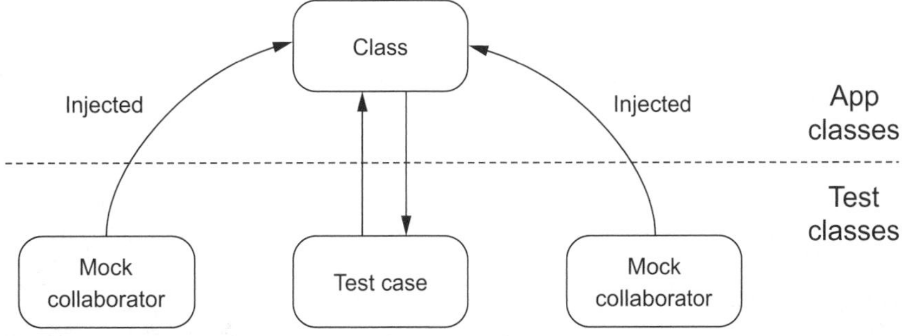

Figure 9.2 Structure of a unit test

run them. Another advantage of unit tests is that they can be run using your IDE's standard unit test integration, so you don't have to use the Grails `test-app` command.

The downside is that the usual Grails DI (for services, for example), the in-memory database, and the HTTP request/response handling aren't available. As a result, you often have to resort to mocking the collaborators of your class (see figure 9.2), something that we look at in more depth in section 9.2.

In the best of cases, unit tests are *black-box* tests that have no knowledge of the internals of the class under test. This makes them robust to changes in the internals of the method under test. Unfortunately most of your classes will have collaborators that need to be mocked, which results in tests that need to change when the code under test changes.

INTEGRATION TEST PHASE

Tests that run in the integration phase effectively run inside the application. GORM is initialized and works against whatever data source(s) you configure for the test environment (see figure 9.3). Your services are automatically injected into the controllers, services, and domain classes that depend on them. And any plugins you've installed are loaded. The only thing missing is the full HTTP request/response handling, although mock versions of the request and response objects are available.

Doing all this setup means that the tests have an initial startup cost that depends on the size of the project and the number of plugins installed. Using the interactive console helps reduce that initial hit after the first time you run the integration tests, but they still don't run as quickly as the unit tests.

Integration tests ensure your components work together correctly in the back end of the application. Those components may even be external to the application, perhaps as RESTful web services.

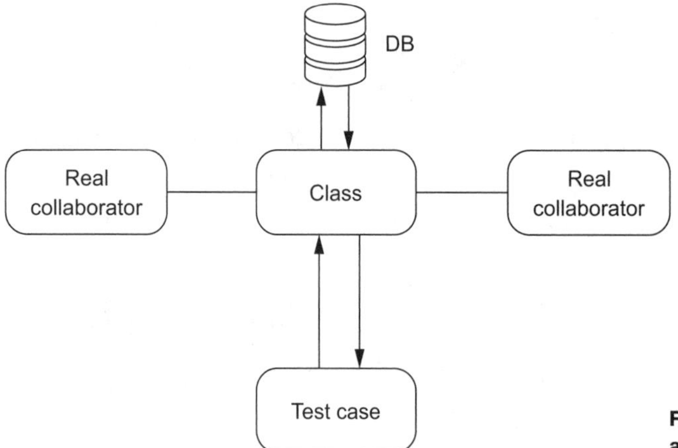

Figure 9.3 Structure of an integration test

FUNCTIONAL TEST PHASE

The functional phase of the tests starts your application in an embedded servlet container using a method similar to the `run-app` command (see figure 9.4). Your test cases no longer run inside the application—hence they can't call methods on the services directly, for example, but interact with the application via the HTTP protocol. Mostly they're used to test the UI of the application. If these pass and you have good coverage, you can feel safe in the knowledge that the application is going to work for your users.

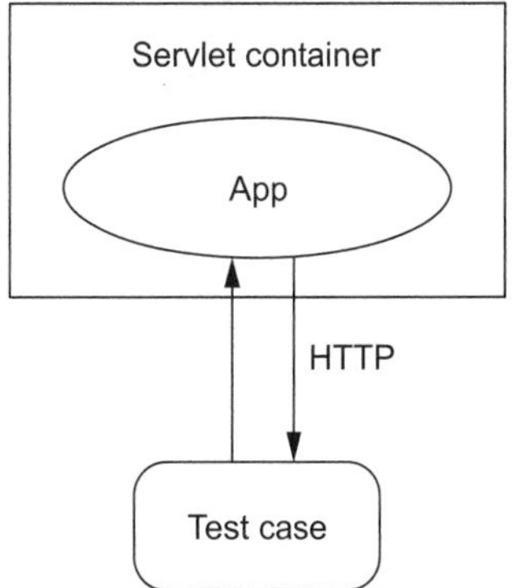

Figure 9.4 Structure of a functional test

Such UI testing isn't as simple as testing a bunch of methods with defined arguments and return values, but it's a critical part of application testing. Functional tests mimic what the user sees and does and are the main way to test your views.

TESTING STRATEGY

All of these test phases raise a big question: which phase should you use for any given test? No hard and fast rules exist for this, so we'll discuss what you should aim for as part of a testing strategy. The strategy you develop will then inform what type of test you should use for any given situation.

First, you want feedback as early as possible in your development cycle because that improves your productivity. As an extreme example, imagine that a bug can only be reproduced in a User Acceptance Testing (UAT) environment. Coding a fix may take only a matter of seconds, but it could take 15 minutes or more to get the app through to UAT to verify if it works. If the fix doesn't work, you have to go through another 15+ minute cycle to verify another fix. And so on. You definitely want to keep that code-test-verify cycle to a minimum. See figure 9.5.

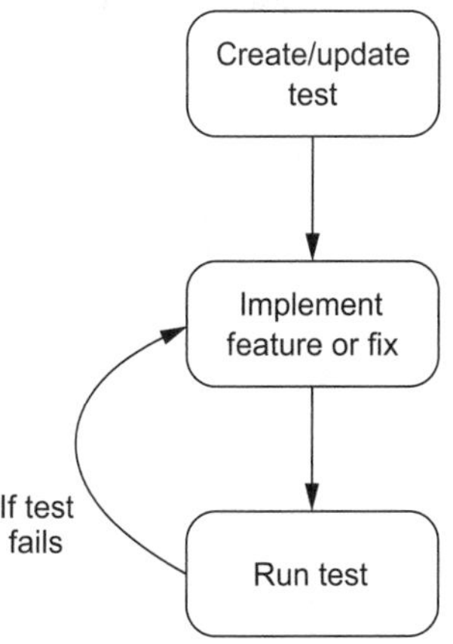

Figure 9.5 Testing strategy

Second, you don't want to change your tests every time the code under test changes. It's not uncommon for tests to depend heavily on the implementation of the code under test, such that any non-trivial change requires a fix to the corresponding test. After fixing a test for the umpteenth time, you'll be ready to throw it away completely!

Unfortunately, these two aims often come into conflict. The faster-running unit tests, particularly with mock collaborators, give quick feedback but break easily when the code changes. Integration tests are more robust, but slower running. The difference is even starker when comparing unit tests to functional ones.

Bearing all that in mind, we have guidelines to help you decide the best approach for your project.

1. *Always have functional tests.* These verify that the interface your users or clients interact with works as expected, replicating the user experience. This is usually the most important aspect of an application or system.
2. *Prefer black-box unit tests.* The more knowledge a test case has of the internals of its associated class, the more likely it is to break when the code is refactored. The most common manifestation of such knowledge is through mock objects. Once the number of mocks in a test rises above 1, the disadvantages of unit testing start outweighing the benefits.
3. *Use the interactive console.* It's important to keep the code-test-verify cycle as short as possible, so use the interactive console. All types of tests run significantly faster from it!

Functional tests are typically orthogonal to the other two types, so the main decision you need to make is what testing library to use (we'll discuss this in section 9.3). If you're having trouble deciding whether to write a unit test or an integration test for a particular class, the safest option is the integration test.

9.2 Understanding Grails unit tests and mocks

Imagine that your user registration controller action from chapter 7 not only saves a new `User` instance to the database but also sends a confirmation email via a service. As figure 9.6 demonstrates, both `User` and the email service are collaborators of the controller handling the user registration. And both collaborators depend on resources that are external to the application, such as the database and a mail server.

If you want to test the `register()` action, you have two options:

1. Write an integration or functional test that has a database and mail server.
2. Write a unit test and mock the collaborators, replacing them with fakes.

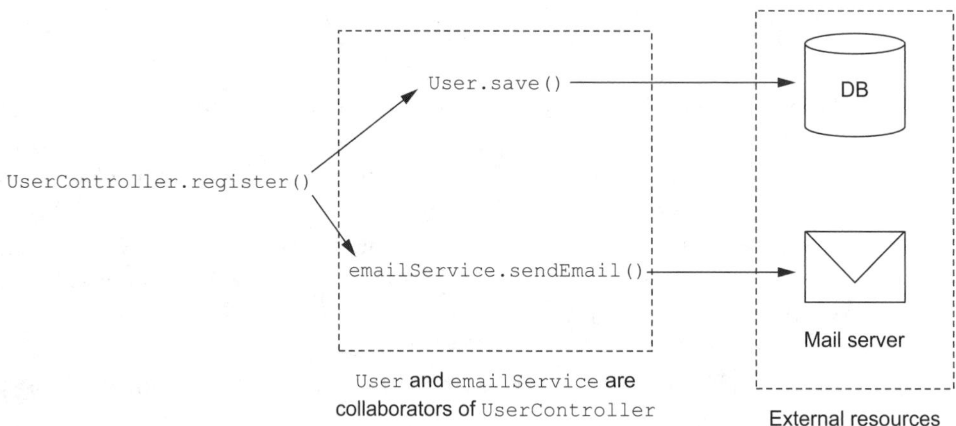

Figure 9.6 The user registration flow, including the controller's collaborators

Functional tests are useful, and we'll talk about them in the next major section of the chapter. For the moment, we'll focus on the unit test approach. You've already seen several examples of unit tests that mock particular types of collaborators, even if you didn't realize it at the time. Now we'll dive into the fundamentals of mocking in Grails unit tests so that you can handle any situation you'll face in the future.

The way you mock a particular collaborator depends on its type. If you go back to the user registration example, `User` is a domain class that Grails itself enhances to provide database persistence. Grails can mock that behavior because it knows what that behavior should be. The email service, however, is either written by your team or provided by a plugin. Either way, Grails has no knowledge of it and you must manually mock the behavior yourself.

Let's start with the built-in artifact mocking, because that's the form you're most familiar with from the many example unit test specifications you saw in previous chapters.

9.2.1 *Mocking core Grails artifacts*

Grails wires artifacts together and connects them to external systems. Domain classes are linked to a database, controllers are bound to an HTTP request and response, and so on. But when you're testing those artifacts from a unit test, none of that magic happens and the code doesn't work. That's where the Grails unit-testing framework comes in.

The framework provides a set of annotations that allow you to mock the enhanced behavior of selected Grails artifacts and use those artifacts as if they are in a running application. The annotations also add state and utility methods to the test case to make testing easier. As an example, let's take a look at part of `PostControllerSpec` in the following listing.

Listing 9.1 Using `PostControllerSpec`

```
...
@TestFor(PostController)
@Mock(User)
class PostControllerSpec extends Specification {

    def "Get a users timeline given their id"() {
        given: "A user with posts in the db"
        User chuck = new User(
                loginId: "chuck_norris",
                password: "password")
        chuck.addToPosts(new Post(content: "A first post"))
        chuck.addToPosts(new Post(content: "A second post"))
        chuck.save(failOnError: true)

        and: "A loginId parameter"
        params.id = chuck.loginId

        when: "the timeline is invoked"
        def model = controller.timeline()

        then: "the user is in the returned model"
        model.user.loginId == "chuck_norris"
```

Test annotations add the special Grails methods to artifacts, such as save() on domain classes.

@TestFor also adds params, controller, and model properties to the test case.

```
        model.user.posts.size() == 2
    }
}
```

How does this work? Does it even matter? We think it does matter because you'll inevitably need to do things in your unit tests that aren't explicitly shown in the book's examples or in the Grails user guide. We're going to delve under the hood and provide the glue between the book's examples, the Grails user guide, and the Grails API documentation.

The first key question is how the annotations add state and behavior to the test cases. You have to remember that these annotations need to work with different types of testing libraries, such as JUnit and Spock, so inheritance won't work without duplication. Instead, Grails uses a lesser-known Groovy feature: mixins.

MIXING EXTRA BEHAVIOR INTO CLASSES

Mixins are a feature borrowed from Ruby that allow you to mix the state and behavior from one class into another, effectively providing something similar to multiple inheritance. For straight Groovy you can do this through the `@Mixin` annotation. You can see it in action in the following listing by running the code in the Grails or Groovy console UI.

Listing 9.2 Using the `@Mixin` annotation

```
class Greeter {
    String message

    void greet(String name) {
        println message + ' ' + name
    }
}

@Mixin(Greeter)                      <- Adds the state and behavior of the Greeter class into Cowboy
class Cowboy {
    Cowboy() {
        this.message = "Howdy"       <- Accesses the mixin's properties
    }
}

def cowboy = new Cowboy()
cowboy.greet("Peter")                <- Calls a Greeter method on the Cowboy instance
```

You'll also find that the `this` reference in `Greeter` refers to the object that it's mixed into. If you add the line

```
println "'this' class: ${this.getClass()}"
```

to the `Greeter.greet()` method, you'll see

```
'this' class: class Cowboy
```

printed to the console.

That's all well and good, but none of your unit test specifications use the `@Mixin` annotation. That's because the `@TestFor` and `@Mock` annotations automatically mix special classes into your test case. These mixin classes serve two purposes:

- To enhance specific artifact classes so that they work standalone
- To provide properties and methods to help with verifying the state of the target system

To put this into context, think about what happens when you use `@TestFor` to test a controller class: the controller class magically gets the methods and properties it expects, such as `render()` and `session`, while your test case gets direct access to `session`, `request`, and other properties. Let's find out exactly where these properties and methods come from.

THE GRAILS UNIT TEST MIXINS

Each of the core artifact types has its own mixin class, all of which are shown in the class diagram in figure 9.7 along with the main methods and properties that get mixed into

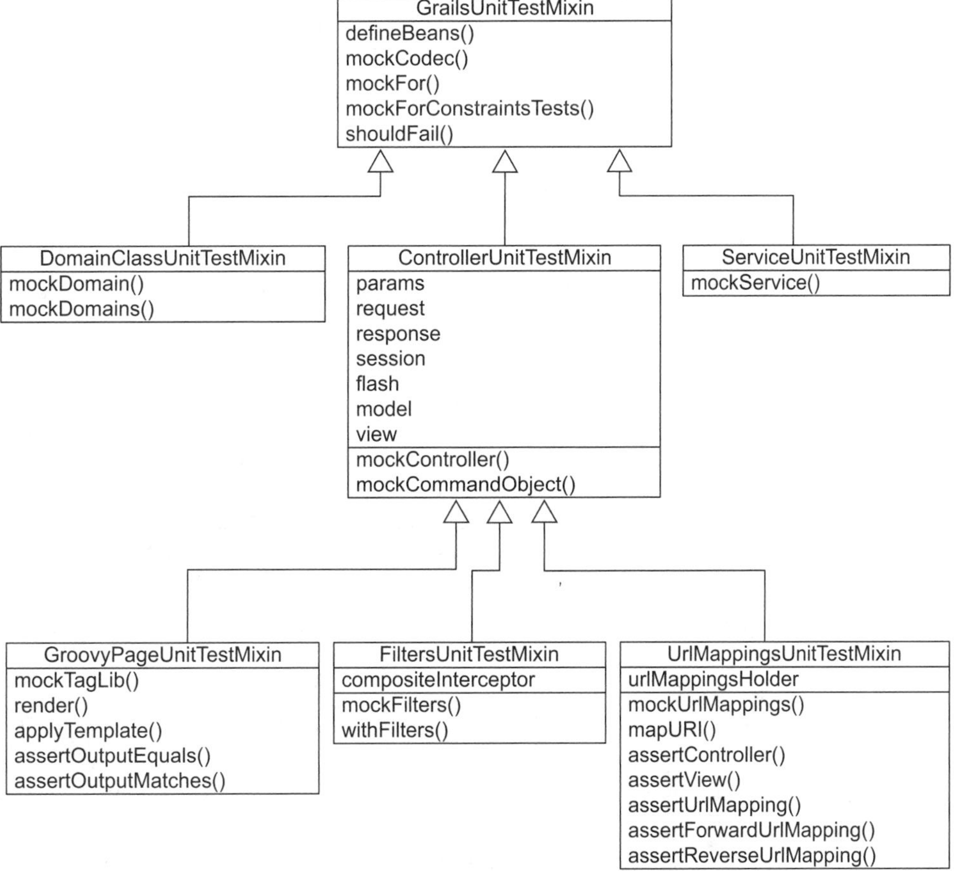

Figure 9.7 The unit test mixin hierarchy

your test cases. When you give the `@TestFor` and `@Mock` annotations one or more classes, the appropriate mixins for those classes are added to the test case.

Mixing these classes into your test case is only half the story. The annotations also ensure that the relevant `mock*()` methods are called so that each artifact class is correctly enhanced (`save()`, `delete()`, and so on, are added to domain classes).

To help you better understand what's going on, we reproduced `PostControllerSpec`, but this time we included the hidden, mixed-in code as italics in the following listing. In reality, it's not the real generated code, because that's liable to change between releases, but it does give you a good idea of what's going on.

Listing 9.3 Showing mixed-in code for `PostControllerSpec`

```
package com.grailsinaction

import ...

@TestFor(PostController)
@Mock(User)
@Mixin([ControllerUnitTestMixin, DomainClassUnitTestMixin])
class PostControllerSpec extends Specification {

    private PostController controller

    @Before
    void setupControllerUnderTest() {
        this.controller = mockController(PostController)
        mockDomains(User)
    }

    def "Get a users timeline given their id"() {
      given: "A user with posts in the db"
      User chuck = new User(
              loginId: "chuck_norris",
              password: "password")
      chuck.addToPosts(new Post(content: "A first post"))
      chuck.addToPosts(new Post(content: "A second post"))
      chuck.save(failOnError: true)

      and: "A loginId parameter"
      params.id = chuck.loginId

      when: "the timeline is invoked"
      def model = controller.timeline()

      then: "the user is in the returned model"
      model.user.loginId == "chuck_norris"
      model.user.posts.size() == 2
    }
}
```

Mixins added by both @TestFor and @Mock.

@TestFor adds a property, creates a new instance of the type under test, and enhances that instance.

@Mock mocks its classes.

Added to domain classes via mockDomains().

Added to test case via ControllerUnitTestMixin.

As you can see, the Grails unit test mixins do most of the heavy lifting. The critical code is inside those `mock*()` methods. Still, you must remember that these are unit tests and the mock implementations won't always behave exactly as the real ones do. The mock GORM implementation, as an example, doesn't support transactions or optimistic locking. If a unit test isn't behaving as you expect, use integration or functional tests to verify the expected behavior. You may have hit a corner case where a mock implementation doesn't match the real one.

The test mixins are the foundation for the built-in mocking of core Grails artifacts, but they don't help with the mocking of generic collaborators. What do you do when you need to mock out behavior that's added by a plugin at runtime? Or perhaps you want to mock a service that's tied to an external system, such as a mail server. In the next section you'll look at how Spock's built-in mocks can help with these scenarios.

9.2.2 Mocking normal collaborators with Spock

Lightweight, in-memory objects are your friends in unit testing. Consider strings: do you ever think about mocking them? No! You create them and pass them round. Difficulties arise only when a class is in one of the following categories:

- It depends on a tree of other collaborators
- It's expensive in memory or time to instantiate or use
- It's tied to external systems

Most Grails artifacts fall into at least the last of these categories, hence Grails comes with out-of-the-box support for mocking them. But Grails applications often have or depend on normal classes too, which can also fall into one of these categories. When those classes are collaborators of classes you're testing, you'll want to mock them out.

Many articles and bits of documentation exist about using mocking libraries in Java or Groovy libraries, all of which apply to Grails applications, too. There isn't a shortage of mocking libraries either. Our current preference is Spock's built-in mocking support, which we briefly introduced in chapter 7. We'll take a more extensive look at that while also investigating when and why you want to use mocks.

MOCKING SERVICES

In chapter 7 you used a mock object in place of a real `PostService` instance to test the `PostController` class. In fact, it wasn't strictly necessary to mock the service because you already mocked the `User` and `Post` domain classes in the unit test, and those were the only ties that `PostService` had to external systems. In addition, the service didn't have other collaborators. You could easily instantiate a new `PostService` instance rather than creating a mock. But it makes a nice, simple example, and it often makes sense to mock services as many of them have other collaborators or interact with other types of external systems, such as mail servers.

Let's take another look at the test case in question, as shown in the following listing.

Listing 9.4 Mocking services using `PostService`

```
...
class PostControllerSpec extends Specification {
    ...
    def "Adding a valid new post to the timeline"() {
```

```
        given: "a mock post service"
        def mockPostService = Mock(PostService)
        1 * mockPostService.createPost(_, _) >>
                        new Post(content: "Mock Post")
        controller.postService = mockPostService

        when:  "controller is invoked"
        def result = controller.addPost("joe_cool", "Posting up a storm")

        then: "redirected to timeline, flash message tells us all is well"
        flash.message ==~ /Added new post: Mock.*/
        response.redirectedUrl == '/users/joe_cool'
    }
}
```

Specifies required interaction

Creates new PostService double (as in stunt double)

What you should take away from this example is that you can readily mock classes (not only interfaces), and that mock objects serve two purposes:

1 To provide data to the calling controller (a new `Post` instance in this case)
2 To verify that certain interactions (typically method calls) take place

Any mock object that performs only the first function is, in reality, a stub, a special kind of mock. Used as test fixtures, these mock objects provide data as needed to the object under test. If that's what you need, you can use Spock's `Stub()` method instead of `Mock()` to make your intention clear, although it's not necessary.

In this example, are you interested only in providing data to the controller? Definitely not! The call to `createPost()` is critical to the correct behavior of the `addPost` action because that's how the new post gets persisted. There's no question that you want to verify that the service method is called exactly once and that its content argument is the same as the post text provided to the action.

You need to ask yourself when using stubs or mocks whether or not you care about a particular interaction. If you do, use a mock and give it a cardinality (the number before the `*`). Otherwise, a stub is simpler to set up and more robust to change. The problem with verifying interactions is that your tests become highly dependent on the internal implementations of the classes under test. Add only the truly important interactions to your specifications.

MOCKING DYNAMIC PROPERTIES AND METHODS

Services are mocked in much the same way as you mock collaborators in a normal Java application. But Grails isn't your run-of-the-mill Java web framework, so you might think that it presents unusual challenges. You're correct.

One of the most common challenges comes from the use of plugins. You'll see a few of them in action in the next chapter, but for now, imagine that the Mail plugin adds a dynamic `sendMail()` method to your controller classes that you then use, as shown in the following listing.

Listing 9.5 Adding `sendMail()` to controller classes

```
class UserController {
    ...
```

```
    def register2(UserRegistrationCommand urc) {
        // Register the user
        ...
        sendMail {
            to urc.email
            subject "Registration complete"
            body """\
${urc.fullName},

You are now registered with Hubbub under the login ID '${urc.loginId}'.

Welcome to the conversation!
"""
        }
    }
}
```

Call to dynamic method added by Mail plugin can't be mocked in the standard way.

The `sendMail()` method is similar to `render()` and `redirect()` in that it appears to be part of the controller without explicitly being declared. As you saw previously, the solution for `render()` and `redirect()` is to use the `@TestFor` annotation. But that won't work in the case of `sendMail()` because it's being added by a plugin—it's not a core part of Grails.

You can work around this by explicitly mocking the `sendMail()` method in the test using a standard Groovy technique for adding behavior to classes at runtime. Let's see it in action in the following listing, which shows a theoretical test case for the code in listing 9.5.

Listing 9.6 Using a Groovy mock

```
@TestFor(UserController)
@Mock([User, Profile])
class UserControllerSpec extends Specification {
    ...
    def "Registration command object for #loginId validate correctly"() {

        given: "a mocked command object"
        def urc = mockCommandObject(UserRegistrationCommand)

        and: "a set of initial values from the spock test"
        urc.loginId = loginId
        urc.password = password
        urc.passwordRepeat = passwordRepeat
        urc.fullName = "Your Name Here"
        urc.email = "someone@nowhere.net"
        urc.validate()

        and: "a mocked sendMail() method"
        def sendMailCalled = false
        UserController.metaClass.sendMail = { Map args ->
            assert args.to == "glen@bytecode.com.au"
            assert args.subject == "Registration complete"
            sendMailCalled = true
        }

        when: "the register action is invoked"
        controller.register2(urc)
```

Mail plugin adds `sendMail()` to controller, so you mock that method.

```
        then: "an email is sent"
        sendMailCalled
        ...
    }
    ...
}
```

Verifies `sendMail()` method is called.

This is an ugly solution to the problem, but it works. You have to manually insert assertions into the mock method if you want to verify its arguments and you also have to manually track whether the method is called. Generally speaking, it's best if you don't call dynamic methods directly like this in controllers. If you can use something like a service instead (the Mail plugin provides one), then do so.

Despite Spock's power, you need to understand the limitations of unit tests. If you find that a test has more setup code than anything else, consider switching to integration tests. This is particularly true if the object under test has a high ratio of interactions with collaborators compared to its own logic.

Ultimately, unit tests help support day-to-day development and keep you focused on small parts of the code base, but they don't represent validation of what the end user sees and interacts with. The only way to do that is through browser-based functional tests, which you'll spend the rest of the chapter looking at.

9.3 Testing the application as a whole

The main mechanism for interacting with user-facing Grails applications is via a browser. That browser displays HTML in combination with CSS and JavaScript. If you want your users to have a bug-free experience, you need to test the HTML generation and the JavaScript code. That's where functional tests come in.

As we mentioned previously in the chapter, functional tests rely on running the application within a servlet container and interacting with it using HTTP. But HTTP is a low-level protocol, so dealing with your application at that level involves work. Fortunately, many tools and libraries allow you to test at the level of HTML documents, making your life easier. The question then is which tool should you use?

Continuing our relatively opinionated approach to Grails development, you'll use only one tool in this chapter: Geb. The origins of the name are lost in the sands of time, but it's one of the most popular and actively developed functional testing tools around. It also has Spock integration, which gives it bonus points in our book. Let's see how to incorporate it into a Grails project and use it for tests.

9.3.1 Introducing browser-based testing with Geb

Several different types of functional testing tools exist. Various tools allow you to develop and run your test suite from within the browser itself (Selenium IDE, for example), while others skip the browser entirely and run headless, without any visual component (HtmlUnit and PhantomJS are examples of this type). Geb falls somewhere between these two types. It's a developer-focused tool, so you write code-based test cases. But it can launch a browser and test its interaction with your application. It can even use

HtmlUnit and PhantomJS in place of a browser. We'll discuss those options later. For now, let's see it in action so you can understand how it works and how to use it.

ADDING GEB TO YOUR PROJECT

Geb is a set of JAR dependencies and a Grails plugin. Adding it to a project means putting the relevant entries into your BuildConfig.groovy file, as shown in the following listing.

Listing 9.7 Using Geb

```
grails.project.dependency.resolution = {
    ...
    def gebVersion = "0.9.2"
    def seleniumVersion = "2.41.0"

    dependencies {
        test "org.gebish:geb-spock:$gebVersion"        <-- Adds Geb/Spock integration

        test "org.seleniumhq.selenium:selenium-support:$seleniumVersion"
        test "org.seleniumhq.selenium:selenium-firefox-driver
          ➥ :$seleniumVersion"
    }                                                   Uses Firefox for functional tests

    plugins {
        ...
        test ":geb:$gebVersion"        <-- Adds Geb Grails plugin
    }
}
```

Once these dependencies are added, you can start writing test cases straightaway.

WRITING YOUR FIRST GEB TEST

As with unit and integration tests, the source files for functional tests get their own home. In this case, that home (test/functional) isn't created when you first create the application. Nor is there a core Grails command to create a functional test case. You need to create the directory structure and source files yourself.

Let's start with a simple Geb test that loads the timeline for the user "phil" and verifies that the page title is correct and that the expected number of posts is displayed. The first step is to create the directory structure and source file for the test case: test/functional/com/grailsinaction/TimelineFunctionalSpec.groovy. If you're lucky, your IDE can do this for you, as long as you add test/functional as a source folder.

As you can see from listing 9.8, the initial test case looks like a normal Spock test apart from funky syntax that looks a little like what you may have seen with jQuery or another similar JavaScript library. The test case loads the timeline for a particular user, "phil", and checks that the level three heading (`<h3>`) above the "new post" text area contains the expected text.

Listing 9.8 A basic Geb functional test case

```
package com.grailsinaction

import geb.spock.GebReportingSpec
```

```
class TimelineFunctionalSpec extends GebReportingSpec {
    def "Check that timeline loads for user 'phil'"() {
        when: "we load phil's timeline"
        go "users/phil"

        then: "the page displays Phil's full name"
        $("#newPost h3").text() ==
                "What is Phil Potts hacking on right now?"
    }
}
```

Loads URL (relative to your application's base URL) (callout on `go "users/phil"`)

Uses a CSS selector to select nodes in displayed HTML page (callout on the `$("#newPost h3")` check)

When you run this via

```
grails test-app functional:
```

you'll see a Firefox window pop up. That's because Geb loads the requested URL in Firefox before querying the browser about the HTML content returned by the server. Best of all, the browser executes any JavaScript included by the HTML, so you can verify content that's added dynamically as well as the static content returned by the server. In an age when more and more applications are using techniques such as client-side (JavaScript) templates, that's important.

Listing 9.8 is straightforward because all it does is verify the state of a page. What if you want to model user interactions? Suppose you want to make sure that a user can post a new message to Hubbub and that the message appears in the timeline right away. Let's see what a corresponding Geb test looks like.

MODELING USER INTERACTION

Geb allows you to interact with all types of HTML fields, buttons, and links so you can mimic and test user interaction with your application. It's all done through a similar syntax to the previous example with CSS selectors identifying HTML elements that you're interested in and methods that interact with those elements.

We'll start by showing you how to test what happens when a user posts a new message via the timeline page. Figure 9.8 has the page and the underlying markup.

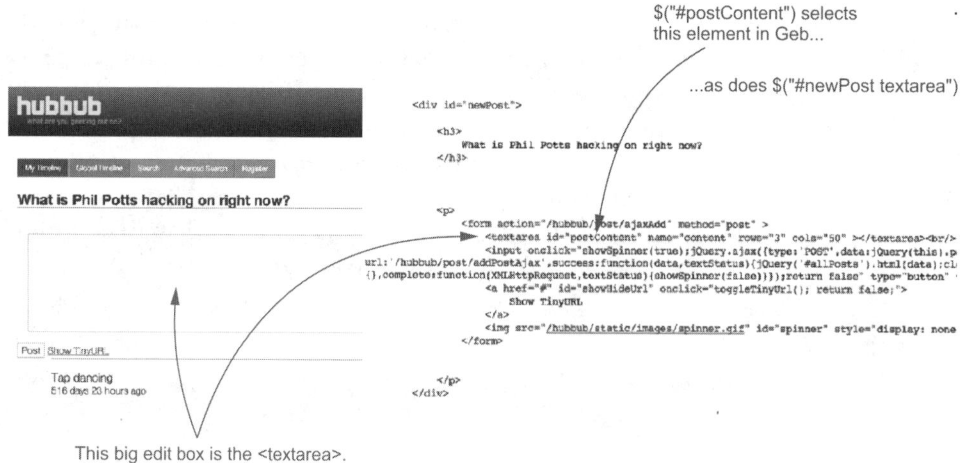

Figure 9.8 The markup for posting a new message

You can also see what selector you're going to use to get hold of that all-important `<textarea>` element.

To verify that a user can post a message, you're going to log in, load the My Timeline page, enter text into the text area, and click on the Post button. That's several interactions you need to perform via Geb. Let's add a new feature method to `TimelineFunctionalSpec` in the following listing to demonstrate that.

Listing 9.9 Verifying a user can post a message

```
def "Submitting a new post"() {
    given: "I log in and start at my timeline page"
    login "frankie", "testing"
    go "users/phil"

    when: "I enter a new message and post it"
    $("#postContent").value("This is a test post from Geb")
    $("#newPost").find("input", type: "button").click()

    then: "I see the new post in the timeline"
    waitFor {
        $("div.postText", text: "This is a test post from Geb").present
    }

    private login(String username, String password) {
        go "login/form"
        $("input[name='loginId']").value(username)
        $("input[name='password']").value(password)
        $("input[type='submit']").click()
    }
}
```

Needs to log in before posting (annotates `login "frankie", "testing"`)

Sets the content of the text area (with ID postContent) (annotates `$("#postContent").value(...)`)

Simulates pressing the Post button (annotates `$("#newPost").find(...).click()`)

Waits for the new post to appear in the page (annotates the `waitFor` block)

Factors out common interactions into methods (annotates `private login(...)`)

The `value()` and `click()` methods you see in the example are two of the available methods that simulate user actions, but they cover most of your needs. If you think about it, the majority of user interaction with web applications is through setting the values of form fields and clicking on buttons and links.

Listing 9.9 also introduces a vital part of Geb that allows you to test Ajax requests. By itself, Geb has no way to know when an Ajax request completes. If you want to verify the page content after the request completes, you need to specify a `waitFor` condition. The `waitFor()` method is similar to Groovy's `find()` in that it takes a closure whose return value is either true or false. In this case, the method continues waiting until either the closure returns true or the timeout limit is reached (5 seconds by default).

You kill two birds with one stone in listing 9.9 by making the content that you're interested in, the new post, part of the condition itself. If the new post fails to appear in the timeline, the test fails due to a timeout exception. But there's nothing stopping you from adding extra assertions after the `waitFor()`.

That's Geb in a nutshell. You should now be comfortable selecting nodes from an HTML page and interacting with them or verifying their content. The next step is for you to understand what's happening under the hood so you can make effective use of the tool and diagnose problems that you may encounter in the future.

9.3.2 Understanding how Geb works

It's hard to use anything effectively without understanding how it works. To that end, you'll look briefly under the covers of Geb and we'll explain its model of selectors and actions in further detail.

LOOKING UNDER THE HOOD

Geb is a framework built on top of Selenium WebDriver, which combines an API for interacting with a browser and a set of drivers that implement that API. Until now you've only used the Firefox driver, but several others exist, including separate ones for Chrome, iPhone, and Android. The basic structure is shown in figure 9.9 .

Why mention WebDriver? Geb does hide most of the details of Selenium WebDriver behind its own API, but sometimes problems manifest at a lower level. When that happens, it's good to know that you can do a web search for Selenium WebDriver, not Geb. It also helps explain the names of the dependencies you need to include for the different drivers.

One thing that stands out in figure 9.9 is that Selenium WebDriver can work through a real browser or it can effectively access the application directly over HTTP using HtmlUnit or PhantomJS. These are libraries that act as in-memory browsers and make for fast tests because Selenium WebDriver doesn't have to start a heavyweight browser as an external process. On the downside, experience suggests that HtmlUnit isn't ready for rich web interfaces with JavaScript, resulting in test failures for pages that work in other browsers. Some people have had success with PhantomJS, but there isn't enough data to support a recommendation.

When deciding whether to use an in-memory browser, we recommend that you compare its results to those obtained using a driver for a real browser. If the results match, great! You can then confidently use it for the development phase. But be sure to use one or more of the other drivers before your application goes off for user-acceptance testing or production.

MASTERING THE GEB SELECTOR MODEL

The previous section introduced you to the Geb notation that consists of a special `$()` function to select nodes from an HTML page. This is the only low-level API you'll use

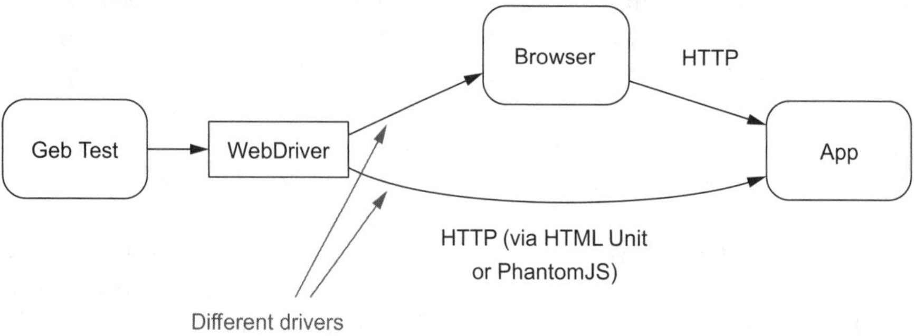

Figure 9.9 How Geb works

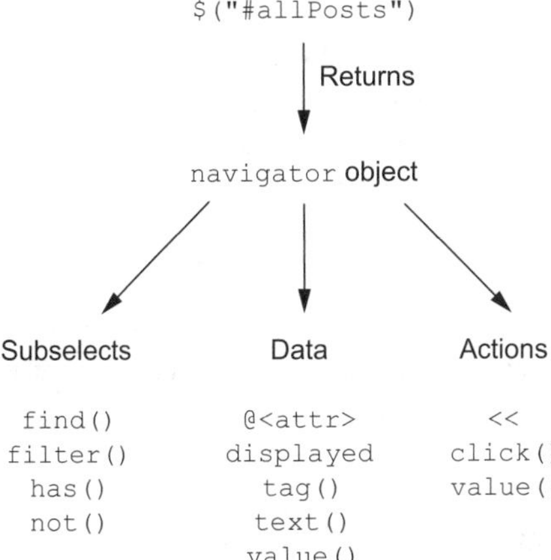

Figure 9.10 What you can do with the `navigator` object returned by `$()`.

in your Geb tests (you'll look at the higher-level page object API in the next section). If you understand the `$()` function and what to do with it, you're well-placed to write good, solid Geb tests.

The `$()` function gives you a `navigator` object (in Geb parlance) that you can then use to

- Select subelements of the HTML
- Perform user actions (such as clicking)
- Extract data

Figure 9.10 shows the most useful properties and methods in each category.

You'll look at subselects, data extraction, and user actions in more detail shortly, but first you need to learn how to use `$()` itself.

THE SELECTOR SYNTAX

The `$()` function has three main parts: a CSS selector string, an index, and constraints. Together, these provide a flexible mechanism for selecting the HTML elements that you're interested in. Figure 9.11 is a quick example demonstrating all three parts in unison.

All three parts are optional—`$()` with no arguments represents the entire document—but you'll find yourself almost always specifying at least a CSS selector. We won't go into the details of CSS selectors here, but if you're not familiar with them,

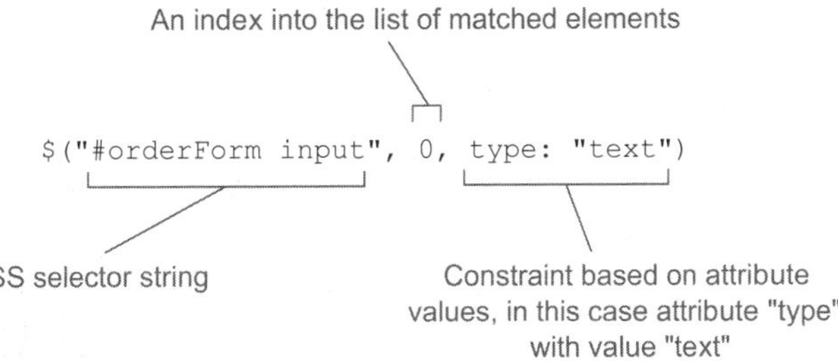

Figure 9.11 Example of the selector syntax

you should learn how to use them. It's difficult to do web application development these days without that knowledge, as CSS selectors are used in not only CSS but also JavaScript libraries and testing libraries such as Geb.

The named arguments of `$()` allow you to filter the matching elements further by constraining them to having particular values for certain HTML attributes. In figure 9.11 the name of the attribute is `type` with a value of `"text"`, which constrains the selector to `<input>` elements of type "text".

Geb understands one special attribute in this syntax: `"text"` (not to be confused with the attribute *value* you saw). This example only matches `<h3>` headings whose content is the same as the given text:

```
$("h3", text: "Understanding how Geb works")
```

In other words, the left-hand side of the colon is either text or the name of an HTML attribute.

The last part, the index, allows you pick individual elements from the list of elements matched by the other two parts. If only one matching element exists, the index is redundant. This does raise the question of whether there's any guaranteed order in which `$()` returns matching elements. The guarantee is that the order of the matched elements is the same as the order in which they appear in the HTML page.

Now that you know how to get hold of an initial list of nodes via the `$()` function, let's see what you can do with those nodes.

SELECTING SUBELEMENTS

Although the `$()` function is powerful for selecting nodes, you may want to further refine the selection, or use it as the base for traversing HTML nodes. Table 9.3 describes methods useful for such tasks. Check out the Geb user guide (www.gebish.org/manual/current/) for more details and a complete list of the properties and methods on navigator objects.

Table 9.3 Selection-focused navigator methods

Method	Description
`filter(cssSelector)`	Filters the element list for those elements that match the given CSS selector. It removes items from the list that *don't* match.
`find(cssSelector)`	Finds all child elements that match the given CSS selector.
`has(cssSelector)`	Similar to `filter()`, but only retains the items that have *child* elements matching the given CSS selector.
`not(cssSelector)`	Similar to `filter()`, but retains the items that don't match the given CSS selector.
`parent()`	Selects the immediate parent element of each item in the selected element list.
`previous()/next()`	Select the previous and next siblings of each item in the selected element list.

All these methods return another list of elements, or more specifically a navigator object. Both `find()` and `filter()` also accept the same arguments as `$()`: a CSS selector, an index, and named arguments. `not()` and `has()` only accept a CSS selector string.

EXTRACTING DATA

Verifying that a page contains what you expect requires a way to access the page content. That's where the properties and methods in table 9.4 come in. They give you access to the textual content of elements, attribute values, and other useful data.

Table 9.4 Data extraction properties and methods of the navigator object

Method/property	Description
`@<attr>`	Returns the value of the specified attribute on the first item in the element list. `<attr>` refers to the attribute name. You could use `$().@name` to get the value of the "name" attribute.
`display`	Returns `true` if the first item in the element list is visible, otherwise `false`.
`classes()`	Returns a list of the CSS classes for the first item in the element list.
`tag()`	Returns the tag name of the first item in the element list, for example, "p" for the `<p>` element.
`text()`	Returns the text content of the first item in the element list.
`value()`	Returns the value of a form element, such as a text field or text area. The value depends on the type of the form element. For text fields, this returns the text content (`text()` isn't appropriate in this case because `<input>` tags are empty HTML elements).

As you can tell from the descriptions of these properties and methods, they apply only to the first matching element of the navigator object. This is convenient for the many occasions when you expect a single element to match your criteria, but what do you do if you want to extract information from all matching elements? No problem: you can use Groovy's spread-dot (`*.`) operator. This returns a new list containing the information you want for each matching element in the navigator object. The following:

```
$(".postEntry")*.tag()
```

returns a list of `"div"` strings, one for each `<div class="postEntry">` element in the page.

PERFORMING ACTIONS

The last category of navigator methods relates to mimicking user interaction with the application. As the user interactions are fairly limited, you don't have many methods to learn. You saw two of them in action previously in the chapter. Table 9.5 summarizes those and a couple of others.

Table 9.5 Action-based methods on the navigator object

Method/property	Description
`<<(keysString)`	Sends key presses to the selected elements.
`click()`	Simulates the user clicking an element, be it a button, a link, or anything else that has a click handler.
`value(newValue)`	Sets the value of a form field, such as a drop-down list or a text area.
`<fieldname> = newValue`	This is a shortcut for `value()` that allows you to directly set the value of the field with name `fieldname`. For example, `$("form").username = "chuck_norris"` sets the value of the form field named "username".

All the properties and methods we've shown you in these three categories are part of the low-level Geb API, and you can find out more information about those and others in the Geb manual. With few exceptions, anything a user can do in a browser can be simulated with Geb.

Let's shift our focus from the low-level API because although it's essential, it's not a good idea to use it directly in test cases. We explain why and describe Geb's built-in solution next.

9.3.3 *Using page objects for maintainability*

Currently, you have one functional test class in Hubbub, and it performs checks on the timeline page. At this scale, using the low-level Geb API is fine because you don't have many opportunities to reuse selectors or other bits of code. As you expand the test suite, though, you need to think about how the test cases are likely to evolve and what they test.

WHAT'S THE PROBLEM?

The first thing to understand is that functional tests are interested in verifying the *behavior* of an application. Yes, part of that involves checking the state of different pages, but you're primarily interested in the user interactions that can take place across several pages.

Consider a user entering the URL for My Timeline into the address bar of a browser so they can post a new message. You first want to make sure that the user is redirected to the login page. Once the user enters the correct credentials, you want to ensure that the My Timeline page is shown correctly. Then you want to simulate posting a new message followed by verification that the My Timeline page is still displayed but also includes the new message.

Even in this one short sequence, you'll check the state of a page twice. The timeline page also features in many other functional tests, as does the login page. Do you want to manually use the `$()` function each time you need to verify that a page is displayed correctly? No, because any time someone changes the markup for a page, every test that checks the content of that page needs to be updated!

The Geb solution is based on something called *page objects*. These put the pages behind an abstraction such that your functional tests deal with pages, while the page objects handle the interactions with the markup. With this approach, only the page object needs to be updated when the markup for a page changes. That makes for much more maintainable tests.

What does this page object mechanism look like?

INTRODUCING THE PAGE OBJECT

Conceptually, a page object is a model that represents a page of your application. When you interact with a page object, you're not dealing directly with HTML elements but with logical parts of the page, such as a login form or a post entry in a Hubbub timeline. To show you what we mean, the following listing shows a Geb page object for the Hubbub timeline (located at test/functional/com/grailsinaction/pages/TimelinePage.groovy).

Listing 9.10 Sample page object

```
package com.grailsinaction.pages

import geb.Page

class TimelinePage extends Page {

    static url = "users"

    static content = {
        whatHeading { $("#newPost h3") }
        newPostContent { $("#postContent") }
        submitPostButton { $("#newPost").find("input", type: "button") }
           posts { content ->
               if (content) $("div.postText", text: content).parent()
               else $("div.postEntry")
        }
    }

    static at = {
        title.startsWith("Timeline for ")
        $("#allPosts")
    }
}
```

All page objects must extend geb.Page.

❶ Specifies the URL for this page relative to the application's base URL.

❷ Defines the page model, usually via the `$()` function.

❸ Specifies the conditions that an HTML page must satisfy to be interpreted as this page.

The three key parts of this definition are: the URL ❶ (we'll talk about the `to()` and `via()` methods shortly), the page model defined by the content block ❷, and an `at` checker that determines whether the current HTML document matches this page ❸. The exact role of each part will become clearer as we demonstrate how to use the page.

> **Why not $("title")?**
>
> You might think you can select the `<title>` element using the `$()` function and grab its content with `text()`. That's not the case because `text()` only works for content that's visible to the user in the page. The title isn't visible as part of the page.
>
> Rather than use `$("title")`, you can take advantage of the `title` property that's available on all page objects.

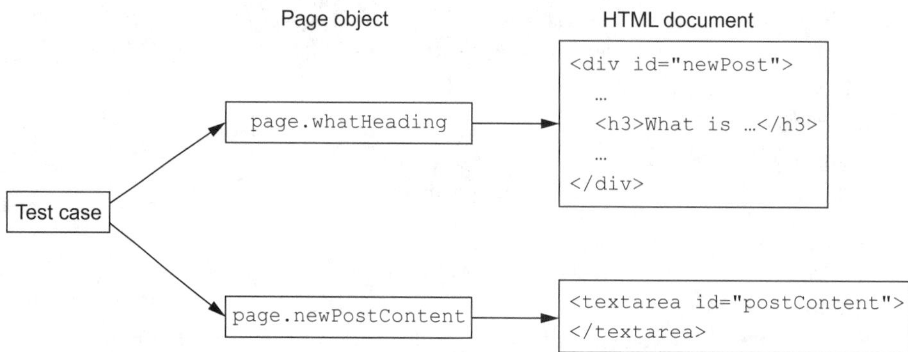

Figure 9.12 A test case uses the defined model of a page, and the model provides the binding to markup.

Perhaps the most critical part of a page object is the content model. Figure 9.12 shows how the model acts as an abstraction between your test cases and the HTML content of the pages being displayed. The idea is that you give important parts of the page (the stuff you interact with in the tests) names that you reference in your tests. You then bind those names to markup, usually with the `$()` function. Note that the closures for each name aren't required to return a navigator object—they can return anything you want.

Now that you have an idea what a page object is, let's see how you can refactor your timeline functional test to use the page object you just defined.

USING PAGE OBJECTS IN TESTS

On your first iteration of the timeline functional test, you used the `go()` method to open a particular URL and then the `$()` function to interrogate the page to verify it displayed the correct content. You now replace those functions with a new set geared toward page objects. The following listing shows a new functional specification testing the same thing as the previous one, but using page objects.

Listing 9.11 Sample page object in a test

```
package com.grailsinaction

import com.grailsinaction.pages.*            <-- Imports page object classes so you can reference them directly
import geb.spock.GebReportingSpec

class TimelinePageFunctionalSpec extends GebReportingSpec {
    def "Check that timeline loads for user 'phil'"() {
        when: "we load phil's timeline"
        to TimelinePage, "phil"                         <-- Opens timeline page for user "phil"

        then: "the page displays Phil's full name"
        whatHeading.text() == "What is Phil Potts hacking on right now?"   <--
    }
}
```

Verifies heading via the relevant model element in TimelinePage (the current page)

You can see from the listing that the test is more readable, because you're now dealing with names (`TimelinePage`, `whatHeading`) rather than URLs and CSS selectors. Using names improves comprehension, which makes it easier not only to understand what's going on and how the application is supposed to behave, but also to maintain the code.

The test introduces new syntax that we'll look at more closely so you can use page objects effectively in your own tests. We'll start with how to load the pages.

NAVIGATING TO PAGES

The mechanism for navigating to URLs represented by page objects is simple. Your page object declares a static `url` property (which can be either an absolute or relative URL) and then in your tests you use the `to()` method and pass the page object's class as the argument:

```
to TimelinePage
```

This method is provided by the abstract Geb super class and effectively invokes `go()` behind the scenes. It also performs an implicit verification on the resulting page to make sure that it *is* the timeline page. Remember the `at` block in `TimelinePage`? It looked like this:

```
static at = {
    title.text().startsWith("Timeline for ")
    $("#allPosts")
}
```

Geb turns each line of the closure into an assertion (like Spock does for the expressions in a `then:` block) and executes them whenever an `at` check is performed, such as at the end of the `to()` method. You can also force an `at` check at any time by calling the `at()` method like so:

```
at TimelinePage
```

In both the implicit and explicit cases, the `at` check throws an assertion error if any of the conditions are unsatisfied, which usually means the current page isn't the one you're expecting.

One issue with the `to()` method is that it can't handle redirects. Imagine that you want to navigate directly to Hubbub's My Timeline page. If you use `to()`, it attempts to verify that the timeline page is displayed. But what should happen is that the test browser is redirected to the login page. In this case, `to()` throws an exception because the current page is the login page, not My Timeline.

> **The current page**
>
> We refer to the "current page" several times in this section. Each time a new page is loaded, either through the `to()` or `via()` methods, or after a link is clicked, that page becomes the current page. All properties and methods in a Geb test then resolve against that page object.

(continued)

It's important to understand that the page object may not match the currently loaded HTML document. That's why `at` checkers are so important: they ensure that tests fail fast when the HTML document doesn't match the expected page

The solution to this problem is the `via()` method. This behaves like `to()` but doesn't perform an implicit `at` check. To verify that you're redirected to the login page, combine `via()` with `at()`:

```
via TimelinePage
at LoginPage
```

The basic usage of `to()` and `via()` is straightforward. Now consider a more awkward scenario: the timeline page can display the timeline for different users, but each user has a different URL of the form /users/<loginId>. This doesn't fit the model of a single static URL defined in the page class unless you want to tie the page object to a particular user. Fortunately, Geb has you covered.

The `to()` and `via()` methods take additional arguments that are concatenated with / and appended to the URL defined in the page object. Your `TimelinePage` has

```
static url = "users"
```

and when you invoke `to()` like this

```
to TimelinePage, "phil"
```

the test browser navigates to the URL /users/phil (relative to the application URL, for example, http://localhost:8080/hubbub). If you want to add query parameters to the URL, use named arguments. For example,

```
to TimelinePage, "phil", max: 10, offset: 0
```

navigates to /users/phil?max=10&offset=0. And as far as syntax goes, you have everything you need to solve 98% of your page navigation needs. For the rare occasions when you need more flexibility, Geb allows you to customize the way the `to()` arguments are converted into a path.

TIP See the section "Advanced Page Navigation" in the "Pages" chapter of the Geb manual[1].

Once you've navigated to a page, you can interact with it either by picking out bits of its content or filling out forms and clicking on things. How you do that depends on how you define the content model of the page.

1 Advanced Page Navigation, http://www.gebish.org/manual/current/pages.html#advanced_page_navigation.

CREATING A RICH CONTENT MODEL

As you saw previously, you define a content model through a DSL that binds a name to content in an HTML page. In the example

```
static content = {
    whatHeading { $("#newPost h3") }
    ...
}
```

you're binding the name `whatHeading` to a Geb navigator object that matches a particular level three heading. In this case, the closure associated with the name returns a navigator object, but it can return anything. To access this returned value directly from your Geb test case, treat it as a property:

```
then: "the page displays Phil's full name"
whatHeading.text() == "What is Phil Potts hacking on right now?"
```

As `whatHeading` is bound to a navigator object, we call `text()` on the property to get the element content.

Such content definitions are straightforward, because you effectively bind a name to fixed markup on the page. It's the same as when you declare a URL in a page object: you have a one-to-one mapping between the two sides. And as with the URLs, this can be limiting when markup can be different based on data provided to the page. That's where parameterization comes in.

You've already seen a parameterized content definition in `TimelinePage`. Here it is again to refresh your memory:

```
static content = {
    ...
    posts { content ->
        if (content) $("div.postText", text: content).parent()
        else $("div.postEntry")
    }
}
```

It looks similar to the other content definitions, but with an explicit argument on the closure. This argument allows you to parameterize the definition. In this case, the `posts` definition returns the Hubbub post that has the given content or all the posts if the argument is empty. With this definition in place, you can fetch the markup for a specific post using this code in your test:

```
then: "the new post is displayed"
!posts("This is a test post from Geb").empty
```

Rather than referencing the content definition as a property as you did previously, you use a method with arguments that match the parameters of the content definition closure. In this case, the `content` argument of the closure gets the value `"This is a test post from Geb"`.

The content definition isn't only about retrieving data from a page. Because it can and often does return a `navigator` object, you can also use it to set form fields, click on links, or perform any of the actions we discussed previously. Bringing this all together, the second test for `TimelinePageFunctionalSpec` becomes what's shown in the following listing.

Listing 9.12 Submitting a new post

```
...
def "Submitting a new post"() {
    given: "I log in and start at my timeline page"
    login "frankie", "testing"
    to TimelinePage, "phil"

    when: "I enter a new message and post it"
    newPostContent.value("This is a test post from Geb")
    submitPostButton.click()

    then: "I see the new post in the timeline"
    waitFor { !posts("This is a test post from Geb").empty }
}

private login(String username, String password) {
    to LoginPage
    loginIdField = username
    passwordField = password
    signInButton.click()
}
...
```

No CSS selectors are in sight! And the content model can be used the same way in any other functional test cases. If any markup changes in a page, update the content definitions of the page object and smile as your tests pass.

We leave it as an exercise for you to create the `LoginPage` class (in the same package as `TimelinePage`). If you run into trouble, you can find an example implementation in the chapter source.

Significant changes to a page may result in the content definition no longer reflecting the structure correctly. When that happens, you may have to update the content model in a breaking way, such as changing content definition names or what they return. When that happens, your test cases will need to be fixed. But remember that such changes to a UI happen much less frequently than simple tweaking of markup. And page objects completely remove the trauma of the latter.

On modules

Geb modules are to page objects as Grails partial templates are to views. They have content definitions like page objects but no URL. They represent parts of pages rather than whole pages. They're particularly useful when the same block of markup is used on different pages.

> ***(continued)***
>
> Modules are well covered in the Geb manual and are defined in a similar way to page objects, so we don't cover the detail here. One useful tip is to define a module for each of your GSP partial templates.

Geb is a rich framework for functional testing built on top of the well-established tool Selenium WebDriver. At this point, not only can you write Geb tests for normal pages and Ajax-based ones, but you can also more easily diagnose problems and use testing techniques that are more advanced.

Ultimately, end-to-end testing isn't easy, but it rewards you with confidence in releasing new versions of your application. The investment in time is well worth it, and as with other things in life, the more you practice developing Geb tests, the easier it becomes to write and maintain them.

9.4 Summary and best practices

Some people take to testing with a vengeance and vigorously follow TDD principles. For others, it's more of a chore. Grails can't really change that, but it does reduce the effort required to write, manage, and run the tests for your application. Spock is a big help, too, by encouraging you to formulate your tests in a specific way.

The key point to remember is that each test phase has its place. The unit tests execute quickly and are great for testing the logic in a class independently of everything else in the application. Integration tests allow you to easily test services and everything they depend on without worrying about HTTP requests and HTML. Functional tests ensure that everything is working properly as a whole.

The following guidelines will help you get the most out of your testing:

- *Always write functional tests.* If you test at only one level, make sure it's the functional level. This is the best way to ensure your application works as a whole. We still recommend that you write unit and integration tests where appropriate because they will save you time in the long run by providing quicker feedback on errors.
- *Get in the habit.* Practice makes perfect and the more tests you write, the easier it becomes. Once testing becomes a habit, it won't feel like a chore and you'll reap the benefits of a more reliable application.
- *Make testing easy.* The testing tools we have mentioned in this chapter aim to make testing easier. But you will always find that applications have their own difficulties, such as spawning external processes or integrating with web services. It's easy to avoid testing such things because they are difficult. Doing so will leave big gaps in your test coverage. Invest the time to make things easy to test so developers aren't tempted to skip writing them.
- *Make use of other tools.* We have only covered a few tools in this chapter. Other tools can help improve your productivity and the reliability of your apps. For example,

CodeNARC can pick up likely sources of bugs from static analysis of your code, while the Code Coverage plugin and Clover can check your test coverage.

This ends our coverage of the core features of Grails, which form the basis of all Grails applications. During this journey we've seen plenty of core features that are implemented via plugins, such as the scaffolding and the database access. Plugins are such a fundamental part of application development with Grails that we look at how the plugin system works in the next chapter.

10 Using plugins: just add water

This chapter covers

- Integrating email support
- Taking advantage of caching
- Migrating database structures
- Adding full-text search

Few things in life do exactly what you want, and unsurprisingly Grails is no different. Fortunately, a wealth of Java tools and libraries are out there to help you implement almost any feature you could want. Because Grails is inherently a Java-based framework, you can use almost any Java library out there. Many of them are robust and mature, so why reinvent the wheel?

You can use Java libraries as is, but there can be big benefits to having an adapter between Grails and the library that makes it easier to use and quicker to set up. This is the purpose of the Grails plugin system. The idea is that functionality is bundled into modules that can be loaded by the framework and integrated into the system. That functionality may be full-text search, tag clouds, or a fancy new UI technology. In fact, many of the features of Grails are implemented as plugins themselves, including GORM.

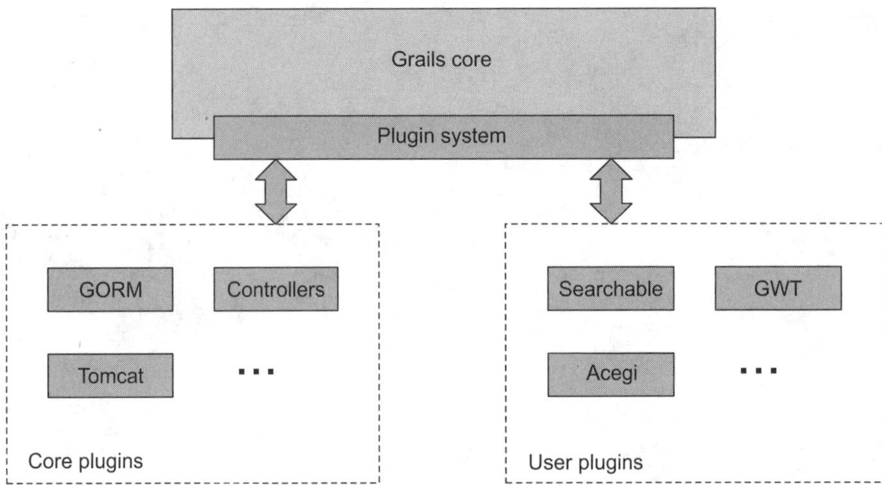

Figure 10.1 The plugin architecture

You can see how the plugins relate to Grails and each other in figure 10.1. If you're familiar with Eclipse or any of the other Java-centric IDEs, their plugin systems are analogous to Grails's own.

The upshot of all this is that anyone can provide extra functionality by writing a plugin, and that's what many people have done. You'll see how easy it is to install these plugins into your applications, effectively giving them a shot of steroids. From section 10.2 to the end of the chapter, you'll explore available popular and cool plugins.

10.1 Taking advantage of others' hard work

When might you want to install a plugin? If you find yourself with a feature requirement that doesn't sound specific to your application—one that's not directly related to your business logic—look for existing plugins that promise to do the job for you. If you'd use a separate library or tool to do the job in a plain Java project, then a plugin is probably the best solution in Grails. Remember, it's rarely a good idea to reinvent the wheel.

Take Hubbub. You want to send emails from various parts of the application, such as a user registration module or a daily email digest module, but emailing isn't what Hubbub is about. The feature is outside the core of Hubbub and is common to different types of applications. That makes it an ideal plugin candidate, and you won't be surprised to learn that an Email plugin already exists.

Once you've decided that there may be a plugin that does what you need, it's time to find the appropriate one.

10.1.1 Finding plugins

The two main sources of information about plugins are the Grails Central Plugin Repository and the Grails website.

THE GRAILS PLUGIN REPOSITORY

Grails has a couple of commands that can be used to query for plugin information, both of which work against what's known as the Grails Plugin repository. This is a centralized online storage area that hosts many of the available Grails plugins, making it easy for Grails to query for, install, and upload them. As you'll see in chapter 20 (available online as bonus content), you can even set up your own local repository.

For now, we're interested in the querying capabilities:

```
grails list-plugins
```

This command produces output similar to this:

```
Plugins available in the grailsCentral repository are listed below:
-------------------------------------------------------------
acegi                <0.5.3.2>         --  Acegi Plugin
activemq             <0.4.1>           --  Grails ActiveMQ Plugin
...
```

As the `list-plugins` name suggests, this command lists all the plugins in the repository. For each one, it displays the name, latest version, and a short description. You may notice that some plugins show both <> and an empty descriptions field. In many cases, this is a sign that the plugin was added to the repository before Grails 1.0, and it hasn't been updated. Proceed with extreme caution since such plugins will almost certainly not work with modern Grails versions.

> **Under the hood**
>
> The Grails plugin repository is implemented as a Maven repository accessible via HTTP, so you need internet access. The structure of the directories and files in the repository follows conventions that allow Grails to download specific versions of a plugin.
>
> If you need to configure an HTTP proxy, run this command:
>
> ```
> grails set-proxy
> ```
>
> Enter the details as requested. The list of plugins is cached locally in a file called plugins-list-grailsCentral.xml, which is typically located in $HOME/.grails/2.x/.

The list of plugins is long. If you run on a Unix-like system, such as Mac OS X or Linux, we suggest that you pipe the output through grep, like so:

```
grails list-plugins | grep "mail"
```

This isn't possible on Windows (unless you use Cygwin), but the plugins are listed alphabetically, so you shouldn't have much trouble browsing the list.

Now that you have the list, what's next? You want to find out whether there's a plugin that makes it easy to send emails from Hubbub, so look for anything to do with "mail." It shouldn't take you long to find an entry in the list for the Mail plugin, which according to its description "provides mail support to a running Grails application." That looks like the ticket.

Once you have the name of a plugin, you can find out more about it with this `plugin-info` command:

```
grails plugin-info mail
```

You receive results similar to this:

```
--------------------------------------------------------------------------
Information about Grails plugin
--------------------------------------------------------------------------
Name: mail          | Latest release: 1.0.1
--------------------------------------------------------------------------
Provides Mail support to a running Grails application
--------------------------------------------------------------------------
Author: Grails Plugin Collective
--------------------------------------------------------------------------
Author's e-mail: grails.plugin.collective@gmail.com
--------------------------------------------------------------------------
Find more info here: http://gpc.github.com/grails-mail/
--------------------------------------------------------------------------

This plug-in provides a MailService class as well as configuring the
necessary beans within the Spring ApplicationContext.

...
```

The important information here is the location of online documentation (http://gpc.github.com/grails-mail/, in this example) and the long description, which should provide enough information to decide whether or not the plugin is suitable. See the "Don't choose a dead (or dying) plugin" sidebar for more information.

Although the Grails Plugin repository makes life easy for the user, not all plugins are available through it. Those that aren't can often be found via the Grails website.

THE GRAILS WEBSITE

Along with plenty of other useful information for the discerning Grails developer, the main Grails website has a page that lists plugins by category. It also has documentation for many of them, which means that searching for plugins on the website can be fruitful. The downside to the website is that it relies on users and plugin authors to keep it up to date, so its information may be out of date, incorrect, or nonexistent for some plugins.

You can find the categorized list at http://grails.org/plugins/. Here you can search for plugins and their reference information. You can even see usage stats and vote for the plugins you think are the best.

What should you do if you can't find what you're looking for either via the Grails commands or the website? As a last resort, you can always ask your question on Stack-Overflow (http://stackoverflow.com) and tag it as a Grails question. The community is friendly and responsive.

Once you find a plugin you want to use, you can install it into your application.

> **Don't choose a dead (or dying) plugin**
> Many plugins in the Grails plugin system are no longer maintained by their original author—such is life in an open source ecosystem. Always check how active a plugin is before committing yourself to it. Look for date of last update, popularity within the plugin portal, or even the date of recent commits on the project GitHub site before you go banking your next world-beating application on dead code.

10.1.2 *Installing plugins via the (deprecated) install-plugin command*

As with almost any piece of software, you have to install a plugin before you can use it. Back in the Grails 1.x days, Grails had a simple command that would do this for you:

```
grails install-plugin <plugin name>
```

Provide the name of the plugin you want, and Grails would fetch the latest version from the Grails plugin repository and install it locally. Use the name displayed by the `list-plugins` command—in our previous example, the name is mail.

Although this feature was initially fantastic for productivity, as the Grails ecosystem grew it ended up being a world of pain when different plugins included other plugins as their dependencies. The feature was deprecated in Grails 2.0 and replaced with a more comprehensive Maven-style dependency mechanism using /grails-app/conf/BuildConfig.groovy. You still see older tutorials reference the install-plugin mechanism, but we take you through the best way to install plugins for maximum future compatibility.

10.1.3 *Installing plugins via BuildConfig.groovy*

Under Grails 2.x, the best way to install plugins is via /grails-app/conf/BuildConfig .groovy. To install a plugin here, you need to know the name of the plugin along with the version you want to install. You can get that information through the `grails plugin-info` command that we introduced you to in the last section. If you run that command for the Mail plugin using `grails plugin-info mail` you see a section marked Dependency Definition:

```
Dependency Definition
--------------------------------------------------------------------------------
    :mail:1.0.1
```

This section tells you the information you need for including the plugin in your project. In the following listing, let's edit the Hubbub /grails-app/conf/BuildConfig.groovy to add the definition for the Mail plugin at the end of the plugins block:

Listing 10.1 Adding the Mail plugin definition

```
plugins {

      runtime ":hibernate:$grailsVersion"
      runtime ":jquery:1.8.3"
      runtime ":resources:1.1.6"
      runtime ":database-migration:1.3.2"
```

```
        build ":tomcat:$grailsVersion"

        compile ':cache:1.0.1'
        compile ':mail:1.0.1'
    }
```

We explain the different dependency scopes in detail in chapter 17, but for now, you added the plugin in `compile` scope because you need the classes and services supplied by the Mail plugin when you're writing updates to Hubbub.

> **Where are my plugins?**
>
> You've installed a plugin or two, but where did Grails put them? Although you don't need to know where they are, they can be a great source of instruction and inspiration when you decide to write your own plugins.
>
> By default, Grails stores plugins in
>
> `$HOME/.grails/<grailsVersion>/projects/<project>/plugins`
>
> where `$HOME` represents the current user's home directory, `<grailsVersion>` is the version of Grails used to install the plugin, and `<project>` is the name of the project you installed it into.
>
> Global plugins go into a slightly different place because they aren't associated with a particular project:
>
> `$HOME/.grails/<grailsVersion>/global-plugins`
>
> In chapter 20 (available online) we show you how to control where Grails stores project plugins.

10.1.4 Plugin dependencies

Many plugins are self-contained, meaning that everything they require is either available through Grails or packaged in the plugin. Other plugins that are more complex may require features provided by other plugins—they depend on those other plugins, which may in turn depend on other plugins.

Figure 10.2 shows a (rather contrived) example of plugin dependencies for a Grails application. As you can see, managing the plugins and their dependencies yourself would be labor-intensive, and that's why Grails manages them for you. When you install a plugin, Grails automatically checks what plugins it depends on and installs those that haven't been installed.

Consider figure 10.2 and imagine you want to install Plugin A. When you compile your application after adding a /grails-app/conf/BuildConfig.groovy entry for Plugin A, Grails automatically fetches and installs Plugins D, E, F, and G because Plugin A depends on them either directly or indirectly. Alternatively, if you have Plugin B installed, then Grails installs only Plugins D, F, and G—Plugin E is already installed because of B.

As a user of plugins, all of this is transparent to you. It's okay if you don't understand what's going on at this stage. One thing to be aware of is that if you install a plugin from

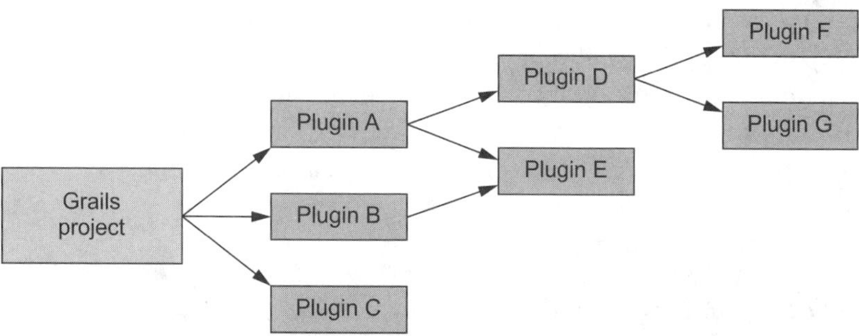

Figure 10.2 Example plugin dependencies for a project

a zip archive rather than a plugin repository, Grails still attempts to install its dependencies from the repository. This may not be a problem for you, but it's useful to know.

10.1.5 Applying your knowledge: the Hubbub extreme makeover begins

Now that you have a feel for how plugins are installed, uninstalled, and otherwise managed, it's time to apply all that theory to a real project. You're going to spend the rest of this chapter being introduced to several popular Grails plugins and giving Hubbub an extreme makeover, adding popular features you're likely to use in your own applications, such as caching, email integration, and full-text search.

Once you get a feel for how plugins can quickly add features to your application, you'll find yourself addicted to the near-instant gratification that this style of functionality reuse provides. Let's start with using that Mail plugin in Hubbub.

10.2 Adding mail support

If your application offers any sort of user sign-up capability, it won't be long before you need to implement email support. Whether you need to send sign-up welcome emails, respond to forgotten-password messages, or support a daily digest, having email capability is now a standard requirement. Grails offers the Mail plugin to make sending email simple. You can send mail from controllers or services and even use complex GSP views to create fancy HTML emails.

To refresh your memory, you installed the Mail plugin by adding it to /grails-app/conf/BuildConfig.groovy:

```
plugins {
    compile ':mail:1.0.1'
}
```

After you install the plugin, you need to add two lines of configuration to tell the plugin where to find your mail server and what the default From address should be. Let's update your /grails-app/conf/Config.groovy file:

```
grails.mail.host="mail.yourserver.com"
grails.mail.default.from="hubbub@grailsinaction.com"
```

The default `From` address is optional. You can always specify your own `From` address each time you invoke the Mail plugin, but it makes sense to set it here because you'll have less maintenance later on if you need to change it.

If you have different mail servers for different environments, you can nest this value inside the development/test/production sections of Config.groovy so that you have environment-specific values.

Adding configuration properties for your own code

You might wonder how the Mail plugin reads values from Config.groovy and how you can add your own property settings to your application.

Let's imagine Hubbub has a setting for enabling a proxy server. In your Config.groovy file, add a value for the property:

```
hubbub.proxy.enabled = true
```

If you need access to settings from a controller (or any artifact that supports DI), you can declare a `grailsApplication` object on your controller and Grails will inject it for you. Once you have that object, you can get to your setting with a line like this:

```
def grailsApplication
...
if (grailsApplication.config.hubbub.proxy.enabled) {
        /* do proxy stuff */
}
```

TIP You might worry whether the Mail plugin is up to supporting your mail server setup. Fear not, ample configuration options are available for the plugin, including custom ports and SSL connections. Consult the Mail plugin page for the complete set of configuration options. A common configuration choice for development is to use your Gmail for your SMTP server. If that's your plan, a configuration like this would suffice.

```
grails {
    mail {
        host = "smtp.gmail.com"
        port = 465
        username = "your_username@gmail.com"
        password = "your_password"
        props = ["mail.smtp.auth":"true",
                 "mail.smtp.socketFactory.port":"465",
                 "mail.smtp.socketFactory.class":
                    "javax.net.ssl.SSLSocketFactory",
                 "mail.smtp.socketFactory.fallback":"false"]
    }
}
```

With your configuration done, it's time to send your first email.

10.2.1 Sending mail inline

The Mail plugin gives you two basic options for invoking the mail service:

- Via a `sendMail()` method dynamically added to each controller and service in your application
- By calling the `mailService.sendMail()` method from within a controller or service that has `mailService` injected

TIP Both of these mechanisms call the same code, so the choice is about which style of injection you prefer (and perhaps which method works better with your mocking and testing strategy, but more on that later).

Let's start with the service-based mechanism (since, as we demonstrated in chapter 9, that will make things easier to mock for any unit tests we might write down the track). For your first email, let's send a "welcome aboard" sign-up message to your `UserController`, as shown in the following listing.

Listing 10.2 Sending a welcome email

```
def mailService

def welcomeEmail() {
    if (params.email) {
        mailService.sendMail {
            to params.email
            subject "Welcome to Hubbub!"
            text """
            Hi, ${params.email}. Great to have you on board.
            The Hubbub Team.
            """
        }
        flash.message = "Welcome aboard"
    }
    redirect(uri: "/")
}
```

Defines an injection point for the Mail service

Calls the sendMail method on the injected mailService with mail params

Uses multiline string to send mail body inline

Using the inline version of `mail` is a matter of passing in a closure with the appropriate values for `to`, `subject`, and `text` (or `html` if you're sending HTML email). You can also provide `cc` and `bcc` fields, and you can comma-delimit a list of addresses. In listing 10.2, you used a Groovy multiline string (`"""`), which laid out the email inline with your controller code.

Handling multipart MIME messages and attachments

We covered the text and HTML options for sending plain text or HTML emails. But what if you want to send a multipart MIME email containing both text and HTML and let the user's email client decide the one to render? In this scenario you can provide an email body for both `text()` and `html()`, but make sure you also set the multipart property to `true`.

> ***(continued)***
> Similarly, you need to set the multipart property to `true` if you add attachments to your emails, which you can do by invoking the `attach()` method and passing in a `File`, `InputStream`, or `byte[]`. See the Mail plugin docs for further details.

That's fine for simple scenarios, but you don't want layout logic embedded in a controller. It's time to move all your layout logic into a GSP to make things more maintainable.

10.2.2 Using a view as your mail body

Having an embedded email layout in your controller classes means you can't take advantage of the HTML editor in your IDE. It's also harder to get your graphic designer's input into the process. Fortunately the Mail plugin lets you delegate your UI output to a view. Let's take it for a spin.

First, let's create a standard Grails view to host your content (`/grails-app/views/user/welcomeEmail.gsp`). You'll include CSS styling too, because it's available, and set the content type to `text/html` so a rich HTML email is sent. The following listing shows the email template.

Listing 10.3 A template view for your email, with CSS styling

```
<%@ page contentType="text/html"%>
<html>
<head>
    <title>Welcome Aboard</title>
    <style type="text/css">                    <-- Provides CSS style for mail
        body {
            font-family: "Trebuchet MS"
        }
    </style>
</head>
<body>
     <h1>Howdy!</h1>
    <p>
       Hi, ${email}. Great to have you on board.      <-- Uses variables provided by controller
    </p>
    <p>
       <strong>The Hubbub Team.</strong>
    </p>
</body>
</html>
```

With your content in place, you need a way to wire it to your controller action. This is handled by custom attributes on the `sendMail` tag. The following listing shows the updated action.

Listing 10.4 An updated welcome action that defers to the view for rendering

```
def welcomeEmail(String email) {
    if (email) {
        mailService.sendMail {
            to params.email
            subject "Welcome to Hubbub!"
            html view: "/user/welcomeEmail", model: [ email: email ]
        }
        flash.message = "Welcome aboard"
    }
    redirect(uri: "/")
}
```

You passed the `view` name and the `model` attributes via the HTML (or text) tag. You're already inside the `UserController`, so you can use a relative `view` name for the corresponding GSP (minus the .gsp extension). If you send email from a service or a Quartz job, you need to specify the full path to the view (in this example, it would be `/user/welcome-Email`) because Grails has no servlet request to work with.

Figure 10.3 shows your welcome email in action, sending your rich HTML email to the user's inbox.

Now that you implemented your mail-sending infrastructure, it would be nice to test it. Fortunately Grails gives you several ways to get there.

10.2.3 Testing mail operation

You could always write a unit test with metaclass magic to mock out the `sendMail` call on your controller, but you wouldn't get your template rendered. A nicer solution is to take advantage of one of the Grails SMTP mocking plugins that lets you mock out a mail server entirely with an in-memory replacement. Several are available, but you'll use the Dumbster plugin (http://grails.org/plugin/dumbster) because it's actively maintained and has first-class support for integration with the Mail plugin.

The Dumbster plugin works by sparking up a mock SMTP server on a known port (using the standard Java Dumbster library), then directly injecting itself into the Mail

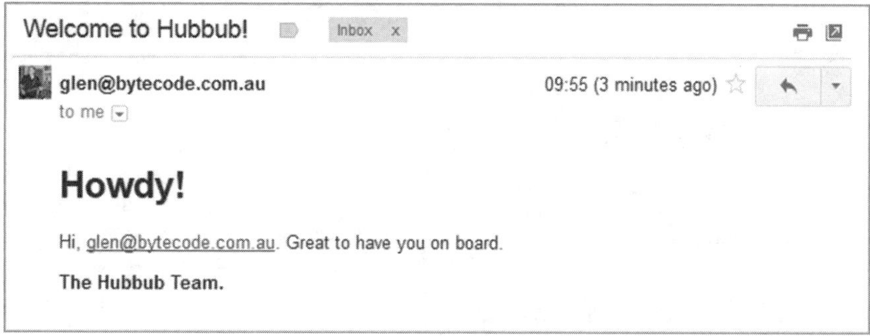

Figure 10.3 A new message arriving with suitable markup

plugin's Spring wiring to point to that mock mail server. Integrating the Dumbster with your current setup is a one-line configuration setting for whatever environment you'd like to enable it.

Let's add the plugin to our /grails-app/config/BuildConfig.groovy and start implementing. You'll add it to the `test` scope because you only need this plugin active when running your tests, and you don't want to inadvertently ship a mock SMTP server with your final application!

```
plugins {

    // ... other plugins omitted
    test ':dumbster:0.2'

}
```

But pulling in the plugin is only part of the story. For sensible reasons, the plugin is disabled by default. (You don't want to accidentally enable a mock mail service in your production deploys!) You need to enable it by changing /grails-app/conf/Config.groovy. Let's turn it on for the test environment:

```
environments {
    test {
        dumbster.enabled = true
    }
}
```

Once the plugin is installed and enabled, you have a new Dumbster Spring bean that you can inject into your tests. Because you want your Spring beans in play for testing (so you're exercising your Mail plugin with Dumbster integration), you'll write an integration test rather than a unit test (remember that unit tests won't spark up any Spring infrastructure).

Let's refresh your /test/integration/com/grailsinaction/UserIntegrationSpec with the new test code shown in the following listing.

Listing 10.5 Testing mail sending using the Dumbster plugin

```
class UserIntegrationSpec extends IntegrationSpec  {

    def dumbster                                          // 1 Injects Dumbster Spring bean into test

    def "Welcome email is generated and sent"() {

        given: "An empty inbox"
        dumbster.reset()                                  // 2 Clears existing mock messages from Dumbster

        and: "a user controller"
        def userController = new UserController()

        when: "A welcome email is sent"
        userController.welcomeEmail("tester@email.com")   // 3 Sends email via UserController action

        then: "It appears in their inbox"
        dumbster.messageCount == 1                        // 4 Confirms inbox count rises to 1
```

```
        def msg = dumbster.getMessages().first()
        msg.subject ==  "Welcome to Hubbub!"
        msg.to == "tester@email.com"
        msg.body =~ /The Hubbub Team/
    }
}
```

❺ **Fetches first message and checks its details**

In this example you inject your Dumbster instance into your integration test using standard Spring injection ❶. With the Dumbster bean in play, you first clear any cached messages ❷, then commence invoking your controller action to send the mail ❸. Because that email ends up in the Dumbster object, you can now query it for an increased message count ❹, and even pull off the message and check that the To/Subject/Body fields are correct ❺.

If you need convincing, run the test from the command line with `grails test-app UserIntegrationSpec` and confirm that your message is delivered as promised. That completes your tour of the Mail plugin. Next on the list is adding full-text search capability using the Cache plugin.

10.3 Caching for performance: making everything snappy

Since Grails 2.1, Grails has shipped with a built-in Cache plugin (which wraps the standard Spring caching infrastructure) that takes care of all those places where you have expensive computed values that you like to keep for a while.

If you're running on Grails 2.0 and keen to take advantage of the new Cache plugin, you need to add a new entry to your /grails-app/conf/BuildConfig.groovy, but current versions of Grails already have the line you need:

```
plugins {
    // ... other plugins omitted
    compile ':cache:1.0.1'
}
```

Note that you want to have the plugin in `compile` scope because it exposes annotations that you may want to employ on your controllers.

The Cache plugin gives you the infrastructure to cache the outcome of controller and service methods, and even provides a standard set of view-tier taglibs giving you all the common caching infrastructure that your app may need.

Even more importantly, the Cache plugin also provides the core caching API that you can extend and customize. Using one of the other Grails caching plugins, such as `cache-ehcache`, `cache-redis`, and `cache-gemfire`), builds on the core plugin. These plugins give you the ability to switch the underlying caching implementation with no source-level changes to your application.

10.3.1 The core caching annotations

The Cache plugin provides three easy-to-use annotations that make caching your method calls straightforward: `@Cacheable`, `@CachePut`, and `@CacheEvict`. You supply the cache name to the annotation (and optionally a cache key in certain circumstances).

Let's imagine you want to cache your global timeline (because you're under so much load) so that the method only gets refreshed periodically:

```
class PostController {

    import grails.plugin.cache.*

    @Cacheable('globalTimeline')
    def global() {

       // ...render the global timeline
    }
```

The global timeline is shared across all users, so you can use the `@Cacheable` annotation and give it the name of the cache in which to store the outcome. You then configure your `globalTimeline` cache to expire every minute or so and let the underlying cache be refreshed with the most recent entries.

But what about the scenario in which you want to cache a given user's timeline and refresh it every time they create a new post? Sounds like just the scenario to introduce you to the @`CachePut` and @`CacheEvict` tags. Let's start by getting your timeline into a per-user cache:

```
@Cacheable('userTimeline')
def personal(String loginId)  {

    // ...lookup personal timeline by loginId
}
```

In this scenario, when a request comes in for a personal timeline, you return the value from a `userTimeline` cache using the parameter `loginId` as the cache key (you can supply your own cache key if you like, but it will default to a concatenation of the parameters to the method). You could rework the `personal` method with a custom key to achieve the same result:

```
@CachePut(value='userTimeline',key='#loginId')
def personal(String loginId)  {

    // ...lookup personal timeline by loginId
}
```

With your personal timelines now cached for high performance, it makes sense to think about refreshing them only when the user posts new content. Enter the `@CacheEvict` annotation that looks after evicting items from the existing cache:

```
@CacheEvict(value='userTimeline', key='#session.user.loginId')
def addPostAjax(String content) {
    // ...add new post to users timeline
}
```

In this example, you use the user's account, which is stored in the session (so you don't let people invoke `addPostAjax()` on behalf of someone else). `@CacheEvict` also offers a handy `allEntries=true` configuration option if you ever need to "go nuclear" and clear out an entire cache as an admin function:

```
@CacheEvict(value='userTimeline', allEntries = true)
def clearUserTimelineCache() {
    // ... other audit functions here
}
```

By combining `@Cacheable`, `@CachePut`, and `@CacheEvict`, you end up with a comprehensive configuration-based caching solution that's super easy to maintain. But what if you need to access fine-grained configuration data? If you need programmatic access, you need to look at the CacheManager API.

10.3.2 Working with the CacheManager API

If you need to do fine-grained cache operations and wish to make calls on the underlying cache, the Cache plugin exposes a `grailsCacheManager` object for injection. This object gives you methods such as `getCache(name)` and `getCacheNames()`, and inspection methods such as `cacheExists(cacheName)` and `destroyCache(cacheName)`. The most common use case is to get access to the underlying cache instance programmatically such as:

```
Cache myCache = grailsCacheManager.getCache("myCache")
myCache.evict("someKey")
myCache.put("someKey", "newValue")
myCache.clear()
```

Although you typically won't need such low-level calls, it's good to know that you can get access to the underlying cache instances directly if your business logic requires it.

10.3.3 Leveraging other members of the Cache plugin family

Out of the box, the Grails-cache plugin provides in-memory caching with only manual cache eviction. If this sounds a little minimalist for a Cache plugin, that's by design. For more sophisticated caching use cases, the core plugin was designed to be extended by other caching plugins that let you configure all sorts of caching facilities without changing your source code.

A popular choice for more sophisticated caching configuration is to extend the cache plugin with the Ehcache plugin that offers a dizzying array of caching configuration use cases. First, let's add the plugin to our `BuildConfig.groovy`:

```
plugins {
    compile ":cache-ehcache:1.0.0"
}
```

NOTE The Ehcache extension plugin declares a dependency on the version of the cache-core plugin that it requires, so if you add Cache-ehcache to your plugins, you can safely remove the standard cache plugin.

With your Ehcache plugin installed, you can configure how you want both your named and global caches to operate. All the configuration work happens, as you might expect, in /grails-app/conf/Config.groovy.

You can consult the Cache-ehcache documentation for a complete set of current DSL configuration values, but the Ehcache plugin's default cache config should give you an idea of how the plugin hangs together (and how flexible the configuration options are), as shown in the following listing.

Listing 10.6 Structure of a Cache plugin

```
grails.cache.config = {
  defaultCache {
     maxElementsInMemory 10000
     eternal false
     timeToIdleSeconds 120
     timeToLiveSeconds 120
     overflowToDisk true
     maxElementsOnDisk 10000000
     diskPersistent false
     diskExpiryThreadIntervalSeconds 120
     memoryStoreEvictionPolicy 'LRU'
  }

  cache {
     name 'myDailyCache'
     timeToLiveSeconds 60*60*24
  }
}
```

You can see from the listing the Cache-ehcache plugin gives you an amazing array of configuration options, but perhaps the most critical ones are `timeToLiveSeconds` (how long things will live in the cache before they're automatically evicted), and `diskPersist` (whether you want your cache to survive an app server restart). Consult the grails-cache-ehcache online docs (http://grails-plugins.github.com/grails-cache-ehcache/) for a comprehensive discussion of all the available options.

> **Caching and serializable**
> For the standard in-memory cache, there's no requirement for you to mark the cached objects as serializable (because they're stored in an in-memory `HashMap`). For certain configurations of the enhanced cached plugins (such as Ehcache with distributed caching), your objects will need to be marked serializable to be persisted across the wire.

Also don't forget that you can configure your caching on a per-environment basis (like anything else in Config.groovy). You might want to use memory-only caching in dev, but overflow to disk in your QA and production environments.

10.3.4 The cache taglibs: caching in the view

We've encouraged you to "think MVC" throughout your Grails journey: business logic in the services, routing and marshaling in the controller, and rendering in the view.

With that style of architecture, you might wonder why would I need to even cache anything in the view if all my logic is happening in services?

Well, one great reason to cache in the view tier is to cache the output of your custom taglibs to make sure the view renders snappily. Another useful case is when you need to invoke view-layer templates (which might themselves be performing calls to other custom taglibs). The cache plugin provides two versatile taglibs to solve these particular common cases: `<cache:block>` for caching arbitrary blocks of view-layer tags, and `<cache:render>` for caching the invoking of view-layer templates. Let's look at each.

The simplest to understand is the `<cache:block>` tag, which globally caches whatever content appears inside the tag. For example:

```
<cache:block >
    Hubbub currently has ${ com.grailsinaction.User.count()} registered users.
</cache:block>
```

That's fine for global data. What about the case where you want to cache on a per-user basis? What if, for example, you had an `<h:followers>` taglib that displayed the list of followers for the current user? It would be no use caching this data globally because it changes for each user of the system. Let's imagine you have an `<h:followers>` tag that renders all the followers for a user in Hubbub. You want to render and cache the list once per user. In that case, you can take advantage of the key attribute to simulate a per-user cache:

```
<cache:block key="${session.id}">
    <h:followers for="${session.user}"/>
</cache:block>
```

Your list of followers will be calculated once and preserved for the life of the session. These procedures generate in-memory cache action, so to avoid a different set of performance problems you might want to think about where you apply any per-user caching.

You had no trouble getting your caching up and running, but what about invalidating the cache when you want to change the values? As you saw in the previous section, if you're using one of the extensions to the core cache plugin (such as Cache-ehcache), cache invalidation can be configured in Config.groovy at various levels of granularity. To be honest, that's certainly the best way to go, and it gives you the most robust outcome. If, however, you're using the Cache plugin on its own, cache invalidation is handled through a Grails service that's supplied by the Cache plugin called GrailsCacheAdminService.

To invalidate your caches, declare an instance of variable for injection, then invoke either the `clearBlocksCache()` (to clear all your `cache:block` sections), or the `clearTemplatesCache()` (to clear all your `cache:render` sections). If you're interested in the internals, all these methods do is clear the named cache blocks that hold the results of those taglibs. For example, the `clearBlocksCache()` method on the service uses the `@CacheEvict` tag to wipe out the named cache used in the taglibs:

```
@CacheEvict(value="grailsBlocksCache", allEntries=true)
def clearBlocksCache() {}
```

The same applies to `clearTemplatesCache`. If you need to configure a more robust block and template caching solution, you now know the cache names to apply your configuration to!

Now that you explored a great set of practical Grails caching tools, it's time to turn your attention to keeping your domain model structure in sync with your database table structure using the Database Migration plugin.

10.4 Database migrations: evolving a schema

In your sample application you haven't yet learned how to evolve your database to cope with changes (for example, introducing or refactoring domain objects and their fields). You set your `dbcreate` option to update in /grails-app/conf/DataSource.groovy and forgot about it:

```
production {
    dataSource {
        dbCreate = "update"
        // ... other settings
    }
}
```

That's worked great so far. What's to worry about?

For one thing, the standard update mechanism doesn't know anything about column renames, so if you ever decide to refactor your field names or types in your domain objects, you're in for manual work in your database console to keep your data in sync.

What you want is a database-agnostic way of describing your database change sets so that you can always migrate your database from its current form to the latest schema. Enter the Grails Database Migration plugin (http://grails.org/plugin/database-migration)—purpose-built Grails integration of the popular Java Liquibase library for database migrations (www.liquibase.org).

Starting with Grails 2.1, the Grails database migration plugin now ships out of the box with Grails, and is fast becoming the safest (and most popular) way to keep your database in sync with your domain objects. Let's install it and start experimenting.

10.4.1 Installing and configuring the plugin

If you run on a version previous to Grails 2.1, you need to install the plugin using the standard /grails-app/conf/BuildConfig.groovy mechanism. For older versions of Grails, the plugin can be installed manually via:

```
plugins {
    runtime ":database-migration:1.3.2"
}
```

Once you have the plugin installed, make sure you turn off Grails's database schema-syncing feature in your /grails-app/conf/DataSource.groovy. You may remove the `dbCreate` line entirely or set it to `none` explicitly to disable the feature. Here's the updated setting for Hubbub:

```
production {
    dataSource {
        dbCreate = "none"
        // ... other settings
    }
}
```

Our one final configuration change is to automatically run all new database migrations when the application starts up. This is turned off by default (to ensure you don't accidentally clobber your production database), but it's so convenient to use that you're going to turn it on right from the get-go through a small modification to /grails-app/conf/Config.groovy:

```
grails.plugin.databasemigration.updateOnStart = true
grails.plugin.databasemigration.updateOnStartFileNames = ['changelog.groovy']
```

These two entries tell the plugin to automatically update all outstanding database migrations mentioned in changelog.groovy as the application boots. You'll dive into the details of all those changes shortly!

In fact, with the plugin installed and your configuration in place, it's time to establish a baseline for your schema; later, you'll generate `changeSets` from this baseline.

10.4.2 Establishing a baseline

The general workflow for the database migration plugin is to: (1) establish a baseline schema for your first release, then (2) generate a changelog entry for each domain class modification you make.

All of the database migration commands are prefixed with `dbm-`; to create your initial migration changelog file, use the following command:

```
grails prod dbm-create-changelog
```

This file creates a skeleton changelog file in /grails-app/migrations/changelog.groovy. This file is your parent file, loaded by the Dbmigration plugin on Grails startup. From here, you can create new child changelog files to represent all of the database changes you introduce in a particular release.

Let's start by creating a changelog file that represents your baseline database schema.

```
grails prod dbm-generate-changelog --add changelog-0.1.groovy
```

If you run this from the command line, you generate a new file in /grails-app/migrations/changelog-0.1.groovy, and the plugin automatically updates your /grails-app/migrations/changelog.groovy file to reference the new file. The following listing shows an extract from the freshly minted changelog-0.1.groovy file.

Listing 10.7 `changeSet` files capture database schema changes in a given release

```
changeSet(author: "Glen (generated)", id: "1383967582482-6") {    <- changeSets have unique IDs.
    createTable(tableName: "USER") {    <- changeSet commands perform database changes.
        column(autoIncrement: "true", name: "ID", type`: "BIGINT") {    <- All types and constraints are expressed in DB-agnostic terms.
            constraints(nullable: "false", primaryKey: "true",
     primaryKeyName: "CONSTRAINT_27")
        }

        column(name: "VERSION", type: "BIGINT") {
            constraints(nullable: "false")
        }

        column(name: "DATE_CREATED", type: "TIMESTAMP") {
            constraints(nullable: "false")
        }

        column(name: "LOGIN_ID", type: "VARCHAR(20)") {
            constraints(nullable: "false")
        }

        column(name: "PASSWORD", type: "VARCHAR(8)") {
            constraints(nullable: "false")
            }
        }
}
```

Notice from the `changeSet` that each entry has a unique ID and issues a database command (such as `createTable`, in this case). Expressing this information in a database-agnostic format means you can express database refactoring operations (even complex ones) without worrying about what kind of database the end user is configured to use. This is useful when you have different databases in development and production (not ideal, but a common reality in a commercial setting).

Should I use Groovy or XML migrations?

The Database Migration plugin supports two mechanisms for describing your migration: a Groovy DSL (as shown in listing 10.7) or the native Liquibase XML format. The Groovy version is more commonly used in Grails circles, and supports a few more complex migration options (such as embedded code in your migrations), so you'll stick with that version here. But if you have previous Liquibase experience, you might find the XML more appealing. See the Database Migration manual for more details about XML support.[1]

But how does the Database Migration plugin know which migrations it has processed and which ones are new? It knows through its own internal DATABASECHANGELOG table. When the plugin processes changes, it creates new entries in that table to show the migration `ids` it has processed.

[1] Bert Beckwith, "Database Migration Plugin—Reference Documentation," version 1.4.0, http://grails-plugins.github.io/grails-database-migration/docs/manual/.

If you're starting with a fresh, empty database and want to leave all table creating to the plugin, you can run your baseline creation with:

```
grails prod dbm-update
```

This command processes all outstanding `changeSets`, writes entries in the DATABASECHANGELOG, and gets everything in sync. In fact, you could issue a `grails prod run-app` and get the same result because you automatically apply all fresh migrations on application startups based on your settings in section 10.4.1. It's probably better, though, to first get a feel for what's happening by running these commands manually.

The `dbm-update` command is great if you start from a blank database, but what if you already have your tables created in the database? How can you tell the Database Migration plugin to sync its changes in its DATABASECHANGELOG table with your existing structure? For that you need to run the following command:

```
grails prod dbm-changelog-sync
```

which marks all your migration scripts as successful in the DATABASECHANGELOG, ensuring those migrations aren't rerun on the current database.

And with those few commands, you've learned how to establish your baseline schema. But things get interesting when you start taking advantage of the handy migration commands that ship out of the box. Let's explore the common example of creating new domain objects and refactoring existing ones.

10.4.3 Implementing common migrations

Imagine you enhance your Hubbub user profile domain class to keep a linked `twitterId` field, perhaps via a change such as the following:

```
class Profile {
    // other fields omitted...
    String twitterId
}
```

To capture this change in your new workflow, you complete the following steps:

1. Make the domain class changes for the new addition.
2. Run `grails prod dbm-gorm-diff --add changelog-0.2.groovy` to add your new migration to the changelog.
3. Either issue a `run-app` to apply the changes, or manually run `grails prod dbm-update` to apply the changes from the command line.

First, let's create the new changelog to see how things work. Run `grails prod dbm-gorm-diff --add changelog-0.2.groovy`, and then look at the output in /grails-app/migrations/changelog-0.2.groovy, as shown in the following listing.

Listing 10.8 Creating a new domain class field (changelog-0.2.groovy)

```
databaseChangeLog = {

    changeSet(author: "Glen (generated)", id: "1383972018405-1") {
        addColumn(tableName: "profile") {
```

```
            column(name: "twitter_id", type: "varchar(255)") {
                constraints(nullable: "true")
            }
        }
    }
}
```

Here you can see your new column added to the changeSet. But what if you want to rename the column? Let's say you change your profile twitterId field to be twitterName.

The plugin can't keep track of a field's old and new names, but it does provide a rich set of database migration commands for writing your own changeSets by hand. Here you've updated your changelog-0.2.groovy by hand to cope with the new change, as shown in the following listing.

Listing 10.9 A changelog to renaming twitterId to twitterName (changelog-0.2.groovy)

```
databaseChangeLog = {

    changeSet(author: "Glen (generated)", id: "1383972018405-1") {
        addColumn(tableName: "profile") {
            column(name: "twitter_id", type: "varchar(255)") {
                constraints(nullable: "true")
            }
        }
    }

    changeSet(author: "Glen (by hand)", id: "1383972018405-2") {     ❶
        renameColumn(tableName: "profile",                            ❷
            oldColumnName: 'twitter_id', newColumnName: 'twitter_name')   ❸
    }
}
```

❶ Creates new changeSet, gives it a unique id

❷ Calls renameColumn refactoring

❸ Provides old and new names for column

In the changelog in the example, you create a new changeSet and supply a unique id ❶. Inside this new changeSet, you use the renameColumn refactoring ❷ and supply the old and new names for the column ❸. Using this method, you can preserve any existing data in the column while migrating the name to match your domain class. A quick run of grails prod dbm-update and your database reflects the change.

What about removing entries? This is a scenario where the plugin can keep track of changes (because the column still appears in the database, but is missing from the domain class). Let's remove your twitterName field, and run a grails prod dbm-gorm-diff --add changelog-0.3.groovy. In this case you see a new changeSet with the dropColumn command invoked as shown in the following code.

```
databaseChangeLog = {

    changeSet(author: "Glen (generated)", id: "1383973002263-1") {
        dropColumn(columnName: "TWITTER_NAME", tableName: "PROFILE")
    }
}
```

You've seen how to create, rename, and remove fields from domain classes. But you might wonder what other kinds of refactorings are available in the plugin (including changing data types, renaming database objects, loading reference data, or even running arbitrary sql). The plugin exposes all the standard Liquibase refactorings, so the best place to look is in the Liquibase reference documentation at www.liquibase.org/documentation/changes.

10.4.4 Groovy-based migrations

One unique feature of the database migration plugin over standard Liquibase is the ability to run arbitrary Groovy code as part of the migration. In fact, there's even support for full GORM access from within the `changeSet`, which is powerful, but has important gotchas (see the "Why shouldn't I use GORM domain classes in my migrations?" sidebar.)

You can take advantage of Groovy-based migration by using the `grailsChange` block inside your ever-familiar `changeSet`. To give you even finer-grained control, the `grailsChange` block is further segregated into a range of lifecycle events (`init`, `validate`, `change`, `rollback`, `confirm`, `checksum`), allowing you to do fine-grained migration rollbacks and confirmations. You can consult the manual for details of each of the event types, but you're likely to spend 99% of your time in the `change` closure, which is responsible for performing the migration, so let's spend our energy there.

Depending on the lifecycle event you chose to bind to, you're given access to standard variables (typically backed by Spring beans), which you can use in performing your migration magic. As we said, the most common event you'll want to bind to is the `change` event, and table 10.1 shows the most important objects that are injected and available to you in your migration code.

Table 10.1 Objects available to migration code

Variable	Description
`ctx`	Spring `ApplicationContext` object (useful for grabbing other Spring beans)
`sql`	A `groovy.sql.Sql` instance already configured to use the current connection
`connection`	Current JDBC Connection instance
`application`	`GrailsApplication` (useful for grabbing current environment and config settings)

There's almost nothing you can't do with all that power at your disposal! In listing 10.10, you use the injected `sql` object (a `groovy.sql.Sql` object configured to use the current data source connection) to perform arbitrary sql fiddling on your datasource.

In this case, imagine you have to write a migration that resets all users's passwords to a random string. You iterate over all your users, using Groovy to generate the random string password on the way.

Listing 10.10 Using a Groovy-based migration to change passwords

```
changeSet(author: "Glen (hand-coded)", id: "1383973002263-2") {
        grailsChange {
```

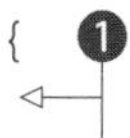

Marks this migration as containing Groovy/Grails code

```
            change {

                println "Resetting all passwords..."

                def allUsers = sql.rows("select * from user")
                println "Resetting passwords for ${allUsers.size} users"

                Random random = new Random(System.currentTimeMillis())
                def passwordChars = [ 'A'..'Z', 'a'..'z',
➥ '0'..'9' ].flatten()

                allUsers.each { user ->
                    StringBuilder randomPassword = new StringBuilder()
                    1.upto(8) { randomPassword.append(
                        passwordChars.get(random.nextInt
                        (passwordChars.size())))
                    }
                    println "Random password is ${randomPassword} for
➥ user ${user.login_id}"
                    sql.execute "update user set password = ? where id = ?",
                            [ randomPassword.toString(), user.id]

                }
                println "Done resetting passwords..."

            }
        }
    }
```

❷ Creates collection of user rows from db

❸ Iterates over each user row

❹ Generates new password of 8 random chars

❺ Updates user table with new passwords

There's a fair bit of custom code happening here, but if we break it down, you'll soon get the hang of it. First we mark this migration as a Grails change ❶ to ensure that our `sql` object gets injected. Then in the body of our change block, we create a collection of existing users from rows in the User table ❷. We then iterate over those users ❸, generating a new password for each user ❹. Finally, we update the User table with the new password ❺, using the user `id` from the current user iteration.

> **Why you shouldn't use Grails domain objects in your migrations**
>
> The GORM support in the database migration plugin is incredibly powerful. And the temptation to use a few dynamic finders to sort reference data seems like a no-brainer. Be warned!
>
> If your migrations use Grails domain class properties, you're making a contract with the plugin that the properties you reference will be there for all time. (Because they must exist at the time the migration runs, they can never be renamed or removed in your application.) If you ever change any property's references in the GORM migration and then attempt to create your database from scratch on a new machine, the migration will fail because the object no longer has those fields.
>
> Our advice is to avoid this feature. You can find other ways to rename and remove fields using the standard Liquibase refactorings.

With your exploration of Groovy-based migration complete, it's time to turn your attention to our next major plugin effort—implementing full-text search with the Grails Searchable plugin.

10.5 Full-text search: rolling your own search

With users flocking to its social networking goodness every day, Hubbub post volumes are going to skyrocket. And users will want to search.

In the good old days, people implemented website search logic using SQL queries (such as `post.content like %grails%`), but that isn't sufficient for today's requirements. Using SQL `like` queries can be inefficient, and it's increasingly complex as the number of searched fields grows. For most full-text searches, the user wants to search multiple fields, which effectively rules out SQL.

Fortunately, clever folks have implemented full-text indexing and search engines that handle indexing database contents and provide convenient ways to search. One of the most popular Java full-text solutions is Lucene, and its higher-level abstraction library Compass.

The Grails Searchable plugin wraps these full-text search libraries to give you a simple and transparent way to implement searching. Whenever you save a domain object (such as with `post.save()`), the plugin adds the object to the full-text index. When you delete or update an instance, the plugin alters the index accordingly. When you want to search, you call `Post.search("your search terms")`, and you have a list of hits. There's also a completely customizable domain-specific language (DSL) for specifying the domain class properties that are indexed.

Let's kick things off by installing the plugin. Add the plugin (and its helpers for spellchecking and hit highlighting) to your /grails-app/conf/BuildConfig.groovy:

```
plugins {
        compile ':searchable:0.6.6'
        compile 'org.apache.lucene:lucene-spellchecker:2.4.1'
        compile "org.apache.lucene:lucene-highlighter:2.4.1"
}
```

With the plugin installed, you can configure the objects you want to be searchable. That requires thinking.

> **The state of search on Grails**
>
> Several full-text search plugins are available for Grails at the time of writing, including Searchable, Elasticsearch and Apache Solr. Although (by far) the most popular at this time is Searchable, the libraries underlying Searchable (Compass) have been deprecated.
>
> The author of Compass has gone on to implement the popular Elasticsearch distributed search engine, which also has a Grails plugin, but, unfortunately, the plugin isn't actively maintained. The company behind Elasticsearch now has a product roadmap for Grails support, so the plugin may well find a fresh life by the time you read this.

> ***(continued)***
>
> Fortunately the Elasticsearch plugin uses an API that's largely compatible with Searchable, so whatever effort you put into learning Searchable is likely to benefit you down the track if Elasticsearch becomes a popular replacement.

10.5.1 Making objects searchable

The first step in using the searchable plugin is determining the objects to index. In the case of Hubbub, users want to search on `Post` object content (to see posts matching a term) and also on the `User` object (does my friend "Joe Cool" have an account?).

The simplest way to add your `Post` and `User` objects to the searchable index is to add a `searchable` property, like this:

```
class User {
    static searchable = true
    ...
}
class Post {
    static searchable = true
    ...
}
```

When a domain class is marked `searchable`, the plugin indexes its primitive fields (strings, dates, numbers, and collections of those). Later in this chapter, you customize which fields are indexed, but for now you'll stick with the defaults.

Your basic search capability is now implemented. If you start up Hubbub, you can use the provided Searchable page to search your index. Open http://localhost:8080/hubbub/searchable and take it for a spin, as demonstrated in figure 10.4.

Not too bad for five minutes' effort, but there's still work to do. The data is being searched, but the output isn't what you want. It found the user and post information relating to "glen", but you need to skin the output with your Hubbub style, and it would be nice to format the link results to use your preferred permalink format (/user/profile/glen for profile info, and /users/glen for all the posts). Also, the user probably only wants to search for posts (Find a Post) or users (Find a Friend).

Let's step outside the default search page and create a custom search page. Create a custom search controller first, and then we'll put some effort into the view:

```
grails create-controller com.grailsinaction.Search
```

You'll start your implementation by offering a search of all posts because that's the more common option. Listing 10.11 shows a first attempt at a custom search controller.

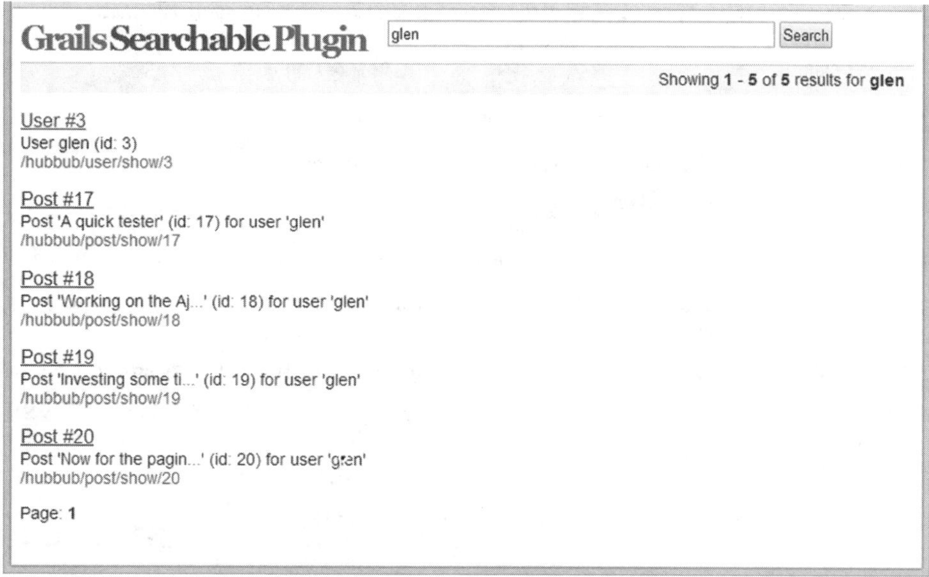

Figure 10.4 The default Searchable interface is usable from the get-go.

Listing 10.11 Custom search controller

```
package com.grailsinaction
class SearchController {
    def search() {
        def query = params.q
        if (!query) {
            return [:]
        }
        try {
            def searchResult = Post.search(query, params)   ❶ Invokes new search method
            return [searchResult: searchResult]
        } catch (e) {
            return [searchError: true]
        }
    }
}
```

As you saw previously, searchable adds a dynamic `search()` method ❶ to each domain class. It has two parameters: the query string and a map of options. Typically the options map contains values for maximum hits per page, offset for pagination, and sorting order. For now, you'll pass in the `params` object and worry later about passing in explicit options.

The `search()` method returns a map containing metadata about the search, along with a list of domain classes matching the criteria. Table 10.2 gives a breakdown of what's available.

Typically, in the view, you iterate over the results field, displaying each of the hit objects (and perhaps get fancy with keyword highlighting). You can also use the `total` and `max` values to display the diagnostics ("returned 10 of 326 hits," for example).

Table 10.2 The `searchResult` return value gives you a wealth of query information.

Field	Description
`total`	The total number of matching results in the index
`results`	A list of domain class instances matching the query
`max`	The maximum number of hits to return (typically used to paginate; defaults to 10)
`offset`	The number of entries to skip when returning the first hit of the result set—used for pagination
`scores`	A list of raw result confidence for each hit (a floating point value between 0.0 and 1.0)

With your controller ready to go, you need to put together a small /views/search/search.gsp file to let the user enter values and display the results from the search. Ignore pagination for now and get started with a bare-bones approach, as shown in the following listing.

Listing 10.12 A first custom search form

```
<html>
    <head>
        <title>Find A Post</title>
        <meta name="layout" content="main"/>
    </head>
    <body>
        <h1>Search</h1>
        <g:form>
            <g:textField name="q" value="${params.q}"/>
            <g:submitButton name="search" value="Search"/>
        </g:form>
        <hr/>
        <g:if test="${searchResult?.results}">
            <g:each var="result" in="${searchResult.results}">     <-- Iterates over search results
                <div class="searchPost">
                    <div class="searchFrom">
                        From
                <g:link controller="users"
                   action="${result.user.loginId}">               Creates links to
                           ${result.user.loginId}                 user profile
                </g:link>
                        ...
                    </div>
                    <div class="searchContent">
                        ${result.content}                         <-- Displays matching
                    </div>                                            post content
                </div>
            </g:each>
        </g:if>
    </body>
</html>
```

If you get results, iterate over them and render them in `div`s. That lets you apply CSS styles to the results. Figure 10.5 shows your first customized search in action.

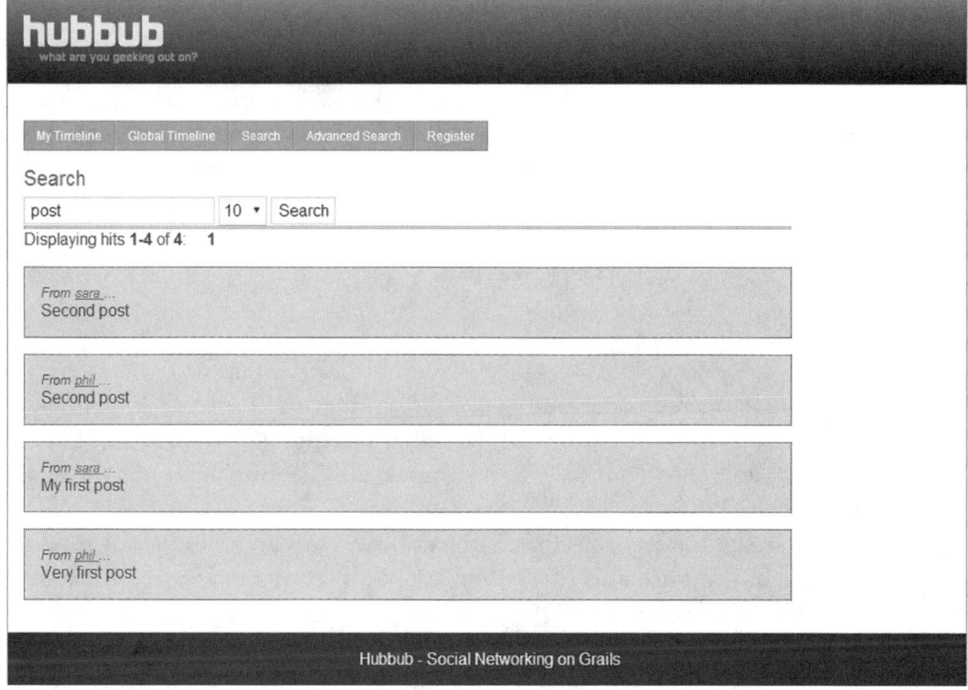

Figure 10.5 Your first custom search form in action

Those results look nice but don't include keyword markup. It's time to explore what searchable offers for help with that feature.

When you display search results, users probably want the keyword hits highlighted.

10.5.2 *Highlighting hit terms*

Searchable gives you the power to implement keyword markup, but it requires work with closures. The following listing shows the updated controller code, which highlights the hits.

Listing 10.13 An updated search controller with hit-term highlighting

```
package com.grailsinaction
class SearchController {
    def search() {
        def query = params.q
        if (!query) {
            return [:]
        }
        try {
            params.withHighlighter = {highlighter, index, sr ->     ❶
                // lazy-init the list of highlighted search results
                if (!sr.highlights) {     ❷
                    sr.highlights = []
                }
```

❶ Introduces withHighlighter closure

❷ Provides empty highlights collection if no matches

```
                // store highlighted text;
                // "content" is a searchable-property of the
                // Post domain class
                def matchedFragment = highlighter.fragment("content")      ❸
                sr.highlights[index] = "..." +
                    (matchedFragment ?: "") + "..."                        ❹
            }
            def searchResult = Post.search(query, params)
            return [searchResult: searchResult]
        } catch (e) {
            return [searchError: true]
        }
    }
}
```

❸ Obtains highlighted content

❹ Surrounds highlight with ellipses

The updated search code uses the `withHighlighter` closure ❶, which takes a `highlighter` object (used to hold the word that was highlighted along with its surrounding text), an `index` counter (used to track the hit number), and the search result object itself.

You create a new `highlights` object on each search result if it doesn't already exist ❷, and you use it to hold the marked-up version of the search result (the version with the keyword highlighted).

For each result, you retrieve the fragment of the `Post`'s `content` field that matched the search ❸, and you surround it with ellipses ❹ to show it's an extract. The matched fragment contains the word that was matched plus a few surrounding words for context. The matched word is surrounded in `<b>` tags by the plugin.

The following listing shows your updated view code that extracts those matching phrases and renders them in the browser.

Listing 10.14 Updated view code for handling hit terms

```
<g:each var="result" in="${searchResult.results}" status="hitNum">       ❶
    <div class="searchPost">
        <div class="searchFrom">
            From
            <g:link controller="users" action="${result.user.loginId}">
                ${result.user.loginId}
            </g:link>
            ...
        </div>
        <div class="searchContent">
                                ${raw(searchResult.highlights[hitNum])}    ❷
        </div>
    </div>
</g:each>
```

❶ Iterates each result with hitNum counter

❷ Displays matching hit in searchContent div

This code uses a `status` attribute ❶ in the `<g:each>` tag. Then it accesses the `hitnum.Hits` marked up with the `searchContent div` ❷. Notice that we use the `${raw()}` construct ❷ to ensure that our hit highlighting markup isn't HTML-escaped. Figure 10.6 shows the results of searching for "work".

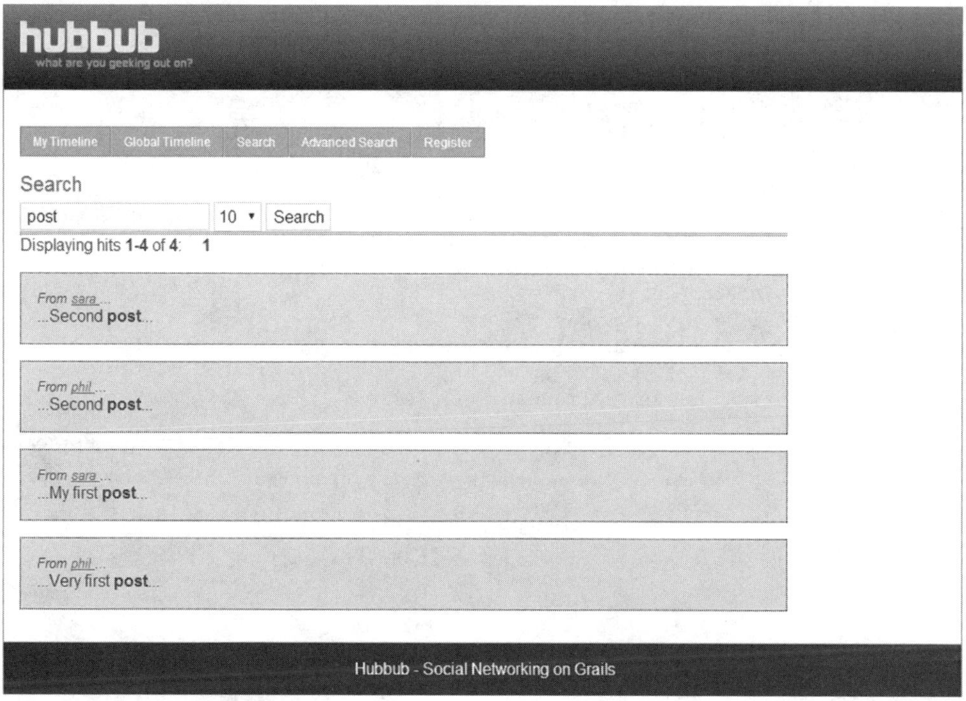

Figure 10.6 Hit-term highlighting in action

With hit-term highlighting set up, the search is starting to look useful. But you don't want your search page to display thousands of hits, so it's time to implement pagination.

10.5.3 Implementing pagination

You explored the first page of your results. You haven't specified the `max` property for your searches, and the Searchable plugin defaults to returning the first ten. It's time to give users control over how many results are returned per page. The good news is that you can use the same pagination control you saw in chapter 6.

Let's first add a combo box to let the user choose the number of hits to be displayed per page. If you call the field `max`, `searchable` will pick it up for free, which means no changes to your controller code. Here's the updated form:

```
<g:form>
    <g:textField name="q" value="${params.q}"/>
    <g:select name="max" from="${[1, 5, 10, 50]}"
              value="${params.max ?: 10}" />
    <g:submitButton name="search" value="Search"/>
</g:form>
```

The back-end controller is unchanged, but you need to make UI changes to the results section of your page to use the paginating aspects of the output (the total number of matching results, which page you're on, and so on).

Handling the case when there's only one page of results makes this trickier than it should be. The following listing shows the updated GSP.

Listing 10.15 Displaying marked-up hit terms

```
<g:if test="${searchResult}">
Displaying hits
    <b>${searchResult.offset+1}-
       ${Math.min(searchResult.offset + searchResult.max,
     searchResult.total)}</b> of
    <b>${searchResult.total}</b>:
    <g:set var="totalPages"
        value="${Math.ceil(searchResult.total / searchResult.max)}"/>
    <g:if test="${totalPages == 1}">
        <span class="currentStep">1</span>
    </g:if>
    <g:else>
        <g:paginate controller="search" action="search"
            params="[q: params.q]"
            total="${searchResult.total}"
            prev="&lt; previous" next="next &gt;"/>
    </g:else>
    <p/>
</g:if>
```

Provides pagination for search results

If there's only one page to display, you don't invoke the `paginate` tag at all. But if you're spanning pages, you need to tell the tag the total size of the result list. As you'll recall from chapter 6, the tag manages its own state and looks after creating the necessary links to navigate to next and previous pages.

Figure 10.7 shows it in use.

Your paginating search capability is done. With that feature implemented, you've learned enough of the basics to implement the most common features you'll need in your own search facilities. But there's more `searchable` power to explore. It's time to look at advanced features.

10.5.4 Customizing what gets indexed

In your exploration of search, you relied on the default indexing rules; you marked your domain classes as `searchable`. But when you index data, it's useful to control what gets stored. It's pointless indexing a million password fields, because you never want them exposed in a search. You also want to be careful not to index data that's under high concurrency (for example, a `clickCounter` field stored on every domain object), because you open yourself up to complex locking and exception handling around concurrent updates to the index.

Figure 10.7 Implementing pagination on your search

Fortunately searchable exposes a more complete DSL for fine-grained index creation, so you can configure what's searchable. Let's upgrade your User object to make sure passwords never get indexed:

```
class User {
    static searchable = {
        except = ['password']
    }
    // more stuff...
}
```

Two common operations on the searchable DSL are except (index all fields except these) and only (only index these).

Customizing the index location

When you install the Searchable plugin, it adds a new command to install its configuration file. If you don't install a custom version, it uses default values. Most of these defaults are fine, except that the index file location defaults to the current user's home directory. This isn't what you want in production.

To install a custom config file, use the following command:

```
grails install-searchable-config
```

This creates the /grails-app/conf/Searchable.groovy file, which lets you customize the location of your index files (and other options—see the comments in the created file). For example, you might have a special location for index files on your production servers:

```
compassConnection = new File(
        "/var/indexes/${appName}/${grailsEnv}"
    ).absolutePath
```

You can override the locations for the development, test, and production environments as in Config.groovy.

With your index now set up, it's time to explore providing a fuzzy search facility.

10.5.5 Query suggestions: did you mean "Grails"?

One of the coolest features in Google is the suggest-query capability. Can't remember how to spell zucchini and spell it zukini? Google shows you results, but it also prompts you, "Did you mean zucchini?" Searchable gives you that feature for free if you tell it what domain classes are subject to the check.

To enable this, use the searchable DSL introduced in the previous section. Let's change your Post domain class to mark it searchable for the suggest-query option, which uses the spellCheck option:

```
static searchable = {
    spellCheck "include"
}
```

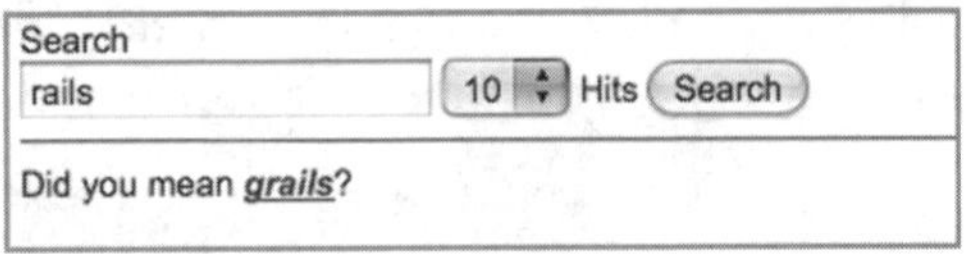

Figure 10.8 The Searchable suggest-query feature in action

Once the domain class is marked to use the suggest feature, you pass in the `suggestQuery` option to your search code. Here's your updated search action using the new parameter:

```
params.suggestQuery = true
def searchResult = Post.search(query, params)
```

Although the controller changes were fairly painless, you have more work in the view to display the suggested terms. Use internal `searchable` classes to do this. Perhaps one day this will be wrapped up in a `searchable` taglib, but for now here's how to display the search term:

```
<g:if test="${searchResult?.suggestedQuery}">
<%@ page import="org.codehaus.groovy.grails.plugins.
           ➥ searchable.internal.util.StringQueryUtils" %>
<p>Did you mean
<g:link controller="search" action="search"
    params="[q: searchResult.suggestedQuery]">
        ${StringQueryUtils.highlightTermDiffs(
            params.q.trim(), searchResult.suggestedQuery)
        }
</g:link>?
</g:if>
```

You've done all the work, so it's time to run your app and give it a test. Figure 10.8 shows a search for a popular competing web framework.

Although `suggestQuery` makes for a great demo, you haven't yet explored one core feature of search. What if you want to constrain the query to match items only within the current user's posts? To implement that, you need to explore how search subcomponents work.

10.5.6 Searching across relationships

You already explored how the indexing process handles domain classes that are in relationships with one another. You discovered that if a domain class has a relationship to another (a `User` has many `Posts`) and the related domain class is also marked `searchable`, the index will also contain that relationship data. That's good, because you can navigate from parent to child without concern.

But what if you want to search all `Posts` that belong to a particular user? You need a way of storing fields from the related `User` object in the index related to the `Post` data. `searchable` handles that relationship with `component`.

We'll show you the syntax first, and then break down what's happening behind the scenes. The following code shows your updated `Post` object's searchable mapping.

```
class Post {
    static searchable = {
        user(component:true)              <-- Allows searching Post objects
        spellCheck "include"                  based on user criteria
    }
    static belongsTo = [ user : User ]
    // ...other stuff
}
```

You told searchable that you want to store all the fields of your User object with the index for each Post. When the index is stored in this manner, you can search against the Post object, using constraints from the User object (for example, to find all posts where loginId is "glen").

To implement this, let's update the search UI to handle the new option:

```
<g:if test="${session.user}">
    Just My Stuff:
    <g:checkBox name="justMine" value="${params.justMine}"/>
</g:if>
```

You also update your search controller to handle the check box. The simplest way to do this is to append a constraint to the submitted query. You can do this with Google-style restrictions, by appending +loginId:glen at the end of the query, for example.

The following code updates your controller to automatically add the constraint when the check box for justMine is checked:

```
if (params.justMine) {
    query += " +loginId:${session.user.loginId}"
}
def searchResult = Post.search(query, params)
```

You now have your constrained user search. Using strings to do this is fine for simple search restrictions, but it can open up security issues when trying to restrict sensitive searches. The user could work all kinds of evil on the submitted query-String, so you have to be careful to remove all the nasties using handcrafted regular expressions.

For those scenarios, a better option is to use the full-blown searchable SearchBuilder DSL. You could, for example, rework the preceding search using must() specifiers, which the user can't tinker with. For example, you could do something like this:

```
def searchResult = Post.search params, {
     must(queryString(query))
     must(term("loginId", session.user.loginId))
}
```

Using the SearchBuilder DSL offers a much safer approach for guaranteeing the constraint applies to the final query. Check out the searchable SearchBuilder DSL on the Grails wiki for more information.[2] Be warned the DSL can be tricky to use, so you might want to familiarize yourself with the Compass API that it's built on first.

---

[2] Query Builder, www.grails.org/Searchable+Plugin+-+Searching+-+Query+Builder.

> **Debugging indexes with Luke**
>
> Luke (https://code.google.com/p/luke/) is a tool for viewing your index files to see exactly what's being stored. If you've having trouble working out how all of the `component` settings affect index creation, download (or Web Start) Luke, and point it at your index directory.
>
> The Documents tab is handy for debugging search DSL issues—it lets you step through each element in the index and see exactly which keywords are stored.

The `searchable` plugin is complex but powerful. Take the time to explore the online docs and see the configuration options available.

10.6 Summary and best practices

We covered many plugins in this chapter, and you got a thorough grounding in a host of popular features that you're likely to add to your next application.

We introduced you to the basics of how plugins are installed and bundled and covered integrating email into your application. Then we explored the new Grails caching infrastructure and showed you how to tune the performance of your Grails app using clever caching strategies.

Finally, we explored numerous searchable options for making your app's full-text search facility hum. It's a big chunk of information to take in, but your app's usability has increased tremendously.

Here are a few best practices to take away from the chapter:

- *Install plugins via BuildConfig.* Opt for the new BuildConfig.groovy mechanism when installing plugins. It gives you more control over how your plugin dependencies are configured, and the older `install-plugin` command is deprecated.
- *Use mail config.* Set the `mail.grails.default.from` attribute in Config.groovy so there's a single place to maintain your From address. Then you no longer need to use the From field when invoking mail services.
- *Apply caching judiciously.* If you identify queries or complex logic that can be easily cacheable to improve performance, take advantage of the built-in caching annotations. Then install a robust cache such as Ehcache to give you more flexible cache configuration options.
- *Customize search config.* Always install a custom searchable config file so you can place your index data somewhere sensible.
- *Index selectively.* Be careful which fields you include in your index. Watch out for sensitive data, as well as data that's under high concurrency (if you index your `clickCounter` field, only bad can come of it).

Now that you've had a good look at some popular Grails plugins, we'll spend next chapter learning about adding security to your application using the popular Grails Spring Security plugin.

11 Protecting your application

This chapter covers

- What security means
- How to protect against common attacks
- How to implement access control
- Advanced security techniques

Hubbub looks good now, so perhaps it's ready to go public. The problem with going public, however, is that it's a big bad world out there with plenty of agents who might want to hack user accounts, steal passwords, or perform a denial of service on your site. It's a sad fact of life, but you need to make sure that Hubbub can survive in the wild, which means hardening it against attacks.

Security is a huge field that includes business processes, identification, network hardening, systems setup, and more. We mention this because it's worth bearing in mind that what you'll focus on in this chapter is a small, Grails-centric bit.

We'll cover the two most important aspects of security for Grails developers: handling user input and implementing access control. These represent the most common vulnerabilities and the most common requirement of web applications, respectively. You'll also learn about Secure Sockets Layer (SSL) and how to set that up.

11.1 Dealing with untrusted data and networks

If you look at the Open Web Application Security Project (OWASP) Top 10,[1] you see that four of the top ten security risks in 2013 involve an attacker submitting malicious data to a web application: injection attacks, cross-site scripting (XSS), cross-site request forgery (CSRF), and invalid redirects and forwards. These security risks force you to verify everything sent over HTTP or sanitize it before use. Fortunately, Grails has several features that help with this. In this section, we show you how to validate user input, escape your output (HTML and otherwise) when it includes user-provided data, and use form tokens to protect against both double submissions and CSRF attacks.

11.1.1 Validating user input

Imagine that you want to search in Hubbub for all posts that have been tagged "grails." Millions of such posts exist because it's a cool topic to discuss, and if Hubbub attempted to return *all* of them, the request would punish both the server and the client. To prevent this, Hubbub returns 50 by default. But a user can override this by passing a `max` URL parameter, and if you don't validate the value of that parameter, your application could attempt to return a billion search results. Outcome? Boom! You have a denial of service (DoS).

This is one example where trusting the data sent by the user can result in bad things happening to your application. One solution is to validate the data before using it. Grails gives you a couple of ways to do this:

- Manually check values before use and fall back to a default or raise an error
- Use command objects

For simple cases such as the `max` parameter from the previous example, the first option is fine because the extra code is minimal. For example,

```
def search() {
    def max = params.max?.toInteger() ?: 50
    max = Math.min(max, 500)
    def results = Post.findAllByTag("grails", [ max: max ])
    ...
}
```

Limits number of results to absolute maximum of 500

If you implement something similar with command objects, you'd likely end up with code such as the following listing.

Listing 11.1 Result of using command objects to validate data

```
class PostController {
    ...
    def search(SearchCommand cmd) {
```

Grails implicitly calls validate() on command object at start of method.

[1] "OWASP Top 10 (2013)," https://www.owasp.org/index.php/Top_10_2013-T10.

```
        if (cmd.hasErrors()) {
            render status: 400, text: "Invalid search parameters"
            return
        }

        def results = Post.findAllByTag(cmd.tag, [ max: cmd.max ])
        ...
    }
    ...
}

class SearchCommand {
    String tag
    int max
    int offset

    static constraints = {
        max min: 0, max: 500
        offset min: 0, max: 500
    }
}
```

Returns 400 Bad Request response indicating invalid parameters.

Embeds parameter value limits as validation constraints.

It appears that manually checking the input values is the way to go because the command object version has more code and it returns an error rather than falling back gracefully to a safe default value. As a one-off, the manual check works nicely.

Now imagine that you have other controller actions that need to validate the `max` parameter. The manual check would then need to be repeated and you could easily end up with manual validation checks littered across controller actions. On the other hand, the command object declares the validation rules in the standard Grails way and can be reused for any number of actions. In addition, command objects enforce types. In the previous listing that means a user can't submit text for the `max` property because the command object requires a number and so its validation would fail.

> **SQL injection attacks**
>
> A common attack vector is through SQL injection. The attacker submits data to the application that contains specially crafted SQL. The application then builds a SQL string from that data without first escaping it and then submits that string to the database. The result may be a leak of confidential data or a DoS.
>
> With Grails, you don't have to worry about this particular problem as long as you use dynamic finders, Where queries, the criteria API, or HQL with named or positional parameters. All of these automatically escape input values. Don't construct any HQL or SQL via string concatenation!

For the simplest cases, manual validation of parameters works fine. But in reality, any simple case typically stops being simple sooner or later. As soon as you find yourself repeating validation across multiple actions or requiring more than a couple of validation checks in a single action, you should switch to command objects. In fact, you're unlikely to go wrong if you use command objects right from the start.

Command objects aren't only useful for validating input. In the next section, we discuss vulnerabilities related to automatic binding of parameters to domain instances and how command objects help protect against the corresponding attack.

11.1.2 Data binding

In 2012, the GitHub website was attacked through a known exploit of Ruby on Rails, the web framework used to build the site. No serious damage was done, as the attacker's intention was to highlight the dangers of the exploit to the Rails community. The source of the exploit was a feature known as mass assignment—something you can also see in Grails via code such as `new Post(params)`. The fundamental problem is that such data binding blindly copies values to a target domain instance's properties and an attacker can provide values for properties that shouldn't be modified.

Imagine that Hubbub's posts require moderation. You add an additional `moderated` flag to the `Post` domain class that's initially set to `false`. You then make sure that the page for creating a new post has no option to set that flag. It's easy to think you're safe, but there's nothing stopping a user from sending their own HTTP POST request to the relevant URL using a tool such as telnet. Hubbub could receive this request:

```
POST /hubbub/post/update/13 HTTP/1.1
Host: localhost:8080
Content-Type: application/x-www-form-urlencoded

content=You+all+suck!&moderated=1
```

Sets the moderated flag

If the corresponding controller action that handles this request then does something like this:

```
class PostController {
    ...
    def save() {
        def post = new Post (params)
        ...
        // Validate and save the new post
        ...
    }
}
```

Binds all parameters, including moderated if it appears in request

the attacker's request bypasses your moderation mechanism. That's not good.

In this case, the simplest solution is to explicitly exclude the `moderated` property from automatic binding, via the `bindable` constraint in the `Post` domain class:

```
class Post {
    // Other Post properties
    ...
    Boolean moderated = false

    static constraints = {
        ...
        moderated bindable: false
    }
}
```

Prevents automatic binding to moderated property

You can use this constraint in any domain class, and it's an easy win for existing code because you don't have to rewrite your controllers. Unfortunately, you have to remember to add the constraint—forgetting to do so automatically opens a security hole in your application.

An alternative approach is to decouple the domain model from the user input by using command objects. The command object only has to include the properties that are allowed by a particular action, eliminating the problem of malicious extra parameters in the request. And as you saw in chapter 7 (section 7.3.1), you can easily bind the command object to a domain instance. For example:

```
def update(PostCommand cmd) {
    if (!cmd.hasErrors()) {
        def post = new Post(cmd.properties)
        ...
    }
    ...
}
```

Binds command object to new domain instance

The `properties` property works equally well with the `bindData()` method, too.

The major downside to command objects is that you feel like you're duplicating information when a command object matches a domain class closely. But convenience is usually the enemy of security, as you can see from the mass assignment feature. Using a command object also allows you to evolve the domain model independently of the UI, which makes application maintenance easier.

Before you move on from the risks of not validating user input, here's one temptation you want to avoid: putting your data validation only in the browser (via JavaScript, Flash, or whatever). Yes, validating in the client and on the server is tedious repetition, but remember that an attacker doesn't have to use a browser to use your application. They can easily craft HTTP requests via telnet or another tool, bypassing the client validation.

Sometimes you don't use the input data directly, so there's no point in validating it. For example, do you want to validate Hubbub's posts? If so, what rules would you use? All you do is store them in the database and then display them at a later date. Such scenarios are the source of a whole class of attack: XSS. Protecting against such attacks requires a whole different approach.

11.1.3 Escaping output

In XSS, the attacker takes advantage of the lack of validation to provide HTML and/or JavaScript in whatever content they are submitting. If the web application then regurgitates that content as is, the browser parses it, and if there's any JavaScript content, executes it. This can lead to all sorts of weird and wonderful behavior, such as alert boxes popping up every time someone accesses your application. Often it can mean defacement of your website or exposure of sensitive data.

The solution is to escape the content before displaying it in the browser, for example, by replacing angle brackets with the `<` and `>` HTML entities. This prevents the browser from parsing the content as HTML and potentially executing malicious JavaScript. How do you escape your content and safeguard your website?

As of Grails v2.3, you don't need to do anything. Let's look at the fragment of GSP that renders a Hubbub post:

```
<div class="postEntry">
  <div class="postText">${post.content}</div>        <-- Content inside ${} is automatically escaped
  <div class="postDate">${post.dateCreated}</div>
</div>
```

Even if someone submits JavaScript in a Hubbub post, it has no effect. The HTML in the page would look something like this:

```
<div class="postEntry">
  <div class="postText">
&lt;script&gt;alert('Got ya!');&lt;/script&gt;
  </div>
  <div class="postDate">Wed Feb 05 10:41:43 GMT 2014</div>
</div>
```

Sometimes this is too safe. Imagine that you have a content management system (CMS) where the author of a website wants to include HTML tags in one or more of their pages. Those tags should not be escaped, otherwise their pages will look awful. In that case, you have two options:

- Use a special `raw()` method when rendering the content in a GSP page:

  ```
  <section name="pageContent">${raw(page.content)}</section>
  ```

  The method disables any currently active escaping and renders its content as is. This should be done only with trusted user input.
- Disable the automatic escaping of content through a couple of configuration settings:

  ```
  grails.views.gsp.codecs.expression = 'none'     <-- Applies to ${} expressions
  grails.views.gsp.codecs.scriptlet = 'none'      <-- Applies to <% %> expressions
  ```

  We recommend you take this path only with extreme caution because it's easy to miss bits of a page that need escaping, and can introduce an XSS vulnerability.

How do you escape an expression after you disable the automatic behavior? Grails implements the automatic escaping through a set of classes called codecs. These allow you to escape (or encode) arbitrary strings, as well as unescape (or decode) them. The default automatic behavior results in the HTML codec being applied to the result of `${}` expressions. You can also do this manually via special methods added to the `String` class. Imagine that you switched off the automatic expression escaping for Hubbub. In that case you need to use this code to render each post:

```
<div class="postEntry">
  <div class="postText">${post.content.encodeAsHTML()}</div>   <-- Encodes post content
  <div class="postDate">${post.dateCreated}</div>
</div>
```

Each codec class adds its own pair of methods to the String class: encodeAs<Codec>() and decode<Codec>() (note the lack of As in the latter method name). The HTML codec is obviously the most common one, but table 11.1 lists several of the most useful ones that come with Grails.

Table 11.1 Useful codecs provided by Grails

Codec class	Added methods	Description
HTMLCodec	encodeAsHTML() decodeHTML()	Escapes HTML, replacing angle brackets and ampersands with the corresponding HTML entities.
Base64Codec	encodeAsBase64() decodeBase64()	Converts bytes to Base64 format for mail attachments and the like.
URLCodec	encodeAsURL() decodeURL()	Encodes characters according to the x-www-form-urlencoded content type. Should only be used to encode text for the query string part of a URL, not for the path.
MD5Codec	encodeAsMD5()	Creates an MD5 hash of the string.
SHA256Codec	encodeAsSHA256()	Creates an SHA256 hash of the string.

Best of all, codec escaping is idempotent. You can call a method such as encodeAsHTML() as many times as you like; it never double encodes. You'll never have < become < and then < through a second call to encodeAsHTML().

Before Grails v2.3

Times were dark in previous versions of Grails. Although there was automatic escaping of GSP expressions, that behavior was disabled by default. Even if you switched it on via this config setting:

```
grails.views.default.codec = "html"
```

there was no fine-grained way to disable it for individual expressions. It could also easily break views provided by plugins as there was no double-encoding protection. If you wanted to disable automatic escaping (assuming it was enabled), your only option was to add this to the top of your GSP files:

```
<%@page defaultCodec="none" %>
```

which disables the default codec for the entire view or partial template.

One thing you need to be wary of is *incorrect* encoding. Imagine you have a script element in your view:

```
<script>
alert('${ myMessage }');      <-- Automatically encodes result using default codec (HTML)
</script>
```

You don't want Grails to automatically encode `myMessage` as HTML. Otherwise, the alert box will display "Hello & goodbye" for a value of "Hello & goodbye"! You should either use the `<g:javascript>` tag, which switches the default codec to JavaScript, or explicitly encode the string:

```
<script>
alert('${ myMessage.encodeAsJavaScript() }');
</script>
```

Explicitly encodes myMessage as JavaScript instead of HTML

As you can see, Grails has your back as far as XSS prevention goes, while still giving you flexibility when you need it. You've also seen the main aspects of Grails' encoding support and you can check out the user guide for information on how tag libraries and other aspects of view rendering factor into the XSS prevention mechanism.

A vulnerability that's closely related to XSS attacks is something called CSRF. You look at this next.

11.1.4 CSRF and form tokens

When a request comes in, for example to update a user's Hubbub post, how do you know that the request is coming from someone with the authority to do that? Normally you require the user to authenticate first, but logging in for every request leads to a poor user experience. That's why a session for the authenticated user is created and an associated cookie stored in the browser.

As you can see from figure 11.1, a CSRF attack hijacks the session cookie to post data to your application as the victim.

All an attacker needs to do is get the user to load a page on a site (1 & 2) that automatically submits a form to your application (3), and the browser will automatically ensure that the victim's session cookie is added to the request. As far as the bank's website is concerned, the request to transfer funds is coming from the user!

Several approaches exist for protecting your application against such forged requests, but the most common is to include a unique token in the form displayed by

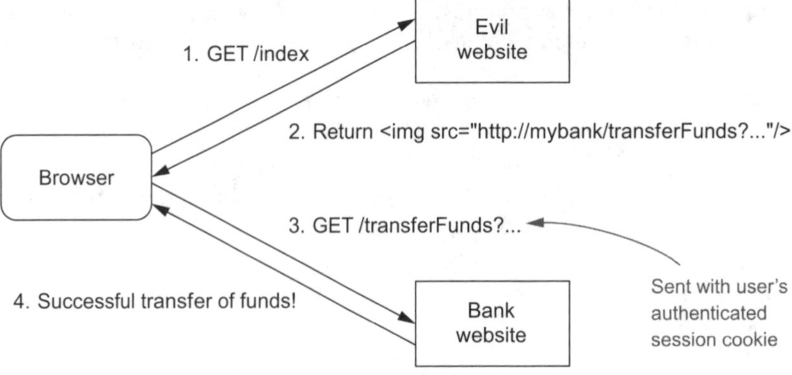

Figure 11.1 An example CSRF attack in which a malicious website gets the browser to send an authenticated request to a bank site to transfer funds

your application. When the browser submits the form, your application checks the unique token against the one it's expecting. Unless the tokens are easily guessable, there's no way for an attacker to submit the forged request with the correct token.

This may sound like a fair bit of work and it would be if you had to code it yourself. Fortunately, Grails has a built-in mechanism: the `useToken` attribute on the `<g:form>` GSP tag along with the `withForm()` controller method. This feature was originally introduced to prevent double-submissions of forms (remember those "Please don't click on the submit button more than once!" messages?), but it also happens to be the perfect antidote to CSRF.

Assuming that your imaginary form for editing an existing post now has the `useToken="true"` attribute, the corresponding controller action looks like the following listing.

Listing 11.2 Using tokens to block CSRF

```
def update(PostCommand cmd) {
    withForm {                                          // Ensures request has valid token
        if (!cmd.hasErrors()) {
            def post = new Post(cmd.properties)
            ...
        }
        ...
    }.invalidToken {
        render "Invalid or duplicate form submission"   // Renders error message if no or incorrect token is submitted
    }
}
```

One downside to using this approach is that you effectively prevent REST requests to this endpoint. No need to worry. You can have separate endpoints (actions) to handle REST requests and it's easier to authenticate a REST client per request than a real end user, making CSRF a nonissue. We'll talk about this more in the next chapter.

All that's left in terms of data transfer is to ensure confidentiality of the data that travels between the browser and your application.

11.1.5 Protecting your data in transit

It's easy to forget that the data traveling between a user's browser and your application server often takes a tortuous and unsecured route. Running the command `traceroute` (on Unix-like systems) or `tracert` (on Windows) against a host name such as grails.org shows you how many pieces of equipment the data goes through, any of which could be compromised. And don't forget that a user may be in an airport or other public place using unsafe Wi-Fi. That's why it's important to encrypt any confidential data.

As you're no doubt aware, the standard solution on the web is SSL. We won't go into the details of how it works, but we think it's important that you understand how to set it up for a Grails application. And that depends on how you deploy your application.

LOCAL DEV MODE

When you develop your application, you want things to be simple. That's why enabling SSL is trivial when you use the `run-app` or `run-war` commands: add the `--https` argument when calling them:

```
grails --https run-app
```

All you need to do then is access your application via an HTTPS URL, such as https://localhost:8443/hubbub/. Note that the scheme, https, and the port, 8443, are different from the usual ones. To control the port number used, add the `grails.server.port.https` setting to BuildConfig.groovy, or pass the following on the command line:

```
grails -https -Dgrails.server.port.https=8184 run-app
```

If you do run Hubbub or your own application like this, notice that your browser doesn't seem too happy when accessing it. Figure 11.2 shows you what Firefox thinks of Hubbub over HTTPS. Behind the scenes, Grails creates a self-signed SSL certificate

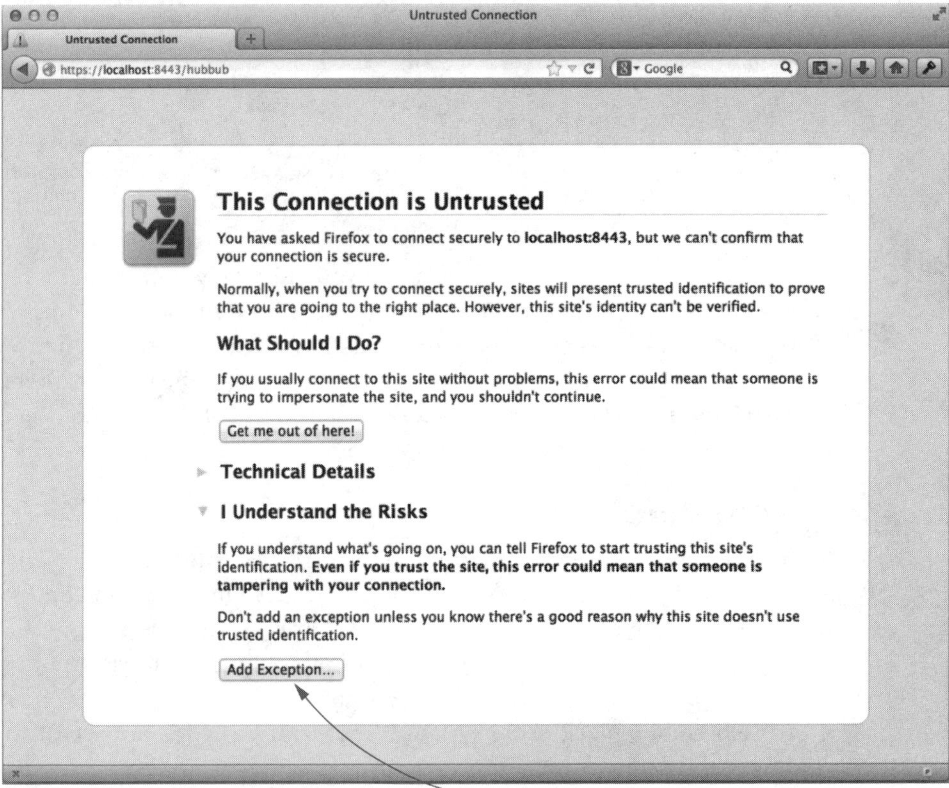

Figure 11.2 Trying to access Hubbub via HTTPS with Firefox—the browser doesn't like the self-signed certificate

on demand. Such a certificate in effect says, "trust me because I say so"—hardly something to inspire confidence. It's fine for local development but not a production deployment.

PRODUCTION

As you can see from figure 11.2, SSL is about more than encrypting data. It's also about trust and verifying the identity of both the server and (less commonly) the client. If you want users to trust your website, then you have to get your SSL certificate signed by what's known as a certificate authority (CA). Examples of companies that provide this service are VeriSign, Thawte, Comodo, and GoDaddy. It's worth shopping around. Be sure to use a CA that most browsers recognize and trust by default, otherwise the user will see warning messages.

How do you get your certificate signed by one of these CAs? Every provider gives explicit instructions for doing this, but the general procedure is something like this:

1. Create a private key for your server using the JDK's `keytool` command.

   ```
   keytool -genkey -alias my.domain -keyalg RSA -keystore
   <path_to_keystore>
   ```

2. Generate a certificate signing request (CSR).

   ```
   keytool -certreq -keyalg RSA -alias my.domain -file certreq.csr
   ➥ -keystore <path_to_keystore>
   ```

3. Send the CSR to the CA.
4. Wait for them to send you a signed certificate back, and then import it into your keystore using `keytool`.

   ```
   keytool -import -alias my.domain -keystore <path_to_keystore>
   ➥ -file <path_to_certificate>
   ```

One thing to bear in mind is that if your version of the JDK doesn't trust your CA by default, your application won't work with HTTPS requests. You then have to get the CA's root (or chain) certificate and import it into your keystore:

```
keytool -import -alias root -keystore <path_to_keystore> -trustcacerts
➥ -file <path_to_root_cert>
```

New versions of the JDK occasionally include extra trusted CA certificates, so it's worth checking whether yours has been added when you upgrade your version of the Java runtime. It makes life easier.

After you sign a server certificate in your keystore, it's up to you to ensure your server is configured appropriately. Tomcat 7.0 requires you to add a `<Connector>` element to your server.xml configuration file that includes the location of the keystore and the username/password pair for accessing the certificate. After that's done, you're good to go!

Malicious users will always be out there waiting to take advantage of vulnerabilities in your application, but by following the guidance on input validation, data binding, escaping output, and form tokens, you'll be as safe as you can be. It also helps that good security practice such as the use of command objects is good architectural practice, too!

The topics we covered here apply principally to URLs that everyone has access to, but many applications want at least part of an application accessible only to selected users, such as the employees of the company or subscribers to a service. That requires a different type of security based on access control, which we look at next.

11.2 Access control

Many applications need to know who the user is, either because they're storing information that should be visible only to certain (known) people or because they need to restrict access to part or all of their functionality. Maybe they need to track who does what. In Hubbub, for example, you're not interested in anonymous posts: when a user posts a new message, Hubbub needs to know who posted it. You also want to make sure that only a user can modify their own profile. Nobody else should be allowed to do so, except perhaps a system administrator.

This is what access control is all about. It can range from making sure that only real people (as opposed to bots) can access an application to using complex rules based on multiple permissions, projects, and groups. Hubbub falls firmly into the first category, but we try to provide enough information that you can readily go beyond the basics.

11.2.1 What is it and what can we use?

Access control breaks down into two main aspects:

- Is the person you're communicating with who they say they are (authentication)?
- Do they have the rights to perform a given action (authorization)?

Simple access control can be implemented via standard Grails filters and the session as we did in chapter 7, but you should use one of the available security plugins. Rolling your own security solution usually ends in tears, unless your business is security. With that in mind, here are the main candidates for security solutions in Grails:

- *Authentication plugin*—The Authentication plugin is a lightweight authentication implementation with no dependencies on any third-party libraries. It's good for websites that require registered users but don't have complex authorization requirements.
- *Shiro plugin*—The Shiro plugin provides full-featured access control and cryptography via the Apache Shiro library. The Java library is mainly maintained by Stormpath.
- *Spring Security plugin*—Formerly known as Acegi Security, Spring Security is a well-known and widely used security framework for Java applications. It provides the most comprehensive suite of authentication options of the three plugins listed here. Newcomers often find it difficult to understand, but the plugin does a great job of hiding much of the complexity.

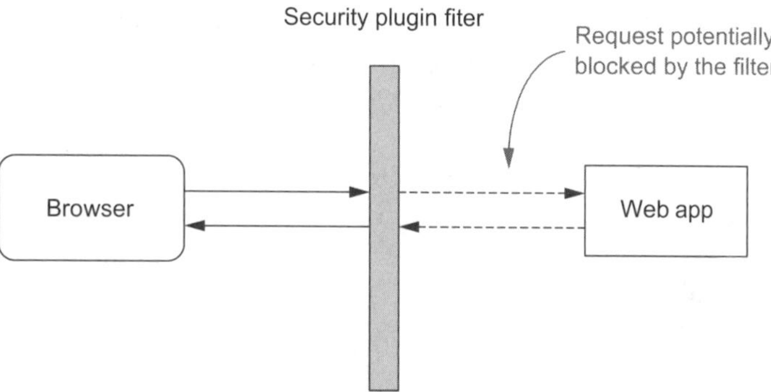

Figure 11.3 How the typical Grails security plugin fits into the request/response cycle

A couple of options we haven't listed here are the standard Java Authentication and Authorization Service (JAAS), which comes as part of the JDK, and the access control specification defined by Java Enterprise Edition (Java EE) and implemented by Java EE containers such as JBoss. Although both are standards, they aren't widely used in the Grails community. JAAS in particular is difficult to use and understand.

Regardless of which plugin you use, it operates as a gatekeeper to your web application, as illustrated in figure 11.3. It decides whether a particular request is allowed through to the application based on a set of rules that you configure. Those rules may require the user to authenticate or may result in an access denied page.

A question of terminology

The phrase "authentication and authorization" is fairly common and means much the same as access control, but the latter is currently the preferred term in security circles. Different security frameworks also tend to have their own jargon, which can make comparing them difficult. If in doubt, pick a library or framework that you understand.

We can't cover all these plugins in one chapter, so we concentrate on the Spring Security plugin as it's powerful and well maintained. Many of the ideas we discuss apply equally to the other plugins, so you shouldn't have trouble using them in combination with their documentation.

11.2.2 Getting started with Spring Security

Access control is impossible without identifying the current user. Hubbub does this by requiring users to enter their user ID and password on the login page and then storing the corresponding `User` instance in the HTTP session (assuming authentication is successful). Let's replace this basic mechanism with the more full-featured Spring Security.

The first step as usual is to install the plugin by declaring it in BuildConfig.groovy:

```
plugins {
    ...
    compile ":spring-security-core:2.0"
}
```

You may find the name of the plugin confusing, but it makes sense when you realize that the various Spring Security plugins provide different sets of features, such as Twitter and Facebook-based authentication. You'll see those later in the chapter, but for now the core plugin does everything you need (and more).

After you update the `BuildConfig.groovy` file and run the `grails refresh-dependencies` command (this is required before running any of the commands provided by the plugin), you're ready to set up access control for your application. If you create a new application from scratch, you can get started quickly by running

```
grails s2-quickstart org.example User Role Requestmap
```

This creates four domain classes in the `org.example` package: `User`, `Role`, `UserRole`, and `Requestmap`. It also creates a login page and everything else you need to authenticate users and protect URLs.

In the case of Hubbub, you already have a `User` domain class that you don't want to overwrite. Rename User.groovy (under the domain folder) to TempUser.groovy so it isn't overwritten and run the same command:

```
grails s2-quickstart com.grailsinaction User Role
```

Note that you leave out the `Requestmap` argument because you don't want to store URL rules for Hubbub in the database. If you want to change your URL rules at runtime, then it's best to include `Requestmap`. The plugin's documentation explains how to use runtime request maps.

Now you have User.groovy and TempUser.groovy. How do you reconcile them? The new `User` class should include everything from the generated class and everything from `TempUser` except:

- The `username` property should be replaced by `loginId`
- The `password` property becomes `passwordHash`

The Spring Security Core plugin doesn't force property names on you, but it does need a property for the username and the hash of the password (you should never store plain text passwords in your database). You can see the final `User` domain class in the following listing with additional changes that we explain afterward.

Listing 11.3 The Spring Security-enabled `User` domain class

```
package com.grailsinaction

class User {

    String loginId                          // Renames username property to loginId
    String passwordHash                     // Renames password to make it explicit you're storing password hash
    boolean enabled = true
    boolean accountExpired
    boolean accountLocked
    boolean passwordExpired

    Date dateCreated                        // Adds existing User properties missing
                                            // from Spring Security-generated class
    static hasOne = [ profile : Profile ]
```

```
    static hasMany = [ posts : Post, tags : Tag, following : User ]

    static transients = ['springSecurityService']

    static constraints = {
        loginId size: 3..20, unique: true, blank: false
        tags()
        posts()
        profile nullable: true
    }

    static mapping = {
        posts sort: "dateCreated", order: "desc"
    }

    Set<Role> getAuthorities() {
        UserRole.findAllByUser(this).collect { it.role } as Set
    }

    String toString() { return "User $loginId (id: $id)" }
    String getDisplayString() { return loginId }
}
```

Removes password constraints as Spring Security stores password hash.

Removes beforeInsert and beforeUpdate event handlers.

After you make these changes, you can (and should) remove the TempUser.groovy file, leaving a simple domain model of a user having zero or more roles.

> **Don't forget data migrations!**
> Because you're modifying a domain class and adding extra ones, you'll have to add the corresponding migrations. You can find examples in the chapter source on GitHub.

One important modification to the original code generated by the Spring Security Core plugin is the removal of the event handlers `beforeInsert()` and `beforeUpdate()`. You do this because modifying field values before they're persisted to the database causes behavior around validation that's difficult to understand. It's also confusing from the developer's perspective because there's a discrepancy between the initial value set and the one stored.

The safest choice is to factor out user creation into a service that explicitly encodes incoming passwords using the `springSecurityService` bean. For the chapter source on GitHub, we've taken a less ideal but simpler approach: explicitly encoding passwords in `BootStrap` and `UserController` via the `encodePassword(String)` method on the `springSecurityService` bean.

With these big changes to the `User` domain class coming in, it's not only the application code that needs updating. The existing tests don't work now, either! It would take too much space to show all the updated code here, so we'll describe the changes you need to make to the tests, and then you can look at the source code on GitHub to see the result. Here's the short list of things you need to do:

- *Tests involving validation failures should use* `loginId` *rather than password.* Because you now have a `passwordHash` property with no constraints, any test relying on the old constraints causing validation failures must be updated. You can use the `loginId` property to trigger validation failures instead.

- *Integration tests should not compare passwords.* Several integration tests check the value of the `password` property, but the property has been renamed and now contains a hash. You shouldn't query or test on the password hash, so we updated the chapter source to remove those tests that do.
- `UserControllerSpec` *must mock the security service.* As `UserController` now uses `springSecurityService` to encode the passwords, this service must be mocked in the corresponding unit test.
- *Unit tests creating* `User` *instances must use* `passwordHash`. Several unit tests instantiate `User` objects. These should initialize the `passwordHash` property rather than `password`. The value doesn't have to be a valid hash.

Password hashing

The Spring Security plugin stores password hashes (using bcrypt by default) rather than the plain text password. Ideally, you should use a strong hashing algorithm with a salt and multiple iterations in case an attacker ever gets hold of the data in the user table.

You can manually control when password encoding takes place by directly using the `encodePassword()` method on the `springSecurityService` bean.

Now that you have the domain model to support your access-control system, you're almost ready to implement rules for determining who can do what. The only thing left to do is configure the plugin to use the `loginId` and `passwordHash` properties in place of `username` and `password`. Add the following entry to grails-app/conf/Config.groovy, preferably after the user domain class name setting (we've used `g.p.s` to save space but you'll need the full `grails.plugin.springsecurity` in your Config.groovy):

```
g.p.s.userLookup.userDomainClassName = "com.grailsinaction.User"
g.p.s.userLookup.usernamePropertyName = "loginId"
g.p.s.userLookup.passwordPropertyName = "passwordHash"
```

Adds lines to Config.groovy

Several other configuration options allow you to use nonstandard class and property names, all of which are well documented in the plugin's user guide. You can, for example, change the name of the `enabled` property as well.

> **NOTE** Version 1.2.x and earlier of the Spring Security plugin defaults to a value of `false` for `enabled`. When creating new users, be sure to initialize the property to `true` first, otherwise those users won't be able to log in.

Spring Security is primed and ready, blocking access to most parts of the application. All you have to do now is tell it what URLs need protection so that users can access at least some parts of the application without logging in.

11.2.3 Protecting URLs

You'll start with a simple security model for Hubbub: all pages require an authenticated user except the home page, the global timeline, and all the user pages (such as registration and user search). The plugin gives you three options for specifying this information:

- *Static config*—The rules are declared in Config.groovy.
- *Dynamic*—The rules are stored in the database as `Requestmap` instances.
- *Annotations*—The rules are declared using annotations in controllers and services.

As we mentioned previously, the dynamic option is useful if you want to change the access control rules at runtime. Annotations are simple and convenient and allow you to work at the controller and action level, rather than the URL. They're also convenient for securing service methods.

For Hubbub, you're going with the old-fashioned static-config approach, partly because URL-based rules are common, partly because it keeps all the security information together, and partly because we need to talk about the ordering of rules. It also allows you to protect pages or resources that aren't backed by an action, such as images.

Let's look at the configuration you'll use to implement the required access control. Listing 11.4 shows the extra settings you need to add to Config.groovy so that all users have access to the home and login pages, but only authenticated users can see the rest of the application. These rules also make sure that all JavaScript, CSS, and image files are publicly visible. Note that the `s2-quickstart` command adds a `controllerAnnotations.staticRules` setting that you need to replace with the `interceptUrlMap` one.

Listing 11.4 Spring Security configuration for Hubbub's simple access-control model

```
grails.plugin.springsecurity.securityConfigType = "InterceptUrlMap"

grails.plugin.springsecurity.interceptUrlMap = [
    '/': ['permitAll'],
    '/post/global': ['permitAll']
    '/user/**': ['permitAll']
    '/login/auth': ['permitAll'],
    '/**/js/**': ['permitAll'],
    '/**/css/**': ['permitAll'],
    '/**/images/**': ['permitAll'],
    '/**': ['isFullyAuthenticated()']
]
```

Tells Spring Security to use static URL rules

Unrestricted access

Open access to static resources

Everything else requires authenticated user

A couple of things aren't apparent from this listing:

- All URLs require an authenticated user by default if there is no matching rule.
- The URL patterns in the configuration must be all lowercase.

A URL such as http://localhost:8080/hubbub/starPost/showAll should be specified in the configuration as

```
'/starpost/showall'
```

You must be careful with the order of these rules, because Spring Security uses the first one that matches the request URL. If you put the rule

```
'/**': ['ROLE_USER']
```

first, all pages of your application would require an authenticated user with that role regardless of the rules that come after. The more specific the URL pattern in a rule, the earlier it should go in the list.

Hubbub is now secured against anonymous access. If a user doesn't have an account, they can't post any messages. Try it out by starting the server and pointing your browser at http://localhost:8080/hubbub/timeline. You're redirected automatically to the plugin's login page, shown in figure 11.4.

You can try to log in using one of the existing users, such as `frankie` with a password of `testing`, but this results in a server error. You still need to integrate the login with the rest of the application because most pages currently expect to find a `User` instance in the session.

Before you do that, let's look at that Remember me option on the login page. It's a feature we're sure you're familiar with from various websites, and it suits Hubbub well. The application doesn't need a high degree of security, so allowing users to see their timeline and post new messages without logging in every time is a big win. The problem right now is that if you come back to Hubbub after a period of time (30 minutes, by default), you'll find you can't access the application. You can test this by changing

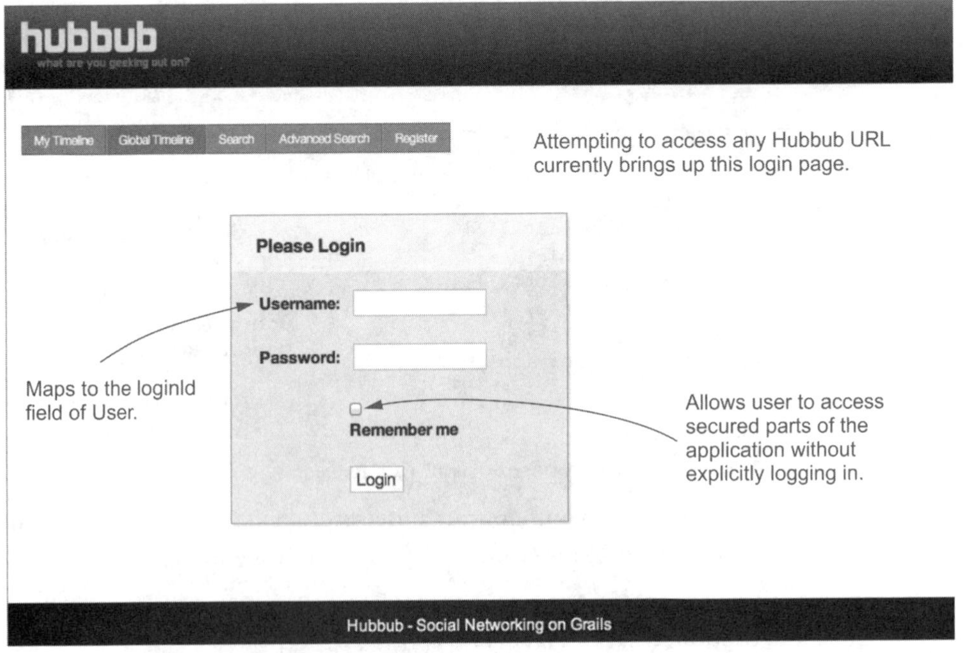

Figure 11.4 The Spring Security plugin's standard login page

the session timeout in src/templates/war/web.xml to 1 or 2, restarting the server, logging into the application with the Remember me option selected, waiting a couple of minutes, and then accessing one of the protected pages.

> **Diagnosing problems**
> Problems with Spring Security rules can often be diagnosed by seeing what requests and responses are shuttling between the browser and your application. It's a good idea to use your browser's developer tools for this. Look out for redirects (response codes 301 or 302), nonauthenticated users (401), and access denied (403).

Behind the scenes, Spring Security allows the user through because it remembers them, despite the user session timing out. Unfortunately, the user isn't allowed to access any of the pages because a fully authenticated user is required, meaning one who has explicitly logged in at the beginning of the session. The result is that Spring Security redirects the user to the /login/full page, which happens to also require a fully authenticated user. You end up with an infinite loop of redirects.

> **WARNING** Never allow the user to select the Remember me option if the application doesn't support it. Remove the option from the plugin-provided default login page if you're using that page.

Okay, so it was foolish to have only the /login/auth URL open to anonymous access. In reality, you should grant anonymous access to /login/** and /logout/**. But the configuration we showed previously was useful in highlighting the kinds of strange behavior that you might see due to misconfigured rules.

As it happens, you do want to support Remember me in Hubbub. Replace the /login/auth rule with this:

```
'/login/**': ['permitAll'],
'/logout/**': ['permitAll'],
```

and change the last rule to this

```
'/**': ['isAuthenticated()']
```

That's it! The Remember me feature now works, the browser won't get stuck, and users no longer need to authenticate every time they visit Hubbub.

Now that you sorted out that particular problem, let's see how to wire Spring Security into the rest of Hubbub.

11.2.4 Getting hold of the current user

The access control isn't fully working yet, but that won't take long to fix. The first thing to do is sort out the user's timeline page, which is currently generating a 500 error because it can't access the logged-in user.

You have a couple of options. You could store the `User` instance in the session when the user logs in. That requires you to copy the LoginController.groovy file from the plugin to the app's controllers directory and modify it. This is wasted effort, however, because you can get the current user from Spring Security directly. Also, why use up valuable session space if you don't have to? Instead, go with the second option: get the user from Spring Security.

All the information you need is provided by the `springSecurityService` bean, so you can inject into whichever classes need access to the current user. The bean is useful, so we've documented several of its properties and methods in table 11.2.

Table 11.2 A summary of useful methods provided by the plugin's `springSecurityService` bean

Method	Description
`currentUser`	Property that returns the domain instance representing the current user.
`isLoggedIn()`	Returns `true` if the current user is logged in, otherwise `false`.
`encodePassword(pwd[, salt])`	Encodes the given password with the configured hash algorithm, returning the hash; this hash can be stored in the `password` field of the user domain class. You can optionally pass in a salt for the hash algorithm.
`isAjax(request)`	Returns `true` if the given `HttpServletRequest` appears to be an Ajax one.

As you can probably guess, you want to use the `currentUser` property to get hold of the `User` instance. One thing to be aware of is that the property returns `null` if the user isn't logged in or remembered. The following listing shows the changes you need to make in `PostController` as italics.

Listing 11.5 Using `PostController` to get the `User` instance

```
class PostController {
    ...
    def postService
    def springSecurityService
    ...
    def personal() {
        def user = springSecurityService.currentUser
        render view: "timeline", model: [ user : user ]
    }
    ...
    def addPost(String content) {
        def user = springSecurityService.currentUser
        try {
            def newPost = postService.createPost(user.loginId, content)
            ...
        }
        redirect(action: 'timeline', id: user.loginId)
    }
```

Fetches current user from Spring Security instead of HTTP session

```
    def addPostAjax(String content) {
        def user = springSecurityService.currentUser
        try {
            def newPost = postService.createPost(user.loginId, content)
            def recentPosts = Post.findAllByUser(
                user,
                [sort: 'dateCreated', order: 'desc', max: 20])
            ...
    }
    ...
```

That fixes the controller, but if you try to access the Global Timeline page, you won't see the text box for submitting a new post. The global.gsp view tests whether the HTTP session contains a `user` variable, which is no longer the case. Your first thought may be to use the `springSecurityService` bean from the view (an ugly solution) or add the user to the view's model (a better idea).

The best approach is to use Spring Security Core's handy tag library instead, which provides what you need. Instead of code such as

```
<g:if test="${session.user}">
    ...
</g:if>
```

in global.gsp, you can use the following tag to check whether or not a user is logged in

```
<sec:ifLoggedIn>
    ...
</sec:ifLoggedIn>
```

If you need access to the User instance for the logged in user, then you do need to provide it through the view's model. That's what we do in the chapter source on GitHub.

While we're on the subject of GSP tags, you can add the following block to any of your layouts; it allows users to log out at any time:

```
<sec:ifLoggedIn>
  <g:form name="logoutForm" controller="logout" action="index">
    <g:submitButton name="signOut" value="sign out"/>
  </g:form>
</sec:ifLoggedIn>
```

As you can probably guess, the `ifLoggedIn` tag only writes out its contents if the user is logged in via Spring Security. In this case, the content is a form and button that submit to the index action of the logout controller, which is provided by the plugin. You use a form because the plugin only allows POST requests for logging out by default, although this can be changed in your application configuration.

The access control is working nicely now. Only authenticated (or remembered) users can access the /post/timeline page, and new posts are correctly associated with the currently logged-in user. You can even provide a button allowing the user to log out. What more do you need?

One problem is that you now have two login pages, so it's good to get rid of one. Let's keep the old one because it has better styling right now and hook it up to the Spring Security authentication mechanism.

11.2.5 Using a custom login page

The process of configuring the plugin to use your home page for login is easy. Add these entries to Config.groovy:

```
g.p.s.auth.loginFormUrl = "/login/form"
g.p.s.failureHandler.defaultFailureUrl = "/login/form"
g.p.s.successHandler.defaultTargetUrl = "/timeline"
```

The first option makes sure that Spring Security redirects to the previous login page when authentication is required, and the second tells Spring Security to load the user's timeline page by default after a successful login. This second option doesn't apply if a user attempts to access a protected page and is redirected to the login page to authenticate. In that case, Spring Security redirects to the page the user was originally trying to access.

It would be nice if that was all you need to do, but the existing login form won't work as it is. The username and password fields need to have special names—ones that are recognized by Spring Security, and the form needs to be submitted to a different URL. On the bright side, this gives you an opportunity to add a Remember me box. The following listing shows the new form in grails-app/views/login/form.gsp.

Listing 11.6 Adding a Remember me box

```
<g:form uri="/j_spring_security_check" method="POST">
    <fieldset class="form">
        <div class="fieldcontain required">
            <label for="j_username">Login ID</label>
            <g:textField name="j_username" value="${loginId}"/>
        </div>
        <div class="fieldcontain required">
            <label for="j_password">Password</label>
            <g:passwordField name="j_password"/>
        </div>
        <div class="fieldcontain required">
            <label for="_spring_security_remember_me">Remember me</label>
            <g:checkBox name="_spring_security_remember_me"/>
        </div>
    </fieldset>
    <fieldset class="buttons">
        <g:submitButton name="signIn" value="Sign in"/>
    </fieldset>
</g:form>
```

Submits user credentials to /j_spring_security_check URI. No other URI works.

The username field must be called j_username.

The password field must be called j_password.

One last thing you should do is rename your `LoginController` because Spring Security Core provides a controller with the same name. Rename your controller `AuthController` and move the views from grails-app/views/login to grails-app/views/auth. To ensure that the /login/form URL continues to work, add this URL mapping:

```
"/login/form"(controller: "auth", action: "form")
```

Also delete the LameSecurityFilters.groovy file, because you're no longer using it for access control.

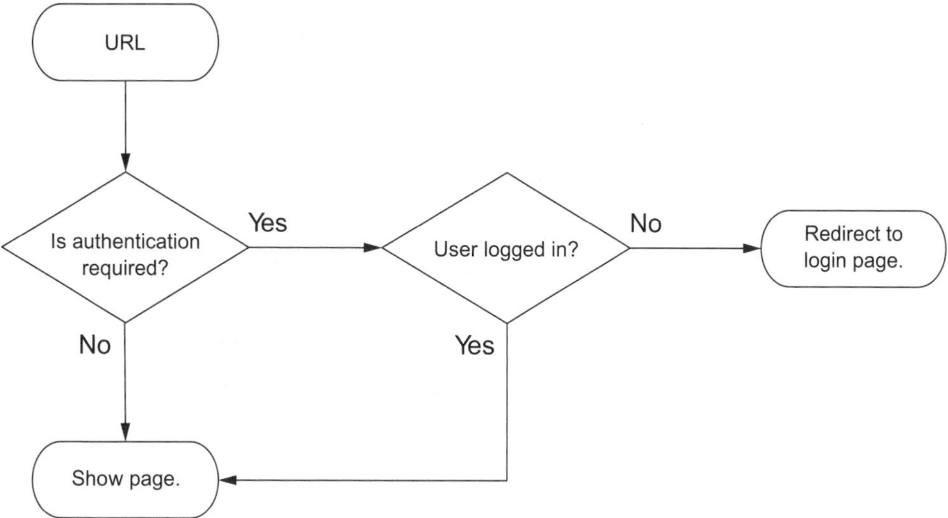

Figure 11.5 A simple access-control logic flow that we want to functionally test

Now that everything is working and you have basic access control in place, it's time to consider how to test this. You do want to make sure that it's working properly and that future changes don't break anything!

11.2.6 Testing access control

Spring Security, like other security frameworks, uses a combination of servlet filters and other types of interceptors to control access to an application. That means if you want to test your access control at the page level, functional tests are the only game in town.

Figure 11.5 shows the logic you want to test. It's not comprehensive, but it does illustrate what you're trying to achieve with your tests. You want to make sure that all the conditions work and that application pages are displayed when you expect them to be.

Writing a test to confirm the behavior shown in the diagram is straightforward, and you can see the resulting code in the following listing. As in chapter 9, you're using the Geb plugin to access particular URLs, but now most of those URLs are protected.

Listing 11.7 A functional test to verify the access-control behavior

```
package com.grailsinaction

class AccessControlFunctionalSpec extends spock.lang.Specification {
    void "Anonymous access to home page"() {
        expect: "Unauthenticated user can access global timeline"
        to GlobalTimelinePage
    }
```

Allows anonymous access

```
    void "Anonymous access to restricted page"() {
        when: "Unauthenticated user accesses a user's timeline page"
        via TimelinePage, "phil"                                    Denies
                                                                    anonymous
        then: "the user is redirected to the login page"           access
        at LoginPage

        when: "the user logs in"                                    Checks login
        login "frankie", "testing"                                  failure

        then: "he or she can access the timeline page"
        to TimelinePage, "phil"
    }

    private login(String username, String password) {
        to LoginPage
        loginIdField = username
        passwordField = password
        signInButton.click()
    }
}
```

This functional test should also give you a good idea how to modify the existing functional tests so that they work. Remember, the timeline page for a specific user now requires authentication and the login page has different names for its fields. You'll need to update both `TimelineFunctionalSpec` and `LoginPage`.

Everything is now working, and you have a system in place that you can grow as needed. And remember, much of the work involved has come from the use of existing domain classes and views. The process is much simpler and quicker if you accept the defaults that the plugin provides. That said, by doing it the hard way, you explored several facets of Spring Security and the plugin that stand you in good stead for the future.

In the remainder of the chapter, you look at more advanced techniques that help you with a variety of security requirements and add useful refinements to Hubbub.

11.3 Further exploration of Spring Security

Spring Security is a powerful framework with various options for authentication and authorization, many of which the plugin exposes to you. It's impossible to discuss everything you can do with Spring Security in a single chapter—a book would be more appropriate—so rather than attempt the impossible, in this section we introduce common scenarios that require extra work.

11.3.1 Tightening restrictions on access

Spring Security uses the concept of authorities for assigning and determining rights: who can do what. Its implementation is surprisingly powerful, but because the concept of authorities is abstract, it's difficult for people to understand.

The plugin sidesteps this problem by only dealing with named authorities called roles. These are simple—they're names. A user is assigned any number of roles, which gives them the right to access URLs restricted to any of those roles. Table 11.3 demonstrates how rule requirements combine with role assignments to determine whether a user has access to a particular URL. If any of the roles the user has match any of the required roles, access is granted. Note that in these examples, `ROLE_USER` and `ROLE_ADMIN` are strings. Also, if a user has no role, then they can't even log in.

Table 11.3 How role requirements and rule assignments relate to each other

Rule requires	User has	Access granted?
`ROLE_USER`	`ROLE_USER`	Yes
`ROLE_ADMIN`	`ROLE_USER`	No
`ROLE_USER,ROLE_ADMIN`	`ROLE_USER`	Yes

How are roles assigned? By linking a `Role` instance to a `User` instance either programmatically, as you do in `BootStrap` in the example Hubbub source code, or via a user-management UI. The latter is ideal if you want to assign or revoke user privileges at runtime.

Spring Security expressions

The URL rules can use expressions as well as the string constants. For example, `ROLE_USER` can be replaced with `hasRole("ROLE_USER")`. We use these expressions in the chapter source code. Find out more in the Spring Security user guide.[2]

A typical `Role` instance might have a name of `ROLE_USER` and a description of "A known, registered user of the system." You can then make that role a requirement for any given URL by adding it to the corresponding rule in Config.groovy:

```
'/profile/**': ['ROLE_USER']
```

This raises the question, what's the difference between `IS_AUTHENTICATED_REMEMBERED`, `IS_AUTHENTICATED_FULLY`, and `ROLE_USER`?

- `IS_AUTHENTICATED_REMEMBERED`—Built into Spring Security. Allows any user who's authenticated or remembered.
- `IS_AUTHENTICATED_FULLY`—Built into Spring Security. Allows any authenticated user. Does not allow *remembered* users.
- `ROLE_USER`—User-defined role that only allows access to users who've been assigned it. Applies whether the user is authenticated or remembered.

Let's consider a more concrete example. Say you're using the user-management UI provided by the Spring Security UI plugin. You don't want everybody to have access to

[2] Expression-Based Access Control, http://docs.spring.io/spring-security/site/docs/3.1.x/reference/el-access.html.

it because modifying user information and adding, deleting, or disabling accounts are highly sensitive operations. What do you do?

First, you create a new role, in BootStrap.groovy for example, with the name `ROLE_ADMIN` and assign it to a user:

```
def role = new Role(authority: "ROLE_ADMIN", description: "A super user.")
def admin = new User(loginId: "dilbert", ...).save()
role.addToPeople(admin)
role.save()
```

Then, you restrict access to the user-management URLs to that role:

```
grails.plugins.springsecurity.interceptUrlMap = [
    '/': ['permitAll'],
    '/user/**': ['ROLE_ADMIN'],
    '/role/**': ['ROLE_ADMIN'],
    ...
]
```

That's all there is to it. Your user-management UI is now restricted to administrators only.

All straightforward, we think you'll agree. But there's one fly in the ointment. Imagine that users can edit their profiles. You can limit access to the edit profile page by role, but then anyone with the required role can access everyone's profile, definitely not what you want! This is where you hit the limits of Spring Security and have to implement a solution yourself.

The easiest way to add this kind of feature is via Grails filters. All you have to do is configure a `before` interceptor on the profile controller that checks whether the current user is the owner of the requested profile. The following listing contains such a filter, which goes into grails-app/conf/com/grailsinaction/SecurityFilters.groovy. If the current user's ID doesn't match the one given in the request URL, access is blocked.

Listing 11.8 Restricting access to a single user via a Grails filter

```
package com.grailsinaction

class SecurityFilters {
   def springSecurityService

   def filters = {
      profileChanges(controller: "profile", action: "edit|update") {
         before = {
            def currLoginId = springSecurityService.currentUser.loginId
            if (currLoginId != Profile.get(params.id).user.loginId) {
               redirect controller: "login", action: "denied"
               return false                          <-- Blocks access if
            }                                            profile isn't current
            return true                                  user's one
         }
      }
   }
}
```

As you can see, the filter is simple. The main thing is to ensure that it returns `false` if the current user shouldn't be allowed access to the page or submit data to the update action.

You've now finished with the authorization side of things. Role-based schemes work for many types of applications. For those occasions when you need finer-grained access control, you might want to look into either the Spring Security ACL plugin, which supports access control lists (ACLs), or the Spring Security Shiro plugin, which allows you to use Shiro's simpler permission system.

If you're done with authorization, what's left? The final feature we'll add to Hubbub is social authentication, because let's face it, users don't like maintaining multiple user accounts with multiple passwords.

11.3.2 Social authentication

The authentication you used so far is based on storing users and their passwords in the database. Although this is one of the most common approaches, it isn't the only one. Spring Security (and, by extension, the plugin) supports many schemes via what it calls *authentication providers*. You may be surprised to learn that Hubbub is already using three of them:

- `AnonymousAuthenticationProvider`
- `RememberMeAuthenticationProvider`
- `GrailsDaoAuthenticationProvider`

It's the last of these that utilizes your `User` domain class for authentication and authorization. But do you need to maintain your own identity management?

Let's think about what you want for Hubbub right now. The plan is to take over the world, or at least displace Twitter from its position at the top of microblogging services. That means at least allowing Twitter users to access Hubbub immediately, so why not let them authenticate with Twitter and bypass creating new accounts in Hubbub? Maintaining an account for every website or application you use is one of the more frustrating things online today.

Grails is blessed with several plugins that add social authentication to Spring Security, such as Spring Security Twitter, Spring Security Facebook, and Spring Security OAuth. We won't look at all of these, but after you see one, the rest are fairly easy to understand and use. It helps that most of them use OAuth (http://oauth.net/) in one form or other under the hood.

Before you can implement Twitter authentication in Hubbub, you need to register the application with Twitter. It's not obvious how to do this, so we show the flow of screens in figure 11.6. Go to https://dev.twitter.com/, log in, and then follow the links in figure 11.6.

After the Hubbub application is registered, you have access to the all important consumer key and secret. You can't connect to Twitter without them! You can now switch back to Grails and start incorporating Twitter authentication by first adding the Spring-Security-Twitter plugin to your dependencies:

```
compile ":spring-security-twitter:0.6.2"
```

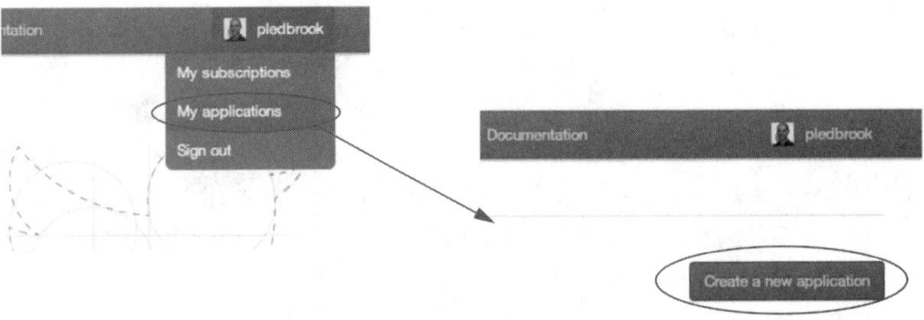

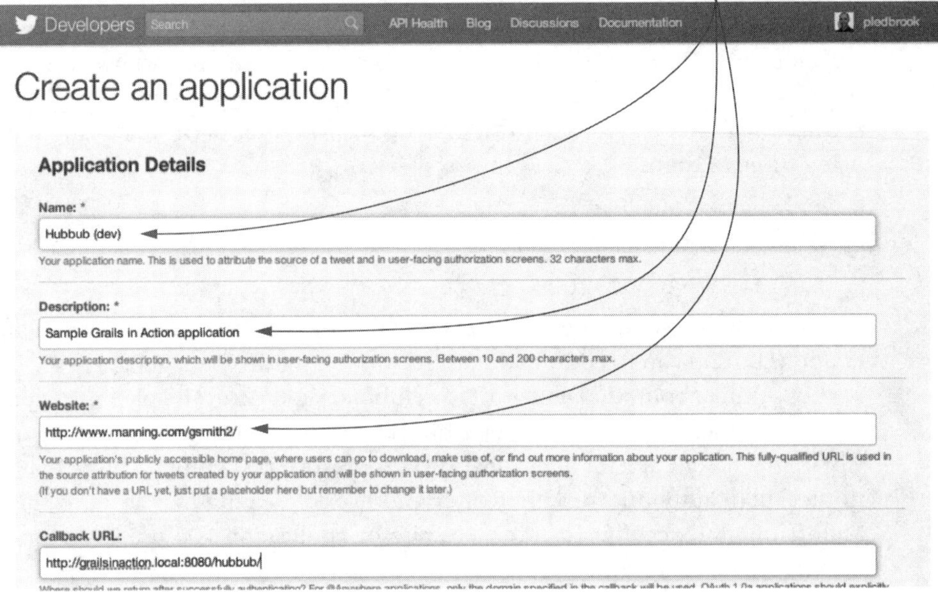

Figure 11.6 The sequence of screens for registering a new application with Twitter

Then run the `compile` command (to install the plugin), followed by

```
grails s2-init-twitter
```

This asks for several pieces of information:

```
> Enter your Twitter API Key hubbub
> Enter your Twitter API Consumer Key testuser483498
> Enter your Twitter API Consumer Secret ksfhekfhaekrhsdfsfahhreg
```

The API Key isn't that important and you can enter "hubbub" as shown in the example. But the other two fields, the Consumer Key and Consumer Secret, require the values that Twitter provides when you register the application.

The `s2-init-twitter` command installs a few files into your project and adds configuration settings to the end of Config.groovy. Those settings comprise the app key, the Consumer Key, and the Consumer Secret. At this point, you have a decision to make. Config.groovy is normally included in source control, which means that anything in it becomes public knowledge. That makes it a bad location for passwords and secrets.

Now, you may consider your source control system private and safe, so perhaps putting secrets in it isn't a problem. But you don't want to do that for Hubbub because its source is on GitHub and available to everyone. What you're going to do is move those settings into a separate file that's not kept in source control. First, add these lines to the beginning of Config.groovy:

```
grails.config.locations = [ "classpath:${appName}-config.groovy",
                            "file:./${appName}-config.groovy" ]
```

The `grails.config.locations` setting tells Grails where it can find extra configuration files. Locations that begin with `file:` represent files on the local filesystem and those that begin with `classpath:` represent paths relative the application's classpath.

The reason you have two locations like this is so that it works with both `run-app` and production deployments. By putting a `hubbub-config.groovy` file in the project directory, you can make extra settings available to the application when using `run-app` and `run-war`. But when you package the application as a WAR file and deploy it to Tomcat, you can put the configuration file into the Tomcat lib directory, which automatically goes onto the application classpath. We talk more about such external configuration files in chapter 17.

Next, you move the `grails.plugin.springsecurity.twitter.*` settings from Config.groovy to hubbub-config.groovy (which goes into the root directory of the project):

```
grails.plugin.springsecurity.twitter.app.key='Hubbub'
grails.plugin.springsecurity.twitter.app.consumerKey='...'
grails.plugin.springsecurity.twitter.app.consumerSecret='...'
```

And finally, you enable the Sign in with Twitter feature by adding the following lines to your login page.

Listing 11.9 Enabling the Sign in with Twitter feature

```
<html>
<head>
  <meta name='layout' content='main'/>
  <title><g:message code="springSecurity.login.title"/></title>
  <g:external dir="css" file="twitter-auth.css"/>       <-- Includes CSS to style Sign in with Twitter link
  ...
</head>
<body>
<div id='login'>
  <div class='inner'>
    <div class='fheader'>
      <g:message code="springSecurity.login.header"/>
    </div>
    <twitterAuth:button/>          <-- Adds Sign in with Twitter link to page
  </div>
  ...
```

```
</body>
</html>
```

Everything is now in place and all that's left is try it out. But if you run the application and try to log in via Twitter (assuming you have a Twitter account), you find that it doesn't work. What's going on?

When you run the application normally, via `run-app`, you point your browser at localhost or 127.0.0.1. Browsers are absolutely fine with this, but Twitter isn't. You need a nonlocalhost domain. The way to do this is to invent a local domain, grailsinaction.local, and bind it to the IP address 127.0.0.1 in the hosts file. On Mac OS X or Linux, you'd have a line such as the following in the /etc/hosts file:

```
127.0.0.1        localhost grailsinaction.local
```

On modern versions of Windows (XP and above) you can find the equivalent file at %SystemRoot%\system32\drivers\etc\hosts, where %SystemRoot% is typically C:\Windows.

Now if you point your browser at http://grailsinaction.local:8080/hubbub/ and ensure that the callback URL registered with Twitter is the same, you can log into your local Hubbub instance via Twitter! Unfortunately, some of the pages won't display because they expect a properly configured profile, which doesn't get created for Twitter-authenticated users. For seamless integration, you should add a Grails filter that checks whether the authenticated user has a profile, and if not, redirects that user to a page for filling in the required profile information.

You can breathe a sigh of relief—you made it! This chapter covered a good portion of information on security, but there's even more to learn. Don't worry, though; you've got a solid foundation on which to build your knowledge in this area.

11.4 Summary and best practices

Security is a complex subject that often requires the average developer to think in new ways. You saw several examples of the types of attacks that your Grails applications might face, but our focus is more on the prevention techniques you should apply rather than the attacks that they counter. While developing, it's easier to remember to validate all your inputs rather than to protect against SQL/code/whatever injection attacks.

We urge you to think about the access-control rules you set up. A framework such as Spring Security can make it easy to add access control to an application, but it's no more secure than the rules you define. Make sure you understand the application's specific requirements before implementing its access control.

Another important point to think about is how secure the application needs to be. How sensitive is the information in it? What are the consequences if an attacker manages to masquerade as a genuine user? You can implement security checks, but are they worth the associated cost in development time and possible user inconvenience? For example, Hubbub doesn't contain particularly sensitive information, but it should make it difficult to post messages as other people. On the other hand, a banking application requires far more checks and should make sure that no one can even see user-specific information.

Here are ideas and guidelines to help you protect your application:

- *Remember the motto: "strength in depth."* If you have only a single layer of security around your application, an attacker who gets through has untrammeled access to the whole application. You should also perform input validation in your controllers and use the query options that autoescape parameters, for example.
- *Know your trust boundaries.* A trust boundary is a point of communication where one side is trusted and the other isn't. It's at these trust boundaries that you must be particularly vigilant, scrubbing data that comes in and making sure data going out is safe.
- *Test, test, test!* Make sure that the application isn't susceptible to common types of attack by using functional tests and automated tools like OWASP's WebScarab.[3]
- *Obfuscation isn't a substitute for proper security.* Hiding or mangling information can be useful—after all, there's no point in advertising anything that might help an attacker. But if you rely on obfuscation, you run a high risk of compromise. It's complementary to other techniques, not a substitute.
- *Develop with security in mind.* Remember that security is a process and a mindset. In order for your application to be secure, you have to consciously consider the potential effects of the code you write.
- *Perform code reviews.* Similar to the way code reviews help weed out coding mistakes and movements in the direction of the "ball of mud" design pattern, they can also pick up security flaws. There's nothing like a second pair of eyes when it comes to catching these things.
- *Use existing tools and frameworks.* No matter how vigilant you are errors will creep in. Security tools and frameworks are battle-tested and in wide use, so vulnerabilities are quickly found and quashed. Why risk your application by using homegrown solutions?

We'd like to reiterate that several security frameworks are available for Grails, so if you need one, we think it's worth a little research to make sure you pick the right one for you.

With all this security knowledge under your belt, you can now consider opening up your applications and allowing access to software clients, and not only human users via their web browsers.

---

3 "WebScarab (Next Generation) Project," https://www.owasp.org/index.php/OWASP_WebScarab_NG_Project.

12 Exposing your app to other programs

This chapter covers

- Implementing RESTful services in Grails
- Applying authentication to API calls
- Exporting services to remote clients

Now that you've added access control to Hubbub, your application is ready for the big, bad world. Your users can start conversations and kick off a big hubbub. Does that mean there's nothing more to add? No. An important feature of web applications these days is an API.

Do you ever wonder why Twitter and Facebook became so popular? Sure, people like socializing, and people gravitate to where everyone else is. But how did they gain critical mass in the first place? By being first to market? Well, Facebook came after MySpace and still managed to supplant it.

They're successful for many reasons, but one of the most important is that they're open platforms. Think about all the websites that include Twitter feeds on their home page, or all the pages that have the "share via Twitter/Facebook" links. And never forget the popularity of games such as Farmville on Facebook, games that are created by companies independent of Facebook itself. Such integration

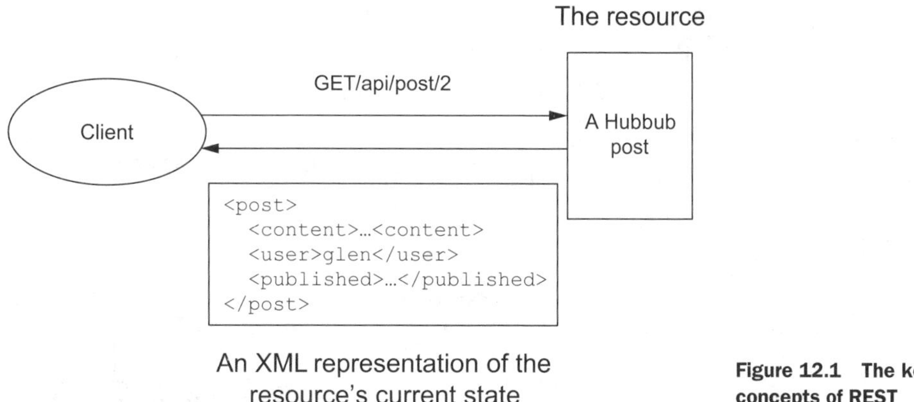

Figure 12.1 The key concepts of REST

with external sites and applications is a key element of a *sticky* platform, which refers to how well the platform attracts and retains new users.

Given that application-to-application integration is important to the success of a project, a fundamental requirement for the project is to have a public API. Ideally an API that's both usable and well documented. For web applications such as Hubbub, the dominant form of API is a REST-based interface.

12.1 Creating a REST interface

In this section, we introduce the basic elements of REST and then show how to get an initial REST interface into Hubbub. This approach makes it easy to get going, and you can start playing with the interface straightaway, using any number of tools. We also mention how to get those tools and how to use them.

12.1.1 What is REST?

HTTP is the language of the web, but it also embodies an architectural style called REST that works for any client/server communication. The incredible success of the web in its current form is a major reason why REST is so popular. Its flexibility and scalability have been proven many times over.

The idea of REST is that an application is a collection of resources that can be operated on by a few methods. In a wiki, each page is a single resource that you can fetch, modify, or delete. You can even create new pages. Each method (except delete) involves transferring the contents of a particular page between the client (the browser) and the wiki. The data in the requests and responses is a representation of the page's state. Another example of REST comes from Hubbub (see figure 12.1), in which a client retrieves an existing post and also creates a new one.

For a web application such as Hubbub, the methods you can use to operate on a resource are already provided by HTTP. The four basic verbs (or methods) available are:

- GET—Retrieves a resource
- POST—Creates a new resource

- PUT—Updates an existing resource or creates a new one with a known ID
- DELETE—Removes a resource

The first two are common among normal web applications because browsers use them regularly. Every time you open a web page, the browser is issuing a GET request, and when you submit a form the information is typically sent as a POST.

> **POST versus PUT**
>
> A common source of confusion in REST revolves around when you should use POST and when PUT. According to the specification,[1] PUT is used for creating and updating resources *at a given* URL.
>
> In Grails, the ID of a new resource often isn't known before it's created, so PUT doesn't have a URL to work against. Instead, you perform a POST to the parent URL, say /posts, which creates a subordinate resource, such as /posts/10.
>
> In the case of an existing resource, you know the ID, so you should use PUT to update it.

Those are your REST methods, so what about the resources themselves? First, you need to know how to identify them when using the methods. Once again, HTTP provides the solution: URLs. Ideally, those URLs should have the following attributes:

- *Unique to a resource*—Each URL should only represent a single resource. A single URL should not identify two different posts. You can have multiple URLs per resource, but we think it helps avoid confusion if you don't.
- *Long-lived*—A URL should always point to the same resource, preferably until the end of time. That may sound like too much to ask for, and the HTTP specification acknowledges this with temporary and permanent redirects. Yet you should endeavor to ensure that your URLs *are* long-lived, or you might get a bad reputation for broken links—one of the banes of the web.

> **Good URL design**
>
> We highlight only two recommendations for URLs here, but they aren't the only contributing factors to good URL design. It can be argued that URLs should also be short, easy to understand, and easy to remember. These principles aren't directly related to REST, but they can help users and developers. To find out more, search for "good URL design" on the web.

The last element of REST, but certainly not the least, is the resource data itself. More often than not, the data is stored in a database. When a client requests a particular resource, the REST implementation converts that data into a representation the client

---

1 "HTTP/1.1 method definitions," http://www.w3.org/Protocols/rfc2616/rfc2616-sec9.html.

can handle. The most common formats for such data representation are JSON and XML. The former is particularly popular for rich JavaScript clients because it's trivial to parse and use from JavaScript.

In essence, REST is about resource identifiers (your URLs), methods for interacting with resources (the HTTP verbs), and the resource data in an easily consumable and producible form (typically JSON or XML). With that background, you're ready to implement your first REST interface for Hubbub.

12.1.2 Implementing a quick API

Grails provides several mechanisms for implementing a REST interface for an application with many opportunities for customization. The quickest approach is to mark up one or more of your domain classes as resources using the following annotation:

```
package com.grailsinaction

import grails.rest.Resource

@Resource(uri="/posts")        <-- Adds JSON and XML REST endpoints at the URL /hubbub/posts
class Post {
    ...
}
```

This will create an implicit controller that provides JSON and XML endpoints at the URL /hubbub/posts. At least, it would if you didn't already have a `PostController` class. To try this out, rename the PostController.groovy file temporarily (to PostController.groovy.tmp, say), start the server, and point your browser at /hubbub/posts. You'll see an XML representation of all the posts in the database. You'll see the same data in JSON form if you use the URL /hubbub/posts.json (the .json suffix forces the content type to application/json).

This URL doesn't only allow you to retrieve the posts from the database. You can also retrieve individual posts, create new ones, and modify them. It depends on which URL and HTTP method you use. Table 12.1 shows you which actions are associated with which URL/method combinations.

Table 12.1 Standard REST URL and HTTP method mappings

URL	HTTP method	Controller action	Description
/posts	GET	index	Retrieves all posts.
/posts	POST	save	Creates a new post initialized with the given data.
/posts/5	GET	show	Retrieves only the post with the given ID.
/posts/5	PUT	update	Updates a particular post with the given data.
/posts/5	DELETE	delete	Deletes a particular post.

If all you want to do is expose your domain model via a cheap and cheerful REST interface, this is perfect. It doesn't work so well if you want to have an HTML UI as well or want to decouple the REST API from the domain classes. That means you need to use a different approach for Hubbub.

Beyond the `@Resource` annotation, the key parts of a Grails application involved in REST implementation are the URL mappings and the controller actions. Let's start with the URLs. Until now, you've only seen one-to-one mappings between URLs and controller actions. That's because a standard HTML-based application only ever accepts one of GET or POST to a particular URL. With a REST interface, each URL can support more than one HTTP verb. Enter the `resource` attribute for URL mappings:

```
"/api/posts"(resources: "postRest")
```

This single entry creates the same mappings as you saw in table 12.1. You could use the URL /posts, but we prefer to keep the REST API for the application separate from the browser-focused UI. Because of that, you'll also create an extra controller rather than reusing `PostController`. You can certainly use a single controller for JSON, XML, and HTML if you want, but there won't be much duplication between the separate controllers if you use services and we like the flexibility to evolve the HTML and REST interfaces independently.

> **resources vs resource**
>
> The previous URL mapping example used the parameter `resources`. Unfortunately there's also a `resource` parameter (the singular form) that has slightly different mappings. Just one extra or missing character can break your application. Be careful.
>
> The singular form is for singleton resources, meaning that there aren't multiple instances of the resource. Application configuration could be a singleton resource.

That's all you need to do on the URL mapping side. The next step is to implement the corresponding controller actions so that they return the appropriate content. As in previous chapters, start your implementation by first creating the controller and its unit test:

```
grails create-controller com.grailsinaction.PostRest
```

Next, write the unit test that specifies how the controller should work. This unit test is different from previous controller tests because you aren't concerned with any views. Instead, you want to submit JSON and XML data and verify the resulting JSON and XML. The following listing contains a subset of the full unit test (which can be found on GitHub), but it covers all the important techniques for unit testing a RESTful controller.

Listing 12.1 A unit test for our REST controller

```
package com.grailsinaction

import grails.plugin.springsecurity.SpringSecurityService
import grails.test.mixin.TestFor
import grails.test.mixin.Mock
import spock.lang.Specification
```

```
@TestFor(PostRestController)
@Mock([User, Post])
class PostRestControllerSpec extends Specification {

    void setupSpec() {
        defineBeans {
            springSecurityService(SpringSecurityService)
        }
    }

    void "GET a list of posts as JSON"() {
        given: "A set of posts"
        initialiseUsersAndPosts()

        when: "I invoke the index action "
        controller.index()

        then: "I get the expected posts as a JSON list"
        response.json*.content.sort() == [
                "A first post",
                "A second post",
                "Preparing for battle",
                "Soaking up the sun" ]
    }

    void "GET a list of posts as XML"() {
        given: "A set of posts"
        initialiseUsersAndPosts()

        when: "I invoke the show action without an ID and requesting XML"
        response.format = "xml"
        controller.index()

        then: "I get the expected posts as an XML document"
        response.xml.post.content*.text().sort() == [
                "A first post",
                "A second post",
                "Preparing for battle",
                "Soaking up the sun" ]
    }

    void "POST a single post as JSON"() {
        given: "A set of existing posts"
        def userId = initialiseUsersAndPosts()

        when: "I invoke the save action with a JSON packet"
        request.json = '{"content":"A new post!","user":{"id":' +
                userId + '}}'
        controller.save()

        then: "I get a 201 JSON response with the ID of the new post"
        response.status == 201
        response.json.id != null
    }

    private initialiseUsersAndPosts() {
        def chuck = new User(loginId: "chuck_norris",
                             passwordHash: "password")
        chuck.addToPosts(content: "A first post")
```

Ensures springSecurityService bean is injected into User domain instances

Checks JSON response, where json property is map that replicates structure of JSON data

Requests XML response (works with withFormat() method)

Checks XML response, using GPath syntax

Passes JSON string as request content

Tests HTTP status code of response; 201 indicates successful POST

```
        chuck.addToPosts(content: "A second post")
        chuck.save(failOnError: true)

        def bruce = new User(loginId: "bruce_lee",
                             passwordHash: "iknowkungfu")
        bruce.addToPosts(content: "Soaking up the sun")
        bruce.addToPosts(content: "Preparing for battle")
        bruce.save(failOnError: true, flush: true)

        return chuck.id
    }
}
```

This code demonstrates several important techniques: submitting JSON and XML data, specifying a preferred content type for the response, and checking JSON and XML responses. JSON responses are generally easier to deal with than XML responses because JSON objects become Groovy maps and JSON lists become Groovy lists.

The XML responses have a different structure, but we can still use dynamic property access and the like via GPath notation. This is a generic Groovy feature that allows you to select elements and attributes by their names and navigate through the hierarchical structure of the document with dot (.) notation. GPath is beyond the scope of this book, but you can easily find out more online. To help you get started, we break down the GPath expression from listing 12.1 in figure 12.2.

The new unit test is failing because you haven't implemented the necessary controller actions. Let's rectify that in the following listing with a short `PostRestController` implementation.

Listing 12.2 A quick and simple REST controller

```
package com.grailsinaction

import grails.rest.RestfulController

class PostRestController extends RestfulController {
    static responseFormats = ["json", "xml"]

    PostRestController() {
        super(Post)
    }
}
```

- Implements all REST actions (`import grails.rest.RestfulController`)
- Specifies which content types the controller should handle (`static responseFormats`)
- Tells REST controller which domain class to scaffold (`super(Post)`)

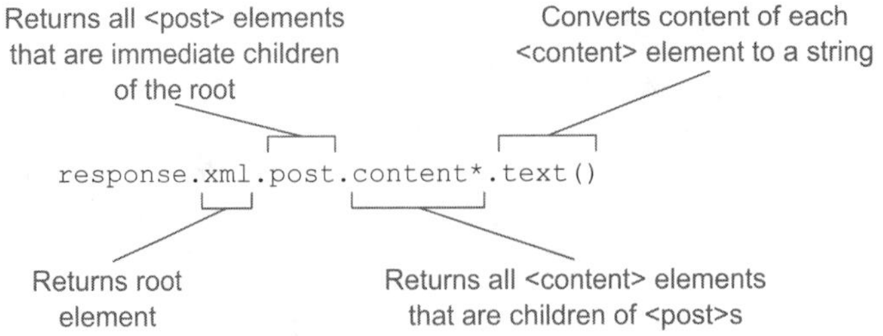

Figure 12.2 Anatomy of a GPath expression

Congratulations! You now have a fully functional REST API for Hubbub's posts that supports both JSON and XML. A client can easily specify what content type it wants through a number of mechanisms:

- A suffix on the end of the URL, such as .json or .xml
- A `format=<type>` URL parameter, for example `format=json`
- The Accept header of the HTTP request

This does raise the question of how you try the API out. You can perform GET requests from the browser, but what about adding or updating Hubbub posts? Fortunately, there are plenty of tools out there that you can use. We like the browser-based ones such as the Poster extension for Firefox or the REST Console app for Chrome. You can also use curl from the command line or something like the Spring REST Shell.[2]

As a quick test, try submitting the following request content to the URL http://localhost:8080/hubbub/api/posts. Be sure to set the request content type to application/json!

```
{"content":"A new post via REST", "user":{"id":7}}
```

You can then go to the timeline page in your browser to verify that the post was added. Note that you can submit data in a different format than you want it returned, for example, by submitting JSON and requesting XML in the response. This is rarely useful, though.

The format of the data in such requests is fixed, corresponding to the properties of the domain class and its associations. The best way to discover what structure you should use for your own POST and PUT requests is by looking at the content returned by a GET. For example, pointing your browser at /api/posts/1.json (and logging in) results in

```
{"class":"com.grailsinaction.Post",
 "id":1,
 "content":"My first post",
 "dateCreated":"2007-05-12T10:08:22Z",
 "tags":[],
 "user":{"class":"User","id":6}}
```

Normal domain class properties become JSON fields.

Associations become nested JSON objects.

This contains more than you need when attempting to create a new Hubbub post via the REST interface since Grails can infer the type of domain class to instantiate from the URL. Grails also automatically assigns an ID and creation date. Hence you can ignore the `class`, `id`, and `dateCreated` fields.

The content returned by the /api/posts/1.xml URL isn't much different:

```
<post id="1">
  <content>My first post</content>
  <dateCreated>2007-05-12 11:08:22.664 BST</dateCreated>
  <tags/>
  <user id="6"/>
</post>
```

Normal properties (except id) become elements.

Associations become nested elements.

[2] "Spring REST Shell project," https://github.com/spring-projects/rest-shell.

In the case of XML, the name of the root element is immaterial. When submitting XML data via a POST, you could use `<root>`, `<post>`, or even `<jelly>`.

There's one big problem with the API as it stands: any changes to the domain classes immediately result in changes to the generated JSON and XML. Public APIs should be stable with minimal and controlled changes, whereas the persistence model embodied by the domain classes should be allowed to change freely as it's an internal model. You ideally want to decouple the public API from the internal persistence model and we look at how to do that in the next section.

12.2 Improving the API

What makes a good API? Here is a list of what we think are the most desirable attributes:

- Consistent and well-behaved URLs
- Stable data representations
- Informative error handling

The core Grails support has the first of these well covered. Each HTTP method on a resources URL does the appropriate thing. And for those HTTP methods that don't make sense, such as a PUT on /api/posts, Grails returns a suitable error status code (405 Method Not Allowed). You'll also discover in this section that Grails handles validation errors well, but you can still improve the general error handling. Before we get to that, the most critical aspect you need to deal with is stable data representations.

12.2.1 Handling data representations

As the API's implementer, you're happy. It was easy to set up and it does lots of things right. But let's look at it from a user's perspective. Consider the response from a `GET` request to /api/posts.xml:

```
<?xml version="1.0" encoding="UTF-8"?>
<list>
  <post id="13">
    <content>Pilates is killing me as well</content>
    <dateCreated>2013-02-26 15:31:41.28 GMT</dateCreated>
    <tags />
    <user id="7" />
  </post>
  ...
</list>
```

First, the name of the root element leaves something to be desired, although the name is generally irrelevant when consuming XML. Second, the timestamp for each post isn't great for parsing, particularly with a three-letter time zone rather than a UTC offset. Most importantly, this schema is tied to the domain model.

You may remember that in chapter 3 you moved the `homepage` property from the `User` class to `Profile`. It's useful to have the flexibility to refactor the domain model like that, otherwise it tends to become harder and harder to work with. But think about the impact that such a change would have on the XML and JSON generated for a `User` instance. It goes from something like

```
<user id="5">
  <loginId>phil</loginId>
  <homepage>http://philisgreat.blogspot.com/</homepage>
  ...
</user>
```

to

```
<user id="5">
  <loginId>phil</loginId>
  <profile>
    <homepage>http://philisgreat.blogspot.com/</homepage>
    ...
  </profile>
  ...
</user>
```

A small change, but it would break any client that relied on the old schema. And old applications abound, so even if you wait two years before making such a breaking change you'll probably affect someone—perhaps a paying customer who'll become irritated (to put it mildly) and either go elsewhere or sue you.

The problem here is that APIs should change slowly and with as few breaking changes as possible, but a persistence model should be free to adapt to changing requirements on a potentially frequent basis. This friction between the two leads to a simple rule: decouple the resource representations from the internal persistence model.

Serializing the persistence model without any control results in an unstable API that clients will refuse to use after a while. What should you do? The choices boil down to these three:

- Imperatively generate the XML and JSON
- Copy the persistence model information into a different, more stable object hierarchy and serialize that
- Customize the marshaling of the domain model objects

The first option uses builders or similar to generate the text representation of the domain model. This approach has the advantages of full control of the XML or JSON generation and clarity in how the serialization happens. It's easy for developers to track the code from the response rendering back to the serialization, but you're duplicating work that the Grails converters already do.

The second option requires maintaining a separate model and copying data from the domain model to this intermediate one. It's similar to the old data transfer object (DTO) technique, although in this case the intermediate model may be different from the domain model. Decoupling the UI and public API from the domain model in this way has significant advantages, but works best when the two models are noticeably different.

We don't have space to cover examples of all three techniques, so we focus on the third one, particularly as it's the most Grails-specific option. This approach works with the existing serialization mechanisms, while allowing for a good degree of control.

The idea is to register custom marshalers for your classes, which control how instances of those classes are turned into JSON or XML. This sounds like a nontrivial amount of work, but, in fact, the simplest scenario is straightforward. Consider that you want the XML representation of Hubbub posts to look like

```
<post id="13" published="2013-02-26T15:31:41">
  <message>Pilates is killing me as well</message>
  <tags>
    <tag>personal</tag>
  </tags>
  <user>phil</user>
</post>
```

This is a similar schema to the existing one, but note the change from `<dateCreated>` to `<published>`, the replacement of the user instance ID with the login ID, and the renaming of `<content>` to `<message>`. To use this, you need to register a custom marshaler for the `Post` class. To keep things simple, register it in BootStrap.groovy, as shown in the following listing.

Listing 12.3 Registering the marshaler in BootStrap.groovy

```
import com.grailsinaction.*
import grails.converters.*
import java.text.SimpleDataFormat

class BootStrap {
    def init = { servletContext ->
        def dateFormatter = new SimpleDateFormat("yyyy-MM-dd'T'hh:mm:ss")

        XML.registerObjectMarshaller(Post) { Post p, converter ->
            converter.attribute "id", p.id.toString()
            converter.attribute "published",
                    dateFormatter.format(p.dateCreated)
            converter.build {
                message p.content
                user p.user.loginId
                tags {
                    for (t in p.tags) {
                        tag t.name
                    }
                }
            }
        }

        environments {
            ...
        }

        createAdminUserIfRequired()
```

Starts serialization for given Post instance

Uses Groovy markup builder syntax to generate XML

```
    }
    ...
}
```

In this case, the custom marshaler uses the second argument of the closure, the converter instance, to render XML directly via Groovy's markup builder syntax (see appendix C). Best of all, the custom XML will be generated whenever a `Post` instance is serialized using XML, no matter where this happens.

You can also customize the JSON that's generated through the same mechanism, albeit somewhat more simply. For JSON, the custom marshaler returns a map or a list of maps representing the object data. The next code generates similarly structured JSON to the XML you saw in the previous listing.

```
JSON.registerObjectMarshaller(Post) { Post p ->
    return [ id: p.id,
             published: dateFormatter.format(p.dateCreated),
             message: p.content,
             user: p.user.loginId,
             tags: p.tags.collect { it.name } ]
}
```

Returns map containing data to serialize

As you can probably work out from the code, because JSON is a representation of maps and lists, the previous code converts a `Post` instance into

```
{"published":"2013-02-26T15:31:41",
 "message":"Pilates is killing me as well",
 "tags":["personal"],
 "user": "phil"}
```

And because you aren't using the converter to generate JSON (you rely on its default handling of maps), you don't need the second argument on the closure for `registerObjectMarshaller()`.

You can do the same with the XML converter (return a map), but its default handling of maps is nasty. You end up with XML such as this:

```
<post>
  <entry key="published">2013-02-27T09:12:27</entry>
  <entry key="message">Pilates is killing me as well</entry>
  <entry key="user">phil</entry>
  <entry key="tags" />
</post>
```

Nobody wants to use such an API! You're better off using the markup builder syntax for XML custom marshalers.

Using this approach of custom marshalers, you can happily change the domain model as the need arises. Any time the domain model changes, you update the custom marshalers to generate the same JSON and XML as before. That said, you don't really want to cram all your custom marshaling into your `BootStrap` class. You're better moving it into a separate class. Create the file src/groovy/com/grailsinaction/MarshallerRegistrar.groovy and set its content to that shown in this listing.

Listing 12.4 Registration of custom marshalers

```
package com.grailsinaction

import java.text.SimpleDateFormat
import javax.annotation.PostConstruct

class MarshallerRegistrar {
    @PostConstruct
    void registerMarshallers() {
        JSON.registerObjectMarshaller(Post) {
            ...
        }
        ...
    }
}
```

Declares that registerMarshallers() will be called immediately after object's constructor

Registers a marshaler as before

You can register as many marshalers as you want in this class. Once you've added it to the project, you need to make sure that `registerMarshallers()` is called on application startup. You do that by registering it as a Spring bean. We look in more detail at Spring in chapter 14, but for now add the following to the file grails-app/conf/spring/resources.groovy:

```
import com.grailsinaction.MarshallerRegistrar

beans = {
    hubbubMarshallerRegistrar(MarshallerRegistrar)
}
```

Declares registrar as a Spring bean

This short bit of code guarantees that all your custom marshalers will be registered when the application starts up. At least it should. Check issue GRAILS-11116[3] to see whether your version of Grails supports this.

Renderers vs. converters

Converters are Grails's built-in mechanisms for serializing objects to XML and JSON. You don't need to use them if you don't want to. If you'd prefer to use an external library for the serialization, such as Jackson for JSON, you can implement and register a custom *renderer*. This gives you full control over how the serialization is done. The Grails user guide gives you plenty of information on creating custom renderers.

By default, Grails registers XML and JSON renderers that delegate to the converters for the actual serialization.

Custom marshalers give you a degree of decoupling between the persistence model and the public REST API, but both the model and the API may evolve to such a point that custom marshalers can no longer do the job. You then need to consider one of

---

[3] "Custom marshaller registrar bean does not work," http://jira.grails.org/browse/GRAILS-11116.

the other options we mentioned previously, such as using an intermediate model that matches the API.

You should be able to keep the API stable from now on, which your users will appreciate. What they won't appreciate is that the REST API doesn't behave the same way as the HTML UI. Remember that your `PostController` is delegating much of the business logic to `PostService`, whereas the REST API bypasses the service. You need to rectify this so that all interfaces to your application behave consistently.

12.2.2 Customizing the controller

The `RestfulController` class you're currently using for the REST API is incredibly useful for getting started quickly. It's akin to the scaffolding for the browser UI. And as with the scaffolding, you'll eventually need to write your own actions for most applications.

Fortunately, Grails makes it easy to create your own REST controllers without using `RestfulController`. The key is to implement the standard REST actions (`index`, `show`, `save`, and so on) and return data in the requested format. Let's dive straight into the implementation and go from there. The following listing shows part of the new controller implementation (you can find the rest of it on GitHub). We'll focus on the `index` and `save` actions here.

Listing 12.5 The new REST controller implementation

```
package com.grailsinaction

class PostRestController {
    def postService
    def springSecurityService

    def index() {
        respond Post.list()
    }

    def save(Post post) {
        if (!post.hasErrors()) {
            def user = springSecurityService.currentUser
            def newPost = postService.createPost(
                    user.loginId,
                    post.content)
            respond newPost, status: 201
        }
        else {
            respond post
        }
    }
    ...
}
```

- Generates the list of posts in the format requested by the client. (`index`)
- Only command objects or domain classes work with JSON/XML requests. (`save(Post post)`)
- Returns new post with HTTP status 201.
- Renders validation errors in requested format.
- Other actions: show, update, delete.

A lot of the work is done by the `respond()` method, which determines what content type to return to the client and performs the serialization of its argument. In fact, `RestfulController` uses the `respond()` method under the hood, so the custom marshalers you created still work.

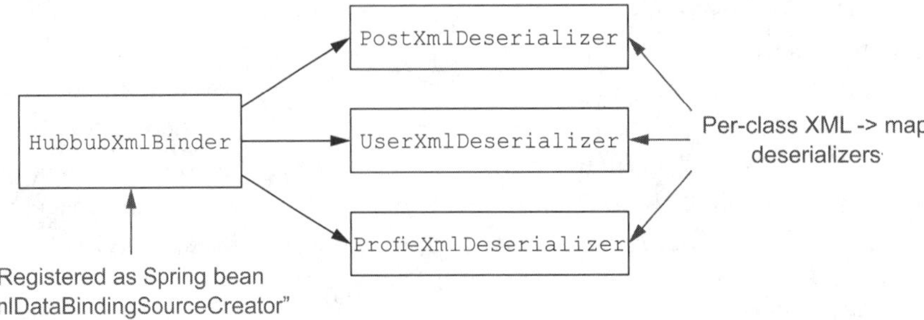

Figure 12.3 Potential class structure to handle per-domain class data binding

It's also worth noting that when a user submits JSON or XML content, it's not bound to the `params` object, nor does Grails bind the content to typed action arguments unless the type is a command object or domain class. In fact, the data binding doesn't use the converters we discussed in the previous section.

The standard Grails data binding is based on a set of classes that implement the `DataBindingSourceCreator` interface. These are registered against content types and there are default implementations for application/json and application/xml. The problem for Hubbub is that you can't have different implementations for different data classes, unlike with converters. You could implement your own data binding classes as shown in figure 12.3, but that's extra work.

It's simpler to use a command object that matches the serialized form you want. And as we discussed in the previous chapter, it's safer to use command objects from a security standpoint. To handle a POST request of the form

```
<post>
  <message>I'm trying out the new REST API!</message>
</post>
```

you need to modify the REST controller. We highlight the changes in italics in the following listing.

Listing 12.6 Using a command object to control the accepted data format

```
class PostRestController {
    ...
    def save(PostDetails post) {                 <- Uses command object for action argument
        if (!post.hasErrors()) {
            def user = springSecurityService.currentUser
            def newPost = postService.createPost(
                    user.loginId,
                    post.message)                <- Extra data from command object to create new post
            respond newPost, status: 201
        }
        else {
            respond post
        }
    }
}
```

```
class PostDetails {
    String message                              <-- Command object uses
                                                    property name matching
    static constraints = {                          XML element name
        message blank: false, nullable: false
    }
}
```

This is good enough for now because you decoupled the data representations from the domain classes. And yet it's not ideal because you don't have full control over the XML structure. The current code doesn't support binding attributes to command object properties. In other words, clients can't send requests of the form

```
<post message="A new Hubbub post"/>
```

You're trading flexibility for convenience. If you want more control, which would make sense for a large and popular API, you should create your own `DataBindingSourceCreator` implementations as described in the Grails user guide.

When making these changes to the controller, you'll have to update the unit test for the class. The controller is now using both the Spring Security service and the post service, and the format of the JSON accepted by the `save` action has changed.

The last step in improving the REST API for Hubbub is to set up better error handling, even though Grails already does a good job in this regard.

12.2.3 Reporting errors

Imagine using a library that provides a `sendMail()` method, perhaps something like the Mail plugin for Grails. You incorporate it into your application, run your functional tests (because you wrote those before deploying to production), and then discover that the emails you fire off aren't being sent. Puzzled, you debug through your code and notice that the "to" addresses are invalid. It appears that the email API you use swallows errors related to invalid email addresses, quietly failing without providing any feedback.

How long is it before you decide to switch to a different library or do it yourself? The API could throw an `InvalidAddressException` or give feedback in another way, and yet it doesn't. The result is a wasted half-day trying to find out what's going on. We've all been there. A REST API is no different: feedback is important in allowing developers to fix problems with their API clients quickly and effectively.

Given that error reporting is important, what extra work do you need to do for the Hubbub API? Grails already deals with the most common scenarios, but you may not realize what it's doing. We'll look at its default behavior first.

A well-implemented API should always send the appropriate HTTP status code with every response. That code is normally 200, which is the default status code for Grails responses. But as you'll see in table 12.2, even successful responses sometimes have a non-200 status. For example, a POST should set the status to 201 if it successfully creates a new resource.

Table 12.2 Common HTTP status codes and when to use them

Code	Short name	Description
`200`	`OK`	The request completed normally.
`201`	`Created`	A new resource was created. The `Location` response header should contain the "most specific" URI of the new resource, and the response content should include a list of possible URIs.
`301`	`Redirected Permanently`	The resource moved to a different URI permanently.
`302`	`Found`	This indicates a temporary redirect. The `redirect()` method works by returning this status code.
`400`	`Bad Request`	The content of the request is incorrect or malformed. Use this code when the wrong XML message is used for a particular URL or when the message contains invalid XML.
`401`	`Unauthorized`	The client isn't authorized to access the resource. This code is only valid if one of the standard HTTP authentication methods, such as `Basic`, is used.
`403`	`Forbidden`	The request isn't allowed. Often used by access control libraries to indicate an authenticated user does not have access rights.
`404`	`Not Found`	The resource wasn't found. Everyone knows this one!
`405`	`Method Not Allowed`	The HTTP method of the request isn't allowed for the target URL. The response should include an `Allow` header listing the allowed methods.
`406`	`Not Acceptable`	The server can't return the resource in any format requested by the client via the `Accept` header.
`415`	`Unsupported Media Type`	The server doesn't recognize or understand the request's content type.
`422`	`Unprocessable Entity`	Part of the Web DAV specification, the server recognizes the content type of the request and the content isn't malformed, but the server can't deal with the request content anyway. Often used for data that fails validation rules.
`500`	`Internal Server Error`	This usually indicates an error in the server code. Servlet containers typically return 500 if there's an uncaught exception.

Both the `@Resource` annotation and `RestfulController` have a save action that will return a status code of 201 if the save is successful. Any validation errors will result in a 422 and the content of the response will include the detail of those errors using Vnd.Error[4] syntax, which has both JSON and XML forms. You can easily reproduce the same effect in your own actions and that's exactly what the code in listing 12.6 does. To return a 201, you pass a `status: 201` argument to the `respond()` method. As for

[4] Vnd.Error specification, https://github.com/blongden/vnd.error.

returning a 422, `respond()` does that automatically if its primary argument has a populated `errors` property.

Grails will also handle requests that use an unsupported HTTP method for a URL. If you try to send a DELETE request to /posts, you'll see a 405 status. This will happen regardless of what you have in your controller: Grails uses the URL mappings to determine whether a URL accepts a particular HTTP method.

At the time of writing, Grails doesn't deal with 406 and 415 responses automatically. Fortunately, you can easily add your own support. Create a new Grails filter, for example, via the `create-filters` command, and set its content to what's in the next listing.

Listing 12.7 Grails filter to handle 406 and 415 errors

```
package com.grailsinaction

class RestFilters {
    def filters = {
        contentType(controller: "postRest") {        // Only applies to the REST controller
            before = {

                if (!(request.format in ["json", "xml", "all"]) &&     // Tests the request content type
                        !(request.method in ["DELETE", "GET", "HEAD"])) {
                    render status: 415,
                           text: "Unrecognized content type"
                    return false
                }

                if (!(response.format in ["json", "xml", "all"])) {    // Tests the response content type
                    render status: 406,
                           text: "${response.format} not supported"
                    return false
                }
            }
        }
    }
}
```

There isn't much else for Hubbub to do with regard to error handling. All that's left is the handling of server-side errors, as represented by 5xx status codes. When the server throws an exception that bubbles up out of the controller, you see an informative HTML page describing what the exception was and where it occurred. This is great for you as the developer of the server because it makes debugging easy. But REST clients expecting JSON won't be happy with such a page.

To ensure that even server-side errors don't cause problems for clients, you should create an error controller if you don't already have one and make it format-aware, as shown in the following listing.

Listing 12.8 Making the error controller format-aware

```
package com.grailsinaction

class ErrorController {
    def internalServer() {
```

```
        def ex = request.exception.cause          // Fetches exception that triggered error handler
        def body = new ErrorDetails(
                type: ex.class.name,
                message: ex.message)
        respond body, view: "/error"              // Renders exception details in requested format
    }
    ...
}

class ErrorDetails {
    String type
    String message
}
```

To finish this off, make sure that you map the HTTP status codes to the appropriate error controller actions in UrlMappings.groovy by replacing:

```
"500"(view:"/error")
```

with

```
"500"(controller: "error", action: "internalServer")
```

You now have all your bases covered as far as error-handling goes. You saw how to respond to both client errors (4xx status codes) and server errors (5xx), such that clients can easily find out what went wrong. That's all there is to it, and that completes the API from a usability and feature perspective.

In an ideal world you've done enough, but this isn't an ideal world, and you have to deal with trust issues and an evolving application. That means dealing with access control, API versioning, and testing.

12.3 Securing and maintaining the API

You dealt with testing and security in previous chapters, but what you've seen so far is geared toward HTML-based applications. REST APIs have different requirements that affect the way you approach these topics. In this section, we'll look at those requirements and develop solutions for them, starting with security.

12.3.1 Configuring API security

When it comes to security, API usage is interesting. Most access control is focused on end users and whether or not they're allowed to access certain pages. Sometimes this also applies to APIs, but it depends on the software client that's accessing the API.

TYPES OF REST CLIENT

Two authentication scenarios to consider are shown in figure 12.4:

- *User authentication*—The client application acts as an intermediary agent for an end user.
- *Client authentication*—The client application acts as a client in its own right.

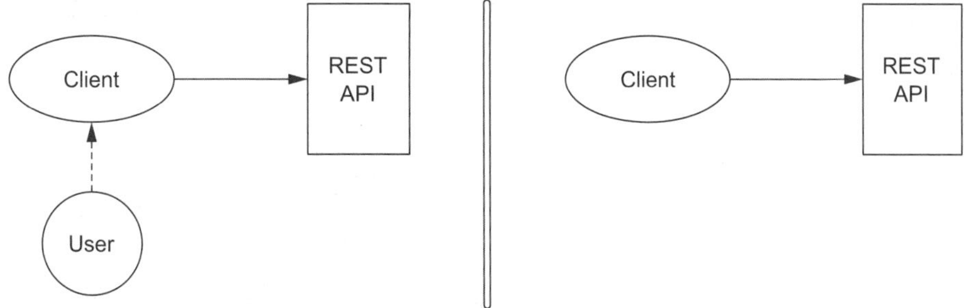

Client acts as intermediary between user and API. It's the user that is authenticated.

Client is autonomous and consumes the API. The client itself needs to authenticate, as if it were a user.

Figure 12.4 The roles that a client application can have

As an example of the first scenario, consider the Twitter applications that exist on various platforms. These clients access the Twitter API on behalf of the users, who must log in before they can write tweets, see direct messages, and so on.

You'll also find websites and applications that pull data from Twitter to perform statistical analysis or another job. These are examples of the second scenario, in which the software doesn't need access to an end-user account because it's dealing only with public data. And that's the key difference: whether or not the software requires an end user to authenticate with your application.

If your API doesn't require end-user authentication, you could dispense with authentication altogether, with the caveat that this only works for data that's freely available via the REST API. If you do need to limit access, it's best to use a client ID with an API key. This is similar to a username and password, but the API key is a random, unique string generated by your application. In fact, the API key can act as the identity as well as the password, so you could eliminate the client ID, too. Implementing support for API keys is beyond the scope of the book, but you can do it with Spring Security by creating a custom security filter that verifies API keys sent in a custom HTTP header.

Certain sites and applications want software clients to use an API key even when their data is public, but this is mainly for tracking purposes. It's also an easy way to restrict the number of requests a single client can make. Previously, Google required an API key for its Maps application, but as of v3 of their JavaScript client that's no longer the case. If you want to throttle clients without requiring an API key, you can always do it based on the client IP address.

That leaves you with end-user authentication. At the moment, Hubbub's authentication relies on a redirect to a login page when a user attempts to access a secure page. This is fine for a browser, but it's a complete pain for any other type of client. The application also maintains user state (who is logged in) in the HTTP session, something else that's inconvenient for nonbrowser clients. No, we definitely need an alternative approach, the simplest of which is HTTP Basic Authentication.

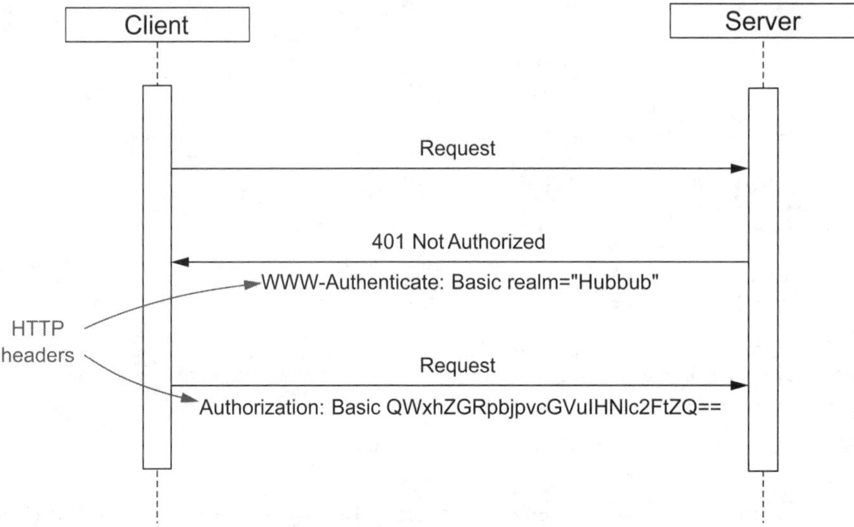

Figure 12.5 The sequence of requests and responses that make up HTTP Basic Authentication

About HTTP Basic Authentication

Basic Authentication involves clients sending user credentials in the headers of a request (see figure 12.5). A client must send the credentials with every request that goes to a restricted URL.

It's a simple scheme, but it has weaknesses to address:

- The credentials are sent in plain text.
- Authentication must be done for each request.

The first problem is easily solved by requiring clients to use SSL when accessing the API, a topic we covered briefly in the previous chapter. The second issue is more problematic because we deliberately try to keep the authentication process relatively slow, which makes it harder for attackers to use brute force to crack passwords. Slower authentication doesn't noticeably impact the experience of a user who logs into the browser-based version of the application, but it can have a much more noticeable effect on software clients that send hundreds of requests a second to your API.

This is where things get interesting. Whose credentials should the application send? It could be that the client itself has credentials if it needs to access restricted resources. If it's acting on behalf of a normal end user, should it send the user's credentials instead? The disadvantage of doing that is the slow authentication due to the salted hash algorithm used for standard logins.

For the rest of this section on security, we focus on enabling HTTP Basic Authentication for software clients that have their own identity and access rights. It's simpler than dealing with end-user authentication via a client intermediary and allows us to cover the Grails-specific bits.

> **OAuth and end-user authentication**
>
> One of the primary aims of OAuth is to provide a mechanism by which a user can authenticate directly against a target service, to give another application access to his or her information via that target service's API. This may sound like the ideal solution for end-user authentication, but it's geared toward client *web applications*. The application needs to both redirect the user to the target website (Twitter, for example) and have a URL that the target website can redirect the user back to. It doesn't work well for standalone applications.

On the basis that we've decided to add Basic Authentication to Hubbub, how do you go about enabling it? The first port of call is the Spring Security plugin.

ADDING BASIC AUTHENTICATION VIA SPRING SECURITY

By default, the plugin and its login controller only support one authentication provider at a time, but you can change this fairly easily. Even better, you can control which authentication providers are active for particular URLs. This is immensely useful for you because you want Basic authentication active on API URLs and normal form-based (login page) authentication on all the rest. To achieve this, add the following extra bit of security configuration to Config.groovy:

```
grails.plugin.springsecurity.useBasicAuth = true
grails.plugin.springsecurity.basic.realmName = "Hubbub"

grails.plugin.springsecurity.filterChain.chainMap = [
    '/api/**': 'JOINED_FILTERS',
    '/**': 'JOINED_FILTERS,-basicAuthenticationFilter,
➥  -basicExceptionTranslationFilter'
]
```

Basic Authentication requires realm name. We recommend the app name.

The first two lines enable Basic authentication, and the rest configure the URLs for which it's active. `JOINED_FILTERS` is a plugin alias that represents all enabled plugin providers, which includes Basic authentication at this point. You explicitly disable the Basic authentication provider for the rest of the URLs by prefixing the filter names with a hyphen (-). Note that the filter chain configuration is distinct from the URL access control rules you saw first in chapter 11 under the `interceptUrlMap` configuration option.

Figure 12.6 may help you understand the filter chain configuration. It shows how Spring Security applies a chain of filters to every request, each one handling a different authentication mechanism. And the order is important: the first filter that handles a request can prevent the later filters from getting a look in. You can't have the Basic authentication filter returning a 401 *and* the standard login filter redirecting to the login form.

Now your API is protected by Basic Authentication, but as we mentioned previously there's still an issue in that authentication of the user occurs on every request. Anything you can do to speed up the authentication process is helpful. This is where generated API keys can help: because they're random and long, they're much harder to crack using brute-force methods compared to user-selected passwords or passphrases. The difficulty with this approach is in configuring Spring Security to do a different, faster credentials check for API keys as opposed to the salted hash approach for normal usernames and passwords. We won't go into the details here, but you have to do a couple of things:

1. Create a separate authentication manager for Basic authentication that verifies API keys.
2. Configure the Basic authentication bean so that it uses the custom authentication manager.

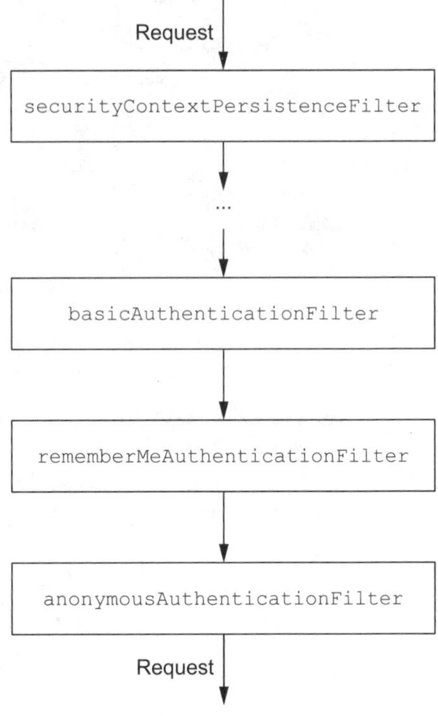

Figure 12.6 Example Spring Security filter chain

The authentication manager itself isn't particularly complicated, because it needs to authenticate a given set of credentials. As with normal passwords it's a good idea to compare a hash of the API key in case the database is compromised, but a straightforward SHA-256 hash without salt and only a single iteration is fast, and because API keys are generated and random, rainbow tables won't help attackers reverse engineer the key.

Taking the API key approach also means adding the admin UI elements required to generate API keys and make them available to clients. You should also consider adding support to revoke API keys and regenerate new ones in case a key is compromised.

With authentication in place and communication with the API protected with SSL, you can start considering the long term and how to handle API changes.

12.3.2 Versioning the API

Once you have a user base for your API, evolving the API without breaking existing clients becomes a primary concern. You have to think about what sorts of changes are likely to break clients and whether and how to incorporate them.

WHY VERSION AN API?

Any changes that involve adding data to resources without changing the existing structure can normally be incorporated without any concerns whatsoever. Most JSON and XML parsing ignore the extra data. The difficulty arises when clients use schemas (yes, there's even a schema language for JSON), which makes it much harder to modify the structure of the data without breaking clients.

As a simple example of the kind of change we're talking about, imagine that you want to include the number of times a `post` has been shared through others' Hubbub accounts. The XML would probably look like this:

```
<post id="13">
  <content>Pilates is killing me as well</content>
  <published>2013-02-26T15:31:41</published>
  <tags>
    <tag>personal</tag>
  </tags>
  <user>phil</user>
  <sharedCount>10</sharedCount>
</post>
```

An additional element that doesn't break existing XML parsing, but may be invalid according to the resource's XML schema.

It's a breaking change for any client that uses a schema. Removing elements, restructuring them, or changing the format of data (for example, dates) will also break existing clients, even if they don't use a schema. Imagine that you want to include both the user's login ID and his or her full name in the post's representation. The JSON looks like this:

```
{"published":"2013-02-26T15:31:41",
 "content":"Pilates is killing me as well",
 "tags":["personal"],
 "user": {"id":"phil", "name":"Phil Smith"}}
```

User field is now an object rather than a string.

Existing clients break because they assume that the `user` field is a simple string. You need a strategy for dealing with changes like this.

The first question you need to ask yourself is whether you want to maintain the old API. Ideally you keep it alive for a reasonable time after introducing breaking changes so that clients have time to upgrade. But keeping it alive for several years is typically impractical: the underlying domain model often changes to such a degree that it's no longer feasible to generate the resource representations for deprecated APIs.

Looking at it from a different perspective, it's easy to maintain an old/legacy/deprecated API as long as you can generate the resource representations through simple custom serialization. But if you find yourself retaining old bits of the domain model or other code, then it's probably time to drop the old API.

IMPLEMENTING API VERSIONS

Given that you want to introduce breaking changes in the data representation of a resource and that you still want existing clients to work, what are the next steps? You have several options:

- Serve the new representation at a different URL.
- Use the existing URL, but return either the new or old representation based on a query parameter or `Accept-Version` HTTP header.
- Create custom MIME types for each API version and register custom renderers for those MIME types.

The first option is fairly common in the wild with many APIs including a version number in the URL. This is fine, but remember that different URLs represent the locations of different resources, not different *representations* of a resource. Such an approach often runs counter to the principles of REST. On the other hand, using the `Accept` header means working with custom media types—an approach that involves more work than URL versioning.

As far as we can tell, the jury is still out on what the ideal approach is. Grails has support for all three, so it's a case of use whatever works for you. Nonetheless, you need to decide what to do for Hubbub's API. Let's keep it simple and rely on a URL query parameter to determine the version.

All you have to do is honor the v parameter in the backing controller. One potential approach is to use different marshalers for different API versions. This works well when the data model doesn't change much, only the data representation. For big data model changes, you should probably look at a different URL scheme, different controllers, and perhaps different services.

For the case where you change the user field in the JSON from a string to an object, you can register a new custom marshaler. You can register only one *default* marshaler per type, which doesn't help if you want to support both versions of the JSON. Fortunately, you can register marshalers in named configurations as well.

Your first step is to register a second JSON marshaler alongside the existing one, as shown in the following listing. The new code is in italics.

Listing 12.9 Registering a second JSON marshaler

```
JSON.createNamedConfig("v1") { cfg ->
    cfg.registerObjectMarshaller(Post) { Post p ->
        return [ published: dateFormatter.format(p.dateCreated),
                 message: p.content,
                 user: p.user.loginId,
                 tags: p.tags.collect { it.name } ]
    }
}

JSON.createNamedConfig("v2") { cfg ->
    cfg.registerObjectMarshaller(Post) { Post p ->
        return [ published: dateFormatter.format(p.dateCreated),
                 message: p.content,
                 user: [id: p.user.loginId,
                        name: p.user.profile.fullName],
                 tags: p.tags.collect { it.name } ]
    }
}
```

Registers previous marshaler with name "v1".

Creates new configuration called "v2".

v2 marshaler renders user's login ID and full name.

The next step is to activate the appropriate converter configuration based on the "v" URL parameter. That requires a small change to `PostRestController`, as shown in the following listing.

Listing 12.10 Activating the marshaler if client requests version 2 of the API

```
package com.grailsinaction

import grails.converters.*
...
class PostRestController {
```

```
    def index(String v) {
        def configName = 'v' + (v ?: 1)
        re
        JSON.use(configName) {
            respond Post.list()
        }
    }
    ...
}
```

Determines configuration to use based on API version requested

Activates named configuration

With those two changes, you can now serve different JSON depending on which version of the API the client has requested. You can also do exactly the same for the XML generation as well by creating the named configuration on the `XML` converter class.

This isn't the best solution to the problem, so we recommend that you try the options Grails supports. The most flexible approach is to create dedicated mime types for your resources and register different renderers for the each version of a mime type.

Managing version changes to the API is an important factor in keeping users happy, but you still need to ensure that both old and new clients work. That means maintaining proper test coverage of the API.

12.3.3 Implementing functional testing

A stable API that you can evolve requires end-to-end testing. Unit tests are good for day-to-day development, but the internals are likely to change much more frequently than the public API. You need a guarantor of the API's stability. The easiest way to achieve this is through functional tests.

In chapter 9, we introduced you to functional testing with Geb. Using a jQuery-like syntax, you can interrogate the HTML pages coming back from the server and verify their content. That doesn't help in this case because you're dealing with JSON and XML in the REST API, but such content is easier to test than HTML and doesn't require any special tools. In fact, all you need is a client library for sending JSON and XML requests to the server and something to enable the functional test phase.

As far as enabling the test phase goes, that's already done by the Geb plugin. But if you're not using Geb, if your application is a pure REST API, then you can install the Functional Spock plugin instead and follow the rest of this section as is.

The next step is to choose the client library and make sure it's added as a dependency. You don't absolutely need a dedicated library for testing REST APIs, but using one does make your life easier. You'll go with the groovy-wslite library for your tests (you don't need a plugin), but the Grails HTTP Builder and Rest Client Builder plugins are both viable alternatives. To use groovy-wslite in your tests, you need to add it as a test dependency in BuildConfig.groovy:

```
dependencies {
    ...
    test "com.github.groovy-wslite:groovy-wslite:0.7.2"
}
```

Note this is a straightforward JAR dependency and doesn't go in the plugins section. That's all you need. Now you can create your functional tests. To demonstrate how this works, you'll reproduce the unit test from listing 12.2. The following listing contains the functional test code that goes into the PostRestFunctionalSpec.groovy file in the test/functional/com/grailsinaction directory (you'll need to create the file manually).

Listing 12.11 A functional test for your REST API

```
package com.grailsinaction

import spock.lang.Specification
import wslite.http.auth.HTTPBasicAuthorization
import wslite.rest.*

class PostRestFunctionalSpec extends Specification {
    @Shared def restClient =
            new RESTClient("http://localhost:8080/hubbub/api/")

    void setup() {
        restClient.authorization =
                new HTTPBasicAuthorization("frankie", "testing")
        restClient.httpClient.sslTrustAllCerts = true
    }

    void "GET a list of posts as JSON"() {
        when: "I send a GET to the posts URL requesting JSON"
        def response =
                restClient.get(path: "/posts", accept: ContentType.JSON)

        then: "I get the expected posts as a JSON list"
        response.json*.message.sort()[0..1] == [
                "Been working my roundhouse kicks.",
                "My first post" ]
    }

    void "GET a list of posts as XML"() {
        when: "I send a GET to the posts URL requesting XML"
        def response =
                restClient.get(path: "/posts", accept: "application/xml")

        then: "I get the expected posts as an XML document"
        response.xml.post.message*.text().sort()[0..1] == [
                "Been working my roundhouse kicks.",
                "My first post" ]
    }

    void "POST a single post as JSON"() {
        when: "I POST a JSON document to the posts URL"
        def response = restClient.post path: "/posts", {
            type ContentType.JSON
            json message: "A new post!"
        }

        then: "I get a 201 JSON response with the ID of the new post"
        response.statusCode == 201
        response.json.id != null
    }
}
```

Creates single REST client used by all tests in this spec that targets test server

Uses json property on the response to access data as maps and lists

Uses xml property to get XML data as GPath syntax

Sends POST data as JSON using closure argument

The structure of the tests isn't that different between listings 12.1 (the unit test specification) and 12.8, but this time you're sending real HTTP requests to a live server rather than invoking controller methods directly. The response data is still available through those special `json` and `xml` properties though, meaning that it's easy to verify its content.

> **Functional tests without Geb plugin**
>
> If you were to remove the Geb plugin and all your Geb tests, Grails would stop running the `PostRestFunctionalSpec` that you created. That's because you have to register the fact that you have functional tests, along with the location of the test directory. Grails does this automatically for unit and integration tests, but not functional tests.
>
> The Geb plugin performs this registration for you. Since the registration process depends on the libraries that you are using and your version of Grails, we recommend depending on the Geb plugin anyway to ensure that your REST functional tests run. If you don't use Geb, consider the Functional Spock plugin we mentioned earlier.

It's worth bearing in mind that the tests in listing 12.8 rely on the sample data created by the `BootStrap` class when the test server starts up. Refer to chapter 9 for more information on dealing with test data and avoiding side effects between tests. Another interesting aspect of the test is the `setup()` method: this configures the REST client to trust all SSL certificates. This isn't important in these particular tests, but if you run with HTTPS enabled, it's vital. That's because the test server uses a self-signed certificate that the REST client will reject by default, resulting in all the tests failing.

Listing 12.8 only contains a small sample of the functional tests that you need for your REST API, but it shows you how to exercise the API through HTTP requests using different HTTP methods. The mechanics for testing PUTs and DELETEs are no different. In real life you want more extensive testing of the data returned, but that's a case of using more queries on the returned JSON or XML.

Hubbub now has a fully fledged REST API for posts that has tests at both the unit and functional level, a level of security via basic authentication, and a plan for dealing with versioning. And all of that can easily be transposed to your own projects. The mechanics are simple, so you can focus on making your API easy to use and full of value to your users.

12.4 Summary and best practices

Giving software clients access to your application requires a different approach from the usual HTML-based UIs. Real users require data presented in a manner that's easy to read and understand, software clients only care about the data and want to extract what they need easily.

We focused in this chapter on implementing the REST architectural pattern, which is ideally suited to web applications and is supported by Grails out of the box. By leveraging the HTTP protocol, you can easily create a secure and reliable API for your application that other applications can use.

Despite the focus on REST in this chapter, you should be aware that other options are available. For example, you can use operation-oriented protocols such as SOAP and Java RMI. Various Java libraries and Grails plugins (such as the CXF plugin) use these; remember that any documentation and articles that apply to Java applications also apply to Grails.

We finish with a few guidelines on REST development and how best to implement REST APIs in Grails:

- *Know your clients.* Is your API going to be used only by a rich, JavaScript UI that your team or another one in the company is developing? Or will it be used for integration into other websites? Perhaps autonomous software clients will use it for analysis. The type of clients you need to support affects your policies on security and legacy API support as well as how stable the API is. If you only have a rich UI using the API, you have more room to introduce breaking changes as the UI is typically kept up to date with the API.
- *Decouple the API from the persistence model.* When you have a public API and no control over the clients, it's important to keep the API stable. The best way to achieve this is to decouple the API from the persistence model through custom marshalers, command objects or Grails services that generate the data representations as required.
- *Use the appropriate HTTP methods.* Map the HTTP methods to actions that conform to the expectations and requirements of the methods. For example, don't map `GET` to an action that adds, removes, or modifies data on the server. Doing so breaks the contract defined by HTTP.
- *Make use of HTTP status codes.* It's easy to return a status code of 200 for all requests and use the content of the response to determine whether a request was successful. Easy, but bad practice. You give up a flexible and well-defined mechanism for error reporting—one that can be understood by any HTTP client (such as a browser).

From interapplication communication, we move on to internal communication systems that enable you to coordinate either different parts of an application or multiple internal applications or subsystems.

13 Single-page web applications (and other UI stuff)

This chapter covers

- Why single-page apps are popular
- Advanced Grails layouts and Ajax facilities
- How to manage Grails UI resources
- Modern web app architecture with AngularJS

In chapter 12, we took you through the basics of designing and implementing RESTful API endpoints in your Grails application. And one of the most common consumers of those RESTful endpoint is likely to be a rich web-client application. In this chapter you build exactly that—adding rich desktop-like services to your Grails web tier that leverage today's hottest JavaScript frameworks and latest web app architecture trends.

But before you leap into the code, let's consider "What exactly are Single-Page Applications (SPA) and why are they so popular?" Probably the greatest driver that spiked all the interest in SPAs was the release of Gmail. There had been numerous webmail solutions before Gmail, but here was a web-based mail client that had the look and, more importantly, the feel of a desktop application. It dynamically updated your inbox without all that nasty page refresh flickering you were used to, it offered a rich viewing experience for reading and replying to mail items, and it was amazingly fast and responsive. It was like using a desktop mail client. But in a browser!

SPAs such as Gmail have become the gold standard for modern web application development because they attempt to deliver all the richness of a full desktop GUI application, but hosted in the convenience of a ubiquitous browser. The huge win for users is that they can access these rich applications from wherever they are and on whatever device they happen to have with them. And because SPAs are hosted on a single page with portions of the screen refreshing as needed, users typically experience a much snappier and more visually appealing application experience.

If you're going to deliver this rich experience to clients, you need to manage JavaScript, CSS, and HTML artifacts. Fortunately, that whole area is significantly improved in Grails 2. Let's take a tour.

13.1 Revisiting Grails web resource management

You can't avoid it: SPAs are JavaScript heavy. To pull off those seamless page updates and a responsive user experience, there's going to be event magic happening behind the scenes.

If you attempted to write SPAs in the days of Grails 1, you included truckloads of JavaScript (typically pulling in bags of YUI or Dojo JavaScript libraries for all the widgets you needed on a particular page).

Grails 2 changes all that with the introduction of the Resources plugin that we first mentioned to you in the heat of chapter 8. The new resource infrastructure, which ships with all Grails 2 applications by default, attempts to address several important challenges that affect SPAs:

- Making it easy to pull in CSS/JavaScript libraries and their dependencies
- Ensuring JavaScript resources are imported to a page in a performance-efficient manner
- Minifying and bundling JavaScript and CSS resources for optimized production deployments
- Seamlessly handling static resources (such as JavaScript libraries served from a CDN)
- Providing a pipeline for resource generation that other resource-aware plugins can participate in
- Standardizing the manner in which plugins can expose their own resources to an application

The first step in taking advantage of this amazing new resource management infrastructure is to declare your web resources (such as CSS and JavaScript files) in the new resource DSL. Let's get you up to speed.

13.1.1 Defining your resources

In the new Grails Resources world, you no longer reference CSS/JavaScript files in your pages. Instead, you abstract away all your required resources in modules that you define in /grails-app/conf/ApplicationResources.groovy. It's in these modules that you specify the physical CSS/JavaScript files that make up a particular module. Using this approach gives you several important benefits:

- Your page markup is much smaller because you need to reference only the module name, not the tons of CSS/JavaScript that it might represent.
- When you update the version of a JavaScript library, you need to do it in only one place, not throughout every page in your application that uses it.
- The Resources plugin can render those files uncompressed in dev (where you're debugging them), but compress them when you deploy your WAR file (or even reference a CDN version in production!).
- You can define modules to be dependent on other modules, and the Resources plugin ensures that you only ship one copy of each JavaScript file to your client's browser (optimizing page load time).

You're probably curious what the resources DSL looks like and how you can define your own resources. Let's look at the default resource configuration that you find in any new Grails application:

```
modules = {
    application {
        resource url:'js/application.js'
    }
}
```

Hmm. Kind of unimpressive, isn't it? By default, Grails only defines one module called `application`, which contains a single JavaScript resource called js/application.js (found relative to your web-app directory, so it lives at /web-app/js/application.js. The sum contribution of application.js is to conditionally display an Ajax spinner during Ajax operations.

Let's think of a more common use case for your SPA. You're planning to use AngularJS (http://angularjs.org/) for the JavaScript MVC framework, Restangular (https://github.com/mgonto/restangular) for all the REST backend integration with AngularJS, and Lo-Dash (http://lodash.com/) for JavaScript utils such as filtering arrays and the like.

First, you download the uncompressed versions of those files (handy for debugging) and drop them in your /web-app/js directory. You also need a new empty JavaScript file called hubbub.js, which hosts all the custom logic you develop this chapter. After all that's set up, your /web-app/js directory should look something like figure 13.1.

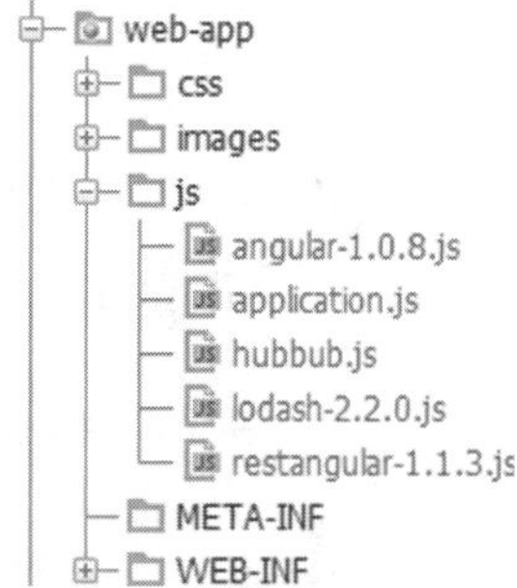

Figure 13.1 The JavaScript resources you downloaded to /web-app/js/, plus an empty hubbub.js

With the JavaScript files now in place, you can define module entries for each of them. Set up files in their own modules and with dependencies so you can later pick and choose the modules you wish to bundle with your page. The following listing shows how to define the needed modules.

Listing 13.1 Defining modules for angular.js, Restangular, and lodash.js

```
modules = {

    application {
        resource url:'js/application.js'
    }

    angularjs {
        resource url:'js/angular-1.0.8.js', disposition: 'head'
    }

    restangular {
        dependsOn 'angularjs'
        resource url:'js/restangular-1.1.3.js'
    }

    lodashjs {
        resource url:'js/lodash-2.2.0.js'
    }

    baseCss {
        resource url:'/css/main.css'
        resource url:'/css/hubbub.css'
    }

    core {
        dependsOn 'baseCss'
        dependsOn 'restangular,lodashjs,application'
        resource url: '/js/hubbub.js'
    }

}
```

Notice how in the core module you used the `dependsOn` construct to pull in your `basecss`, and also to pull in Restangular, lodash.js, and your application.js as dependencies. Because Restangular depends on the AngularJS module, that's pulled in, too.

All this bundling means that you need to specify in your target pages that you want the core module, and the resources infrastructure will drag in everything you need. Should you ever need to change library versions in the future, you can drop in the new library/web-app/js, update the single reference in the relevant module, and be done. And if you have pages that don't need a kitchen sink include, you can cherry-pick whichever modules you need on the page in question. Simple and flexible.

Your modules are defined, so it's time to update your page markup to take advantage of them. You do that in the next section.

> **Why not use the AngularJS resources plugin?**
>
> The introduction of the Resources plugin has spawned a slew of resource library plugins for all the common JavaScript frameworks. Among them is an AngularJS resources plugin (http://grails.org/plugin/angularjs-resources) that's actively maintained with the latest AngularJS library files. You can pull in these types of plugins via `BuildConfig` and you'll have prebuilt modules defined that you can `r:require` in your page.
>
> We haven't opted for that strategy for a few reasons. The first is that we want to teach you how these resource modules work for yourself, so you're not dependent on a plugin for the next library you want to integrate.
>
> But more importantly, if you opt for a Resources plugin for your library of choice, you often limit yourself to the version of the library the plugin offers. The AngularJS plugin is frequently updated, but many aren't. If we empower you to do your own configuration, you can mix and match the libraries and versions you want to use.

13.1.2 Using resource modules in your view tier

Using resource modules in your GSP layer is normally a two-step process:

1. Add markup to your layout templates as placeholders where the resources should be placed
2. Update your page templates to specify the modules you want to pull in for particular pages

Let's look at your current master template for Hubbub, which lives at /grails-app/views/layouts/main.gsp, as shown in the following listing.

Listing 13.2 The existing Hubbub template in main.gsp

```
<!doctype html>
<html>
<head>
  <title>Hubbub &raquo; <g:layoutTitle default="Welcome" /></title>
  <g:external dir="css" file="hubbub.css"/>
  <g:external dir="css" file="main.css"/>
  <nav:resources/>
  <g:layoutHead/>
  <r:layoutResources/>
</head>
<body>
  <div>
    <div id="hd">
      <g:link uri="/">
        <g:img id="logo" uri="/images/headerlogo.png" alt="hubbub logo"/>
      </g:link>
    </div>
    <div id="bd"><!-- start body -->
      <nav:render group="tabs"/>
      <g:layoutBody/>
    </div>  <!-- end body -->
```

External CSS references are good candidates for modules.

Calls layoutResources in head and body.

```
    <div id="ft">
      <div id="footerText">Hubbub - Social Networking on Grails</div>
    </div>
  </div>
  <r:layoutResources/>
</body>
</html>
```

Call layoutResources in head and body.

The calls that you need to make sure are in your master template are the `<r:layout-Resource>` entries that need to appear in both the `<head>` and `<body>` sections of your HTML. Why in both places? Because the Resources plugin optimizes your page layout with where it places those CSS and JavaScript references.

The Resources plugin typically places the CSS entries in the `<head>` element of your layout and the JavaScript files at the end of the `<body>` element. It takes this approach because your browser blocks when parsing those large JavaScript files and you want that block to happen after the browser renders the page to the client (and your end user is busily distracted for a few minutes taking in all that lovely information).

What if I want to override where my resources go on the page?

Control freak, eh? We get it, and so does the Resources plugin. You might have JavaScript files that you specifically want to load at the head of the page. In fact, AngularJS is one library that prefers to be in your `head` section so you can avoid any FOUM (flash of unstyled content—where AngularJS's templates appear before they're filled in by the JavaScript).

In those cases you can take advantage of the `disposition:` attribute when specifying your module resource. You may have noticed that we ensured AngularJS was loaded in the page `<head>` by defining it as:

```
angularjs {
    resource url:'js/angular-1.0.8.js', disposition: 'head'
}
```

You'll quickly refactor your layout page to pull in those base CSS modules, but you won't drag in all the modules because you don't want every page in the application to need to pull in all that base JavaScript (see the following sidebar on caching).

The way you pull a resource module into a particular page is via the `<r:require>` tag—telling it the module or modules you wish to include. Let's update your base layout to use the `baseCss` module you defined previously. Here's what the new `<head>` element of your /grails-app/views/layouts/main.gsp layout looks like with a `r:require` tag:

```
<head>
  <title>Hubbub &raquo; <g:layoutTitle default="Welcome" /></title>
  <r:require module="baseCss"/>
  <nav:resources/>
  <g:layoutHead/>
  <r:layoutResources/>
</head>
```

Although the visual layout of the page looks identical to its preresources format, if you do a "view-source" on the newly minted page, you'll see that the Resources plugin has concatenated your `baseCss`-dependent files into a single file to ensure fewer requests and better performance. It now looks like this:

```
<link href="/hubbub/static/bundle-bundle_baseCss_head.css"
     type="text/css" rel="stylesheet" media="screen, projection" />
```

And if you use your browser tools, you'll see in the development environment that it's an ordered concatenation of the dependencies one after another. In a production environment, you typically install the zipped-resources and cached-resources plugins to handle minification and unique URL hashing (even across redeploys).

How the Resources plugin impacts caching

We suggested that you be careful about dragging in more modules than you need on a particular page because your browser needs to download all that extra JavaScript on the page render. And that's good advice. But not the whole story.

Truth be known, the way the Resources plugin sets up its cacheable JavaScript endpoints, if you put all that JavaScript in your base template, it would only be downloaded once by the browser—on the first page view. After that initial request, that JavaScript bundle would then be cached by the browser on every subsequent page request throughout the application with virtually no performance penalty until you edit one of those dependent JavaScript files (at which point the Resources plugin would generate a fresh cacheable JavaScript URL for your bundle).

It doesn't change our advice to pull in only the bundles you need, but it's nonetheless helpful to understand what the resources infrastructure is doing behind the scenes.

Now that you're cross-configuring your resource modules and their dependencies and know how to `require` them into your target GSP pages, let's put them to use by writing AngularJS code that consumes all those RESTful services you wrote in the previous chapter.

13.2 RESTful clients with AngularJS

AngularJS has become a popular modern JavaScript framework for building single-page web applications. Previous frameworks, such as Backbone.js and KnockoutJS, pioneered the idea of rich JavaScript web tier apps, with JavaScript data binding and templating, while interacting and syncing with RESTful back-end services.

AngularJS evolved from JavaScript MVC frameworks with a system that:

- Provides a simple, declarative HTML templating language that's easy to extend.
- Has a powerful two-way data binding system so your UI and JavaScript business objects always stay in sync.
- Requires no messing with the browser DOM. AngularJS looks after all the trickiness or refreshes the page bits under its control, so you don't have to worry.

- Has a large and growing ecosystem of extension modules.
- Is backed and used by Google. What else can you say?

Writing AngularJS is also an excellent way to demonstrate all the common things you may want to do in your next Grails-based SPA. Remember that this isn't a book on AngularJS, and we can cover only so much. If you want more than the basics, which we'll cover, you can find heaps of great books, tutorials, and videos to help you learn AngularJS. We recommend you check out the Learn section of http://angularjs.org/. With disclaimers out of the way, let's hack your first async Hubbub timeline!

13.2.1 Configuring your Grails app for AngularJS

The road to your first AngularJS single-page edition of Hubbub starts with creating a new controller action and GSP view to host your new markup. We pull in all the data for your new page via back-end REST calls, so there won't be much to pass through. Let's add a single page action to your `PostController` class so you can start UI markup:

```
def singlepage() {
    def user = params.id ? User.findByLoginId(params.id) :
              ➥ springSecurityService.currentUser
    if (!user) {
        response.sendError(404)
    } else {
        [ user : user ]
    }
}
```

You passed the current user object through to your singlepage.gsp file, so you could set up the page title, but otherwise you request everything that you need from the RESTful service that you built in chapter 12.

Let's put in the shell of your singlepage.gsp for now, then talk about how you can integrate AngularJS into the picture, as shown in the following listing.

Listing 13.3 A minimalist /grails-app/views/post/singlepage.gsp to get started

```
<html>
    <head>
        <title>Timeline for ${user.profile ?
            ➥ user.profile.fullName : user.loginId}</title>
        <meta name="layout" content="main"/>
        <r:require module="core"/>                    ❶ Pulls in supporting JavaScript modules
    </head>
    <body>
        <div id="newPost">
            <h3>
                What is ${ user.profile ?
            ➥ user.profile.fullName : user.loginId } hacking on right now?
            </h3>
        </div>

    </body>
</html>
```

Well, that certainly is minimalist! You declared your core module ❶, and pulled in all the JavaScript you needed. But before you write any AngularJS code, you have to get your document setup AngularJS-ready. AngularJS applications like to have an app-name configured on the `ng-app` attribute of their HTML root element (the namespace was chosen because ng sounds like "Angular"), so you want something such as:

```
<html ng-app="Hubbub">
```

The only trouble is that you can't add that definition to the `<html>` element of your singlepage.gsp, because it'll be overwritten by the layout definition of `<html>` in your /grails-app/views/layout/main.gsp. Conversely, you can't add it to the `<html>` element in your main.gsp layout, because it'll appear on every page in your app!

You have to perform Grails SiteMesh kung fu to get the magic happening. In your template, define the header as:

```
<html ${pageProperty(name:'page.htmlAttrs')}>
```

Which tells Grails to merge in any page-level properties defined as `htmlAttrs` on your target page. If there aren't any, it leaves this section blank. Let's update your new singlepage.gsp file with the required attribute:

```
<html>
    <head>
        <title>Timeline for ${user.profile ?
              ➥ user.profile.fullName : user.loginId}</title>
        <meta name="layout" content="main"/>
        <content tag="htmlAttrs">ng-app="Hubbub"</content>     <-- Defines the value of the htmlAttrs element for merging
        <r:require module="core"/>
    </head>
    ...
</html>
```

Now that you defined your `htmlAttrs` element, it'll be merged in the render. Point your browser at http://localhost:8080/hubbub/post/singlepage and do a view-source to see your new markup in action:

```
<html ng-app="Hubbub">
```

Bingo! With your document now configured for AngularJS, let's pull in your first set of `POST` via a RESTful service.

13.2.2 Your first AngularJS controller: pulling in a RESTful timeline

In chapter 12, you developed a `PostRestController` that did all the heavy lifting of adding/updating/deleting/listing the posts held in Hubbub. Let's write a bit of AngularJS code to pull in the timeline.

Your first step in writing AngularJS code is to define an `ng-controller` that's responsible for scoping the section of the page where AngularJS binds data and responds to rendering events.

In the following listing, let's start with the markup in singlepage.gsp, then dive into the backing JavaScript.

Listing 13.4 Adding your first AngularJS controller to singlepage.gsp

```
<div ng-controller="PostsCtrl">

        <div id="newPost">
            <h3>
                What is ${ user.profile ?
            ➥ user.profile.fullName : user.loginId } hacking on right now?
            </h3>
        </div>

        <div class="allPosts" ng-cloak>
            <div class="postEntry" ng-repeat="post in allPosts">
                <div class="postText">{{post.message}}</div>
                <div class="postDate">{{post.published}}
                        ➥ by {{post.user}}</div>
        </div>

</div>
```

1. Links this block to Angular controller object
2. Prevents browser from displaying unstyled markup
3. Iterates over allPosts list of this controller
4. Renders attributes of each post to browser

You introduced a few `ng-*` attributes to your elements. What do they do? The `ng-controller` element ❶ binds an Angular controller to this portion of the DOM. That means you can do things in the controller that affect the markup of this section of the document (and vice versa).

After a controller is bound, you can access variables and methods that the controller exposes and perform markup operations based on them. Because you don't want the browser displaying anything until the template is finished rendering, use the `ng-cloak` directive ❷ to stop any unwanted flickering of the browser.

In ❸ you do an iteration over the controller's `allPosts` property and create a new `div` for each post in the timeline using AngularJS's distinctive double-brace templating ❹. How does the matching controller give you all those posts? Let's look in your /web-app/js/hubbub.js in the following listing to find out.

Listing 13.5 Your first AngularJS controller

```
angular.module('Hubbub', ['restangular']).config(
    function(RestangularProvider) {
        RestangularProvider.setBaseUrl('/hubbub/api');
    }
);

function PostsCtrl($scope, Restangular) {

    var postsApi = Restangular.all("posts");
    $scope.allPosts = postsApi.getList();

}
```

1. Registers Hubbub with AngularJS, importing Restangular module
2. Defines PostsCtrl, injecting scope and Restangular
3. Configures Restangular URL with REST service endpoint URL
4. Points REST client at posts endpoint in API
5. Requests list of posts

Let's take it slow so you can see everything that's going on here. First, you register your application with AngularJS ❶ and import the `Restangular` module into play. You can configure modules after you import them, so configure Restangular to know the base API URL for all your REST calls ❷.

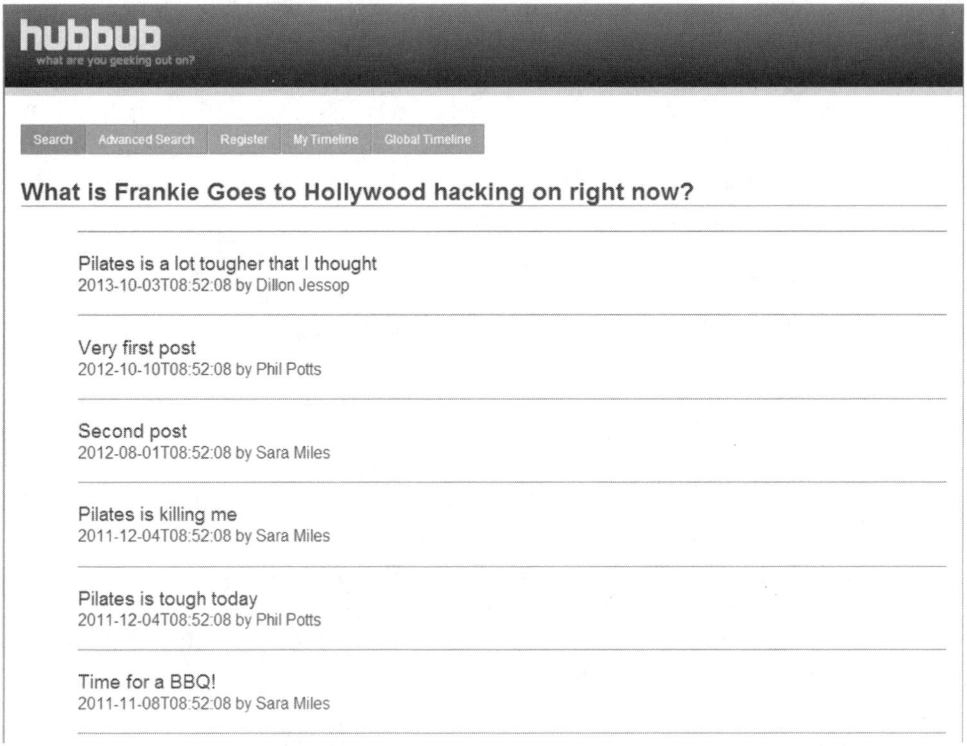

hubbub
what are you geeking out on?

Search | Advanced Search | Register | My Timeline | Global Timeline

What is Frankie Goes to Hollywood hacking on right now?

Pilates is a lot tougher that I thought
2013-10-03T08:52:08 by Dillon Jessop

Very first post
2012-10-10T08:52:08 by Phil Potts

Second post
2012-08-01T08:52:08 by Sara Miles

Pilates is killing me
2011-12-04T08:52:08 by Sara Miles

Pilates is tough today
2011-12-04T08:52:08 by Phil Potts

Time for a BBQ!
2011-11-08T08:52:08 by Sara Miles

Figure 13.2 Your first async timeline using AngularJS

With the config done, you define your `PostsCtrl` controller ❸, providing arguments for AngularJS to inject the current scope and a `Restangular` object for your REST calls. Then create an endpoint where you can request a list of `post` objects ❹. (Restangular offers the `all()` method if you expect a list or the `one()` method if you expect a single `post` object.) At this point your URL resolves the /hubbub/api/posts.

Finally, you request that list of objects ❺ and assign it to a variable in your controller scope (so your markup can read it). Behind the scenes Restangular sends a `GET` request to http://localhost:8080/hubbub/api/posts and parses the list of `post` objects it returns. That's the list you iterated in listing 13.4. As shown in figure 13.2, to see it in action, point your browser at http://localhost:8080/hubbub/post/singlepage.

Well done! You wrote your first set of RESTful AngularJS code and saw how data is bound between the UI and the back-end JavaScript. Your timeline is static for now; you'll fix that shortly. But what fun is a dynamic timeline if you can't create new posts? Let's allow users to create posts RESTfully, then circle back to the timeline business.

13.2.3 *Creating a new post via REST*

Creating a new post is a great way to show off AngularJS's amazing two-way data binding services, while also demonstrating how you can interact with your back-end Grails

REST service using different HTTP verbs. Recall from the previous chapter that the common REST verbs are GET (for requesting objects), POST (for creating new objects), PUT (for updating objects), and DELETE (for removing objects).

You want to implement POST to your RESTful back end to create a post, but before that you need content to send there. Let's put together your first AngularJS form, and bind it to your controller. Here's a little posting form to add to singlepage.gsp that uses your existing styling:

```
<form >
    <textarea id='postContent' ng-model="postContent"></textarea>
    <button type="button" ng-click="newPost()">Post</button>
</form>
```

Your new form introduces two new AngularJS directives: ng-model and ng-click. You might already know what they do! The ng-model directive tells AngularJS that it should bind the value in the text area to a postContent variable on the controller. If you change that value in the backing JavaScript, or in the text area itself, AngularJS makes sure the other side is updated.

The ng-click directive tells AngularJS to invoke the newPost() function on your controller when the user clicks the button. Let's look at the backing code to see how you can extract that new post content and send it to your Grails REST endpoint, as shown in the following listing.

Listing 13.6 Creating your first post via REST

```
angular.module('Hubbub', ['restangular']).config(
    function(RestangularProvider) {
        RestangularProvider.setBaseUrl('/hubbub/api');
    }
);
function PostsCtrl($scope, Restangular) {

    var postsApi = Restangular.all("posts");
    $scope.allPosts = postsApi.getList();

    $scope.newPost = function() {
        var postApi = Restangular.one("posts");          <-- 1 Sets up /hubbub/api/posts endpoint to receive a POST
        var newPost = { message: $scope.postContent };   <-- 2 Creates new JSON content to send
        postApi.post(null, newPost).then(function(response) {   <-- 3 Posts new post to back end
            $scope.allPosts = postsApi.getList();        <-- 4 Refreshes list when post succeeds
            $scope.postContent = "";
        }, function(errorResponse) {                     <-- 5 Handles any errors that occur
            alert("Error on creating post: " + errorResponse.status);
        });
    }

}
```

Your controller has certainly grown. You defined your newPost handler and pointed it at the appropriate URL endpoint ❶. Notice you used one() because you're sending a single post object this time, not a list. You then constructed the JSON of your new post ❷, and called Restangular's `post()` method ❸ to perform an HTTP `POST` of your new JSON.

Normally all of that posting happens asynchronously. In listing 13.5 you didn't care about waiting around. In the case of listing 13.6, however, you need to know when the post has finished updating so you can refresh your list of posts.

That's why you invoke the `then()` method ❸, which takes two arguments that are callback functions: the first is called for a successful post (in which case you refresh your post list and clear out the new post text area ❹), the second if an error condition is encountered, in which case, you pop up an error dialog ❺.

Now's a great time to point your browser at http://localhost:8080/hubbub/post/singlepage and post your first RESTful post!

13.2.4 Communicating between controllers

You've grown your `PostsCtrl` controller by jamming in new functionality, but you can't keep tracking this way without it leading to a big mess. Time to clean things up and separate out one controller to look after handling new posts and another controller to look after managing your timeline.

First let's change your form markup to introduce its own controller, which you call `NewPostCtrl`:

```
<form ng-controller="NewPostCtrl">
          <textarea id='postContent' ng-model="postContent"></textarea>
          <button ng-click="newPost()">Post</button>
</form>
```

Then move your timeline renderer into the PostsCtrl on its own.

```
<div ng-controller="PostsCtrl">
        <div class="allPosts" ng-cloak>
            <div class="postEntry" ng-repeat="post in allPosts">
                <div class="postText">{{post.message}}</div>
                <div class="postDate">{{post.published}}
                     ➥ by {{post.user}}</div>
            </div>
        </div>
</div>
```

You then move all the code that creates now posts into the `NewPostCtrl`, and let the `PostsCtrl` refresh its timeline. For that to happen, you need a way for `NewPostCtrl` to notify the `PostCtrl` when it's updated the posts. That gives us a reason to talk about how AngularJS handles events. First, let's look at the updated controller code, as shown in the following listing.

Listing 13.7 Propagating client-side events with AngularJS

```
angular.module('Hubbub', ['restangular']).config(
    function(RestangularProvider) {
        RestangularProvider.setBaseUrl('/hubbub/api');
    }
);
```

```
function PostsCtrl($scope, Restangular) {

    var postsApi = Restangular.all("posts");

    $scope.allPosts = [];

    $scope.refreshPosts = function() {                                      ❶
        postsApi.getList().then(function(newPostList) {
            $scope.allPosts = newPostList;
        }, function(errorResponse) {
            alert("Error on refreshing posts: " + errorResponse.status);
        });
    }

    $scope.$on('newPost', function() {                                      ❷
        $scope.refreshPosts();
    });

    $scope.refreshPosts();                                                  ❸

}

function NewPostCtrl($scope, $rootScope, Restangular) {                     ❹

    $scope.newPost = function() {
        var postApi = Restangular.one("posts");
        var newPost = { message: $scope.postContent };
        postApi.post(null, newPost).then(function(response) {
            $rootScope.$broadcast("newPost", newPost);                      ❺
            $scope.postContent = "";
        }, function(errorResponse) {
            alert("Error on creating post: " + errorResponse.status);
        });
    }
}
```

❶ **Moves post refreshing into reusable function**

❷ **Triggers refresh of post list on any newPost event**

❸ **Refreshes all posts the first time controller loads (first page view)**

❹ **Injects $rootScope, the parent of all scopes**

❺ **When new post is created, broadcasts newPost event to all scopes**

It seems like new code in there, but mostly you rejiggered the code you've already seen, tidying up a few things along the way. You moved the `refreshPosts()` operation into a reusable function with error handling ❶, which you call the first time the controller loads ❸. You also started listening for any `newPost` events ❷ (which is a name you made up to represent when the user creates a post in the system), and you trigger a refresh of your post list when that event occurs.

The other side of your change revolves around raising an event ❺ (or *broadcasting*, in AngularJS terms) whenever the user creates a new post, implementing logic to broadcast an event when new posts are created, and re-rendering the timeline when that event is consumed. In this case, you want all other controllers to know about the event, so you broadcast it via the AngularJS `$rootScope` (the parent of all other scopes), which you need to inject when defining your new controller ❹.

With your two controllers in place, you've seen the basics of fetching and creating posts with Grails and AngularJS. You'll take a small detour to improve your Hubbub posting UI experience and to learn a few new ways to apply AngularJS to the client side, then you'll circle back to complete your CRUD tour.

13.2.5 Better posting with live UI feedback

In your exploration of AngularJS, you focused on the RESTful integration with your Grails service. But when writing SPAs, you also need to think of making a compelling user experience on the client side.

You don't offer users too many data entry experiences in Hubbub, except for generating new posts. But you can certainly improve that experience. Suppose users have an input limit of 140 characters on their posts. Let's add a UI facility that counts down the number of remaining key presses.

The markup is simple. You add a small HTML `span` to hold the current value and then bind it to your back-end controller. First the markup in singlepage.gsp:

```
<form ng-controller="NewPostCtrl">
    <textarea id='postContent' ng-model="postContent"></textarea>
    <button ng-click="newPost()">Post</button>
    <span id='charsRemaining'>{{charsRemaining()}}</span>
</form>
```

You call a function on your `NewPostCtrl` to get the remaining characters so you can calculate that value dynamically on the fly. Let's implement the controller code in hubbub.js:

```
function NewPostCtrl($scope, $rootScope, Restangular) {

    $scope.postContent = "";

    $scope.charsRemaining = function() {
        return 140 - $scope.postContent.length;
    }

    // ... other code omitted
}
```

❶ **Initializes postContent to non-null value on first run**

❷ **Dynamically calculates remaining characters**

You initialized the `postContent`, which is bound to the text area, to an empty string when the controller starts ❶ because this eliminated any noisy null-checks later on. Other than that, your `charsRemaining` function ❷ takes the current length of the text area away from 140 and returns that as your `charsRemaining`. You style that `<span>` element in your hubbub.css so it appears as an unobtrusive light gray element next to your post button. Let's see it in action in figure 13.3.

That looks fantastic, but let's take it to the next level. You don't want users to click the Post button if they type in more than 140 chars (or if they have no chars in their post because a blank post breaks your Grails domain class validation rules). Let's put in code to stop them entering long or empty posts.

First, change the Post button definition to include an `ng-disabled` call to check whether or not the button should be disabled:

```
<button ng-click="newPost()"
      ng-disabled="postInvalidLength()">Post</button>
```

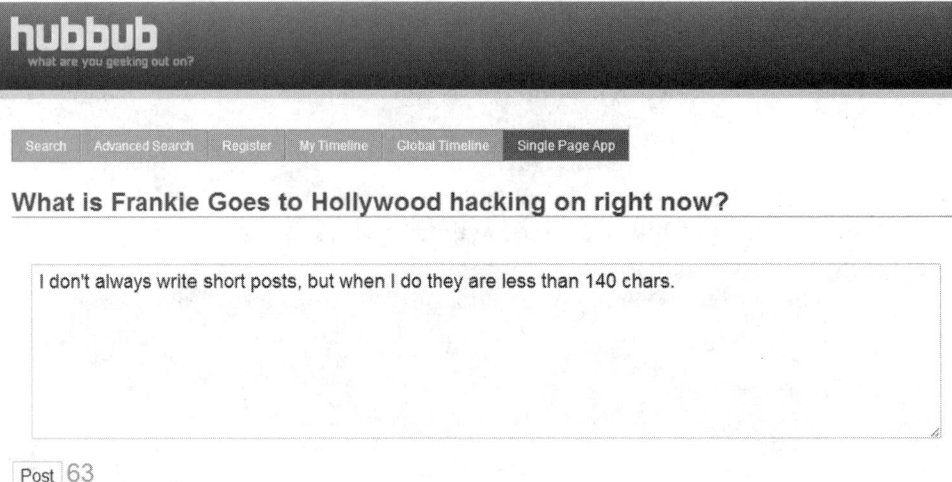

Figure 13.3 Your unobtrusive click counter lets you know you have 63 chars remaining.

Then implement that tweet logic that determines whether the button is grayed out in your `NewPostCtrl`:

```
$scope.postInvalidLength = function() {
    return $scope.postContent.length == 0 ||
       $scope.postContent.length > 140
}
```

And with that function in place, the Post button is now disabled (appears gray) when the post is empty, enabled (not gray) while the char count is <= 140 chars, then gray again after 140 chars. You're ensuring the user enters only valid data before you make any expensive remote calls.

> **The many validators of AngularJS**
> You rolled your own little AngularJS validation routines because the logic was specific to our application. For the basic cases, AngularJS includes a range of built-in validation directives such as `ng-maxlength`, `ng-minlength`, and `ng-pattern`. Check out the AngularJS docs for details.

Given that 140 chars is a tough limitation for posters, wouldn't it be nice if you gave users helpful visual feedback as they approach the character limit (and cue them to start abbreviating)? This sounds like a good time to look into AngularJS's CSS integration.

AngularJS's `ng-class` construct lets you set the CSS style class of an element based on any valid AngularJS expression. Let's reuse that `charsRemaining` function you used in the character counter to change the color of the text area when the character count gets tight:

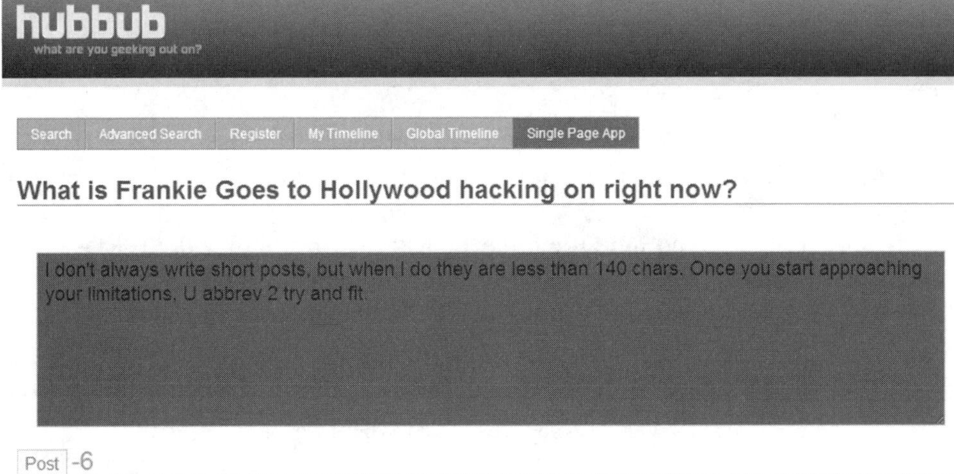

Figure 13.4 Maxing out the field length brings the red text area of doom

```
<textarea id='postContent' ng-model="postContent"
      ng-class="{'charsLow' : charsRemaining() < 12,
                 'charsOverflow' : charsRemaining() < 0}"></textarea>
```

Add styling to hubbub.css to define your `charsLow` class as a bright yellow, and your `charsOverflow` as an intrusive red:

```
.charsLow      { background-color: yellow !important; }
.charsOverflow { background-color: red !important; }
```

Notice that you mark these CSS styles as `!important` only to make sure you trump your other base styling that affects the color of focused text areas (you probably won't have this need typically). Now users have strong visual cues when their constraints approach. Let's see it in action in figure 13.4.

And with your snazzy posting UI in place, and validation logic in your AngularJS toolbox, you can return to learning about how to RESTfully edit existing posts. While you're at it, you'll apply all you've learned so far to implement in-place editing of your existing posts.

13.3 Advanced RESTful CRUD: implementing in-place editing

You performed RESTful `GET`s to your `PostRestController`'s `list()` action and even created new posts with a RESTful `POST` to your `PostRestController`'s `save()` action. Let's finish off your RESTful client exploration of CRUD operations by creating the UI elements to work with updates (RESTful `PUT`s to your `PostRestController`'s `update()` action), and deletes (RESTful `DELETE`s to your `PostRestController`'s `update()` action).

One way you can pull those final two operations together is by offering the user a way to update and delete their posts directly from their timeline. Let's make it super easy by watching when the user moves their mouse over an existing post, then automatically making that post editable.

13.3.1 Implementing UI switching

The easiest way to create the visual appearance of a post becoming editable is to switch between two `div`s. You generate the markup for both the "view post" `div` ❺ and the "edit post" `div` ❸ side by side when you generate the timeline, but then you show only one and hide the other depending on whether the user is mousing over the element.

Let's take a look at the code, as shown in the following listing.

Listing 13.8 Marking up for in-place editing

```
<div class="allPosts" ng-controller="PostsCtrl" ng-cloak>

   <div class="postEntry"
      ng-repeat="post in allPosts" ng-controller="EditPostCtrl"
      ng-mouseenter="activate()"
      ng-mouseleave="deactivate()">

     <span ng-show="isEditState">
         <textarea class="inplacePostEdit"
             ng-model="editedContent"></textarea>
         <button ng-click="updatePost()">Update</button>
         <button ng-click="deletePost()">Delete</button>
     </span>

     <span ng-show="!isEditState">
         <div class="postText">{{post.message}}</div>
         <div class="postDate">{{post.published}}
              by {{post.user}}</div>
     </span>

   </div>

</div>
```

❶ Iterates over each available post
❷ Activates or deactivates editing based on mouse entry
❸ Provides a span for the edit state
❹ Invokes update routines when user clicks buttons
❺ Provides span for the view (nonedit) state

Given that all this in-place editing needs state tracking, you introduce a new `EditPostCtrl` ❶ that looks after the editing for a particular post. One important nuance is that because this controller is defined on an `ng-repeat`, AngularJS creates a new instance of this controller for each iteration of the repeat.

When the mouse enters or leaves the post, call an `activate()` or `deactivate()` routine ❷, which flips the edit state of the post from on to off as appropriate. The remaining two spans conditionally render the "edit post" ❸ or the "view post" ❺ based on that edit state.

Your edit mode also sports buttons to update and delete posts ❹, which you'll implement shortly. But before you dive into the update/delete function, let's take a look at the following listing, which implements enough of your `EditPostCtrl` to turn on your UI elements as appropriate.

Pilates sure is tough today
2013-10-03T05:50:47 by Frankie Goes to Hollywood
Who's heading off to the gym?
2013-10-03T05:50:43 by Frankie Goes to Hollywood
Look at me, I'm nearly editable!
Update
Delete

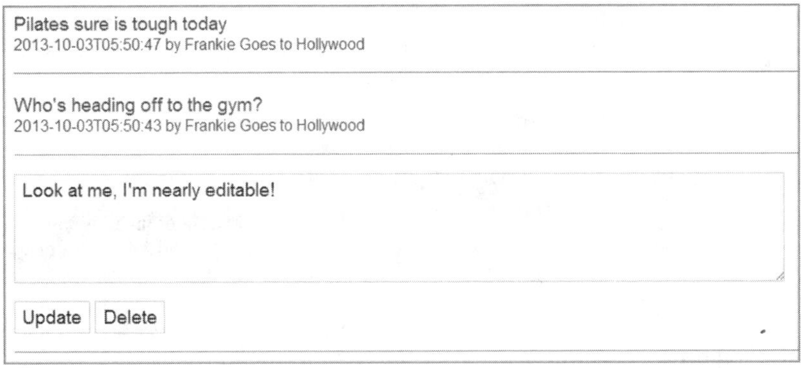

Figure 13.5 The new in-place editor with Update and Delete on mouse-over

Listing 13.9 Your first cut at adding in-place editing to hubbub.js

```
function EditPostCtrl($scope, $rootScope, Restangular) {

    $scope.isEditState = false;

    $scope.editedContent = $scope.post.content        <-- Binds textarea field to original post content

    $scope.activate= function() {
        $scope.isEditState = true;
    }

    $scope.deactivate= function() {
        $scope.isEditState = false;
    }
    // ... we'll implement our update() and delete() here later
}
```

The first cut lets you flip the UI between edit and view mode. Let's head over to http://localhost:8080/hubbub/post/singlepage and give it a workout.

That looks good, but you haven't implemented the connection to your back-end Grails `PostRestController` actions.

13.3.2 *Introducing an update feature*

Let's fill out the `EditPostCtrl` with the new methods. We'll start with the update routine (`updatePost`) because it has a tricky corner case. In the case of an error when the user updates a post, you want to set the post content back to what it was before the edit. Let's implement your safe update inside your `EditPostCtrl` in the following listing.

Listing 13.10 Implementing post updating in your `EditPostCtrl`

```
$scope.originalContent = $scope.post.content      <-- Saves original post content
$scope.editedContent = $scope.post.content          (1) for later revert if required

$scope.updatePost = function() {

    isEditState = false;
```

```
        $scope.post.message = $scope.editedContent;          <-- ❷ Transfers updated content to post
PUTs    $scope.post.put().then(
updated     function() {
post to         $scope.isEditState = false;
RESTful     }, function(errorResponse) {
service ❸       $scope.post.message = $scope.originalContent;      <--
                alert("Error saving object:" + errorResponse.status);
            }
        );                              In case of failed update, sets
                                        edited text to original ❹
    }
```

In this listing, you save the original post content from the get-go ❶ in case you ever encounter a REST failure and need to revert. When the user clicks the Update button, you transfer the contents of the bound text area onto your post object ❷, then issue a `put()` call to send it to the back end ❸.

Where does that `put()` method come from? Remember, you fetched this object from Restangular when you built the original timeline. Restangular decorates each object it returns with methods using all the standard RESTful verbs (`get()`, `post()`, `put()`, and so on).

TIP Check out the Restangular docs for a detailed look at what's available: https://github.com/mgonto/restangular.

If things go horribly wrong, revert your change ❹ to the content of the post (remember AngularJS uses that post content when rendering the "read" view of timeline, so leave it tidy).

And your update is in! Time to press on to your final feature: deleting posts!

Wrangling Restangular with custom RESTful endpoints

We're using a custom JSON mapper, but the default Grails RESTful Post endpoint would expect the JSON of the post to be wrapped in a nested element called `Post`. Although, this practice is common in both Grails and Rails applications, most RESTful APIs on the web take the JSON of the post natively without the nesting. Either way, Restangular has you covered.

The easiest way to accommodate the special nesting is to register a Restangular request interceptor in your application to do the wrapping for you automatically so you can get on with business. The interceptor wraps every `PUT` request inside an element with a wrapper of the same name. For example, it wraps the payload of a `post` object of

```
{ content: "my new post" }
```

as

```
{ post : { content: "my new post" } }
```

(continued)

In case you need to do this in your own applications, here's the updated configuration with a `RequestInterceptor`.

```
angular.module('Hubbub', ['restangular']).config(
    function(RestangularProvider) {
        RestangularProvider.setBaseUrl('/hubbub/api');
        RestangularProvider.setRequestInterceptor(
            ➥ function(elem, operation, what) {
            var retElem = elem;
            if (operation === 'put') {
                var wrapper = {};
                wrapper[what.substring(0, what.length -1)] = elem;
                retElem = wrapper;
            }
            return retElem;
        });
    }
);
```

Your last, big in-place editing feature is the delete of an existing post.

13.3.3 Finalizing lifecycles with delete

You already have the button for a delete feature; after you write the backing logic in your `EditPostCtrl`, you're done. Let's see how it works in the following listing.

Listing 13.11 Implementing a delete function on `EditPostCtrl`

```
$scope.deletePost = function() {

    isEditState = false;

    $scope.post.message = $scope.editedContent;
    $scope.post.remove().then(                           ❶ Calls remove() method to
        function() {                                       issue RESTful delete() call
            $rootScope.$broadcast("deletePost", $scope.post);
        }, function(errorResponse) {
            alert("Error saving object:" + errorResponse.status);
        }
    );                                        Broadcasts global deletePost
                                              event to all listeners ❷
}
```

The delete operation is much more straightforward than update. You made a call to the `remove()` method ❶ of your post and when that completes, you broadcast a `deletePost` event ❷ so that your `PostsCtrl` (which looks after the timeline) can remove the post you deleted from its timeline. Notice that you pass the deleted post as one of the attributes of the event. That will be important when you consume the event in your `PostsCtrl`. Let's see how you implement that:

```
$scope.$on('deletePost', function(event, postToDelete) {
    $scope.allPosts = _.filter($scope.allPosts, function(nextPost) {
        return nextPost.id != postToDelete.id
    });
});
```

In your `PostsCtrl`, you listen for the `deletePost` event then use a simple JavaScript utility routine provided by Lo-Dash to filter your posts list and remove the deleted post placed on the event.

> **NOTE** You could've called your `$scope.refreshPosts()` routine and refetched the entire timeline from the server (which would now be missing the deleted post), but that seems expensive for what you need.

And with that change, your in-place editing capability is now complete. Congratulations on hardcore AngularJS hacking. There's so much more AngularJS we didn't have room to cover in this chapter: creating your own custom directive tags, working with AngularJS services, and integrating JavaScript testing frameworks such as Jasmine. Make sure you take time to browse the AngularJS site (http://angularjs.org/) if you want to see more of what this productive new framework has to offer.

13.4 Summary and best practices

You spent this entire chapter in the UI tier: marshaling objects around the browser and interacting with back-end RESTful services. Although we can't cover everything about SPAs, we've given you a broad exposure to the tools and techniques available to build rich and responsive SPAs. You now have jumping-off points to start your own explorations into this exciting technology.

Before we leave the UI layer and return to the hardcore middle-tier world of transactional Spring beans, let's review a few key best practices from this chapter:

- *Use the Resources plugin to abstract your libraries.* The Resources plugin saves maintenance time because you can update JavaScript libraries in one place rather than scattering the updates throughout your application.
- *Optimize your resource dependency bundling.* Rather than define massive "kitchen sink" dependencies in the resources DSL, structure your resources so you can cherry-pick the libraries (or collection of libraries) you need for a particular page. It pays off in page-load time.
- *Investigate Resources plugins, but don't be wedded to them.* You can get Resource plugins that pull in the resources for all the common JavaScript libraries, but not all of them are actively updated. Often it's better to pull down the version of a library that you want to use and do your own resource configuration.
- *Avoid massive JavaScript controllers.* The same rules that apply to all software development thinking still apply to JavaScript. It can be tempting to add "a few more features" to a particular controller, but you end up with a page-scoped controller that's a mess of responsibilities. Refactor, refactor, refactor.

- *Don't forget about eventing.* One of the most powerful features of AngularJS is its integrated eventing model. It provides a loosely coupled way for your controllers to communicate, and using the provided `Eventbus` can lead to clean solutions.
- *Go deeper with Angular.* As you saw, AngularJS has a gentle learning curve after you master a few key concepts. Take advantage of the wealth of AngularJS resources on the web to level up your web-framework knowledge. It pays off in whatever framework you use next.

In the next chapter, we take a break from the UI tier and jump back in the middle-tier world of Spring and transactions.

14 Understanding Spring and transactions

This chapter covers

- Introducing the Spring framework
- Working with transactions
- Mastering transactions

As you've seen throughout the book, Grails isn't only about giving you the tools to write web applications. It also provides the means to structure your application in a standard way, whether that's through a service layer or a more asynchronous, message-oriented architecture as described in chapter 15. This isn't by chance: the middle tier of your application (the business logic) is important because it normally provides the real business value.

The reason Grails works so well in this area is that it's built on top of the incredibly popular and powerful Spring framework. We mentioned it in passing a few times, and it tends to remain invisible when your Grails applications don't have complex business logic. You happily rely on services being automatically injected into your controllers and other artifacts. Yet when an application does increase in complexity, you won't want to miss out on the help Spring can provide.

Understanding the basics of Spring is essential to writing flexible and maintainable Grails applications. Fortunately, Grails gives you a gradual learning curve to

Spring that we take advantage of in this chapter to dig deeper and tease out the key features that will help you day to day. We also look at maintaining data integrity through transactions, which is one of the core features of Spring.

> **NOTE** If you're already a Spring aficionado, we suggest you skim the introduction and give the section on services a brief review.

This look into the workings of Spring starts with an introduction about what it is and how Grails's "Spring by convention" feature, the service, fits into the whole package.

14.1 Spring fundamentals

Since its birth many years ago (version 1.0 was released in 2004), Spring has simplified the development of enterprise applications, from transaction support to messaging and more. Its core, though, is a DI framework, which you need to understand for the rest of Spring to make sense.

14.1.1 What is dependency injection?

A while back, a new paradigm emerged in application architecture called inversion of control (IoC)[1]. The principle is simple. Instead of each object creating and initializing the objects it depends on itself, you have a container that instantiates, initializes, and wires together objects. Figure 14.1 illustrates the difference between the two approaches.

The traditional approach

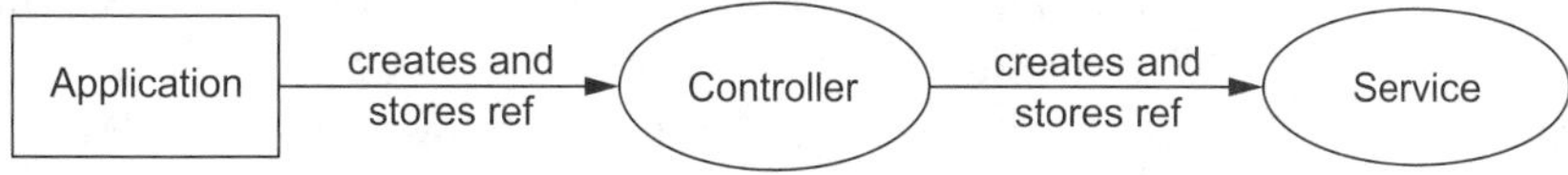

The IoC approach

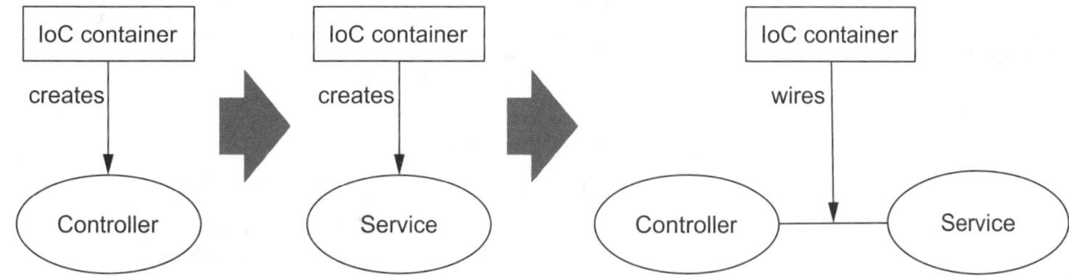

Figure 14.1 Inversion of control compared to the traditional approach of dependency management: all objects are created by the IoC container rather than by the objects themselves.

[1] For a more complete description of IoC, see http://en.wikipedia.org/wiki/Inversion_of_Control.

DI is a specific form of IoC and probably the only one you'll ever see. It may seem from figure 14.1 that the IoC pattern introduces unnecessary complexity, but the approach has significant advantages. The key benefit is that object plumbing can be complex and IoC moves that complexity out of the class, leaving pure, unadulterated business logic. This makes it easier to understand what a class is doing and helps keep classes clean and manageable. Secondary benefits exist, too:

- *Easy testing*—As objects expect a container to inject their collaborators (through a constructor or setter methods), unit tests can easily set up mock collaborators and inject them manually.
- *Flexible topographies*—Letting a container manage the wiring of objects together means that it's easy to change implementations, even at runtime. For a standard deployment you may want to use a mail service based on SMTP, but when you deploy to a cloud you may have to use one based on HTTP. Both services should implement the same interface, but you can switch between them via a little configuration (rather than explicitly coding it yourself).
- *Simple Aspect-Oriented Programming (AOP)*—It can be difficult to explain AOP, but the idea is that you can wrap methods with other code that executes before and after the method itself. This is effectively how transactional services work in Grails: a bit of code provided by Grails starts a transaction before each service method is called and then another bit of code commits the transaction after the method completes. You just specify which methods on which classes should be decorated with transactional behavior.

If you're new to the IoC approach, you need to learn to let go and let Spring handle the nitty-gritty of object management. If you fight it, you'll have an unhappy development experience. If you embrace it, you'll learn how much simpler it can make your life.

How do you get Spring to manage your objects for you? None of the classes you've seen so far include any references to Spring. That's because most of it happens by convention, as you see in the next section.

14.1.2 Beans by convention

When your Grails application starts up, it creates a host of Spring beans, most of which you won't see directly. Together, they form the backbone of your application. Perhaps more important, all the standard artifacts in your project also become Spring beans (controllers, tag libraries, services, and so on). This makes it easy to wire the various components together, as you've already seen in the Hubbub code.

If you remember, your `PostController` delegates the hard work to `PostService`, and yet at no point does the controller instantiate the service. The following listing shows the start of `PostController`.

Listing 14.1 The start of `PostController`

```
package com.grailsinaction

class PostController {
    static scaffold = true
    ...

    def postService
    def springSecurityService

    def home() {
        if (!params.id) {
            params.id = "chuck_norris"
        }
        redirect(action: 'timeline', params: params)
    }
    ...
}
```

The controller's actions work because both the controller and the service are Spring beans. Not only does Spring instantiate the controller and service, but it also assigns the service object to the controller's `postService` property. This property assignment is an example of what Spring calls autowiring: objects are wired together via a convention. In Grails, the default is to autowire by name, so all you need to do is declare a property with the same name as a Spring bean.

Autowiring by type

Experienced Spring developers know that you can also autowire beans by type. Spring assigns whatever bean matches the type of a given property (so it won't work with `def` properties!). It's difficult to switch to this behavior for artifacts, but you'll see later that you can easily autowire your own beans by type if you define them yourself.

This raises a good question: what are the names of the Spring beans in the application? In the case of services, the bean name is the class name but with a lowercase first letter. Hence `PostService` becomes `postService`.

The other types of artifacts also have names, but those names are deliberately obtuse so that you can't automatically wire them into other beans. Controllers are the HTTP request handlers and aren't geared toward being used directly by other objects. Domain classes are designed to be instantiated directly, and so on. In fact, services are the only standard artifacts that are specifically designed for other beans to depend on. That's part of the reason the typical Grails application architecture consists of controllers delegating to services, which in turn use GORM to access the database. This is shown in figure 14.2.

Any named bean can be injected in this way into any other bean. We mentioned previously that Grails sets up a bunch of beans, and we list a few of the more useful ones in table 14.1. Of these, `grailsApplication` is the one you're most likely to use. It

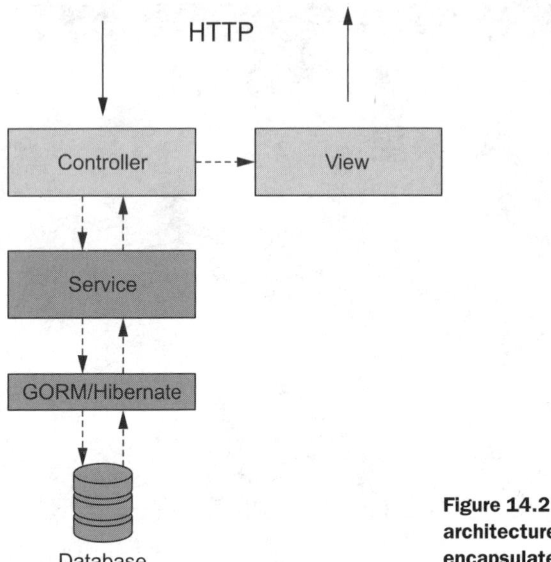

Figure 14.2 Typical Grails application architecture using services to encapsulate business logic

provides access to information about the various artifacts in the application as well as the Spring application context (via `grailsApplication.mainContext`) and the run-time application configuration (via `grailsApplication.config`).

Less commonly, you may want to use the native Hibernate API in addition to GORM. If that's the case, you can declare a `sessionFactory` property and use that. Want to parse GSP pages yourself? Consider using the `groovyPagesTemplateEngine` bean. And last but not least, the `messageSource` bean allows you to manually look up the appropriate text for a given message code.

Table 14.1 Useful Spring beans in Grails

Bean name	Type	Provided by
grailsApplication	`DefaultGrailsApplication`	Grails core
sessionFactory	`SessionFactory`	Hibernate plugin
groovyPagesTemplateEngine	`GroovyPagesTemplateEngine`	Controllers plugin
messageSource	`ReloadableResourceBundleMessageSource`	I18n plugin

That's only a taste of what's available; almost every plugin adds its own beans to the mix. You saw the `springSecurityService` and `mailService` beans used in Hubbub. Be sure to check the documentation for every plugin you use so that you know about any services or other types of Spring bean that they provide. They can prove remarkably useful.

You should now understand how a Grails application hangs together via a DI framework (Spring) and how you can easily inject services and other Spring beans into your various artifacts. This is an important step in embracing the Spring way of doing things. We now go a step further and show you concrete benefits of this approach within the context of Hubbub.

14.1.3 Customizing an application at runtime

One of the biggest benefits of using Spring (other than easy database transactions, which we cover in the next section) is that it's easy to switch implementations of various beans at runtime. Why would this be useful?

Let's say you want to deploy Hubbub to a cloud platform. We look at these in chapter 18, but for now assume that the cloud platform you choose doesn't allow access to SMTP servers. That makes sending emails via the Mail plugin rather difficult, because it relies on SMTP. One option is to use an HTTP-based email service for the cloud deployment, while using the Mail plugin's `mailService` bean for local development and any corporate deployments. The road to achieving this starts with the application context.

The Spring application context

We mentioned the idea of an IoC container several times in this chapter, but we never said which part of Spring is the container. It's called the application context, and it's the object against which you register bean definitions and then, once it's initialized, you can query it for specific beans by name or by type. You can find out more about this useful object through its API documentation.[2]

Let's make this discussion more concrete by showing you how to work with the application context. Spin up the Grails console inside the Hubbub project and run this simple script:

```
def svc = ctx.getBean("postService")
svc.createPost("nobody", "Some post")
```

Okay, so it throws an exception, but it's an exception (`"Invalid User Id"`) that only the `PostService` implementation throws. You plucked your Hubbub `PostService` instance directly from Spring's IoC container rather than injecting it into a property. Also, notice how the argument to `getBean()` matches the corresponding property name on `PostController`. That's because you typically retrieve beans by their names.

Most of the time, you won't want to work directly against the application context like this because normal DI satisfies most needs. Occasionally it's useful to get a direct reference to the application context, in which case you can use one of these standard techniques:

---

[2] For more on the ApplicationContext API, see http://static.springsource.org/spring/docs/3.2.x/javadoc-api/org/springframework/context/ApplicationContext.html.

- Add a `grailsApplication` property to your bean and access its `mainContext` property
- Get a reference from the servlet context:

  ```
  import org.springframework.context.ApplicationContext
  import org.springframework.web.context.support.WebApplicationContextUtils
  ApplicationContext appCtx =
          WebApplicationContextUtils.getWebApplicationContext(servletContext)
  ```

- Fetch the Grails application from a static holder class:

  ```
  import org.codehaus.groovy.grails.commons.ApplicationHolder
  def grailsApp = ApplicationHolder.application
  def appCtx = grailsApp.mainContext
  ```

These are in order of preference. The static holder class is less than ideal because static references can be difficult for the JVM to clean up. Alas, it's sometimes the only way.

Going back to the idea of using an HTTP-based email service for cloud deployments, how do you register a different `mailService` implementation? And equally important, how do you ensure that your custom mail service implementation is only used if the application is deployed to the cloud? The answer lies in a special file: grails-app/conf/resources.groovy.

DEFINING YOUR OWN BEANS

You can turn any of the classes in your application, even those provided in JARs, into Spring beans. That doesn't necessarily mean you should, but it makes sense to do it for singletons and any objects that are collaborators of other objects. To demonstrate how, you start with a couple of dummy classes for sending email via HTTP, both of which go into the directory src/groovy/com/grailsinaction/mail:

```
package com.grailsinaction.mail

class HttpMailService {
    HttpMailClient client

    def sendMail(Closure mailDetails) {
        ...
    }
}
```

Extracts addresses and mail body from closure, populates MailDetails instance, and then passes to client

and

```
package com.grailsinaction.mail

class HttpMailClient {
    String emailServiceUrl

    void send(MailDetails details) {
        ...
    }
}
```

Converts details into HTTP request that it sends to emailServiceUrl

The exact details of these classes don't matter for this discussion, although you can find real implementations in the source code for this chapter on GitHub. The key point is how you replace the standard `mailService` bean provided by the Mail plugin with your `HttpMailService` implementation. Let's do that in the following listing. Open up grails-app/conf/spring/resources.groovy and add the following.

Listing 14.2 Using the `HttpMailService` implementation

```
import com.grailsinaction.mail.*

beans = {
    mailClient(HttpMailClient) {
        emailServiceUrl = "http://my.server/mail"
    }

    mailService(HttpMailService) {
        client = ref("mailClient")
    }
}
```

- Creates bean with name mailClient of type HttpMailClient
- Initializes bean's emailServiceUrl property
- Wires the mailClient bean into mailService bean by name; this is manual, as opposed to autowiring

Your own `mailService` bean overrides the `mailService` bean provided by the Mail plugin. Now, any time your application calls the `sendMail()` method, the email is sent by your dummy HTTP mail service.

You aren't done yet. Remember that you only want to use the HTTP mail service for cloud deployments. Fortunately, resources.groovy is a Groovy file, so you can put a condition in there. Imagine that you can determine that the application has been deployed to the cloud by checking for the existence of a `cloud.deployed` system property:

```
...
beans = {
    if (System.getProperty("cloud.deployed")) {
        mailClient(HttpMailClient) { ... }

        mailService(HttpMailService) { ... }
    }
}
```

We hope you're impressed! This is a great way to change the topography of your application at runtime based on whether you deploy to the cloud, run user acceptance tests, or do anything that doesn't fit with the standard setup.

> **Load order**
>
> Both resources.groovy and resources.xml are loaded after all the core Grails and plugin beans are defined. You can refer to core and plugin beans from your resources files, but plugins can't see the beans you define.
>
> More important, you can override beans that have already been defined by a plugin. If you define a bean named `messageSource`, it will be used instead of the bean defined by the i18n plugin.

This example with the HTTP email service also provides an opportunity to show off further runtime configuration options. Not only can you set the value of the `emailServiceUrl` property on `HttpMailClient` in resources.groovy, but you can also do it from Config.groovy!

BEAN PROPERTY OVERRIDES

First of all, why might it be useful to put bean configuration into Config.groovy? That file is packaged with the application in the same way as resources.groovy, so there doesn't seem to be an immediate advantage. Well, imagine that you're using a Grails plugin that defines a set of beans and you want to configure a property on one of those beans, perhaps a URL or a simple flag. If the plugin doesn't expose a specific configuration option for that property, your only option is to use the bean property override syntax.

Let's say you want to change the URL used by the `mailClient` bean from within Config.groovy. Add a `beans` block containing the bean name and the properties you want to set, such as:

```
beans {
    mailClient {
        emailServiceUrl = "http://my.other.server/mail2"
    }
    ...
}
```

Bean name block contains the property overrides.

You can override multiple beans in this block.

And you can use the standard environment blocks and `if` conditions with this technique to provide different values at runtime based on certain criteria. Bean property overrides are particularly effective when used in combination with the externalized configuration we present in chapter 17 (under per server configuration), because then you can have different values for different deployments without having to repackage the WAR file.

There's far more to Spring and the Grails integration of Spring than we can possibly deal with in this chapter, so it's worth learning more through books such as *Spring in Action* (Manning Publications). The fourth edition, by Craig Walls, will be published in 2014. The Grails user guide also gives solid coverage of the syntax for resources.groovy, so once you fully understand the underlying concepts, you'll easily work out how to implement what you need. We have also included a mapping between Spring's XML format and Grails's resources.groovy syntax in appendix C.

We've shown you the IoC aspects of Spring and how powerful they can be, but that's not all Spring provides. One of the most important features it gives you is simple database transactions, which we look at next.

14.2 Using transactions with GORM

In particular fields, transactions are a big deal. Microsoft created Microsoft Transaction Server (MTS) and then Component Services (COM+) to make developing transaction-based applications easier than they used to be. Enterprise JavaBeans (EJBs) and their servers were also designed with transactions in mind. What are transactions? Let's start with a definition:

> **DEFINITION** A *transaction* is a unit of work in which either everything is done or none of it. It isn't possible for only part of the work to have been done once the transaction is complete.

As a practical example, consider a user who's transferring funds between accounts. This might involve a credit to one database record and a debit to another. A transaction ensures that the two updates either both succeed or both fail. You can't have an inconsistent state where one account has been credited but the other hasn't been debited. That would spell trouble for the bank. Transactions are therefore a way of ensuring data integrity, hence the acronym summarizing their behavior: Atomicity, Consistency, Isolation, Durability (ACID).

Transactions are a useful tool for many types of applications because applications are often written with an implicit assumption that the data they store is valid. If database updates only partially complete, that assumption breaks down and the applications fail. Without further ado, let's look at how to use transactions within a Grails application.

14.2.1 Easy transactions with services

To investigate the properties of transactions, we have to add transactional behavior to Hubbub. It's not naturally a transaction-oriented application, but we know the feature we need to demonstrate transactions.

Let's say users can reply to others' posts by including the string `@<user ID>` in their own message. You'd like to keep track of these replies and to whom they're directed, so you're going to introduce a new domain class, `Reply`:

```
package com.grailsinaction

class Reply {
    Post post
    User inReplyTo
}
```

Next, you want to make sure that every time a user posts a reply, a corresponding `Reply` instance is created. There's a constraint though: if Hubbub doesn't recognize the user ID specified in the message, it shouldn't even commit that post to the database. You could check the user ID before saving the post, but that doesn't help in demonstrating transactions. Instead, you first save the message and *then* check the user ID. You'll understand why soon.

> **NOTE** To see the correct behavior, you should use a database that supports transactions, such as PostgreSQL, H2, or MySQL with the InnoDB engine. Nontransactional databases, such as MySQL with MyISAM tables, won't work as expected.

Where do you add the code for all this? It's time to dust off your old friend `PostService`. The beefed-up implementation, in which you create replies, is shown in the following listing.

Listing 14.3 The reply-aware post service

```
package com.grailsinaction
...
@Transactional
class PostService {
    Post createPost(String loginId, String content) {
        def user = User.findByLoginId(loginId)
        if (user) {
            def post = new Post(content: content)
            user.addToPosts(post)
            if (!post.validate() || !user.save(flush: true)) {
                throw new PostException(
                    message: "Invalid or empty post", post: post)
            }
            def m = content =~ /@(\w+)/
            if (m) {
                def targetUser = User.findByLoginId(m[0][1])
                if (targetUser) {
                    new Reply(post: post, inReplyTo: targetUser).save()
                    return post
                }
                else {
                    throw new PostException(
                        message: "Reply-to user not found", post: post)
                }
            }
        }
        throw new PostException(message: "Invalid User Id")
    }
}
```

Required for consistent behavior; (explained in next section)

Finds "@ ... " in post

Checks target user exists

As you can see, the post service saves the new post, looks for a reply-to user ID, and checks that the user exists. If so, a new `Reply` is saved; otherwise an exception is thrown. With the service now ready for prime time, what do you need to do to make it transactional? Nothing!

The `@Transactional` annotation on the class ensures that all public methods in a service are transactional. If you post a message containing `@dilbert` (assuming Dilbert isn't a user in Hubbub), not only would you see an exception trace in the browser, but you also discover that the post hasn't been saved. Why not try it out and see for yourself? Run the application and then try posting these two messages:

```
@glen hi there mate!
@dilbert do you really exist?
```

The first appears in your list of posts, but the second doesn't—as you expected. This raises an interesting question: how does Grails know that the transaction should be rolled back (not committed)? Because the method throws an exception. Grails (or more accurately, Spring) turns any runtime exception it catches into a failed transaction.

> **Under the hood**
>
> The `@Transactional` annotation used by `PostService` triggers an AST transformation that adds code to start a transaction at the beginning of the method and code to commit or roll back the transaction at the end.
>
> If you don't use Grails's `@Transactional` annotation, service methods are still transactional by default but are implemented using Spring's AOP mechanism: each service is wrapped by a proxy (via `TransactionProxyFactoryBean`). When you have a reference to a service, it's in fact a reference to that proxy. The same happens if you use Spring's `@Transactional` annotation (which is different from the Grails one).
>
> Transactions themselves are controlled by a `transactionManager` bean that's an instance of Spring's `HibernateTransactionManager` by default. You can override this in one of the resources.* files if you need a special transaction manager or custom settings.

Let's now add a dynamic scaffolding controller for the `Reply` domain class so you can check whether the replies are being saved:

```
grails create-scaffold-controller com.grailsinaction.Reply
```

You can then load the associated "list" view to verify the existence or absence of the replies. You're now in a position to demonstrate to yourself the more surprising behavior related to transactions in Grails.

One common problem that people encounter is related to exception handling. To see what we mean, change the line

```
throw new PostException(message: "Reply-to user not found", ...)
```

in `PostService.createPost()` to read

```
throw new Exception("Reply-to user not found")
```

All you changed was the exception type, but now when you try to post the `@dilbert` message, the new post appears in the list (after a refresh)! Why did that happen?

The default behavior for Spring mimics that of EJB containers: transactions are rolled back automatically only for runtime exceptions and errors. It expects you to handle checked exceptions yourself. That's because Java forces you to deal with checked exceptions (or declare them on the method). Groovy, on the other hand, lets you treat checked exceptions as if they are runtime exceptions, so it's not immediately obvious why transactions aren't rolling back. That can lead to wasted time if you're not aware of the issue.

What if you don't want your service to have transactional behavior? Remove the `@Transactional` annotation from the class and set the static `transactional` property to `false`:

```
class PostService {
    static transactional = false
    ...
}
```

To see what effect this has, make sure that you revert the previous change (the service method should throw a `PostException` again rather than an `Exception`), and then start the application. Try to post the `@dilbert` message again. Notice any difference? The message appears in the list! Even though Dilbert isn't a recognized user ID (and a runtime exception is thrown), the post is saved to the database. You no longer have transactional behavior.

> **Testing transactions**
>
> Integration tests run inside a transaction by default, which is then rolled back after each test finishes. This ensures that data changes don't affect other tests, but it means you can't check whether or not transactions are rolled back. If you want to test transactional behavior, you need to add a static `transactional` property to your test:
>
> ```
> static transactional = false
> ```
>
> The alternative is to use functional tests for this job.

Now that you've dealt with the basics of transactions, let's go back to listing 14.3 and find out why `save(flush: true)` is required. It's all down to how transactions and the underlying Hibernate session interact.

14.2.2 Transactions, the session, and me

The way Hibernate works can be confusing for newcomers. It's a powerful library with a fair bit of corresponding complexity. When you add transactions into the mix, it's time to reach for the aspirin. Part of the confusion comes when the Hibernate session appears to exhibit transactional behavior. If an exception is thrown after a `save()`, the data may not be persisted to the database. But notice the use of the word "may": you have no guarantees and, hence, it's most definitely not transactional.

The Hibernate session is, in reality, a special type of cache that sits in front of the database. That's why it's sometimes also known as the *first-level cache* (and now you know why the second-level cache is so called). When you save a domain instance, all you're doing is updating this in-memory cache. The data isn't committed to the database until the cache and database are synchronized, a process known as *flushing* in Hibernate. You can see all this in figure 14.3.

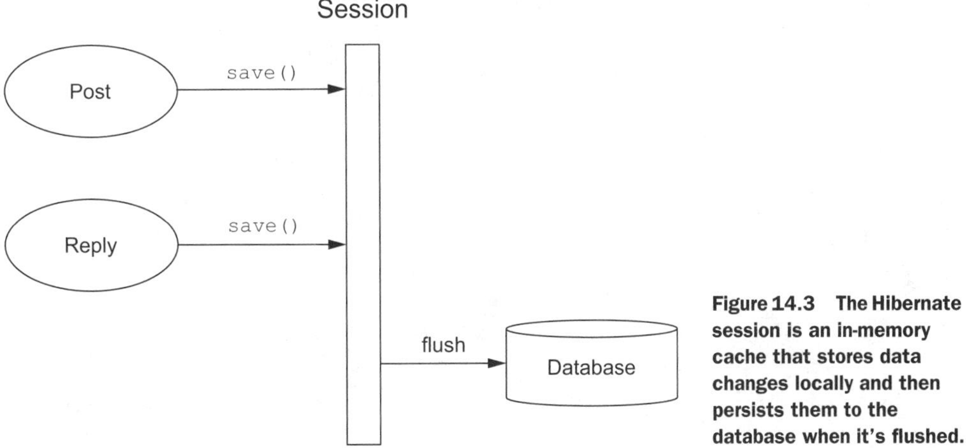

Figure 14.3 The Hibernate session is an in-memory cache that stores data changes locally and then persists them to the database when it's flushed.

If an exception is thrown before the flush happens, none of the changes to the domain instances in the session are persisted to the database. The trouble is, you don't know exactly when a flush will occur unless you explicitly force it, for example, through the `flush: true` argument to `save()` and `delete()`.

When is this session thing created? How long is it kept alive? How are objects added to it? These are important questions and understanding the answers will help you when your GORM usage goes beyond the basics—a common occurrence.

In answer to the first two questions, the session is created at the start of a request and kept alive until the response is finished. That said, you can't save or modify domain objects once the corresponding controller action has finished because at that moment the session switches to a read-only mode. If you're interested in how this all happens, check out the sidebar.

Under the hood

Grails uses a custom version of a Spring web interceptor to ensure that a session is open before an action executes. The Spring class is `OpenSessionInViewInterceptor`, but Grails modifies it slightly by changing the `flush` mode of the session to `manual` after an action returns but before the view is rendered. This allows views to access lazy-loaded collections and relationships, but it prevents them from making any changes that will be automatically committed to the database.

That leaves the third question: how are objects added to the session? The most obvious way is through the `save()` method. In addition, any object returned in a query or via the `get()` method is also automatically added to the session. That means you don't have to explicitly save an object to persist its changes, as shown in figure 14.4.

The main thing to be aware of is that making changes to the database is a two-stage process: you update your domain objects (or save new ones), then flush the session.

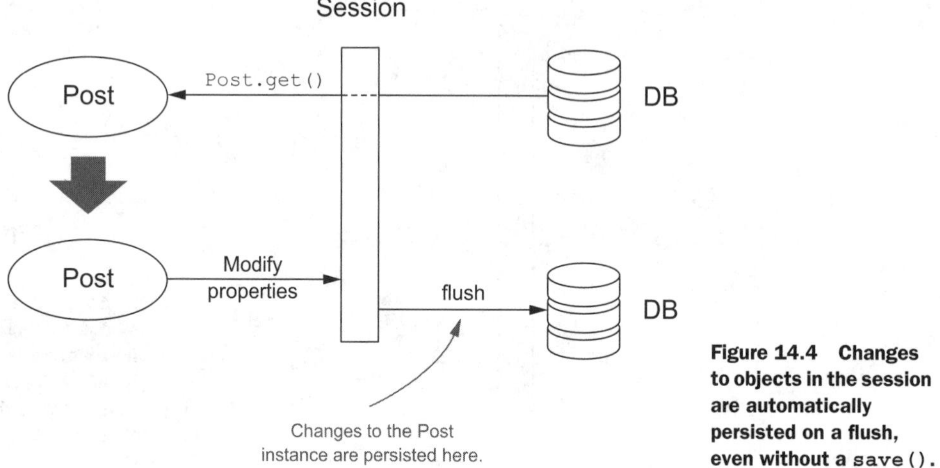

Figure 14.4 Changes to objects in the session are automatically persisted on a flush, even without a `save()`.

The next question is how do transactions fit into this model? Keep in mind the following key points:

1. Transactions operate at the database level.
2. A flush isn't the same as a transaction commit.
3. A transaction creates a new session for the life of that transaction unless one already exists.
4. Committing a transaction forces a flush of the session.

These properties make transactions easy to use because the behavior is consistent. You don't have to worry about whether a Hibernate session exists because a transaction always creates one. You don't have to worry about when changes are persisted to the database because it's always at the point when the transaction is committed. Transactions are particularly useful if you start your own threads because they don't have a session immediately available to them.

> **WARNING** When a transaction flushes the session, *all* the changes associated with that session get persisted to the database, including any that were made before the start of the transaction. We recommend that you only ever change or save domain objects within transactions to ensure consistent and expected behavior.

One question that might be bugging you at this point is what happens when you have transactions within a transaction? Let's say that our post service (in transaction mode) calls *another* transactional service method. Does the second method start its own transaction? Does it have any impact on the original transaction? The answer is that nested transactions join their parent by default, so there's only ever one transaction in progress (the parent). This behavior is configurable.

There's no doubt that services are a convenient way to work with transactions and the benefits we described in this section help explain why they form part of the standard Grails application architecture. That doesn't mean there aren't other valid architectures you might want to use, and there may be cases where you need finer-grained control over transaction boundaries and how child transactions are handled. We finish this section with a quick look at alternative techniques for using transactions in a Grails application.

14.2.3 Fine-grained transactions

When might you want more control over what goes into a transaction? One possibility is that you may want to update the database from a controller directly, because that particular change only happens in that one place. Or perhaps you want to execute multiple transactions within a single service method.

Let's say you want to move the post creation code back into the controller, but you still want it to run in a transaction. This isn't recommended practice, but we do it for demonstration. You can either apply the `@Transactional` annotation to the action or use the `withTransaction()` static method that's available on all domain classes. You can see the resulting code for the latter approach in the following listing. For the sake of brevity, we removed part of the variable checks.

Listing 14.4 Using `withTransaction()` for fine-grained transactions

```
import org.springframework.transaction.TransactionStatus
class PostController {
    ...
    def addPostAjax(String content) {
        Post.withTransaction { TransactionStatus status ->      <-- Starts new transaction, whose boundaries are start and end of closure
            def user = springSecurityService.currentUser
            user.addToPosts(content: content)
            user.save()
            def m = content =~ /@(\w+)/
            if (m) {
                def targetUser = User.findByLoginId(m[0][1])
                if (targetUser) {
                    new Reply(post: post, inReplyTo: targetUser).save()
                }
                else {
                    status.setRollbackOnly()      <-- Rolls back changes without throwing exception
                }
            }
        }
        ...
    }
    ...
}
```

Although we still recommend that you use a transactional service instead, this neatly demonstrates how you can quickly add a transaction to a block of code. The key is the `withTransaction()` method, which accepts a closure as an argument. Everything inside that closure is run within a transaction. An additional benefit of this approach is that you have access to the Spring `TransactionStatus` instance, which allows you to manually roll back the transaction without throwing an exception.

> **Which domain class for withTransaction()?**
>
> One thing that might puzzle you is why we call `withTransaction()` on the `Post` domain class rather than `User`. In fact, it doesn't matter which domain class is used—the type has no effect. You could even use `Tag`, which isn't used within the transaction block. It's best to use a domain class relevant to the code in the transaction to avoid unnecessary confusion.

On the other hand, the `withTransaction()` method doesn't allow you to control how the transaction behaves in relation to parent or child transactions. For that, you can use Grails's `@Transactional` annotation. This can be attached to any method of any class (such as a service). Here's a modified version of `PostService` that disables the standard transactional behavior and uses the annotation instead:

```
package com.grailsinaction

import grails.transaction.Transactional

class PostService {
    static transactional = false

    @Transactional(rollbackFor=Exception)
    Post createPost(String loginId, String content) {
        ...
    }
}
```

Disables standard Grails service transactions (annotates `static transactional = false`)

Configures transaction for createPost() that rolls back on checked as well as runtime exceptions (annotates `@Transactional(rollbackFor=Exception)`)

For versions of Grails prior to 2.3, you can use Spring's `@Transactional` annotation instead, which is in the `org.springframework.transaction.annotation` package.

You can also use the annotation to control the transaction isolation level and propagation semantics for advanced use cases, although they're rarely needed. The only thing you need to be aware of if you use the Spring annotation (as opposed to the Grails one) is that calling transactional methods from the same class effectively disables the transaction. To show what we mean, look at the following listing.

Listing 14.5 Disabling a transaction

```
import org.springframework.transaction.annotation.Transactional

class MyService {
    static transactional = false

    void nonTransactionalMethod() {
        transactionalMethod()
    }

    @Transactional
    void transactionalMethod() {
```

No transaction for this method ... (annotates `void nonTransactionalMethod()`)

... so this call doesn't run in a transaction. (annotates `transactionalMethod()`)

```
        ...
    }
}
```

This unusual behavior—a method marked as `@Transactional` that doesn't run in a transaction—only happens when a nontransactional method calls a transactional one within the same class. If `transactionalMethod()` were called from a different object, there would be no problem. It's one of those things to be aware of and is related to how Spring implements transactions.

Transactions are important to many applications, and it's great that Grails makes them easy to use. Even better, you always have other options if the defaults don't meet your needs. We gave you a peek under the covers of the Hibernate session and how it interoperates with transactions because we think that knowledge is important when diagnosing persistence problems and getting the persistence to work the way you need it to.

14.3 Summary and best practices

As you saw, Spring is a fundamental part of Grails, and although you can happily develop simple applications without ever being aware of its existence, you should take advantage of it as your application grows. Fortunately, this is easily done with services and the automatic DI that Grails provides.

When you start using Java libraries and integrating your application with other Java systems, you find that services don't help. For the integration to work well, you have to define your own beans using the resources.xml and resources.groovy files, so that they can be easily slotted into the various Grails artifacts. If you do this type of integration, we recommend you become more familiar with Spring itself, either through the online documentation or a book. The framework contains far more than the classes related to the core IoC container.

Grails transaction support is one example of other features Spring brings to the table, and you saw how easy they are to use. If you write an application that performs updates to a database, you ought to familiarize yourself with transactions and the effects they have on reliably saving and modifying domain objects.

What recommendations do we make for your projects?

- *Put your business logic into services.* Not only does this conform to the separation of concerns design principle, resulting in code that's easier to understand, maintain, and test, but you can also easily reuse the functionality for web service gateways, remoting interfaces, and the like.
- *Make important singleton objects Spring beans.* Lifecycle management and DI mean that any singleton objects benefit hugely from becoming Spring beans. Use the resources.* files to define beans for classes under the src directory or in JAR files.
- *Prefer Spring DSL.* Whether or not you're a fan of XML, the advantages of defining Spring beans in code are massive, with support for conditions, loops, and environment-specific definitions.

- *Update the database within a transaction.* Making changes to the database outside of a transaction means that you have to be aware of how the Hibernate session operates, or you can easily end up with inconsistent data. Transactions are so easy to set up, why not use them?

  Note that there's an overhead associated with transactions, so if you need to perform a high volume of updates, you may need to come up with a different solution. This is specialized, though, so it's unlikely to affect you.

With your application structured along these guidelines, you'll find that further development, testing, and maintenance become easier than you have a right to expect.

In the next chapter, which begins the final part of this book, you'll see how Spring makes it easy to integrate messaging into your applications. This is important as more and more projects rediscover messaging as a way to scale applications and break them into manageable, decoupled parts.

Part 4

Advanced Grails

In part 4, we'll introduce some of the most advanced features that Grails has to offer. You'll learn about performance tuning, legacy integration, database transactions, custom build processes, and even how to develop and publish your own plugins.

Chapter 15 walks you through events, messaging, and scheduling tasks. We'll work with Platform Core's lightweight messaging and JMS messaging. Then we'll implement queues and topics, schedule jobs using Quartz and cron, and use Quartz for advanced scheduling tasks.

In chapter 16, we build on your GORM experience with relational data by looking deeper into how GORM supports nonrelational data sources such as the emerging NoSQL movement. You will see an example of how to integrate Grails with key-value, document-oriented, and even graph datasets.

Build infrastructure is an important part of professional software development, and chapter 17 takes you deep inside the Grails build system. You start by learning how to add your own Grails commands. Then we teach you how to integrate your Grails build with the most commonly used build tools in the Java space. We also give you strategies for handling data migration as your application grows, demonstrating how third-party plugins can help.

Chapter 18 explains how the cloud is becoming an important part of all of our deployment futures, so we'll survey all the popular cloud deployment options for Grails apps. We'll then focus on Cloud Foundry, a very popular Grails cloud deployment service.

By the end of part 4, you'll have taken your Grails skills to a whole new level. You'll be ready to write the next uber-scalable, world-changing Web 2.0 social networking application. Remember us when you hit the big time.

15 Understanding events, messaging, and scheduling

This chapter covers

- Working with Platform Core's lightweight messaging
- Working with JMS messaging
- Implementing queues and topics
- Scheduling jobs using Quartz and cron
- Using Quartz for advanced scheduling tasks

In chapter 14, you investigated how Spring integrates with Grails, including the trickier uses of transactions. In this chapter, we keep you in that enterprise headspace by looking at sending intraapplication messages. In particular, you examine how different components in an application can communicate *internally* while different events in the application's lifecycle unfold. One of the most popular ways of doing that is via messaging queues, an architecture sometimes referred to as *message-oriented middleware* (MOM).

If you've been around enterprise circles for a while, you've probably used or heard of MOM architectures. You may think it's a heavyweight old-school technology that won't die. Nothing could be further from the truth. In fact, with the birth of service-oriented architectures (SOAs), Enterprise Service Bus (ESB), and the rise of massive social networking sites, you're experiencing an explosion of interest in messaging architectures.

You may wonder why these styles of architecture have had such a resurgence in recent years. From Twitter to Facebook to LinkedIn, if you look behind any of today's big web applications, you find that they're backed by an extensive messaging infrastructure. These messaging architectures are prevalent at high-volume sites for three reasons:

- They lead to loosely coupled architectures, so you can replace parts of your infrastructure without any client downtime.
- They're highly scalable, so you can add more components to process work on your queue.
- They offer a reliable transport that ensures your messages and transactions aren't lost in the system.

In this chapter, you add a messaging system to Hubbub so you can create a link between Hubbub and Jabber, a popular instant messaging (IM) system. After you're done, you can post messages to your Hubbub account via your IM client; you'll also bridge the other way so you'll be notified of your friends' Hubbub posts in your IM client. Along the way, you learn the ins and outs of all the common messaging scenarios and get ideas how to apply them to your current projects.

The Java Message Service (JMS) API is a popular approach to asynchronous messaging, and you'll get a close-up look at it in later sections, but the new Grails Platform Core infrastructure also offers a compelling and lightweight solution for intraapplication messaging. In particular, if you're after lightweight application eventing architecture, Platform Core offers an incredible array of features implemented in a typical Grails convention-over-configuration paradigm. For these reasons, we'll begin with an introduction to features of the Platform Core infrastructure; we'll also demonstrate the kind of messaging applications that make it an ideal choice.

But messaging isn't the only asynchronous game in town. In many situations, a lightweight scheduling solution is all you need. Kicking off a daily backup? Sending out daily digest emails? Regenerating your full-text index? Every developer needs to deal with these kinds of scheduled events occasionally, and Grails offers a robust and easily configurable scheduler based on the popular Quartz framework. You'll look at the different ways you can schedule jobs: how to write daily-digest-type jobs, how to turn them off and on while your application is running, and how to manage scheduling in clustered environments.

You'll get into the details of scheduling later in the chapter. For now, sink your teeth into Platform Core.

15.1 Lightweight messaging with Platform Core

One of the most exciting new features in Grails v2.x is the introduction of the Platform Core infrastructure developed by Marc Palmer and Stephane Maldini. Designed as a set of shared services that applications and plugins can use, this plugin includes common application infrastructure features such as a menu navigation API, common security API, configuration API, and, our focus for the next section, a new lightweight message API called the Events API.

The Events API is a simple, lightweight, and extremely flexible set of services for generating and consuming application events in both a synchronous and asynchronous manner. But why is that handy?

Well, one of the original intents of the Platform Core plugin was to provide a way for plugins to notify both the application and other plugins that a particular event occurred. Think of a Grails Security plugin. When the plugin logs the user in or out of the application, other services and plugins (such as an Audit plugin) may also want to be notified that the event occurred so the user can log out. The UI may also like to listen in on this event so it can notify any followers of the user that they are online or offline. The Events API provides a perfect way to implement this kind of logic while keeping all the parts of the system loosely coupled.

In this scenario, the login process raises or fires an event, while the other plugins and services declare a listener to observe any events generated by the app. Neither sender nor listener is aware of the other, which makes it extensible for situations that you never imagined when you first raised the event.

Enough theory about event-driven architecture, let's implement eventing! You'll implement a basic security audit service, then enhance it to take you through more sophisticated uses of events.

15.1.1 Installing Platform Core

The first step in your journey is to install the Platform Core library. Add the latest Platform Core plugin to your /grails-app/conf/BuildConfig.groovy to bring the plugin into your application:

```
plugins {
    ...
    compile ":platform-core:1.0.RC5"
    ...
}
```

After the plugin is installed and running, it automatically enhances all your controllers, domain classes, and services with a new `event` method that you can use for raising events. Let's make the magic happen.

15.1.2 Sending off an event

The most common approach for sending off an event is known as *fire-and-forget*. With this strategy, you generate or raise an event, but you don't care if anyone is listening, or you aren't expecting any kind of return value. That's certainly the case here, so let's augment your login listener to generate your first event, as shown in the following listing.

Listing 15.1 Raising an event from `PostService`

```
class PostService {
    static transactional = true

    Post createPost(String loginId, String content) {
        def user = User.findByLoginId(loginId)
        if (user) {
            def post = new Post(content: content)
            user.addToPosts(post)

            if (post.validate() && user.save()) {
                event 'onNewPost', post                    ❶ Raises new event
                return post
            }
            else {
                throw new PostException(
                   ➥ message: "Invalid or empty post", post: post)
            }
        }

        throw new PostException(message: "Invalid login ID")
    }
}
```

In this example, you take your new `Post` and place it on the event bus ❶ using topic name `onNewPost`. With that one new line in place, the Events API generates a new event asynchronously for each new `Post` that passes validation.

> **Map-style events**
>
> The most common format for raising an event is
>
> ```
> event topicName, message
> ```
>
> This is the format used in the previous example. But the plugin offers an alternative syntax with a richer set of map-style configuration options that developers may find more flexible:
>
> ```
> event topic: 'onNewPost', data: [ post: post,
>         timestamp: new Date(), source: this.class ]
> ```
>
> Using this syntax requires more work at the receiving end but does give you a higher level of flexibility with the content of your generated events. We'd tend toward wrapping the data portion in its own self-describing event object rather than go free-style with a map, but it's good to know you have the freedom to innovate.

With your `onNewPost` event topic now sitting on the event bus, it's time to implement your new `AuditService` to listen for your messages.

15.1.3 Listening for an event

As you might anticipate, Platform Core offers convenient conventions to make listening a breeze, as shown in the following listing.

Listing 15.2 Listening to an event via conventions in an `AuditService`

```
package com.grailsinaction

class AuditService {

    static transactional = false

    @grails.events.Listener
    def onNewPost(Post newPost){
        log.error "New Post from:
            ➥ ${newPost.user.loginId} : ${newPost.shortContent}"
    }
}
```

❶ Ensures no participation in existing transaction (static transactional = false)

❷ Marks method as Eventbus listener (@grails.events.Listener)

❸ Matches method name and type to raised event topic and content (def onNewPost(Post newPost))

To listen for an event, you first annotate a method with the `@grails.events.Listener` annotation ❷. You then give the method a name that matches the event's topic and provide an argument that takes the event's message type ❸. This code takes advantage of Platform Core's convention-over-configuration mechanism for event handing. By declaring a method with the same name as the event topic you raise (`onNewPost`) and annotating it as a listener, you're automatically invoked every time an event of that type is raised.

You mark your new audit service nontransactional ❶ so you don't get Hibernate in a tangle with your asynchronous work on the incoming objects.

To name your event handlers something other than the event topic, use a configuration option on the annotation. The following method is analogous to the previous example but uses a custom method name:

```
@grails.events.Listener(topic = 'onNewPost')
def myCustomPostEventMethodName(Post newPost){
    // your logic here
}
```

15.1.4 Using namespaces to integrate GORM and events

You have your audit service up and running and auditing all your `Post` events because you made changes to your `PostService`. But what if you want to use your audit service to monitor GORM-related activities, such as creating, updating, or deleting domain objects in the system, without making many changes to your existing services?

You could certainly use the standard GORM event support built into Grails, perhaps by wiring up a custom event-listener to domain class changes through a Spring bean (we talk about such magic in the Advanced GORM kung fu, chapter 19 [available online as bonus content]), but when it comes to GORM, it turns out that the Platform Core plugin already performs much of that heavy lifting by exposing all existing GORM events on the `Eventbus`. To make sure all those different events don't clash with any existing events in your application, the plugin introduces the notion of a *namespace*.

Namespaces give you a way to qualify the events that you raise or listen to so they don't clash with any application or plugin events of the same name. In the case of GORM, the plugin uses a custom GORM namespace to make light work of listening to any of the events that might be interesting.

Let's imagine you want to audit any changes to your `User` or `Post` objects. In the following listing, you enhance your audit service to listen to any GORM `save` or `update` events that occur on your `User` and `Post` objects, but only for changes made by a logged-in user (so you wrap your calls in a test for `isLoggedIn()`).

Listing 15.3 Using the GORM namespace to listen to domain class changes

```
package com.grailsinaction

class AuditService {

    static transactional = false

    def springSecurityService

    @grails.events.Listener
    def onNewPost(Post newPost){
        log.error "New Post from: ${newPost.user.loginId} :
     ${newPost.shortContent}"
    }

    @grails.events.Listener(namespace = 'gorm')
    void onSaveOrUpdate(User user) {
        if (springSecurityService.isLoggedIn()) {
            log.error "Changes made to account ${user.loginId}
              ➥ by ${springSecurityService.currentUser}"
        }
    }

    @grails.events.Listener(namespace = 'gorm')
    void onSaveOrUpdate(Post post) {
        if (springSecurityService.isLoggedIn()) {
            log.error "New Post Created: ${post?.content} by
                   ➥ ${springSecurityService.currentUser}"
        }
    }
}
```

❶ Listens on specific GORM namespace

The Platform Core plugin gives you conventions for all the common persistence event types that GORM exposes (`beforeInsert`, `beforeUpdate`, `beforeDelete`, `afterInsert`, etc.). If you follow conventions and name your method after the exposed event name, then take an argument of the type of domain class you are interested in; the plugin makes sure you're called at the appropriate time.

If the standard convention name doesn't suit, you can customize the name by taking advantage of the event topic name:

```
@grails.events.Listener(namespace = 'gorm', topic = 'onSaveOrUpdate')
void logAllAccountChanges(User user) {
    log.info "Changes made to account- ${user.name} by
        ➥ ${springSecurityService.currentUser}"
}
```

Rejecting GORM events

Depending on the GORM event type that you listen to (for example, `beforeInsert`, `beforeUpdate`), you can use return types to reject the update. If you wanted the audit service to reject any changes made by the admin user, you could use the following code:

```
@grails.events.Listener(namespace = 'gorm')
boolean beforeUpdate(User user) {
    if (springSecurityService.principal.username.equals("admin")) {
        return false   // veto admin changes
    }
    // rest of your code...
}
```

Remember that adding lots of GORM custom event listeners can complicate your code paths during debugging, so use with discretion.

15.1.5 Aggressive listening: using wildcards

We gave you the tools to listen in on a single event, but what happens when you want to listen more aggressively (for example, to every event that occurs)? The Platform Core has your back! You can listen to the event message itself then pull it apart for all the gory details. Let's get a little wild with your `AuditService` listener and use `EventMessage` to catch everything:

```
@Listener(topic = '*', namespace = 'gorm')
void beforeEachGormEvent(EventMessage message) {
    log.info "gorm event $message.event on domain $message.data.class"
}
```

To listen to only particular events, tighten up the wildcards, for example

```
topic="before*"
```

listens to only `before` events.

15.1.6 Integrating Spring Security using the grailsEvents bean

The Platform Core plugin automatically decorates your controllers, domain classes, and services with an event bean for raising events. But what do you do when you're living outside those constraints and need to raise an event?

Fortunately, the plugin exposes a Spring bean, `grailsEvents`, which you can access through the Grails `applicationContext` or by configuring resources.groovy (see chapter 14 for more information). You'll take advantage of the `applicationContext` to make the Spring Security plugin generate events on user login.

The Spring security plugin has its own internal events that you can listen in on by configuring /grails-app/conf/Config.groovy. Let's hook into the Spring Security events and use the `grailsEvents` bean to raise an event on the bus:

```
grails.plugins.springsecurity.useSecurityEventListener = true      <-- 1 Turns on events in Spring Security plugin
grails.plugins.springsecurity.onAuthenticationSuccessEvent =
{ evt, appCtx ->
    appCtx.grailsEvents.event 'security', 'onUserLogin' , evt      <-- 2 Raises Platform Core events
}
```

The `grailsEvents event()` method takes three arguments: the namespace, the topic, and the event itself. In this scenario, you raise an `onUserLogin` event on the `security` namespace with the native Spring event as the payload.

Let's augment your `AuditService` to listen in on the user login process:

```
import org.springframework.security.authentication.
➥ event.AuthenticationSuccessEvent
class AuditService {

    def springSecurityService

    // other methods here

    @grails.events.Listener(namespace = "security")
    def onUserLogin(AuthenticationSuccessEvent loginEvent){
        log.error "We appeared to have logged in a user:
            ➥ ${loginEvent.authentication.principal.username}"
    }

}
```

If you want, you can even drill into that `loginEvent` to log out the remote IP address of the login or other Spring-specific security mechanisms. But we leave that as an exercise for you.

The Platform Core eventing infrastructure is incredibly powerful. You now have under your belt all the common use cases (generating events, listening to events, interacting with GORM, and working with the `grailsEvents` bean).

We don't have space here to show you everything the plugin exposes (event filtering using the DSL, dynamic listeners, collating asynchronous replies, and much more). The online documentation is excellent, and we highly recommend you check it out to take your eventing knowledge to the next level.

For now, it's time to turn your attention from lightweight messaging to the more heavyweight industrial-strength messaging you typically find in enterprise Java shops.

15.2 A hitchhiker's guide to JMS messaging

Messaging has been around for ages, but its predominant use has been in large enterprise scenarios, so you may never have been exposed to how this style of architecture works. In this section, we discuss the basics of how messaging works and get you sending and receiving JMS messages. Buckle up!

15.2.1 Learning to think in async: identifying messaging candidates

Often, time- and resource-intensive procedures in your application don't need to be done immediately. One example is generating a PDF flight itinerary and emailing it to the user. When the user books the flight, you tell them you'll email the PDF to them, but the work doesn't have to be done that instant. Generating the PDF is likely to be CPU-intensive, and you don't want to hold up every user's web experience while the server is bogged down generating one user's PDF. Realistically, the PDF can be generated and emailed any time in the next minute or so, but it needs to be done reliably.

This is a classic example of a candidate for messaging, and this "do it soon" approach is known as *asynchronous processing*. Here's how it might work behind the scenes: when the user requests a flight itinerary, a message is placed on an itinerary message queue. That can be done immediately, and you can report to the user that the PDF is in the mail. Another process, perhaps even on a different server (inside a firewall, with access to a mail server), retrieves the itinerary request off the queue, generates the PDF, and emails it to the user. Figure 15.1 shows the PDF request flowing through the queue to the target process.

One of the cool parts of this asynchronous approach is that the messaging server persists the messages on the queue, so the messages remain until a client is available to service them. If generating PDFs is a bottleneck, you can have many clients listening on the queue to partition the work of generating and mailing PDFs, and the messaging server preserves the transactional semantics, making sure requests are removed from the queue after they're serviced.

Now that you understand where asynchronous systems can make sense, it's time to get acquainted with key implementation terminology. Let's implement your first queue-based feature for Hubbub.

15.2.2 Messaging terminology: of producers, consumers, queues, and topics

Before you implement messaging, you need to understand basic JMS terminology. All the plugin documentation and sample articles assume you know what producers, queues, and topics are, so we first cover those and give you a feel for which situations lend themselves to which messaging techniques.

First, the JMS market uses two types of actors:

- *Producers*—Producers generate and place messages on the queue.
- *Consumers*—Consumers pull entries off the queue.

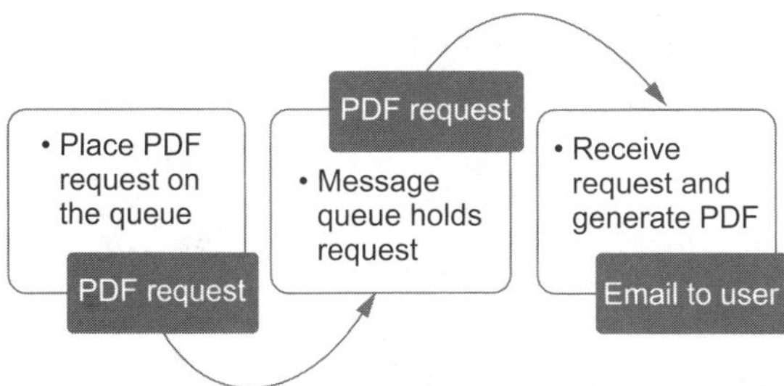

Figure 15.1 A PDF request flows through a message queue to a target process.

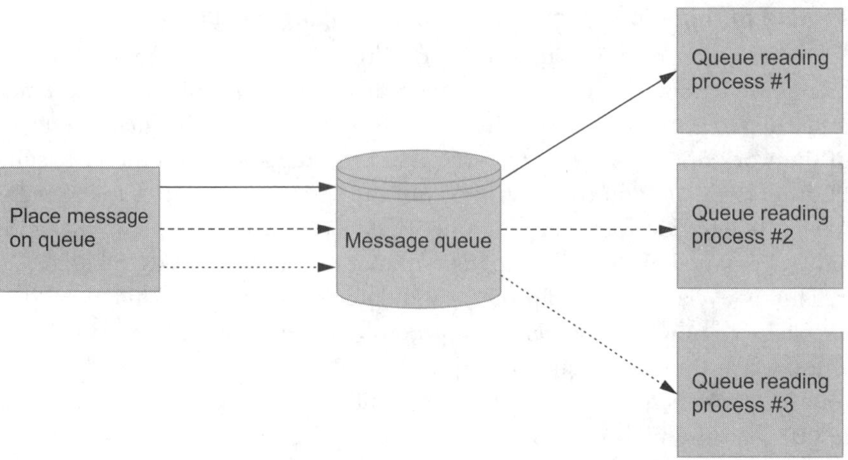

Figure 15.2 Message queues operate from point to point, with each message going to a single process.

In the PDF example, the web application (the producer) posts new PDF requests to the queue, and the PDF-emailing application (the consumer) pulls them off.

How do consumers and producers communicate? JMS offers two main communication models:

- *Queues*—Queues operate on a FIFO (first in, first out) principle, where each message that a producer places on a queue is processed by one (and only one) consumer. This is sometimes known as point-to-point messaging (see figure 15.2).
- *Topics*—Topics use a broadcast model where all listeners on the topic get a copy of the message. The producer places one message on the queue, but that message is duplicated and shuffled off to many consumers simultaneously (see figure 15.3).

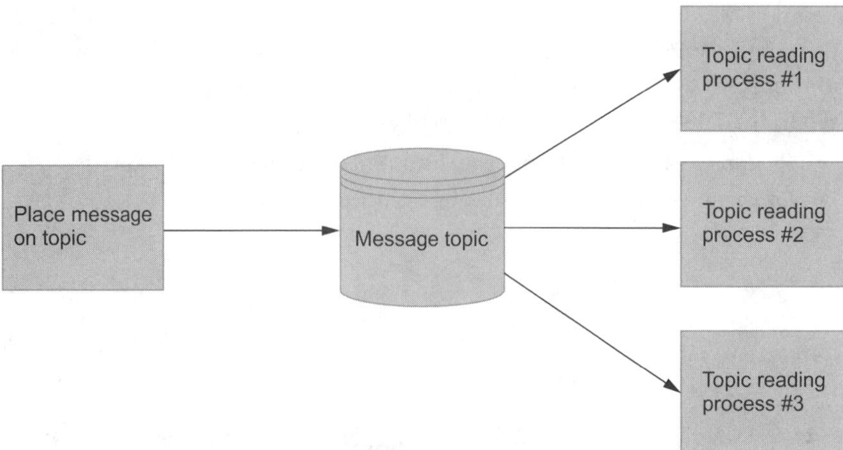

Figure 15.3 Topics broadcast all messages to all clients.

One example that may work well with a topic-style architecture is a network-monitoring application. For example, when a device in the system experiences an outage, a monitoring application can broadcast on a topic to notify other system components to use an alternate device. In this scenario, all listeners on the topic process the incoming message.

In the PDF example, you want your PDF-generation messages processed once, so you should use a queue. With the theory out of the way, let's get the JMS plugin up and running.

> **When to topic, when to queue?**
>
> You looked at sending and receiving JMS messages via a queue. Using a queue made sense in this case, because you wanted your messages to be processed only once.
>
> Topics are ideal for broadcast scenarios in which you want all listeners updated about a particular event. Imagine writing a network-monitoring system to track when your services go up or down. The node responsible for probing servers may want to let everything else in the system know when a server crashes. Topics are ideal for this kind of broadcast scenario.

15.2.3 *Installing and configuring the JMS plugin*

To implement a basic messaging system for Hubbub, the first step is installing the JMS plugin. Edit your /grails-app/conf/BuildConfig.groovy to include the necessary dependency:

```
plugins {
    ...
    compile ":jms:1.3"
}
```

Next, choose a messaging provider.

> **About message service providers**
>
> The dominant vendors in the industry provide open-source (ActiveMQ, Open MQ, HornetQ) and commercial (IBM WebSphere MQ) providers.
>
> The Java EE specification requires that an application server ship with a JMS container, so the decision may have been made for you (GlassFish, for example, is a great JMS server that ships with Open MQ). But if you plan to deploy to a servlet container (such as Tomcat or Jetty), you're free to choose any provider you like.

Only small differences in configuration exist between the vendors, so let's use ActiveMQ, a popular open-source messaging provider.

Create a dependencies entry in /grails-app/conf/BuildConfig.groovy to pull in your message provider jar from Maven central:

```
dependencies {
        compile 'org.apache.activemq:activemq-core:5.7.0'
}
```

NOTE If you get a message saying "Compilation error: java.lang.NoClassDefFoundError: javax/jms/MessageListener" when installing the JMS plugin or when running the first time after installing, you need a JEE JAR file in the lib directory of your Grails application. This JAR file defines the JMS interfaces and supporting classes. If you're using Open MQ, you can use jms.jar. If you're using ActiveMQ, use activemq-all-5.1.0.jar.

INSTALLING AND STARTING ACTIVEMQ

ActiveMQ is open source, free, and popular—it's currently the messaging stack used by LinkedIn (http://hurvitz.org/blog/2008/06/linkedin-architecture).

To install it, download a copy of ActiveMQ from http://activemq.apache.org/, and unzip it into your preferred installation location.

No configuration is required, so start /activemq/bin/activemq from a new command prompt. After the startup process completes, you can access the ActiveMQ console via the browser at http://localhost:8161/admin/ (the default username is "admin" with a password of "admin"). Figure 15.4 shows the interface in action.

The ActiveMQ console lets you browse your queues and topics to make sure your messages are getting through; we explore that later. Now that the messaging server is running, it's time to configure Hubbub to point to it.

CONFIGURING YOUR PROVIDER

After installing the JMS plugin and starting your messaging server, you may need to do two additional tasks to set it up:

- Configure your messaging service in /grails-app/conf/spring/resources.groovy.
- Provide custom JMS configuration in /conf/Config.groovy to override the JMS plugin's defaults.

Let's tackle the message-service configuration first. Each JMS provider supplies a connection factory class that's responsible for establishing connections to your JMS provider.

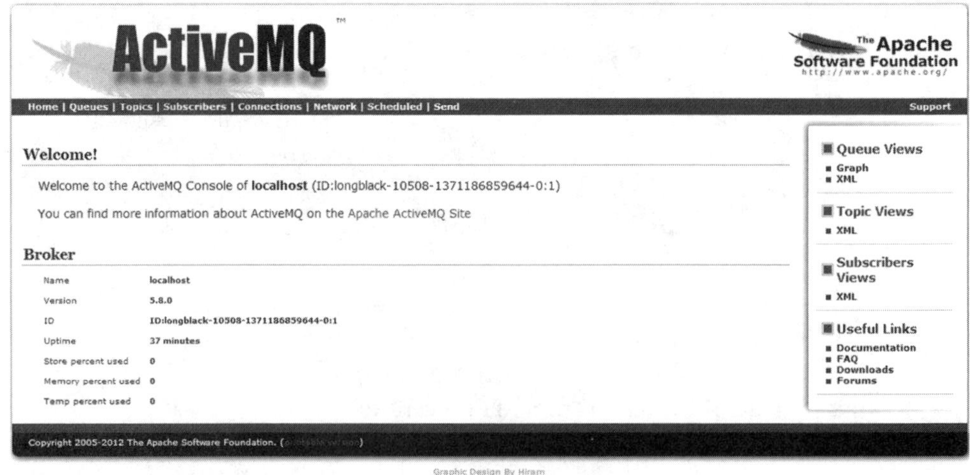

Figure 15.4 The ActiveMQ console is available via a browser interface.

For ActiveMQ, the connection factory needs the hostname and port of the messaging server, so let's update resources.groovy as shown in the following listing to give the plugin the information it needs.

Listing 15.4 Updating resources.groovy to connect to ActiveMQ

```
import org.apache.activemq.ActiveMQConnectionFactory
import org.springframework.jms.connection.SingleConnectionFactory

beans = {
    jmsConnectionFactory(SingleConnectionFactory) {
        targetConnectionFactory = { ActiveMQConnectionFactory cf ->
            brokerURL = "tcp://localhost:61616"
        }
    }
}
```

Imports broker factories

Defines broker connection

Configures broker endpoint

Many JMS applications may require further tuning to individual queue or topic configurations. The JMS plugin has you covered with an extensive array of fine-grained configuration options that you can apply under a `jms { }` configuration key in /grails-app/config/Config.groovy. Consult the online documentation at http://gpc.github.io/grails-jms/docs/manual/ for all the available options.

You're configured and ready to go. It's time to harness the power of the JMS plugin to send JMS messages.

15.3 Using the Grails JMS plugin

The Grails JMS plugin provides a simple way to both send to and receive from JMS topics and queues. Like most Grails plugins, it uses a sensible convention-over-configuration approach to make sure you're sending messages, not configuring queues (although overrides exist for all the conventions if you want to set up your own queue names).

In this section, we cover the basics of getting messages onto a queue and reading them off by beefing up Hubbub with an IM gateway.

15.3.1 Our killer Hubbub feature: IM integration with Jabber

Let's consider what messaging features to implement for Hubbub. A cool one is IM integration, so for Hubbub let's write a simple IM gateway to bridge to the popular IM networks. Specifically, let's write a messaging gateway for Jabber, a popular open source IM system that can gateway to other clients (AIM, Yahoo! IM, and so on).

If a Hubbub user registers his IM account, you can let them post from their favorite IM client; if they're online, you can even send back to them posts from users on their timeline to keep them up to date in real time. When the user adds a new post, you put it on a messaging queue (to be broadcast to any followers that are IM active). Similarly, if the user sends an IM message to the Hubbub bot, you put it on an incoming queue to be posted on the Hubbub website. You use the IM transport to read and send. Figure 15.5 shows your basic architecture with messages flowing between Hubbub and the gateway through the queue.

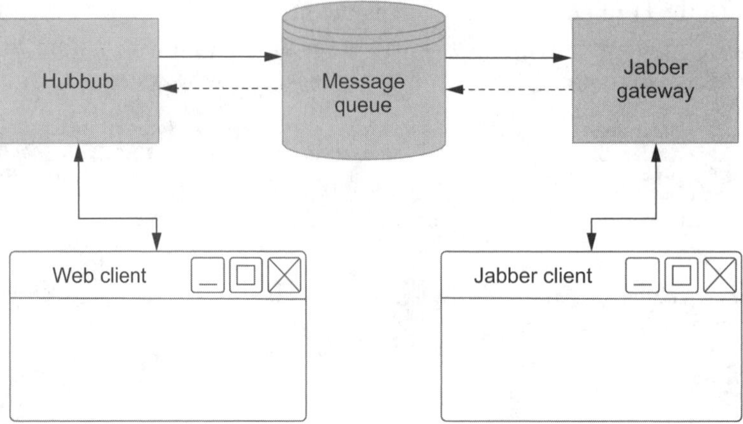

Figure 15.5 Your Jabber gateway architecture

Before you can implement your gateway, you need to look at what's involved in putting outgoing messages on a JMS queue.

15.3.2 Sending JMS messages

The JMS plugin provides a `jmsService` that you can inject into your service and controller classes, giving you a range of JMS-related methods. The method you invoke on your `jmsService` object depends on whether you send your message to a queue or a topic. Table 15.1 lists the methods for each destination type.

Table 15.1 Method names for each destination type

Destination	Method
Queue	`sendJMSMessage()`
	`sendQueueJMSMessage()`
Topic	`sendPubSubJMSMessage()`
	`sendTopicJMSMessage()`

Queues and topics each have two methods, but they're aliases to one another, so feel free to use whichever makes more sense to you. For your examples, use `jmsService.sendQueueJMSMessage()` for queues and `jmsService.sendTopicJMSMessage()` for topics because they make things explicit (which is a good thing for other developers).

Whether you're dealing with queues or topics, the method parameters are the same. The first parameter is the destination name (the name of the queue or topic in your messaging server), and the second is the payload of the message. ActiveMQ doesn't require that you precreate queue names, but your provider may differ. Optional third and fourth parameters in the latest versions of the plugin support JMS message templating and custom postprocessing of messages after creation, but in practice their use is less common, so explore these parameters if and when you need them.

In the following example, you add a `JabberService` class that sends your messages. You'll place a `Map` holding all of your relevant message data on the queue.

```
package com.grailsinaction
class JabberService {
   def jmsService

    void sendMessage(post, jabberIds) {
        log.debug "Sending jabber message for ${post.user.userId}..."
        jmsService.sendQueueJMSMessage("jabberOutQ",
                [ userId: post.user.userId,
                        content: post.content,
                        to: jabberIds.join(",") ] )
    }
}
```

Places Map on the queue

All the infrastructure is in place, but nothing is available to read off the queue. Let's write a test harness to generate traffic. The following listing shows a basic test case to exercise the service.

Listing 15.5 Exercising your Jabber service with an integration test

```
package com.grailsinaction
import grails.plugin.spock.IntegrationSpec
class JabberServiceIntegrationSpec extends IntegrationSpec {

    def jabberService

    def "First send to a queue"() {
        given: "Some sample queue data"
        def post = [user: [userId: 'chuck_norris'],
                content: 'is backstroking across the atlantic']
        def jabberIds = ["glen@grailsinaction.com",
                "peter@grailsinaction.com" ]

        expect:
        jabberService.sendMessage(post, jabberIds)

    }
}
```

Make sure you started ActiveMQ, and then give the test case a run with `grails test-app integration: Jabber*`. This test shows that you can put elements on a queue.

After the test finishes, point your browser to the ActiveMQ console at http://localhost:8161/admin. Figure 15.6 shows your Queues menu so you can see your new `jabberOutQ` queue.

You can click individual messages to see that everything arrived safely. Figure 15.7 shows what you see when you inspect the contents of an individual message.

All your message details look in order, and your `Map` of data is persisted on the queue awaiting a listener to retrieve it. But before you look at how to read messages, let's detour into what types of payload you can put on a queue.

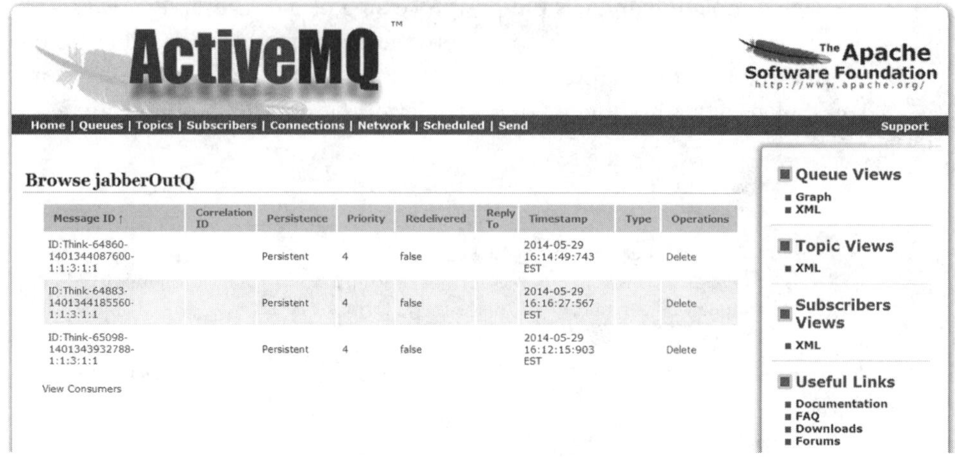

Figure 15.6 Browsing the Jabber queue using ActiveMQ's web interface

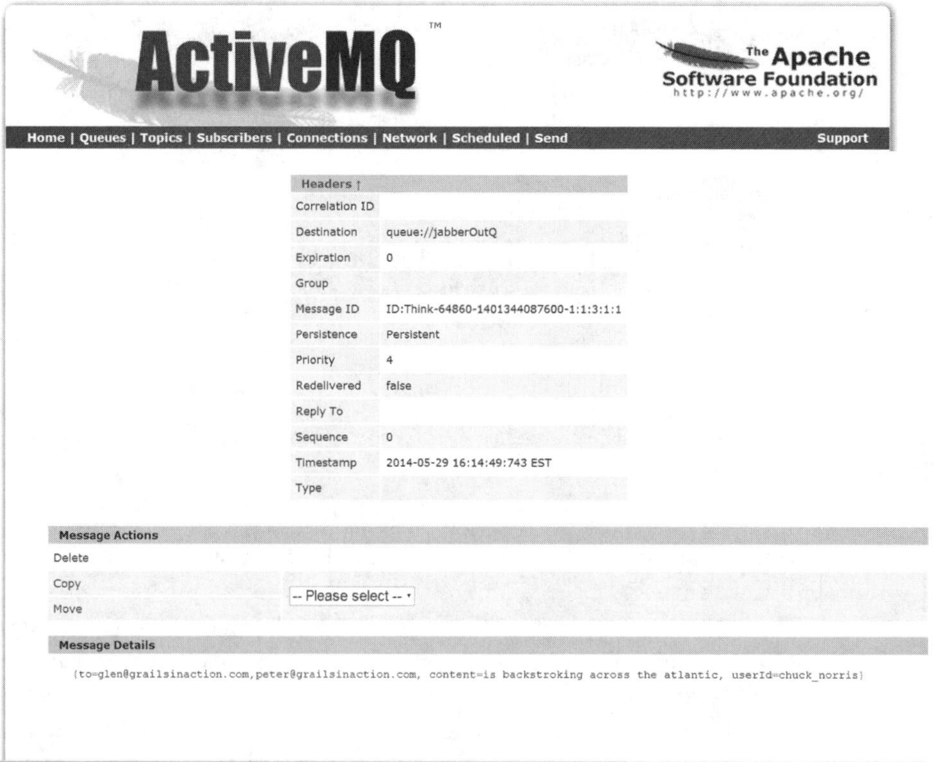

Figure 15.7 Inspecting a message on the queue

You've seen map messages put on a JMS queue, and you may wonder what sorts of things are queue-able. You can send several basic JMS data types to a destination. They're listed in table 15.2.

Table 15.2 The basic data types for JMS messages

Type	Example
`String`	`"Message from ${user.name}"`
`Map`	`[ name: "glen", age: "40", job: "stunt programmer" ]`
`byte[]`	`image.getBytes()`
`Object`	Any object that implements `Serializable`

Although many people prefer to use XML payloads in the `String` data type, we find the `Map` style message the most flexible. Using a `Map` allows you to easily add new properties to objects you send to a destination without worrying about breaking any parsing code elsewhere in the system.

> **How does type conversion work?**
> If you've worked with JMS before, you know that JMS supports its own type system (`TextMessage`, `MapMessage`, `BytesMessage`, and so on). The JMS plugin does the conversion of payload data to the appropriate type for you, leaving you to get on with building your application.
>
> Behind the scenes, the JMS plugin uses the standard Spring JMS `Template` class. By default, this class delegates all type conversion to Spring's `SimpleMessageConverter`, which handles marshaling the basic types listed in table 15.2.

You did the hard work of getting everything on your queue, so it's time to implement the queue-reading side of things so you can get your work done.

15.3.3 Reading the queue

By taking advantage of a convention-based model, the JMS plugin makes the reading process straightforward. For the basic implementation, you need to do four things:

- Add an entry to your service class to expose it as a queue or topic listener.
- Add an additional property to name the queue you wish to listen on.
- Provide an `onMessage()` method to handle incoming messages.
- Override conventions (when required) to match your queue names and the quantity of listener threads.

Let's cover each of those steps to get you up and running.

IMPLEMENTING YOUR FIRST ONMESSAGE()

First, only services can be exposed as JMS endpoints. To let the plugin know that a service is a JMS endpoint, include the following line in your class definition:

```
static expose = ['jms']
```

The expose property is used by a number of remoting plugins (XFire, Remoting, Jabber), and you can happily mix and match SOAP and JMS endpoints in the same service class.

Next, add an onMessage() method that the plugin can call when new messages arrive. That gives you a complete messaging class. The following listing implements the new feature.

Listing 15.6 Handling an incoming message in the service

```
package com.grailsinaction
class JabberService {
    static expose = ['jms']
    static destination = "jabberInQ"
    static sendQueue = "jabberOutQ"

    def jmsService

    void onMessage(msg) {
        log.debug "Got Incoming Jabber Response from: ${msg.jabberId}"
        try {
            def profile = Profile.findByJabberAddress(msg.jabberId)
            if (profile) {
                profile.user.addToPosts(new Post(content: msg.content))
            }
        } catch (t) {
           log.error "Error adding post for ${msg.jabberId}", t
        }
    }
    void sendMessage(post, jabberIds) {
        log.debug "Sending jabber message for ${post.user.userId}..."
        def msg = [userId: post.user.userId,
                content: post.content, to: jabberIds.join(",")]
        jmsService.sendQueueJMSMessage(sendQueue, msg)
    }
}
```

❶ Names queue to listen on

❷ Injects JMS service for sending operations

❸ Catches error conditions

Notice that you specify the destination property of the queue ❶. Following convention, the JMS plugin takes the queue name from the service, so your JabberService defaults to a queue name of Jabber. In this example, you want your incoming and outgoing queue names to follow a different standard, so you overwrite the destination property to tell the plugin what name you want.

With your endpoint set up, you inject your JMS service ❷ so you can send messages.

Finally, you're particular about handling exception cases ❸. Certain messaging servers get upset if clients don't behave well when reading from open connections, so you make sure that you terminate nicely when experiencing stray or malformed messages.

With all your basic logic in place for sending and receiving messages, it's time to spark up an integration test to make sure everything is wired together as you expect, as shown in the following listing.

Listing 15.7 Integration test for JMS operation

```
package com.grailsinaction

import grails.plugin.spock.IntegrationSpec

class JabberServiceIntegrationSpec extends IntegrationSpec {

    def jabberService
    def jmsService

    def jmsOutputQueue = "jabberOutQ"

    static transactional = false

    def "Send message to the jabber queue"() {
        given: "Some sample queue data"
        def post = [user: [userId: 'chuck_norris'],
                content: 'is backstroking across the atlantic']
        def jabberIds = ["glen@grailsinaction.com",
                "peter@grailsinaction.com" ]
        def msgListBeforeSend =
             jmsService.browse(jabberService.sendQueue)        ❶

        when:
        jabberService.sendMessage(post, jabberIds)

        then:
        jmsService.browse(jabberService.sendQueue).size() ==   ❷
                msgListBeforeSend.size() + 1

    }
}
```

❶ **browse() lets you peek at messages on queue.**

❷ **Confirms message queue is now one message longer.**

Your integration test introduces you to the `browse()` method ❶ of the `jmsService`. This method lets you inspect the contents of a queue without altering it (typically called peeking at a queue). This method returns a collection of messages, which you can count using `size()` to determine that one new message appeared on the queue ❷.

To confirm that your message-sending operation works as expected, issue the command line command:

```
grails test-app integration: Jabber*
```

Don't forget that after you run the test, you can also browse the JMS queue via your web browser at http://localhost:8161/admin/. With confirmation that your JMS messages are happily being sent, it's time to turn your attention to how you can consume them. Let's think about your Jabber gateway.

PULLING OUT THE STOPS: IMPLEMENTING A JABBER GATEWAY APPLICATION

Now that your messaging interface is up and running in the web-facing portions of Hubbub, it's time to write an application to interface with the Jabber protocol. To make things simple, write your gateway application as a separate Grails application and use the JMS and Jabber plugins to interface with the rest of the internet.

To install the Jabber plugin, use the normal Grails plugin installation mechanism, and edit your /grails-app/conf/BuildConfig.groovy:

```
plugins {
    ...
    compile ":jabber:0.1"
}
```

The Jabber plugin works much like the JMS plugin you're familiar with, albeit with a more opinionated injection strategy. The Jabber plugin identifies any service class marked with an `expose = ['jabber']` property and automatically adds a `sendJabberMessage()` method. If the service offers an `onJabberMessage()` closure, the plugin calls it when any Jabber message arrives on the configured queue. But before your Jabber plugin can function correctly, you need to point it to a Jabber server. Your next job is to edit /grails-app/conf/Config.groovy and add your Jabber configuration entries. You'll use Google Talk for now because it supports the Jabber protocol (though they're talking about removing it one day).

```
chat {
    serviceName = "gmail.com"
    host = "talk.google.com"
    port = 5222
    username = "your.email@gmail.com"
    password = "your.password"
}
```

After installing the JMS and Jabber plugins and tidying up your configuration, the whole application is implemented in a single service class as shown in the following listing.

Listing 15.8 A gateway service reads and writes Hubbub messages to Jabber

```
package com.grailsinaction
class GatewayService {
    static expose = ['jabber', 'jms']                    // 1 Marks service as JMS and Jabber-aware
    static destination = "jabberOutQ"                   // 2 Sets JMS queue name
    static sendQueue = "jabberOutQ"

    def jmsService
    void onMessage(msg) {                                // 3 Receives incoming JMS messages
        log.debug "Incoming Queue Request from:
➥      ${msg.userId} to: ${msg.to} content: ${msg.content}"
        def addrs = msg.content.split(",")
        addrs.each {addr ->
            log.debug "Sending to: ${addr}"
            sendJabberMessage(addr, msg.content)         // 4 Sends message to Jabber queue
        }
    }
    void onJabberMessage(jabber) {                       // 5 Receives incoming Jabber messages
        log.debug "Incoming Jabber Message Received
➥      from ${jabber.from()} with body ${jabber.body}"
```

```
        def msg = [jabberId: jabber.from, content: jabber.body]
        jmsService.sendQueueJMSMessage(sendQueue, msg)
    }
}
```

❻ Sends message to JMS queue

NOTE The complete source for the application is included with the source code for this chapter under the name jabber-gateway.

Your `GatewayService` starts with the configuration for receiving both JMS and Jabber messages ❶. It then sets up the name of the JMS queue (`destination`) to listen on ❷. It then implements `onMessage()` for JMS messages ❸ and takes incoming JMS messages and sends them to a Jabber destination that it pulls from the message ❹.

The service implements `onJabberMessage()` ❺, which receives Jabber messages and places them on the message queue for Hubbub to process and add to users' timelines ❻.

With those 20 or so lines of code, you implemented a two-way gateway from Jabber to JMS! As you can see, harnessing the power of plugins can lead to massive reductions in the code you need to maintain.

That covers the basics of messaging. It's now time to explore a more lightweight alternative for your asynchronous needs: Grails scheduling.

15.4 Scheduling tasks with Grails

You looked at messaging architectures and saw easy ways to take advantage of their asynchronous approach to making systems simpler, more scalable, and more flexible. But getting such a reliable and well-performing architecture requires infrastructure.

Sometimes you want a simple asynchronous solution to run a function at a scheduled time (for example, a daily report, an index update, or a daily backup). For those scenarios, Grails offers a fantastic, easy-to-use scheduling capability, and it's time to explore it in depth.

15.4.1 Writing a daily digest job

Grails's support for scheduling operations is handled by the Quartz plugin. Quartz is a popular Java library (http://www.quartz-scheduler.org/) with robust and powerful scheduling capabilities, and the Quartz plugin gives you a simple, Grails-style way to access all that power. Let's use it to send a daily digest email to each Hubbub user, outlining all the activity on their followers' timelines for the past day.

Start by installing the plugin. Edit your grails-app/conf/BuildConfig.groovy to contain the following:

```
plugins {
    ...
    compile ":quartz:1.0.1"
    ...
}
```

With the plugin installed, you notice that two new commands are available (which you can see via the `grails help` command):

```
grails create-job
grails install-quartz-config
```

The first is used to create new job templates (much like `grails create-service`), and the second installs a custom Quartz configuration file (which is only needed for advanced use cases such as clustering; we'll talk more about it later).

To create your daily digest email, you need to create a new job that runs each night:

```
grails create-job com.grailsinaction.DailyDigest
```

This newly created job class is located in grails-app/jobs/com/grailsinaction/DailyDigestJob.groovy.

The simplest way to use jobs is to specify a `timeout` value in milliseconds. Every time an interval of `timeout` passes, the plugin invokes your job. The following listing shows the shell for your daily digest job.

Listing 15.9 A basic daily digest job (using `timeout` style)

```
package com.grailsinaction

class DailyDigestJob {

    static triggers = {
      simple startDelay: 60 * 1000,
             repeatInterval: 24 * 60 * 60 * 1000
    }

    def execute() {
        log.debug "Starting the Daily Digest job."
        // ... do the daily digest
        log.debug "Finished the Daily Digest job."
    }
}
```

Runs job once per day

Delays first run for one minute

Notice that you also add a `startDelay` field, which is the initial wait period before the plugin invokes your job. This is handy if you have tight timeouts (a few seconds), but you want to make sure the rest of your Grails application finishes bootstrapping before the first job fires.

At this stage, you may be tempted to implement your business logic in the job class. This is supported, but it's never a good idea. Because jobs support the same injection-based conventions as other artifact classes, it's much better to call an injected service rather than implement the process inline. Using an injection-based approach makes things much more testable, and it fosters code reuse. Your newly created job is refactored in the following listing to tidy things up.

Listing 15.10 A basic daily digest job

```
package com.grailsinaction

class DailyDigestJob {
```

```
    def dailyDigestService

    static triggers = {
      simple startDelay: 60 * 1000,
             repeatInterval: 24 * 60 * 60 * 1000
    }

    def execute() {
        log.debug "Starting the Daily Digest job."
        dailyDigestService.sendDailyDigests()          <- Encapsulates logic in service class
        log.debug "Finished the Daily Digest job."
    }

}
```

By defining your `dailyDigestService` field, the Quartz plugin makes sure everything is nicely wired together before any jobs start.

Now that your daily digest is running, it's time to rethink your scheduling mechanism. Until now, you've been using simple Quartz scheduling, which is fine for jobs that need to fire every so many seconds. But you may prefer your daily digest to be sent out at the same time each day: perhaps 1 a.m. when things are quiet on the servers. To get that kind of calendar-based flexibility, you need to get acquainted with the cron scheduler.

15.4.2 Fine-grained scheduling with cron

If you have any kind of UNIX background, you're probably familiar with the cron service. Cron is a UNIX facility that allows you to schedule jobs to run on certain days at certain times, or on a particular day of the week or month, with all kinds of flexibility. With that flexibility comes a rather arcane syntax that only a hardcore command-line fiend could love. Figure 15.8 shows the basic components of a cron expression.

As shown in figure 15.8, each field of the cron expression refers to a different time period. This example tells cron to run the job at 1 a.m. every Monday.

Cron expressions give you incredible scheduling power, but the syntax is certainly something to wrestle with. All fields in a cron expression can take numbers, wildcards (*), ranges (5–15), sets (5, 10, 15), or increments (10/15). The month and day-of-week fields are special cases where you can use special literals. For months, you can use expressions such as `JAN-MAR`, and for the days of the week, you can use expressions such as `MON-FRI`.

It's much easier to understand cron expressions when you see a few in action. Table 15.3 lists common expressions.

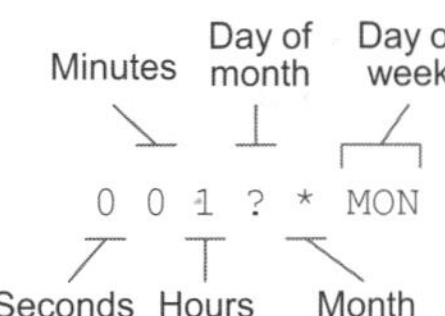

Figure 15.8 The basic components of a cron expression

Table 15.3 A series of basic cron expressions

Expression	Description
`0 0,45 1 ? * MON-FRI`	Every weekday at 1 a.m. and 1:45 a.m.
`0 0/15 1 ? * MON`	Every 15 minutes from 1 a.m. to 1:45 a.m. on a Monday
`0 0 10-12 1 * ?`	10 a.m., 11 a.m., and 12 p.m. on the first of the month
`0 0 0 1 1 ?`	Midnight on New Year's Eve

TIP The Quartz website has a comprehensive reference to cron expressions and more examples.[1]

With that bit of dangerous knowledge under your belt, let's reimplement your daily digest service so that it runs at 1 a.m. each weekday. The following listing shows the new version of your job.

Listing 15.11 A basic daily digest job with custom cron settings

```
package com.grailsinaction

class DailyDigestJob {

    def dailyDigestService

    static triggers = {
      cron cronExpression: "0 0 1 ? * MON-FRI"     <-- Supplies cron-style expression to Quartz job
    }

    def execute() {
        log.debug "Starting the Daily Digest job."
        dailyDigestService.sendDailyDigests()
        log.debug "Finished the Daily Digest job."
    }

}
```

That covers the basic scheduling operations available in Grails. It's time to explore more advanced options for putting the scheduler to work.

15.5 Advanced scheduling

You covered much of the common scenarios for Grails scheduling, and you're probably full of ideas for adding these jobs to your next Grails application. But there's still plenty to explore. In this section, you create, trigger, and control jobs programmatically, and you add an administrative UI so you can control them directly from your application. You also look at sharing data between job runs or sharing jobs in a cluster. By the time you finish, you'll know the fine points (and gotchas) of all these scenarios.

---

[1] Check out the tutorials section of the website for a comprehensive walkthrough: http://www.quartz-scheduler.org/documentation/quartz-2.1.x/tutorials/crontrigger.

Let's start by getting acquainted with how the scheduling plugin handles stateful and re-entrant jobs.

15.5.1 Dealing with re-entrance and stateful jobs

By default, the Quartz plugin creates a new instance of your job class and calls it each time your job runs. But you may have situations when you don't want two instances of your job to fire at the same time.

Imagine you have an SMS notifier for Hubbub. A timer job fires every 10 seconds to see if any unsent SMS messages exist; if messages exist, it shuffles them off to an SMS web service that sends them. But what happens if the SMS service takes 60 seconds to time out? Your job might fire again, and again, and again within the same minute, resulting in multiple (annoying) message sends. You could work around this by keeping a `processed` field on the message itself, or use a JMS queue for the sending; assuming you ruled out those options, you'll want a way to make sure your job never runs concurrently.

The Quartz plugin protects against concurrency via the `concurrent` property. The following listing demonstrates this feature.

Listing 15.12 Using the `concurrent` property to stop re-entrance

```
package com.grailsinaction

class SmsSenderJob {

    def concurrent = false

    static triggers = {
      simple repeatInterval: 10000 // execute job every 10 seconds
    }

    def execute() {
        log.error "Sending SMS Job at ${new Date()}"
        Thread.sleep(20000)                                   <-- Simulates web service delay
        log.error "Finished SMS Job at ${new Date()}"

    }
}
```

If you run this application, you see that even though the timeout is specified to run every 10 seconds, the simulated delay means it runs only when the job isn't already running. Here's the output of this sample SMS job:

```
2013-06-24 10:14:44,665 ERROR grailsinaction.SmsSenderJob  - Finished SMS Job
     at Mon Jun 24 10:14:44 EST 2013
2013-06-24 10:14:54,653 ERROR grailsinaction.SmsSenderJob  - Sending SMS Job
     at Mon Jun 24 10:14:54 EST 2013
2013-06-24 10:15:14,654 ERROR grailsinaction.SmsSenderJob  - Finished SMS Job
     at Mon Jun 24 10:15:14 EST 2013
2013-06-24 10:15:24,654 ERROR grailsinaction.SmsSenderJob  - Sending SMS Job
     at Mon Jun 24 10:15:24 EST 2013
2013-06-24 10:15:44,655 ERROR grailsinaction.SmsSenderJob  - Finished SMS Job
     at Mon Jun 24 10:15:44 EST 2013
```

```
2013-06-24 10:15:54,653 ERROR grailsinaction.SmsSenderJob  - Sending SMS Job
     at Mon Jun 24 10:15:54 EST 2013
2013-06-24 10:16:14,656 ERROR grailsinaction.SmsSenderJob  - Finished SMS Job
     at Mon Jun 24 10:16:14 EST 2013
```

It's important to understand that if a job is scheduled to run, but another instance is already running, the new job is skipped rather than batched up to run later.

Another consequence of marking a job as not concurrent is that the plugin creates the job as a Quartz `StatefulJob`. That means a shared state area, called a `jobDataMap`, is available for you to share information with subsequent jobs. In your SMS gateway example, you might use a counter to keep track of the number of failed sends, and raise a warning when a large number of jobs times out. The following listing shows how to implement this.

Listing 15.13 A stateful job gets a persistent context to work with

```
package com.grailsinaction

class SmsSenderWithTimeoutJob {

    def concurrent = false

    static triggers = {
      simple repeatInterval: 10000 // execute job every 10 seconds
    }

    def execute(context) {
        log.error "Sending SMS Job at ${new Date()}"
        def failCounter = context.jobDetail.jobDataMap['failCounter'] ?: 0
        log.error "Failed Counter is ${failCounter}"
        try {
            // invoke service class to send SMS here & reset fail count
            throw new RuntimeException("Simulate SMS service failing")
        } catch (te) {
            failCounter++
            log.error "Failed invoking SMS Service. Fail count is
                       ${failCounter}"
            if (failCounter == 5) {
                log.fatal "SMS has not left the building."
            }
        }
        context.jobDetail.jobDataMap['failCounter'] = failCounter
        log.error "Finished SMS Job at ${new Date()}"
    }
}
```

1. Provides the execute() entry point for when trigger fires
2. Serializes incremented failCounter value

In this example, notice that you changed your `execute()` method to take a Quartz `jobContext` argument (1). Additionally, note that you can store any kind of `Serializable` object in the context (2): numbers, dates, strings, collections, and so on. Try it out to see the counter value being passed into subsequent executions.

You've explored stateful jobs and looked at how to handle re-entrance. But what if you want to take control of scheduling programmatically?

15.5.2 Pausing and resuming stateful jobs programmatically

The Quartz scheduler lets you pause and resume individual jobs, groups of jobs, or the entire scheduler. In order for your job to be easily controllable, you need to place it in a group. The following listing shows your first crack at a pausable job.

Listing 15.14 The `group` property makes it easy to control jobs programmatically

```
package com.grailsinaction

class ControllableJob {

    def concurrent = false

    def group = "myServices"                    <-- Sets group property to control job programmatically

    static triggers = {
      simple repeatInterval: 5000 // execute job every 5 seconds
    }

    def execute(context) {
        log.error "Controllable job running..
     ${context.jobDetail.key.dump()}"
    }
}
```

Notice that you specify a group attribute on the job. Later, you'll use the scheduler to gain access to this job via its group name.

For now, you need a way to get a handle on the scheduler itself. It comes as no surprise that this can be done via the standard Grails injection pattern. In the following listing, you create a controller to tinker with your jobs programmatically.

Listing 15.15 A controller for pausing and resuming jobs programmatically

```
package com.grailsinaction

class JobAdminController {

    def jobManagerService                       <-- 1 Obtains handle to Quartz Job Manager service

    def index = { redirect(action:'show') }
    def show = {
        def status = ""
        switch(params.operation) {              <-- 2 Determines which operation user selected
            case 'pause':
                jobManagerService.pauseJob("com.grailsinaction.ControllableJob",
                                  "myServices")
                status = "Paused Single Job"
                break
            case 'resume':
                jobManagerService.resumeJob("com.grailsinaction.ControllableJob",
                                  "myServices")
                status = "Resumed Single Job"
                break
            case 'pauseGroup':
                jobManagerService.pauseJobGroup("myServices")
                status = "Paused Job Group"
                break
```

```
            case 'resumeGroup':
                jobManagerService.resumeJobGroup("myServices")
                status = "Resumed Job Group"
                break
            case 'pauseAll':
                jobManagerService.pauseAll()
                status = "Paused All Jobs"
                break
            case 'resumeAll':
                jobManagerService.resumeAll()
                status = "Resumed All Jobs"
                break
        }
        return [ status: status ]
    }
}
```

Your `JobAdminController` introduces a few important aspects of job control. First, you define the `jobManagerService` property to inject the scheduler ❶. The `switch` statement demonstrates the different ways you can pause and resume jobs—by name, by group, or globally ❷.

In the following listing, you add a basic UI so you can drive the scheduler. Let's add a grails-app/views/jobAdmin/show.gsp.

Listing 15.16 A basic web UI for interacting with our jobs

```
<html>
    <head>
        <title>Job Admin</title>
        <style>
            div#status {
                margin: 1em;
                padding: 1em;
                border: 1px solid blue;
                background: lightblue;
            }
            body {
                font-family: "Trebuchet MS",Helvetica;
            }
        </style>
    </head>
    <body>
        <h1>Job Admin</h1>
        <g:if test="${status}">
            <div id="status">
                ${status}
            </div>
        </g:if>
        <g:form action="show">
            <fieldset>
                <legend>Job Admin Operations</legend>
                <label for="operation">Select an operation:</label>
                <g:select id="operation" name="operation"
                       from="${ [
```

```
                        'pause', 'resume',
                        'pauseGroup', 'resumeGroup',
                        'pauseAll', 'resumeAll'
                        ] }" />
                <g:submitButton name="go" value="Go"/>
            </fieldset>
        </g:form>
    </body>
</html>
```

Open http://localhost:8080/hubbub/jobAdmin/show to see this admin UI in action, as shown in figure 15.9.

Looking at the Grails output to the command line, log messages show that `Controllable-Job` (and your other jobs) can be started and stopped via the admin UI. This kind of control comes in handy for the administrative section of your applications, when you want the ability to pause scheduled jobs when dealing with emergency situations (such as your SMS service provider going down).

You've looked at handling stateful and re-entrant jobs, but what happens to your scheduled jobs and their `jobDataMaps` when the application server is restarted? And what happens when you want to run your jobs in a cluster? For these sorts of cases, you need to learn how Quartz handles persistence.

15.5.3 Job persistence with JDBS storage

The default storage mechanism for Quartz is the `RAMJobStore` class, and as you can probably guess from the name, it's fast, but it isn't persistent. If you restart your server, all of your jobs terminate, and any persistent data in your `jobDataMaps` is lost. If you want your stateful jobs persistent, you need to swap out that `RAMJobStore` for something permanent, such as a `JDBCJobStore`.

To do that, you need to create a Quartz plugin config file:

```
grails install-quartz-config
```

The preceding command writes a new file in /grails-app/conf/QuartzConfig.groovy that lets you enable JDBC storage. It looks like this:

```
quartz {
    autoStartup = true
    jdbcStore = false
}
```

When `jdbcStore` is set to `true`, your job state is persisted in the database. But before that can happen, you need to create the required tables.

Job Admin

Paused All Jobs

Job Admin Operations

Select an operation: pauseAll Go

Figure 15.9 Pausing a job via your new admin UI

The SQL to create the tables is found in /plugins/quartz-{version}/src/templates/sql/ inside the Quartz plugin. SQL scripts are available for all the common databases, so use your favorite database admin tool to import the scripts and create the tables.

After your database has the required tables, modify QuartzConfig.groovy to turn on Quartz persistence:

```
quartz {
    autoStartup = true
    jdbcStore = true
}
```

Job persistence is now enabled, but one final change is required before you can rerun your application and see if the job state of your counter job survives a restart of the application.

By default, all Quartz jobs are marked as `volatile`, which means their state won't be persisted to the database. Let's set that right now by marking one of our jobs as nonvolatile, as shown in the following example.

```
class SmsSenderWithTimeoutJob {
    def concurrent = false
    def volatility = false
    def execute(context) { ... }
}
```

You're in business. Let's restart your application and see your job write out its counters.

> **Going deeper into Quartz configuration**
>
> Sometimes the default configuration options the Quartz plugin exposes aren't detailed enough. For instance, if you want more fine-grained control over transaction management inside your jobs, or you'd like to customize the table names that Quartz uses for DB persistence. The heavy lifting is done by adding a /src/java/quartz.properties file to your project, and then taking advantage of the numerous Quartz details config options you can find discussed on the Quartz website. To enable Quartz clustering support, add entries such as these:
>
> ```
> org.quartz.jobStore.isClustered=true
> org.quartz.jobStore.clusterCheckinInterval=60000
> ```
>
> If you want to see persistence in action on your local H2 DB, you need to change your data source `url` property to a persistent version, such as this:
>
> ```
> jdbc:h2:devDb;MVCC=TRUE;LOCK_TIMEOUT=10000
> ```

With your exploration of persistent jobs complete, you've finished your tour of Grails's messaging and scheduling features. Let's wrap things up with best practices to take away.

15.6 Summary and best practices

You covered much asynchronous territory in this chapter. We introduced you to the nature of asynchronous technologies and the sorts of applications they're well suited to. You then toured basic messaging terminology and jumped in the deep end with Platform Core eventing for lightweight messaging to implement an audit service. You then took a deep dive on the JMS plugin.

After applying your JMS plugin skills to build a Jabber gateway for Hubbub, you moved on to explore the lightweight asynchronous options of Grails scheduling. You used cron-style expressions to implement a daily digest email and discussed programmatic uses of scheduling.

It's time to review best practices:

- *Consider eventing architectures.* An eventing approach can provide an extensible, decoupled system. Platform Core gives you all the tools you need for lightweight eventing, so consider whether your app can fit that approach.
- *Painless GORM events.* Platform Core takes a sane approach to GORM event handling without complex configuration. If you need to listen to GORM events, choose Platform Core over custom configuration.
- *Know your application server.* Your application server probably already ships with a JMS provider, and it's time to try using it. If you run on a servlet container, Open MQ and ActiveMQ are the best options.
- *Choose queues or topics.* Use queues when you want a message to be processed by one listener, and use topics for broadcast scenarios.
- *Favor maps.* Favor map-style messages on queues and topics—they give you greater flexibility to evolve your API over time.
- *Override convention when needed.* Don't be afraid to override default settings (such as destination names) if it makes your system easier to maintain. It's nice to know what a destination is used for by looking at its name (such as `sms-IncomingQueue` and `smsOutgoingQueue`).
- *Know your throughput.* Set the number of queue listeners to match your expected throughput. Don't guess—do basic profiling to see what your system is capable of under load.
- *Use your console.* The ActiveMQ admin console gives you good insight into what's happening on your queues—take advantage of it.
- *Separate business logic.* Don't put business logic in Quartz job classes. Use service injection to wrap your logic in service classes that are more testable and more reusable.
- *Favor cron.* Cron-style expressions are concise and expressive and give you more consistency than straight timeout values.
- *Name your job groups.* Always give your jobs a group attribute so you can get easy programmatic access to them later on.
- *Be cluster-aware.* If you run in a cluster, you can take advantage of Quartz database persistence to share state and partition the work between nodes.

In the next chapter, you work with NoSQL and discover how to use it with Grails to make your relational and NoSQL data coexist.

16 NoSQL and Grails

This chapter covers

- Why NoSQL is worth considering
- How GORM interacts with NoSQL stores
- Key/value stores with Redis
- Document-oriented data storage with MongoDB
- Graph databases with Neo4J

In chapter 15, you worked on events, messaging, and scheduling tasks. In this chapter we take you on a tour of all the popular Grails NoSQL solutions, and give you a good sense of what makes sense where. You also learn how your relational and NoSQL data can happily co-exist (remembering that NoSQLstands for Not Only SQL). By the end of this chapter, you'll understand the brave and shiny new world of NoSQL solutions and know which ones are worth exploring in your next enterprise project.

16.1 The problem with PostgreSQL (or when to choose NoSQL)

You've used GORM with our favorite relational databases throughout the entire book, so why bother to look elsewhere? We hear you. There's a huge amount to be said for sticking with workhorse technologies that are battle-tested and proven in the real world. Relational technology has been with us since Codd and Date's work in the 1960s, and we've all had professional experience with modern, fast relational databases. There's nothing wrong with using PostgreSQL—we highly recommend it if it suits your data storage needs. And then there's the catch…

If you haven't hit them already in your professional life, situations occur where you're willing to make a trade-off between the standard relational ACID model (and its normalized transactional goodness) and something that offers either one of the following:

- Much greater performance on the kinds of large datasets you deal with
- Much more flexible and extensible data structures than your typical normalized relational tables will permit

If you've ever tried to shoehorn a document-based structure into a relational model (where each document may have its own unique set of properties), you've already felt the pain of fighting city hall. In these scenarios, using a document-oriented database that supports these structures out of the box (such as MongoDB) makes sense. Cleaner code, cleaner data, better performance. What's not to love?

Similarly if you've ever tried to cram a tree or graph structure (such as a directory tree) into the relational model, it's a world of complex joins and indirections and various parent/child columns, and it becomes difficult to overcome the impedance mismatch. In those scenarios, having a database that "speaks graph natively" (such as Neo4j) is what you want. Traversing the tree is fast, the structures are logical and easy to move around, and no dodgy abstractions are required.

What kinds of data-storage operations does NoSQL bring to the table? In this section we take you on a rock-star tour of the finest tools in the NoSQL market.

16.2 Types of NoSQL databases (and typical use cases table)

Before we dive into the most common NoSQL options, let's survey popular products in the NoSQL world and the types of data that they excel at storing (see table 16.1). If nothing else, it's worth noting the terminology used for any NoSQL explorations you do down the road.

Table 16.1 NoSQL databases and types of data they contain

Type of NoSQL database	Common products	Typical examples of data stored
Key-value store	▪ Redis ▪ Memcached ▪ Voldemort ▪ Basho Technologies Riak ▪ Tokyo Tyrant	Persistent hash tables, session tokens, global state, counters (such as API meters)
Document-oriented store	▪ MongoDB ▪ Apache CouchDB ▪ Apache Jackrabbit ▪ Elasticsearch	User profile data (with free-form fields), survey and questionnaire data, "objects" with their properties

Table 16.1 NoSQL databases and types of data they contain *(continued)*

Type of NoSQL database	Common products	Typical examples of data stored
Graph database	▪ Neo Technology Inc. Neo4j ▪ Orient Technologies OrientDB	Social network graphs (Facebook graphs), directory and tree structures, query link depth on related data
Column database	▪ Apache HBase ▪ Apache Cassandra ▪ Google Bigtable	Time series data

Now that you've seen the common types of NoSQL solutions, it's time to explore the field with one of the most common NoSQL services deployed today: a key/value server called Redis.

16.3 Using Redis to work with key-value stores

You might think of a key-value NoSQL store as a massive persistent hash table: you send it your key/value pairs to hold, and you pull back your values by key later on. The advantages of doing this in a NoSQL store rather than in your own app is that you don't have to worry about

- The app-server crashing/restarting
- Writing anything to disk to save your hash state
- Configuring any kind of persistent caching solution (such as the ones we looked at in chapter 15)
- Providing an API for other applications to share your hash table data

One extremely popular hash table for these kinds of operations is Memcached. It's lightweight, easy to set up and replicate, and lightning fast because it stores data only in memory. It's also common on cloud services and runs great in both Windows and UNIX-like environments. The only snag is that it isn't persistent, so your data never survives a restart.

Then Redis came along—a better Memcached than Memcached! It offers all the benefits of Memcached (memory-based, single-threaded, lightning fast), but adds a truckload of compelling features to boot (persistence, master/slave replication, lists, sets, queues and unions, and all with transactionality). Being backed by a big vendor (VMware), it also feels like it's going to be stable, supported, enhanced, and around for while!

Tons of high-traffic sites use Redis (think GitHub, Digg, Stack Overflow, and Disqus to name a few), and the technology is rock solid. Thanks to its popularity, you also find it deployed on all the popular cloud environments (Heroku, OpenShift, and Cloud Foundry)

16.3.1 Installing your own Redis server

If you're not running your app on one of the existing cloud services (and chances are you won't be for your first iteration), you need to install a local copy of Redis to test

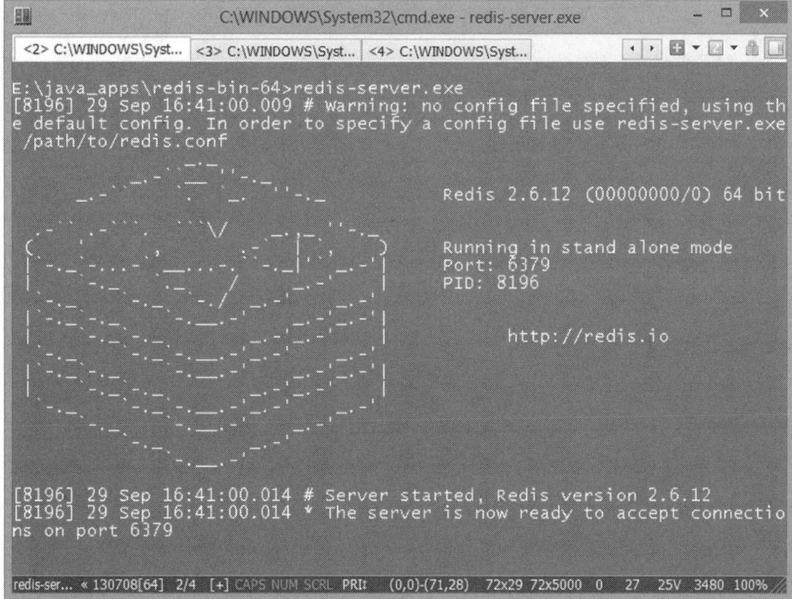

Figure 16.1 The Redis welcome screen

against. Fortunately, it's easy to install and available for all your favorite OSes. Head over to www.redis.io/ to download a copy for your target OS. If you're on Windows (which you will be in this chapter), grab the Microsoft version of Redis that you find on its GitHub site. You want redisbin.zip (32-bit Windows) or redisbin64.zip (64-bit Windows), which you'll find at https://github.com/MSOpenTech/redis/tree/2.6/bin/release.

Windows users can simply unzip the binary and they're ready to roll. No further setup is required. Linux and OS X users will need to Untar/zip their distro of choice, then run a `make` to place a compiled Redis binary in `./src` subdirectory. You can start up your local Redis by running the `redis-server` executable in your installation directory. You're greeted with the famous Redis ASCII art shown in figure 16.1.

With your Redis server installed and started, it's time to learn a few of the basic Redis commands using the command-line client.

16.3.2 Using Redis operations

With Redis installed, the best way to experiment with the service is to use the `redis-cli` executable found in the same directory where you unzipped the service. Start it up and experiment with the common Redis commands listed in table 16.2. Running these yourself will acquaint you with the commands you'll use via the Redis Grails API in the next section.

Table 16.2 Redis commands and descriptions

Command samples	Description

`set name glen`
`get name`
`exists glen`
	Placing a value in the cache, reading it's current value, and testing for it's existence

`incr hitcount` `decr hitcount`	Incrementing and decrementing a counter

`rpush users glen`
`lpush users peter`
`lrange users 0 1`
`lpop users`
`rpop users`
	Lists can be pushed, popped, and inspected from either left or right side

`hset email glen glen@bytecode.com.au`
`hget email glen`
`hvals email`
`hkeys email`
	Hashtables are supported natively

`sadd fruit orange`
`smembers fruit`
`sinter fruit citrus`
`sdiff fruit citrus`
`sunion fruit citrus`
	Sets ensure uniqueness and support common set operations such as intersection, diff, and union

As you can see, Redis goes beyond caching and returning simple values. It also has first-class support for atomic integer operations (perfect for counters), lists, hashes, and sets. You explore more of that goodness in the next few sections.

Diving deeper into Redis

To learn more about all the available Redis commands, we recommend you check out the excellent online reference at http://redis.io/commands. If you want to see everything that Redis via Groovy has to offer, we highly recommend all the amazing Redis presentations given by Groovy great Ted Naleid; they're linked off the Grails Redis plugin page at http://grails.org/plugin/redis.

16.3.3 Installing the Redis plugin (including pooling configuration)

The first question that you need to ask is "which Grails Redis plugin?" because two are available:

1. *Grails Redis plugin*—Provides a nice wrapper for the underlying Jedis library, with much Grails goodness baked in (taglibs, Grails service, annotations, and so on). See http://grails.org/plugin/redis.
2. *Grails Redis GORM Plugin*—Offers GORM support for Redis, including the ability to store Grails domain objects in Redis and use the standard GORM goodness

you're used to, including dynamic finders, criteria queries, named queries, and so on. See http://grails.org/plugin/redis-gorm.

To be honest, the low-level API of the Redis plugin makes more sense for what you need because Redis isn't the ideal place to store and query GORM objects (and the base Redis plugin offers better Grails support for all the common places you typically want to interact with Redis from Grails).

Let's add the latest Redis plugin to your /grails-app/conf/BuildConfig.groovy, so you'll be ready to cache up a storm.

```
plugins {
    ...
    compile ":redis:1.3.3"
    ...
}
```

With the plugin installed, your application is equipped with a range of Redis enhancements including

- A `redisService` Spring bean that wraps all the low-level Redis API, as well as many Grails-specific convenience methods.
- A `redisPool` Spring bean that gives you low-level access to a pool of Redis connections (though typically you let `redisService` transparently handle all pooling for you).
- A `redis:memoize` taglib that lets you cache sections of your GSP pages (with timeout).
- A series of Redis-backed annotations, such as `@Memoize`, `@MemoizeList`, `@MemoizeHash`, `@MemoizeDomainObject`, `@MemoizeDomainList`, that return a cached object (or fetch the object and cache it if required).

Do you notice all the "`@Memoize`"ing happening around here? Perhaps we'd better introduce you to the simple meaning behind this complex term.

16.3.4 Simple, expiring key/value caching: what is all this @Memoize stuff?

One of the most common ways to use Redis is to cache your expensive data values and calculations. The quickest and easiest way to do this in Grails is using the range of handy annotations that ship with the Redis plugin. They all have an `@Memoize` prefix, which might be a new term for you, but don't be scared off, a quick example clears things up.

If you haven't yet come across this computer science term, it's a concise way to refer to an optimization technique you've probably already seen (and used) when you looked at the Cache plugin in chapter 10. Consider something such as this:

```
@Memoize(key = "#{user.loginId}", expire = "60000")
def performExpensiveUserProfileOperation(User user) {
    log.info "${user.loginId} not in cache,
              ➥ performing expensive calculation"
    return user.doSomeExpensiveOperation()
}
```

The first time the `perfomExpensiveUserProfileOperation` method is invoked with a given user, the expensive calculation is performed and the value is cached in Redis based on the user's `loginId`. The second time the method is called with the same user as an input, the cached value is immediately returned (thereby skipping the expensive calculation).

The `expire` parameter specifies that you want this value cached for up to 60 seconds only (the value is specified in milliseconds), and after that you want to expire the value from the cache and recalculate it. You might hear this called the TTL (time-to-live) of the value.

Under the covers, the Redis plugin looks at all the interactions with the back end to set and get the keys based on the user's `loginid`, but the flexibility of the annotation allows you to use whatever keys you like.

The `@Memoize` annotation is perfect for all your service classes that perform data lookups and calculations. But what if you need to cache in the view tier? Well, the Redis plugin provides the taglib you need.

16.3.5 *Working with the Redis taglib*

When we introduced the Cache plugin in chapter 10, we showed you the `cache:cache` taglib, which allows you to cache a portion of a GSP into an in-memory cache for later reuse. Remember this old chestnut for caching the user count?

```
<cache:block>
    Hubbub currently has ${ com.grailsinaction.User.count()} registered users.
</cache:block>
```

In this case you don't specify a timeout because you configured the underlying cache with a set timeout value.

The Redis plugin gives you the same capability, but this time it's backed by a Redis store, so you can safely use it in clusters, and it happily survives restarts. It comes as no surprise that the Redis plugin embraces a similar semantic:

```
<redis:memoize key = "hubbubCount", expire = "60000">
    Hubbub currently has ${ com.grailsinaction.User.count()} registered users.
</redis:memoize>
```

In this case you need to provide a key to use in the Redis store, and, optionally, an expire value, otherwise the value lives forever.

> **Backing the standard Grails Cache with Redis**
> You may wonder whether it's possible to use Redis to back the standard Grails Cache plugin. The answer is yes! A special Grails plugin called the Grails Redis Cache plugin (http://grails.org/plugin/cache-redis) plugs into the existing Grails cache beans and backs them with Redis. Check out the plugin page for more details.

16.3.6 Beyond the basics: working with the Redis service object directly

We showed you the most common use cases for interacting with key/value stores such as Redis—storing and retrieving expiring values in a persistent cache. But when we introduced Redis, we said it could do more than that. We talked about sets, lists, hashes, and atomic integers. It's time to unleash all that power. The Redis plugin provides you with the lower-level `redisService` Spring bean for such operations.

For your Redis enhancements to Hubbub, we're going to introduce a `StatsService` object responsible for keeping various stats on Hubbub's operation (such as the number of posts made today and the highest posting users).

Let's get your scaffolding in place for your service object with your familiar `grails create-service com.grailsinaction.Stats`. For your stats object, it would be nice to hook into any new Post objects created in the system, which should make you think about the Platform Core Events capabilities we introduced in chapter 15.

Let's hook your `StatsService` into any newly created posts and keep a cache of the number of posts created today, as shown in the following listing.

Listing 16.1 A `StatsService` storing daily totals in Redis

```
package com.grailsinaction

class StatsService {

    static transactional = false

    def redisService                                          // 1 Injects redisService for Redis integration

    @grails.events.Listener
    void onNewPost(Post newPost){

        String dateToday = new Date().format("yy-MM-dd")
        String redisTotalsKey = "daily.stat.totalPosts.${dateToday}"   // 2 Works out daily unique Redis key for caching

        log.debug "New Post from: ${newPost.user.loginId}"

        redisService.incr(redisTotalsKey)                     // 3 Increments post count for today

        log.debug "Total Posts at: ${redisService.get(redisTotalsKey)}"   // 4 Logs out current totals

    }
}
```

To take advantage of standard Grails injection, you inject the `redisService` ❶ that the plugin provides. Use this service object to invoke any of the standard Redis operations included in the Redis command reference we introduced you to previously (http://redis.io/commands. See the following sidebar for more information on how this service works under the hood).

With your service acquired, you need to work out which key to use in Redis to store your daily post counts. Let's use the current date as a key ❷ with `yy-MM-dd` qualifiers, for example, daily.stat.totalPosts.13-09-30 indicates September 30, 2013.

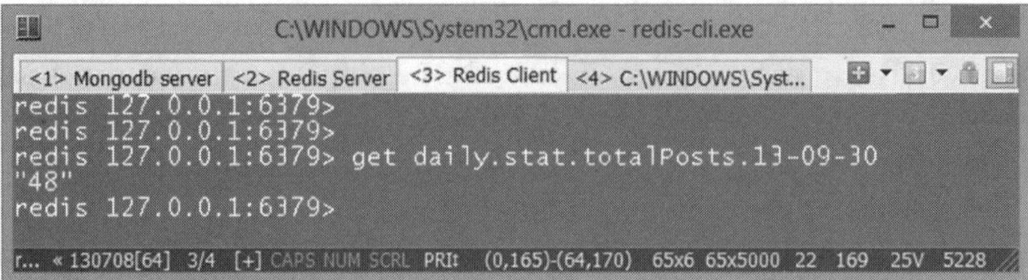

Figure 16.2 After you create a few posts in Hubbub, you can use the Redis client to get your current values.

With a Redis service handle and your key calculated, incrementing the posts for the day is a simple matter of invoking the `incr` method ❸. This is atomic and inherently thread-safe (because all Redis servers are single-threaded).

For fun, you log out the current value of this counter ❹ to make sure your changes stick. You could instead use your command-line Redis client, as shown in figure 16.2, to inspect the value.

Wow, 48 posts already. It's been a good day of testing.

> **Why doesn't my IDE autocomplete redisService methods?**
>
> You may wonder why your IDE isn't autocompleting the various methods on the `redisService` such as `incr`. The reason is that the plugin is implemented using Groovy's `methodMissing` metaclass feature (the same techniques that GORM uses for dynamic finders).
>
> The plugin literally catches any method you invoke on the service, then looks for a matching method in the underlying Jedis Java library. It's easier to enhance the plugin with new features that appear in the underlying library but harder for you to find out exactly which method you need to call!

It's nice to have your daily stats in place, but it would be even nicer if you could break them down by top posters of the day. And that sounds like a perfect way to introduce you to one of Redis's most powerful data structures: the sorted set.

16.3.7 Top posters with Redis sorted sets

In your Redis explorations you looked at caching simple values (such as strings), and worked with the atomic counter support offered by `incr` (and `decr`). But one of Redis's most powerful features is its support for lists, sets, and hashes. Users have even described Redis as "a collection of data structures exposed over the network."

If you had a "Top Posters of the Day" feature, you'd need to keep a set of user IDs and their counts. You can easily do that in a hash, but Redis offers first-class support for these kinds of counting tables through sorted sets. Every entry in a Redis sorted set records a name and a score. You can then efficiently perform various operations on the order sets, such as retrieving the list ordered by score (in either direction), retrieving values higher/lower than a given score, finding the score for a given entry, incrementing and decrementing scores for a given name, and so on.

In your Post of the Day sample, you take advantage of these sorted sets to keep a `loginId` along with a count of posts for the day. To keep it simple, you key the whole ordered set off the current date (as you did for the daily totals stat).

To increase the score of an element in a sorted set, use the Redis command `zincrby` (the `Z` is used to prefix all sorted set operations). To invoke the command (and the Grails method), use the following arguments:

```
ZINCRBY cacheKey incrBy name
```

To increment the count of posts for `chuck_norris` by 1 on September 30, 2013, you issue this command:

```
redisService.zincrby("daily.stat.totalPosts.13-09-30", 1, "chuck_norris")
```

To retrieve the current value of that element, use the `ZSCORE` method:

```
redisService.zscore("daily.stat.totalPosts.13-09-30", "chuck_norris")
```

With a basic knowledge of sorted sets under your belt, let's dive into the implementation, as shown in the following listing.

Listing 16.2 A `StatsService` with total posts by user per day

```
package com.grailsinaction

class StatsService {

    static transactional = false

    def redisService                                    ❶ Injects redisService for Redis integration

    @grails.events.Listener
    void onNewPost(Post newPost) {

        String dateToday = new Date().format("yy-MM-dd")
        String redisTotalsKey = "daily.stat.totalPosts.${dateToday}"

        redisService.incr(redisTotalsKey)

        String redisTotalsByUserKey = "daily.stat.totalsByUser.${dateToday}"

        redisService.zincrby(redisTotalsByUserKey,
                             1, newPost.user.loginId)      ❸ Increments post count for user's daily tally
        int usersPostsToday = redisService.zscore(redisTotalsByUserKey,
     newPost.user.loginId)
        log.debug "Incremented daily stat for ${newPost.user.loginId} to
     ${usersPostsToday}"

    }
}
```

❷ Works out daily unique Redis key for caching daily sorted set

❹ Fetches current daily post count for user

Once again, you take advantage of your injected `redisService` ❶ to do all the low-level work. You calculate your key using the current date with namespacing ❷, then you get to work incrementing the count for the current user ❸. If the user doesn't have a current value in the set, Redis assumes the current value is zero and increments it to one.

To prove to yourself the value is persisting, you fetch the current value for the user ❹ and log it out. This isn't necessary in prod code. In the real scenario, you'd fetch those values; you can use the `zrevrangeWithScores` method to fetch back a list in reverse sorted order (highest to lowest). Jedis returns these as an ordered list of tuples, in which you can get at each element using the `element()` and `score()` methods with code similar to the following listing.

Listing 16.3 Getting back an ordered list of top posters for the day

```
def getTodaysTopPosters() {
        String dateToday = new Date().format("yy-MM-dd")
        String redisTotalsByUserKey = "daily.stat.totalsByUser.${dateToday}"
        def tuples = redisService.zrevrangeWithScores(
                           redisTotalsByUserKey, 0, 1000)
                                tuples.each { tuple ->
           log.debug("Posts for ${tuple.element} -> ${tuple.score}")
        }
        return tuples
    }
```

❶ Fetches ordered list of top posters (highest to lowest)

❷ Iterates list outputting name and score

Using your `redisService`, you grab and reverse-order the list from your sorted set (reverse in the sense that it's ordered highest to lowest). This routine takes two arguments ❶: the first is the minimum count to retrieve. Because no one gets into this set without at least one post, you set this value to zero. The second is the maximum score to retrieve (which you set to 1,000 as an arbitrarily high value).

In this case you log out the results ❷, which sends the list to your console:

```
DEBUG grailsinaction.StatsService  - Posts for frankie -> 12.0
DEBUG grailsinaction.StatsService  - Posts for phil -> 10.0
DEBUG grailsinaction.StatsService  - Posts for graeme -> 4.0
```

And now that you're across common sorted set operations, this completes your whirlwind tour of Redis.

Additional Redis features to explore

We whetted your appetite for all the goodness available in Redis via Grails but recommend that you look through the online Redis plugin documentation on GitHub (https://github.com/grails-plugins/grails-redis), which has full coverage of all the available Redis annotations (and detailed configuration guides for pooling, pipelining, and other advanced features).

If you want to explore further how to integrate GORM with Redis, we recommend you also check out Grails's Redis GORM plugin (http://grails.org/plugin/redis-gorm) to see how you can augment domain classes for storage in Redis via GORM. It's a little fiddly at the moment, but many of the common GORM operations are well supported.

It's time to branch out into the document-oriented world of MongoDB.

16.4 Using MongoDB to work with document-oriented data

Your second set of NoSQL technologies to explore revolves around document-oriented NoSQL, in which the biggest player is MongoDB.

> **MongoDB: company and open-source community**
> MongoDB Inc. (formerly 10gen) builds and supports MongoDB, the open-source database (www.mongodb.org), and MongoDB Enterprise, the commercial edition of MongoDB (www.mongodb.com).

Document-oriented stores specialize in storing data items as self-contained objects rather than as key/value pairs. They provide fast ways to query and update these documents (and because they don't typically need to do any joins, the performance implications of querying documents can result in lightning-fast responses).

Aside from the potential speed improvements, what's so attractive about document-oriented databases and MongoDB in particular?

- *MongoDB is schemaless.* In a relational model, you have to decide your table structure and list of column names ahead of time, because refactoring columns can be a pain later. In MongoDB, every document can have its own custom set of fields, and you can change them (including adding and removing fields) whenever you like. That's amazing flexibility that you can let your database grow with your software.
- *MongoDB offers easy scalability options.* Scaling out to a cluster of relational databases can be tricky business. Deciding on sharing strategies remains a black art. MongoDB was designed with scalability in mind. Add more MongoDB servers to your config and MongoDB redistributes your documents for optimal load sharing and failover.
- *MongoDB is fast on Big Data.* MongoDB is short for "hu*mongo*us DB" and ships with a rich indexing model designed for storing gigantic datasets. Running MongoDB servers on commodity hardware is likely to give you more fast storage than you can ever use.
- *MongoDB offers native support for files and other large binary content.* Need to store pictures or other binary content in your database? MongoDB has built-in support for storing large files and their metadata.
- *Ubiquitous cloud services.* Most of the popular cloud operators (such as Heroku, OpenShift, and Cloud Foundry) all offer native MongoDB support on their cloud offerings. Companies such as MongoLab and MongoHQ offer "Mongo as a service" on a per-month, hosted-service basis.
- *Zero-cost kickoff, with great vendor support.* MongoDB is free under the Affero General Public License (AGPL) to use and run, but you can also purchase great

commercial support from MongoDB Inc. You don't have to skimp on big vendor backing if it's important to your scenario.

What do MongoDB documents look like? Let's work through an example, to give you an idea of what this document business is all about. Imagine you're storing a user's questionnaire results in your data store. Instead of a typical relational model (where you'd need to have a table with userid, question number, and question response), MongoDB stores the whole set of data in a single related document that it represents in a JSON format similar to the following code:

```
{
    "_id" : ObjectId("5248d92ae102251e9e94eb4b"),
    "title" : "q1",
    "question" : "What is your favourite colour",
    "answer" : "orange"
}
```

As you can see, this is the JSON that you know and love from your Ajax work in part 2 of the book, and which we dived even deeper into in chapter 13 when we looked at single-page web applications).

Internally, MongoDB stores documents in a special binary version of JSON known as BSON. But to the outside world, documents present as standard JSON that you can use with all the JSON tools you're used to. Because this is such a ubiquitous data format, developers are drawn to MongoDB because they can use their familiar tools and libraries.

But you aren't limited to "flat" documents of properties; you can also nest documents within one another as subdocuments. Imagine a blog system where you want to keep all the comments with their respective blog entry:

```
{
    title: "MongoDB rocks!",
    author: "Glen Smith",
    content: "I've been experimenting with MongoDB and it looks amazing",
    created:  ISODate("2013-09-30T14:00:00Z"),
    comments: [
        {
            comment: "Yeah, looks really promising",
            author: "Joe User",
            created: ISODate("2013-09-30T15:00:00Z")
        },
        {
            comment: "Cool. I must check it out",
            author: "Jill User",
            created: ISODate("2013-09-30T16:00:00Z")
        }
    ]
}
```

In addition to the ability to nest documents within documents and query them efficiently, you can structure your data in whatever way makes the most sense to your particular application without having to worry about any kind of schema definition up front.

We hope by now we piqued your interest in this bold, new document-oriented world. Let's take a small detour to introduce MongoDB terminology, then you'll create and query documents of your own.

16.4.1 Learning MongoDB terminology

In the relational world, you talk about tables and rows. But tables and rows don't make sense in a document-oriented world. Table 16.3 introduces the way MongoDB thinks about storage.

Table 16.3 MongoDB terminology

Relational database term	MongoDB equivalent
Database	Database
Table	Collection
Row	Document
Field	JSON property on a document
Primary key	Primary key
Index	Index

We'll walk you through working with collections and documents, but first, let's get all your tools and servers set up.

16.4.2 Getting set up: installing a MongoDB server

First you need to grab a MongoDB server for your platform of choice. It's a free download at www.mongodb.org/downloads.

After you unzip the installation, create a data directory to hold your MongoDB database data. By default, this directory is located at C:\data\db on Windows, and /data/db on UNIX and derivatives. You need to create this directory before you spark up MongoDB. Alternatively, you can tell MongoDB where your data directory is by passing in `--dbpath c:\my\custom\path`, but we assume you'll use the defaults.

To launch the MongoDB daemon, head into the bin directory of your unzipped MongoDB server, and run the `mongod` command as shown in figure 16.3.

It's time to fire up a client and connect to it.

16.4.3 Creating your first database

MongoDB ships with a command-line client called, well, `mongo`, which you'll find in the same bin directory as the MongoDB server. To create your first database, complete the following steps:

1 Start up the `mongo` client:

```
E:\java_apps\mongodb-win32-x86_64-2008plus-2.4.6\bin>mongo
MongoDB shell version: 2.4.6
connecting to: test
```

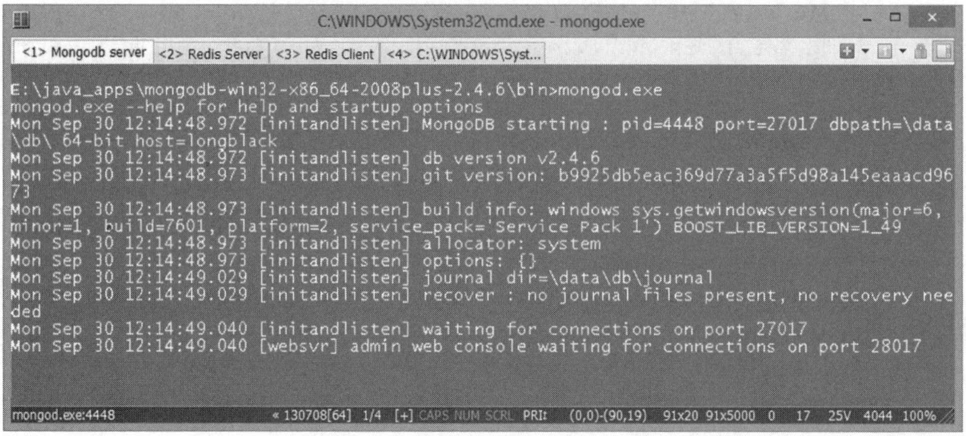
C:\WINDOWS\System32\cmd.exe - mongod.exe
<1> Mongodb server
<2> Redis Server
<3> Redis Client
<4> C:\WINDOWS\Syst...
E:\java_apps\mongodb-win32-x86_64-2008plus-2.4.6\bin>mongod.exe
mongod.exe --help for help and startup options
Mon Sep 30 12:14:48.972 [initandlisten] MongoDB starting : pid=4448 port=27017 dbpath=\data\db\ 64-bit host=longblack
Mon Sep 30 12:14:48.972 [initandlisten] db version v2.4.6
Mon Sep 30 12:14:48.973 [initandlisten] git version: b9925db5eac369d77a3a5f5d98a145eaaacd9673
Mon Sep 30 12:14:48.973 [initandlisten] build info: windows sys.getwindowsversion(major=6, minor=1, build=7601, platform=2, service_pack='Service Pack 1') BOOST_LIB_VERSION=1_49
Mon Sep 30 12:14:48.973 [initandlisten] allocator: system
Mon Sep 30 12:14:48.973 [initandlisten] options: {}
Mon Sep 30 12:14:49.029 [initandlisten] journal dir=\data\db\journal
Mon Sep 30 12:14:49.029 [initandlisten] recover : no journal files present, no recovery needed
Mon Sep 30 12:14:49.040 [initandlisten] waiting for connections on port 27017
Mon Sep 30 12:14:49.040 [websvr] admin web console waiting for connections on port 28017
mongod.exe:4448
« 130708[64] 1/4 [+] CAPS NUM SCRL PRI: (0,0)-(90,19) 91x20 91x5000 0 17 25V 4044 100%

Figure 16.3 Launching the MongoDB server

2 Create a new database called "quiz" by switching to it with the `use` command:

```
> use quiz
switched to db quiz
```

MongoDB creates the database automatically when you switch to it. Once in a database, you create a `responses` collection to house all your response documents (remember, a collection is analogous to a table in relational parlance). Collections are automatically created when the first document is inserted into them.

3 Use the `insert` method on the `responses` collection to pass in your JSON objects, which represent each document:

```
> db.responses.insert({ title: "q1",
    ➥ question: "What is your fave color", answer: "orange" })
> db.responses.insert({ title: "q1",
    ➥ question: "What is your fave color", answer: "blue" })
> db.responses.insert({ title: "q1",
    ➥ question: "What is your fave color", answer: "green" })
```

With your collection populated with documents, you can give MongoDB queries to resolve, such as the count of documents in a collection:

```
> db.responses.count()
3
```

Or, if you're chasing the equivalent of a SELECT * FROM RESPONSES, you can display all the documents MongoDB has in a collection using the `find()` command:

```
> db.responses.find()
{ "_id" : ObjectId("5248e2dbb97b0d6acea283bb"),
    "title" : "q1", "question" : "What is your fave color",
    "answer" : "orange" }
```

```
{ "_id" : ObjectId("5248e2e6b97b0d6acea283bc"),
    "title" : "q1", "question" : "What is your fave color",
    "answer" : "blue" }
{ "_id" : ObjectId("5248e2edb97b0d6acea283bd"),
    "title" : "q1", "question" : "What is your fave color",
    "answer" : "green" }
```

Notice that MongoDB automatically assigns an `ObjectId` element to the documents after they're inserted. This is a unique key for the object in the database.

What if you want to qualify your finds? No sweat. Pass in the argument(s) you want to constrain to your `find()` call, and MongoDB does the heavy lifting. Here's the equivalent of a SELECT FROM RESPONSES WHERE ANSWER='green':

```
> db.responses.find({answer: 'green'})
{ "_id" : ObjectId("5248e2edb97b0d6acea283bd"),
    "title" : "q1", "question" : "What is your fave color",
    "answer" : "green" }
```

Robomongo instead of the command line

If messing about on the command line seems tedious to you, we understand. Fortunately, you have a range of MongoDB GUIs and web apps that can make all this experimenting less painful. If a rich GUI takes your interest, we recommend you check out Robomongo (http://robomongo.org/). It's free and available on all the major platforms.

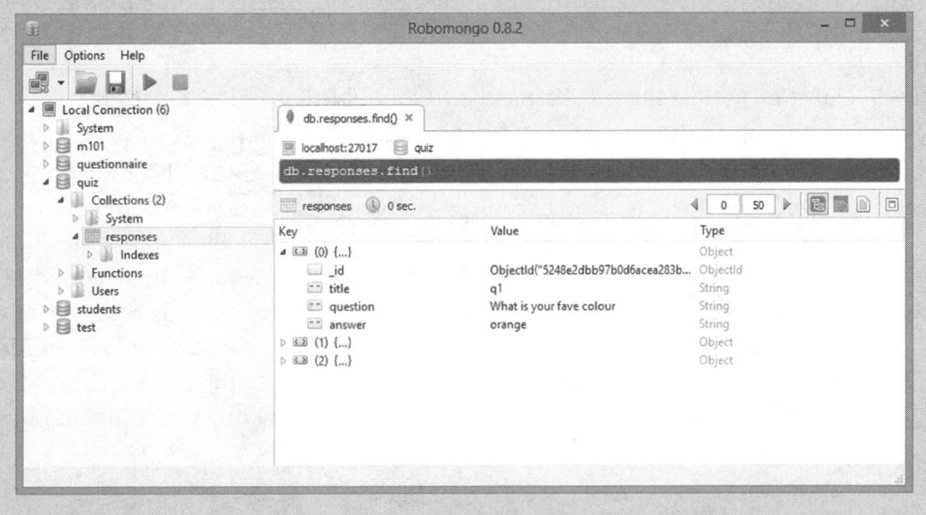

Robomongo is a GUI-based management tool for MongoDB.

Now that you've experimented with the MongoDB console, let's look at how to integrate Grails into this document-oriented world. Start by installing the MongoDB plugin.

16.4.4 Installing the MongoDB plugin

As you might imagine, the first step in making Hubbub MongoDB-ready is to install the Grails Mongo plugin (http://grails.org/plugin/mongodb). Add the latest MongoDB plugin to your /grails-app/conf/BuildConfig.groovy so you can get cracking on your Grails integration effort:

```
plugins {
    ...
    compile ":mongodb:1.3.0"
    ...
}
```

If you run MongoDB on your local host and the default port, no further configuration is required. If you connect to an external cloud-hosted solution, you can always customize your MongoDB server as shown in the following code:

```
grails {
  mongo {
        host = "yourRemoteService"
        port = 27017
        // or replicaSet = [ "server1:27017", "server2:27017"]

        databaseName = "hubbub"
    }
}
```

With the plugin installed (and optionally configured), it's time to point your domain classes toward MongoDB.

16.4.5 Polyglot persistence: Hibernate and MongoDB working together

If you use only MongoDB for your persistence engine, you can safely remove the Hibernate plugin entirely from your /grails-app/conf/BuildConfig.groovy. However, in your case, you're going to augment your existing Hibernate solution with new domain classes that are stored in MongoDB. This strategy is sometimes called *polyglot* persistence because you use several persistence engines in a single application.

One immediate candidate for your MongoDB integration is your `AuditService`. At the moment you log out your audit data to a file, but if you persist it in MongoDB, a range of query operations are available that you can expose to your admin users.

First up, in the following listing, let's create an `AuditEntry` domain object to hold your audit data.

Listing 16.4 Defining an `AuditEntry` object to store in MongoDB

```
package com.grailsinaction

import org.bson.types.ObjectId

class AuditEntry {

    static mapWith = "mongo"
```

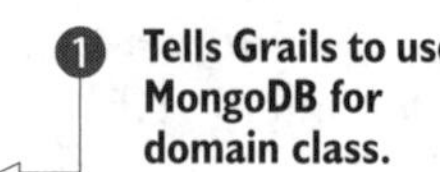
1 Tells Grails to use MongoDB for domain class.

```
    ObjectId id                         <-- ❷ Defines ObjectId to let Mongo assign its own IDs.
    String message
    String userId
    Date dateCreated                    <-- ❸ Autotimestamping works fine for Mongo.

    static constraints = {
        message blank: false
        userId blank: false             ❹ Custom collection name (defaults to class name).
    }

    static mapping = {
        collection "logs"               <-- ❹
        database "audit"                <-- ❺ Custom database name (defaults to app name).
        userId index:true               <-- ❻ Indexes common query fields and increases performance.
        version false                   <-- ❼ Turns off versioning.
    }
}
```

This GORM domain class looks remarkably like any other GORM domain class. Aside from the `mapsWith` ❶ property (which is only required because you're getting Hibernate and MongoDB to coexist in one app), it consists of all the field definitions, autotimestamp fields ❸, constraints block, and indexing operations you know and love.

You'll notice, however, a few artifacts that are unique to how MongoDB-GORM interacts. You supplied an ID field ❷ declared as type `org.bson.types.ObjectId` (see the following sidebar). You also provided a custom mapping block to tune exactly where and how MongoDB stores this domain class. In this block you specified the MongoDB collection name ❹ and database name ❺, which, if not specified, defaults to the `classname` and `appname` respectively.

Even though you're in NoSQL land, for best performance you still need to index any fields that are likely to be common query candidates ❻, and because you won't ever edit or update an `AuditEntry`, you probably want to turn off versioning ❼.

> **What's with the ObjectId?**
>
> Normally you don't declare an ID field on Grails domain classes—you let Grails assign one for you. This causes a snag in MongoDB-land, however, because if you don't declare an ID, Grails stores an ordinal `Long` as the ID, which breaks MongoDB advantages such as autosharing. The best strategy is to declare it as an `org.bson.types.ObjectId` and let MongoDB assign an ID to that string when the object is stored (much like you saw in your console examples).

After all the plumbing is in place, persisting objects using the standard GORM APIs works. Here's your enhancement to the existing audit service to log all new post creations back to MongoDB:

```
@grails.events.Listener
    def onNewPost(Post newPost){
        log.error "New Post from: ${newPost.user.loginId} :
              ➥ ${newPost.shortContent}"
```

```
        def auditEntry = new AuditEntry(message: "New Post:
              ➥ ${newPost.shortContent}",
              userId: newPost.user.loginId)
        auditEntry.save(failOnError: true)
    }
```

With all the familiar `save()` semantics you're used to, you'd think this was heading into a relational data source if you didn't know the backstory. Let's run a few posts and see where these domain classes end up.

With a quick browse of the database in Robomongo, you can see your new entries persisting nicely in figure 16.4.

Notice the collection name is set to `logs` and the database name to `audit` as configured in the domain class (see listing 16.4). Also notice that MongoDB assigned an appropriate `_id` field on the document using its standard semantics.

Until now you've stored objects as you would with any relational back end. Now it's time to explore GORM's support for MongoDB's schemaless operations.

16.4.6 Stepping outside the schema with embeddables

One of the great advantages of document databases is storing all the data related to an object within a single document—typically through a kind of embedded subdocument. Fortunately the MongoDB GORM plugin knows all about this style of operation, so let's explore the support for these embedded documents.

One of the simplest forms of embedding is taking advantage of standard lists and maps on your domain classes. Imagine that when you store your `AuditEntry` domain classes, you want to dump out not only the name of the operation happening now, but also everything you know about the object under audit (such as all the properties of a newly created post). But you need that to be generic for all the kinds of objects you may audit in the future.

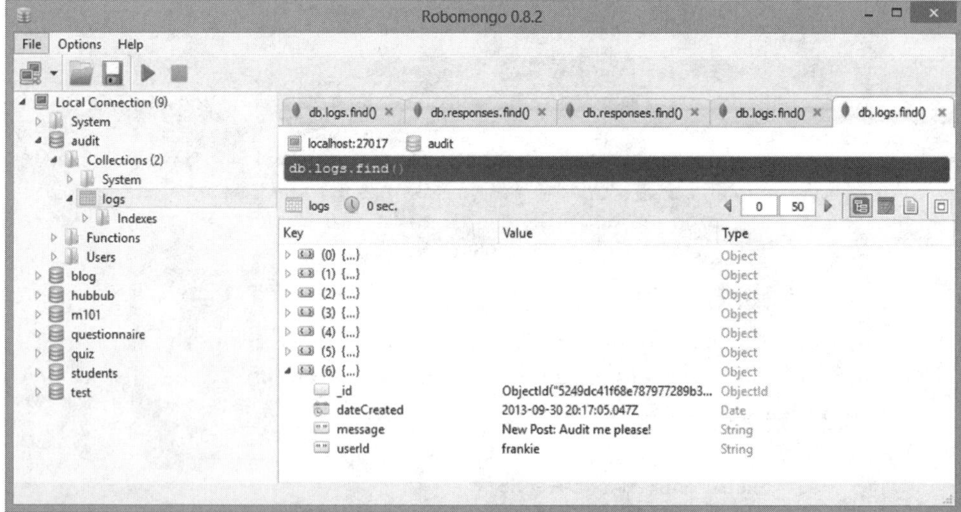

Figure 16.4 New entries in Robomongo

Let's capture the details of the object being audited in your `AuditEntry` via a `details` `Map`. Most of the domain class is omitted, but you'll get the gist:

```
class AuditEntry {

    ObjectId id

    // ...other fields omitted

    Map details

}
```

Now that you have your embedded `Map` object, it's a simple matter to dump out all the properties of the object under audit directly to that map. Something like a straight properties assignment should do the trick:

```
@grails.events.Listener
def onNewPost(Post newPost){
    def auditEntry = new AuditEntry(message: "New Post:
        ➥ ${newPost.shortContent}", userId: newPost.user.loginId)
    auditEntry.details = newPost.properties
    auditEntry.save(failOnError: true)
}
```

If you browse the next newly minted `AuditEntry`, you see your embedded `details` properties object as a subdocument, as shown in figure 16.5.

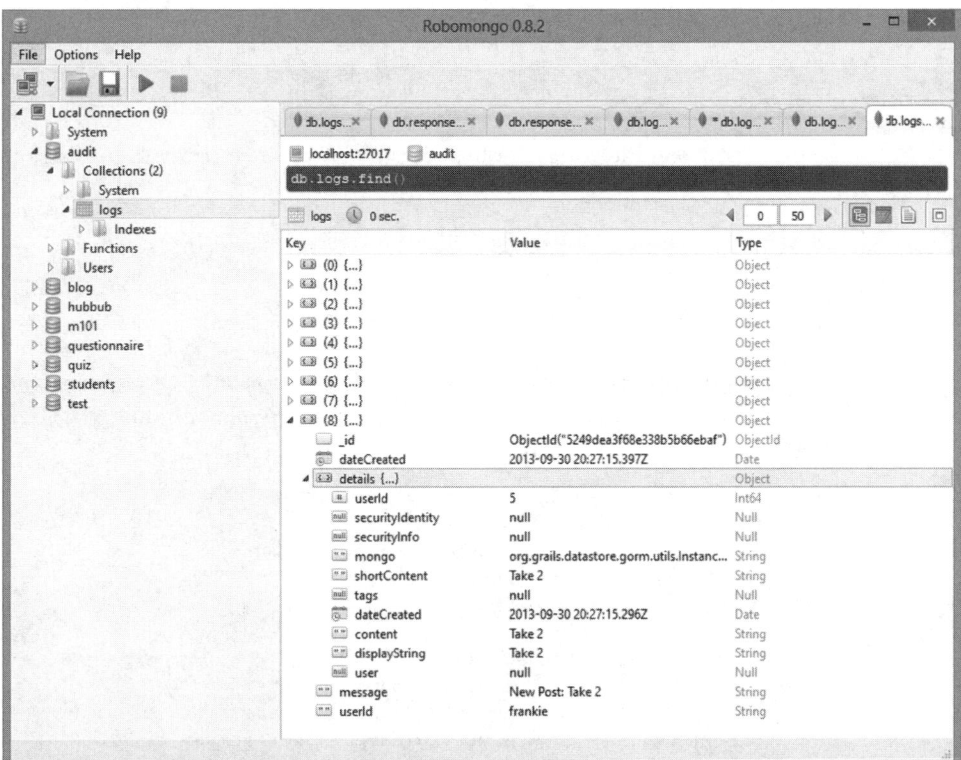

Figure 16.5 Embedded details as a subdocument

In this case, you probably made things too "noisy" with overhead fields. You're better off whitelisting properties (as you feel appropriate) during the assignment to tidy things up. Perhaps something like this:

```
auditEntry.details = newPost.properties['userId',
    'shortContent', 'dateCreated']
```

But what if you want to go beyond embedded maps and embed domain classes? Turns out the MongoDB plugin takes advantage of GORM's standard embedded annotation.

Let's enhance your `AuditEntry` to be taggable. You can tag each audit entry with one or more tags to allow pick up of audit entries that relate to object creation, object access, deletion, and so on. Here's your enhanced `AuditEntry` with the new modeling:

```
class AuditEntry {

    static mapWith = "mongo"

    ObjectId id
    String message
    String userId
    Date dateCreated

    Map details

    static hasMany = [ tags : AuditTag ]      <-- Uses standard hasMany to say you linked objects

    static embedded = ['tags']      <-- Marks tags as embedded

}
```

Now you need to define your simple `AuditTag` and you're ready to persist:

```
package com.grailsinaction

class AuditTag {

    String name

}
```

Once again, after the plumbing is in place, all your normal GORM persistence operations work in the standard relational manner. Here's an enhanced `AuditService` method to add tags to your logging:

```
@grails.events.Listener
def onNewPost(Post newPost){
    def auditEntry = new AuditEntry(message:
        "New Post: ${newPost.shortContent}",
    userId: newPost.user.loginId)
    auditEntry.details = newPost.properties['userId',
        'shortContent', 'dateCreated']
    auditEntry.addToTags(new AuditTag(name: "post"))
    auditEntry.addToTags(new AuditTag(name: "create"))
    auditEntry.addToTags(new AuditTag(name: "user-driven"))
    auditEntry.save(failOnError: true)
}
```

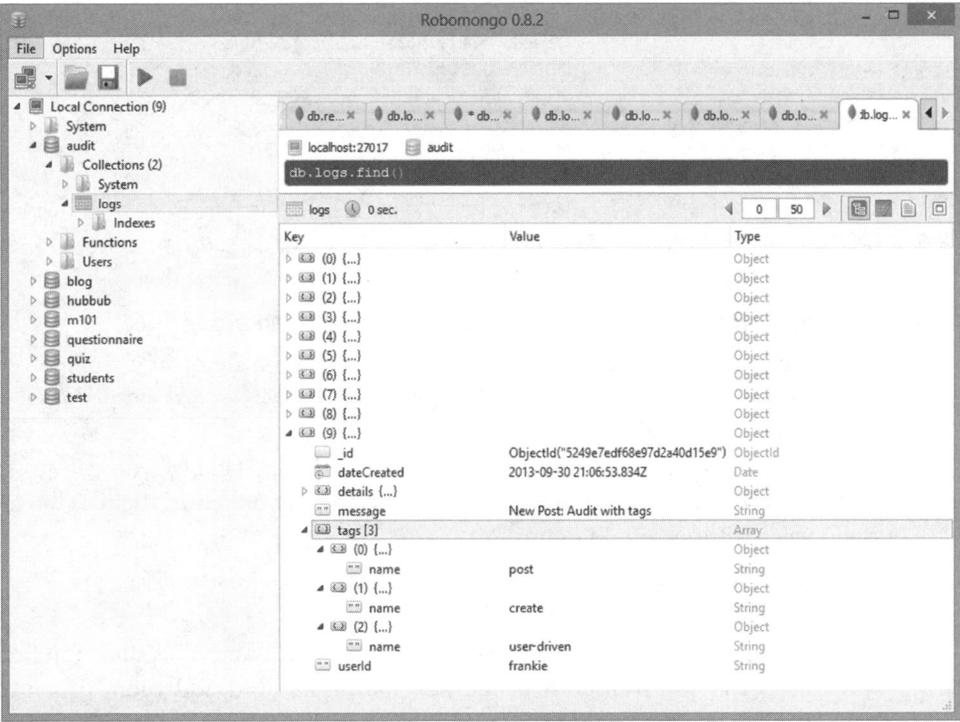

Figure 16.6 Tags nested in subdocuments

Notice you use the standard GORM `addToTags` infrastructure to work with your embedded collection of tags. Once you create a few audits, browse Robomongo to confirm your new tags are nicely nested inside a set of subdocuments, as shown in figure 16.6.

Your three tags seem to be nicely embedded there. You explore how to take advantage of querying those subdocuments in a later section.

> **How does MongoDB store non-embeddable Grails relationships?**
>
> You may wonder what happens when MongoDB/GORM encounters related domain classes (such as `oneToMany`) that aren't marked as embedded. By default, the plugin stores the objects as two separate documents, then uses a MongoDB structure known as a DBRef to provide the link between them.
>
> Remember this has performance implications; you'll now do more than one fetch operation to retrieve the related documents when required (which can happen either lazily or eagerly depending on how you configure your plugin).

Now it's time to turn your attention to one of the most interesting aspects of working with a schemaless database: dynamic attributes.

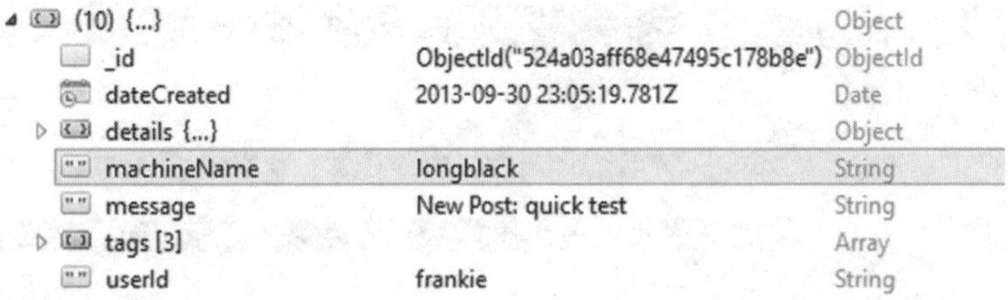

(10) {...}		Object
_id	ObjectId("524a03aff68e47495c178b8e")	ObjectId
dateCreated	2013-09-30 23:05:19.781Z	Date
details {...}		Object
machineName	longblack	String
message	New Post: quick test	String
tags [3]		Array
userId	frankie	String

Figure 16.7 Your newly minted audit object now in a MongoDb collection

16.4.7 Dynamic attributes: making up properties as you go along

You've mostly dealt with scenarios where you create a field on a domain class, and then populate it with values. But MongoDB domain classes are happy to have properties dynamically created on them.

To store a `machineName` property on your next `AuditEntry`, you can pretend that the property exists and assign it without having any matching field. This is entirely valid, even without a field definition

```
auditEntry.machineName = InetAddress.localHost.hostName
auditEntry.save(failOnError: true)
```

and your new property is persisted directly to the audit object, as shown in figure 16.7.

You can create your own properties at runtime and add them to your domain object as you go. You could do something like this

```
def dynamicProps = [
    "os-name"       : System.getProperty("os.name"),
    "os-version"    : System.getProperty("os.version"),
    "os-java"       : System.getProperty("java.version")
]
dynamicProps.each { key, value ->
    auditEntry[key] = value
}
auditEntry.save(failOnError: true)
```

which creates the property names dynamically at runtime, as shown in figure 16.8.

You've comprehensively explored all the common dynamic data storage aspects that MongoDB brings to the table. But what about querying all that dynamic data? In the next section you see how MongoDB/GORM makes that painless.

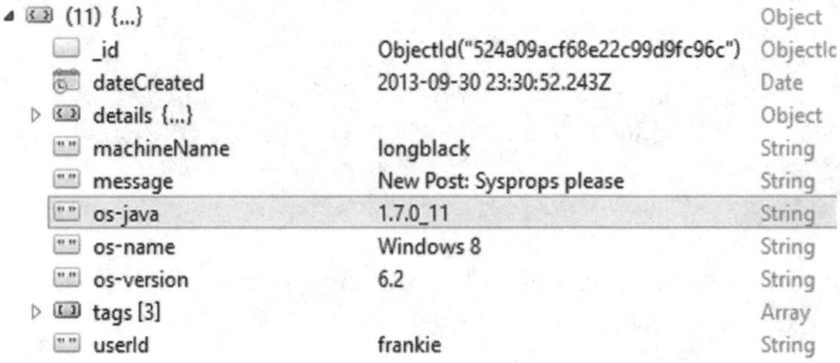

(11) {...}		Object
_id	ObjectId("524a09acf68e22c99d9fc96c")	ObjectIc
dateCreated	2013-09-30 23:30:52.243Z	Date
details {...}		Object
machineName	longblack	String
message	New Post: Sysprops please	String
os-java	1.7.0_11	String
os-name	Windows 8	String
os-version	6.2	String
tags [3]		Array
userId	frankie	String

Figure 16.8 New property names created at runtime

16.4.8 Querying MongoDB via standard GORM

This should probably be one of the smallest sections in the book because most of your standard GORM mechanisms apply to MongoDB querying: dynamic finders, criteria queries, named queries, and query by example. You can't use Hibernate's proprietary HQL (or any other Hibernate-specific API), but it's a small price to pay.

The truly amazing thing is that all these query methods work fine with dynamic MongoDB properties. Remember that dynamic `machineName` property you added to `AuditEntry`? You can query on it via normal query APIs

```
def entries = AuditEntry.findByMachineName('longblack')
```

and it returns the full-blown `AuditEntry` objects you expect. You can iterate them in a Grails view to prove how ubiquitous the access is

```
<h1>Recent Audits From Machine: Longblack</h1>
<ul>
    <g:each in="${com.grailsinaction.AuditEntry.
        ➥ findByMachineName('longblack')}" var="auditEntry">
        <li>${auditEntry.message} -
            ${auditEntry.userId} -
            ${auditEntry.dateCreated}
        </li>
    </g:each>
</ul>
```

What if you want to find all the `AuditEntries` that have an embedded tag? Again, all the standard criteria and `where` queries work as you expect. If you want to find all `AuditEntries` with an embedded tag named `post`, you can use a regular `where` query:

```
def entries = AuditEntry.where {
            tags.name == "post"
}.list()
```

and `entries` contains a `List` of `AuditEntry` objects that you can manipulate in whatever way makes sense for your application.

But what if you want to go lower level and do raw MongoDB querying without going through GORM? Even in those scenarios the plugin has you covered. Let's go native.

16.4.9 Working with low-level MongoDB querying

In addition to the GORM standard API, the plugin enhances your domain class with a `collection` property giving you access to the underlying MongoDB collection via the low-level GMongo API. Be warned, though, you're now working with MongoDB objects and not GORM domain classes.

To repeat your previous query using raw MongoDB querying, you can enter

```
def entries = AuditEntry.collection.find(tags: [ name: 'post' ])
```

which returns a list of `DBObjects` (that you can treat as a `Map` if you're reading values). If you need to convert your results back to a domain class, the plugin registers type converters for you, so go ahead and jump in

```
def entries = AuditEntry.collection.find(tags: [ name: 'post' ])
entries.each { entry ->
    AuditEntry auditEntry = entry as AuditEntry
    // and you have yourself a domain class
}
```

If you need to go even lower than the query layer, Grails also injects a GMongo object (https://github.com/poiati/gmongo) on any service and controller classes that define a MongoDB property.

With an injected GMongo instance, you can be as hard-core MongoDB as you like. How about a Mongo Map-Reduce function that counts the number of audit entries per user and then stores that in a new collection called `auditCounts`? The following listing shows an enhancement to your `StatsService` to do that, and then returns a map of `userId` to `auditCount` to boot!

Listing 16.5 Enhancing `StatsService`

```
class StatsService {

    def mongo                                         <-- Declares MongoDB handle for injection

    def countAuditMessageByUser() {

        def db = mongo.getDB("audit")
        def result = db.logs.mapReduce("""            <-- Maps function to pair data values
    function map() {
        emit(this.userId, this.message)
    }
""",
                """
    function reduce(userId, auditMessages) {          <-- Reduces function to count number of audit entries
        return auditMessages.length
    }
""",
                "auditCount", [:]                     <-- Stores result in a collection called auditCount
        )

        def countMap = [ : ]

        db.auditCount.find().each { counter ->        <-- Transforms auditCount collection to map of userId to count
            countMap[counter._id] = counter.value
        }

        return countMap
    }

    // rest of StatsService omitted.

}
```

As you can see, the sky is the limit with an injected MongoDB instance. Here you pass in a `Map` function (in JavaScript because it runs inside MongoDB itself) that maps all the `AuditEntries` in your database as a tuple of `userId` and `message`. You then feed those tuples into your `reduce` function (which is handed a `userId` along with an array of matching messages), and you return a count of those messages back to MongoDB.

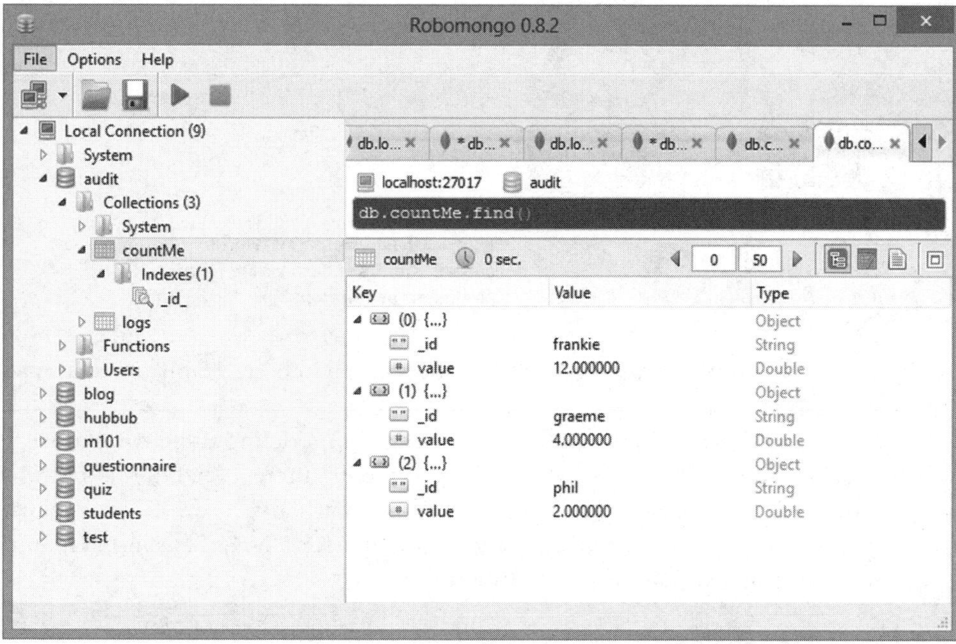

Figure 16.9 The results of our MapReduce operation

After all that Map/Reducing, you're left with a collection of documents that map a `userId` to a count of entries that MongoDB stores in a collection you named `auditCount`. If the collection already exists, MongoDB wipes it out on the next run. You can even browse the results in Robomongo (see figure 16.9).

With insanely hard-core Map/Reduce code under your belt, you're probably deeper into MongoDB than you ever planned to be in an introductory Grails book! Let's spend the last section of the chapter exploring another interesting take on the NoSQL story: graph databases with Neo4j.

16.5 Using Neo4j to work with graph-oriented data

Neo4j is your final stop on your NoSQL explorations, and we chose it because it models data and relationships in a completely different way than anything you've encountered so far. You've seen the relational model, key/value model, and document model, but Neo4j introduces you to modeling data as a graph of connected data.

It's probably been a while since you've played with graph data structures, though you use them behind the scenes every time you use a social networking application such as LinkedIn, Facebook, or Twitter. Let's reintroduce them to you using Hubbub as an example.

When one Hubbub user follows another, you create a link in the database that you model as `firstUser.addToFollowing(targetUser)`. With each user following several

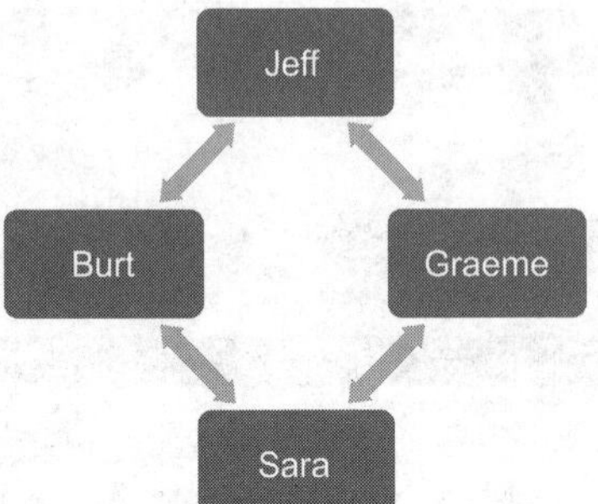

Figure 16.10 Social networks contain graphs of data where items are linked by relationships.

other users in the system, you soon end up with a web or "graph" of relationships such as the one shown in figure 16.10.

Graph databases such as Neo4j specialize in modeling these types of relationships and provide high performance tools for querying them. Need to find out which users are within three degrees of separation from a particular user? That's expensive to do in a relational data source but bread and butter for Neo4j. Let's install it and whip up a social graph visualization for Hubbub.

16.5.1 Installing and configuring the Neo4j plugin

Your first step in getting Hubbub into graph database territory is to install the Grails Neo4j plugin (http://grails.org/plugin/neo4j). A quick update of your /grails-app/conf/BuildConfig.groovy should sort that out. At the time of writing, the current version is 1.0.1, so add it to your list of plugins:

```
plugins {
    ...
    compile ":neo4j:1.0.1"
    ...
}
```

By default the Neo4j plugin sparks up an embedded version of Neo4j server that runs in the same JVM as your Grails app. That's perfect for your experimentation, but you can always override the defaults by customizing your /grails-app/conf/Config.groovy. The default place in which the plugin stores your Neo4j database is /var/neo4j, so if you're on a local Windows box, tweak that to something that makes more sense:

```
grails {
    neo4j {
        type = "embedded"
        location = "/data/neo4j"
    }
}
```

With the plugin installed and optionally configured, let's get under way teaching you Neo4j parlance as you implement Hubbub's social graph searcher.

16.5.2 *Neo4j domain classes: combining with Hibernate*

You can use Neo4j as your primary data source, if you like. In that case, as in MongoDB, it's a matter of removing your Hibernate plugin from /grails-app/conf/BuildConfig.groovy and you're ready to run. No special domain class markup is required.

In this case, let's supplement your existing Hibernate (and MongoDB) domain classes with a few Neo4j-specific domain classes. The way you mark a domain class for persistence in Neo4j is similar to what you did with MongoDB—add a custom `mapsWith` property.

Let's create a domain class that you can use to keep the social networking graph for Hubbub. Let's start with the minimal set of data you might keep to store a graph—`userIds` and their relationships:

```
package com.grailsinaction

class UserGraph {

    static mapWith = "neo4j"

    String loginId

    static hasMany = [ following : User ]

    static constraints = {
        loginId blank: false
    }
}
```

Now that you have your domain class in place, you need code to populate it with real data so you have something to query. Let's write the glue to perform the synchronization.

16.5.3 *Populating Hubbub's social graph*

You need a way to sync your domain class with your existing user relationships. Let's create a `GraphController` to house all your graph interactions, and perhaps put in a scrappy little `sync()` method to convert your list of users and their followers into a graph of `UserGraph` objects, as shown in the following listing.

Listing 16.6 Creating a `GraphController` and `sync` method

```
package com.grailsinaction

class GraphController {

    private UserGraph getOrCreateMatchingUserGraph(User user) {

        UserGraph matchingGraphUser = UserGraph.findByLoginId(user.loginId)
        if (!matchingGraphUser) {
            matchingGraphUser = new UserGraph(loginId: user.loginId)
            matchingGraphUser.save(failOnError: true)
            if (user.profile?.fullName) {
                matchingGraphUser.fullName = user.profile.fullName
            }
        }
        return matchingGraphUser

    }
```

```
    def sync() {

        log.debug("Starting sync process...")

        int syncCount = 0
        int linkCount = 0

        UserGraph.list()*.delete() // go nuclear
        User.list().each { user ->

            UserGraph matchingGraphUser =
                getOrCreateMatchingUserGraph(user)
            user.following.each { nextFollowing ->
                UserGraph matchingFollow =
    getOrCreateMatchingUserGraph(nextFollowing)
                matchingGraphUser.addToFollowing(matchingFollow)
                linkCount++
            }
            syncCount++
        }
        render text: "<html>Sync complete. Synced ${syncCount} users with
    ${linkCount} links at ${new Date()}</html>",
            contentType: "text/html"

    }
}
```

Nothing particularly exciting is going on there. You use standard GORM domain logic with the odd `addToFollowing()` and `save()` calls. Under the covers the Neo4j plugin persists all those objects for you.

You may notice that you use dynamic properties (as you did in MongoDB) to store the user's full name on the `UserGraph` node because that comes in handy for rendering later on. One gotcha with the current version of the plugin is that dynamic properties can be set only after `save()` is called, hence the unusual placement in your source code.

It's time to experiment with walking the tree and rendering nodes.

16.5.4 Walking and visualizing the graph with Cypher

Neo4j offers two ways to query the graph in object style:

- Its own SQL-like query language called Cypher
- A code-centric mechanism exposed via a traversal API

All Neo4j domain classes are enhanced with several variations of the `cypher()` and `traverse()` methods to make things easy.

You start your journey using the Cypher query language to find friends of friends of a user. The idea is that you can pass in a user, find all their friends, then find all the friends that are friends with them. In a relational world, you'd need many joins, but as you'll see, Neo4j makes that a one-liner.

Let's implement the `friendsOfFriends()` action in your graph controller, as shown in the following listing, then we'll show you how it all hangs together.

Listing 16.7 Implementing `friendsOfFriends()` in your graph controller

```
def friendsOfFriends() {

        if (params.id) {
            UserGraph startingUser = UserGraph.findByLoginId(params.id)   ❶
            if (startingUser) {
                def resultsTable = startingUser.cypher(
                    "start myself=node({this})
                     MATCH myself-[:following]->friend-[:following]->fof
                     WHERE fof.loginId <> myself.loginId
                     RETURN myself, friend, fof")   ❷
                [resultsTable: resultsTable]   ❸
            } else {
                response.sendError(404)
            }
        } else {
            response.sendError(404)
        }

    }
```

❶ Finds matching UserGraph using GORM dynamic finder

❷ Runs Cypher query to find followers of followers

❸ Passes results to view

This is familiar territory. You grab the user's ID off the incoming URL and attempt to find a matching `UserGraph` in your Neo4j database using standard GORM dynamic finders ❶. If you can locate them, you invoke the Neo4j `cypher` method ❷ on that domain class instance, passing it complex-looking Cypher code (which we'll get to in a moment). Finally, you pass any results, which are returned as a table-like structure, through to the view for rendering ❸. We'll look at that rendering code in a minute, but for now, let's break down that Cypher query so it becomes less magical.

First, let's reformat the query so you can see the individual clauses:

```
start myself=node({this})
MATCH myself-[:following]->friend-[:following]->fof
WHERE fof.loginId <> myself.loginId
RETURN myself, friend, fof
```

If you restate each clause in plainer English, this query says, "Start at the current node, which I'm going to now alias as 'myself'. Then match all the nodes that have a 'following' relationship with me, and alias them as a 'friend'. Then match all the nodes that have a 'following' relationship with 'friend', and alias them as 'fof' (friend of friend). Make sure that my fof.loginId doesn't match my own loginId because I don't want to display cases where my friends follow me back. Finally, return a table with three columns: myself, friend, and fof."

Phew! It's a mouthful of a query, but let's make it clearer by putting it to use in a view. To render a table that outputs you, your friend, and their friends, you iterate that `resultsTable`. The following listing shows what you may find in a friendsOfFriends.gsp.

Listing 16.8 Creating a view for the `resultsTable`

```
<h1>Friends Of Friends</h1>
    <table>
        <tr>
            <th>User</th><th>Is A Friend Of</th><th>Who Is A Friend Of</th>
        </tr>
        <g:each in="${resultsTable}" var="row">
             <tr>
<td><g:link action="friendsOfFriends"
    id="${row.myself.loginId}">${row.myself.fullName}
</g:link></td>
<td><g:link action="friendsOfFriends"
     id="${row.friend.loginId}">${row.friend.fullName}
</g:link></td>
<td><g:link action="friendsOfFriends"
    id="${row.fof.loginId}">${row.fof.fullName}
</g:link></td>
             </tr>
        </g:each>
    </table>
```

Each of the rows in that `resultsTable` exposes you, your friend, and friend-of-friend objects whose properties you can inspect to get back your underlying attributes. What you iterate here are the underlying node objects. If you want to get back to the matching domain objects (for example, for manipulation), you can take advantage of another domain class convenience method and call `UserGraph.createInstanceForNode(row.myself)`, which gives you back the domain class instance matching this node.

You create links on each of those users so you can keep exploring who's linked to whom. You also used that dynamic `fullName` property that you previously squirreled away on each node. Figure 16.11 shows the view in action for `loginId` jeff (http://localhost:8080/hubbub/graph/friendsOfFriends/jeff):

That's an impressive way to browse relationships and only scratches the surface of what Cypher can do. If you want to go deeper, fantastic docs (with working examples) are on the Neo4j site (http://docs.neo4j.org/chunked/milestone/cypher-introduction.html).

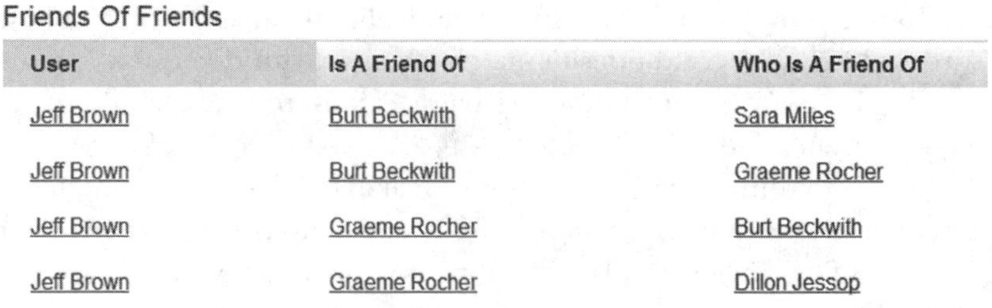

Friends Of Friends

User	Is A Friend Of	Who Is A Friend Of
Jeff Brown	Burt Beckwith	Sara Miles
Jeff Brown	Burt Beckwith	Graeme Rocher
Jeff Brown	Graeme Rocher	Burt Beckwith
Jeff Brown	Graeme Rocher	Dillon Jessop

Figure 16.11 Viewing the friends of Jeff

Querying friends of friends is impressive, but what if you want to walk the entire object graph displaying every relationship? For that use case it may be time to drop down to the Neo4j traversal API to see what's achievable in code.

16.5.5 Walking the entire graph

You've experimented with the Cypher query language through the domain class instance `cypher()` method, and now let's look at the API equivalent by seeing what's possible through the `traverse()` method.

Let's implement a `walk()` action on your graph controller that starts at a given node, and then traverses its `following` relationships until it runs out of nodes. Depending on your starting node, and who's following whom, you may even see the entire system!

The following listing shows what your `walk()` action looks like.

Listing 16.9 Using `walk()` to find relationships

```
import org.grails.datastore.gorm.neo4j.GrailsRelationshipTypes
import org.neo4j.graphdb.*

def walk() {

        if (params.id) {
            UserGraph startingUser = UserGraph.findByLoginId(params.id)
            if (startingUser) {
                def followingRel = startingUser.node.relationships.
                    ➥ find { it.type.name == 'following' }
                def nodeList =
     startingUser.traverse(Traverser.Order.BREADTH_FIRST,
                        StopEvaluator.END_OF_GRAPH,
                        ReturnableEvaluator.ALL,
                        followingRel.type, Direction.OUTGOING)
                [nodeList: nodeList]
            } else {
                response.sendError(404)
            }
        } else {
            response.sendError(404)
        }

    }
```

The `nodeList` returns a list of all the `UserGraph` nodes that Neo4j found by traversing outward links. But it's no fun if you can't see them, so let's add a walk.gsp view so you can see exactly what's happening, as shown in the following listing.

Listing 16.10 Viewing the list of users

```
  <h1>Walking The Graph</h1>
    <table>
        <tr>
            <th>User</th><th>Following</th>
        </tr>
```

```
        <g:each in="${nodeList}" var="node">
            <tr>
                <td><g:link action="walk"
                     id="${node.loginId}">${node.fullName}</g:link>
                </td>
                <td>
                    <ul>
                    <g:each in="${node.following}" var="following">
                        <li>
                            <g:link action="walk"
             id="${following.loginId}">${following.fullName}</g:link>
                        </li>
                    </g:each>
                    </ul>
            </tr>
        </g:each>
    </table>
```

In this view you display the node you found, and all the nodes that node follows. Figure 16.12 shows the output for user jeff.

If you notice carefully, the table can be read from the top down. Jeff follows Burt and Graeme, so they're the next two nodes you see in the table. Then rinse and repeat all the way down.

In this graph, Dillon is followed by Graeme, but Dillon himself doesn't follow anyone. If you click the Dillon link, you shouldn't see any outgoing links in your traversal. In fact, figure 16.13 shows exactly what that output looks like.

Using the traversal API offers you powerful features. You traversed OUTGOING relationships, but you can traverse INCOMING, OUTGOING, or BOTH depending on how you want to navigate your tree.

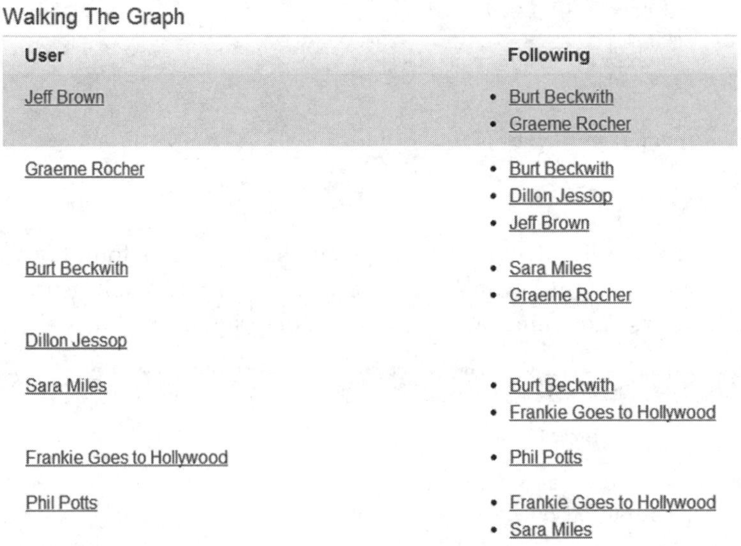

Walking The Graph

User	Following
Jeff Brown	• Burt Beckwith • Graeme Rocher
Graeme Rocher	• Burt Beckwith • Dillon Jessop • Jeff Brown
Burt Beckwith	• Sara Miles • Graeme Rocher
Dillon Jessop	
Sara Miles	• Burt Beckwith • Frankie Goes to Hollywood
Frankie Goes to Hollywood	• Phil Potts
Phil Potts	• Frankie Goes to Hollywood • Sara Miles

Figure 16.12 Viewing all the friends linked to Jeff

Walking The Graph

User	Following
Dillon Jessop	

Figure 16.13 Viewing a friend with no outgoing links

With a good sense of what's achievable via Neo4j's low-level API, it's time to wrap up your tour of popular NoSQL technologies in Grails.

16.6 Summary and best practices

We covered NoSQL territory in this chapter, introducing three of the most dominant NoSQL technologies available in the space today:

- *Redis*—for persistent key/value storage
- *MongoDB*—for document-oriented storage
- *Neo4j*—for graph-based storage and traversal

No doubt your head is spinning! This chapter was designed to give you a basic level of exposure to all three types of stores, so you can decide which ones you may like to explore further. Before we leave back-end territory and move on to testing and compiling in chapter 17, let's review a few key best practices from this chapter:

- *Redis is a data-structure server.* While you can use Redis as a persistent hash table, it shines when you take advantage of its high-performance data structures, such as lists, hashes, and sorted sets.
- *Use Redis to back Grails caching.* Now that caching services are built into the Grails platform, don't forget you can easily back your caches with Redis via the Grails Redis Cache plugin.
- *Experiment with MongoDB native queries via query tools.* Using a GUI tool such as Robomongo gives you freedom to experiment with Mongo queries or browse the results of previous Grails database operations. Don't be afraid to use these GUI tools to learn more about optimizing your Mongo queries. This approach can save you time.
- *Always provide an ObjectId field on your MongoDB domain classes.* Remember that if you don't provide your own `ObjectId` field, Grails supplies a long-based one. This can hamper your clustering options later, so bite the bullet and put an `ObjectId` ID field on all your domain classes from the get-go.
- *You can always fall back to GMongo.* The Grails Mongo integration is complete, but if you ever hit an edge case not supported out of the box, don't forget that you can always drop back to straight GMongo code and do anything you need to.
- *Consider a graph database.* If your application works with graph-based data structures (such as your social networking app Hubbub), consider storing your data

the way it wants to be stored. You end up with less code to maintain, and you won't have to worry about endless tuning of relational databases.

- *Learn Neo4j's Cypher query language.* Using Cypher to query a graph gives you a fast and self-describing mechanism for rich graph queries. Take the time to work through the Neo4j documentation and learn the basics of the language. The docs are great, and in-browser tools in the documentation let you experiment. It's worth the investment.

In the next chapter, we explore the processes involved in compiling, testing, and running your app.

17 Beyond compile, test, run

This chapter covers

- Managing dependencies
- Packaging and deploying your application
- Using continuous integration
- Integrating multiproject builds

Grails gives you all the tools you need to build your web application and run it, as we've shown throughout the previous chapters. The ability to make changes and see their effect immediately in a running server makes for a productive development environment. At a certain point, though, you need to deploy your application into a production setting: `grails run-app` isn't going to cut it. It won't scale or perform efficiently.

Getting to the point of deployment can potentially be a single-step process (use the Grails `war` command to create the artifact of deployment), but most projects have more to them. Systems often consist of multiple projects that depend on one another, and you typically have multiple teams working on them. Building the software then becomes a process of pulling all these components together, verifying that they work, packaging them, and deploying one or more of the components to production.

In this chapter, we look at the parts of the build process that we haven't discussed in previous chapters and yet are significant factors in using Grails for nontrivial projects. This starts with how you manage your dependencies—a surprisingly tricky subject—before touching on continuous integration systems and application deployment. Later in the chapter, you see how to incorporate Grails applications into multiproject builds using tools such as Maven and Gradle.

17.1 Getting to deployment

Grails applications are fundamentally based on Java servlet technology, so to run them in production you need to create what's known as a Web Application Archive (WAR) file and deploy it into a servlet container, such as Tomcat or Jetty (among others). As we mentioned at the beginning of the book, even when you execute the `run-app` command, you're starting an instance of Tomcat.

> **Grails 3.0**
>
> It's likely (although not certain) that Grails 3.0 will break the dependence on Java servlet technology, allowing you to run Grails applications in different ways. You'll still have the ability to create servlet-based applications, but it'll be one of several options.

Creating the WAR file (the unit of deployment) is as simple as running the following command:

```
grails war
```

What else is there to talk about? The most important topic is controlling what goes into the WAR file. Few things are worse than taking an application that works fine under `run-app`, deploying it as a WAR file, and discovering that the application doesn't work because the WAR contains conflicting versions of a library. This is where dependency management comes in.

17.1.1 Managing your dependencies

If there's one area of the Java ecosystem that consistently causes developers grief, it's library dependencies. It's absolutely wonderful that you can use prebuilt libraries that provide time-saving features. Why reinvent the wheel? And Java has a plethora of libraries that you can use, as well as all the Grails plugins that people have created.

Trouble arises because many of those libraries require other libraries to function. Add in all the possible versions of each library and you create a rather messy mix. To understand what we mean, let's look at a few of the dependencies in a normal Grails application. Figure 17.1 shows a partial dependency graph demonstrating how multiple versions of a single library can end up being pulled in by an application.

This isn't normally a problem because Grails automatically picks the most recent version of a library from the dependency graph and uses that. Any other versions are

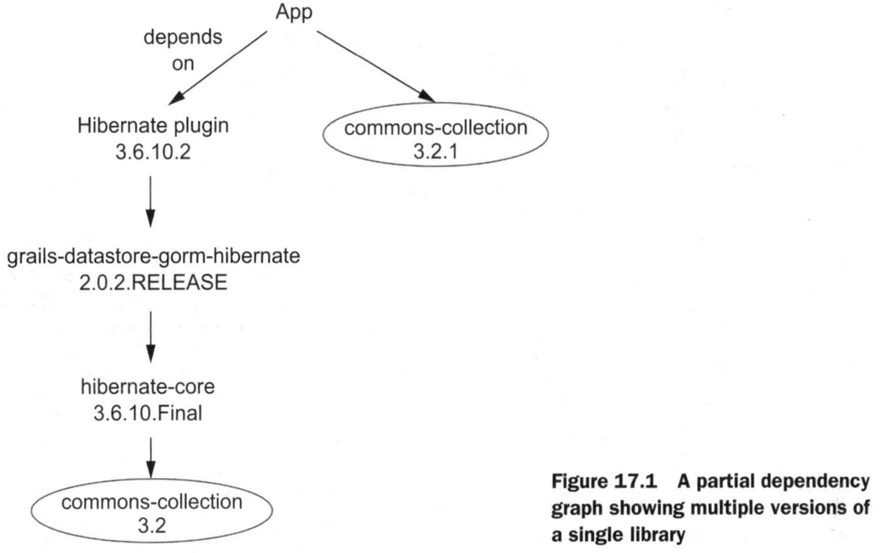

Figure 17.1 A partial dependency graph showing multiple versions of a single library

"evicted" from the dependency graph so that you only ever have one version in your application. Based on figure 17.1, Grails uses only version 3.2.1 of the Apache Commons Collection library. If Grails automatically evicts older versions, what's the issue? Here are several problem scenarios:

- A newer version of a library breaks other libraries (or your app)
- Spock versions
- Snapshot handling (pre-Grails 2.3)

Let's look at each of these and work out how to resolve the problems.

NEW VERSIONS BREAKING YOUR APPLICATION

In an ideal world, libraries wouldn't introduce breaking changes into their APIs except in major version changes, such as from 3.x to 4.0. As you know, though, the world is far from ideal. Libraries do introduce breaking changes in new minor or patch versions, either accidentally or intentionally. When this happens, your application either fails to compile (if the relevant code is type-checked) or fails at runtime. This isn't good.

If you explicitly declared this dependency yourself, then you can easily revert to an older version. But imagine what happens if you introduce a new dependency that has the problematic library as a transitive dependency? It's a newer version, and so Grails evicts the old (working) version and uses the new (broken) one.

A real-life example of this was SLF4J, the logging API used by Grails. Certain method signatures in its API changed between versions 1.5 and 1.6 that meant code compiled with version 1.5 failed to work with 1.6. At the time, Grails used SLF4J 1.5 and yet it was easy to add a separate library or plugin to a project that included SLF4J 1.6 as a transitive dependency. The result? You got either `NoSuchMethodErrors` or `MissingMethodExceptions` when any logging took place.

SPOCK VERSIONS

Prior to Grails 2.3, you had to use a Spock plugin to write Spock tests in your Grails application, and for Grails 2.2, the corresponding dependency declaration was slightly more complex than the average:

```
dependencies {
    test "org.spockframework:spock-grails-support:0.7-groovy-2.0"
    ...
}

plugins {
    test ":spock:0.7", {
        excludes "spock-grails-support"
    }
    ...
}
```

Excludes transitive version (0.7-groovy-1.8), which doesn't work with Grails 2.2, and provides correct version.

The base Spock library is tied to particular versions of Groovy and so is Grails. The default dependencies of the plugin are fine with Grails 2.0 and 2.1 (which use Groovy 1.8), but Grails 2.2 switched to Groovy 2.0, which explains why you need to perform the previous exclusion.

> **Which version of Spock?**
>
> The rule is simple: if you're using Grails 2.0 or 2.1, you need the -groovy-1.8 JAR, the default for version 0.7 of the Spock plugin. If you're using Grails 2.2, you need the -groovy-2.0 JAR. Grails 2.3+ comes with Spock as a core dependency, so you don't need the plugin.

Fortunately, Spock is one of the few libraries that has different JARs for different versions of Groovy, making it a special case.

WORKING WITH SNAPSHOT VERSIONS

It's occasionally necessary to live on the bleeding edge and use development versions of libraries, whether it's because they have a specific bug fix you need or a particular feature. Whatever the reason, one of the most common ways to use development versions is through *snapshots*.

A snapshot is a version for which the underlying JAR can change. You should never (and rarely can these days) publish a different JAR under an existing release version, such as 2.1.1. After a release version is published, that JAR is forever tied to that particular version number. This rule doesn't apply to snapshots: you can publish new builds of a JAR under existing snapshot versions. The idea is that if you include a snapshot as a dependency, you always get the latest published JAR for that version.

Take caution when using snapshot dependencies. They lead to volatility in your application (it can readily break when a new snapshot is published), and before Grails 2.3, it was difficult to ensure that you got the latest published JAR. Grails 2.3 introduced a new dependency resolution engine that fixes this problem, so you generally don't have to worry. Regardless, we strongly recommend against using snapshot dependencies unless you have to.

> **The twin resolution engines**
>
> Grails 2.3 introduces and defaults to a new dependency resolution engine based on Maven rather than Apache Ivy. This results in much more reliable behavior, but you don't get the flexibility of the previous engine. Nor do you get the HTML report from the `dependency-report` command (the dependency information is printed to the terminal instead).
>
> Despite the limitations, we do recommend sticking to the new resolution engine as it makes for a much smoother experience.

Note that milestone releases, such as M1, alpha1, RC1, and so on, don't behave in the same way as snapshots, so they're safe to use. Libraries and tools are still subject to change between milestone releases, but at least you can control exactly which version you depend on.

As we said, the new dependency resolution engine in Grails 2.3 solves the major problems with snapshot dependencies, but how do you resolve issues that fit into the other two categories? The answer is through exclusions, an example of which you saw with the Spock plugin.

RESOLVING DEPENDENCY ISSUES

In many areas of software development, the process of fixing problems starts with diagnosis. Dependency management is no different, and Grails gives you the tool you need: the `dependency-report` command.

Prior to Grails 2.3, this command generated an HTML report that you could open in the browser. It now prints the report to the console. In both cases, you get information about what dependencies are in which scopes. This is crucial in determining whether you have any unexpected or duplicate versions of particular dependencies. It also enables you to ultimately see which of your direct dependencies pulled in the problematic one.

After you identify the source of the problem, it's easy to solve: exclude that particular transitive dependency. As you saw previously, this is what you do with the Spock plugin:

```
plugins {
    test ":spock:0.7", {
        excludes "spock-grails-support"
    }
}
```

Exclusions go in closure argument

Excludes named modules (can take multiple arguments)

You could be even more precise and specify the dependency's group, not only its module name:

```
plugins {
    test ":spock:0.7", {
        exclude group: "org.spockframework",
                module: "spock-grails-support"
    }
}
```

Excludes by group and module. Note "exclude" isn't plural.

This can be necessary when projects publish their projects under a new group but with the same module name. It's rare, though.

These exclusions work on normal JAR dependencies as well as plugins. They also apply to all transitive dependencies, regardless of how far down the dependency tree those dependencies are. All in all, dependency exclusions are the go-to tool for controlling your dependency tree and solving dependency-related issues. We'd now like to round off this section by explaining what those dependency scopes (compile, test, and so on) mean.

UNDERSTANDING DEPENDENCY SCOPES

If you come from a Maven background, then the dependency scopes used by Grails will be familiar:

- `compile`—All the dependencies required to compile your application. If you use classes directly from a library, that library should be declared as compile scope, even if it's also a transitive dependency. This makes it clear to other developers that you're using the classes from that library and avoids the problem associated with the library no longer being a transitive dependency at a certain point.
- `runtime`—Everything required to run the application, even if the classes aren't used directly by your code. This automatically includes everything in `compile` scope, so you don't need to repeat your dependency declarations. A common runtime dependency is a JDBC driver.
- `test`—All the dependencies that are needed when testing the application via `test-app`. It includes everything in the `runtime` scope (and by extension `compile`, too). You normally only declare things in the `test` scope if they're used directly by your test cases.
- `provided`—This is an unusual scope in that the associated dependencies are required to compile the application but aren't needed at runtime. The classic example is the servlet-api JAR when you use classes like `HttpServletRequest`. At runtime, the servlet container provides these classes instead, so you don't need the JAR.
- `build`—Unknown in Maven, this scope contains the things you need for the Grails commands themselves. It's often used to include plugins (such as Release) that provide extra build commands. It's unusual to specify JARs as build dependencies unless you write your own build scripts.

These separate dependency scopes ensure that the compilation and runtime classpaths contain only those JARs required for the associated activity. This reduces the

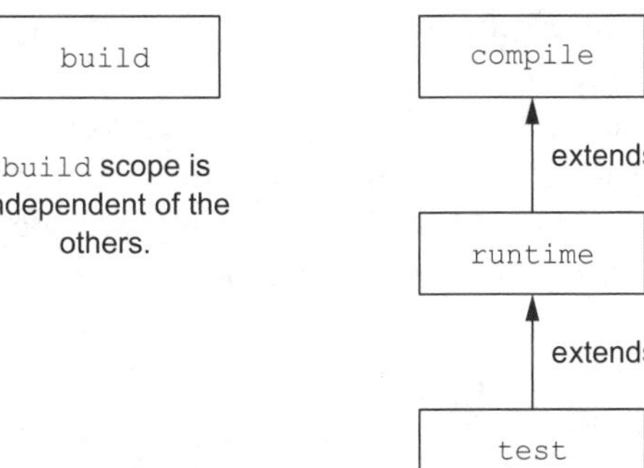

Figure 17.2 The relationship between dependency scopes

chances of conflicting JARs and improves performance because Groovy has fewer JARs to search when looking for classes. Note also that certain scopes effectively inherit from others, which helps keep the number of dependency declarations down. We show the relationship between the scopes in figure 17.2. If you're ever in doubt, it's usually safe to use the `compile` scope.

Be aware of the following issues when it comes to the scopes:

- *Evictions don't happen across unrelated scopes.* If the `build` dependencies are merged with the `runtime` dependencies, and each scope has a different version of a particular dependency, the resulting classpath includes both versions because eviction doesn't happen between `build` and `runtime`. But eviction does happen between related scopes, such as `compile` and `test`, or `compile` and `runtime`.

  Imagine that you declare `commons-compress` version 1.5 as a build dependency and your `runtime` scope has `commons-compress` 1.2 through a transitive dependency. If the dependencies from both scopes are merged into a single classpath, that classpath includes both version 1.2 and version 1.5 because no eviction takes place. This raises the question of which JAR the `commons-compress` classes are loaded from. The answer is that it depends which JAR is first in the classpath, and there are no guarantees about what that order is.

  Fortunately this isn't an issue if you use Grails 2.3. Nor is it an issue for Grails 2.2 if you add this configuration setting to your BuildConfig.groovy:

  ```
  grails.project.fork.run=true
  ```

- *You can compile and run against different library versions.* This may seem strange because we said that evictions occur between related scopes, but it's possible to compile your application against version 1.6 of SLF4J and run it with version 1.7. This happens if the highest version of the library is 1.6 in `compile` scope, but 1.7 in `runtime`. This may cause problems if any breaking changes exist between the two versions.

As we mentioned, dependencies are a surprisingly tricky subject and older versions of Grails have more problems than more recent ones. Despite that, and no matter what version of Grails you use, you can resolve your dependency pains after you get the hang of the dependency report and how to use exclusions.

Dependencies are also a fairly common source of the old "it works for me" problem in team development. This is typically a result of one developer having the required library in their dependency cache, although the application's dependency tree does not include it. One great way to find these problems early on is through a process called continuous integration (CI).

17.1.2 Continuous integration and deployment

In the last few years, we've started to see a new approach to deploying applications: continuous delivery. The idea is to push new features and fixes to your production systems frequently, from every couple of days to many times in a single day (GitHub has had more than 100 deploys in a single day). This isn't to say that continuous delivery is appropriate for all projects, nor is it something that can be achieved solely through Grails. But the automation necessary for continuous delivery is incredibly useful for all projects.

One of the most important factors is test coverage. You can't deploy new versions quickly and easily unless you have a high level of confidence that a new version works correctly. You need fully automated unit, integration, and functional tests that give close to full coverage of the code. We've already covered testing, but when you have multiple teams working on a single project, how can you be sure that all their work is properly integrated before testing and deploying? The most common solution is CI.

SETTING UP A CI SERVER

Once upon a time, new application versions were delivered infrequently and there was a code-freeze period during which multiple teams would attempt to merge (or integrate) their separate development streams together. It was often a painful and time-consuming process because the different developments diverged significantly over time.

CI alleviates this particular issue by ensuring that all the development streams are merged and tested on a frequent basis, typically on a separate build server, as shown in figure 17.3. Every time new code is committed to a set branch, the server compiles the

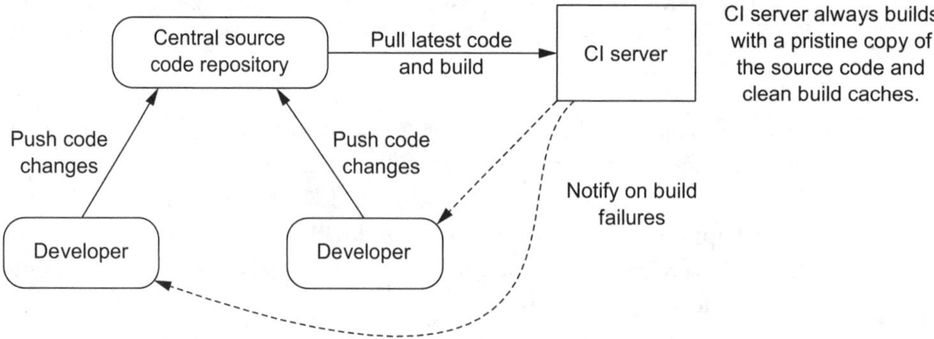

Figure 17.3 A typical CI setup

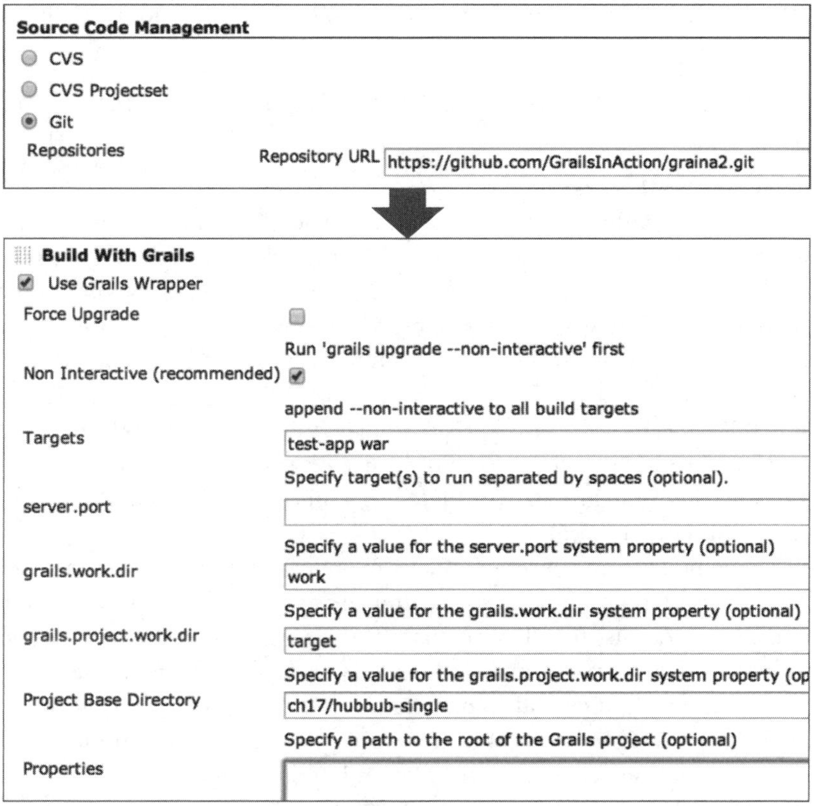

Figure 17.4 The configuration settings for a Grails application on the Jenkins CI server

application and runs the tests, then packages the app. The advantage to this approach is that integration problems are picked up early when they're relatively easy to resolve.

As a Grails developer you now have many options for a CI server, including hosted or installed on your own systems. A few have dedicated support for Grails, but in reality, you can use any build server that supports Java because of the Grails wrapper.

In figure 17.4, we show you the settings for a Grails application on a Jenkins instance (http://jenkins-ci.org/) because it's one of the most popular Java-oriented CI tools. Although Jenkins has a Grails plugin, we configure the build server to use the Grails wrapper because this approach is more widely applicable.

When configuring a Grails application to build on a CI server, you only need to do a few specialized things:

- Configure the build to run the Grails wrapper (`grailsw`).
- Use `grails.work.dir` and `grails.project.work.dir` values that are relative to the project directory. This ensures they're cleaned properly between builds. They can be passed in as system properties, for example:

```
./grailsw -Dgrails.work.dir=target test-app war
```

- Make sure the build server knows where to find the test reports as these are in a nonstandard location.

That's all there is to it. Otherwise a Grails application is handled like a normal Java web application.

CUSTOMIZING THE WAR PACKAGE

When you want to deploy your application to a servlet container, typically you first package it as a WAR file. This is a ZIP file containing your application classes, resources, dependencies, and web configuration. Normally the only thing that you need to worry about is whether you're packaging the application for the appropriate environment. Unlike the `run-app` command, the `war` command defaults to the production environment.

Not much typically goes wrong, but you may find extraneous JARs in the WAR file, particularly if you use an older version of Grails. It's not uncommon for JARs related to testing to find their way into it. Fortunately, it's simple to filter out files from the WAR file using a build event handler.

The Grails build system fires events in many circumstances, such as each time a build target executes—both before and after the execution. Other significant parts of the build trigger events, too. Unfortunately, the Grails build system is poorly documented, which is a shame because the build system gives you great flexibility to add your own Grails commands and hook into its events. Still, the `CreateWarStart` event in the following example is useful in its own right and helps you understand articles and forum postings online that describe other handy events.

To get started, create the file scripts/_Events.groovy (if it doesn't already exist). The scripts directory is where you put all your custom build scripts if you choose to write them. The underscore (_) prefix tells Grails to ignore the file rather than turn it into a command. For example, the file scripts/DeployToTomcat.groovy adds a Grails command called `deploy-to-tomcat`. Note the transformation from camel case to hyphenated lowercase.

Once you have the _Events.groovy script, add the handler inside it:

```
eventCreateWarStart = { String warName, File stagingDir ->
    println "About to package the WAR file from ${stagingDir}"
}
```

As you can see, the handler is a closure assigned to a script variable whose name matches the pattern `event<eventName>`. To verify that the handler works, run the Grails `war` command and look for the message you're printing. If you don't see it, the likely problem is either a misnamed _Events.groovy file or a misnamed `eventCreateWarStart`.

You can probably guess what happens next: because the event is passed the location of the staging directory from which the WAR is created, you can remove files from that directory to keep them from going into the WAR. You can even add files if you want, although this is less common.

Common libraries that you don't want in your WAR file but are often packaged in it include:

- *commons-logging*.jar*—Grails uses SLF4J for logging, rather than Apache Commons Logging.
- *h2*.jar*—Unless you use the H2 Database Engine for production, you don't need the database in your WAR!
- *hsqldb*.jar*—Unless you use it for production (not recommended), this shouldn't be included.
- *spring-test*.jar*—Why would you want a testing library inside your application?
- *Junit*.jar*—Same as for spring-test*.jar.

To delete these files, you have two options: use either the JDK classes or the equivalent Ant tasks via Groovy's Ant Builder. To use the JDK classes, the code looks like the following listing.

Listing 17.1 Using JDK classes to delete files

```
eventCreateWarStart = { String warName, File stagingDir ->
    def exclusions = [
        "commons-logging-1.1.1.jar",
        "h2-1.3.173.jar",
        "hsqldb-1.8.0.10.jar",
        "spring-test-3.2.5.RELEASE.jar",
        "junit-4.11.jar"]
    new File(stagingDir, "WEB-INF/lib").eachFileRecurse { File f ->
        if (f.name in exclusions) {
            f.delete()
        }
    }
}
```

Deletes any files found in WEB-INF/lib whose name is in exclusion list

This works fine, but it's not convenient if you don't know the exact names of the files you want to delete. It's easy to remember the base name (commons-logging, junit), but what about the version number of a JAR? And what happens when you upgrade the app or change a dependency that results in the version number changing on one of your exclusions? Using a pattern-based approach is generally superior, which is why you often see Ant Builder used instead. The following listing takes this approach.

Listing 17.2 Using Ant Builder to delete files based on a pattern

```
eventCreateWarStart = { String warName, File stagingDir ->
    def exclusions = ["commons-logging",
                      "h2",
                      "hsqldb",
                      "spring-test",
                      "junit"]
    ant.delete {
        fileset(dir: new File(stagingDir, "WEB-INF/lib").canonicalPath) {
            for (basename in exclusions) {
```

ant variable is available in all scripts; delete is Ant task.

```
                    include name: "${basename}-*.jar"
                }
            }
        }
    }
```

Ant provides useful tasks around file manipulation (among other things), all of which are built around the powerful file set concept. If you want to write your own build scripts and event handlers, it's well worth consulting the Ant manual (http://ant.apache.org/manual/) to learn which Ant tasks are available.

Bear in mind that Ant is based on XML, which means that all the task definitions in the manual are given in XML. We're obviously not using XML in the previous example, so how do you convert between the two syntaxes? It's a simple one-to-one mapping based on the markup builder syntax (see appendix C). In XML form, the `delete` task looks like this:

```
<delete>                                                    <-- Methods map to XML elements and closures to nesting
    <fileset dir="stagingDir/WEB-INF/lib">
        <include name="commons-logging-*.jar"/>             <-- Named arguments map to XML attributes
        <include name="h2-*.jar"/>
        ...
    </fileset>
</delete>
```

As you can see, the Groovy nature of the build scripts together with the `AntBuilder` object result in a powerful and flexible approach to build that allows you to do most anything you want. Before you move on to other things, though, we leave you with a word of warning.

> **USE AT YOUR OWN RISK** As we mentioned previously, the Grails build system is poorly documented, so you're somewhat on your own. In addition, it's likely that Grails 3.0 will switch to a Gradle-based system that may result in your having to manually migrate any custom scripts and event handlers you create. We recommend you keep the number of build customizations to a minimum and focus on those that provide real value.

This technique of adding an event handler to the WAR creation is particularly powerful when combined with using shared JARs in Tomcat, as you see next.

DEPLOYING TO TOMCAT

If deploying a Grails application to a servlet container is as simple as creating a WAR file, why talk about Tomcat specifically? It's because Tomcat is a common platform that provides a couple of bonus features that developers take advantage of: shared libraries and per-deployment configuration.

The idea behind shared libraries is that you may want to deploy multiple Grails applications to a single servlet container instance. If you try this with a normal Grails WAR file, you typically run into PermGen memory issues (unless you use the Java 8 JVM). Every application gets its own copy of all the classes—and Grails uses many classes.

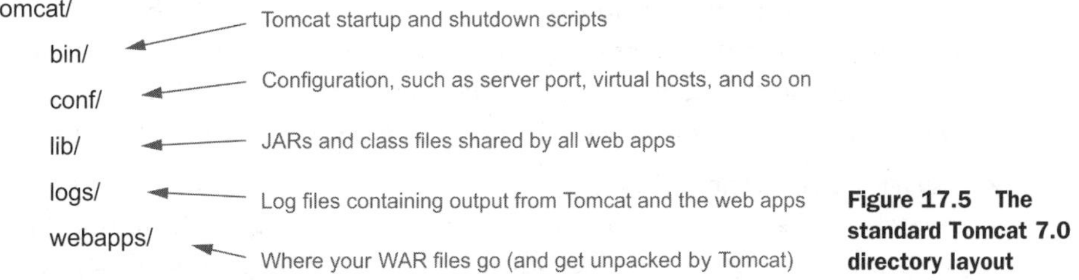

Figure 17.5 The standard Tomcat 7.0 directory layout

You can partially solve this problem by putting many of the JARs common to Grails applications in Tomcat's lib directory, as shown in figure 17.5. When you do this, you have only one copy of the classes in those JARs regardless of how many Grails applications are deployed in the container. That's a big saving on memory usage! It's a partial solution because you can't put all the common JARs into the shared directory, but you can at least deploy more than one application to the container.

The big question is this: Which of the base JARs that are common to most Grails applications can be shared? The answer is all of them except the Grails-specific ones. Grails still uses static holder classes for various objects, including the `grailsApplication` bean, and those static variables are shared between all Grails web apps running in Tomcat if the Grails JARs are shared.

Assuming that you want to split out the shared JARs, how do you do it? The `war` command has no built-in feature, unfortunately, so you have to do it manually. The answer is to use the `CreateWarStart` event, as shown in the next listing.

Listing 17.3 Splitting shared JARs

```
eventCreateWarStart = { String warName, File stagingDir ->
    if (grailsEnv == "production") {
        def sharedLibsDir = "${grailsSettings.projectWorkDir}/sharedLibs"

        ant.mkdir dir: sharedLibsDir
        ant.move todir: sharedLibsDir, {
            fileset dir: "${stagingDir}/WEB-INF/lib", {
                include name: "*.jar"
                exclude name: "grails-*"
            }
        }

        println "Shared JARs put into ${sharedLibsDir}"
    }
}
```

Now all you need to do is place the JARs from the sharedLibs directory into Tomcat's lib directory and deploy your (now much slimmer) WAR to Tomcat! For real applications you should refine this so that only the general Grails dependencies are included in the sharedLibs directory, not the project-specific ones.

The lib directory is also the key to setting up per-deployment configurations. Remember that the application's runtime configuration goes into the Config.groovy file, which is then compiled and packaged into the WAR file. This is fine as far as it goes, but it means that no matter where the WAR file is deployed, it has the same configuration, such as the database connection settings, mail server hosts, and so on. Do you want to create a different WAR for every target server? We didn't think so.

PER SERVER CONFIGURATION

Fortunately Grails allows you to pull configuration settings in from other locations at runtime, including from the classpath and from the filesystem. It happens through the `grails.config.locations` setting, which every new Grails application has commented out at the top of Config.groovy. Its most common form is the following, which you saw at the end of chapter 11:

```
grails.config.locations = [
    "classpath:${appName}-config.groovy",
    "file:./${appName}-config.groovy"
}
```

Loads file from classpath if it exists

Loads file from current working directory

This code loads additional configuration files from both the classpath and the current working directory. If the files don't exist, that's fine: you see a warning, but otherwise the application works as before. This behavior is important because for local development, you can put an <appName>-config.groovy file in the project root with your own custom settings, which takes effect when you execute `run-app`, and for Tomcat deployments you can put an <appName>-config.groovy file in the Tomcat lib directory.

This sounds like a great idea, we hear you say, but what about the database connection settings? They have to go in DataSource.groovy, right? In fact, they don't. You can also put them in Config.groovy or in one of these external configuration files we're talking about. The DataSource.groovy and Config.groovy are merged at runtime into a single configuration object used by the entire app. The only reason to have a separate file is to make it easier to locate the important database settings.

> **Order of precedence**
>
> Any settings in external configuration files override those in Config.groovy or DataSource.groovy, so you can still have useful per-environment defaults in those files.

You can achieve a similar result through environments, but you still need to repackage the WAR every time you make a change to the environment's configuration settings. An additional benefit of external configuration files is that they allow you to keep sensitive information, such as usernames, passwords, and API keys, out of source control or at least out of public source control. That's the reason we used this technique for the Twitter API credentials in chapter 11.

You can deploy Grails applications to multiple platforms, for example, to the cloud, as we discuss in chapter 18, but it's still common enough for companies to use dedicated Tomcat instances that there's a good chance these tips will help you out.

As you've seen, there's plenty of flexibility for building and deploying standalone Grails applications, and if that's all you need to do, you're good to go. The requirements change when you integrate a Grails application into a larger system, or when a Grails application depends on one or more other components that are separate projects. In these cases, consider more generic and powerful build tools.

17.2 Integrating Grails with Maven

It's becoming more and more common for applications or systems to be built from independent, composable parts. A Grails REST-based service could be one of those parts used by several other services or applications. It's also common to bundle features into reusable JARs and plugins. The aim is to improve maintainability, keep a clear separation of responsibilities, and make it easier to independently deploy and update different parts of the system.

When your projects are set up this way, you need to use a dedicated build tool that can handle all the different parts of the system. The Grails build system is fine for standalone applications, but the way it works makes it effectively useless for building multiple interdependent projects.

In this section we discuss how to incorporate Grails projects into builds based on Maven, and in the next section we look at Gradle. The former is prevalent in the Java space while Gradle is growing rapidly and will almost certainly become the built-in tool for Grails 3.0. Apache Ant is also an option, but few new projects are adopting it, and it's certainly showing its age. It also has no built-in support for multiproject builds.

Maven & Gradle vs. Grails

Although both Maven and Gradle integrate fairly well with the Grails build system, you do lose features. It's a rare occurrence that you can use the Grails command line (and its interactive console) once you set up build integration. You may also find that certain plugins don't work, particularly those that provide their own Grails commands.

Switching to an alternative build tool is not to be undertaken lightly, but you gain benefits within a multiproject environment.

Maven is a popular build tool in the Java space that brought us build by convention, transitive dependency management (along with Apache Ivy), and a central dependency repository (Maven Central). It's so common now in Java enterprises that if you want to use Grails for any projects within such companies, you need to integrate with Maven.

It's out of this book's scope to explain how Maven works or why you want to use it, so we focus purely on building a Grails project with Maven. That's what your company's build managers are interested in. We start by converting Hubbub into a Maven project to keep things simple, but we follow that up by turning Hubbub into a multiproject build—that's the real use case for choosing Maven rather than the Grails commands.

17.2.1 Creating a single-project POM

Every Maven build starts with a Project Object Model (POM) file. The POM describes the project and defines any custom logic required to build it. The idea is to have as little custom logic as possible by keeping your Java projects as close to the Maven conventions as they can be. The difficulty with Grails is that its projects are about as far from those conventions as the moon is from the Earth! Fortunately, Grails provides help to reconcile these two competing, opinionated views of project structure and build logic. It all starts with a simple command:

```
grails create-pom com.grailsinaction
```

This creates a pom.xml file in the root of the project that you can test by running

```
mvn clean compile
```

You perform a `clean` because Maven puts its files in the target directory, which is where the generated files from the Grails commands go by default. You may see build errors if you don't `clean` first. It's also worth noting that the Maven plugin creates a plugins directory in the root of the project. This is where Maven installs the Grails plugins for the project.

TIP You should delete the grails-app/controllers/TwitterAuthController.groovy file because it isn't needed and may cause compilation issues.

> **Dependency issues**
>
> If you run into apparent dependency problems, such as Maven using the wrong version of a dependency or missing one, run `mvn dependency:tree` and compare its output to that of `grails dependency-report`. Assuming the project builds with the Grails command line, you can identify where the problem lies and update the POM appropriately by adding exclusions or any missing dependencies.

Now that you can build the project with Maven, let's look at the POM that was created. The first interesting part is the project info:

```
<groupId>com.grailsinaction</groupId>
<artifactId>hubbub</artifactId>
<packaging>grails-app</packaging>
<version>0.2</version>
```

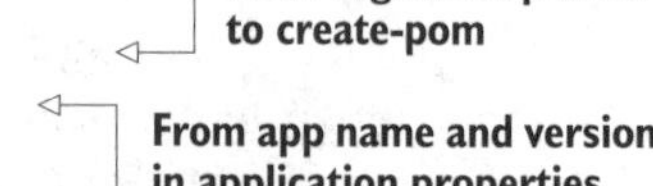

The part that sticks out is the packaging: `grails-app`. You may expect a packaging of type `war` because that's what a Grails application ultimately produces, but the WAR file is built differently from the standard Maven approach and can cause problems with other Maven plugins that work with the `war` packaging type.

The rest of the POM is standard, and the dependencies section contains all the JARs and plugins defined in BuildConfig.groovy. It also includes custom repository declarations. It gets more interesting in the plugins section because that's where the POM incorporates the Grails Maven plugin:

```
<plugin>
    <groupId>org.grails</groupId>
    <artifactId>grails-maven-plugin</artifactId>
    <version>${grails.version}</version>          <-- grails.version property is defined in POM.
    <configuration>
        <fork>true</fork>                         <-- A value of true avoids out-of-memory errors.
    </configuration>
    <extensions>true</extensions>
</plugin>
```

It's the plugin that understands the `grails-app` packaging type and integrates the appropriate Grails commands into the Maven build phases. Table 17.1 shows you which commands are matched to which phases. You can tell which commands are used by looking closely at the console output from the Maven build—the Grails output and Maven output are interleaved.

Table 17.1 How the Grails build commands fit into the Maven phases

Maven phase	Grails command
`initialize`	`create-app/create-plugin` (depending on packaging type)
`clean`	`clean`
`compile`	`compile`
`test`	`test-app unit:`
`package`	`war/package-plugin` (depending on packaging type)
`integration-test`	`test-app integration: functional:`

As you can see, you can start with a POM (no Grails project at all) and then run `mvn initialize` to create the skeleton project based on the packaging type. And if the project structure already exists, nothing happens.

This is great if all you need is the standard build phases, and they certainly cover the most common tasks. But remember that the Grails build system provides additional commands to ease your workload, such as `create-domain-class`. Such commands don't fit into the Maven build cycle, so how do you execute them? You have two options: use custom Maven goals directly or use the Grails build system instead.

The Grails Maven plugin does more than integrate the Grails commands into the Maven build lifecycle. It also provides access to most of the standard Grails commands via Maven goals that start with the prefix `grails`. To run the `create-domain-class` command, for example, use the following Maven goal:

```
mvn grails:create-domain-class -DdomainClassName=com.grailsinaction.Post
```

You can find a full list of commands to use with this syntax in the Grails user guide.[1] Although it doesn't contain goals for every command, you'll find a reference to a get-out-of-jail-free card: the exec goal. This allows you to execute any arbitrary Grails command, including those provided by plugins, although at the time of writing there are problems with the feature.[2]

Let's say you want to run the s2-quickstart command provided by the Spring Security Core plugin (yes, you've already run it, but it's a useful example). You can run this command:

```
mvn grails:exec -Dcommand=s2-quickstart -Dargs="org.example User Role"
```

The args parameter should be the complete set of arguments that you'd have passed to the grails command, hence the value is quoted. You can also use this goal to integrate arbitrary Grails commands into the different phases through the Maven plugin configuration. A short example is given in the Grails user guide, so we won't go further into that here. It's a Maven feature rather than a Grails one.

Although you have complete access to the Grails commands through Maven, you do lose out on the interactive console, and the exec goal is clunky. To get around that, Grails allows you to use the normal Grails commands while pulling the dependency information from a POM. To enable this support, add the following line (the one in italics) to your dependency resolution configuration in BuildConfig.groovy:

```
grails.project.dependency.resolution = {
    inherits "global"
    pom true
    log "warn"
    ...
}
```

Tells Grails to use POM as sole source of dependency information.

After you do this, you can use the Grails command line as before, including the interactive console. It's like getting the best of both worlds! When doing this, you should remove all the dependency declarations from BuildConfig.groovy except the ones marked build. Grails should ignore them, but at the time of writing it doesn't appear to.[3]

Before Grails 2.3

Using the POM to declare your application's dependencies works well with Grails 2.3, but that's because that version uses Maven's Aether dependency resolver by default. Previous versions of Grails used Ivy, which doesn't work well with POMs. If you use a pre-2.3 version of Grails, you're unlikely to get much success with the pom true setting.

1 Grails User Guide—Command line reference, http://grails.org/doc/latest/guide/commandLine.html#antAndMaven.

2 "grails:exec goal does not work for plugin-provided scripts," http://jira.grails.org/browse/MAVEN-217.

3 "pom true is resolving plugins from BuildConfig.groovy," http://jira.grails.org/browse/GRAILS-10569.

It's surprisingly easy to build a Grails project using Maven. Grails helps you create the initial POM and the Maven plugin does the rest of the work. That said, we won't lie: it's not always going to be smooth and easy. The two build systems are different and the integration can never be perfect. Here are a couple of things to bear in mind when using the two together:

- Maven has no concept of a build scope, so these dependencies have to be maintained in BuildConfig.groovy
- The Maven Release plugin automatically updates the project version in the POM, but this doesn't sync to application.properties. You can find a discussion of this issue online.[4]

Considering the impedance mismatch between the two, it doesn't make sense to use Maven for a standalone Grails project. In contrast, it does make sense when you build multiple projects together.

17.2.2 Multiproject Maven builds

Many software systems are composed of multiple libraries and applications that can be built separately or together. The main reasons for this are to allow for effective reuse and to improve maintainability. By decomposing a monolithic application into modular parts, you allow developers to work on smaller, easier to understand pieces.

When taking this approach, it makes sense to have a build tool that can build all the parts of an application together. Maven allows you to do this through parent POMs, and this mechanism is fully supported in Grails. In fact, Grails has a built-in command, `create-multi-project-build`, to help you to get started quickly. Before you use that, though, how are you going to split Hubbub into multiple projects?

Most projects in Java land can be broken down into collections of JAR libraries, where each library is a separate project. You can do this with Grails, too, but the framework provides a more interesting unit of modularity: the plugin. Writing a Grails plugin may seem like an intimidating prospect at this stage, and we certainly don't expect you to write something such as the Spring Security Core plugin yet. But as you'll see shortly, you already know how to develop simple plugins because they're Grails applications with optional extras.

To demonstrate both a multiproject Maven build and a minimal plugin-oriented architecture, you'll move Hubbub's user management code into a plugin. That includes the domain classes, controllers, and views that are associated with registering new users and managing their profiles. Because access control and user management are so closely linked, you'll also declare the Spring Security plugins as dependencies of your User Management plugin. You can see a broad overview of the structure you end up with in figure 17.6. And you can look at the complete chapter code on GitHub to see exactly which files end up where in this structure.

---

[4] Nicholas Hagen, "Grails 2.1 and Maven Integration: Simple Project," July 11, 2012, http://www.znetdevelopment.com/blogs/2012/07/11/grails-2-1-and-maven-integration-simple-project/.

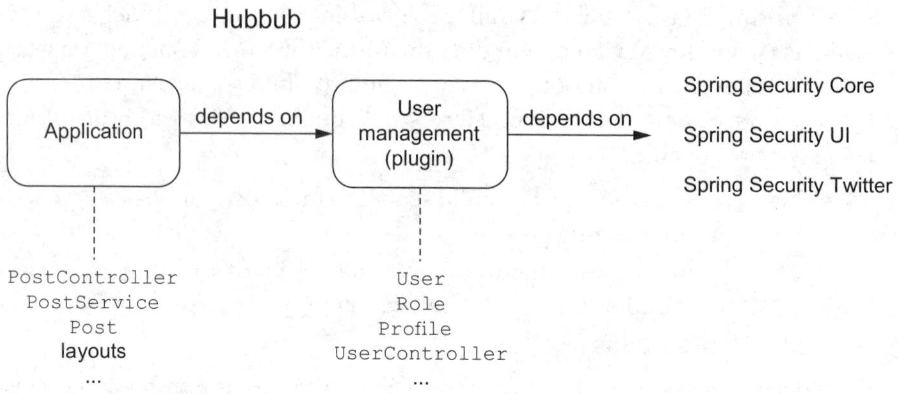

Figure 17.6 How Hubbub is split into an application and a User Management plugin

The first step in splitting up Hubbub is to create a new directory structure, with the application and plugin in a shared parent project directory. Set up the following directories:

```
hubbub
   +- user-mgmt
   +- app
```

You effectively move the current application down one level to a new app directory, so app now contains the application.properties file, the grails-app directory, and all the other files and directories that form the Grails application.

Next, to create the plugin, run this command from the hubbub directory:

```
grails create-plugin user-mgmt
```

This creates a new user-mgmt directory that should look familiar when you peek inside: it looks much like a Grails application with an additional UserMgmtGrailsPlugin.groovy file in the root. We'll look closely at that plugin descriptor in chapter 20 (an online bonus chapter), but for now move the user management classes from the application to the plugin:

```
app/grails-app/domain/com/grailsinaction/User.groovy
```

becomes

```
user-mgmt/grails-app/domain/com/grailsinaction/User.groovy
```

Here's a complete list of the files you need to move across:

- User.groovy (grails-app/domain/com/grailsinaction)
- UserRole.groovy (grails-app/domain/com/grailsinaction)
- Role.groovy (grails-app/domain/com/grailsinaction)
- Profile.groovy (grails-app/domain/com/grailsinaction)
- TwitterUser.groovy (grails-app/domain/com/grailsinaction)
- UserController.groovy (grails-app/controllers/com/grailsinaction)
- ProfileController.groovy (grails-app/controllers/com/grailsinaction)
- ImageController.groovy (grails-app/controllers/com/grailsinaction)

You can now try to build everything by running `mvn compile` in the parent directory, but this quickly demonstrates that the plugin doesn't yet compile: the `User` domain class still has references to the `Post` and `Tag` domain classes. This is typical of the tight coupling that litters monolithic applications, and it's an example of the kind of references you need to fix to move successfully to a decoupled, multiproject architecture.

Let's take a cheap and cheerful approach to solve this particular problem and create a `HubbubUser` class in the application (not the plugin) that extends `User` and has the references to the other classes:

```
package com.grailsinaction

class HubbubUser extends User {
    static hasMany = [ posts : Post, tags : Tag, following : User ]
}
```

Be sure to also remove the `hasMany` line and the `tags` and `posts` constraints from the plugin's `User` class!

It's important to be aware that inheritance introduces extra columns into the user table, so if you have existing data you have to do a database refactoring. It's better to go with a solution that doesn't affect the underlying database table, but that requires too much work for this example. You should certainly avoid such quick fixes for real applications, as they typically reintroduce coupling.

You're almost done, but if you run `mvn install` (and wait a while—it has much to do), you notice that you still have one or two problems:

1. The build complains about a missing `EnvironmentAware` class.
2. The tests may complain about a missing `persistenceInterceptor` bean (depending on the Grails version).

Nobody ever said this would be easy! The first problem results from Maven's eviction strategy. The ActiveMQ dependency has a dependency on an older version of Spring (3.0.x) than Grails uses (3.2.x) and Maven decides to evict the 3.2.x version of the spring-context JAR, leaving the 3.0.x version. Unfortunately, 3.0.x doesn't have that `EnvironmentAware` class.

The solution in this case is to add an exclusion to the ActiveMQ dependency in the POM, as shown in the following listing.

Listing 17.4 Adding an exclusion to the ActiveMQ dependency

```
<dependency>
    <groupId>org.apache.activemq</groupId>
    <artifactId>activemq-core</artifactId>
    <version>5.7.0</version>
    <scope>compile</scope>
    <exclusions>
        <exclusion>
            <groupId>org.springframework</groupId>      | Excludes spring-context JAR,
            <artifactId>spring-context</artifactId>     | ensuring Grails's version is used
        </exclusion>
```

```
    </exclusions>
</dependency>
```

The second problem relates to dependency scopes. At the moment, the Hibernate plugin, which provides the `persistenceInterceptor` bean, is included as a runtime dependency. As far as Maven is concerned, that means it's not required for the tests. This is different from the Grails approach, which puts all the runtime dependencies onto the test classpath in addition to the compile and test dependencies. The simplest solution here is to change the Hibernate plugin dependency to `compile` scope in the POM.

With the plugin project set up, you can direct your attention to the application. The changes you need to make are minimal:

- Remove the Spring Security dependencies from the app's POM.
- Add the user-mgmt plugin as a dependency.
- Adjust the POM to use a parent POM, if you have one.

Here's the POM dependency declaration:

```
<dependency>
    <groupId>com.grailsinaction</groupId>
    <artifactId>user-mgmt</artifactId>
    <version>0.1</version>
    <scope>compile</scope>
    <type>zip</type>
</dependency>
```

Now that you have the projects building, there's not much more to say about the Maven integration. As with any multiproject Maven build, you can put common information into a parent POM if you want. In the chapter source, the parent POM contains the `grails.version` property plus a couple of other shared properties.

It's also worth bearing in mind that you cannot run `grails:*` goals in the application until all its project dependencies are built and available either in the local Maven cache (via `mvn install`) or a Maven repository. Even if the goals don't need those projects to run, Maven won't let you execute them unless all the application's dependencies can be resolved, so be sure to use `mvn install` on the parent POM nice and early!

The Maven integration had many changes for the Grails 2.1 release, and the introduction of the Aether transitive dependency resolution engine has improved that integration further. It's now viable to manage your Grails projects with Maven, particularly as part of multiproject builds. As we said, that doesn't mean the rough edges are gone, but the workarounds you need are fewer than before and are feasible.

Not everyone's a fan of Maven and it certainly lacks flexibility to express nonstandard builds. That's why users are shifting to an alternative solution: Gradle. Next we look at what it takes to get a Grails project building with this relatively new tool.

17.3 Grails with Gradle

Not everyone has heard of Gradle. It's a build tool that attempts to solve many of the problems with Ant and Maven and is gaining traction in many parts of the Java universe. It's likely to become even more popular now that it's the de facto tool for building Android projects. Gradle also happens to use Groovy as the language for describing builds, which is convenient for people like us who work with Groovy and Grails.

Perhaps the most important reasons for covering Gradle integration are

- Gradle has a semiofficial plugin that allows you to build Grails projects.
- Grails 3.0 is likely to move to Gradle for its build system.

Let's start along the same path you took with Maven by first creating a Gradle build that works for the standalone application and then switching to a multiproject build with a Grails application and a plugin. You'll need to install Gradle before trying the samples from this section, so if you don't already have it, head over to http://www.gradle.org for the download and installation instructions. Alternatively, use the Groovy enVironment Manager (GVM) at http://gvmtool.net to install Gradle.

17.3.1 Building a standalone app

Every Gradle build starts with a build file: build.gradle. This file contains the description of the build as well as any custom tasks that need to be performed. For a Groovy project, the simplest build looks like this:

```
apply plugin: "groovy"

version = "1.0-SNAPSHOT"
```

Loads tasks and conventions for Groovy project

Sets project's version

Plugins are Gradle's mechanism for convention-based builds, which result in streamlined build files. In this example, as long as you put source code into the src/main/groovy directory and tests into src/test/groovy, you can compile the project, run tests, and build a JAR with no additional information.

A Grails application is different from a standard Groovy project, so it needs a special plugin: the Grails plugin for Gradle.[5] This plugin provides access to all the standard Grails commands in a consistent manner. You'll create a build file for the original standalone Hubbub application—you can use the source code for chapter 14 as a starting point.

Create a build.gradle file in the root of the project and add the content shown in this listing.

[5] Project page for the Grails Gradle plugin, https://github.com/grails/grails-gradle-plugin.

Listing 17.5 Creating a Gradle build file for Hubbub

```
buildscript {
    repositories {
        maven { url "http://repo.grails.org/grails/core" }
    }

    dependencies {
        classpath "org.grails:grails-gradle-plugin:2.0.1"
    }
}

apply plugin: "grails"

repositories {
    grails.central()
}

dependencies {
    bootstrap "org.grails.plugins:tomcat:7.0.47"
    compile "org.grails.plugins:hibernate:3.6.10.6"
    ...
    test    "org.grails.plugins:dumbster:0.2"
}

group = "com.grailsinaction"
version = "1.0-SNAPSHOT"

grails {
    grailsVersion = "2.3.7"
    groovyVersion = "2.1.9"
    springLoadedVersion = "1.1.4"
}

tasks.withType(org.grails.gradle.plugin.tasks.GrailsTask) { Task t ->
    t.jvmOptions {
        jvmArgs "-Xmx384mx", "-XX:MaxPermSize=256m"
    }
}
```

Annotations:
- Declares dependencies required to run the build.
- Specifies dependency containing Grails plugin for Gradle.
- Configures this as Grails build.
- Manually configures standard Grails repositories.
- Declares same project dependencies as BuildConfig.groovy. Plugins must include groupId.
- Tells plugin which version of Grails to use.
- Makes sure Grails build system has enough memory to run.

The list of dependencies is long, so we cut most of them out of the code in listing 17.5. You can find the complete list in the chapter source on GitHub. The key dependency for any Grails project is the Tomcat plugin, and if you're using a database, you also need the Hibernate plugin.

After this build file is in place, you can execute several core tasks:

- `init`—Creates a fresh Grails application in the current directory if one doesn't already exist
- `clean`—Removes all the generated classes and other files
- `test`—Executes all your Grails tests
- `assemble`—Packages the application as a WAR file

This seems like a limited set of tasks, and indeed it is. That's because the plugin gives you direct access to the Grails commands using a simple naming convention. Every Grails command can be executed through the following pattern:

```
gradle grails-<grailsCmd>
```

If you want to start the development server, you could run this command:

```
gradle grails-run-app
```

This even starts your application with automatic reloading enabled! You can also pass arguments through to the underlying Grails commands via a `grailsArgs` property:

```
gradle grails-create-controller -PgrailsArgs=org.example.User
```

This example creates a new `org.example.UserController` class using the standard `create-controller` command. You can access any Grails command this way, even those provided by plugins.

Still, this syntax is slightly more verbose than with the standard Grails command line, particularly if you regularly pass the same set of arguments to a given command. The most obvious example is when running the tests: you might want to regularly run the unit and integration tests together without the functional tests. The Gradle invocation for this is the command:

```
gradle grails-test-app -PgrailsArgs="unit: integration:"
```

Do this often enough and you'll get frustrated. Fortunately, Gradle allows you to create aliases for such invocations through its custom-task mechanism. Every `grails-*` task is implemented via the class `GrailsTask` (which is provided by the plugin), so you can define your own tasks using that type. Here you effectively alias the previous `test-app` command by defining a new task at the end of build.gradle:

```
task stdTest(type: org.grails.gradle.plugin.tasks.GrailsTask) {
    env = "test"
    command = "test-app"
    args = "unit: integration:"
}
```

You can then execute the custom task from the command line:

```
gradle stdTest
```

You can also incorporate these tasks into the larger build. Let's say you want to run the unit and integration tests whenever the application is packaged via the `assemble` task. All you have to do is add these lines after the `stdTest` task is declared:

```
tasks.'grails-war'.mustRunAfter stdTest
assemble.dependsOn stdTest
```

The first line ensures that the `grails-war` task executes after `stdTest` *if they both run.* The second line adds `stdTest` as a dependency of `assemble` so that whenever the latter is executed, so is the former. This is the kind of powerful technique you can use with Gradle that isn't possible with Maven.

There isn't much more to the core behavior of the plugin. You can see how to execute any Grails command via Gradle tasks and integrate those into a more complex build. Now, let's follow the path you took with Maven and demonstrate how to use Gradle with a multiproject build.

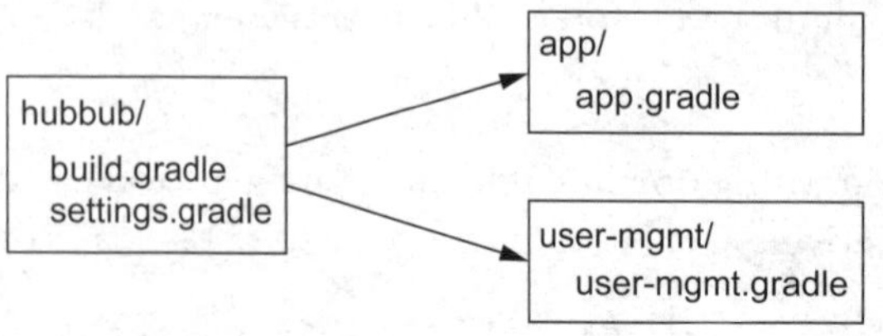

Figure 17.7 Hubbub multiproject directory structure with Gradle files

17.3.2 Building a multiproject app

In the previous section on Maven, you split Hubbub into an application and a plugin to demonstrate multiproject Maven builds. You can use that same structure for the multiproject Gradle build. Figure 17.7 shows the structure you're after, along with the relevant Gradle files.

Let's start with the parent directory and the settings.gradle file. This is where you specify what directories take part in the build. It also allows you to set the overall name of the project. Here's the code:

```
include "app", "user-mgmt"

rootProject.name = "hubbub"

for (p in rootProject.children) {
    p.buildFileName = p.name + ".gradle"
}
```

- Specifies subprojects for this build
- Sets name of parent project
- Changes build file to use for subprojects from build.gradle to <projectName>.gradle

The settings.gradle file holds configuration information about the overall build, but it doesn't describe *how* to build any of the parts. For that, you need build files. You can see in figure 17.7 that you have three build files: one for each subproject plus a parent build file. This raises the question of what that parent build file is for.

When you have a multiproject build, you often want to share information between the projects. In this case, you have two Grails projects, so you want to make sure that they both use the same version of Grails. The parent build is where you can put this shared information. It's like the parent POM in Maven.

Let's look at the parent build file, build.gradle in the root of the project, and see what we can use it for, as shown in the following listing.

Listing 17.6 Writing a top-level build.gradle

```
import org.grails.gradle.plugin.tasks.GrailsTask

buildscript {
    repositories {
        maven { url "http://repo.grails.org/grails/core" }
    }

    dependencies {
        classpath "org.grails:grails-gradle-plugin:2.0.1"
    }
}
```

- A buildscript can be defined only in root (parent) project; automatically applies to all subprojects.

```
subprojects {                                                      Applies block to all
    if (project.file("grails-app").exists()) {                     subprojects.
        apply plugin: "grails"

        repositories {                                             Conditionally applies Grails
            grails.central()                                       plugin based on existence
        }                                                          of grails-app directory.

        dependencies {
            compile "org.grails.plugins:hibernate:3.6.10.6"        All Grails projects
            runtime "org.grails.plugins:tomcat:7.0.47"             have these default
        }                                                          dependencies.

        grails {
            grailsVersion = "2.3.7"
        }

        tasks.withType(GrailsTask) { Task t ->
            t.jvmOptions {
                jvmArgs "-Xmx512m", "-XX:MaxPermSize=256m"
            }
        }
    }

    group = "com.grailsinaction"
    version = "1.0-SNAPSHOT"
}
```

It's a fairly long bit of code, but you're already familiar with most of it because the bit inside the `subprojects` block corresponds to much of the content of the standalone project's build.gradle file. Rather than duplicate the plugin declaration, repositories, dependencies, and Grails version in the build file of each individual Grails project, you can apply the same settings in one go via the root project's build.gradle. If you then add another Grails project at a later date, it also picks up these base settings, saving copying and pasting.

All that's left for the subprojects themselves, app and user-mgmt, are the dependencies. Specifying normal JAR or plugin dependencies is no different from the standalone Hubbub project. The interesting case is where you have one project depending on another, such as app depending on user-mgmt. Setting this up requires more extra work than you may expect.

The starting point is the project being depended upon—user-mgmt in your case. As things stand, Gradle doesn't know what the output of building a Grails plugin is. That means you can't use a standard Gradle project dependency. You have to tell Gradle what artifacts it produces (the packaged plugin as a ZIP file) and any transitive runtime dependencies it has. These are required to use the plugin in the main application.

Fortunately it only takes a few lines of code in the plugin's build file to set this up. The following listing goes inside the user-mgmt/user-mgmt.gradle file.

Listing 17.7 Defining artifacts and dependencies for Gradle

```
configurations {                                                   Adds runtime and
    getByName("default").extendsFrom runtime, archives             archives configurations
}                                                                  to default.
```

```
dependencies {
    bootstrap "org.grails.plugins:release:3.0.0"
    bootstrap "org.grails.plugins:rest-client-builder:2.0.0", {
        exclude module: "grails-core"
    }

    compile "org.grails.plugins:spring-security-core:2.0-RC2",
            "org.grails.plugins:spring-security-ui:1.0-RC1",
            "org.grails.plugins:spring-security-twitter:0.6.2"
}

artifacts {
    archives file("grails-user-mgmt-${version}.zip"), {
        builtBy tasks.'grails-package-plugin'
    }
}
```

Release plugin allows you to publish your plugin.

Tells Gradle what the generated artifact is, what's required to build it, and what configuration it's in.

The two key parts of the build file are the beginning and the end. When you have an inter-project dependency like this code

```
dependencies {
    compile project(":user-mgmt")
    ...
}
```

Gradle checks the configuration named default in the target project (user-mgmt) for any artifacts. This default configuration doesn't have anything in it at the beginning, so you attach the runtime and archives configurations to it. Anything in those configurations is added to the including project (app).

The last bit of the build file tells Gradle that the plugin package should be added to the archives configuration. It also tells Gradle that the artifact is built by the task `grails-package-plugin`. That's an important piece of information; otherwise when you build the project that depends on the user-mgmt plugin, how does Gradle know what to build and how to do it?

The last and simplest part of the puzzle is to set up the app project to depend on user-mgmt, which is done by adding the following line (in italics) to the dependencies in app/app.gradle:

```
dependencies {
    compile project(":user-mgmt")
    ...
}
```

you can see the rest of the application dependencies in the chapter source code on GitHub.

After all the pieces are in place, you can build any part of the project. If you try to build the application via the following:

```
gradle :app:assemble
```

You see Gradle build the User Management plugin first before packaging the application WAR—the way you want it to! This approach scales to as many subprojects as you want, typically needing only small build files per project.

The main downside to the Gradle integration is that you can't use the Grails command line interchangeably with Gradle tasks. There's no equivalent of the `pom: true` option provided by the Maven integration. That said, you have access to everything you need for building your Grails projects via Gradle, and you benefit from the stronger dependency management and multiproject support that Gradle offers over the standard Grails build system. Those features alone make Grails 3.0.0 an enticing prospect if it does eventually use Gradle natively for its build system.

17.4 Summary and best practices

Building nontrivial software is often a complex task, and we've shown you in this chapter several of the issues you need to consider. Transitive dependency resolution has made developers' lives better in that you no longer need to trawl web pages to find out what JARs you need to compile and run your application, but it introduces its own problems. You need to learn how to diagnose and resolve problems with dependency conflicts and library duplication.

It's also important to keep software manageable, which tends to argue for modularization. The Grails build system doesn't scale well for this, hence we looked at both Maven and Gradle. These tools are designed to cope with large-scale software and are worth considering even if you lose the convenience associated with the Grails build system and its interactive console.

That leaves us with a few suggestions to round off this chapter:

- *Make use of dependency reports and exclusions.* Dependency reports are your friend in terms of diagnosing class loading issues related to incorrect dependencies, and exclusions allow you to fix those problems. It's not fun, but it has to be done!
- *Use a CI server.* This is an absolute must if you have a team, otherwise the delay in discovering errors due to merging code from multiple developers costs you unnecessary development time and energy. CI also ensures that developers push code on a fairly frequent basis.

  A CI server is even beneficial for one-man-band operations because it's easy to commit code without running tests. It also ensures that your build doesn't become dependent on stuff you have lying around in various local caches.
- *Externalize sensitive or deployment-specific configuration.* Packaging configuration in with a WAR file makes it less easy to transfer that WAR to an alternative environment. It's also important to keep sensitive information out of source control.
- *Use Maven or Gradle for multiproject development.* This is a case of using the right tool for the right job. After you go beyond a single monolithic application, the Grails build system is less easy to work with.

In this chapter, we talked about topics related to deployment, and that's where we head next. But rather than talking about traditional deployments on dedicated hardware, we look at the phenomenon called the cloud.

18 Grails in the cloud

This chapter covers

- Understanding cloud platforms and their providers
- Assessing the impact cloud platforms have on your applications
- Deploying Hubbub to Cloud Foundry

One of the big questions for any web developer is where to deploy your applications. The traditional approach in the Java world is to run servlet containers on dedicated hardware. This is fine for enterprises that can invest in that up-front cost, but it's a significant investment for startups and lone developers. It's been with much envy that we've looked on the PHP world with its huge array of cheap hosting options.

Cloud platforms are changing the game, making cheap and easy hosting available to many web development communities, even Java's. It's easy to be cynical about this because the cloud has become a marketing and business buzzword, something that solves everyone's IT problems as if by magic. The truth is definitely more complex, but the underlying technologies of the cloud continue to change the way IT systems are run.

We start by explaining what the cloud is so that you have context for the rest of the chapter. And if you plan to make any decisions about whether to use a cloud platform, you should understand how it works. We then compare a few of the best-known platforms for hosting Java (and hence Grails) web applications. Finally, we explain how cloud platforms affect the way you develop your applications, because assumptions you make at the moment don't apply to the cloud.

18.1 Getting to know the cloud

The cloud is many things to many people. For the people who maintain IT infrastructure, it's a way to easily manage hardware resources and allocate them to applications and other bits of software. For consumers, it's a remote location where their music and videos are kept. For developers, it's a place to deploy applications. The cloud concept has several layers.

Understanding how these layers fit together helps you make decisions on whether to use the cloud and helps explain why the cloud places certain restrictions on the way your applications work. That's why we start by looking at what makes up the cloud.

18.1.1 What is the cloud?

You're used to physical computers. You interact with them every day to do your work, whether they're desktop computers or laptops. Your computer has a CPU, memory, a hard drive or flash drive for storage, and miscellaneous bits and pieces. You boot it up, and it has applications and files on it. This isn't the cloud. But physical computers are still the foundation of the cloud because computer software needs CPUs, memory, and storage.

To understand what cloud computing is, we go back several years when VMware Inc. introduced the world to *virtualization*: the idea that you could run a complete OS with its own applications, networking, and storage (the guest OS) within another OS that has direct access to the hardware (the host). In effect, virtualization software broke the link between the OS and the physical computer such that it was no longer a one-to-one mapping. You can see an example configuration in figure 18.1 where the host OS has two guest OSes running inside it.

Each guest OS runs in a VM that abstracts away the physical hardware and allows you to move or copy the OS from computer to computer. The VM contains all the installed software and can even save the memory state at the point the VM is suspended. Suddenly you can run a server anywhere and on any hardware (as long as the hardware supports the VM).

This led to the first stage of cloud computing: infrastructure as a service (IaaS).

IAAS CONCEPTS

In the IaaS world, you never access the hardware directly. Instead, you set up VMs and let the IaaS run them. It's up to the IaaS to determine which bits of hardware a VM uses. It's similar to the way Java applications run; you package your application as a

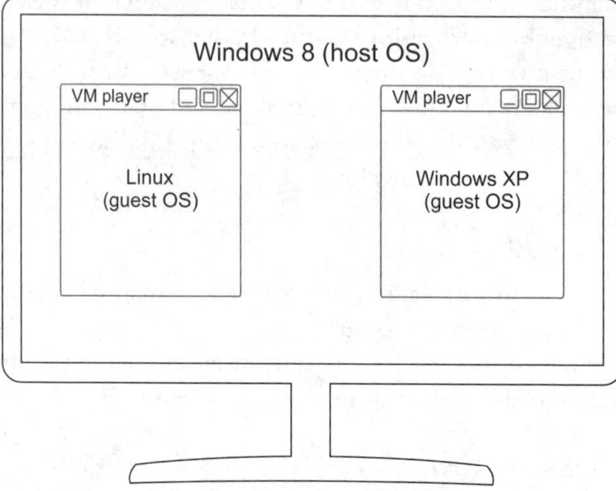

Figure 18.1 The origins of virtualization with two guest OSes running on a single host OS

JAR and then let the JVM run it on the host OS and hardware—the VM corresponds to the JAR and the IaaS corresponds to the JVM.

You can have as many instances of a VM running as you want. The IaaS provider manages the physical hardware and typically runs special software to host your VMs. That software ensures that your VMs have access to the CPU power, memory, and disk space that they need. Figure 18.2 gives you the basic structure of an IaaS setup.

You have several options for hosting if you don't mind configuring VMs, installing the software you need on them, and then deploying your application.

IAAS PROVIDERS

The best-known IaaS provider is Amazon through its Amazon Web Services (AWS), but it's not the only public provider: Microsoft has its Azure cloud and Google has Compute Engine.

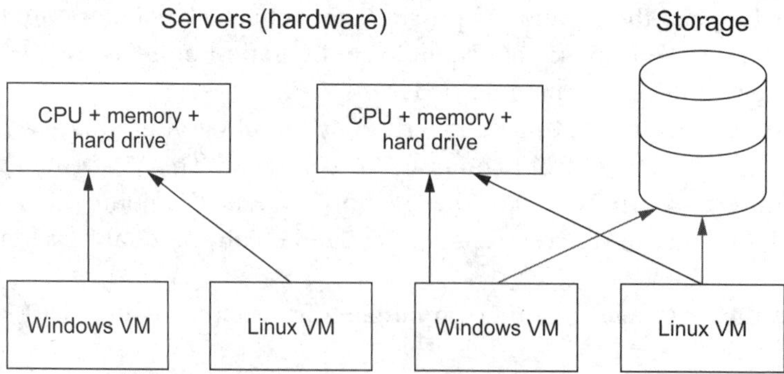

Figure 18.2 How IaaS works

AWS is where companies such as Netflix and Spotify run their back-end services. It's split into several services; the main ones are shown in figure 18.3.

The big benefit of an IaaS is that you don't buy any hardware (a capital cost) either up-front or as the demand on your application grows. Nor do you have to manage that hardware.

Another significant benefit of an IaaS is that you can readily scale your application as the load on it changes—if you design your application for that. Imagine that your company starts a new marketing campaign that results in a big spike in traffic (the dream of every marketer). To handle the load, you can increase the number of VMs running your application and spread the load across them. If and when the traffic drops again, you can reduce the number of VMs. This is a cost-efficient way to handle variable traffic.

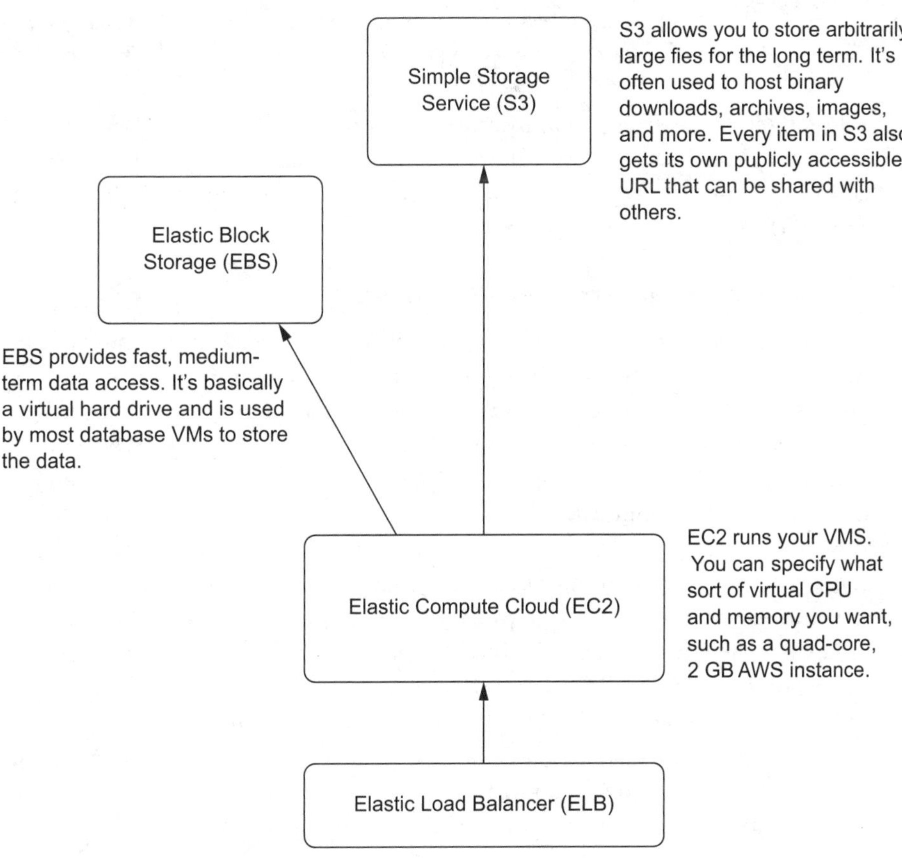

Figure 18.3 The core services provided by AWS

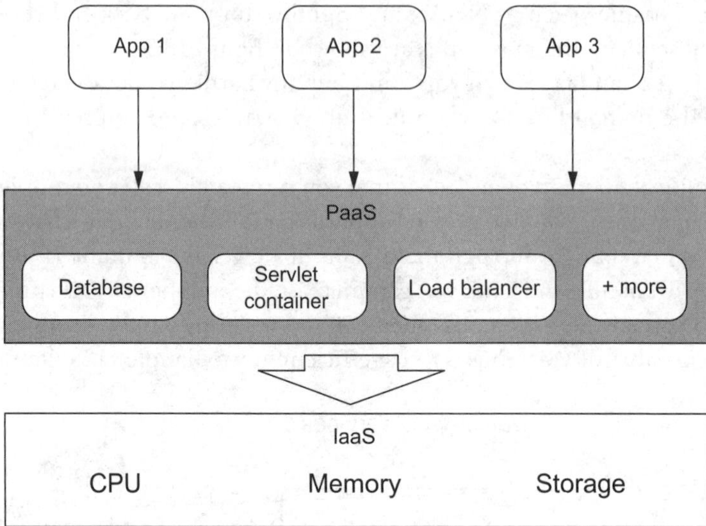

Figure 18.4 The basics of PaaS

Yet many software houses don't want to manage even that much. Wouldn't it be better if you could one-click deploy a new application? That's what the second stage of cloud computing promises via a new breed of cloud implementations dubbed platform as a service (PaaS).

18.1.2 The new kids on the block—PaaS providers

Where IaaS abstracts away the hardware infrastructure, PaaS abstracts away the software infrastructure. You don't need to worry about setting up runtimes, servlet containers, or databases. Instead, you specify what type of application you want to run (a servlet-based one or perhaps a Ruby web application) and the services you need (such as a database or a message broker). Figure 18.4 shows how a PaaS fits between an IaaS provider and your applications.

It's these PaaS systems that we focus on for the rest of the chapter because they're the growth area at the moment and the most appealing platforms for application hosting due to the simplicity of deployment. Enterprises are even evaluating such platforms for their own internal hosting to simplify IT infrastructure management and make it easier and quicker to deploy applications. We start with a quick look at several of the more popular public providers and discuss their unique selling points.

PaaS is still in its early phases, and yet many public clouds are available for your use. Which one should you go with? At the time of writing, this space has no hard and fast winners. Instead, you should consider several factors:

- *Can you run your application on a given cloud platform?*—Your application may have special requirements, be it specific data stores or the need to have a persistent filesystem. Such requirements often affect which cloud platforms you can use or even if you can use one at all. We discuss filesystems and other restrictions in the last section of this chapter. It's also worth bearing in mind that certain cloud platforms may not even support Java.

- *Where will your applications run?*—Data privacy concerns and other issues influence where companies are willing to host their software. In particular, many companies and institutions are concerned about hosting in the US. Another potential consideration is where the majority of your users are. If they're in Europe, hosting an application on the US West Coast may result in latency that adversely affects the user experience.
- *Are you stuck with the provider you initially pick?*—One promise of the cloud should be that you can move your applications between providers easily. Currently, that's far from the case. It's easy (and sometimes required) to use services specific to a particular provider. But as soon as you do, you tie yourself to that provider unless you perform major work on your application. And no one wants to waste valuable engineering time on that.
- *How much will it cost?*—Almost every cloud provider charges differently. In addition to pricing levels, a provider may charge for number of CPUs, CPU usage, memory usage, and so on. This can make it difficult to compare providers based on price only. Running costs can be high, so it's worth investing time trying to work out your needs and how much it's going to cost.

Let's look at a few of the contenders.

GOOGLE APP ENGINE

App Engine was one of the first publicly available PaaS systems. Originally it only allowed you to host Python-based applications on Google's servers, but Java support was added. It's a proven system that scales well. The downside is the number of restrictions on your application:

- Some JDK classes are unavailable.[1]
- You can't write to files on the local filesystem; in effect you have no local filesystem.
- Several APIs are unsupported, including pure JDBC, JMS, and JNDI.[2]

In addition to restrictions, the platform is sticky because it provides its own APIs for such things as an image service, task queues (for background jobs), and full-text search. We've heard recommendations that you also use the native API for BigTable (Google's data store) instead of JPA or JDO. The mismatch between the relational model of the latter and BigTable's column model results in extra pain for you.

On the positive side, all the restrictions make it much more likely that your application will scale if and when necessary. Google's core services are good, too. The search and image services could well be worth the cost of vendor lock-in and the loss

---

1 See Google's whitelist of usable classes, https://developers.google.com/appengine/docs/java/jrewhitelist.

2 For a list of the level of compatibility of Java technologies and App Engine, see https://code.google.com/p/googleappengine/wiki/WillItPlayInJava.

of GORM, JMS, and so on. It's also worth bearing in mind that the platform finally supports a relational database offering: Cloud SQL based on MySQL.

CloudBees

Whereas the other platforms we talk about offer application hosting only, CloudBees provides much more. If you want, CloudBees can host your source code and build it on its CI servers (based on Jenkins) before deploying your application to its cloud. It's Java-only at the moment, although there appears to be experimental Node.js support. The Java focus is good for Grails developers, though.

Beyond deployment of WAR files, CloudBees also offers several essential services:

- *MySQL*—The only relational database available at the time of writing
- *SendGrid*—Sending email
- *Solr*—Full-text indexing and search
- *RabbitMQ*—(Non-JMS) message broker

This list is likely to change, but it gives you an idea of what's available. Many of these services are provided by third parties.

Almost uniquely among PaaS systems, CloudBees also supports sticky sessions. Once a user starts an HTTP session on a particular application instance, they always hit that instance. This makes life simpler if your application or one of its libraries uses the session. Be aware that it can scale badly if you have many concurrent users.

CloudBees's public cloud currently runs on AWS—although only in the North American and EU regions. Your application can also access any other services on AWS, not only those provided through CloudBees's service integration. That opens up other options. You can also run your own CloudBees instances as a private PaaS, either on OpenStack or HP's cloud services infrastructure.

Heroku

Heroku started life as a cloud solution for Ruby-based web applications. It has now evolved into a general-purpose cloud platform that supports many different languages, runtimes, and frameworks. It runs exclusively on AWS and uses Git for deployment. The idea is that you push your source code to Heroku and the platform then builds and deploys your application based on its type. If your application has special build requirements, then you can develop a buildpack for it. The basic mechanics are shown in figure 18.5.

This reliance on Git and command-line-based tools may put off those with a Windows background. Otherwise, it's a flexible and easy-to-use hosting solution with big-money backing (Salesforce). It also has one of the largest selections of services to choose from through the Heroku marketplace, not to mention that you can use any service on AWS.

Cloud Foundry

The last of the PaaS offerings we look at is an open source product. Originally created within VMware, Cloud Foundry is now primarily developed by EMC-VMware spinoff Pivotal and, like Heroku, constitutes a multilanguage and multiframework PaaS. The

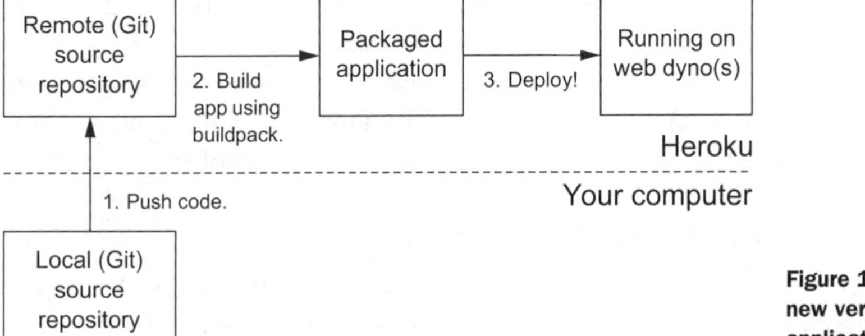

Figure 18.5 Deploying new versions of an application to Heroku

key difference is that anyone can run their own Cloud Foundry PaaS instance from their own data center.

Pivotal is one of several public providers that runs your applications on AWS or elsewhere. And no matter the provider, you use the same tools. Cloud Foundry also uses the same system of buildpacks as Heroku, which allows you to use frameworks that aren't supported by the core system.

One thing to be aware of is that Cloud Foundry has two distinct versions in the wild: version 1 and version 2. Each has its own tools for deployment and the versions are incompatible. Moving from a version 1 instance to a version 2 instance, even if it's the same provider, means redeploying your application to the new system and potentially migrating any data you have. We definitely recommend using a version 2 (or greater) provider.

As we mentioned, these aren't the only PaaS providers out there, and many of the differences between them are marginal (Google App Engine stands out as an exception to this). It's also important to recognize that this is a rapidly changing field, so anything we say here is likely to be out of date fairly quickly. That makes choosing a provider difficult, particularly if you're not familiar with PaaS systems in general. Remember to ask yourself these key questions:

- Can you run your application with the prospective cloud provider?
- Where (geographically) will your application run?
- Are you stuck with the provider once you pick it?
- How much will it cost?

Your answers may even lead you to go with an IaaS provider so you have more control over the software infrastructure for your project.

What's it like using one of these platforms? In the next section, we focus on deploying Hubbub to a PaaS to see what's involved with the deployment process and what changes you have to make to the application so that it works effectively in the cloud.

18.2 Running in the cloud

Before you can deploy Hubbub to a PaaS and run the application in the cloud, you first need to choose a provider. That means looking at Hubbub's requirements to see which PaaS is the best fit. Next, you should assess the application to identify any changes you need to make so it can run in the PaaS.

No hard and fast rules exist for these two steps because every application is different. Using Hubbub as an example, we'll cover many of the common cases you're likely to encounter and walk you through the thought process involved.

18.2.1 Choosing a cloud provider and assessing Hubbub

We demonstrate many Grails features in the book, and this makes Hubbub a moderately complex application. Putting the application in the cloud affects many of those features in one way or another. Several of these are handled perfectly well by all the cloud providers:

- *GORM/Hibernate*—How do you wire up the application to a cloud database?

  All of the cloud platforms we mentioned provide one or more relational databases to choose from.
- *Mail*—Can you use SMTP to send emails, as you're already doing?

  All the platforms allow you to send email via SMTP, usually through a service such as SendGrid (Google App Engine and AWS have their own email sending services).
- *Quartz*—How do you ensure that the daily digest job only runs once, no matter how many application instances you have?

  To ensure that each job is only ever executed by one application instance, the Quartz plugin needs a relational database in which to persist its jobs. This feature is already configured in Hubbub, and because Quartz uses whichever database is configured for GORM, you need only wire up the relational database provided by the cloud platform.
- *Events*—Should an event in one application instance propagate to others?

  It depends on the event, but if an event results in an update of the *internal state* of the application, you want it propagated. That requires something such as an external message broker or some other service that receives and sends messages, such as Redis. All the platforms have at least one of these options.

Other features require more thought:

- *Caching*—You want the cache shared among all application instances, but distributed Ehcache requires multicast, which isn't available on cloud platforms.

  No cloud provider supports Ehcache out of the box, so you need a substitute that works in a distributed way.
- *Spring Security*—The library in itself isn't an issue, but it does rely on HTTP session support. If you want more than one application instance for Hubbub, you need either session affinity (sticky sessions) or distributed sessions.

  Only two of the providers provide an out-of-the-box solution.

- *JMS*—You need a message broker to forward your messages, preferably one that supports the JMS API.

  JMS is a problem because none of the providers offer a JMS-compliant message broker.

Table 18.1 summarizes the potential solutions to these conundrums.

Table 18.1 Cloud provider support by feature

Feature	App Engine	CloudBees	Heroku	Cloud Foundry
Caching	Custom caching service; use JCache API	Use AWS caching service	Redis with official Cache plugin implementation	Redis with official Cache plugin implementation
HTTP sessions	N/A	Sticky sessions	N/A	Sticky sessions
JMS	N/A	CloudAMQP with RabbitMQ plugin	CloudAMQP with RabbitMQ plugin	CloudAMQP with RabbitMQ plugin

Both Redis and Memcached are fast key-value stores that can be used with the Grails Cache plugin. The main difference from the Grails integration perspective is that the Redis plugin is supported by Pivotal. The Memcached plugin is community-contributed and therefore riskier to use.

On the HTTP sessions front, it's definitely best to use any built-in support that a cloud platform provides. For platforms that don't have such support, you could instead use the Grails Database Session plugin. It can be used on any platform that has a relational database and effectively provides a distributed HTTP session for your application. The big questions are how well does it work, and how well is it maintained?

As you can see in table 18.1, it looks like you have to switch from JMS for messaging. Fortunately, RabbitMQ (which CloudAMQP is based on) does everything you need, and the corresponding plugin works in a similar fashion to the JMS one. As we mentioned earlier, a cloud message broker also helps with propagating your events between different application instances.

Cloud Foundry stands out as having everything you need without much extra work. For the rest of the chapter, you're going to rework Hubbub to run on Cloud Foundry and use it as your demonstration platform. Please note that you must consider many factors when choosing a cloud provider, and each has its pros and cons. You should always perform your own analysis.

18.2.2 Getting familiar with the platform

Before you update Hubbub and deploy it to Cloud Foundry, let's work with something simple to get familiar with the platform's tools and deployment mechanism. The Quote of the Day application from chapter 1 is ideal as the only external service it requires is a relational database.

Start by editing the content of the QOTD home page (grails-app/views/index.gsp) as shown in the following listing. We'll explain the reasons for the changes later in this section.

Listing 18.1 Changing the QOTD home page

```
<!DOCTYPE html>
<html>
  <head>
    <meta name="layout" content="main"/>
    <title>Environment information</title>
    <style>pre { white-space: pre-wrap; }</style>        <-- Wraps text in <pre> blocks
  </head>
  <body>
    <h2><g:link controller="quote" action="random">Main App</g:link></h2>
    <h2>Environment variables</h2>
    <h3>VCAP_APPLICATION</h3>
    <pre>${System.getenv("VCAP_APPLICATION")}</pre>
    <h3>VCAP_SERVICES</h3>
    <pre>${System.getenv("VCAP_SERVICES")}</pre>
    <h3>VCAP_APP_HOST</h3>
    <pre>${System.getenv("VCAP_APP_HOST")}</pre>
    <h3>VCAP_APP_PORT</h3>
    <pre>${System.getenv("VCAP_APP_PORT")}</pre>
  </body>
</html>
```

Displays contents of several environment variables

Next, you need to make sure your quotes get persisted to a database. You may think of sticking with the file-based H2 that QOTD is already configured for. That's a bad idea. To understand why, think about where the data is stored. In the case of a file-based H2, it's on the local filesystem, which works fine on dedicated hardware. The problem with cloud-based systems is that the local filesystem is *ephemeral*, and as such it doesn't have a guaranteed lifetime. As an example of this, the filesystem is typically reset every time you restart the application. When that happens, you lose any data on it.

The solution is to use a database service provided by the cloud platform. Let's use a PostgreSQL service on Cloud Foundry. All you need to do is add the PostgreSQL JDBC driver to the application, so open the BuildConfig.groovy for QOTD and add this dependency:

```
dependencies {
    ...
    runtime "org.postgresql:postgresql:9.2-1003-jdbc4"     <-- Adds PostgreSQL database driver
}
```

At this point you should ask yourself why you're not updating the data source configuration. How's the application going to connect to the database otherwise? Cloud Foundry is unique among cloud platforms in that it understands certain libraries and frameworks enough that it can automatically configure them. In the case of Spring-based applications (which Grails apps are), Cloud Foundry looks for a bean of type `javax.sql.DataSource` and sets its properties based on whichever relational database is bound to the application.

The end result is that you can deploy your Grails application, bind a database service to it, and run it. Your application uses that database automatically as if by magic.

Believe it or not, the application is now ready for deployment to the cloud! All you need is access to Cloud Foundry-based hosting, which may be a public provider such as Pivotal or your company's own Cloud Foundry instance. We went through the Pivotal registration process (https://console.run.pivotal.io/register), but Pivotal isn't the only public provider. Try a web search for "cloud foundry hosting." Whoever you register with, be sure to note your username and password because you need them to deploy applications.

> **Cloud Foundry versions 1 and 2**
> Cloud Foundry has two distinct versions of its code base: version 1 and version 2. A Cloud Foundry provider can implement one or the other, but not both. Always check which version a prospective provider uses as it affects the way applications are deployed. It's best to stick with version 2 implementations if you can.

Once you create an account, you're ready to deploy the application. The normal way to deploy applications to Cloud Foundry is via a command-line tool: `cf`[3]. Once the tool is installed, run this sequence of commands in the root directory of your Grails application:

```
cf login -a <API URL>
grails war
cf push <app name> -p target/<WAR name> -m 650M
```

The URL you specify for the `login` command depends on what provider you're using. For Pivotal, this is api.run.pivotal.io. The application name is anything you want, so long as it's unique within your account. It makes sense for this value to match the name in application.properties, but it doesn't have to. And there you have it: a (hopefully) successful deployment to a Cloud Foundry instance. If a deployment isn't successful, try these commands:

- `cf logs <app name>`—Displays the startup logs for your application
- `cf events <app name>`—Reports significant events that occur during the startup and running of your application
- `cf files <app name> app/.tomcat/logs/stacktrace.log`—Prints the application's stacktrace.log file, which may include exceptions that don't make it into the application's startup log

---

[3] You can find instructions on how to install it in the Cloud Foundry docs at http://docs.cloudfoundry.org/devguide/installcf/install-go-cli.html.

Common deployment issues include too little memory allocated for the application and failed configuration of the services the application needs. In the sequence of commands, you specify that the application should be started with 650 MB of memory, which is enough for the QOTD application. If you encounter issues, be sure to verify that the application runs locally before attempting to fix it on the cloud. It's much easier to solve issues with a locally running application!

Now that the application is running, let's look at the home page. Previously, you modified it to display environment variables. Here are those variables with some example partial and full values highlighting the most interesting pieces of information:

- *VCAP_APPLICATION*

  ```
  {...,"host":"0.0.0.0","port":61371, ...,
   "limits":{"mem":768,"disk":1024,"fds":16384},
   ...,"application_name":"qotd",...}
  ```

- *VCAP_SERVICES*

  ```
  {"elephantsql-n/a":[{"name":"elephantsql-51d59",
   "label":"elephantsql-n/a","tags":["postgres","postgresql","relational"],
   "plan":"turtle","credentials":{"uri":"postgres://..."}}]}
  ```

- *VCAP_APP_HOST*

  ```
  0.0.0.0
  ```

- *VCAP_APP_PORT*

  ```
  61371
  ```

The first two have a high density of data, but don't worry about trying to understand all the information. The key point is that this is how Cloud Foundry tells the application to connect to the services that are bound to it and what port the application runs on. You didn't have to interpret this information yourself because Cloud Foundry managed the configuration of your application.

All the cloud platforms use either environment variables or Java system properties to pass in the service connection information. Cloud Foundry gives you the information as a JSON string. Other platforms use multiple environment variables or system properties, making the data more accessible. Whichever platform you're on, you can easily use this information to configure data sources and other data connections. Imagine Cloud Foundry didn't automatically configure your data source. To do it manually, you could update your production connection settings in `DataSource.groovy` as shown in the following listing.

Listing 18.2 Updating production connection settings

```
production {
    dataSource {
        dbCreate = null

        def jsonReader = new groovy.json.JsonSlurper()
        def serviceData =
                jsonReader.parseText(System.getenv("VCAP_SERVICES"))
```

Parses VCAP_SERVICES as JSON

```
        driverClassName = "org.postgresql.Driver"
        url = "jdbc:" +
                serviceData.'elephantsql-n/a'[0].credentials.uri
        ...
    }
}
```

Pulls PostgreSQL connection URL from parsed JSON

Remember that the configuration files ending in .groovy are ultimately code, so you can read environment variables and system properties directly within them. It's a powerful feature! And it's typically the approach you use on cloud platforms that don't support auto-reconfiguration of Spring beans.

Configuring other data stores

You can treat nonrelational data stores the same way you do relational databases. Cloud Foundry can automatically configure Redis and MongoDB if you use the corresponding plugins. For other data stores, you should parse the information in the VCAP_SERVICES environment variable to get the relevant connection settings. The Cloud Foundry docs for Ruby & Node.js give useful examples.

With that familiarization exercise out of the way, let's get on with adapting Hubbub for the cloud. You need to set up caching, email, and messaging with RabbitMQ. As for the other considerations we mentioned previously, the relational database is set up in the same way as the QOTD app, and the session affinity is taken care of by the platform. In other words, Spring Security will work.

18.2.3 Adding cache support

When you cache data, you want to make sure it's consistent. This is usually done by automatically clearing a cache when the application updates the corresponding data—you saw this in action with the `@CacheEvict` annotation in chapter 10. The trouble is that each update happens only on one application instance, so the other instances don't see the changes. If each app instance has its own cache, those caches get out of sync, as shown in figure 18.6. Note that this problem isn't unique to the cloud and affects any setup with clustered instances of an application.

This problem has two main solutions:

- Use a distributed cache
- Use events to ensure that every update is propagated to every app instance

You currently use an in-memory Ehcache implementation for Hubbub, but we mentioned previously that the distributed version doesn't work in the cloud due to the lack of multicast support. You have an event bus, so you could theoretically synchronize in-memory caches in each application instance via events. The downside is that it requires you to effectively move Hubbub to an event-based architecture. That's not a bad plan, but it takes more work than the solution we suggest: Redis as a cache.

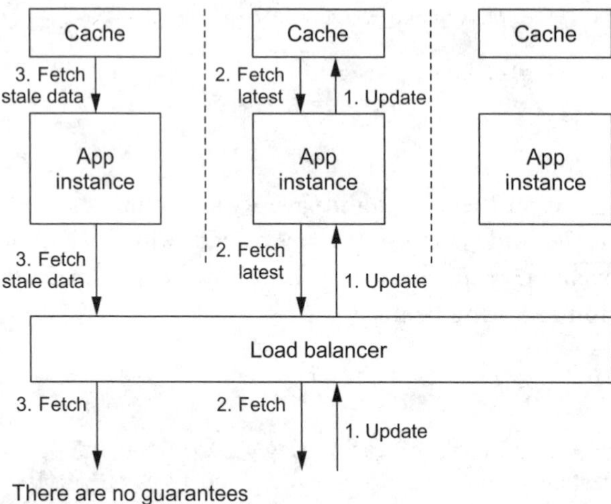

Figure 18.6 The trouble with clustered application instances and caching

As you saw in chapter 16, Redis is a fast key-value store. It also has TTL support, which means that its keys can expire. These attributes make it a great candidate for caching data. Hence there's a Redis implementation of the standard Grails Cache plugin you saw in chapter 10. Thankfully, Cloud Foundry has a Redis service that you can use.

How do you set up Redis as the cache provider? Easy! Add this dependency to the plugins section of BuildConfig.groovy:

```
plugins {
    ...
    runtime ":cache-redis:1.0.0"
}
```

Because you haven't fine-tuned the Ehcache configuration, it's literally a drop-in replacement. When you deploy the application to Cloud Foundry, the plugin is automatically reconfigured to use the bound Redis service. If auto-reconfiguration isn't available (for example, if you're using a different cloud provider), you can configure the Redis connection settings in Config.groovy:

```
grails {
    cache {
        redis {
            database = 0
            hostName = "localhost"
            port = 6379
        }
    }
}
```

Values should be extracted from relevant system properties/ environment variables

That's all it takes. You can now tackle the question of how to send emails when the application is in the cloud.

18.2.4 Sending emails

You currently use the Mail plugin to send emails. Under the hood, this uses the standard JavaMail API with SMTP to do the work. Fortunately, most cloud platforms have SMTP access to a mail service, either through a third-party (such as SendGrid) or through its own (such as Google App Engine). All you need to do is configure the Mail plugin appropriately.

In the case of Cloud Foundry, you bind an instance of the SendGrid service to the application and pull the connection details out of the `VCAP_SERVICES` environment variable. The basic JSON content describing the service is on the Cloud Foundry website[4] and looks like the following listing.

Listing 18.3 Configuring the Mail plugin

```
{ sendgrid-n/a: [
  { name: "mysendgrid",
    label: "sendgrid-n/a",
    plan: "free",
    credentials: {
      hostname: "smtp.sendgrid.net",
      username: "QvsXMbJ3rK",
      password: "HCHMOYluTv"
    }
  }
]}
```

You parse this in Config.groovy and extract the credentials information in the following listing. The code is standalone and can go anywhere in Config.groovy as long as it's not nested in any other configuration settings.

Listing 18.4 Extracting mail credentials

```
...
def vcapServices = System.getenv("VCAP_SERVICES")
if (vcapServices) {
    def servicesData =
            new groovy.json.JsonBuilder().parseText(vcapServices)
    def sendGridCreds = servicesData.'sendgrid-n/a'[0].credentials

    grails.mail.host = sendGridCreds.hostname
    grails.mail.port = 587
    grails.mail.username = sendGridCreds.username
    grails.mail.password = sendGridCreds.password
}
else {
    grails.mail.host = "127.0.0.1"
}

grails.mail.default.from = "hubbub@grailsinaction.com"
...
```

Only configures for CF if VCAP_SERVICES exists.

Extracts mail server credentials from JSON.

SendGrid service uses port 587.

[4] JSON configuration format for SendGrid: http://docs.run.pivotal.io/marketplace/services/sendgrid.html.

When the application is deployed to Cloud Foundry, it automatically uses the bound SendGrid service to send emails. There's nothing more to do.

Next, let's tackle the biggest job in this whole process of putting Hubbub into the cloud: refactoring the application to use RabbitMQ instead of JMS for messaging.

18.2.5 Messaging in the cloud with RabbitMQ

Changing the API you use to do something, particularly in a mature application, is never to be undertaken lightly. In the case of Hubbub, you can either do that or try to use the JMS API with a message broker that doesn't properly support it. An example of the latter is AWS Simple Queue Service (SQS). Both approaches have their problems, but the refactoring for RabbitMQ shouldn't be too hard due to the similarities in the Grails APIs between JMS and RabbitMQ. The main downside of this approach is that RabbitMQ doesn't have an embedded version you can use. You have to install it separately. We won't go into the details here as the RabbitMQ web site has good installation instructions for all the common platforms. Once it's installed and running, you need to configure your application to use the message broker.

CONFIGURING RABBITMQ

Before you can configure your application to use RabbitMQ, you first need to add the following plugin dependency:

```
plugins {
    ...
    compile ":rabbitmq:1.0.0"
}
```

Next, you specify the connection settings for the broker. You did this for JMS by adding a bean definition to the resources.groovy file. That's not necessary for RabbitMQ. Instead, you put the settings in Config.groovy:

```
rabbitmq {
    connectionfactory {
        username = "guest"
        password = "guest"
        hostname = "localhost"
    }
}
```

These are the typical settings for a locally installed RabbitMQ server, but what about the Cloud Foundry connection settings? As you may have guessed, you don't need to do anything here because Cloud Foundry automatically reconfigures the plugin to use the bound RabbitMQ service at runtime.

REFACTORING THE MESSAGING SERVICES

The next step in the migration from JMS is to update the Grails services that send and respond to messages. In the main Hubbub application, that means `JabberService`, as shown in the following listing.

Listing 18.5 Updating `JabberService` to use RabbitMQ

```
package com.grailsinaction

class JabberService {
    static rabbitQueue = "jabberInQ"

    static sendQueue = "jabberOutQ"

    void handleMessage(msg) {
        log.debug "Got Incoming Jabber Response from: ${msg.jabberId}"
        try {
            def profile = Profile.findByJabberAddress(msg.jabberId)
            if (profile) {
                profile.user.addToPosts(new Post(content: msg.content))
            }
        }
        catch (t) {
            log.error "Error adding post for ${msg.jabberId}", t
        }
    }

    void sendMessage(post, jabberIds) {
        log.debug "Sending jabber message for ${post.user.userId}..."
        def msg = [ userId: post.user.userId,
                    content: post.content,
                    to: jabberIds.join(",") ]
        rabbitSend(sendQueue, msg)
    }
}
```

Specifies which queue to pull messages off (replaces destination property).

Executes when message received (replaces `onMessage()`).

Sends message to given queue. `rabbitSend()` is available in all Grails artifacts.

One thing to bear in mind is what other apps are processing the messages. Currently, the code is serializing maps in a Java-specific way. If you need to work with non-Java apps, you should consider passing the messages around in JSON, XML, or some other standard text-based format.

Updating GatewayService

You need to update `GatewayService` in the jabber-gateway application the same way you updated `JabberService`. We leave that as an exercise for you to do on your own. Alternatively, you can see the necessary changes in the chapter source code on GitHub.

With these changes in place, you can deploy the two applications (Hubbub and Jabber Gateway) to Cloud Foundry and bind the same instance of a CloudAMQP service to both of them. That service routes the messages between the apps.

RabbitMQ is also a good solution if you want to propagate events between application instances. You don't need to do it for Hubbub, but it wouldn't be difficult to convert events to JSON messages, which are then converted back into the events in the receiving application instances.

We do think that RabbitMQ is a solid alternative to JMS for messaging. The underlying model of exchanges and queues is different from JMS (which is based on queues and topics), but it's more flexible. The plugin also makes queue- and topic-style messaging straightforward, as you saw. If you're thinking of deploying to the cloud, consider using RabbitMQ right from the start because it saves any potential issues with a migration later on.

18.2.6 Other features to consider

You implemented the library and service-specific changes that you need, but that's not the end of the story. Consider these conundrums:

- How do you make the Twitter credentials available to the application so users can log in via Twitter? The same goes for Jabber settings.
- How do you get existing data into and out of the cloud database?

You need answers to these questions before you can safely deploy Hubbub to the cloud.

WORKING WITH A SENSITIVE CONFIGURATION

Credentials can be packaged into the WAR file, but that generally means putting them into Config.groovy, which should go into source control. That's far from ideal, and you solved this problem in chapter 11 by putting the settings into an external configuration file that you can place directly on the server. That's not possible with the cloud because you don't have access to the filesystem. And as we mentioned previously, the filesystem can effectively be reset at any time. You need an alternative solution.

You could put an external configuration file in one of the data stores you bind to the application. While certainly viable, we prefer consistency with the rest of the platform: let's inject the connection settings as a JSON string in an environment variable! This works even if the application has no data store bound to it.

Both the Twitter and Jabber credentials have associated config settings, so it's nice to use those setting names in JSON as well. Your goal is to inject JSON, similar to what's shown in the following listing, into the runtime configuration of the application.

Listing 18.6 Example JSON to inject into the runtime configuration

```
{ grails: {
    plugins: {
      springsecurity: {
        twitter: {
          app: {
            key: "Hubbub",
            consumerKey: "bd782bsdfj249tuni2ng",
            consumerSecret: "wefnin42048hgnirgn30g8hnerglsh943"
          }
        }
      }
    }
  },
```

Equates to grails.plugins.springsecurity.twitter.app.key in Config.groovy

```
  chat: {
    serviceName: "gmail.com",
    host: "talk.google.com",
    port: 5222,
    username: "your.email@gmail.com",
    password: "your.password"
  }
}
```

Equates to chat.serviceName in Config.groovy

We'll now show you a trick that loads the JSON string from an environment variable and merges the data into the main application configuration. You treat the JSON string as another source of external configuration, like the hubbub-config.groovy file currently in the root of the project. This trick may look scary, but you don't need to understand how it works at this point. As your understanding of Groovy deepens, you'll eventually understand what's happening. Add these lines to the end of Config.groovy:

```
ConfigLoader.addEntries(loadJson(fetchJson()), this)

def fetchJson() { return System.getenv("GRAILS_APP_CONFIG") }
def loadJson(content) {
    return content ? grails.converters.JSON.parse(content) : [:]
}
```

Merges JSON into app's runtime configuration

Parses JSON string into nested maps and lists

Next, create the file grails-app/util/ConfigLoader.groovy and set its contents to the following:

```
class ConfigLoader {

    static void addEntries(Map data, obj = null) {
        data?.each { key, value ->
            if (value instanceof Map) {
                addEntries(value, obj.getProperty(key))
            }
            else obj.setProperty(key, value)
        }
    }
}
```

Sets property value on app's config object

Note that this class is deliberately not in a package to eliminate having to import it in Config.groovy, where it's used.

With this trick in place, you can put any configuration you like into the JSON string and it's merged into the application's runtime configuration. You can also use this technique to override settings that are already in Config.groovy.

You need to provide the JSON configuration as an environment variable, but how you do this depends on the cloud platform you use. In the case of Cloud Foundry, you can use the `set-env` command:

```
cf set-env qotd GRAILS_APP_CONFIG '...'
```

The tricky bit is getting the JSON content into a form that you can put on the command line. We usually opt for writing that content into a text file in its pretty form (across multiple lines with indenting), and then join all the lines together. We then copy the resulting single line of text and paste it into the command line. It's not the prettiest approach, but works fairly well.

IMPORTING AND EXPORTING DATA

The other conundrum we mentioned was how to get data into and out of data stores. Again, how you do this depends on what cloud platform you use. Certain platforms have nice web UIs for importing and exporting data. Others give you access to the data store itself. Cloud Foundry falls into the latter category and allows you to access any service using the tools you want.

The first step in accessing a service is to get its public URL. To do this, go to the Cloud Foundry web console and click the Manage link of the service you want to access (see figure 18.7). In the case of PostgreSQL, this loads a page showing the URL of every PostgreSQL service you have in your account.

Once you have the connection URL, you can use it directly in any PostgreSQL tool. To export the data from the database, run

```
pg_dump --no-owner postgres://... > data.sql
```

where the shortened argument is the URL.

To import data, run this command:

```
psql postgres://... < data.sql
```

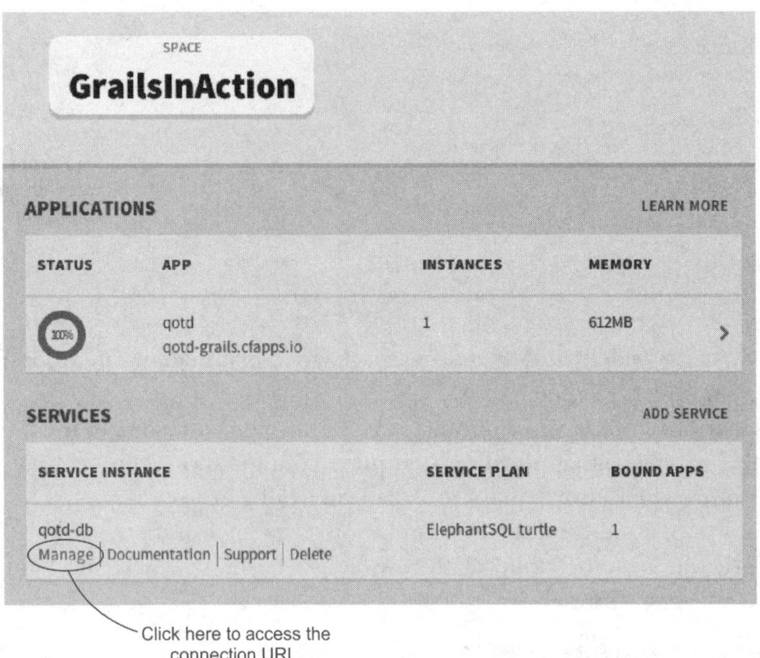

Figure 18.7 How to access the connection URL from the Cloud Foundry web console

You can also use this URL with the database migration plugin by configuring the application's production data source with the remote URL and running the update commands manually. As a result, you don't need to rely on automigration on application startup, which is good because the process can be slow and on particular platforms may result in the application being killed for not starting quickly enough.

Like Cloud Foundry, the other cloud platforms provide appropriate tooling to do the administration you need. Differences exist, however, so we recommend you give at least a few of the platforms a try to see how they compare on that front.

Now that you've configured Hubbub to run on the cloud, your job here is done. Although we focused on deploying to Cloud Foundry, most of the information we presented is applicable to other platforms, too. When combined with the documentation provided by the cloud platforms themselves, you can deploy any application to any platform.

18.3 Summary and best practices

Whether you think the cloud is the greatest thing since sliced bread or just a passing fad, it's not going away any time soon. Its advantages in terms of reduced capital costs (hardware infrastructure) and simpler IT administration are too great to ignore. It's now at the stage where enterprises run their own internal clouds.

In this chapter we introduced a few cloud providers to get you started, but more are out there. The big beast in this space is Amazon with its AWS offering—an IaaS offering used by several of the PaaS providers. Amazon even offers its own PaaS-like system in the form of Elastic Beanstalk. You're certainly not short of choices these days.

If you do decide to deploy to the cloud, the big decision you face is whether to go for IaaS or PaaS. That's why we took the time to explain both of them. PaaS gives you an easier mechanism for deploying and running applications at the cost of losing fine-grained control over the software setup and configuration. You should consider IaaS if you have special requirements in terms of load, throughput, data storage, or anything else that means controlling low-level configuration.

We also showed you the steps involved in migrating an existing Grails application to the cloud because the cloud forces certain restrictions on you. This leads us to the first of several best practices:

- *Decide early whether you're likely to deploy to the cloud.* You don't have to commit to the cloud right at the beginning of a project. But remember that such a deployment affects the way you architect your application and what libraries and services you use, so it's best to factor those constraints in at the beginning. Modifying an application after the fact can be an extremely painful and slow process.
- *Evaluate the cloud providers on a case-by-case basis.* Each project has unique needs, as do the teams and companies that develop them. Be sure to factor those needs into the decision on which cloud to use. At the moment, it's typically not easy to move your application and data from one provider to another. You can reduce the risk of needing to do this if you put time into the initial evaluation phase.

- *Code for multiple instances.* Even though you may think your application will only ever run one instance, why lose out on the benefits of the cloud by restricting your ability to scale up the application? And by thinking in terms of multiple instances, you're less likely to code in a way that doesn't work well on the cloud, such as storing files locally via the `File` class!
- *Take care with the pricing.* It seems at the moment that the cloud providers have different pricing models, so it can be hard to compare them directly. The main thing to be aware of is that Spring/Java applications in general, and Grails apps in particular, require a fair bit of memory to run. That means any pricing based on memory usage may hurt your wallet.

The cloud is an exciting development in IT and a great way of hosting web applications in particular. Now is definitely the time to start investigating the options and experimenting with various applications. Although the cloud places certain restrictions on your application, they're not that onerous and, as you've seen, it can be easy to get an application up and running.

That's one of the core aims of the framework: Grails let's you create simple web applications in short order. This leads some to view the framework as limited. But that apparent simplicity hides power that's hard to master.

We believe that you now have a solid platform on which to build your Grails experience. You should have a good understanding of the core features of Grails, such as controllers, domain classes, views, and custom tags. We hope that you also have an idea of the flexibility available to you through Spring and the plugin system. You aren't limited to a single architectural style or type of web application.

appendix A Groovy reference

It's not always easy to find the information you want about Groovy, so we've incorporated a short reference here that includes useful information in an easily digested form. It focuses on two Groovy features: operator overloading and the extension methods that Groovy adds to the core Java class library.

A.1 Operator overloading

Groovy allows you to support operators on your own classes, such as `+`, `*`, `<<`, and so on. The mechanism for this is straightforward: implement methods with specific names. If you want to support adding two matrices together with the `+` operator, you can implement `plus()`:

```
class Matrix {
    ...
    Matrix plus(Matrix other) {
        ...
    }
}
```

Even if you don't implement any of the operator methods yourself, it's important to know the mappings for at least two reasons:

- *API documentation shows the methods of a class.* You have to infer from the method name and signature whether or not a class supports a particular operator.
- *Exceptions display the method name when an operator is incorrectly used.* The mappings allow you to work out that an operator is the source of a problem.

Table A.1 gives you an extensive list of operators and their corresponding method signatures.

Table A.1 Operator to method mappings

Operator	Method	Operator	Method
a + b	a.plus(b)	a[b]	a.getAt(b)
a - b	a.minus(b)	a[b] = c	a.putAt(b, c)
a * b	a.multiply(b)	a << b	a.leftShift(b)
a / b	a.div(b)	a >> b	a.rightShift(b)
a ** b	a.power(b)	a++ or ++a	a.next()
a % b	a.mod(b)	a-- or --a	a.previous()
a | b	a.or(b)	+a	a.positive()
a & b	a.and(b)	-a	a.negative()
a ^ b	a.xor(b)	~a	a.bitwiseNegate()

A.2 Groovy JDK methods

Groovy extends the JDK classes with its own set of properties and methods. In table A.2, you can see a small, but useful, subset of those properties and methods. You should familiarize yourself with the rest of the Groovy JDK as soon as possible, as there are plenty of useful and time-saving methods that we don't mention here.

Table A.2 Useful Groovy JDK properties and methods

Name	Class	Description
size()	String array	Returns the length of the string or array. Provides consistency with the standard JDK size() method on Collection and Map.
each(Closure)	Collection String array Map	Iterates over a sequence, executing the given closure for each element in the sequence. The element is passed as the closure argument.
find(Closure)	Collection array	Returns the first element in a collection for which the given closure returns a value of true (according to Groovy Truth).
findAll(Closure)	Collection array	Returns all the elements in a collection for which the given closure returns true. The matching elements are returned as a list.
collect(Closure)	Collection array	Maps all the values in a collection to new values using a single function.
sort(Closure)	Collection array	Sorts a collection based on the value returned by the closure.

Table A.2 Useful Groovy JDK properties and methods *(continued)*

Name	Class	Description
`join(String)`	`Iterable` array	Combines the stringified value of each element together into a single string, using the given string as a separator.
`text`	`File`	Returns the contents of a file as a string. Not recommended for binary files!
`size()`	`File`	Returns the size of a file in bytes.
`withWriter(Closure)`	`File`	One of several `with*()` methods on `File`, this opens the file for writing and passes the Writer object to the closure. When the closure has finished, the file is closed, regardless of whether the closure ended normally or threw an exception.
`abs()`	`Number`	Returns the absolute (positive) value of a number.
`times(Closure)`	`Number`	Executes the given closure *n* number of times.

Some of these methods need examples to clarify their use. Let's say you have a list of `Person` objects that each have `name` and `age` properties. You could pick out the first person with an age greater than 65 with this

```
def person = people.find { it.age > 65 }
```

or you could print all the people's names with this

```
people.each { Person p ->
    println p.name
}
```

The following example returns a list of the people's names, in the same order as the corresponding `Person` objects:

```
def names = people.collect { it.name }
```

You could even extend this to get a comma-separated list of names:

```
def names = people.collect { it.name }.join(", ")
```

Sorting the list of `Person` objects by their names is as simple as this:

```
def sortedPeople = people.sort { it.name }
```

We recommend that you look up the Groovy JDK documentation[1] for more details on these and other properties and methods.

[1] To see what makes the JDK more groovy, see http://groovy.codehaus.org/groovy-jdk/.

appendix B GORM query reference

As you saw in the main chapters, Grails gives you plenty of options when it comes to querying. Of those, in this appendix, we focus on Where and Criteria queries, which are closely related. We detail the syntax for both options and also show you how the criteria map between the two. This will allow you to convert between Where and Criteria queries. For example, you may find the query you need in an online blog post in Criteria query form, whereas you may want to use Where queries exclusively in your code.

B.1 Where queries

You can invoke Where queries in several different ways:

```
def result = <domainClass>.where { <criteria> }.list()
def result = <domainClass>.where { <criteria> }.get()
def result = <domainClass>.where { <criteria> }.find()
def result = <domainClass>.where { <criteria> }.findBy*()
def result = <domainClass>.where { <criteria> }.findAllBy*()
def result = <domainClass>.find { <criteria> }
def result = <domainClass>.findAll { <criteria> }
```

There is such a thing as too much choice! The `where()` method creates a query object but doesn't execute it. You then use `list()` if the query can return more than one result, or `get()` (`find()` is a synonym) if the query only returns a single domain object or `null`. The dynamic finders allow you to execute the query and add further criteria in one step.

The `find()` and `findAll()` methods declare and execute the query in one go. The main disadvantage with these is that the methods are overloaded, with forms for HQL and query by example. This can be quite confusing. We recommend exclusively using `where()` and `whereAny()`.

The actual criteria are declared using Groovy expressions, for example:

```
def bbqPosts = Post.where { content =~ "%BBQ%" }.list()
```

Sorting and pagination is done through arguments to the `list()` method:

```
def posts = Post.where { ... }.list(
        sort: "dateCreated",
        order: "desc",
        offset: 10,
        max: 5)
```

We tabulate the available criteria expressions in the next section, alongside their Criteria query equivalents.

B.2 Criteria queries

Fewer ways exist to invoke Criteria queries compared to Where queries:

```
def result = <domainClass>.createCriteria().list { <criteria> }
def result = <domainClass>.createCriteria().get { <criteria> }
def result = <domainClass>.withCriteria { <criteria> }
def result = <domainClass>.withCriteria(uniqueResult: true) { <criteria> }
```

It's best to stick either to `createCriteria()` or `withCriteria()`. We have no specific recommendations on which of these you should use; it's your personal preference.

The structure of the criteria is based on methods, so if you want all posts containing the string "`BBQ`", you'd use this:

```
def bbqPosts = Post.withCriteria {
    ilike "content", "%BBQ%"
}
```

Unlike for Where queries and dynamic finders, sorting and pagination are specified by methods in the criteria block:

```
def posts = Post.withCriteria {
    ilike "content", "%BBQ%"
    order "dateCreated", "desc"
    firstResult 10
    maxResults 5
}
```

For easy reference, table B.1 gives you an extensive list of Where query operators and their corresponding Criteria methods.

Table B.1 Query criteria mappings

Where query	Criteria query	SQL equivalent
`prop == null`	`isNull(prop)`	`prop is null`
`prop != null`	`isNotNull(prop)`	`prop is not null`
`prop == value`	`eq(prop, value)`	`prop = value`

Table B.1 Query criteria mappings *(continued)*

Where query	Criteria query	SQL equivalent
`prop != value`	`ne(prop, value)`	`prop <> value`
`prop > value`	`gt(prop, value)`	`prop > value`
`prop < value`	`lt(prop, value)`	`prop < value`
`prop >= value`	`ge(prop, value)`	`prop >= value`
`prop <= value`	`le(prop, value)`	`prop <= value`
`prop ==~ value`	`like(prop, value)`	`prop like value`
`prop =~ value`	`ilike(prop, value)`	`prop ilike value`
`prop in [val1, val2]`	`'in'(prop, [val1, val2])`	`prop in (val1, val2)`
`prop in val1..val2`	`between(prop, val1, val2)`	`prop between val1 and val2`
`prop == prop2`	`eqProperty(prop, prop2)`	`prop = prop2`
`prop != prop2`	`neProperty(prop, prop2)`	`prop <> prop2`
`prop > prop2`	`gtProperty(prop, prop2)`	`prop > prop2`
`prop < prop2`	`ltProperty(prop, prop2)`	`prop < prop2`
`prop >= prop2`	`geProperty(prop, prop2)`	`prop >= prop2`
`prop <= prop2`	`leProperty(prop, prop2)`	`prop <= prop2`

appendix C
XML and Spring builders

Groovy allows you to easily generate XML using the `groovy.xml.MarkupBuilder` class. We'll show you the basic mechanics of that class and then look at how Spring's XML configuration format maps to the bean builder syntax used in chapter 14, because the mapping is similar.

C.1 XML generation with MarkupBuilder

Generating XML text is trivial with the `MarkupBuilder` class. We'll demonstrate with a simple example, as shown in the following listing.

Listing C.1 Using `MarkupBuilder` to generate XML text

```
import groovy.xml.MarkupBuilder

def file = new File("test.xml")
def stock = [
    [ quantity: 10, name: "Orange", type: "Fruit" ],
    [ quantity: 6, name: "Apple", type: "Fruit" ],
    [ quantity: 2, name: "Chair", type: "Furniture" ] ]

def b = new MarkupBuilder(file.newWriter("UTF-8"))
b.stock {
    for (entry in stock) {
        item(qty: entry.quantity) {
            name(entry.name)
            type(entry.type)
        }
    }
}
```

Can mix in normal Groovy code. Loops and conditions are common.

This will create the file test.xml containing the content, shown in the following listing.

Listing C.2 Creating the test.xml file

```
<stock>                                    <-- First method call on builder
  <item qty='10'>                              becomes root element
    <name>Orange</name>
    <type>Fruit</type>
  </item>
  <item qty='6'>                           <-- Named arguments
    <name>Apple</name>                         become attributes
    <type>Fruit</type>
  </item>
  <item qty='2'>
    <name>Chair</name>                     <-- Nested methods become
    <type>Furniture</type>                     nested elements, argument
  </item>                                      becomes content
</stock>
```

This ability to convert method calls into elements and named arguments into attributes makes it easy to generate XML, particularly when you factor in loops and conditions.

NOTE `MarkupBuilder` doesn't work with static type checking.

C.2 Bean Builder

Grails's Bean Builder for Spring maps to Spring XML in a similar fashion to `MarkupBuilder` syntax and XML but with key differences. Much of the information about Spring on the web is based on XML configuration, so it's important that you know how to map the XML to Bean Builder syntax. This section explains how that mapping works.

Comparing Spring's XML and Bean Builder formats

Bean Builder supports almost all of the features you'll find in the Spring XML descriptor format. In table C.1, you'll see the equivalent DSL syntax for various XML forms. If you don't understand what a particular form is or what it does, check out the online Spring reference manual, which covers all of these variants and more.

Table C.1 Comparing the Spring XML descriptor format to Bean Builder

Feature	XML	Bean Builder

Bean attributes	`<bean id="ex" class="o.e.Ex"`
	`scope="prototype"`
	`autowire="byType"`
	`init-method="init"`
	`destroy-method="finish"/>`
		`ex(o.e.Ex) { b ->`
		`b.scope = "prototype"`
		`b.autowire = "byType"`
		`b.initMethod = "init"`
		`b.destroyMethod = "finish"`
		`}`

Table C.1 Comparing the Spring XML descriptor format to Bean Builder *(continued)*

Feature	XML	Bean Builder

Lists	`<bean id="ex" class="o.e.Ex">`
	`  <property name="items">`
	`    <list>`
	`      <value>1</value>`
	`      <value>2</value>`
	`      <value>3</value>`
	`    </list>`
	`  </property>`
	`</bean>`
		`ex(o.e.Ex) {`
		`  items = [1, 2, 3]`
		`}`

Static factory methods	`<bean id="ex" class="o.e.Ex"`
	`  factory-method="create"/>`
		`ex(o.e.Ex) { b ->`
		`  b.factoryMethod = "create"`
		`}`

Instance factory methods	`<bean id="ex"`
	`  factory-bean="myFactory"`
	`  factory-method="create"/>`
		`ex(myFactory: "create")`

Remember that you can include normal code inside the Bean Builder DSL. Consider this example, which creates a new bean based on given variables:

```
def serviceName = "security"
def beanNames = [ "transactionInterceptor" ]
"${serviceName}Manager"(org.example.ServiceManager) {
    service = serviceName
    if (isTransactional) {
        interceptors = beanNames.collect { ref(it) }
    }
}
```

This bit of code creates a bean named `securityManager`, but you can see how the service name and bean names can easily be parameterized. The actual bean configuration could be determined at runtime!

NAMESPACES WITH BEAN BUILDER

To show you how to use namespaces, we'll use a simple example based on Spring's Aspect-Oriented Programming (AOP) support. We won't go into detail about what AOP is, but suffice it to say that the following example will time (profile) every method call on the `sessionFactory` bean:

```
beans = {
    xmlns aop: "http://www.springframework.org/schema/aop"
    aop.config {
        aspect id: "profiling", ref: "profileInterceptor" {
            around method: "profile", pointcut: "bean(sessionFactory)"
        }
    }
    profileInterceptor(com.manning.gria.ProfilingInterceptor)
}
```

First, you have to declare the namespace and assign it a prefix (`aop`, in this case), which you do with the built-in `xmlns()` method. You can declare additional namespaces by adding extra named arguments to the method:

```
xmlns aop: "...", context: "...", ...
```

Once you've declared a namespace, you can use a property with the same name as the namespace prefix to access the custom features, as we do for `aop.config` in the preceding example. Note that the `aspect()` and `around()` methods aren't prefixed because they're nested within a method that is. You could also use this syntax:

```
aop {
    config {
        aspect ...
    }
}
```

For more information on the Bean Builder syntax, we recommend the Grails user guide, which gives significant coverage of this topic.

index

Symbols

Numerics

A

D

H

I

M

Q

S

U

V

W

X

Y

RELATED MANNING TITLES

Groovy in Action, Second Edition
by Dierk König, Guillaume Laforge, Paul King, Cédric Champeau, Hamlet D'Arcy, Erik Pragt, and Jon Skeet

ISBN: 9781935182443
700 pages, $49.99
October 2014

Making Java Groovy
by Kenneth A. Kousen

ISBN: 9781935182948
368 pages, $44.99
September 2013

Java 8 in Action
Lambdas, Streams, and functional-style programming
by Raoul-Gabriel Urma, Mario Fusco, and Alan Mycroft

ISBN: 9781617291999
375 pages, $49.99
August 2014

Griffon in Action
by Andres Almiray, Danno Ferrin, and James Shingler

ISBN: 9781935182238
384 pages, $44.99
June 2012

For ordering information go to www.manning.com